CSWE's Core Competencies and Practice Behavior Examples in This Text

Competency	Chapter
Professional Identity	
Practice Behavior Examples...	
Serve as representatives of the profession, its mission, and its core values	1–13
Know the profession's history	2–13
Commit themselves to the profession's enhancement and to their own professional conduct and growth	1, 3–13
Advocate for client access to the services of social work	3–13
Practice personal reflection and self-correction to assure continual professional development	3
Attend to professional roles and boundaries	1, 3
Demonstrate professional demeanor in behavior, appearance, and communication	1, 3–13
Engage in career-long learning	1, 3–13
Use supervision and consultation	3–13
Ethical Practice	
Practice Behavior Examples...	
Obligation to conduct themselves ethically and engage in ethical decision making	1–13
Know about the value base of the profession, its ethical standards, and relevant law	1–13
Recognize and manage personal values in a way that allows professional values to guide practice	1–13
Make ethical decisions by applying standards of the National Association of Social Workers Code of Ethics and, as applicable, of the International Federation of Social Workers/International Association of Schools of Social Work Ethics in Social Work, Statement of Principles	1–13
Tolerate ambiguity in resolving ethical conflicts	3–13
Apply strategies of ethical reasoning to arrive at principled decisions	2, 3–13
Critical Thinking	
Practice Behavior Examples...	
Know about the principles of logic, scientific inquiry, and reasoned discernment	1–3
Use critical thinking augmented by creativity and curiosity	1–13
Requires the synthesis and communication of relevant information	1–13
Distinguish, appraise, and integrate multiple sources of knowledge, including research-based knowledge, and practice wisdom	1–13
Analyze models of assessment, prevention, intervention, and evaluation	3–13
Demonstrate effective oral and written communication in working with individuals, families, groups, organizations, communities, and colleagues	3–13

Adapted with the permission of Council on Social Work Education

CSWE's Core Competencies and Practice Behavior Examples in This Text

Competency	Chapter
Diversity in Practice	
Practice Behavior Examples...	
Understand how diversity characterizes and shapes the human experience and is critical to the formation of identity	1–13
Understand the dimensions of diversity as the intersectionality of multiple factors including age, class, color, culture, disability, ethnicity, gender, gender identity and expression, immigration status, political ideology, race, religion, sex, and sexual orientation	2–13
Appreciate that, as a consequence of difference, a person's life experiences may include oppression, poverty, marginalization, and alienation as well as privilege, power, and acclaim	2–13
Recognize the extent to which a culture's structures and values may oppress, marginalize, alienate, or create or enhance privilege and power	2–13
Gain sufficient self-awareness to eliminate the influence of personal biases and values in working with diverse groups	3–13
Recognize and communicate their understanding of the importance of difference in shaping life experiences	2–13
View themselves as learners and engage those with whom they work as informants	3–13
Human Rights & Justice	
Practice Behavior Examples...	
Understand that each person, regardless of position in society, has basic human rights, such as freedom, safety, privacy, an adequate standard of living, health care, and education	2–13
Recognize the global interconnections of oppression and are knowledgeable about theories of justice and strategies to promote human and civil rights	2, 13
Incorporate social justice practices in organizations, institutions, and society to ensure that these basic human rights are distributed equitably and without prejudice	1–13
Understand the forms and mechanisms of oppression and discrimination	1–13
Advocate for human rights and social and economic justice	1, 3–13
Engage in practices that advance social and economic justice	3–13
Research Based Practice	
Practice Behavior Examples...	
Use practice experience to inform research, employ evidence-based interventions, evaluate their own practice, and use research findings to improve practice, policy, and social service delivery	3–13
Comprehend quantitative and qualitative research and understand scientific and ethical approaches to building knowledge	3
Use practice experience to inform scientific inquiry	3
Use research evidence to inform practice	3

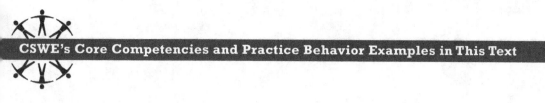

Competency	Chapter
Human Behavior	
Practice Behavior Examples...	
Know about human behavior across the life course; the range of social systems in which people live; and the ways social systems promote or deter people in maintaining or achieving health and well-being	3–13
Apply theories and knowledge from the liberal arts to understand biological, social, cultural, psychological, and spiritual development	4–13
Utilize conceptual frameworks to guide the processes of assessment, intervention, and evaluation	1, 3–13
Critique and apply knowledge to understand person and environment	1, 3–13
Policy Practice	
Practice Behavior Examples...	
Understand that policy affects service delivery and they actively engage in policy practice	2–13
Know the history and current structures of social policies and services; the role of policy in service delivery; and the role of practice in policy development	2, 4–13
Analyze, formulate, and advocate for policies that advance social well-being	2, 4–13
Collaborate with colleagues and clients for effective policy action	2, 4–13
Practice Contexts	
Practice Behavior Examples...	
Keep informed, resourceful, and proactive in responding to evolving organizational, community, and societal contexts at all levels of practice	4–13
Recognize that the context of practice is dynamic, and use knowledge and skill to respond proactively	4–13
Continuously discover, appraise, and attend to changing locales, populations, scientific and technological developments, and emerging societal trends to provide relevant services	4–13
Provide leadership in promoting sustainable changes in service delivery and practice to improve the quality of social services	4–13
Engage, Assess Intervene, Evaluate	
Practice Behavior Examples...	
Identify, analyze, and implement evidence-based interventions designed to achieve client goals	3–13
Use research and technological advances	3–13
Evaluate program outcomes and practice effectiveness	3–13
Develop, analyze, advocate, and provide leadership for policies and services	3–13
Promote social and economic justice	2, 4–13
A) ENGAGEMENT Substantively and effectively prepare for action with individuals, families, groups, organizations, and communities	3–13
Use empathy and other interpersonal skills	3–13
Develop a mutually agreed-on focus of work and desired outcomes	4–13

CSWE's Core Competencies and Practice Behavior Examples in This Text

Competency	Chapter
B) ASSESSMENT Collect, organize, and interpret client data	3
Assess client strengths and limitations	3–13
Develop mutually agreed-on intervention goals and objectives	4–13
Select appropriate intervention strategies	3–13
C) INTERVENTION Initiate actions to achieve organizational goals	3–13
Implement prevention interventions that enhance client capacities	3–13
Help clients resolve problems	3–13
Negotiate, mediate, and advocate for clients	3–13
Facilitate transitions and endings	3
D) EVALUATION Critically analyze, monitor, and evaluate interventions	3

Introduction to Social Work

Through the Eyes of Practice Settings

Michelle E. Martin
Dominican University

PEARSON

Boston Columbus Hoboken Indianapolis New York San Francisco
Amsterdam Cape Town Dubai London Madrid Milan Munich Paris Montréal Toronto
Delhi Mexico City São Paulo Sydney Hong Kong Seoul Singapore Taipei Tokyo

VP and Editorial Director: Jeffery W. Johnston
Senior Acquisitions Editor: Julie Peters
Program Manager: Megan Moffo
Editorial Assistant: Andrea Hall
Executive Product Marketing Manager:
   Christopher Barry
Executive Field Marketing Manager: Krista Clark
Team Lead Project Management: JoEllen Gohr
Team Lead Program Management: Laura Weaver
Project Manager: Janet Portisch
Procurement Specialist: Deidra Skahill

Art Director: Diane Lorenzo
Art Director Cover: Diane Ernsberger
Cover Design: Cenveo Publisher Services
Cover Art: Shutterstock
Media Producer: Allison Longley
Editorial Production and Composition Service:
   Lumina Datamatics Inc.
Full-Service Project Manager: Sudip Sinha
Printer/Binder: LSC Communications
Cover Printer: LSC Communications
Text Font: 10.5/13 DanteMTStd

Credits and acknowledgments borrowed from other sources and reproduced, with permission, in this textbook appear on the appropriate page within text.

Copyright © 2016 by Pearson Education, Inc. or its affiliates. All Rights Reserved. Printed in the United States of America. This publication is protected by copyright, and permission should be obtained from the publisher prior to any prohibited reproduction, storage in a retrieval system, or transmission in any form or by any means, electronic, mechanical, photocopying, recording, or otherwise. For information regarding permissions, request forms, and the appropriate contacts within the Pearson Education Global Rights & Permissions department, please visit www.pearsoned.com/permissions/.

Many of the designations by manufacturers and sellers to distinguish their products are claimed as trademarks. Where those designations appear in this book, and the publisher was aware of a trademark claim, the designations have been printed in initial caps or all caps.

Library of Congress Cataloging-in-Publication Data

Martin, Michelle E.
   Introduction to social work : through the eyes of practice settings/Michelle E. Martin.—
1 Edition.
      pages cm
   Includes bibliographical references and index.
   ISBN 978-0-205-68182-2—ISBN 0-205-68182-4 1. Social service. 2. Social case work—United States.
3. Social service—United States. I. Title.
   HV40.M414 2014
   361.3'2—dc23

                                                                                    2014029748

ISBN 10: 0-205-68182-4
ISBN 13: 978-0-205-68182-2

Contents

PART II: Social Work in Action—Common Practice Settings

8. Homelessness   167

9. Healthcare and Hospice   194

13. International Social Work   288

Preface

Introduction to Social Work: Through the Eyes of Practice Settings was written with the realization that we live in a rapidly changing world, and these changes have dramatically impacted the social work field. Social work is a discipline that touches on virtually every dynamic occurring worldwide that affects people and their surroundings. Social workers provide assistance to people in all dimensions of the client's life. They interact with individuals, families, and communities within a variety of contexts and on a variety of levels, which means that social workers wear numerous hats and must be aware of a vast amount of information.

Social workers are therapists, case managers, social justice advocates, policy experts, and experts on a range of social problems. What other careers require this level of expertise? Social workers working in refugee resettlement must be aware of patterns of global conflict throughout the world. Social workers working in employment assistance must be aware of economic patterns on a micro and macro level, including the impact of globalization on domestic and international employment. Social workers working with children must be aware of child development theory, child- and family-centered intervention strategies, domestic policy and legislation impacting child welfare on national and local levels, and contemporary social problems impacting children (such as cyber-bullying). Social workers must remain abreast of technological advances, including the globalization of communication technologies, which impact their clients in positive and negative ways. Social workers must be aware of contemporary changes in family structures and newer ways of working with families that reflect their changing structures, such as working with blended and same-sex family constellations. These are just a few examples reflecting the breadth of this career.

I have worked in the social services throughout my entire career, and the trajectory of my career has in many respects reflected the changes within the social work field, including evolving from a focus primarily on "domestic" social work on a direct practice level working in traditional practice settings, such as mental health and schools, to a career primarily on a policy and macro level working with international issues, such as conflict and refugees. It is my hope that this book effectively reflects the breadth and complexity of the social work profession, while also reflecting the most recent changes in the world that impact the social work profession.

A CONTEXTUAL AND INTEGRATIVE APPROACH

With regard to the approach and organization of this book, readers will note that I have taken a unique approach to presenting content relevant to the social work profession in that the roles, function, and nature of the work that social workers do is presented contextually and in an integrative manner so that readers will be better able to understand and envision the nature of this profession by looking "through the eyes of practice settings."

The first section of this book is designed to provide a foundation for the rest of the book by providing readers with a very general introduction to the social work profession including its purpose, preparation, practice, and theoretical orientations most often used in social work (Chapter 1); exploring the evolution of social welfare policy and the effect on social work practice (Chapter 2); and identifying and exploring many of the generalist skills and intervention strategies used in the social work profession, as well as the nature of social work ethical standards (Chapter 3). Chapters 4 through 12 focus on a range of practice areas addressing social problems existing in the world today that social workers are most likely to encounter in their careers, such as child welfare (Chapter 4); adolescence (Chapter 5); older adults (Chapter 6); mental health and mental illness (Chapter 7); homelessness (Chapter 8); health care and hospice (Chapter 9); schools (Chapter 10); religion and spirituality (Chapter 11); violence and victim advocacy (Chapter 12); and international social work (Chapter 13), which explores global dynamics, including international human rights violations and the international community's response. Touching the lives of social work students on such a broad scale is an honor, and I hope this book reflects my awareness of the importance of this field—both with regard to its history, its current contributions, and its future.

ACKNOWLEDGMENTS

I would like to thank several people who helped make this book possible. First, and foremost, I would like to thank my family, including my son Xander, my siblings, and colleagues Kathy Clyburn and Charlie Stoops for their valuable input and support.

I would also like to thank the reviewers of this edition: Linda Helmers, Iowa Lakes Community College; Kathryn McKinley, Buena Vista University; Amanda Miller, University of Indianapolis; Karl Mitchell, Queens College CUNY; Elizabeth Patterson, Malone University; Kimberley Zittel-Palamara, Buffalo State College.

Michelle E. Martin

1

Introduction to the Social Work Profession

Purpose, Preparation, Practice, and Theoretical Orientations

LEARNING OBJECTIVES

- Identify and describe three reasons people may need social work intervention.
- Distinguish between the different helping fields and the associated requirements of each ways one can enter the field of social work and the various types of careers within the social work profession.
- Identify the most common degrees and associated licensure level within the social work profession.
- Apply social work foundational theoretical frameworks to client situations experiencing frequently encountered social problems.

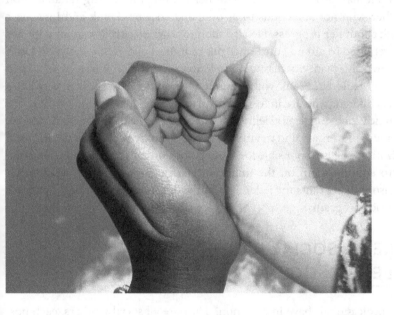

Sara works for a hospice agency, where she spends one hour twice a week with Steve, who has terminal liver cancer and approximately six months to live. He has been estranged from his adult daughter for four years, and Sara is helping him develop a plan for reunification. Sara helps Steve deal with his terminal diagnosis by helping him talk through his feelings of being sick and dying. Steve talks a lot about his fear of being in pain and his overwhelming regret for many of the choices he has made in his life. Sara listens and also helps him develop a plan for saying all the things he needs to say before he dies. During one meeting, she helped him write a list of what he would like to say to his estranged daughter, his ex-wife, and other family members. She is also helping him make important end-of-life decisions, including planning his own funeral. Sara and Steve will continue to meet until his death, and if possible, she will be with him and his family when he passes away.

Gary works for a public middle school, where he meets with six seventh graders every Monday to talk about their feelings. He helps them learn better ways to explore feelings of anger and frustration. Sometimes they play a board game where they each take turns picking a *self-disclosure* card and answering a personal question. Gary uses the game to enter into discussions about healthy ways of coping with feelings, particularly anger. He also uses the game to get to know the students on a personal level, so that they will open up to him more. He dedicates one session per month to discuss their progress in class. The goal for the group is to help the students learn how to better control their anger and to develop prosocial behaviors, such as empathy and respect for others.

Frank works for a county social services agency in the child welfare division, and is working with Lisa, who recently had her three young children removed from her home for physical and emotional neglect. Frank has arranged for Lisa to have parenting classes and individual counseling so that she can learn how to better manage her frustrations with her children. He has also arranged to have her admitted to a drug rehabilitation program to help her with her addictions to alcohol and cocaine. Frank and Lisa meet once a week to talk about her progress. He also monitors her weekly visitation with her children. Frank is required to attend court once per month to update the judge on Lisa's progress on her parenting plan. Successful completion of this plan will enable Lisa to regain custody of her children. Frank will continue to monitor her progress, as well as the progress of the children, who are in foster care placement.

Allison is currently lobbying several legislators in support of a bill that would increase funding for child abuse prevention and treatment. As the social policy advocate for a local grassroots organization, she is responsible for writing position statements and contacting local lawmakers to educate them on the importance of legislation aimed at reducing child abuse. She also writes grants for federal and private funding of the organization's various child advocacy programs.

THE NATURE OF SOCIAL WORK AND ITS NEED IN SOCIETY

What do all these professionals have in common? They are all social workers, each possessing a broad range of skills and having a wide range of responsibilities related to their roles in helping people overcome a variety of social problems. Social work is a growing profession (Doelling, 2004), and is expected to grow at 19 percent over the next decade, representing a faster-than-average pace (Bureau of Labor Statistics, 2014).

Although the responsibilities of social workers can range considerably, the International Federation of Social Workers defines the social work profession as one that

> promotes social change, problem-solving in human relationships, and the empowerment and liberation of people to enhance well-being. Utilizing theories of human behavior and social systems, social work intervenes at the points where people interact with their environments. Principles of human rights and social justice are fundamental to social work. (Hare, 2004)

Human beings have basic needs, such as the need for food, health, shelter, and safety. People also have social needs, such as the need for interpersonal connection and love, and psychological needs, such as the need to deal with the trauma of past abuse or the psychological ramifications of disasters such as a hurricane or house fire. People who are fortunate have several ways to get their needs met. For instance, social and psychological needs can be met by family, friends, neighbors, places of employment, and places of worship, and needs related to food, shelter, healthcare, child care, and housing can be met through employment, education, and family.

But some people in society are unable to meet even their most basic needs because they do not have a supportive network—they may not have a supportive family or they may have no family at all. They may have no friends or have friends who are either unsupportive or unable to provide help. They may have no social support network of any kind, having no faith community, and no supportive neighbors, perhaps due to apartment living or the fact that many communities within the United States tend to be far more transient now than in prior generations. They may lack the skills or education to gain sufficient employment; thus, they may not have health insurance or earn a good wage. Perhaps they've spent the majority of their lives dealing with an abusive and chaotic childhood and are now suffering from the manifestation of that experience in the form of psychological problems and substance abuse and, thus, cannot focus on meeting their basic needs until they are able to deal with the trauma they endured.

> ## Engage Diversity and Difference in Practice
>
> **Practice Behavior: Recognize the extent to which a culture's structures and values may oppress, marginalize, alienate, or create or enhance privilege and power.**
>
> Critical Thinking Question: Social workers work with a range of social problems in order to meet the basic needs of people. These social work delivery systems are critical to facilitate environments that promote growth and learning. What might happen to people in need if social workers were not available to help people in need?

Some people, particularly those who have good support systems, may falsely believe that anyone who cannot meet their most basic needs must be doing something wrong. This belief is incorrect because numerous barriers may exist that keep people from meeting their basic needs, some of which might be related to their own behavior, but more often, the reasons people cannot meet their needs are quite complicated and often lie in dynamics beyond their control. Thus, while some people who are fortunate enough to have great families, have wonderfully supportive friends, have the benefit of a good education, have not experienced racial oppression or marginalization, and have no significant history of abuse or loss may be self-sufficient in meeting their own needs, this does not mean that others who find themselves in situations where they cannot meet their own needs are doing something wrong. Social service agencies come into the picture when people find themselves confronting barriers to getting their basic needs met and their own resources for overcoming these obstacles are insufficient (see Box 1.1).

A tremendous amount of controversy surrounds how best to help people meet their basic needs, and various philosophies exist regarding what types of services truly help those in need. For instance, some philosophies posit that many social welfare programs foster dependence and thus should be stigmatized to discourage liberal use. However, other philosophies posit that a solid social safety net fosters self-sufficiency and what may appear to be dependence is really masked discouragement. Regardless of what philosophy one adopts with regard to social welfare assistance, the primarily goal of social work is to assist people in achieving self-sufficiency and reaching their optimal level of functioning. This means that social workers are committed to helping people develop the necessary skills to become self-sufficient and function at their optimal levels, personally and within society. Thus, although a social service agency may subsidize a family's rent for a few months when they are in a crisis, social workers will then work with the family

---

Box 1.1   Common Obstacles to Self-Sufficiency

- Lack of family (or supportive family)
- Lack of a healthy support system of friends
- Mental illness
- Poverty
- Social exclusion (due to racial discrimination, for instance)
- Racism
- Oppression (e.g., racial, gender, age)

- Trauma
- Natural disasters
- Lack of education
- Lack of employment skills
- Unemployment
- Economic recession
- Physical and/or intellectual disability

Pearson Education, Inc.

---

members to remove any barriers that may keep them from meeting their housing needs in the future, such as substance abuse disorders, a lack of education or vocational skills, health problems, mental illness, or lacking self-advocacy skills necessary for combating prejudice and discrimination in the workplace, for instance.

In addition to a commitment to working with a broad range of populations, including high-needs and disenfranchised populations, and providing them with the necessary resources to get their basic needs met, social workers are also committed to working on a *macro* or societal level to removing barriers to optimal functioning that affect large groups of people. By advocating for changes in laws and various policies, social workers contribute to making strides in reducing prejudice and discrimination related to one's race, gender, sexual orientation, socioeconomic status (SES), or any one of a number of other characterizations that might marginalize someone within society.

Social workers continue to work on all social fronts so that all members of society have an equivalent opportunity for optimal functioning and self-sufficiency. The chief goal of social workers is to help individuals as well as communities function at their maximum potential, overcoming personal and social barriers as effectively as possible in the major domains of living.

> **Assess your comprehension of "The Nature of Social Work and Its Need in Society" by completing this quiz.**

SOCIAL WORKERS: EDUCATIONAL REQUIREMENTS AND PROFESSIONAL STANDARDS

Identify as a Professional Social Worker and Conduct Oneself Accordingly

Practice Behavior: Attend to professional roles and boundaries.

Critical Thinking Question: Social workers engage in a broad range of duties and functions. What are the educational requirements of social workers, and why do they range from state to state?

Each year numerous caring individuals decide to enter the field of social services and embark on the confusing journey of trying to determine what level of education is required for specific employment positions, when and where a license is required, and even what degree is required. There are no easy answers to these questions, because the social services profession is a broad one encompassing many different professions, including human services generalist, mental health counselor, psychologist, social worker, and perhaps even psychiatrist, all of whom are considered social service professionals if they work in a social service agency, working in some manner with marginalized and disenfranchised populations or other individuals who are in some way experiencing problems related to social or systemic issues within society.

Another area of confusion relates to the educational and licensing requirements needed to work in the social work field. What educational degrees are necessary to become a social worker, what level of education is required, and what professional license is needed depend in large part on variables such as specific state and federal legislation (particularly for highly regulated fields, such as educational and healthcare sectors), industry-specific standards, and even agency preference or need. To make matters even more confusing, these variables can vary dramatically from one state to the next; thus, a job that one is qualified for in one state with an Associate of Arts (AA) degree may require a Master of Social Work (MSW) degree and a clinical license in another state. In addition, many individuals may work in the same capacity at a social service agency, each with different professional degrees. Keeping such variability within specific social services fields in mind, as well as differences among state licensing requirements, a very general breakdown of degrees in the mental health field is shown in Table 1.1, along with their possible corresponding licenses, as well as what careers these professionals might be able to pursue, depending on individual state licensing requirements.

While many professionals working in the social services field engage in comparable work, not all are social workers in the legal sense; thus, when I use the term *social worker*, I am referring to the legal definition and professional distinction of a licensed social worker, indicating either a Bachelor of Social Work (BSW) or an MSW level of education, and likely some level of professional licensure.

In the early 1900s, many of those who worked in the social services field were called social workers; yet, as the social work field continued to professionalize, the title of social worker eventually became reserved for those professionals who had either an undergraduate or a graduate degree in social work from a program accredited by the Council on Social Work Education (CSWE), the body responsible for the accreditation of social work educational programs in the United States.

From the 1960s through the 1980s, the majority of social workers had a BSW and could become a licensed social worker. Currently, most states require that social workers have at least a BSW, but the professional standard is an MSW. Most states also require that practicing social workers be licensed, certified, or credentialed by taking a national examination.

Even with the push toward increasing professionalism, the educational and licensing requirements for social workers may range from state to state, or even from community to community (Rittner & Wodarski, 1999). Issues such as the stance of legislators in a particular state, as well as the need for social workers within high-needs communities, may significantly impact educational and licensing requirements. For instance, communities that have a shortage of social workers—such as in high-crime areas, rural communities, and migrant communities in need of bilingual social workers—often require lower levels of education and may not require any licensing (Gumpert & Saltman, 1998).

Other factors that affect educational and licensing requirements for social workers include federal or state governmental licensing requirements pertaining to certain practice settings, such as the healthcare industry (hospitals, hospices, home healthcare), government child welfare agencies, and public schools, that stipulate the requirement for advanced degrees and licensure and/or certain credentials. For instance, in many states,

Table 1.1   Multiple Discipline Degree Requirements

Degree	Academic Area/Major	License/Credential	Possible Careers
BA/BS	Human Services	BS-BCP	Caseworker, youth worker, residential counselor, behavioral management aide, case management aide, alcohol counselor, adult day care worker, drug abuse counselor, life skills instructor, social service aide, probation officer, child advocate, gerontology aide, juvenile court liaison, group home worker, child abuse worker, crisis intervention counselor, community organizer, social work assistant, psychological aide
BA/BS	Psychology, Sociology	N/A	Same as above, depends on state requirements
BSW	Social Work (program accredited by CSWE)	Basic licensing (LSW) depends on state	Same as above, depends on state requirements
MA/MS	Counseling Psychology	LCP (Licensed Clinical Professional—on graduation)	Private practice, some governmental and social service agencies
30–60 credit hours		LCPC (Licensed Clinical Professional Counselor— ~3,000 postgrad supervised hours)	
MSW	Social Work (program accredited by CSWE)	LSW (on graduation)	Private practice, all governmental and social service agencies (some requiring licensure)
60 credit hours		LCSW (Licensed Clinical Social Worker— ~3,200 postgrad supervised hours)	
PsyD 120 credit hours	Doctor of Psychology	PSY# (Licensed Clinical Psychologist— ~3,500 postgrad supervised hours)	Private practice, many governmental and social service agencies, teaching in some higher education institutions
PhD Psychology	Doctor of Philosophy in Psychology	PSY# (~3,500 postgrad supervised hours)	Private practice, many governmental and social service agencies, teaching in higher education institutions
120 credit hours			

Pearson Education, Inc.

school social workers must have an MSW degree, a social work license issued by the state, and an educational credential in school social work. Additionally, most states require hospice social workers to be licensed social workers, thus requiring either a BSW or an MSW degree. But in Illinois, for instance, the Hospice Program Licensing Act provides that a hospice agency can also employ bereavement counselors who have a bachelor's degree in counseling, psychology, or social work with one year of counseling experience. Some states require child welfare workers to be licensed social workers with an MSW, whereas other states require them to have a master's degree in any related field (i.e., psychology, human services, sociology). In states where there is a significant need for bilingual social workers, such as California, educational requirements may be lowered if the individual is bilingual and has commensurate counseling and/or case management experience. Insurance reimbursement is also driving educational and licensing requirements, with some third-party payers reimbursing for services provided by only those service providers with graduate-level education and state licensure (Beaucar, 2000).

The Association of Social Work Boards (ASWB) is legally responsible for regulating the social work profession, developing and maintaining licensing exams for all states, as well as serving as a central clearinghouse of information on the legal regulation of social work. The ASWB has identified professional standards for the practice of social work and defines by law the requirements for each level of licensure as a social worker. There are four levels of practice that states can legally regulate, each with increasingly difficult written examinations (see Table 1.1), but as shown in Table 1.2, not all states recognize each level of practice.

The CSWE is responsible for accrediting and monitoring social work educational programs in the United States, through the development of educational standards that social work educational programs must meet. The current Educational and Policy Accreditation Standards (EPAS) has shifted to a competency-based standard, using an *outcome performance approach* to demonstrate that the curriculum in social work programs illustrates the integration and application of the identified core competencies in practice with individuals, families, groups, organizations, and communities. What this means is that through the use of an integrative learning model (which focuses on the integration of concepts across the entire curriculum), social work students develop competencies in various social work practice behaviors that are deemed important for all social workers to have mastery in (depending on whether they have a bachelor's or master's degree). (See Box 1.2.)

Every social work educational program must provide a comprehensive plan for how they have designed their *explicit* curriculum, which includes the 10 core competencies (with associated practice behaviors), and field education, which according to the CSWE is social work education's *signature pedagogy* (see Box 1.2), reflecting the importance of connecting what's being learned in the classroom with what's occurring in the real-world practice setting. Social work education programs must also provide comprehensive information on its *implicit* curriculum, which includes the inner workings of the program, such as the program's admissions policies and procedures, academic structure, faculty, and commitment to diversity. CSWE's current EPAS also includes an assessment component, which requires social work educational programs to assess student learning to ensure that its curriculum is meeting the competency standards and thus is successfully preparing social work students for their professional careers.

Assess your comprehension of "Social Workers: Educational Requirements and Professional Standards" by completing this quiz.

Table 1.2   ASWB Levels of License Examinations

ASWB License Level	Description
Bachelor's Exam (formerly called Basic Exam)	BSW from a CSWE-accredited school
Master's Exam (formerly called Intermediate Exam)	MSW from a CSWE-accredited school, with no post-degree experience
Advanced Generalist Organization (formerly called Advanced Exam)	MSW with two years of postmaster's supervised experience
Clinical Exam	MSW with two years of postmaster's direct clinical social work experience

Pearson Education, Inc.

Box 1.2   CSWE: 10 Core Competencies in Practice Behaviors

- 2.1.1—Identify as a Professional Social Worker and Conduct Oneself Accordingly
- 2.1.2—Apply Social Work Ethical Principles to Guide Professional Practice
- 2.1.3—Apply Critical Thinking to Inform and Communicate Professional Judgments
- 2.1.4—Engage Diversity and Difference in Practice
- 2.1.5—Advance Human Rights and Social and Economic Justice
- 2.1.6—Engage in Research-Informed Practice and Practice-Informed Research
- 2.1.7—Apply Knowledge of Human Behavior and the Social Environment
- 2.1.8—Engage in Policy Practice to Advance Social and Economic Well-Being and to Deliver Effective Social Work Services
- 2.1.9—Respond to Contexts That Shape Practice
- 2.1.10—Engage, Assess, Intervene, and Evaluate with Individuals, Families, Groups, Organizations, and Communities (CSWE, 2008).

HOW DO SOCIAL WORKERS PRACTICE AND WHAT DO THEY DO?

Since human beings have walked this planet, people have been trying to figure out what makes them *tick*. If we were to construct a historical time line, we would see that each era tends to embrace a particular philosophy regarding the psychological nature of humans. Were we created in the image of God? Are we inherently good? Are personal problems a product of social oppression, or are individuals responsible for their lot in life? Do we have various levels of consciousness with feelings outside our awareness, motivating us to behave in certain ways? What will make us happy? What leads to our emotional demise? These questions are often left to philosophers and more recently to psychologists, but they also relate very much to social work practice because the view of humankind held by social workers will undoubtedly influence how they both view and help their clients.

One of the most common questions social workers are asked in a job interview is about their *theoretical orientation*. I recall a professor in my graduate program cautioning all students to avoid claiming to be eclectic if asked this question in a job interview, because this was a clear indication to any employer that we had no idea what theoretical orientation we embraced. Essentially what this question is addressing is what theoretical orientation social workers operate from as a foundation. In any mental health clinic, one practitioner might counsel from a psychoanalytic perspective, another from a humanistic perspective, and yet another from a cognitive–behavioral perspective. The theoretical orientation of mental health professionals will serve as a sort of lens through which they view their clients. Depending on the theory, a social worker's theoretical orientation may include certain *underlying assumptions* about human behavior (e.g., what motivates humans to behave in certain ways), *descriptive aspects* (e.g., common experiences of women in middle adulthood), as well as *prescriptive aspects* defining adaptive versus maladaptive behaviors (e.g., is it normal for children to experience separation anxiety in the toddler years? Is adolescent rebellion a normal part of adolescent developmental?).

The Application of Models to Student Work video is a resource that explores social work students' perspectives and attitudes about applying theories in practice. Watch this video and ask yourself if you can relate to what these students have to say. Is the prospect of learning a range of theories and applying them when working with clients daunting to you too?

Social Work, Social Media, and Technology

The Internet, particularly social media, has changed the world in many ways, including how social work is practiced. What are some ways you have used the Internet, particularly social media, to engage in social work, even on an informal level?

Most theoretical orientations will also extend into the clinical or direct practice realm by outlining ways to help people become emotionally healthy, based on some presumption of what caused them to become emotionally unhealthy in the first place. For instance, if a practitioner embraces a psychoanalytic perspective that holds to the assumption that early childhood experiences influence adult motivation to behave in certain manners, then the counseling will likely focus on the client's childhood. If the practitioner embraces a cognitive–behavioral approach, the focus of counseling will likely be on how the client frames and interprets the various occurrences in his or her life.

Theoretical Frameworks Used in Social Work

When considering all the various theories of human behavior, it is essential to remember that culture and history affect what is considered healthy thinking and behavior. Common criticism of many major psychological theories is that they are often based on mores common in Western cultures in developed countries (often referred to as the Global North) and are not necessarily representative or reflective of individuals living in developing or non-Western cultures (often referred to as the Global South). For instance, is it appropriate to apply Freud's psychoanalytic theory of human behavior, which was developed from his work with higher society women in the Victorian era, to individuals of the Masai tribe in Africa? Or is it appropriate to use a theory of human behavior developed during peacetime when working with those who grew up in a time of war? Any theory of human behavior one considers using in relation to understanding the behavior of clients should include a framework addressing many systems, such as culture, historical era, ethnicity, and gender, as well as other systems within which the individual operates. In other words, it is imperative that as a part of any evaluation and assessment, social workers consider environmental elements that may be a part of the client's life.

Social workers are often referred to as *generalists*, implying that their knowledge base is broad and varied. This does not mean that they do not have areas of specialization; in fact, in the past 100 years, social workers have increasingly ventured into practice areas previously reserved for other helping professionals, such as psychologists and professional counselors (Rullo, 2001), and even in non–social work arenas, such as business, politics, and international relations. But many believe that regardless of developing areas of specialization, to be most effective, social workers must be competent in working with a broad range of individuals and a broad range of issues, using a wide range of interventions. A conceptual framework that is most commonly associated with the social work discipline is one that views *clients* within the context of their *environment*, specifically focusing on the *transaction* or relationship between the two.

Several theories capture this conceptual framework, and virtually all are derived from general systems theory, which is based on the premise that various elements in an environment interact with each other, and this interaction (or transaction) has an impact on all elements involved. This has certain implications for the hard sciences, such as ecology and physics, but when applied to the social environment, its implications involve the dynamic and interactive relationship between environmental elements, such as one's family, friends, neighborhood, church, culture, ethnicity, and gender, and individual elements, such as one's thoughts, attitudes, and behavior. Thus, if someone asked you who you were, you might describe yourself as a female who is a college student, married, with two high school–aged children, who attends church on a regular basis. You might further describe yourself as having come from an Italian family with nine brothers and sisters and as a Catholic.

On further questioning, you might explain that your parents are older and you have been attempting to help them find alternate housing that can help them with their extensive medical needs. You might describe the current problems you're having with your teenage daughter, who was recently caught *ditching* school by the truancy officer. Whether you realize it or not, you have shared that you are interacting with the following environments (often called ecosystems): family, friendships, neighborhood, Italian-American culture, church, gender, marriage covenant, adolescence, the medical community, the school system, and the criminal justice system.

Your interaction with each of these systems is influenced by both your expectations of these systems and their expectations of you. For instance, what is expected of you as a college student? What is expected of you as a woman? As a wife? As a Catholic? What about the expectations of you as a married woman who is Catholic? What about the expectations of you as a married woman who is Catholic? What about the expectations of you as a married woman who is Catholic? What about the expectations of your family? As you attempt to focus on your academic studies, do these various systems offer stress or support? If you went to counseling, would it be helpful for the practitioner to understand what it means to be one of 10 children from a Catholic, Italian-American family?

Apply Knowledge of Human Behavior and the Social Environment

Practice Behavior: Utilize conceptual frameworks to guide the processes of assessment, intervention, and evaluation.

Critical Thinking Question: Why is it important for social workers to use theories such as the ecological systems theory to understand the feelings and behavior of clients from marginalized and disenfranchised populations?

This focus on transactional exchange between the individual and social forces is what distinguishes the field of social work from other fields such as psychology and psychiatry, although recently, systems theory has gained increasing attention in these latter disciplines as well. Several theories have been developed to describe the reciprocal relationship between individuals and their environment. The most common are *ecological systems theory, person-in-environment* (PIE), and *eco-systems theory.*

Bronfenbrenner's Ecological Systems Theory

Urie Bronfenbrenner (1979) developed the ecological systems, which categorizes an individual's environment into four expanding spheres, all with increasing levels of intimate interaction with the individual. The microsystem includes the individual and his or her family, the mesosystem (or mezzosystem) includes entities such as one's neighborhood and school, the exosystem includes entities such as the state government, and the macrosystem includes the culture at large. Figure 1.1 illustrates the various systems and describes the nature of interaction with the individual. Again, it is important to remember that the primary principle of Bronfenbrenner's theory is that individuals can best be understood when seen in the context of their relationship with the various systems in their lives. Understanding the nature of these reciprocal relationships will aid in understanding individuals and their thoughts, attitudes and behaviors.

Person-in-Environment

Another theory that is similar in nature to the ecological systems theory is referred to as the person-in-environment, or PIE. The premise of this theory is quite similar to Bronfenbrenner's theory, as it encourages seeing individuals within the context of

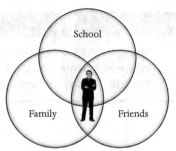

Figure 1.1
Example of Common Eco-Systems
with the Person in the Middle
Source: Pearson Education, Inc.

their environment, both on micro- (i.e., intra- and interpersonal relationships and family dynamics) and on a macro (or societal) level (i.e., the individual is a recently arrived immigrant, who lives in an urban community with significant cultural oppression).

Eco-Systems Theory

Similar to Bronfenbrenner's theory, in eco-systems theory, the various environmental systems are represented by overlapping concentric circles indicating the reciprocal exchange between individuals and their environmental systems. Although there is no official recognition of varying levels of systems (from micro to macro), the basic concept is very similar, and most who embrace this theory understand that there are varying levels of systems, all interacting and thus impacting the person in various ways. It is up to the social worker to strive to understand the transactional and reciprocal nature of these various systems (Meyer, 1988).

It is important to note that these theories do not presume that individuals are necessarily aware of the various systems they operate within, even if they are actively interacting with them. In fact, effective social workers will help their clients increase their personal awareness of the existence of these systems and how they are currently operating within them (i.e., nature of reciprocity). It is through this awareness that clients increase their level of empowerment within their environment and consequently in all aspects of their life.

Case Study 1.1   Evaluating the Environmental Systems

A woman in her forties is feeling rather depressed. She spends her first counseling session describing her fears of her children being killed. She explains how she is so afraid of bullets coming through her walls that she doesn't allow her children to watch television in the living room. She never allows her children to play outside and worries incessantly when they are at school. She admits that she has not slept well in weeks, and she has difficulty feeling anything other than sadness and despair.

Would you consider this woman paranoid? Correctly assessing her does not depend solely on her thinking patterns and behavior, but on the *cultural context* within which her thinking patterns and behavior are situated. If this woman lived in an extremely safe, gate-guarded community where no crimes had been reported in 20 years, then an assessment of some form of paranoia might be appropriate. But what if she lived in a high-crime neighborhood, where *drive-by* shootings were a daily event? What if you learned that her neighbor's children were recently shot and killed while watching television in the living room? Her thinking patterns and behavior do not seem as bizarre when considered within the context or systems in which she is operating.

Social Work Application Activity

[NASW Code of Ethics Guideline: 1.05 Cultural Competence and Social Diversity]	**Using the NASW Code of Ethics located on the NASW national website, and the Ecological Systems and PIE theories, how would you evaluate Case Study 1.1?**

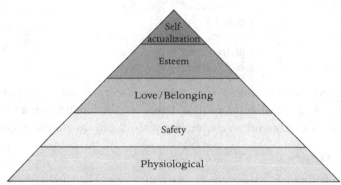

Figure 1.2
Maslow's Hierarchy of Needs
Source: Based on: Maslow, Abraham H.; Frager, Robert D.; Fadiman, James, Motivation and Personality, 3rd Ed., ©1987.

Maslow's Hierarchy of Needs

Another effective model for understanding how many people are motivated to get their needs met was developed by Abraham Maslow. Maslow (1954) created a model focusing on needs motivation. As Figure 1.2 illustrates, Maslow believed that people are motivated to get their most basic physiological needs met first (such as the need for food and oxygen) before they attempt to meet their safety needs (such as the security we find in the stability of our relationships with family and friends). According to Maslow, most people would find it difficult to focus on higher-level needs related to self-esteem or self-actualization when their most basic needs are not being met. Consider people you may know who suffer from low self-esteem and then consider how they might react if a war suddenly broke out and their community was under siege. Maslow's theory suggests that thoughts of low self-esteem would quickly take a backseat as worries about mere survival took hold. Maslow's Hierarchy of Needs can assist social workers in helping clients by recognizing a client's need to prioritize more pressing needs over others.

Assess your comprehension of "How Do Social Workers Practice and What Do They Do?" by completing this quiz.

Summary

This book has been written using an *integrative learning model*; thus, it supports CSWE's EPAS approach to social work education by presenting information in such a way that basic concepts and theories are explored within the context of real-world social work practice settings. This approach allows social work students to more easily see how what they are learning in the classroom applies in the field. For instance, the nature of intervention is often dependent on the specific practice setting where the social worker is providing service, particularly since social work practice settings most often focus on particular social problems (e.g., domestic violence, homelessness, etc.). Thus, how clients and client systems are helped to improve their personal and social functioning (through the application of concepts and theories) will look very different depending on whether services are provided in a school setting, a hospice, a domestic violence shelter, or a prison, each of which exerts different kinds of influence on clients and client systems.

It would be difficult to present an exhaustive list of practice settings due to the broad and often very general nature of social services, and social service practice settings can be categorized in many different ways, including based on social issues or problems (i.e., domestic violence, homelessness), or by target population (i.e., older adults, the chronically mentally ill, children), or even by the area of specialization (i.e., grief and loss, marriage and family, trauma). Regardless of the manner in which practice settings are categorized, there is bound to be some overlap because one area of practice could conceivably be included within another field, and some practice settings could also be considered areas of specialization. For instance, there are religiously affiliated hospices (medical social work and faith-based practice),

some social workers work with both survivors of domestic violence (victim advocacy) and batterers (forensic social work), and adoption is sometimes considered a practice setting unto itself and sometimes it is included under the umbrella of child welfare.

For the purposes of this text, basic concepts and theories will be explored through the application of social work roles and functions within the context of social work within the context of particular social work practice settings general enough to cover as many settings as possible within the field of social work, but narrow enough to be descriptively meaningful. The social work settings and social workers who work in them will be examined by exploring the history of the practice setting and related social problems, the types of clients and client systems most commonly affected, the psychosocial issues most commonly encountered, common modes and types of service delivery, and the most common generalist intervention strategies used within the following practice settings: child welfare, adolescents, older adults, mental health, housing and homelessness, healthcare and hospice, substance abuse, schools, faith-based agencies, violence, victim advocacy and corrections, macropractice, and international social work.

Recall what you learned in this chapter by completing the Chapter Review.

The Evolution of Social Welfare Policy

Effect on Social Work Practice

THE HISTORY OF SOCIAL WELFARE POLICY AND PROVISION IN EUROPE AND THE UNITED STATES

Helping others in need can be traced back to ancient times, but the social work profession in its current context has historic roots dating back to at least the late 1800s. The practice of social work is wholly influenced by social welfare policy, and to be truly effective in helping the poor and indigent, it is essential that all social workers gain a level of social and cultural objectivity so that they can more fully understand both how social welfare policy and legislation has evolved over the years and how the complex relationship between such social welfare policy and legislation and the current prevailing attitudes toward the poor influence one another.

It would be naïve to assume that any current trends in how the poor are perceived and treated developed in a vacuum; thus, a general understanding of the roots of current social welfare legislation, policy, and attitudinal trends is essential to any practicing social worker. The development of the social welfare system in the United States was very much influenced by England's social welfare system; therefore, it is important to understand the evolution of how the poor were treated in England to fully understand how social welfare policy has developed within the United States.

Despite popular contention that social welfare policy practice is evidence based, objective, and free of ideological bias, significant evidence exists indicating that both historic and current economic policy practices are solidly interwoven with moral and religious philosophy, reflecting the cultural mores of the times within a given society (Hausman & McPherson, 2006). Essentially, social policy, particularly policy addressing the social welfare of its citizenry, often reflects dominant philosophical movements and themes, including religious and societal moral codes as well as beliefs about the causes of poverty and the various reasons poverty afflicts certain individuals and populations, and why other individuals and populations do not struggle with poverty on a collective basis (see Box 2.1).

The Feudal System of the Middle Ages

A good place to begin this exploration is England's Middle Ages (around the 11th century), where a system called *feudalism* prevailed as a social structure that also served as a sort of social welfare system. This system of legal and military customs prevailed as England's primary manner of caring for the poor. Under this elitist system, privileged and wealthy landowners called lords would parcel off small sections of their land, which would then be farmed by peasants, also called serfs. Many policy experts frame the feudal system as a harsh but effective method for controlling poverty. However, it has also been characterized as a governmentally imposed form of servitude, since individuals became serfs through both racial and economic discrimination and were commonly born into serfdom with little hope of ever escaping. Serfs were considered the legal property of

---

Box 2.1   Understanding the Social Phenomenon of White Privilege

White privilege is a social phenomenon where Caucasian members of society enjoy a distinct advantage over members of other ethnic groups. White privilege is defined as "unearned advantages of being white in a racially stratified society" and an expression of institutionalized power (Pinterits, Poteat, & Spanierman, 2009, p. 417). White privilege is something that most Caucasians do not acknowledge, leading many of those who benefit from this advantage to take personal credit for whatever they gain through their privilege (Neville, Worthington, & Spanierman, 2001). Unfortunately, this also means that many Caucasians may blame those from groups that do not benefit from privilege for not being as successful. Yet, due to various forms of racial discrimination, it has typically been white people who have benefited most from the best that life has to offer—gaining access into the best educational systems (or being the only ones to obtain an education at all), the best jobs, and the best neighborhoods. Even if white privilege were to end, the cumulative benefit of years of advantage would continue well into the future, just as the negative consequences of years of social exclusion will continue to negatively affect groups who have not benefited from white privilege.

Pearson Education, Inc.

their lord; thus, although lords were required to provide for the care and support of serfs in exchange for farming their land, the lords had complete control over their serfs and could sell them or give them away as they deemed fit (Stephenson, 1943; Trattner, 1998).

Despite the seeming harshness of this system, it did provide insurance against many of the social hazards associated with being poor. It was also complemented by the prevailing belief that there was no shame in poverty. In fact, the commonly held societal more during medieval times was that poverty within society was unavoidable, and the poor were a necessary component of society, in that poverty gave an opportunity to the rich to show their grace and goodwill through the giving of alms to those less fortunate than themselves. Thus, caring for the poor was perceived as a noble duty that rested on the shoulders of all those who were able-bodied. Also, the poor were necessary because without them there would be no servants for the ruling class.

Poor Laws of England

Many economic and environmental conditions led to the eventual phasing out of the traditional feudal system in the mid-14th century to the mid-16th century (1350 through 1550), including several natural disasters, such as massive crop failures, the bubonic plague, and mass urbanization spawned by the Industrial Revolution. The increased demand for factory wage labor in the cities ultimately led to droves of individuals moving to the city to work in factories. This trend, coupled with the decline of the feudal system and the diminishing influence of the church with its complex and effective framework of charitable provision, led to the need for a complete overhaul of the social welfare system in England. Thus, although mass urbanization may have led to freedom from serfdom for the poorest members of English society, it also generated a vacuum in how poverty was managed, creating the necessity for the development of England's earliest poor laws (Trattner, 1998).

Although these social changes were gradual, they led to a dramatic shift not only in how poverty was managed but also how it was perceived. It is always easier to have a gracious attitude and extend a helping hand to someone we know, but such graciousness becomes challenging when the poor are no longer extended family and longtime neighbors, whose personal circumstances are well known; rather they are nameless, faceless strangers living en masse, often from different countries, speaking different languages, and behaving in very different manners (Martin, 2012; Trattner, 1998). The increasingly impersonal nature of caring for the poor, as well as the complexity of life in cities, ultimately led to the belief that the incorporation of punitive measures into relief policy was needed to control begging, vagrancy, and increased crime in the cities. In response, England passed several relief laws during the mid-1500s through the early 1600s, which set forth guidelines for dealing with the poor. England's Relief Act of 1536 placed responsibility for dealing with the poor at the local level and reflected a complete intolerance of idleness. Local law enforcement scoured the cities in search of beggars and vagrants, and once found, a determination was made as to whether they were true victims of poverty (the worthy poor) or legally defined vagrants (the unworthy poor). Legislative guidelines typically stipulated that only pregnant women, individuals who were extremely ill and unable to work, or any person over the age of 60 were considered justifiably poor; thus, they were treated more leniently, including receiving governmental authorization to beg (typically in the form of a letter of authorization). In some cases, the poor were given other forms of sustenance in addition to being allowed to beg. If an able-bodied person was found to be unemployed, they were considered vagrant, and were punished by whippings, naked parading through the streets, being returned to the town of their birth, or incarceration. Repeat offenders were often subjected to having an ear cut off or were even put to death (Beier, 1974; Birtles, 1999).

Clearly, no sympathy was shown to individuals, male or female, who were deemed capable of working but found themselves without a job or any means of support, and little consideration was given to economic difficulties or what is now termed the *cycle of poverty*. Also, little sympathy was extended to children, particularly adolescents who were found begging, and district officials often took these children into custody, placing them into apprenticeship programs, which were later considered to be little different from child slavery. Thus, vagrancy was handled as a criminal matter, and the local authorities provided sustenance only for those deemed unable to work (Trattner, 1998). The earlier English Poor Laws laid the foundation for the Elizabethan Poor Laws of 1601, which acted as a foundation for U.S. social welfare policy.

The Elizabethan Poor Laws

The Elizabethan Poor Laws of 1601 were an organized merging of England's earlier, sometimes conflicting and erratic social welfare legislation, which not only brought order and organization to England's poor laws but also served as the foundation for such legislation in colonial America. Thus, rather than viewing the Elizabethan Poor Laws of 1601 as a single act, it is more appropriate to view it as an evolution of legal acts in a series of previous acts. The Elizabethan Poor Laws of 1601 served to set the stage for poor relief for several centuries and is still considered foundational in contemporary social welfare policy in both England and the United States. This Act established three driving principles as the foundation for social legislation: the belief that the primary responsibility for provision lay with one's family, that poor relief should be handled at the local level, and finally, that individuals should not be allowed to move to a new community if they were unable to provide for themselves financially. Charity included both *indoor* and *outdoor* relief, with the former referring to assistance provided in almshouses and other institutionalized settings and the latter referring to services provided in the home environment of the person in need, including the delivery of food baskets and/or medicines.

It was quite common for community members to bring charges against others if it could be proven that they had moved into the district within the past 40 days and had no means to support themselves. Such individuals would be charged as vagrants by the local officials and returned to their home districts. The underlying notion was that local parishes didn't mind supporting those individuals who had fallen on hard times after years of paying taxes, but they didn't want to be forced to support strangers who came to their district for the sole purpose of receiving aid. Elements of these residency requirements can be found among current U.S. welfare policy; in fact, most welfare reform legislative bills today contain residency requirement language.

Engage in Policy Practice to Advance Social and Economic Well-Being and to Deliver Effective Social Work Services

Practice Behavior: Analyze, formulate, and advocate for policies that advance social well-being.

Critical Thinking Question: Jane Addams believed that advocacy was most effective when advocates lived within the communities they served. Describe how this philosophy influenced the model of social work that serves as a foundation for the profession to this day and how it enables social workers today to be better advocates for their clients.

English colonization of North America began around the 16th century and continued throughout the 17th century. Life in colonial America not only offered tremendous opportunity but also presented significant hardship related to life on the frontier. Many immigrants were quite poor to begin with, and the long and difficult ocean voyage to the New World often left them unprepared for the rigors of life in the United States. Because there was no existing infrastructure in the original 13 colonies (such as religious monasteries or other social welfare programs), relief for the poor consisted primarily of mutual kindness, family support, and distant help from the motherland. Self-sufficiency was a must, and life was not easy on the frontier. But as the population increased within the colonies, the need arose for a more organized form of relief, and it makes sense that the colonies would rely on the English Poor Laws. The colonies adopted not only the social welfare legislation of England but also much of the perceptions of and attitudes about the poor and indigent as well.

Charity Organization Society Movement in the United States

The Charity Organization Society (COS), often considered the genesis of the social work movement, marked one of the first organized efforts within the United States to provide charity to the poor. The COS movement started in about 1870 in response to frustration with the current welfare system that was less of a system and more of a disorganized and often chaotic practice of almsgiving. The COS movement itself was started by a pastor, Rev. S. Humphreys Gurteen, who believed that it was the duty of good Christians everywhere to provide an organized and systematic way of addressing the plight of the poor. Gurteen and his colleagues strongly believed that the indiscriminate giving of alms by many of the relief agencies of that time encouraged fraud and abuse, which in turn encouraged laziness on the part of those who were beneficiaries of relief.

The COS philosophy was built on the concept of voluntary coordination, in which various charities worked within a larger network-coordinating services delivered to the local community. The first COS was created in New York in 1877, and the concept quickly spread to large cities across the nation. Soon, most large cities had at least one COS serving the community, acting as an umbrella organization for smaller agencies and churches offering charity services to the community. The COS practiced what was called *scientific charity*, which embraced social Darwinist philosophies of *intelligent giving* and embraced the notion that charity should work with natural selection, not against it (Gettleman, 1963). A primary motivation of the COS movement was to coordinate charity efforts by serving as an umbrella organization for the myriad of independent and private charities, thus maximizing the best use of material relief (Schlabach, 1969). Outdoor relief, such as cash assistance or indiscriminate giving, was highly discouraged and actually considered evil based on the longstanding belief that such assistance encouraged dependence and laziness, while discouraging self-sufficiency, ultimately leading to increased poverty (Gettleman, 1963; Kusmer, 1973).

In this respect, those involved in the COS movement embraced the concepts of the *unworthy versus the worthy poor*, and it was their goal to determine which category aid recipients fell into and then prescribe what each recipient actually needed. Material aid was provided for those who would not abuse it and other services for those who would. To accomplish this goal, the COSs employed *friendly visitors*, an early version of caseworkers, who visited the homes of aid applicants and attempted to diagnose the reason for their poverty and, if possible, develop a case plan to authentically alleviate their suffering (Trattner, 1998).

A social hierarchy was reflected in the philosophical motivation of the COS leaders, often the community's most wealthy members, who agreed to provide charity to the poor depending on the poor remembering "his place of inferiority" (Gettleman, 1963, p. 319). Yet even the deserving poor did not escape the demands of the Protestant work ethic, which stressed the importance of hard work in order to achieve salvation, or the fatalism of social Darwinism, both of which were deeply imbedded in the COS culture. These philosophical values were clearly reflected in a speech given by Josephine Shaw Lowell, a leader in the COS movement, at a charity conference held in 1895: "Even the widow with little children, if she finds that everything is made easy for her, may lose her energy, may even, by being relieved of anxiety for them, lose her love for the children" (cited in Gettleman, 1963, p. 323). The unworthy poor were often provided with indoor relief only, in the form of placement in an almshouse, and, according to COS leaders, should be allowed to perish according to natural selection. Many in the COS movement argued that to provide charity to those destined to perish was immoral and unkind because it only prolonged their suffering to no good end for either the poor or society (Gettleman, 1963).

Mary Richmond, the general secretary of the Baltimore COS, is often associated with the COS movement because of her passion for social advocacy and social reform. Richmond believed that charities could employ both good economics and compassionate giving at the same time. She became well known for increasing public awareness of the COS movement and for her fund-raising efforts. Her compassion for the poor was the likely result of her own experience with poverty. Orphaned at the age of two and later left by an aunt to fend for herself in New York when she was only 17 years old, she no doubt understood the social components of poverty, and how devastating it could be to one's life. Richmond is also credited for developing the early conception of casework, having written several books and articles on the service delivery model. As a result, the concept of the friendly visitor grew and the debate about material relief continued. Many argued that the best opportunity to truly effect change in those suffering from poverty was through the services of the friendly visitor who could help identify and address any barriers to self-sufficiency (Kusmer, 1973).

Despite the general success of the COS movement, its philosophy was influenced by the Reformation theology that anyone who worked hard enough would be blessed and could rise from the depths of poverty. The country would later realize that it was naïve to presume that poverty was primarily caused by individual failure and that material relief would lead to moral decline. The very hard lesson came during the Depression era—a lesson learned long ago by immigrants and ethnic minorities—that sometimes conditions exist that are beyond an individual's control and that create immovable barriers to self-sufficiency, leading to poverty and destitution.

Jane Addams and the Settlement House Movement

Not all social welfare movements within the United States reflected these harsh philosophical approaches, though. Jane Addams, an advocate for social reform, was responsible for beginning the U.S. settlement house movement in the late 1800s. Addams's social action efforts reflected a far more compassionate approach to poverty alleviation and social inequity. She started the Hull House settlement house in Chicago as an alternative to the more religiously oriented charity organizations, which she perceived as "heartless and overly concerned with efficiency and rooting out of fraud" (Schneiderhan, 2008, p. 3). Addams used a relational model of poverty alleviation based on the belief that the problems of poverty and disadvantage resulted from problems within society, not idleness and moral deficiency (Lundblad, 1995). She advocated for changes within the social structure of society that created barriers to lateral contribution of all members of society, which she viewed as an essential aspect of a democracy (Hamington, 2005; Martin, 2012). In fact, the opening of the first settlement house in the United States was considered the beginning of one of the most significant social movements in U.S. history (Commager, 1961, as cited in Lundblad, 1995).

Addams was born in Cedarville, Illinois, in 1860. She was raised in an upper-class home where higher education and philanthropy were highly valued. Addams greatly admired her father, who encouraged her to pursue an education at a time when women were primarily encouraged to pursue only marriage and motherhood. She graduated from Rockford Female Seminary in 1881, the same year her father died. After her father's death, Addams entered Woman's Medical College in Pennsylvania, but dropped out because of chronic illness. She had become quite passionate about the plight of immigrants in the United States, but due to her poor health and the societal limits placed on women during that era, she did not believe that she had a role in social advocacy.

The United States experienced another significant wave of immigration in the 19th and early 20th centuries (between 1860 and 1910), with 23 million people emigrating from Europe, including Eastern Europe. Many of these immigrants were from non-English-speaking countries, such as Italy, Poland, Russia, and Serbia, did not speak English, and were very poor. Unable to obtain work in the skilled labor force, many immigrants were forced to live in subhuman conditions, crammed together with several other families in deplorable tenements in large urban areas. For instance, New York's Lower East Side had 330,000 inhabitants per square mile (Trattner, 1998). With no labor laws for protection, racial discrimination and a variety of employment abuses were common, including extremely low wages, unsafe working conditions, and child labor. Poor families, particularly non-English-speaking families, had little recourse, and their mere survival depended on their coerced cooperation.

Jane Addams is considered the 'mother of social work' due to her tireless advocacy work.

LIBRARY OF CONGRESS

Addams was aware of these conditions because of her father's political involvement, but she was not sure how to respond. Despondent after her father's death and her failure in medical school, as well as over her chronic medical problems, Addams took an extended trip with friends to Europe, where among other activities, she visited Toynbee Hall, England's response to poverty and other social problems. Toynbee Hall was a settlement house, which was essentially a neighborhood welfare institution in an urban slum area, where trained workers endeavored to improve social conditions, particularly by providing community services and promoting neighborly cooperation.

This concept was revolutionary, in that in its attempt to improve conditions through the promotion of social and economic reform, it actually called for the settlement house workers to reside in the home alongside the immigrant families they helped. In addition to providing a safe, clean home, settlement houses also provided comprehensive care, such as assistance with food, healthcare, English language lessons, child care, and general advocacy. The settlement house movement was different from the traditional charity organizations, in that it had as its goal the mission of no longer distinguishing between the worthy and unworthy poor.

Addams returned home convinced that it was her duty to do something similar in the United States, and with the donation of a building in Chicago, Hull House became the United States's first settlement house in 1889.

Addams and her colleagues lived in the settlement house, in the middle of what was considered a bad neighborhood in Chicago, offering services targeting the underlying causes of poverty such as unfair labor practices, the exploitation of non-English-speaking immigrants, and child labor. Services ranged from child care to education classes. Hull House became the social center for all activities in the neighborhood and even offered residents an opportunity to socialize in the residents' café.

Make a cyber-visit to The Hull House Museum by going to the University of Illinois at Chicago website and navigating to the museum website.

Addams's influence on American social policy was significant, in that it represented a shift away from the fatalistic and metaphysical philosophies of social Darwinism, marking recognition of the need for social change within society to remove barriers to upward mobility and optimal functioning (Martin, 2012). Addams and her counterparts were committed to viewing all individuals equally, to be treated with respect and dignity. She clearly saw societal conditions and the hardship of immigration as the primary cause of poverty, not necessarily one's own moral failing. Focus was placed on making changes in the community, and social inequality was perceived as the manifestation of exploitation, with social egalitarianism perceived as not just desirable but also achievable (Lundblad, 1995; Martin, 2012).

The settlement house movement radically transformed not only how the poor were cared for but also how they were perceived by the majority population. Now, immigrants had a safe place to live, a voice to advocate for them, and a way to better integrate into American society, so that their dream of obtaining a better life for themselves and their children could actually be realized. Addams also lobbied tirelessly for the passage of child labor laws and other legislation that would protect the working-class poor, who were often exploited in factories with sweatshop conditions. She also worked alongside Ida B. Wells, an African American reformer, confronting racial inequality in the United States, such as the extrajudicial lynching of black men.

Although there are no working settlement houses today, the prevailing concept espoused by this model involves recognition of the need for a holistic approach to poverty alleviation that encompasses challenges to social structures, and not just a focus on individual behavioral management. Elements of this concept can still be seen in the current U.S. social welfare system, as well as the current mental healthcare system, yet unfortunately there would be far more future challenges to any philosophical approach to poverty alleviation that considers social inequality as a core reason for poverty, rather than personal moral failing. Thus, despite the overall success of the settlement house movement and the particular success of Addams with regard to achieving social reform in a variety of arenas, the influences of Calvinism, particularly the Protestant work ethic and social Darwinism remained strong, experiencing cyclical decline only during difficult economic times or civil unrest (as experienced in the 1960s).

The New Deal and the Social Security Act of 1935

In 1929 the stock market crashed, leading to a series of economic crises that the United States had never before experienced. For the first time in modern U.S. history, large segments of the middle-class population were unemployed, and within a very short time, thousands of people who had once enjoyed secure lives were without jobs, homes, and even food. This served as a wake-up call for social reformers, many of whom had abandoned their earlier commitment to social activism. In response, many within the social service and advocacy fields started pushing President Hoover to develop the country's first federal system of social welfare.

Hoover was resistant, though, fearing that federal social welfare programs would create dependency and displace private and local charities. He wanted to allow time for democracy and capitalism to self-correct before intervening with broad entitlement programs. But much of the country's population, including many who were literally starving, apparently did not agree, and in 1933, Hoover lost his bid for reelection, and Franklin D. Roosevelt was elected as president.

Roosevelt immediately set about to create dramatic changes in federal policy with regard to social welfare, promising a *New Deal* to the country, where a minimum standard of living was seen as a right, not a privilege. Within his first 100 days in office, Roosevelt passed 13 Acts, including the Civil Works Administration (sometimes referred to as the CWA), which provided over a million temporary jobs to the unemployed; the Federal Emergency Relief Act, which provided direct aid and food to the unemployed; and the Civilian Conservation Core (CCC), which put thousands of young men aged 18 to 25 to work in reforestation and other conservation programs. Yet, as progressive as Roosevelt was, and as compassionate as the country had become due to the realization that poverty could strike anyone, racism was still rampant, as illustrated by Roosevelt placing a 10 percent limit on the enrollment of black men in the CCC program (Trattner, 1998).

By far the most famous of all programs in the *New Deal* and *Great Society* programs were those created in response to the Social Security Act of 1935, which, among other things, created old-age pensions for workers, unemployment compensation, and Aid to Dependent Mothers, Children, and the Blind and Disabled. In total, Roosevelt created 15 federal programs as a part of the New Deal, some of which remain and some of which were dismantled once the crisis of the Great Depression subsided. Although some claim that the New Deal was not good for the country in the long run, it did pull the country out of the Depression, and it provided relief for millions of Americans who may have literally starved had the federal government not stepped in when it did. Programs such as the Federal Deposit Insurance Corporation (FDIC), which provided insurance for bank deposits, helped to instill a sense of confidence in the banking system once again, and the development of the Securities and Exchange Committee (SEC), which regulates the stock market, helped to ensure that a crash similar to the one in 1929 would be unlikely to occur again. In later times, though, the dismantling of some post-Depression financial regulations would contribute to yet another devastating economic downturn—perhaps not as severe as the Great Depression, but more serious and long-lasting than any other recession experienced in the U.S. post–Depression era, particularly because of its global consequences.

> Assess your comprehension of "The History of Social Welfare Policy and Provision in Europe and the United States" by completing this quiz.

INFLUENCES OF AFRICAN AMERICAN SOCIAL WORKERS

A review of the historical elements influencing the development of the social work field would be remiss if the influences of African Americans reformers, particularly African American women in the last part of the 19th century, weren't explored. Black activists had a significant influence on the development of social justice and social work, particularly in the South, filling the vacuum left by a racist society that often created barriers to service in the black community in earlier eras.

Ida B. Wells was an African American reformer and social activist whose campaign against racial oppression and inequity laid the foundation for the civil rights movement of the 1960s. Wells was born in 1862 to parents who were slaves in rural Mississippi, and although her parents were ultimately freed, Wells's life was never free from the crushing effects of severe racial prejudice and discrimination. She was orphaned at the age of 16, and went on to raise her five younger siblings. This experience not only forced her to grow up quickly but also seemed to serve as a springboard for her subsequent advocacy against racial injustice. In Wells's early advocacy career, she was the owner of a black newspaper (the only one of its kind) called *Free Speech*, where she consistently wrote about matters of racial oppression and inequity, including the vast amount of socially sanctioned crimes committed against blacks (Hamington, 2005).

The **African American Women and the Struggle for Civil Rights** video is a resource that provides an overview of the role of African American women in the fight for racial equality in the United States. After watching this video, consider how the actions of these women influenced and contributed to the field of social work.

The indiscriminate lynching of black men was prevalent in the South during Wells's lifetime, and was an issue that Wells became quite passionate about. Black men were commonly perceived as a threat on many levels, and there was virtually no protection of their personal, political, or social rights. The black man's reputation as an angry rapist was endemic in white society, and many speeches were given and articles written by white community members (including clergy) about this "allegedly growing problem". For example, an article published in the mainstream newspaper in the South, the *Commercial*, entitled "More Rapes More Lynchings," cites the black man's alleged penchant for raping white women, stating:

> The generation of Negroes which have grown up since the war have lost in large measure the traditional and wholesome awe of the white race which kept the Negroes in subjection. . . . There is no longer a restraint upon the brute passion of the Negro. . . . The facts of the crime appear to appeal more to the Negro's lustful imagination than the facts of the punishment do to his fears. He sets aside all fear of death in any form when opportunity is found for the gratification of his bestial desires. (Davidson, 2008, p. 154)

Wells wrote extensively on the subject of the "myth of the angry black man," and the myth that all black men raped white women (a common excuse used to justify the lynching of black men) (Hamington, 2005). She challenged the growing sentiment in white communities that black men, as a race, were growing more aggressive and 'lustful' of white women, which she believed was prompted in part by the increasing number of biracial couples. The response to Wells's articles was swift and harsh. A group of white men surrounded her newspaper building with the intention of lynching her, but when they could not find her, they burned down her business instead (Davidson, 2008).

Although this act of revenge essentially stopped her newspaper career, what it really did was motivate Wells even further. After the burning down of her business, Wells left the South and moved to Chicago, where she continued to wage a fierce anti-lynching campaign, often coordinating efforts with Jane Addams. She wrote numerous books and articles on racial inequality, challenging

Identify as a Professional Social Worker and Conduct Oneself Accordingly

Practice Behavior: Advocate for Client Access to the Services of Social Work

Critical Thinking Question: Historically, there have been many influential African American social workers who contributed significantly to the black community, as well as to the development of the social work professionally as a whole. What was the initial motivation that made their grassroots advocacy necessary? Are any of these dynamics still at play in contemporary society, and how can these lessons of the past inform social workers in their perceptions of and advocacy for ethnic minority populations in need?

socially entrenched notions that all black men were angry and violent sexual predators (Hamington, 2005). Wells and Addams worked as colleagues, coordinating their social justice advocacy efforts fighting for civil rights. Together, they ran the Chicago Association for the Advancement of Colored People and worked collectively on a variety of projects, including fighting against racial segregation in schools (Martin, 2012).

Many other key African American social welfare reformers made significant advances in the social work field, particularly with regard to confronting the disenfranchisement and marginalization of African Americans within U.S. society. In the absence of mainstream social work within this population, African American social welfare reformers operated as a tight community, developing close relationships with each other, even though many of them were spread across the United States. Because racism excluded African Americans from receiving many services, including educational opportunities and health services, many early social welfare reformers focused on these two areas, developing 'Negro schools' and healthcare facilities. One such reformer was Modjeska Simkins, who developed healthcare programs for the black community focusing on everything from infant mortality to tuberculosis. Another creative example of social work in the face of extreme opposition was the work of the black sorority Alpha Kappa Alpha, whose members were determined to provide health care services to sharecroppers in Mississippi. When the white community refused to rent them office space, they offered the health care services from cars (Gordon, 1991).

Explore the role of black social work pioneers by going to the National Association of Black Social Workers website.

Other black women who significantly influenced social welfare reform include Anna Cooper, who pushed for increased educational opportunities for blacks, and Jane Hunter, who formed the first black Young Women's Christian Association (YWCA) (Gordon, 1991). Although often unreported and undervalued, African American social welfare reformers not only assisted their own communities but helped the broader community as well by modeling the power of networking and relentlessly pursuing social justice for all, particularly for those who are the subject of social oppression and discrimination.

Assess your comprehension of "Influences of African American Social Workers" by completing this quiz.

GAY RIGHTS: FROM MARRIAGE EQUALITY TO "DON'T ASK, DON'T TELL" REPEAL

Ethnic minorities, women, and immigrants are not the only groups in U.S. society to be used as scapegoats, oppressed and marginalized. The gay community, typically referred to as the LGBTQ (lesbian, gay, bisexual, transgendered, and questioning and/or queer), has long been a marginalized group in the United States (as well as in most countries in the world). Members of the LGBTQ community are often victims of hate crimes, often solely because of their sexual orientation. For years this community has been excluded from many of the social welfare laws designed to protect disenfranchised and socially excluded groups. Yet, in the past three decades, several LGBTQ advocacy organizations, such as the Gay & Lesbian Alliance Against Defamation (GLAAD), have become increasingly vocal about the right of the LGBTQ community to live openly and enjoy the same rights and protections as heterosexuals without fear of reprisal. The specific issues GLAAD has advocated for include the right to be included as a specially protected group in hate crimes legislation, the right of same-sex partners to legally marry (often referred to as marriage equality), and the right to serve openly in the military.

Despite strong opposition from social conservative groups, the LGBTQ community has experienced recent success in response to their efforts. In 2009 President Obama signed into law the Matthew Shepard and James Byrd, Jr. Hate Crimes Prevention Act, which expanded existing hate crime legislation to include crimes committed against individuals based on perceived gender, sexual orientation, and gender identity. Marriage equality is currently a battle fought on both the federal and state levels. In 1996 the Defense of Marriage Act was passed, which defined marriage on a federal level as a union between one man and one woman. Yet many states have now passed laws legalizing same-sex marriage.

Arguments for same-sex marriage are typically based on rights of equality (see Box 2.2). Arguments against same-sex marriages are often based on conservative or religious values that hold same-sex partnerships as sinful and unnatural, and define traditional marriage as being between a man and a woman. There also appears to be a general fear that the normalization of same-sex marriage will lead to the lowering of moral standards in a variety of respects throughout society. Yet advocates of same-sex marriage confront religious arguments by citing research that disputes allegation that same-sex marriage will somehow dilute *traditional* marriage or harm children. They also cite the increasing acceptance among U.S. citizens of same-sex marriage and of same-sex partnerships in general. For instance, according to a series of Gallup polls, in 2009, 63 percent of the U.S. population surveyed stated that they believed that same-sex couples should be able to marry or have a legal civil union, compared to 55 percent in 2004.

Another area of success for the LGBTQ population involves the right to serve in the U.S. military openly. Historically, gays and lesbians were systematically discharged from the military if their sexual orientation was discovered. In December 1993, in response to mounting pressure to change this policy, the Clinton administration compromised by implementing *Don't Ask, Don't Tell* (DADT), an official policy of the U.S. government

---

Identify as a Professional Social Worker and Conduct Oneself Accordingly

Practice Behavior: Advocate for client access to the services of social work.

Critical Thinking Question: How can understanding the history of discrimination and marginalization of the LGBTQ population inform social workers' advocacy on behalf of this population today? If a social worker doesn't agree with the equality movement due to religious beliefs, is it okay not to advocate for LGBTQ populations' access to social work services? Why or why not?

Get updates on the most recent news about marriage equality and other contemporary LGBT issues at the GLAAD website.

Box 2.2   In Defense of Marriage Equality

The GLAAD website lists several protections that marriage offers that are currently unavailable to the LGBTQ population in same-sex partnerships.

- automatic inheritance
- child custody/parenting/adoption rights
- hospital visitation
- medical decision-making power
- standing to sue for wrongful death of a spouse
- divorce protections
- spousal/child support
- access to family insurance policies
- exemption from property tax upon death of a spouse
- immunity from being forced to testify against one's spouse
- domestic violence protections, and more. (GLAAD, 2010, p. 7)

Reprinted by permission from GLAAD. GLAAD Media Reference Guide - In Focus: Marriage, Copyright 2014

that prohibited the military from discriminating against gay and lesbian military personnel as long as they kept their sexual orientation a secret. In other words, military personnel could no longer investigate the sexual orientation of those serving in the military, but if a member of the military admitted to being a gay or lesbian, he or she could legally be discharged from the military. DADT was repealed by Congress in December 2010 pending review by military leadership who were to determine the effect on military readiness, but in July 2011, a federal court of appeals ruling barred further enforcement of the policy, and it was officially repealed by President Obama in September 2011. In May 2012 President Obama officially declared his support for marriage equality,

> **Assess your comprehension of "Gay Rights: From Marriage Equality to 'Don't Ask, Don't Tell' Repeal" by completing this quiz.**

citing his daughters' friends with same-sex parents, and his recognition that he could not defend a position that would prohibit them from having the same right to legally marry as heterosexual parents. Achievements by the LGBTQ population seem to illustrate a movement toward greater acceptance of what some call *alternative lifestyles*, yet there remains considerable resistance to the inclusion of same-sex partnerships into mainstream United States, particularly among social conservatives.

WELFARE REFORM AND THE EMERGENCE OF NEOLIBERAL ECONOMIC POLICIES

A resurgence of earlier negative sentiments toward the poor and their plight began in the mid-1970s, peaking in the 1990s, perhaps in response to increased economic prosperity within mainstream United States. This increased negative attitude toward the poor is reflected in several studies and national public opinion surveys that reflected the general belief that the poor were to blame for their situation. For instance, a national survey conducted in 1975 found that the majority of those living in the United States attributed poverty to personal failures, such as having a poor work ethic, poor money management skills, a lack of any special talent that might translate into a positive contribution to society, and low personal moral values. Those questioned ranked social forces, such as racism, poor schools, and the lack of sufficient employment, the lowest of all possible causes of poverty (Feagin, 1975).

Ronald Reagan capitalized on this negative sentiment toward the poor during the 1976 presidential campaign when he based his platform in large part on welfare reform. In several of Reagan's speeches, he cited the story of a woman from the South Side of Chicago who was arrested for committing egregious welfare fraud.

> **For more information on the myth of the welfare queen, go to the NPR website and search for "The Truth Behind the Lies of the Original 'Welfare Queen'."**

While Reagan never mentioned the woman's race, the context of the story as well as the reference to the South Side of Chicago (a primarily black community) made it clear that he was referring to an African American woman on welfare—thus matching the common stereotype of welfare users (and abusers) (Krugman, 2007). And with that, the enduring myth of the *welfare queen* was born.

Journalist David Zucchino attempted to debunk the myth of the welfare queen in his exposé on the reality of being a mother on welfare, but later stated in his book, *The Myth of the Welfare Queen*, that the image of the African American woman who drove a Cadillac while collecting welfare illegally was so imbedded in American culture that it was impossible to debunk the myth, even though the facts do not back up the myth (Zucchino, 1999). Krugman (2007) also cites how politicians have used the myth of the welfare queen to reduce sympathy for the poor and gain public support for welfare cuts ever since, arguing that while covert, such images clearly play on negative racial stereotypes. They also play on the common belief in the United States that those who receive welfare benefits are poor due to immoral behavior and a lack of motivation to work.

More recent surveys conducted in the mid-1990s revealed an increase in the tendency to blame the poor for their poverty (Weaver, Shapiro, & Jacobs, 1995), even though a considerable body of research points to social and structural issues as the primary cause of poverty, such as shortages in affordable housing, recent shifts to a technologically based society requiring a significant increase in educational requirements, longstanding institutionalized oppression and discrimination against certain racial and ethnic groups, and a general increase in the complexity of life (Martin, 2012; Wright, 2000). The general public's perception of social welfare programs seems to be based in large part on this negative bias against the poor, and the misguided belief that the poor are lazy, immoral, and dependent. In several studies during the 1980s and 1990s, those surveyed claimed support for the general idea of helping the poor, but when asked about specific programs or policies, most became critical of governmental policies, specific welfare programs, and welfare recipients in general. In fact, a 1987 national study found that 74 percent of those surveyed believed that most welfare recipients were dishonest and collected more benefits than they deserved (Kluegal, 1987).

During this same time period a new conservative political movement was born at least in part out of this increasingly negative attitude toward the poor and social programs designed to alleviate poverty. Welfare reform rooted in the Reagan administration in the 1980s ultimately lead to both Republican and Democratic support for drastic welfare reform in 1996. Focus once again shifted from social and structural causes of poverty to personal ones with a renewal of punitive social welfare policies reflecting the paternalistic ideologies of the past (Schram, Fordingy, & Sossz, 2008).

Political discourse in the mid-1990s reflected what is often referred to as economic *neoliberal philosophies*, a political movement embraced by most political conservatives, espousing a belief that capitalism and the free market economy were far better solutions to many social conditions, including poverty, than government programs. Advocates of neoliberalism pushed for social programs to be privatized based on the belief that getting social welfare out of the hands of government and into the hands of private enterprise, where market forces could work their magic, would increase efficiency and lower costs. Yet research has consistently revealed that social welfare services do not lend themselves well to free market theory due to the complexity of client issues, as well as unknown outcomes, lack of competition among social service providers, and other dynamics that makes social welfare services so unique (Nelson, 1992; Van Slyke, 2003).

In 1994, during the U.S. congressional campaign, the Republican Party released a document entitled *The New Contract with America*, which represented "a plan that would reform welfare and, along with it, the behavior of the poor" (Hudson & Coukos, 2005, p. 2). The document, introduced just a few weeks before the 1994 congressional election, President Clinton's mid-term election, was signed by all but two of the Republican members of the House of Representatives, as well as all of the party's congressional candidates. In addition to a renewed commitment to smaller government and lower taxes, the contract also pledged a complete overhaul of the welfare system to root out fraud and increase the poor's commitment to employment and self-sufficiency.

Hudson and Coukos (2005) note the similarities between this political movement in the mid-1990s and the one just 100 years before, arguing that the Protestant work ethic served as the driving force behind both. Take, for instance, the common arguments for welfare reform (policies that reduce and restrict social welfare programs and services), which have often been predicated upon the beliefs that

1. hardship is often the result of laziness;
2. providing assistance will increase laziness (and thus dependence), hence increasing hardship, not decreasing it; and
3. those in need often receive services at the expense of the working population

In an article in *Time Magazine* entitled "100 Days of Attitude," Stacks (1995) captured this "us versus them" dynamic fostered in the debate on welfare reform in the mid-1990s. Stacks described how the country was "up-in-arms" over public assistance program, and this outrage spread quickly through the country. The House held hearings on the state of public welfare in the country in response to the uproar. One of the most inflammatory speeches heard on the House floor was when the U.S. Representative for Florida's 7th congressional district, John Mica compared public assistance users to alligators, arguing that "if you treat the alligator like a pet or a child, it will become dependent." Such perspectives negate the complexity of economic disadvantage often experienced by vulnerable and marginalized populations, and categorize the poor as a homogenous group that is in some significant way different with regard to character from mainstream working society.

The debate about public welfare also reflects the genderized and racialized nature of welfare contributing to institutionalized gender bias and racism. Whether veiled or overt negative bias bestowed upon female public welfare recipients of color negates the disparity in social problems experienced by African American women, including increased incidences of poverty, violence, and untreated child sexual victimization, and their associated psychological and social problems (El-Bassel, Caldeira, Ruglass, & Gilbert, 2009; Martin, 2012; Siegel & Williams, 2003).

Although welfare reform was initiated by a Republican Congress, it was passed by the Democratic Clinton administration, in the form of the Personal Responsibility and Work Opportunity Act (PRWORA) of 1996, illustrating wide support not only for welfare reform but also for the underlying philosophical beliefs about the causes of poverty and effective poverty alleviation methods. PRWORA of 1996 reflects a marked shift away from its predecessor, the Aid to Families with Dependent Children (AFDC), an entitlement program created under the New Deal. Many social welfare advocates believe that the Temporary Assistance for Needy Families (TANF), is punitive in nature, with its strict time limits for lifetime benefits (ranging between three and five years depending on the state), stringent work requirements (often regardless of circumstances), and other measures designed to control the behavior of recipients. Supporters of welfare reform and the passage of PRWORA relied on old arguments citing the need to control welfare fraud and welfare dependency, among a host of other behaviors exhibited by welfare recipients, such as sexual promiscuity and having children out of wedlock (Hudson & Coukos, 2005).

The Christian Right

A powerful voice within the Republican Party that was a big backer of welfare reform is often called the *Christian Right*—a group of individuals, often Evangelical Christians, who espouse what they consider conservative family values. Conservative Christian organizations, such as the Christian Coalition, the Eagle Forum, and Focus on the Family, have wielded considerable influence within the Republican Party beginning in the 1980s, becoming a fringe core of the party in the 1990s (Green, Rozell, & Wilcox, 2003; Guth & Green, 1986; Knuckey, 2005). These groups were instrumental in the call for welfare reform, voicing significant concerns about moral decline in society and citing the need to defend and uphold traditional family values (Reese, 2007; Uluorta, 2008).

Uluorta (2008) points out that far too often "morality within the United States is a highly circumscribed concept that often confines itself to select individual behaviors such as those pertaining to sex and sexuality (e.g., abortion, abstinence), marriage (e.g., gay marriage) and social standing (e.g., welfare reform)" (pp. 253–254). Many within the Christian Right were fervent supporters of welfare reform, and specifically the PRWOA of 1996, because of its focus on behavioral reform, including the promotion of marriage and sexual abstinence (Reese, 2007).

The ability of the conservative Christian movement to mobilize its members into political action is notable. For instance, Uluorta (2008) points out the political lobbying success of Focus on the Family, a conservative Evangelical Christian organization that broadcasts its messages on over 1,600 radio stations and 16 television stations nationwide, has a frequently used website, and disseminates newsletters and political action alerts via email and physical mail to millions of members who are often asked to strongly advocate for the organization's policy positions reflecting its socially conservative values. This level and type of mobilization is of concern to some within the social work fields and others who advocate for a more compassionate approach to helping the poor and disadvantaged, and who recognize the wide range of ways to frame social problems (and their causes), rather than focusing solely on perceived behavioral patterns of those who are struggling. The Christian Right and other socially conservative groups often frame their arguments in terms of tradition, yet their version of American tradition and patriotism often reflects the experiences of the majority population, many of whom have had the cumulative benefit of white privilege (Martin, 2012).

The Tea Party Movement

Another conservative social movement, which appears to overlap at least to some extent with the Christian Right, is the American Tea Party Movement, a social movement and a part of the Republican base that advocates for smaller government, lower taxes (the name of the group is a reference to the Boston Tea Party), state rights, and the literal interpretation of the U.S. Constitution. The Tea Party Movement has quickly gained a reputation for advocating on behalf of conservative policies, similar in many ways to the Christian Right agenda. For instance, Michele Bachmann, a Tea Party member, Minnesota congresswoman, and 2012 presidential candidate, has been criticized for her position on social issues, many of which are based on her conservative Christian values. For example, in a 2006 speech to a Christian youth group, Bachmann asserted that religion was supposed to be a part of government and that the notion of separation of church and state (contained in the First Amendment of the U.S. Constitution) was a myth (Turley, 2011).

Allegations have also been made against some members of the Tea Party Movement for their stance on immigration and racial issues in general. The media has consistently highlighted the racially charged tone at some Tea Party political rallies, pointing out racial slurs on posters, many of which are directed at President Obama's ethnic background, although proponents of the Tea Party complain that the media is exaggerating racist elements at the protests and rallies by seeking out and overfocusing on the more extremist elements of the movement. Although "tea partiers" often deny racist or homophobic values, a recent study showed that about 60 percent of tea party opponents believed that the movement had strong racist and homophobic overtones (Gardner & Thompson, 2010).

Currently the Tea Party is considered a part of the Republican base, but its existence appears to be creating some controversy within the party, particularly among the more moderate GOP base. Whether the Tea Party remains a part of the Republican Party or branches off to its own party will depend on many factors, including whether it can maintain its current momentum and increase the number of supporters.

> **Assess your comprehension of "Welfare Reform and the Emergence of Neoliberal Economic Policies" by completing this quiz.**

A TIME FOR CHANGE: THE ELECTION OF THE FIRST AFRICAN AMERICAN PRESIDENT

The 2008 presidential election was unprecedented in many respects. The United States had its first African American presidential candidate and its first female presidential candidate of a major party. Many people who have historically been relatively apathetic about politics were suddenly passionate about this election for a variety of reasons. Growing discontentment with the leadership in the preceding eight years coupled with a lengthy war in the Persian Gulf region and a struggling economy created a climate where significant social change could take root. Barack Obama's campaign slogans based on hope and change (e.g., "Yes We Can!" and "Change We Can Believe In") seemed to capture this growing discontent.

The fledgling economy of 2007 evolved into an economic meltdown toward the end of the Bush presidency, extending into the Obama administration, evidenced by a plummeting stock market, the near-collapse of the banking industry, and the real estate bubble at a level not experienced since the Great Depression (Geithner, 2009). Some social reformers and economists have advocated for policies that strive to achieve balance between free market forces, which can stimulate the economy by creating a spirit of competition, and a strong nation-state that provides a safety net for all of its constituents.

President Obama and the 111th Congress responded to the economic crisis with several policy and legislative actions, including the passage of the American Recovery and Reinvestment Act of 2009 (often referred to as the Stimulus bill [Pub. L. No. 111-5]). This economic stimulus package, worth over $787 billion, included a combination of federal tax cuts, various social welfare provisions, and increases in domestic spending, designed to stimulate the economy and assist Americans who were suffering economically. It will be some time before economists and the American public come to a consensus on whether the stimulus package was successful in turning the economy around, but early indications appear to suggest that the stimulus package was at least somewhat successful.

In the meantime, the lead-up to the 2012 presidential elections revealed the same debate about the causes of poverty and effective poverty alleviation strategies. After a brief display of compassion toward the poor at the height of the 2008 economic crisis, harsh sentiments reflecting historic stigmatization of the poor were strongly espoused, particularly among potential Republican primary candidates who continued their campaign against 'big government', social welfare programs, and civil liberties in general. The 2012 Republican presidential candidate, Newt Gingrich, even went so far as to challenge current child labor laws, calling them "stupid." In a campaign speech in Iowa in the fall of 2011, Gingrich characterized poor ethnically diverse children living in poor neighborhoods as lazy and having no work ethic. In two different speeches (his initial speech and a subsequent speech where he was asked to clarify his earlier comments), Gingrich suggested that poor children in poor neighborhoods could start work early, perhaps as janitorial staff in their own schools. Describing most poor children in economically challenged neighborhoods, Gingrich stated that these children have

> no habits of working and nobody around them who works . . . they have no habit of showing up on Monday and staying all day or the concept of "I do this and you give me cash," unless it's illegal.

In his follow-up statements, he clarified his earlier comments by stating:

> You have a very poor neighborhood. You have students that are required to go to school. They have no money, no habit of work. . . . What if you paid them in the afternoon to work in the clerical office or as the assistant librarian? And let me get into the janitor thing. What if they became assistant janitors, and their job was to mop the floor and clean the bathroom?

Framing his comments in religious terms, Gingrich concluded by stating:

> If we are all endowed by our creator with the right to pursue happiness, that has to apply to the poorest neighborhoods in the poorest counties, and I am prepared to find something that works, that breaks us out of the cycles we have now to find a way for poor children to work and earn honest money. (Dover, 2011, para 3–5)

Gingrich's sentiments presume a level playing field in society, negating current and historic social forces, such as racial oppression and white privilege that have consistently given one group an unfair advantage for centuries.

Perhaps one of the most significant federal laws to be passed in years is the Patient Protection and Affordable Care Act of 2010 (ACA) signed into law by President Obama in March 2010 after a fierce public relations war waged by many Republicans and health insurance companies designed to prevent its passage. The ACA, which took effect incrementally from 2010 to 2014, is a comprehensive healthcare reform bill. Overall this legislation is designed to make it easier for individuals and families to obtain quality lower-cost health insurance by applying through a central exchange, making it more difficult for health insurance companies to deny coverage. It also expands Medicare in a variety of ways, including bolstering community and home-based healthcare services, and provides incentives for preventative, holistic, and wellness care. With respect to behavioral and mental healthcare, the ACA provides increased incentives for coordinated care and school-based care including mental health care and substance abuse treatment. It also includes provisions that will require the inclusion of mental health and substance abuse

Assess your comprehension of "A Time for Change: The Election of the First African American President" by completing this quiz.

coverage in benefits packages, including prescription drug coverage, and wellness and prevention services. Although the government healthcare marketplace website initially experienced problems making it difficult for people to sign up, according to an April 2014 White House press release, an estimated 8 million people have signed up for private health insurance through the Health Insurance Marketplace (formerly called the exchange).

Summary

As often happens in broad-based economic downturns, the 2007 recession seemed to have led to a softening of antipoverty rhetoric and a political discourse that recognizes the importance of an effective social welfare system for all Americans, yet that empathy appears to be waning, reflected in an increase in discussions of class warfare among politicians in the 2012 presidential election cycle. Discussions of the need for universal healthcare, a federal living wage, and other policies designed to address the economic inequality in the United States will no doubt be ongoing. The debate regarding how capitalism and a free market economy can be balanced with a social safety net for all members of U.S. society continues among politicians (and the public) and shows no signs of abating. Only time will tell where U.S. society ultimately will fall in the philosophical spectrum of individual responsibility and social equity.

Social movements appear to be on the rise, with passionate supporters of both liberal causes, such as marriage equality, and more conservative social movements, such as demands for smaller government and increased restrictions on social welfare programs. Social workers can positively engage in a variety of social movements by advocating for social equality in productive ways that do not contribute to existing polarization.

Recall what you learned in this chapter by completing the Chapter Review.

3

Generalist Skills and Intervention Strategies

Effecting Meaningful and Ethical Change

Mary is the 34-year-old single parent of a five-year-old boy. She has been living with her mother since her own divorce three years ago. This is a negative situation because her mother is verbally abusive toward Mary and her son, abuses alcohol, and smokes inside the home. In addition, their living space is small, and Mary and her son share a bedroom. Mary's original goal was to live with her mother for only six months, but whenever she considers moving out, she becomes overwhelmed with the prospect of not only finding an appropriate apartment but finding child care as well, because despite her mother's abusive behavior, Mary has been relying on her mother for before- and after-school child care while she works. Mary feels trapped but completely powerless to do anything about her situation. During her intake interview, she described her prior counseling experiences, sharing that she quit counseling because whenever she was faced with the prospect of finding an apartment, her fears would snowball into so many fears that she simply couldn't even bring herself to make the first phone call in search of housing. She ended up feeling embarrassed, as if she were letting the counselor down, and just decided she could not deal with any more failures, so she stopped going to counseling. Mary explained that throughout the past several years, her mother has consistently reminded her that she would never make it on her own, that she would surely fail, and that she would end up destroying her life and her son's life. Her mother also told Mary that if she moved out, and ran out of money, she would not bail Mary out again and would instead force Mary and her son to go to a shelter. Searching online to look for a rental advertisement resulted in a flood of worries and concerns—some specific and some she could not even put into words. She worried about everything from whether she would know what to say when calling about an apartment, to whether she would be able to support herself and her son. What if she was laid off from her job and could no longer afford her apartment and had to live in a shelter? What if she couldn't find a babysitter she could afford? What if she found an apartment and got a babysitter, but the babysitter ended up abusing her son worse than her mother did? She read about such things all the time in the newspaper, she reasoned. Or what if she found an apartment, but she had a financial emergency such as her car breaking down, and she started falling behind on her rent and was evicted? She couldn't fathom the thought of moving out and then having to move back in with her mother again, or worse, what if her mother made good on her threat and refused to allow them to move back in with her? Once confronted with this slippery slope of catastrophizing, Mary would resist even taking the first step toward independence and could not bring herself to even look at rental ads. Mary's mood became increasingly melancholy over the years, and after years of verbal abuse from her mother, her ex-husband, and now her mother again, she had no confidence in her ability to emotionally or financially support her son let alone to manage her own life without her mother's assistance. Yet her mother's abuse led to a cycle of depression, despair, and increasing dependence that Mary could not seem to break on her own. We will revisit this vignette later in this chapter as we explore different intervention strategies used by social workers when effecting meaningful change in the lives of their clients.

ETHICS AND THE SOCIAL WORK PROFESSION

Ethics can be defined in many different ways, with most definitions including references to a set of guiding principles or moral values. In a professional context, ethics often refers to a set of standards that provide guidance to individuals within a particular discipline with the goal of assisting them in resolving ethical dilemmas they are likely to face. Regardless of how the concept of ethics is defined, ethical standards, within virtually all contexts, are by definition based on a foundational value system designed to guide us in determining the difference between good and bad behavior. A more basic way of putting it is that ethical standards and principles provide us guidance in what we *ought* to do in any given situation.

What Does It Mean to Be Ethical?

Now you might be asking yourself—I'm a good person, so why do I need a detailed set of ethical standards to tell me what to do? Don't good people behave *well* naturally? The answer may surprise you! Although it may be true that very few people wake up in the morning and say to themselves, "Hey! I think I'm going to lie, cheat, and steal today!" it is true that many people become hysterical or enraged, or are biased, selfish, naïve, or ignorant. In the process of being so very human, they may behave quite unethically as they make decisions based on their urges, desires, passions, personal biases, negative stereotypes, or uninformed opinions.

Ethical values and principles are a necessary part of life, both personally and professionally. Although some may argue that their personal ethical values are not necessarily tied to their professional ethics, a strong argument can be made that they are very much a reflection of one another. Some of you may remember former president Bill Clinton's impeachment hearings, which centered on his perjury in a sexual harassment claim filed against him as well as his inappropriate relationship with a young White House intern. Many of his supporters argued fervently that what he did in his personal life had no bearing on his ability to be a good president. Yet others argued that poor character demonstrated in one's personal life will most definitely play out in one's professional life as well, and any line drawn between the personal and professional domains of life is both arbitrary and illusory.

It would be very convenient if there was one long list of rules and all situations could be perceived in the same manner by everyone. But of course that is not how life works. Most people will argue that there are universal moral principles, particularly relating to such acts as murder, robbery, child abuse, and sexual assault. But even with these seemingly black-and-white moral issues, the gray in life seems to abound. Such is the case when someone kills in self-defense, or someone steals bread to feed a starving child. So, is morality absolute or relative? What I mean by this is, is there an absolute right and wrong in this world? Or is the rightness and wrongness of a decision or action dependent on perspective, context, culture, and one's own self-truth? This is an age-old question and not one that I will answer definitively here. In fact, many moral theorists deal with this dilemma as a core issue, and although some argue for either polar position, most will argue that both are true—there are fundamental moral principles that are universal (e.g., sexually abusing a child is considered wrong in most cultures) and there are many occasions when one must consider the appropriateness of a certain behavior within the context of one's culture (e.g., burping in public, direct eye contact, gender roles, orientation toward authority).

I want to address some of the issues that have the greatest potential of muddying the waters when it comes to determining how we know whether an action is moral or immoral, which in turn will help us determine how we can ensure we're making ethical and moral decisions. We will then apply what we've learned to the professional arena, specifically to the social work profession.

The Conflict Between Ethical Standards and Emotional Desires

Most people will find themselves caught in a tug-of-war between their ethical standards and their emotional desires, or feelings, with the latter often leading to the breaking down of moral behavior at some point in their lives. When I had a counseling practice I often told my clients that feelings and emotions are like the interior design in a house—moving and poignant, even beautiful at times—but truly useful only if protected by the exterior and structure of the house—the walls and roof, which are the protective framework—like our ethical standards, values, and principles. Thus, although human beings are certainly emotional, individuals with high character are not driven to act solely on the basis of their desires and passions, but on their values, which manifest in rules for self-governing.

Individuals who are motivated to act primarily on emotion are often emotionally unstable, at times behaving erratically and impulsively. This is not because their emotions are wrong, but because their values and principles are not well defined and/or developed to contain or regulate their emotions, oftentimes leading to the inability to control their impulses. For instance, an employee might become angry with his boss and feel like striking him in the face, but doesn't because the employee values nonviolence. A person's ethical values should then be the *rudder* of behavior, and although there are certainly times when people will be driven by passion, or will need to follow their hunches, emotions and desires serve people best when they aren't chief in the decision-making process.

Another reason it is important to understand the relationship between our ethical values and our emotions is that we often use our emotions to justify our unethical behavior. Cheating on a test is wrong, unless the test is too hard and we don't like our teacher; adultery is wrong, unless we're in a loveless marriage, are extremely lonely, and fall hopelessly in love with someone else; lying is wrong, unless we need the day off and will get paid only if we say we're sick, even though we're not; violence is wrong, unless we're provoked; and drinking too much alcohol is wrong, unless we've gone two weeks without and just had a very bad day. Thus, one of the primary functions of ethical values is to keep us on a good moral track, particularly when we find our ethical values at odds with our emotional desires and urges. Certainly there are times when emotions should lead, and we certainly do not want to become heartless in our application of rules. When someone is driven to act solely on the basis of their values or self-governing rules, they are often deemed rigid legalists. But when people behave in ways that are solely driven by their feelings and desires, they are often deemed immature, volatile, and impulsive.

Ethical behavior is not just made difficult because of competing emotions and desires, but oftentimes we find ourselves in situations where our values are competing with one another. We value family dinners with our kids, but what if that conflicts with our value of their extracurricular involvement? We value our friendships, but what if they are interfering in our marriage that we also value?

Many times people act in a way that is later perceived to be unethical, but at the time they were committing the act, they may have believed that they were acting in a very ethical manner, but were forced to choose among competing values. Employees who shred documents to protect their employers may very well believe they were acting ethically based on their ethical value of employee loyalty. Yet, they may later be charged with obstruction of justice because someone else perceived their behavior to be immoral and illegal. Perhaps in retrospect these employees may realize that their values were misguided, or they may forever believe as though they were behaving morally and that the government agency that charged them with a legal offense was not.

> The Managing of Personal Values/Code of Ethics video is a resource that provides valuable information on how to resolve ethical dilemmas when personal values collide with NASW Ethical Codes. After watching this video, review the NASW Code of Ethics and consider what ethical standard may conflict with a personal value you have. How would you resolve an ethical dilemma that involved such a conflict?

Resolving Ethical Dilemmas

Ethical mindfulness can often guide social workers with issues related to informed consent (informing clients of their rights and making sure they know all that is involved in engaging in the counseling process), the use of real clients in therapist educational videotapes, and other ethical issues appropriate for discussion and evaluation in order to avoid blatant ethical lapses (West, 2002). But even if everyone agrees that having ethical standards is a good thing, and that constant evaluation is necessary, the next challenge is to determine how to respond when an ethical breach may have occurred.

Kitchener's (1984) ethical decision-making model was designed to guide professionals in navigating the sometimes-murky waters of decision making in difficult situations. The model is based on five moral principles that Kitchener maintains need to be at the heart of any ethical evaluation and can, in a sense, be used as a "litmus test" when attempting to determine whether a certain act was in fact ethical. These moral principles include: (1) autonomy (respects others' free will and independence), (2) beneficence (contributes to the welfare of others), (3) nonmaleficence ("above all do no harm"), (4) justice ("treating equals equally and unequals unequally but in proportion to their relevant differences," p. 49), and (5) fidelity (loyalty and commitment to the process). When a certain act is being evaluated to determine its ethical nature, the model would have the evaluators ask whether the professional acted with free will (autonomy); whether the professional's actions were intended to benefit the client (beneficence); whether the professional's actions involved no evil, illegal, or harmful intentions (nonmaleficence); and whether these acts were carried out in a manner that respected the rights and dignity of all involved parties (justice).

Cultural Influences on the Perception of Ethical Behavior

Cultural context is another very important variable to consider when evaluating the rightness or wrongness of behavior. Garcia, Cartwright, Winston, and Borzuchowska (2003)

Apply Social Work Ethical Principles to Guide Professional Practice

Practice Behavior: Apply strategies of ethical reasoning to arrive at principled decisions.

Critical Thinking Question: The NASW Code of Ethics stipulates that social workers have a responsibility to both clients and the community. Using Kitchener ethical decision-making model, how would you resolve an ethical dilemma where a client's best interest conflicts with the practice setting where the client is receiving services? Consider the following: You are a social worker working at an adoption agency. Currently you are working with a young, pregnant birthmom and her boyfriend, who are seeking pre-placement services. You are also providing services to the pre-adoptive family who has been selected to adopt the baby as soon as it is born. Your agency and the pre-adoptive family have invested a considerable amount of resources in the birthmom, including hours of counseling, medical expenses, housing, and clothing. Two weeks before the birthmom's due date, she leaves a voicemail for you saying that she is unsure about her decision to place the baby for adoption and wants to meet and talk about parenting options, a service your agency does not offer. According to Kitchener ethical decision-making model, what is the most ethical course for you to take in this situation?

Case Study 3.1 Corrie ten Boom

In 1945, when Corrie ten Boom was hiding Jews in her attic during the Holocaust, she chose to lie to the Nazi officers who came to her door questioning her, even though she believed lying to be wrong (ten Boom, Sherrill, & Sherrill, 1974). Corrie was put in a position where she had to choose the higher value. What did she value more? Complete honesty at all costs? Obedience to authority? Personal safety? Or interceding in matters of inhumane cruelty and injustice at all costs? In light of what we now know about Nazi Germany and the Holocaust, Corrie and her family are lauded as heroes, behaving in the highest moral fashion, refusing to stand by and do nothing as an evil government slaughtered millions of innocent people. Yet does this mean that those who did not hide Jews acted immorally? What if you had the opportunity to interview a family who refused to hide a Jewish neighbor? What if this family told you that Nazis used the practice of dressing as Jews and going door-to-door asking for refuge and that the punishment for harboring a Jew was imprisonment in a concentration camp, and likely death? What if this family explained that they believed they behaved morally because their first responsibility was to protect their children? Would you still consider their behavior immoral? Or what about the ruling authorities'

Case Study 3.1 *Continued*

perspective? Corrie ten Boom and her family broke the law. From the authorities' perspective, then, their behavior was immoral. What makes the ten Boom family's behavior moral now? Our belief that the Nazis were evil? So does this mean that if you or I believe that a particular law, or even our entire government, is evil, we'd be justified in disobeying its laws? Many protective parents kidnap their children because they strongly believe that the family courts will not protect the children from the other parent, whom they believe is abusive. If this is true, is the behavior of kidnapping their children in violation of a child custody order justified? Many ethnic minorities believe that if they are pulled over by the police, it is because they are being racially profiled, and they may be unjustly arrested. Does this justify an attempt to flee? Would their behavior be any more or less moral than a slave who escaped before the Civil War?

Of course, these are somewhat rhetorical questions with no clear-cut answers, but I hope you are beginning to see that evaluating ethical behavior in retrospect, when we have the benefit of perspective and outcome, is a far easier task than determining what is truly ethical in the moment. And the lens that we use to evaluate the moral correctness of a behavior is often determined by the outcome—something that those involved in decision making don't have the benefit of knowing or have any control over when acting in the moment. This explains why some people who are initially perceived as highly immoral are later considered heroes, and why some people who authentically believe they are behaving morally end up in prison.

Application of Kitchener's Ethical Decision-Making Model

Was Corrie ten Boom's behavior ethical or unethical? The ruling Nazi government certainly considered her behavior of hiding Jews unethical, which is why she and her family members were arrested. But there are numerous examples of individuals acting contrary to their government's laws, and being considered traitors, yet contemporary perspectives hold them as heroes (consider Martin Luther King Jr. and Nelson Mandela as two examples). Remember, when evaluating the ethical nature of our own or others' behavior, we often do not yet have all of the facts to render a comprehensive ethical assessment. We know now that ten Boom's actions were ethical because we have all of the facts about the evils of the Nazi regime, yet rarely does one have the luxury of having retrospective perspective when in the midst of a moral dilemma—this is why Kitchener's model is so useful when navigating ethical dilemmas.

In evaluating ten Boom's actions in hiding Jews during the Holocaust within the context of Kitchener's five moral principles, it appears as though those she helped were acting *autonomously*, and of their own free will in that they knew the risks involved in accepting ten Boom's assistance. Her behavior was *beneficent* in the sense that it was motivated by her deep desire to help others and contribute to the welfare of society, particularly those who were being persecuted. Her actions reflected *nonmaleficence* in that she refused to engage in harm by standing by and allowing atrocities to be committed against her Jewish friends and neighbors. She was clearly motivated by her commitment to justice in that she elevated her hatred for injustice above her need for personal safety. And finally, she acted out of a sense of loyalty to her religious beliefs that dictated she work against a cruel and evil dictatorship. Thus, according to Kitchener's model, ten Boom's behavior was ethical regardless of the fact that she broke the law by acting contrary to the wishes of the ruling government.

---

discussed a model of ethical decision making that stresses the importance of being culturally sensitive when evaluating any ethical decision-making process. Garcia et al. (2003) challenged the notion that all cultures value autonomy equally, arguing that many cultures operate on a very interdependent basis. They also cautioned that what one culture considers abnormal, another culture considers perfectly normal. But regardless of how one goes about determining what is ethical and how ethical decisions are made (or how unethical decisions are made), it is very important to remember to be sensitive to differing *cultures, genders*, and *generational cohorts*.

Again, it is also very important to remember that oftentimes what appears blatantly unethical in retrospect may have seemed quite ethical, or at the very least somewhat muddy, in the midst. Thus, taking the time to truly understand the behavior from the professional's perspective, keeping issues related to enculturation in mind, is absolutely imperative and undoubtedly very challenging.

Ethical Standards in Social Work

It is because of the difficult nature of determining what constitutes moral behavior— including the balancing of our ethical values and emotional urges, of knowing which competing values to choose in any given situation, of having the benefit of perspective when making moral decisions—that many professions have elected to develop foundational ethical standards and professional values to safeguard from emotion, bias, and misguided commitments serving as the primary motivators in decision making. Many professions begin with some stated set of values or underlying guiding assumptions, oftentimes found reflected in their mission statement, and sometimes, ethical standards are developed from some form of abuse.

Regardless of how standards are developed, virtually all professions rely on some form of ethical standards to maintain integrity and trust within their profession. Numerous professions espouse basic ethical principles, which serve as a foundation for their business practices and standards, but in addition to such values of choice, an increasing number of professions are bound by legally enforced ethical standards, which if violated can result in quite punitive consequences, ranging from professional or financial sanctions (such as license suspension or fines) to a wide range of criminal penalties, including incarceration.

Virtually every professional group operates under a professional organization or licensing entity that enforces ethical codes in some form. The National Association of Social Workers (NASW) has developed a set of ethical standards that govern the social work profession throughout the United States (NASW, 1999; 2002). These standards have established what constitutes appropriate professional conduct for social workers in practice, in terms of how social workers should act in society and how they should treat clients and colleagues. The standards have also established a set of values associated with the profession in general. These guidelines are specific enough to provide a concrete sense of how professional social workers should conduct themselves, but broad enough so as to provide social workers with guidance in managing ethical dilemmas, particularly those that fall somewhere in the gray. In other words, there isn't a prescribed list of do's and don'ts but rather a guiding framework within which social workers can engage in professional decision making in such a way that places the best interests of clients in the forefront.

The NASW Code of Ethics is separated into four sections, the first of which is the preamble, and includes an explanation of the social work profession's mission and core values of service, social justice, dignity and worth of the person, importance of human

Social Work Application Activity

Evaluate Corrie ten Boom's actions in accordance with the NASW Code of Ethics. Do Corrie's activities uphold the Code of Ethics? Do they violate them? How can the NASW Code of Ethics help guide a social worker's activities, particularly during times of public crisis?

relationships, integrity, and competence. The second section, entitled "Purpose of the NASW Code of Ethics," outlines the overall purpose of the Code of Ethics as well as provides some parameters for their application, including how to use the Code of Ethics to resolve ethical dilemmas. The third section, entitled "Ethical Principles," links each core value to an ethical principle, and the final section includes the ethical standards separated into the following six categories:

1. Social Workers' Ethical Responsibilities to Clients
2. Social Workers' Ethical Responsibilities to Colleagues
3. Social Workers' Ethical Responsibilities in Practice Settings
4. Social Workers' Ethical Responsibilities as Professionals
5. Social Workers' Ethical Responsibilities to the Social Work Profession
6. Social Worker's Ethical Responsibilities to the Broader Society

> **Assess your comprehension of "Ethics and the Social Work Profession" by completing this quiz.**

Many social service agencies, insurance companies, and courts, as well as most licensing and regulatory bodies, have adopted the NASW Code of Ethics to manage and enforce the ethical behavior of social workers. If a licensed social worker violates the Code of Ethics and a complaint is filed, the complaint progresses through a peer-review process allowing the profession to discipline its own members.

INFORMED CONSENT AND CONFIDENTIALITY

Before any discussion of generalist skills and direct practice interventions, the important topics of informed consent, confidentiality, and the limits of confidentiality must first be discussed. Informed consent refers to disclosing to clients the nature and risks of the counseling relationship prior to their engaging in these services. According to the NASW, social workers should inform their clients of the purpose of the services, any risks involved, any limits to the services, all associated costs, alternatives to the services (if any), information on how the client can refuse or withdraw from services, and how long the informed consent is valid (NASW, 1999).

Confidentiality is another component of the social worker–client relationship, outlining what clients can expect in terms of what the social worker can and cannot share with others. The commitment to keep whatever clients share private is not merely a clinical issue practiced by most in the mental health field—it is considered so vital to mental health treatment that confidentiality is a legal mandate throughout the United States. Thus, any professional offering counseling-type services must by law maintain confidentiality or face losing their professional license or other sanctions.

The importance of confidentiality is based on the belief that for trust to develop in the counseling relationship, clients must be assured that they have a safe place to discuss their most private thoughts, fears, and experiences. Without such a guarantee, clients might not be willing to discuss their fears that they are not good parents, or about their intermittent desire to abandon their families because they are so overwhelmed in life, or about their histories of child sexual abuse. Knowing that they have a safe place to talk about their most private thoughts with someone who is not personally affected by their feelings, experiences, or choices makes this exploration possible for thousands of individuals, enabling them to become better parents, less overwhelmed in their lives, and gain power over their childhoods of abuse, turning victimization into a survivor mentality. There are *limits of confidentiality*, though, designed to ensure the safety of the client and the general public.

Although there are no national standards on the limits of confidentiality in mental health services, each state has laws that establish exceptions of confidentiality related to both voluntary and involuntary disclosures. These laws determine how and when client information can be disclosed to other treatment providers, insurance companies, and caregivers, and typically require that the client sign an *authorization to release information*, a legal document that provides all relevant information about what information will be released and for what purpose.

In general, the limits of confidentiality also include the counselor's duty-to-warn and duty-to-protect in relation to situations where through direct disclosure clients share that they are a threat to themselves (suicidal) or others (homicidal). For instance, if a client shares with a social worker that he plans on leaving the office and committing suicide, the practitioner has the legal obligation to disclose this information to the client's family or even the police to ensure the client's safety. If a minor client discloses during the counseling session that she is being sexually abused by her uncle, the practitioner is legally obligated to report this information to child protective services to ensure the child's safety.

Disclosures are not always so clear-cut or direct, though, and there are many occasions where social workers find themselves needing to use their clinical skills to determine whether violating confidentiality is the appropriate course of action. For instance, consider the client who *may* be suicidal and who discloses a level of despair that *may* indicate suicidal ideation. Couple this with a disclosure that the client attempted suicide four months before and told no one; that he uses alcohol to "make the pain go away"; and that although he won't admit to a suicide plan, he doesn't always feel safe. A client who makes this type of disclosure—denying any outright plan to commit suicide, but appearing to manifest many signs of suicidal behavior—may very well be at real risk of committing suicide, but might be resistant to sharing this clearly either because of confusion about how he feels (wants to end his life one moment and wants to live the next) or because he already planned to commit suicide and does not want anything or anyone to get in the way.

This scenario requires the practitioner to take a clinical risk—if the practitioner takes no action, the client may indeed commit suicide, but if the practitioner violates confidentiality and the client was not really at risk for suicide, then the counselor–client relationship might be seriously damaged. Because confidentiality laws in most states do not bar professional discussions among practitioners within the same agency, clinical dilemmas are most appropriately explored in clinical supervision, where a team of social workers discusses cases and client issues as a group with the goal of making the best decisions possible about client care.

Another challenging scenario involves a minor-child client who discloses possible abuse—a spanking that seems to the practitioner to go beyond mere discipline, verbal abuse that might meet the criteria of child maltreatment, or some other indication that the child *may* be experiencing abuse at home. Determining when that line has been crossed between appropriate parenting and abuse is a clinical issue, best explored within clinical supervision, but it is important to note that, legally, it is the practitioner who is responsible for complying with disclosure laws, and it is the practitioner's professional license that will be at risk if the appropriate actions are not taken. In some states a failure to report suspected child abuse can result in a range of consequences, such as professional sanctions, or the loss of one's professional license, to criminal charges. Thus, although clinical supervision can be of significant assistance in making these types of clinical decisions, the practitioner must make the final decision on whether to break confidentiality to protect the client's welfare.

Another limit to confidentiality involves a client who discloses during the counseling relationship that he or she has a plan to cause serious and immediate harm to another person. Laws in most states dictate specifically how, when, and to whom this information is to be disclosed. Duty-to-warn laws have been influenced greatly by a tragic incident that occurred on the University of California, Berkeley campus when a student disclosed to a campus psychologist his intent to kill his girlfriend. Although the psychologist informed various individuals, including his supervisor and campus police, he did not inform the intended victim or her family. The client later killed the girlfriend, and the family of the victim sued the university for the psychologist's failure to warn the victim. The case *Tarasoff v. The Regents of University of California* resulted in two decisions by the California Supreme Court in 1974 and 1976 (*Tarasoff I* and *II*, respectively). *Tarasoff I* found that a therapist has a duty to use reasonable care to give threatened persons a warning to prevent foreseeable danger. *Tarasoff II* was more specific in referencing the therapist's duty and obligation to warn intended victims if necessary to protect them from serious danger of violence. Virtually every state in the nation now uses the *Tarasoff* decisions as a foundation for the development of duty-to-warn laws (Fulero, 1988).

Although clients are told about the limits of confidentiality by the written informed consent, they may forget or be confused about what would warrant violation of the confidentiality privilege. Clients who share deeply personal information with their counselors may feel betrayed by the counselor who informs them that a disclosure is going to be shared with someone to protect the client or others. It is vital that this topic be fully discussed during the first counseling session so the client knows what disclosures do and do not limit confidentiality. For instance, disclosures of shoplifting, cheating on one's

Assess your comprehension of "Informed Consent and Confidentiality" by completing this quiz.

taxes, lying to an employer, having an affair, or *feeling* like attacking a coworker do not justify breaking confidentiality, but admissions of plans to kill oneself or someone else, of setting someone's house on fire, or of child maltreatment do require disclosure in accordance with federal and state mandates. Child and adolescent clients in particular may be taken by surprise when their confidentiality is violated; thus, it is often a good idea for the social worker to remind clients of these limits intermittently throughout the counseling relationship.

SKILLS AND COMPETENCIES

Generalist practice has been defined as "a perspective focusing on the interface between systems with equal emphasis on the goals of social justice, humanizing systems, and improving the well-being of people" (Schatz, Jenkins, & Sheafor, 1990, p. 220). Generalist practice is also characterized as having a wide range of skills that are used with a diverse population. Therefore, the skills and intervention strategies referenced in this chapter will be general enough to be applied to a variety of situations and clients. It is important to note, though, that social workers who do not have a license to counsel will not engage in counseling per se. Typically, bachelor's trained social workers are not trained to counsel clients in the traditional and legal sense of the word. Since social workers practice at different degree levels, for the purpose of this discussion, I use the term *generalist practice* in this chapter in reference to engaging in any type of *direct practice* with clients and client systems. If I use the term *counsel*, or *counseling*, it is with the intention that these terms be interpreted in the broadest sense. This may involve the facilitation of support groups, providing general case management services, or discussing a person's problems on the telephone as a crisis hotline worker. Direct practice may also include therapeutic counseling if the social worker has a state license to provide professional counseling services.

More specific skills and intervention strategies will be discussed in successive chapters as they apply to clients seeking services in particular practice settings. Despite the generalist nature of the social work profession, and the fact that in most (if not all) states social workers working on a bachelor's level will not be permitted to work in the capacity of a professional licensed mental health provider, some direct practice with clients will occur in various contexts, as many who work in the helping fields will attest; thus, it is important for social workers on all professional levels to become familiar with some basic theoretical modalities and counseling techniques.

Many of the skills included in this chapter could almost be considered personality characteristics. *Empathy* and *compassion* are powerful and necessary skills and often appear naturally engrained in someone's personality or character. Nevertheless, even if someone is naturally empathetic and a naturally good listener, it is imperative that these skills be sharpened and more fully developed to be truly useful in the social work field. Other skills must be taught. For instance, although some people might be a good judge of character, they need to be taught various clinical assessment skills and techniques.

Sympathy and Empathy

Escalas and Stern (2003) discuss the traditional definition of both sympathy and empathy (commonly confused responses). They define sympathy as sorrow or concern for another's welfare and empathy as a person's absorption in the feelings of another. The difference between these two responses, although seemingly subtle, is significant when one considers that the response of empathy goes one step further, allowing us to actually feel what another person feels.

In a social work setting, empathy involves the willingness and ability to truly understand a client's beliefs, thoughts, feelings, and experiences from the client's own perspective. Sympathy is not a difficult emotional response to muster for the true victims of this world (Greenberg, Elliot, Watson, & Bohart, 2001). Imagine watching the news and hearing about the plight of a young couple whose five-year-old child was recently abducted. Your immediate response would likely be to express feelings of sorrow for them, and you might express concern for their welfare, wondering what will become of the little girl and her family as they search for her. You might stop short, though, of allowing yourself to feel the actual feelings of grief and fear that this couple is no doubt feeling. Allowing yourself to immerse so deeply in what you imagine their feelings to be might hit too close to home, particularly if you have children. You might feel compelled to distance yourself emotionally—to resist putting yourself in their place. You shiver as you watch your own five-year-old playing on the swing set in your backyard and will yourself not to give this situation another thought, lest you find it impossible to sleep tonight.

Effective practitioners cannot limit their emotional responses to sympathy alone; to be effective they must be willing to go on the emotional roller coaster ride with the client, and extend their response to empathy, which in a counseling relationship involves the ability and willingness to experience a client's beliefs, thoughts, and feelings through the client's personal lens. This requires emotional maturity, the ability to be honest with oneself, the capacity for immersing oneself in another's emotional crisis without getting lost in the experience, and being able to keep the focus on the client, not on themselves. I have often referred to the empathetic response in counseling as having the emotional capacity to not only see the client's world through the client's eyes, but also be willing to walk alongside the client through a difficult time. This can be emotionally exhausting, but if I am working with a survivor of sexual assault, and if I want to be truly effective in helping my client navigate through this crisis, then I need to be willing to understand what it feels like to be sexually violated as best I can without having gone through this experience myself—what it feels like to be humiliated and what it feels like to be filled with shame and embarrassment. Thus, although the concept of empathy might seem appealing, many practitioners resist truly empathizing with their clients because it requires them to search their own minds and hearts, to reflect on past hurts, and in this case, past times in their lives where they have been humiliated, shamed, and embarrassed—experiences many are not particularly inclined to revisit.

Another challenge in responding empathetically to clients is when working with clients who do not appear to deserve sympathy or empathy, which makes empathizing with their feelings, even their perceived plight, quite challenging. How do counselors empathize with pedophiles, with parents who abuse their children, or with the drunk driver who drove into a family of five, killing a child? Unlike therapists in private practice who typically have complete control over their caseloads, social workers rarely have such control and are often given a caseload, depending on the practice setting, with clients who the general public might deem undeserving of anything other than a prison sentence.

Looking at the world through the eyes of a serial rapist, a domestic batterer, or a raging alcoholic might be the last thing any sane human being would want to do, but the willingness to do so is a requirement for social workers, who will likely find themselves working with *mandated clients*—individuals who are required by some governmental agency (e.g., the courts, department of probation, child welfare) to seek treatment.

So how does one accomplish this feat, when the behavior of such a client is often morally incomprehensible, or at the least very maladaptive? The first step in developing the ability to empathize with unsympathetic clients is to understand that to empathize with them does not mean you condone their behavior or choices. Consider the last motion picture that you watched. It is the director's job to help the viewer see the world through each of the character's eyes. Considering the role of the director, although not a direct parallel, illustrates the concept of the social worker essentially sitting alongside those in counseling and seeing the world through their eyes. You do not have to agree with their perspective, and you certainly do not have to agree with their actions, but to be a truly effective social worker, you must be willing and able to understand what it feels like to be them.

Although it might not make intuitive sense that a victim of abuse goes on to become the batterer, this dynamic is quite common. The boy who was sexually abused *may* grow up to be a pedophile, the child who was beaten *may* grow up to beat her own children, and the boy who witnessed his father beat his mother *may* grow up to beat his own wife. The nature of this dynamic will be discussed in later chapters, but understanding that most abusive behavior is born out of pain might help the social worker see mandated clients not as monsters, but as broken human beings who have suffered greatly themselves, yet rather than remaining vulnerable so healing could occur, their hearts were hardened to the point where sometimes they become like those who hurt them.

Boundary Setting

Any discussion of empathy and the need for emotional immersion in another's problems must be considered in the context of appropriate boundary setting. Although social work certainly is not the sort of career one can leave at the office, it would be imprudent to become so immersed in a client's problems that practitioners cannot distinguish the difference between their problems and the problems of their clients. It is probably easier to discuss good boundary setting by giving examples of poor boundary setting. The practitioner who counsels a victim of domestic violence and spends the majority of the session talking about her own abusive relationships is not setting good boundaries. The practitioner who becomes so upset about a mother abusing her child that he takes the child home with him is not setting good boundaries. The practitioner who becomes so upset at a client who projects anger in the counseling session that she cries and tells the client how she is having a horrible day and that the client just made it worse is not setting good boundaries. Finally, the practitioner who gets so immersed in his clients' problems that he becomes convinced his clients cannot survive without him is not setting good boundaries.

Personal boundaries are sometimes compared to physical boundaries such as the property line around one's house, porous enough that someone can enter the property but solid enough that a neighbor knows not to set a shed up in another neighbor's yard (Cloud & Townsend, 1992). So too must social workers establish boundaries in their mental, physical, and emotional lives to determine what falls within their domain and responsibility and what does not.

In the social work field, some boundaries are determined by the professional ethical standards. For instance, having a sexual relationship with a client violates an ethical boundary because this type of intimacy can exploit the practitioner–client relationship that grants the practitioner a significant measure of control—even authority—over the client. Violating the prohibition against having sexual relations with a client is so serious that it can result in suspension of one's professional license. Violating this ethical boundary might seem like an obviously bad idea to most people, but it occurs more often than many suspect.

> ## Engage Diversity and Difference in Practice
>
> **Practice Behavior: Gain sufficient self-awareness to eliminate the influence of personal biases and values in working with diverse groups.**
>
> **Critical Thinking Question:** You entered the social work field to help children because when you were young, you were abused as a child and no one advocated on your behalf. In your first job as a social worker at a family agency, you are working with a family seeking services for their teen daughter who is acting out in a rebellious manner. During one of the sessions the daughter complains that her father is "mean" to her and that is why she is acting out. How would boundary setting help you navigate this situation and not overidentify with the daughter?

One reason is that counseling someone of the opposite sex creates a sense of intimacy that can sometimes foster romantic feelings, particularly on the part of the client. Much like the child who develops a crush on a teacher, a client who is depressed and lonely may experience the practitioner's comfort, nurturing, and guidance as intimate love. But a sexual relationship when one party possesses power and control and the other is vulnerable will always result in emotional and physical exploitation. A practitioner who respects this boundary will recognize the clinical nature of the client's feelings and will help the client see that experiencing intimacy can be a very positive experience, but developing a romantic relationship should occur only when it can be truly reciprocal. This is an example of a clearly marked boundary, and it is difficult to step over this boundary line without knowing one is in dangerous territory. However, other boundaries are not so clear and are frequently violated by social workers.

My first job in social services was as an adolescent counselor at a locked residential facility. I was 23 years old, fresh out of college, and excited to finally be making a difference in people's lives. I became too involved in my clients' lives, though, and quickly began to overidentify with the teens on my caseload. I was so flattered by my clients' expressed need for me that I was willing to work any hours necessary to make sure they knew how much I cared. If I worked a 3:00 p.m. to midnight shift, and one of the girls on my caseload told me that she needed me there in the morning, I would make sure I was there at 8:00 a.m., even if it meant getting little sleep. If another counselor called me at home because a teen on my caseload was insisting that she would talk only to me, I dropped whatever I was doing and rushed down to the facility, feeling good that I was so needed.

This sort of behavior on my part indicated several problems. First, it led to a situation where I almost left the field of social services altogether because after three years I was so burned out that I was no longer sure I wanted to be a social worker in any respect. It also encouraged a sense of dependency among the girls on my caseload. Because it felt good to be needed, I neglected one of the fundamental values of social workers: empowering clients to be more self-sufficient. Setting boundaries would have encouraged my clients to develop relationships with other counselors and to rely on themselves and newly developed skills to cope with their struggles.

Since that point in my career I have developed some rules for the road for determining necessary boundaries and for making sure that I consistently enforce them. One rule is that I never work harder than my client. This does not mean that I do not advocate for clients, or that I do not assist clients in performing various tasks, but what it does mean is that I recognize that I am not truly helping clients who are not motivated to change because a counselor who overfunctions in a counseling relationship helps no one. Thus, when I begin to feel exhausted in my work with clients, I recognize this as a potential sign that I may be overfunctioning, perhaps out of impatience and a need to see progress. This recognition tells me that it is time to step back a bit and give my clients room to decide the best course of action for themselves.

I have also come to see my clients' lives as *their* journey, not mine. This conceptualization allows me to view myself as one of many individuals who will come alongside clients and help them at some point along their journeys, just as various people have helped and influenced me along my own life journey. This conceptual framework helps to remind me that my clients have free will to make whatever choices they deem fit. This self-determination means that they can accept my help and suggestions, or they can reject them.

A final conceptualization that can help establish and maintain healthy boundaries in a counseling relationship is to recognize that people grow and change at varying rates and in their own unique ways. Thus, when I am working with someone and it appears as though nothing I am doing or saying is making a difference, I remember that I might be the *seed planter*. Seed planters do just as it sounds—they plant the seeds for future growth, but oftentimes they do not have the benefit of seeing these changes come to fruition. It is often this way when working with adolescents. I rarely witnessed the results of my work with my teen clients, but I had to trust that in 5 or 10 years, something I said, some kindness I showed, some reframing I did would result in healthy personal growth.

It is equally important to recognize the role of the *fertilizer* and the *harvester* in counseling relationships. These are the counselors who come into the lives of clients after the seeds have already been planted. The fertilizer is the practitioner who helps the client do productive work—this is no easy task, but the counselor has the benefit of seeing the results of the counseling and intervention strategies. The harvester is probably the most gratifying role a social worker can have. This practitioner comes along when everything seems to align for the client. The client is ready to make the necessary changes for a healthy life, recognizes past negative patterns in relationships and choices, and has the necessary insight and motivation to effect true change.

I recently had a client who was at this point in her life. Fortunately, I was able to recognize that I could not take full credit for helping her to make the significant realizations and changes she was making in counseling. She'd had several prior counseling experiences, and my role was to help her to merge all that she had previously learned so that she could finally make the necessary, permanent changes in her attitude and approach to life, so that she could be a healthy, happy and productive individual, recognizing her own right to self-determination and dignity and her responsibilities to herself, her family, and her community. If you are working productively with a client but see little to no progress, you may very well be the seed planter. If you are working productively with a client but it seems as though change is still a long way off, then you are probably the fertilizer, and if you are reaping changes left and right with a client, then you may very well be the harvester. Seeing yourself operating as a part of a team, even though you will likely never meet the practitioners who came before you or those who may come after, helps to ease the burden of feeling so responsible for a client's growth, as well as helping to resist the temptation to take full credit for the client's progress.

Assess your comprehension of "Skills and Competencies" by completing this quiz.

THE PSYCHOSOCIAL ASSESSMENT

The process of assessing the psychosocial issues of a client utilizes a combination of numerous skills, such as *patience, active listening skills,* and *good observation skills,* as well as more tangible skills, such as being familiar with how to administer various psychological tests and assessments. The tools for conducting an effective assessment are numerous.

The first session is often spent conducting an *intake interview,* which includes collecting basic demographic information about the client (e.g., age, marital status, number of children, and ethnicity), as well as other pertinent information, including the nature of the identified problem(s), employment status, housing situation, physical health status, medications taken, history of substance abuse, criminal history, history of trauma, any history of mental health problems (including depression, suicidal thoughts, or other mental illness), and any history of mental health services.

When I was in graduate school, I recall being taught that the first five sessions with a client should be focused almost exclusively on assessment, but I quickly realized that if some intervention does not occur during those first few sessions, clients are not likely to return. Unlike many clients who see a clinical psychologist in private practice, many social work clients are in severe crisis, and they often need immediate intervention. Thus, social workers often find themselves jumping in with both feet, sizing up the client and the situation rather quickly so that some intervention strategies can be employed.

This by no means indicates that the assessment process should be shortchanged due to the frequent crisis nature of many social services agencies. Quite the opposite in fact—although it is true that the practitioner will be focusing more on assessment the first few sessions, the process of assessing the mental health functioning, as well as the client's situation, is ongoing and should continue throughout the counseling process. This is important for two reasons. First, before effective intervention strategies can be identified and used, the practitioner needs to know what the client's issues are. In addition, more often than not, new information will continue to emerge long after the formal assessment period is over, and if practitioners assume the assessment is complete, they might overlook important information about the client that emerges later in the counseling relationship.

Patience is imperative in conducting an effective assessment. One reason people enter the field of social work is that they love to figure other people out, but a seasoned professional will not allow this passion to result in a rush to judgment. Social workers should always approach clients with the understanding that the client's perspective is just that— the client's perspective, and that clients, as with all people, are complex beings that often emerge rather slowly (see Case Study 3.2).

Active listening skills involve the ability to attend to the speaker fully, without distraction, without preconceived notions of what the speaker is saying, and without being distracted by thoughts of what one wants to say in response. Active listening in the counseling relationship also includes behaviors such as maintaining direct eye contact and observing the client's body language. It also involves considering virtually everything that the client says as relevant. In fact, it is often the subtle, offhand comment that yields the most information about the client's interpersonal dynamics (see Case Study 3.3).

Good *observation skills* are also an important part of the assessment process because individuals communicate as much through their bodies as they do through their words. Practitioners should observe their clients' eye contact, whether they are shifting uncomfortably in their seats when talking about certain subjects, crossing their arms self-protectively, or tapping their feet anxiously. All these behaviors can be clues or indicators

---

Case Study 3.2   Patience in Action

I used to work with victims of domestic violence—a practice setting that I am passionate about because I am an advocate for those who are vulnerable. I recall one female client who shared stories of her controlling and abusive husband. Her stories seemed valid, and there was nothing in particular that would lead me to believe that she was not telling me the truth. In fact, what she shared about her husband's behavior met many of the hallmark signs of domestic violence relationships—her husband controlled the finances, and she had little or no access to the bank accounts; her husband appeared jealous and possessive, consistently demanding to know her constant whereabouts; and many of the arguments she reiterated to me reflected what appeared to be her husband's critical response to her in all respects, ranging from her housekeeping ability to the way she managed their children. I quickly began to view her low self-esteem and depression as being the *result* of his abusive behavior and counseled her accordingly. Yet several sessions into our counseling relationship, she retold a story, which she apparently did not recall telling me before. This version, though, was considerably different. I knew she was reciting the same story, but this time the events illustrating her husband's abusive behavior were different. I was not sure whether she was simply merging stories accidentally or whether this was an indication that she was not being completely honest with me. I made a note to explore this area further at a later date, and to be more diligent in determining the veracity of her stories. After interviewing her husband and children and spending more time assessing my client, I discovered that she was actually the abusive member of the family! She feared her husband leaving her and seeking custody, and thus, she hoped to enter into a counseling relationship and manipulate the counselor, so that she was perceived as the victim, and the counselor would therefore support her version of events in court. If practitioners are not diligent in thoroughly assessing their clients, they will be far likelier to be manipulated by some of their clients, thus doing more harm than good.

Case Study 3.3   Active Listening Skills in Action

I recall working with one female client on issues related to depression and parenting, who in response to my questions regarding her perception of the origin of her problems spent a considerable amount of time discussing her troubled marriage and her difficulty making friends. In the midst of sharing a particularly painful story about her difficult college years, she made a casual comment about how one of her college roommates said something to her once that reminded her of something her mother always said which was clearly quite painful. If I had not been actively listening, I could have missed the significance of that seemingly unimportant comment. It was stated as a joking aside, but I also noticed her brief pause and a quick, almost imperceptible, sadness in her eyes. The entire exchange lasted no more than a few seconds, but it completely turned the course of my assessment. I made a mental note to revisit the issue of her mother during a later session when we knew each other better and she knew she could trust me. Eventually it became clear that her core emotional issues resided in her tumultuous relationship with her mother, but she had previously been so protective of this relationship that it felt far too unsafe for her to recognize that her primary issues revolved around her relationship with a controlling, shaming mother, and not her husband or friends. Over the course of the next several months I continued to revisit the issue, slowly at first and then more boldly once we were on solid ground in our own relationship, and she was finally able to recognize the hold her mother had on her all these years. Had I not been as attentive, responding instead to only what the client wanted to focus on, we would have spent our time together focusing on residual issues.

of deeper dynamics. Employing good observation skills can also yield information about whether a client is being direct or evasive, genuine or masked, sincere or manipulative, open or guarded.

Bowen's Family Genogram

A more comprehensive assessment tool involves constructing a *genogram* of the client's family. Murray Bowen (1978) developed the family systems theory, which is based on the premise that inter- and intrarelational patterns are transmitted from one generation to the next. Thus, one way to grasp the "big picture" of the client's life is to study this intergenerational transmission as it relates to issues such as communication style, emotional regulation, and various other "rules for living" (e.g., it is good to express emotions, it is bad to express emotions). Bowen believes that the goal for achieving positive well-being is to find the balance between achieving personal autonomy and individuation while maintaining appropriate closeness with one's family system.

Learn how to construct a genogram by conducting an Internet search on Genopro, creating an account, and developing your personal genogram.

Those who are so close to their family system that they cannot make decisions without family approval for fear of being considered betrayers of the family are considered *enmeshed*, and those who find it necessary to emotionally distance themselves to the point of estrangement in order to achieve independence are considered *cut off*.

Most people have some information about their parents, limited information about their grandparents, and oftentimes no information whatsoever about their great-grandparents. They may have grown up hearing one-sided (and unquestioned) versions of family feuds or odd distant relatives, but to gain accurate and valuable information about one's family system, information seeking must be intentional. This can be uncomfortable and may ruffle some feathers, because it is often the family members who have been cut off, or are considered the "black sheep" of the family, who hold the family secrets that will unlock the true underlying dynamics of a family system. Poking around the skeleton closet can often threaten families, particularly in closed family systems, but this information may also hold the key to truly unlocking those well hidden dynamics that have been in place sometimes for numerous generations.

Genograms use a variety of symbols designed to indicate gender, the type of relationship (married, divorced, etc.), as well as the nature of the relationships (cut off or enmeshed). Traumatic events, such as deaths, divorces, and miscarriages, are noted, as are the family's responses to these events (e.g., losses are openly talked about, never discussed, or denied). Typically, shameful events are also relevant, such as out-of-wedlock births (particularly relevant in earlier generations), abortions, extramarital affairs, domestic violence, alcohol abuse, sexual abuse and assault, and job losses. Such events are often kept secret but can affect family members for generations to come. The shame of an extramarital affair and an out-of-wedlock birth that was hushed up several generations back can have a profound effect on how emotions are handled and how feelings are communicated.

I once worked with a woman who struggled to understand why her mother never seemed to accept or approve of her. She had spent years in counseling attempting to understand her mother's and her own intense perfectionism and refusal to accept even the smallest of mistakes. My client was convinced that her mother was ashamed of her, and this belief affected every area of her functioning. A genogram revealed that my client's grandmother was raped, and my client's mother was the product of that rape. Both the grandmother and my client's mother lived their lives in constant shame, and their high expectations of my client were really a reflection of their desire to protect her from the shame they were forced to endure, not some statement of their disapproval of her. It was through the development of a genogram that my client was able to take a few emotional steps back and see her family system with more clarity.

A family genogram provides a structured way to obtain a comprehensive family history so that the practitioner and client can develop a more complete understanding of the family dynamics that are affecting the client in ways perhaps never before recognized or acknowledged. It also provides for an objective and non-shaming way to gain a level of objective understanding of various issues within one's family system that can potentially pave the way for the client to view relationships and various events without personalizing hurtful experiences, including gaining an objective understanding of the nature of conflict-filled family relationships (Prest & Protinsky, 1993).

No longer is the client blaming himself for his father's seeming disapproval or feeling hurt because his mother seemed emotionally distant and rejecting. Instead clients can develop a greater understanding of the broader picture and can see their family members as individual people who are as much a victim of circumstances as the client. Thus, a family genogram is not merely an effective assessment tool, but also a very effective intervention tool that can be used to address long-standing issues that have potentially kept clients in emotional bondage for years.

Psychological Testing

Social workers have numerous other tools at their disposal as well, including various objective assessments tools, such as inventories designed to assess levels of depression, anxiety, social functioning, and personality style. Less objective measures, such as interpretive drawing exercises, free choice drawing, clay manipulation, and structured play therapy, can also be useful. These assessments are particularly effective with clients who are either less verbal, or are dealing with particularly painful emotional issues.

When working with traumatized children, I would often ask them to draw a picture of their families. Although the results always need to be considered cautiously, and in the context of all other information gleaned during sessions, it is always interesting to see how children conceptualize themselves and their various family members. For instance, drawing a picture where the father is significantly larger than the rest of the family might indicate a perception that the father is overbearing. A child who draws himself or herself floating away or standing separately from the rest of the family might indicate a feeling of being disconnected from the rest of the family members. Again, it is essential that social workers use great caution when interpreting subjective techniques, and all assessment material should be considered as a whole, rather than giving too much weight to any one particular measure.

Continuum of Mental Health and Mental Illness

When evaluating someone's level of functioning and mental health status, it is important to recognize that virtually all behaviors occur on a continuum. It is only when a particular behavior occurs frequently enough, and at an intensity level high enough to interfere with normal daily functioning for a significant amount of time, that it becomes the subject of clinical attention. All of us feel sad at times, but if we are so intensely sad that we stop eating and want to stay in bed all day, then we may be suffering from clinical depression. Similarly, many of us become concerned from time to time that our friends might be talking behind our backs or that one of our coworkers is trying to get us fired, but if we're convinced that everyone is out to get us, even people we've never met, then we may be suffering from some form of paranoia.

The *Diagnostic and Statistical Manual of Mental Disorders*, 5th edition *(DSM-V)* accounts for this continuum by including criteria relating to frequency and intensity of psychological experiences. For instance, in order to meet the criteria for major depressive disorder, an individual does not just have to be depressed, but must have a depressed mood nearly every day for at least a two-week period. An individual who meets the criteria for generalized anxiety disorder isn't someone who worries from time to time, but someone who worries *excessively*, more days than not, for at least six months.

The value of services provided depends on the effectiveness of the assessment. A good assessment defines the problem or problems the client is experiencing, develops a needs assessment to determine where the client's strengths and deficits lie, ascertains the client's social support system, and develops an appropriate treatment plan. It is also important to reassess the client at various points in the counseling process to monitor new or previously masked issues, and to make sure that treatment goals are consistent with the assessment (see Box 3.1).

Assess your comprehension of "The Psychosocial Assessment" by completing this quiz.

GENERALIST TECHNIQUES FOR DIRECT PRACTICE

Although the assessment process is ongoing, once the initial assessment is complete, a treatment plan is developed that is designed to address the client's identified issues. There are basic techniques involved in generalist practice that apply in a broad way to most counseling and intervention situations.

Many individuals seeking services at a social services agency will need assistance with developing better coping skills. Regardless of whether the problems experienced

Box 3.1   Case Management vs. Direct Practice

What types of issues do you think are best addressed with direct practice and which are best addressed by case management?

It is important to understand the qualitative differences between case management and direct counseling services. Although both encompass a broad range of activities, they are distinctly different. Direct practice with clients is focused more on an individual's psychological growth and the development of emotional insight and personal growth, whereas case management involves coordinating services with other systems impacting the life of the client. A case manager might coordinate services with a client's school social worker, the housing authority, the local rape crisis center, or even a court liaison, all in an attempt to meet the needs of the client who is interacting in some manner with each of these systems. The goal of the case manager is to assist the client in plugging in to necessary and supportive social services within the community and to learn how to improve the reciprocal relationship or transaction with each of these social systems. These efforts have many purposes and goals, but chief among them is the caseworker's proactive attempt to strengthen and broaden the client's social support network.

Pearson Education, Inc.

by the client are pervasive or more limited, most clients can benefit from learning to manage high levels of stress, learning to prioritize the various problems in their lives, and learning how to manage the current crisis in a way that diminishes the possibility of a domino effect of crises. A crisis with one's child requiring a significant amount of time and attention can quickly result in a job loss, which can in turn result in the loss of housing. Confronting crises effectively, though, can have a positive impact on one's life, including an increase in self-esteem, the development of new and more effective coping skills, the gaining of wisdom and the development of new social skills, and the development of a better overall support system.

Most mental health experts recognize that one of the best opportunities for personal growth is a crisis, due to the possibility of shaking up long-standing and entrenched maladaptive patterns of behavior. Park and Fenster (2004) studied stress-related growth in a group of college students who experienced a stressful event and found that the struggle involved in a life crisis produced personal growth. This is true, though, only for those who expend the necessary energy to work through their struggles in a positive way. Those in the study who remained negative and avoided dealing with the problems born out of the crisis did not take advantage of the growth-producing opportunities and thus did not experience any significant personal growth. Those who worked hard to manage the stress resulting from their crisis and were able to see the crisis as an opportunity for growth often developed better personal life mastery skills and developed a changed and healthier perspective. Recognizing this potential for personal growth provides the practitioner with a framework for assisting clients in developing better coping skills that can not only better assist them in the management of concrete problems but also help them to shift their entire perspective of life struggles in general. For instance, clients who once saw themselves as powerless victims can begin to see themselves as empowered survivors.

Task-Centered Casework

Most of us can relate to feeling completely overwhelmed when facing a life crisis. We know there are things we need to do to manage the crisis, but all we see is a gigantic mountain looming before us. For some, this has a motivating effect, and they attack the mountain until every issue is resolved. But for some, particularly those with a long history of crises, those with poor coping skills, or those suffering from emotional or psychological problems with diminished capacities the mountain can seem virtually insurmountable, and their response may be to shrink away with a feeling of despair and defeat.

A counseling technique called the *task-centered approach*, an intervention strategy developed at the School of Social Services at the University of Chicago (Reid, 1975), works well with clients who feel paralyzed in response to the challenges of various psychosocial problems. Treatment is typically short, lasting anywhere between two and four months, and is focused on problem solving. The client and social worker or caseworker define the problems together and develop mutually agreed-upon goals. Each problem is broken down into smaller and more easily manageable tasks. Goals can be as tangible as finding a new job or as intangible as more effectively managing frustration and anger. Rather than having one broad goal of obtaining a job, a client might have a week-one goal of doing nothing more than looking at the want ads in one or two online job sites and a week-two goal of making one phone call to a prospective employer. Dividing large goals into smaller, specific, stepping-stone goals diminishes the possibility that clients will allow their anxiety to overwhelm them. By focusing on specific problems and breaking them into bite-sized, manageable pieces, clients not only learn effective problem-solving skills but also gain insight into the nature of their problems, develop increased self-esteem as they experience success rather than failure in response to meeting goal expectations, and learn to manage their emotions, such as anxiety and depression, without allowing such states to overtake and overwhelm them.

The counselor or caseworker assists clients in meeting goal expectations through a variety of intervention strategies specific to the actual problem, but can include planning for obstacles, role-playing (where the client can actually act out difficult situations in the safety of the counselor's office as a way of practicing communication, etc.), and mental rehearsal (similar to role-playing but involves the client thinking or fantasizing about some specific situation—such as an upcoming job interview or a difficult confrontation) (Reid, 1975). Revisiting original goals and evaluating client progress are also powerful tools in helping clients experience a sense of personal mastery and empowerment as they are helped to recognize their progress.

Perceptual Reframing, Emotional Regulation, Networking, and Advocacy

Another general counseling method includes the reframing of a client's perception of a situation, emphasizing the importance of viewing various events, relationships, and occurrences from a variety of possible perspectives. For some reason it seems easier for human beings to assume the negative in many situations. Whether considering the intentions of a boyfriend or the prospects of getting a better job, most of us seem to gravitate toward negative assumptions despite many of us perceiving ourselves as optimists. Many people in the midst of a physical or emotional crisis of any proportion will often resort to taking a somewhat polarized negative stance on an issue and would benefit from assistance in seeing situations and relationships from a different perspective. A client's perception that life is unfair and nothing good ever happens to her can be encouraged to see life struggles as normal and even good because they promote positive personal growth.

Case Study 3.4   Example of the Task-Centered Approach

The plight of Mary explored in the opening vignette at the beginning of this chapter serves as an ideal case study for the application of the task-centered approach. Mary's social worker begins her work with Mary by assuring her that there is no rush to accomplish all of the tasks that lay before her immediately by reminding Mary that she is in charge of her own life and can make the choices she thinks are best for her and her son.

During the first two sessions, Mary and her social worker develop realistic goals for her, including securing an apartment when Mary has the funds to ensure financial security. They also develop a detailed budget and determine that Mary will need about three months' salary put away in a savings account to ensure against any realistic financial emergencies. By identifying possible obstacles to Mary achieving independence, decisions are made based on facts and realistic risks, not on undefined and generalized fear. Once goals are developed and obstacles identified, Mary and her social worker agree on tasks to be accomplished by the following week.

Mary's task for the first week is to find apartment rental websites and peruse online ads, and bookmark listings within her price range in her desired neighborhoods. She is told not to call about any of apartments though, even if she finds one that seems ideal. Mary comes to her second appointment with the websites and descriptions of the apartments, and she and her caseworker spend the first portion of the session discussing how Mary felt while reviewing the various apartment rental websites. Mary explained that her initial excitement was quickly followed by intense anxiety, but that when she realized she was not permitted to call on the apartments, even if she had wanted to, she calmed down almost immediately. The next portion of the session is spent on determining tasks for the following week. The first task involves calling about two apartments for informational purposes only. Because Mary has a significant amount of anxiety about calling and talking to a stranger, she and her social worker write a script and rehearse it by doing a role-play, with the social worker playing the part of the potential landlord. Mary's additional task for the week is to talk to her boss and ask for reassurance that her employment is secure.

Mary returned the following week feeling excited. She shares that she called on two apartments, and while she followed the script on the first one, the second call went so well she decided that she did not even need the script. Her discussion with her boss also went well, and he reassured her that her job was, in fact, secure. Mary shares excitedly that her boss was pleased that Mary showed initiative in approaching him and offered her an opportunity to attend some training courses so that she could be promoted. Breaking apart the tasks that lay before Mary into *bite-sized pieces* allowed her to manage her anxiety more effectively and gain valuable experiences that refuted her negative worldview.

For the next three months Mary's counseling proceeds in a similar fashion with weekly tasks that inch her along slowly enough that she does not become overwhelmed by unidentified and general fears, but quickly enough that she gains confidence and courage with each successive step. Ultimately Mary rents an apartment during her fourth month of counseling with three months' income safely tucked away in a savings account, a promotion with a raise, and a reputable and affordable day care.

Clients who feel shame because they were recently fired from a job they despised can be encouraged to see this incident as a disguised blessing opening the door to find a career for which they are far better suited.

Additional intervention goals include assisting clients with *emotional regulation*, teaching them how to sit with their emotions rather than immediately acting on them, developing a better *social support network* so that they can become emotionally independent and self-reliant, and *advocating for clients* who are being oppressed, either within their family systems or in society in general.

Cultural Competence and Diversity

Because social workers work with such a wide range of people, across various cultures, and socioeconomic levels, it is vital that social work education and training be presented in a context of cultural competence and cultural sensitivity. Cultural competence is reflective of a counselor's ability to work effectively with people of color and minority populations by being sensitive to their needs and recognizing their unique experiences and is a required component of working in the social work field.

Most professional organizations require that their mental health professionals obtain cultural competency training based on a foundation of respect for and sensitivity to cultural differences and diversity (Conner & Grote, 2008). Yet cultural competency extends beyond that of ethnic differences. For instance, social workers who undergo cultural competency training will learn the importance of remaining sensitive to populations from different income levels, religions, physical and mental capacities, genders, and sexual orientations, as well as races, and as such, will learn the importance of avoiding what is commonly referred to as ethnocentrism—the tendency to perceive one's own background and associated values as being superior to or more *normal* than others. In recent years, the issue of cultural or multicultural competence has become so important that training protocols have been developed with recommendations that all those who work in the helping fields engage in some form of cultural competency training (NASW, 2000).

Cultural competence is somewhat a general term, though, and is often used synonymously with other terms such as *cultural sensitivity*. Despite the relatively universal belief among social work experts that cultural competence is a vital aspect of practice, very little consensus exists as to what constitutes cultural competency on a practice level (Fortier & Shaw-Taylor, 2000). Although broad themes of respect and sensitivity tend to be universally accepted as foundational to cultural competent practice, the concept of cultural competency has tended to remain as an idea or a general philosophy that has not yet been operationalized in a concrete way. For instance, Cunningham, Foster, and Henggeler (2002) surveyed counselors who considered themselves culturally competent and found that there was a vast difference in terms of which counseling methods they believed were most effective with culturally diverse clients. This last consensus among experts on which specific counseling approaches and counselor responses constituted "cultural competence" makes it difficult, if not impossible, to determine what methods will have the greatest likelihood of having a positive outcome in counseling a particular ethnically diverse client group. Although recent research has attempted to develop what is called *evidence-based practice* with regard to cultural competence, to date there remains very little research on what constitutes *cultural competent practice*. It is for this reason that cultural competency is explored contextually throughout the remainder of this book.

Apply Knowledge of Human Behavior and the Social Environment

Practice Behavior: Critique and apply knowledge to understand person and environment.

Critical Thinking Question: You are a social worker working with a client who has recently emigrated from another county. The client is a different gender than you, is from a completely different culture than you, and practices a different religion than you. What steps can you take to ensure that you develop cultural competency and thus do not approach your work with this client with a sense of ethnocentrism?

Assess your comprehension of "Generalist Techniques for Direct Practice" by completing this quiz.

SOCIAL WORK PRACTICE ON A MACRO LEVEL

When students consider entering the field of social work, they often do so because they want to help people meet their basic needs by counseling them, helping them obtain much-needed services, and teaching them new ways of meeting their needs in the future. In other words, most students think of *direct practice* or *micro practice* with individuals and families when considering a career in the social work profession. But many times the challenges a client is encountering are being caused by some external source—an injustice that is structural or systemic, such as the school system that offers no bus service and therefore inadvertently contributes to low-income students' truancy rates, or a government social welfare policy that inadvertently punishes single mothers who work part-time by cutting their benefits, or a three-strikes law that sends a young ethnic-minority male to jail for 25 years for a third, yet relatively minor, offense. How does the social work professional combat harmful policies that punish when they should reward or unfair legislation that hurts certain segments of the population?

The social work profession is grounded in the notion that people are a part of larger systems and to truly understand the individual one must understand the broader system the individual is operating within. The discussion of Bowen's family systems theory is a good place to start in understanding how systems work, noting that there is a reciprocal dynamic involving both the individual and the system, where each has an impact on the other. Hence, an individual can receive years of counseling and other forms of direct intervention, but until injustices within society are addressed, they will continue to experience difficulty in some manner.

It is important, then, for social workers to recognize that people can be helped by approaching problems on various levels. By way of comparison, if as a social worker you were committed to eradicating violence within society, you might choose to work with survivors of domestic violence in the hope that counseling them might help your clients recognize the signs of abuse and avoid engaging in abusive relationships in the future. This approach would involve *micro practice*—practice with individuals. You might also decide to facilitate treatment groups for batterers, believing that the greatest likelihood of change can be accomplished by addressing the perpetrators of violence in a group setting where each group member can learn from others. This approach would involve *mezzo practice*—practice with groups. But if you decided to address the problem of violence by working with an entire community, locally, nationally, or perhaps even globally, by creating a new program in your agency, by conducting a public awareness campaign to educate the population about the prevalence of violence, or by lobbying for the passage of antiviolence legislation, then you would be conducting *macro practice*—practice with communities and organizations.

Macro practice involves addressing and confronting social issues that can act as barriers to getting one's basic needs met on an organizational level by creating structural change through social action. The most basic themes involved in macro practice include advocating for *social and economic justice* and *human rights* for all members of society to end human oppression and exploitation (Weil, 1996). There are several ways *social change* is accomplished through macro practice, including *program development, community development* through *community organizing, policy practice,* and *international* or *global advocacy.*

Thus, although direct practice is important, working with entire systems to promote positive structural change on all fronts is equally important. Some social workers

Social Work Application Activity

The Importance of Macro Practice

Think about a common social problem that concerns you. What are some ways that social workers may address this problem through macro practice? How do these macropractice intervention strategies complement direct (micro) practice strategies?

Social workers might ask themselves why they should be concerned about what is happening to people in an entire community, in a different part of the country, or in a completely different part of the world. A foundational value of the social work profession is a commitment to social justice and human rights achieved through social action and social change. This is particularly relevant to social workers living in the United States since many clients in need of assistance have emigrated from countries where they were victims of oppression and human rights violations. Working with this type of population requires that social workers have an understanding of the wide range of global issues related to social injustice and human rights abuses, as well as the skills necessary to recognize how these abuses have implications on direct practice with individual clients (Weiss, 2003).

Social workers must also be aware of the history of social injustices and human rights abuses that have occurred within U.S. borders, as well as develop an awareness of what groups are most likely to be targets of discrimination and oppression. For instance, this foundational commitment to social justice is so integral to the social work profession that the professional obligation to social action is reflected in the ethical principles of the discipline. In fact, the NASW (1999) ethical standards go one step further by expanding the social workers' responsibility to the international level stating that "[s]ocial workers should promote the general welfare of society, from local to global levels, and the development of people, their communities, and their environments" (p. 26).

Unfortunately, the social work profession has gradually moved away from its original call to community action, turning instead to a model of individualized care (Mizrahi, 2001). This is likely due to the increased popularity of individual psychotherapies within all the mental health professions in the 20th century. This doesn't mean that macro practice or social advocacy has ceased. Rather, as those in the social work profession have pulled away from community work, other disciplines have moved in to fill the vacuum, such as urban and public planners and those in the political science fields. This pattern has resulted in the social work profession often being out of the loop of community-building and organizing efforts (Johnson, 2004). Concerns have also been expressed regarding the trend of neglecting the subject of macro and community practice in social work educational programs, thus compounding the tendency for social workers to avoid macro practice because many recent graduates feel ill-equipped to enter into social advocacy or policy practice on an organizational level (Polack, 2004).

Social work's movement away from macro practice is apparently an international trend as well because studies generated outside the United States have made some similar observations. For instance, Weiss (2003) cited examples of how many social workers in Israel do not feel competent addressing social issues on a community or global level because the majority of their training focused on practice with individual clients. Weiss encourages those in the social work profession both in Israel and abroad to reengage in policy-related activities and social advocacy on a macro level.

The reality is that social issues such as poverty and human exploitation must be addressed through advocacy efforts for social change on a macro level as well as a micro level, since structural change in society's institutions will determine the quality of clients' everyday lives.

work solely in macro practice in administrative positions or policy practice conducting no direct practice whatsoever, but a great many social workers who are involved in micro practice are also involved in macro practice on at least some level. For instance, when I worked as a victim advocate for a local state's attorney's office, I counseled victims of violent crime. But I also served on a domestic violence advisory coalition that evaluated community concerns and interagency coordination and advocated for social reform; thus, I engaged in both micro and macro practice.

At-risk, Oppressed, and Disenfranchised Populations

Before beginning any discussion on social advocacy efforts, it is important to identify populations that are often the target of social injustice, oppression, and human rights violations. It is challenging to comprise a comprehensive list of at-risk populations because there is some shifting in oppressed people from era to era. For instance, children, although still quite vulnerable, are no longer considered an oppressed group in the same way that they were around the turn of the century when poverty and harsh economic conditions led to thousands of children flooding the streets of New York, leading to a significant reduction in sympathy toward orphaned children.

In essence, an at-risk population can include any group of individuals who are vulnerable to exploitation due to lifestyle, lack of political power, lack of financial resources, and lack of societal advocacy and support. Currently, at-risk and oppressed populations may include ethnic minorities, immigrants (particularly those who do not speak English), indigenous people, older adults, women, children in foster care, prisoners, the poor, the homeless, single parents, lesbians, gays, bisexual transgendered individuals, members of a religious minority, and the physically and intellectually disabled. In addition, in many regions of the world, certain groups of individuals are selected and oppressed due to their ethnic background, religious heritage, and caste (their level of status within society, which in many regions of the world is a level they are born into), and although these individuals may not be in the minority as far as numbers, they typically have little to no political power and are subject to mistreatment and exploitation.

At-risk populations often share unique characteristics not shared by others within a particular culture (within mainstream population and/or those in the majority) (Brownridge, 2009), and it is this uniqueness that can often increase their risk of oppression, discrimination, injustice, and exploitation. At-risk populations are thus *at greater risk* of experiencing a variety of social problems than other populations within mainstream society, which undoubtedly then affect the broader population (even if those in power do not believe so).

Vulnerability increases with what is called *intersectionality*—where an individual possesses more than one social and cultural characteristic of vulnerability, leading to increased risk of disadvantage. The concept of intersectionality was originally applied to race and gender, but is now applied to a variety of marginalizing categories, such as level of disability, sexuality, socioeconomic status, social class, immigration status, nationality, and family status (Knudsen, 2005; Meyer, 2002; Samuels, 2008). An example of intersectionality of vulnerability would be an African American older lesbian who is economically disadvantaged, physically disabled, and struggling with homelessness. This profile reveals a woman who experiences multiple forms of vulnerability to injustice on a variety of levels, likely warranting various types of advocacy (Martin, 2014).

Social forces can combine as well, increasing the risk of discrimination, prejudice, oppression, and injustice. For instance, social conditions such as white privilege (advantage experienced by Caucasians to varying degrees), nativism (a bias against foreign-born residents or those who are perceived as threats to a country's nationalism), xenophobia (an irrational fear of immigrants and foreigners), and other forms of prejudice often combine to increase a group's vulnerability to oppression, marginalization, and exploitation (Martin, 2014). Within the social work field there is a recognition that at-risk populations often need advocacy because many of the challenges that lie before them are created within society through policies, laws, and attitudes that create an *uneven playing field*, where some groups enjoy greater access to benefits (i.e., *privilege*) whereas other groups are systematically excluded from such societal benefits.

A Human Rights Framework: Inalienable Rights for All Human Beings

Before social workers can effectively engage in work on a macro level, whether doing community organizing or more direct social justice advocacy on behalf of at-risk and oppressed populations, they must first become aware of what a just society looks like. What is an ideal society? At the root of any discussion of an ideal society is the assumption that all human beings have inalienable rights simply because they are human. Yet history is replete with examples of egregious human rights violations, often waged in the belief that such actions are justified on some level. Slavery, a caste system that deems one group of people more worthy than another, a patriarchal system that subjugates females within society, the genocide or *ethnic cleansing* of a particular cultural group, and the sale and exploitation of women and children are all examples of the gross mistreatment of individuals, often because there is some defining characteristic about these individuals that makes them different from another group. Such differences are often used to justify their mistreatment, where members of a more powerful group place themselves above the members of a more vulnerable group. Members of a just society recognize that no one group should have oppressive power over another, and that all human beings have basic rights that must be protected. Since some groups of individuals are more vulnerable than others, social workers working in macro practice, particularly on an international level, take responsibility for being the voice of the voiceless (Martin, 2014).

Shared Goals of Effective Macropractice Techniques

Macro practice is a multidisciplinary field shared by those in social work, social sciences, political sciences, and urban planning disciplines. Within the general field of macro practice, models have been developed to frame the various ways of approaching social concerns on a broad level. Although there is a very broad range of theories and models of macro or community practice, most models have at their core the basic goal of societally based social transformation where a community on any level (local, national, or global) incorporates values that reflect the human dignity and worth of *all* its members.

Within most macropractice models, empowerment strategies are used that focus on social and economic development, creating liaisons between community members and community organizations, political and social action, which will likely involve advocating for policy changes that address injustices and inequalities within society (Netting, Kettner, & McMurtry, 2011). Various aspects of macro practice will vary depending on the area of concern and the vulnerable population being targeted, but virtually all models of macro practice include a focus on community development, which can refer to the development of a geographic community, such as a neighborhood or city, or a community of individuals, such as women, immigrants, or children.

Common Aspects of Macro Practice

In the next few sections we will explore some ways in which social workers engage in practice on a macro level, including community development, community organizing, and policy practice. These areas of macro practice are quite general, and you'll likely notice that there is quite a bit of overlap between each but gaining at least a cursory understanding of the different types of macro practice is important so that you can better understand how social work goes from identifying social problems within society to finding ways of effectively addressing them.

Community Development

Community development dates back to the settlement house movement when Jane Addams and her colleagues worked with politicians, various community organizations, political activists, and community members to create a better community for all members. By engaging residents, community leaders, local politicians, and other community organizations, Addams was able to develop a sense of community cohesion, which resulted in several laws being passed that benefited the members of her community, including those who resided in the settlement houses.

Community development in Addams's day is similar in many respects to today, where effective community building depends on the participation of community organizations and community members working together to address issues that are of concern to the entire community (Austin, 2005). The actual issues involved could be anything from addressing crime in the community to educational concerns such as low state test scores, developing an after-school program to combat juvenile delinquency, bringing new businesses to the community to create jobs for community members, or rallying community leaders to develop more open spaces, including parks in densely populated neighborhoods.

A community development approach is empowering because the mutual collaboration of several agencies and area organizations provides support for community members in ways not possible through social service agencies alone. Another empowering aspect of community development is that the collaboration process can create a sense of collective self-sufficiency that often leads to civic pride for community members. In fact, effective community development is based on the conviction that any community is capable of mobilizing "economic, social, and political resources to support families" (Austin, 2005, p. 109).

There are several necessary components of successful community development, including diversity among group members, a sense of shared values among members, positive and collaborative teamwork, good communication, equal participation of all team members, and a good network of connections outside the community. Good community development also depends on the ability to secure enough funding to support group members' activities and efforts. Good networking skills are also essential as are good technology skills because so much of networking in contemporary society is accomplished through email and other technological means (Austin, 2005; Weil, 1996).

Community Organizing

Community development depends on the efforts of community-organizing efforts, which in turn depends on the efforts of community organizers. The first step in community organizing is to create a consensus on what the community needs, in particular what negative issues the community is facing or areas of needed improvement. Once community members agree on the problems to be addressed, community organizers set about to recruit members to join in the effort to create change. It is important to once again note that the term *community* does not necessarily refer to a geographic community, but might also refer to a community of people, such as women, victims of domestic violence, prisoners, or foster care children.

Community organizers can be professional policy makers or licensed social workers, or they can be individual people with a particular passion and calling for social action. A schoolteacher who gets a group of his students together to remove graffiti from public buildings is a community organizer. The single mother of three who organizes a voluntary after-school tutoring program for the kids in her neighborhood is a community organizer. The father of a child survivor of sexual abuse who organizes a campaign to increase prison time for sexual offenders is a community organizer. The licensed social worker whose agency is hired to canvas a neighborhood in an antidrug educational campaign is a community organizer.

Community organizing efforts usually begin around a problem or concern of many people in a community. Once a problem has been identified, community organizers must conduct research to define the issues, understanding how the problem or issue developed and what if any forces exist to keep the problem in place. For instance, the community activist who is organizing efforts to increase the labor rights of undocumented immigrants will likely encounter opposition from factory owners who benefit by paying untaxed low wages to undocumented workers. Thoroughly researching this issue will enable community organizers to identify constituents in the community who will support their cause as well as those who will oppose it. Research will also enable community organizers to identify additional harm done by unfair labor practices not initially identified that might increase the strength of any collating forces.

Once the problem has been identified and research has been conducted, a plan of action must be determined. Community organizers might decide to picket factories where they perceive abuse of undocumented workers; they might decide to distribute press releases and have a press conference to gain media involvement, organize a work walkout, or conduct a letter-writing campaign to local political leaders. Successful community organizers also organize fund-raising efforts to support their social activism. Sources of fund-raising can include a number of strategies, including a direct request for donations, auctions, fund-raising dinners, membership fees, or government grants.

Policy Practice

Policy practice is a narrower form of community practice where the social worker works within the political system to influence government policy and legislation on a local, state, federal, or even global level. The form that policy practice takes depends in large part on the issues at hand, but certain activities in policy practice are consistent despite the issue. This is a relatively new field within social work, with few researchers focusing on policy practice prior to the 1980s. It remains an often neglected area of practice, both within social work education and within social services practice setting. One reason for this may be that effective policy practice relies on a broad range of skills that reaches far beyond the clinical realm (Rocha & Johnson, 1997), although in the past decade, this trend has been reversing.

Policy practice activities center on either reforming current social policy or initiating the development of new policy that addresses the needs of the underserved and marginalized members of society with the primary goal of social justice through social action and advocacy. Policy practice is based on the belief that many problems in society, such as poverty, are structural in nature and can be addressed through making structural changes within society (Weiss, 2003).

Although various approaches to policy practice have been defined within academic literature, Iatridis (1995) has defined several skills necessary for effectively integrating social policy practice into direct service or micro practice. The first skill involves the social workers' ability to understand the nature of social policy, including what it is, how it is developed, its influences and effect on society, as well as how social welfare policies are most often implemented. The second skill involves the ability and willingness to view direct practice from a systems perspective, where individual practice is seen as a part of a greater whole. In other words, social workers engaged in policy practice must be able to link issues confronted in direct service to structural problems in society (i.e., institutionalized racism, laws that oppress certain groups) by using a PIE paradigm (person-in-environment), a concept addressed throughout this text relating to the importance of viewing social issues such as poverty on a societal as well as an individual level. Another equally important skill involves the social workers' commitment to improving social justice within society by working toward a more equitable distribution of the community's resources.

Those who engage in policy analysis research various social issues in an attempt to determine the short- and long-term effects of new policies and legislation. Policy activists and analysts might focus their attention broadly on social injustices in general, or they may focus on more narrow issues such as the quality of mental health delivery systems, or the focus may be extremely narrow such as the social injustices confronted by migrant farm workers seeking healthcare services for work-related injuries. Social workers engaging in policy practice must be able to identify key trends and issues, as well as become familiar with legislation or pending legislation that will affect the area of concern. Let's assume you are involved in policy practice working for an agency concerned with the older adult population. The federal administration's policies regarding Social Security funding would be a matter of great concern to you. Yet if you were involved with policy practice advocating for the rights of the children of undocumented immigrants, you'd be very concerned about possible legislation that would prohibit these children from attending public school. Regardless of the area of concern, policy analysts must be able to identify the *ripple effect* of new policies and legislation to identify their potential harm or benefit to their target population as well as the entire community.

Assess your comprehension of "Social Work Practice on a Macro Level" by completing this quiz.

Summary

Although social workers work with a very wide range of clients presenting with an equally diverse range of psychosocial problems, the skills and intervention techniques they must possess can be broadly applied in generalist practice. Understanding that people are not pathological by nature, but often are responding to real traumas, tragedies, and crises in a natural way (e.g., it is normal to become depressed after experiencing a loss) helps the social worker look for a client's strengths, rather than solely assessing a client's perceived deficits.

The unique nature of the social work encourages practitioners to view the individual as a part of a greater whole; thus, a client's social world is assessed and evaluated holistically, which enables social workers to help their clients better navigate their world. Essentially, social workers are committed to working with displaced, marginalized and oppressed populations, assessing not only clients but also the worlds in which they live. Social workers then apply various culturally competent intervention techniques on a micro, mezzo, or macro level, that encourage, empower, and integrate some of society's most broken and marginalized members helping them to become whole and functional, so that they can function at their optimal level.

Recall what you learned in this chapter by completing the Chapter Review.

Child Welfare Services

Overview and Purpose of Child and Family Services Agencies

In 2001, ABC's news show *Nightline* aired a documentary featuring the horrible plight of the street children of Romania (Belzberg, 2001). After the show, U.S. citizens flooded the network with telephone calls, expressing outrage and horror at the images that flashed across their television screens for almost two hours. The documentary revealed children as young as six years old living on the streets, with no food to eat, with only slightly older children and liquid glue to keep them warm at night. The reporter explained how political events in Romania created a situation where impoverished families could no longer care for their offspring, leading to the streets becoming flooded with marauding children, in desperate search of money and food. These children, who often resorted to pickpocketing and other petty crimes, were considered by most mainstream Romanians to be the scourge of society, pests to be avoided.

The U.S. response was one of literal horror, not only at the conditions in which the children were forced to live but also at the apparent apathy of most Romanians, particularly those in government and the Romanian police force. The documentary showed numerous incidences of police mistreatment, including one young boy whose leg was broken in a scuffle with a police officer. This seeming indifference shocked viewers, who expressed outrage at the heartlessness necessary not only to accept orphans living on the street but to actually perceive these orphans as social pariahs.

These concerned and outraged Americans are apparently unaware that our own recent past includes alarmingly similar conditions and attitudes toward orphans, with only 150 to 200 years separating the United States from Romania in this regard. The United States also experienced several waves of political, economic, and environmental tragedies that resulted in strikingly similar conditions as those described in modern Romania. During the 1700s and 1800s in particular, attitudes toward children were harsh, and many orphaned or uncared for children roamed the streets, particularly in growing urban areas such as New York.

INTRODUCTION TO CHILD AND FAMILY SERVICES

The field of child and family services generally involves the care and provision of children who cannot be appropriately cared for by their biological parents, as well as providing assistance for those who need support in the management and provision of their families. This practice setting is primarily concerned with children in foster care placement, but it may also involve family preservation services and adoption services (see Box 4.1).

The most common psychosocial issues involved in this field are quite broad but almost always involve issues related to abandonment and loss, post-traumatic stress disorder (PTSD), cultural sensitivity, child development, parenting issues, substance abuse, anger management, and the ability to work with a broad range of life stressors and maladaptive responses that might lead to breakdowns within the family.

In addition to the wide range of activities a social worker might engage in within a child and family services agency, there is also an equally wide range of practice settings

---

Box 4.1

A social worker working in a child and family services setting may be involved in the following activities:

- Child abuse investigations
- Child abuse assessments
- Case management and counseling of the child in placement, foster families, and biological parents

- Case management and counseling of families in crisis
- Case management and counseling of potential adoptive parents, adult adoptees, and birth parents

Pearson Education, Inc.

where the social worker might work. The largest practice setting is a state's child protective services (CPS) agency. Social workers also work for not-for-profit agencies, some of which are contracted by the state to provide mandated services to children in substitute care and some of which provide voluntary services to any family in crisis. Within these agencies a social worker may be involved in a number of activities, including counseling, case management, and writing grants for increased funding. Many working in the field of child welfare do so on a volunteer basis, and although these individuals are not paid professionals, the work they do is so vital that their role in the welfare of children must be mentioned.

The child welfare system in the United States has undergone significant changes in the last several hundred years because of numerous factors such as urbanization, indus-

Assess your comprehension of "Introduction to Child and Family Services" by completing this quiz.

trialization, immigration, mass life-threatening illness, changes within the family system, changing social mores (including the reduction of shame associated with divorce, out-of-wedlock births, and single parenting by choice), and the eventual availability of government financial assistance for those in need. Thus, to truly understand the current child welfare system, it is vital to understand its past.

THE HISTORY OF CHILD WELFARE IN THE UNITED STATES

The historical mistreatment of children in Colonial America and England has in many respects served as a precursor for child welfare laws in the United States, including child labor laws. The use of children in the labor market, otherwise known as *child labor*, and the treatment of children who were, for whatever reason, without parents, most often referred to as *orphans* or *street children*, tended to be the primary child welfare issues during Colonial America and England. By exploring only child labor and the treatment of orphans and street children, readers should not presume that other forms of maltreatment did not exist in America's history. Of course, there were many other ways in which children were mistreated—without federal laws protecting children, sexual abuse, physical abuse, and various other forms of maltreatment, such as neglect (physical and emotional), were rampant. The rationale for exploring just two areas of maltreatment (child labor and the treatment of orphans and street children) is based on the fact that they represent a significant departure from how children are treated today and also highlight key areas within child welfare, with regard to early child welfare advocacy and development of laws, policies, and programs intended to protect children.

During Colonial America, all children were expected to work, whether bonded or not. In fact, children as young as six years worked alongside their parents, and children as young as 12 years were expected to work in adult-like capacities, often working in apprenticed positions outside their homes and away from their families. Children of poor families, particularly immigrants, were often forced to work alongside their parents either in indentured servitude or as slaves. In fact, during the many waves of early immigration, individuals, families, and minor children as young as 10 or 11 years often paid for their passage to the United States through a process called *indentured service*. Indentured service contracts required that the servant—most often poor individuals, or families hoping for a better life in America—work off the cost of their travel by working for a master in some capacity once they arrived in America. If a family immigrated to

America in this manner, then their children, regardless of age, were required to work as well.

The economic system of indentured servitude was extremely exploitative. Research indicates that it was the ship owners who would often recruit unsuspecting, yet desperate individuals from other countries, with stories of a life of abundance in America. Many individuals and entire families accepted the call, believing that they could make a better life for themselves in Colonial America. They were told that the terms of their service would last for three years, and then they would be free—free to buy land and to make a life for themselves that was not possible in many European countries (Alderman, 1975). In reality, the cost of their passage would be paid off in only one year, and the remaining years of service were considered free work. Also, masters often treated their bonded labor quite poorly. Servants received no cash wages but were supposed to be provided with basic necessities, which depending upon the nature and means of the master, might include anything from sufficient to meager sustenance and substandard shelter. Thus, while indentured servants were not considered slaves, the treatment of them was quite similar (Martin, 2015).

Although most indentured servants were in their early 20s, Greene (1995) notes that children who immigrated with their families on bonded contracts were expected to work as well and were often treated no differently than their parents. Children were not allowed to enter into bonded labor contracts without the permission of their parents, but very poor and orphaned children, particularly in London, were often kidnapped and sold to ship captains, who then brought them to America and sold them as indentured servants, most often to masters who used them as house servants. Additionally, some local governments would "bind out" poor and orphaned children in early America as a form of poor relief (Katz, 1996). Most local laws favored masters (as virtually all judges were in fact masters themselves) and stipulated that child bonded servants could often be kept until the age of 24, and if they ran away, their treatment became even more abusive and their time in bonded servitude was often doubled (Greene, 1995).

Another form of work that children engaged in, in early America was *apprenticeship*. Apprenticeship involved the training of children in a craft. Some children went to live with the artisan who trained them and others did not. Essentially, apprenticeship involved an artisan taking on an apprentice in early adolescence and teaching him a trade. The apprentice would serve as an assistant to the artisan (Schultz, 1985). Apprenticeships might involve learning to become a barber, making shoes, or woodworking. Children were not paid, and in fact parents often had to pay to have their children apprenticed. Although most apprenticeships did not involve overt exploitation, the practice did reflect the focus on working children, rather than on education. Apprenticeships eventually became less popular as Industrialization began in the late 18th century, as machines were developed, replacing the need for many craftsmen.

Slavery and Child Labor

Indentured servitude eventually waned during the 17th century in favor of slavery, but the binding out of children who were poor and orphaned continued well into the 19th century. During the 300 years of the Atlantic slave trade, over 15 million Africans were brought to the United States through the West Indies or directly from Africa. Among these Africans were many children who were either forced or born into slavery along

Social Work Application Activity

The Long-standing Legacy of Slavery

Do you think that most people in the United States acknowledge the long-standing impact of slavery on the African American population? What other ways has a history of slavery and overt and covert social exclusion impacted this population? What do you believe are at the root of recent federal and state attempts to limit Affirmative Action programs?

There were not as many African slave children born into captivity as one might expect, due in large part to extremely high rates of infant mortality of African slave children resulting from disease and poor nutrition. In fact, the infant mortality of African slave children under the age of four was double that of white children during the time when slavery was legal. Ironically, not only has this trend continued well into the 21st century, but it has gotten worse with infant mortality among African American infants being about three times that of Caucasian infants (CDC, 2002).

with their parents. In time, masters realized that slaves who had once experienced freedom were far more difficult to control than those born into captivity; thus, a market developed for children who could work for a slave owner and essentially grow up as captive slaves and be trained to be a submissive servant. According to Greene (1995), children under the age of about seven were more often sold with their mothers, but once the children were between the ages of 7 and 10, they could and often were sold off and separated from their families, particularly to fill this growing need for young "negro" slave children born into captivity. Slavery was outlawed in 1865 with the passage of the Thirteenth Amendment to the U.S. Constitution, but the plight of African children did not improve significantly immediately (and most social workers would argue that the legacy of slavery creates significant challenges for African American children to this day).

Child Labor During the Industrial Era: Children and Factories

By the mid-19th century, the primary form of labor, particularly child labor, was factory work (Bender, 1975). Orphans or children from poor families were often recruited to work in factories. By the early to mid-19th century, it is estimated that hundreds of thousands of children—some as young as six—were employed in the textile industry, including cotton mills. In fact, some scholars estimated that children were the bulk of the workforce in many factories throughout the 19th century, with some children working six days a week, 14 hours a day (Greene, 1995). Excerpts of autobiographies written by individuals who worked in factories throughout their childhoods reference dismal conditions, with poor sanitation and air quality, repetitive work on machinery that left small hands bleeding, and very long days on their feet, which in many cases significantly shortened the life spans of these child workers (Greene, 1995).

Garment industry sweatshops began to spring up throughout New York and other large cities in the mid- to late-19th century. Although sweatshops eventually occurred in factory-like settings, their origin involved what was called "outwork," where workers sewed garments and other textiles in their homes. Women and children were primarily hired for these tasks as they could be paid a lower wage. As they were paid by the piece, they often worked 14 or more hours per day, seven days a week. Children worked alongside their mothers, because their small fingers enabled them to engage in detail work, such as sewing on buttons, a task that was challenging for adults.

The Orphan Problem and the History of the Foster Care System in Early America

The plight of the orphan did not appear to tug at the heartstrings of the average U.S. citizen during the 1700s and 1800s, not only because of the vast amount of abandoned and orphaned children, but also because during the 17th through the mid-19th centuries, children were not perceived to be in need of special nurturing because childhood was not considered a distinct stage of development until years later. The influence of Puritanical religious thought as well as the general mores of the times led to the common belief that children needed to be treated with harsh discipline or they would fall victim to sinful behaviors such as laziness and vice (Trattner, 1998).

A significant shift in child welfare policy occurred in the mid-1800s, though, when the Civil War left thousands of children orphaned, making tragedy a visitor in some respect to virtually every U.S. family. Coinciding with this increase in concern over the plight of disadvantaged children was a dramatic shift in the way children on the whole were viewed. The evolution of the field of psychology, including developmental psychology in the first quarter of the 20th century, as well as a transition in theology toward a more compassionate and loving God, led to the emerging belief that children were essentially good by nature and needed to be treated with kindness, love, and nurturing to enhance their development so that they could become fully functioning adults (Trattner, 1998).

The Industrial Revolution reduced the need for apprenticeship, and at the same time, stories of abhorrent conditions and mass abuse in almshouses (particularly involving abuses against children) were being widely reported. Settlement house workers, Charity Organization Societies (COSs), and government officials alike were eager to address the problem of orphaned and abused children in the latter part of the 19th century, and the most commonly suggested solution was the creation of institutions designed solely for the care of orphaned and needy children.

Early Orphan Asylums

Even though mortality rates were down in both the United States and Europe in the post-Industrial era (between about 1760 and 1840) (Condran & Cheney, 1982), several factors resulted in an increasing need for orphanages. Poor safety conditions in factories resulted in a relatively high prevalence of work-related injuries and death among the poorest members of society, leaving many children completely orphaned or fatherless (half-orphaned). Coupled with this was a significant influx of poor immigrants in the late 1800s and early 1900s, resulting in a vulnerable segment of society often not having an extended family on which to rely in cases of parental death or disability. This was often true of recently emigrated families, who left their extended families behind in their venture to the New World.

Although some orphanages existed in the 1700s, they did not become the primary means for handling needy and orphaned children until the middle to late 1800s. By the 1890s there were more than 600 orphanages in existence in the United States (Trattner, 1998). Orphanages, or *orphan asylums* as they were often called, did not house just children who lost both parents to death but also became the solution for many of the economic and environmental conditions of the time. For instance, families who were for whatever reason unable to support their children could leave them in the temporary care of an orphanage for a small fee, but if they missed some monthly payments, the children could become wards of the state, and the parents would often lose all legal rights to them (Trattner,

1998). In addition, although infectious disease was nothing new to early America, several infectious disease epidemics spread through urban areas between the mid-1800s and the early part of the 1900s, including smallpox, influenza, yellow fever, cholera, typhoid, and scarlet fever, leaving many children orphaned (Condran & Cheney, 1982).

Despite early perceptions of the orphanage system as a significant improvement over placing children in almshouses or forcing them into indentured servitude, these institutions were not without their share of difficulty, and in time, reports of harsh treatment and abuses were common in orphanages as well. Although some orphanages were government run, the majority were privately run with governmental funding but had little, if any, oversight or accountability. Because the government paid on a per child basis, there was a financial incentive to run large operations, with some orphanages housing as many as 2,000 children under one roof. Obedience was highly valued in these institutions out of sheer necessity, whereas individuality, play, and creativity were discouraged through strict discipline and harsh punishment (Trattner, 1998).

The next wave of child welfare reform involved the gradual shift from institutionalized care to the substitute family foster care system, or the placing out of children into private homes. This trend was prompted by the development of compulsory public education, which meant that the education of an orphan was no longer linked with the provision of housing.

The Orphan Trains

Have you ever wondered where the expression "farming kids out" came from? The origin of this term is rooted in what is called the Orphan Train movement, a program developed by the first agency to utilize in-home placement rather than institutionalized care. The New York Children's Aid Society was founded by Rev. Charles Loring Brace, who recognized the serious problem of children growing up on the streets of New York due to several tragic events from the mid-19th century. Brace estimated that as many as 5,000 children were homeless and forced to roam the streets in search of money, food, and shelter. Brace was shocked at the cruel indifference of most New Yorkers, who called these children "treet Arabs" with "bad blood." He was also appalled at reports of children as young as five years old being arrested for vagrancy (Bellingham, 1984; Brace, 1967).

Brace feared that the temptations of street life would preclude any possibility that these children would grow up to be God-fearing, responsible adults, and he reasoned that children who had no parents, or whose parents could no longer care for them, would be far better off living in the clean open spaces of the farming communities out west, where fresh air and the need for workers were plentiful. Because the rail lines were rapidly opening up the West, Brace developed an innovative program where children would be loaded onto trains and taken west to good Christian farming families. Notices were sent in advance of train arrivals, and communities along the train line would come out and meet the train, so that families who had expressed an interest in taking one or more children could examine the children and take them right then, if they desired. Brace convened committees who would interview families to ensure that they met the standards for qualified adoptive or foster families.

Children on one of the Orphan Train.

RIIS, JACOB A / LIBRARY OF CONGRESS

Survivors of these Orphan Trains have talked about how they felt like cattle, being paraded across a stage. Interested foster parents would often feel the children's muscles and check their teeth before deciding what child they would take. Few parents would take more than one child; thus siblings were most often split up, sometimes without even a passing comment made by the child-care agents or the new parents (Patrick, Sheets, & Trickel, 1990). It was almost as if the breaking of lifelong family bonds was considered trivial compared to the gift these children were receiving by being rescued from their hopeless existence on the streets.

Most children were not legally adopted but were placed with a family under an indentured contract, which served two purposes. First, this type of contract allowed the placement agency to take the children back if something went wrong with the placement. Second, children placed under an indentured contract could not inherit property; thus, farming families could adopt boys to work on the farm or girls to assist with the housework but did not have to worry about them inheriting the family assets (Trattner, 1998; Warren, 1995).

The Orphan Trains ran from 1854 to 1929, delivering approximately 150,000 children to new homes across the West, from the Midwestern states to Texas, and even as far west as California. Whether this social experiment was a glowing success or a miserable failure (or somewhere in between) depends on whom you ask. Some children were placed in wonderful, loving homes and grew up to be happy and responsible adults, who feel strongly that the Orphan Trains were a true blessing. But other survivors of the Orphan Trains shared stories of heartache and abuse. Some tell stories of lives no better than that of slaves, where they were taken in by families for no other reason than to provide hard labor for the cost of bed and board. Others tell stories of having siblings torn from their sides as families chose one child, leaving brothers and sisters on the train. And still others tell stories of failed adoptions, where farming families exercised their one-year return option, sending the children back to the orphanage or allowing the children to drift from farm to farm to earn their keep (Holt, 1992).

Eventually, new child welfare practices caught up with new child development theories, leading to a general focus shifting from work virtue to valuing childhood play. By the early 20th century the practice of "farming out" children received increasing criticism, and the last trainload of children was delivered to its many destinations in 1929. Despite the controversy surrounding the Orphan Train movement and the many similar out-placement programs that followed across the country, even its harshest critics agreed that it was a far better alternative than allowing children to fend for themselves on the streets of New York. Also, despite the program's many shortcomings, including poor oversight and insufficient screening of the families, it is considered the forerunner of the current foster care system in the United States, where children are placed in available private homes, rather than in institutions (Trattner, 1998).

Learn more about the history of the Orphan Train Movement by going to the PBS website and searching for the video "The Brave Journey of an Orphan Train Rider."

Jane Addams and the Fight for Child Labor Laws

At around the same time that Charles Loring Brace was sending New York orphans out west, Jane Addams and her friend Ellen Gates Starr were busy founding Hull House of Chicago, the first U.S. settlement house providing residential and what we is now call "wrap around" services, including advocacy to marginalized populations working in sweatshop conditions in Chicago. Addams was appalled by the conditions of those living in poverty in urban communities, particularly the plight of recently arrived immigrants, who were forced to live in substandard tenement housing and work long hours in factories, often in very dangerous working conditions.

Hull House offered several services for children and their widowed mothers, including after-school care for those children whose mothers worked long hours in factories. Providing comprehensive services to those in need, and living among them in their own community were some of the ways in which Addams became aware of the plight of children forced to work in the factories.

In her autobiography *Twenty Years at Hull-House*, Addams wrote of her first encounter with child labor referring to how during a Christmas party several young girls in attendance refused to eat any of the candy at the party. When she asked the girls why they did not want any candy (a rare treat, particularly for girls at the Hull House), the girls told her that they worked from 7:00 a.m. to 9:00 p.m. in a candy factory and they could not stand the thought of even seeing candy. Addams also wrote about a young boy who was killed in an easily preventable accident where he worked. Addams wrote about her grief and horror when she learned of the indifference of the factory owners who took no effort to remedy the unsafe working conditions and had to pay no damages to the parents because of the documents parents signed giving away all of their rights to damages, even in cases of negligence (Addams, 2011, pp. 198–199).

Addams and her colleagues began an advocacy campaign against sweatshop conditions in Chicago factories early in the Hull House's existence, advocating in particular for the women and children who were most often hired to work in them. Their activism seemed to pay off quickly when the Illinois legislature passed a law limiting the word *day* to just eight hours (from the typical 12- to 14-hour day). Their excitement, however, was soon tempered when the law was quickly overturned by the Illinois Supreme Court as unconstitutional. In her autobiography, Addams discussed how the greatest opposition to child labor laws came from the business sector—businessmen from large corporations (such as Chicago glass companies), who considered such legislation as "radicalism" and who argued that their companies would not be able to survive without the labor of children (Addams, 2011; Martin, 2015).

Addams and the Hull House networked quite extensively joining efforts with trade unions and even the Democratic Party, which in 1892 adopted into its platform union recommendations to prohibit children under the age of 15 years from working in factories. Addams and her Hull House colleagues increased the focus of their activism to the federal level with their support for the *Sulzer Bill*, which when passed allowed for the creation of the Department of Labor. In 1904 the National Child Labor Committee was formed, and Addams served as chairman for one term. In 1912, one of Addams's Hull House colleagues, Julia Lathrop, was appointed chief of a new federal agency by President William Taft, focusing on child welfare, including child labor. As chief of the Children's Bureau, Lathrop was responsible for investigating and reporting on all relevant issues pertaining to the welfare of children from all classes, and she spent a considerable amount of time extensively researching the dangers of child labor (Martin, 2015).

Assess your comprehension of "The History of Child Welfare in the United States" by completing this quiz.

After several failed attempts, federal legislation barring child labor was finally passed in 1938 and was signed into law by President Franklin D. Roosevelt, three years after Addams's death. The Fair Labor Standards Act is a comprehensive bill regulating various aspects of labor in the United States, including child labor. The act defined "oppressive child labor" and set minimum ages of employment and the number of hours children were allowed to work. This act is still in existence today and has been amended several times to address such issues as equal pay (Equal Pay Act of 1963), age discrimination (Age Discrimination in Employment Act of 1967), and low wages (federal minimum wage increases) (Martin, 2015).

OVERVIEW OF THE CURRENT U.S. CHILD WELFARE SYSTEM

Children living in contemporary western societies face very different challenges than children who lived 100 years ago. Child labor laws preclude child exploitation in the workforce, and federal and state social welfare programs now exist, which have helped not only to alleviate poverty but also to protect families from the effect of various catastrophes, such as natural disasters and health pandemics. Also, vulnerable groups of children are far better protected from disparity in treatment through the passage of such federal legislation as the Civil Rights Act of 1964 and the Americans with Disabilities Act.

Despite these advances, there remain serious issues with how some children are treated within U.S. society. For instance, there exists a disparity in treatment of children from certain ethnic groups, such as African Americans, Latinos, and Native Americans. Few truly effective systems are in place to assist runaway and homeless youth. Far too often, adolescents who experienced physical and sexual abuse in their homes are not served well by child protective services, and many choose to live on the streets rather than remain in their homes or trust the "system" to provide for their care. Far too many children are charged as adults for crimes they committed as children, and most of these are children of color—primarily African American boys. African American girls also experience disparity in treatment by organizations charged with the responsibility for their protection. For example, there is a growing recognition that African American girls are far more likely to be victims of domestic sex trafficking; yet, if they are apprehended, rather than being treated as victims, they are far more likely to be charged as prostitutes and sent back to the streets (Martin, 2015).

With regard to child protection and the care of orphaned and abused children, care has slowly transitioned from institutionalized care to primarily substitute family care or foster care over the past 100 years. By 1980, virtually no children remained in institutionalized care in the United States, excluding group homes, treatment centers, and homes for developmentally disabled children (Shughart & Chappell, 1999). Government public assistance programs, which developed in the 1960s, reduced the necessity for the removal of children from their homes due to poverty, because single mothers now had some place to go for financial help in raising their children (Trattner, 1998).

Getting Into the System

The U.S. child welfare system exists to provide a safety net for children and families in crisis. A primary goal of the foster care system is to reunite foster care children with their biological parents whenever possible (Sanchirico & Jablonka, 2000). Federal and state laws have established three basic goals for children in the U.S. child welfare system:

- Safety from abuse and neglect
- Permanency in a stable, loving home (preferably with the biological parents)
- Well-being of the child with regard to their physical health, mental health, and developmental and educational needs

How these goals are met depends on the specific issues involved in each case, but before these various alternatives are considered, it is important to understand how a child enters the child welfare system in the first place. Made-for-television movies might have the public thinking that child welfare workers have the power to remove children from homes with minimal evidence of abuse. Yet, in reality, several criteria must be met to place a child into protective custody, and a child cannot be removed from a family home without a judge's approval. The U.S. Constitution guarantees certain liberties to parents by giving them the right to parent their child in the manner they see fit. But such liberties are balanced by the parents' duty to protect their child's safety and ensure their well-being. If parents cannot or will not protect their children from *significant* harm, the state has the legal obligation to intervene (Goldman & Salus, 2003).

The demographic makeup of children currently in the foster care system differs considerably from the children institutionalized in orphanages in the 1800s, as well as the children of the Orphan Train era. Gone are the days where the majority of children being placed into substitute care were orphaned because of industrial accidents, war, or illness. Instead, the majority of children currently in child protective custody have been removed from their homes because of serious maltreatment. Also, unlike earlier eras when orphanage placements were most often permanent, almost half of all children currently in foster care have the goal of reunifying with their biological parents (U.S. Department of Health and Human Services, 2008).

As of September 1, 2012 (the most recent statistics available), there were approximately 400,540 children in the U.S. foster care system. This represents a decrease of almost 55,000 children in foster care since 2007, and it also represents a continued pattern of a reduction of children in out-of-home placement since 1998 (U.S. Department of Health and Human Services, 2012). But despite this reduction in the number of children in state care, disparity still exists with regard to which ethnic minority groups are more likely to have children in out-of-home placements. For instance, according to the latest statistics, approximately 41 percent of all children in foster care are Caucasian, followed by 29 percent African American children, and 21 percent Hispanic children. These demographics indicate an overrepresentation of African American children in the foster care system because African Americans constitute only 15 percent of the general population, whereas Caucasians constitute 61 percent of the general population.

The average age of children in care is about nine years old, with the greatest number of children in foster care placement being between the ages of 11 and 15 years, followed by children aged one through five years. About half of all children in placement are in non-relative foster care placement, followed by about a quarter of all children who are placed in relative care. The median length of stay in foster care is about 18 months, but it appears that if children aren't returned home, or placed in a permanent home situation in the first 18 months of out of home care, chances increase that they will remain in placement for several years. The greatest number of children who left the child welfare system in 2010 were infants and toddlers under three years of age, as well as those exiting the system at 17 years old and above (U.S. Department of Health and Human Services, 2010).

Current Legislation Impacting the U.S. Child Welfare System

The U.S. Congress has passed several pieces of legislation that support the state's obligation to protect its youngest residents. For instance, the Child Abuse Prevention and Treatment Act (CAPTA) of 1974, which was established to ensure that the maltreatment of children is reported to the appropriate authorities. This act (which was most recently amended in 2010) also provides minimum standards for definitions of the different types of child maltreatment. The Adoption Assistance and Child Welfare Act of 1980 requires that states develop supportive programs and procedures, enabling maltreated children to remain in their own homes with the assistance of family reunification services following out-of-home placements.

Other legislation is aimed at (1) improving court efficiency so that child abuse cases do not languish in the court system for years, (2) providing assistance to foster care children approaching their 18th birthday, and (3) bolstering family preservation programs designed as an early intervention strategy designed to circumvent out-of-home placement (Goldman & Salus, 2003).

In 1997 former President Bill Clinton signed the Adoption and Safe Families Act into law, which amended the Adoption Assistance and Child Welfare Act of 1980. Among the amendments the act now provides incentives for families adopting children in the foster care system and mandates that states provide evidence of adoption efforts. Amendments also set a new accelerated time line for terminating the rights of parents whose children are in foster care placement. As we will see in subsequent sections of this chapter, there are both positive and negative aspects of this legislation. Certainly no one wants abused and neglected children to languish in temporary placement, but expediting the finding of permanent homes should not be at the expense of biological parents' rights to have an appropriate amount of time to meet the state's criteria for regaining the custody of their children. Balancing the rights of the biological parents with the best interest of their child is challenging, particularly in light of the complexity involved in many foster care cases.

Another important piece of child welfare legislation is the Safe and Timely Interstate Placement of Foster Children Act of 2006 (Pub. L. No. 109–239), which made it easier to place children in another state, if necessary. This legislation holds states accountable for the orderly, safe, and timely placement of children across state lines by requiring that home studies be completed in less than 60 days and that the children be accepted within 14 days of completion. This legislation also provides grants for interstate placement and requires caseworkers to make interstate visits, when necessary.

Quite likely, the most significant federal legislation passed recently is the Fostering Connections to Success and Increasing Adoptions Act of 2008 (Pub. L. No. 110–351), which former President George W. Bush signed into law in October 2008. This law amends the Social Security Act by enhancing incentives, particularly in regard to kinship care, including providing kinship guardians financial assistance as well as providing "family connection" grants designed to facilitate and support kinship care. This legislation also includes provisions for education and healthcare particularly for children in kinship care, many of whom were not previously eligible for special assistance programs because they were not in nonrelative care.

Child Abuse Investigations

There are several ways that a child abuse investigation may be initiated, but all have their origin in a concern that a child is being mistreated in some manner. Many professionals, such as counselors, teachers, physicians, and even Sunday school teachers, are required by law to call their state's child abuse hotline immediately if they suspect that a child is being abused or neglected. *Mandated reporters* typically fall into one of several categories and include professionals who work with children as a part of their normal work duties.

Social Work, Social Media, and Technology

Child Abuse and Social Media

In January 2014, the Omaha, Nebraska, police union found a disturbing video posted on a known gang member's Facebook page. The video showed a toddler being sworn at by off-camera adults who were encouraging him to use profanity, which the young boy did prolifically. The police union made the video public on its website to promote conversation about conditions Omaha police face everyday in some communities in the city. Although the Omaha police and prosecutors found nothing in the video that was illegal, they did work with Child Protective Services to identify safety concerns in the home and a decision was made to temporarily remove the child and place him into protective custody. News reports noted how many in the public criticized the police union for their decision to make the video public. What are your thoughts?

Mandated reporters include personnel in the following fields: medical, schools, social services, mental health, law enforcement, child care, and members of the clergy.

Most states have strict laws that define the parameters of child abuse reporting, including delineating what constitutes a reportable concern, the time frame in which a mandated reporter must report the suspected abuse, and the consequences of failing to report suspected abuse, such as the suspension of one's professional license. In fact, in most states, the failure to comply with mandated reporting requirements is a crime (a misdemeanor or even a felony for repeated failures). In many states, the majority of calls made to the child abuse hotline are from mandated reporters, but this does not preclude anyone from calling the child abuse hotline if they suspect that a child is being abused or neglected by a parent or caregiver. Thus, it is not uncommon for neighbors, friends, or even relatives to report suspected child abuse, and those who are not mandated reporters are allowed to call anonymously.

A child abuse investigation is initiated when someone, either a concerned individual or a mandated reporter, places a call to the state child abuse hotline. Because of the intrusive nature of an abuse investigation, federal and state laws exist to protect the privacy of family life. Thus, hotline workers must adhere to strict guidelines regarding what reports can and cannot be accepted. If the report of alleged abuse meets the stated criteria, then the report will be accepted and investigated in a timely manner.

Sequence of Events in the Reporting and Investigation of Child Abuse

For state CPS agencies to receive federal funding, the federal law mandates that all child abuse reports be screened immediately and investigated in a timely manner (CAPTA, 2010). Although federal law does not specify a particular time frame, most states have compliance laws stipulating specific guidelines requiring that reports of abuse be investigated anywhere from immediately after receiving a report for cases involving imminent risk to 10 days in some states for reports with moderate to minimal risk to the child (Kopel, Charlton, & Well, 2003).

Once a hotline worker makes the decision to accept a child abuse report, the case is sent to the appropriate regional agency and assigned to an abuse investigator, who is a licensed social worker or other licensed mental health professional. The actual investigation will vary depending on the specific circumstances of the allegations, but most investigations will involve interviewing the child, the nonoffending parent(s), and the alleged perpetrator. Although the sequence of the interviews might alter depending on the specific circumstances of the case, most investigators prefer to interview the child before the parents or caregivers are aware of the investigation to avoid the potential for influencing or intimidating the child.

Child maltreatment is a crime regardless of who the perpetrator is and should always be reported to authorities, but a state's CPS agency becomes involved when the abuse is perpetrated by someone who is acting in a caregiving role to the child. This includes a parent, a relative, a parent's boyfriend or girlfriend, a teacher, or even a babysitter.

Although each state is charged with the responsibility for defining child abuse and neglect according to state statute, the federal government has developed a definition of what constitutes the minimum standard for child abuse and neglect and has created four general categories of child maltreatment, including neglect, physical abuse, sexual abuse, and emotional abuse (National Clearinghouse on Child Abuse and Neglect, 2005).

Read more about how the U.S. government defines child abuse and neglect by going to the Child Welfare Information Gateway website and navigating to the "Child Abuse and Neglect" section.

The following is the U.S. Health and Human Services' definition of each type of abuse, but again it is important to remember that each state, although bound to this minimum standard, will likely have additional criteria and scenarios that qualify as abuse.

Neglect involves the failure to provide for a child's basic needs. Neglect may be

- Physical (e.g., failure to provide necessary food or shelter or lack of appropriate supervision)
- Medical (e.g., failure to provide necessary medical or mental health treatment)
- Educational (e.g., failure to educate a child or attend to the child's special education needs)
- Emotional (e.g., inattention to a child's emotional needs, failure to provide psychological care, or permitting the child to use alcohol or other drugs)

Because cultural values, standards of care in the community, and poverty may be contributing factors related to caregiving challenges, the existence of some of these problems does not necessarily indicate that the treatment of a child has risen to the level of legal maltreatment. Rather, the manifestation of certain problems within a family system, such as not sending a child to school, may indicate an overwhelmed family's need for information and general assistance. Yet, if a family fails to utilize the information, assistance, and resources provided and if the child's health and/or safety is determined to be at risk, then CPS intervention may be required.

Physical abuse includes physical injury (ranging from minor bruises to severe fractures or death) as a result of punching, beating, kicking, biting, shaking, throwing, stabbing, choking, hitting (with a hand, stick, strap, or other object), burning, or otherwise physically harming a child. An injury is considered abuse regardless of whether the caretaker intended to hurt the child.

Sexual abuse includes activities by a parent or caretaker that include fondling a child's genitals, penetration, incest, rape, sodomy, indecent exposure, and exploitation through prostitution or the production of pornographic materials.

Emotional abuse involves a pattern of behavior that impairs a child's emotional development or sense of self-worth. This may include constant criticism, threats, or rejection, as well as withholding love, support, or guidance. Emotional abuse is often difficult to prove, and, therefore, CPS may not be able to intervene without evidence of significant harm to the child. Emotional abuse is almost always present when other forms of abuse are identified.

The Forensic Interview

In the past 25 years, allegations of child abuse, particularly child sexual abuse, have skyrocketed. Reasons for this include increased public awareness, mandatory reporting requirements, and a significant change in attitudes regarding child abuse, with an increasing sentiment that abuse is no longer a private family matter. Yet, as the pendulum swung, the 1970s witnessed a sort of frenzy in child sexual abuse reporting, and a popular contention among mental health experts was that children were incapable of making false allegations. This belief fostered a sense of over eagerness on the part of some therapists, who sometimes used inappropriate interviewing techniques, with leading questions: "Did he touch you on your privates?," with forced choice: "Did he touch you under your clothing, or over your clothing?", with option posing: "I heard that your uncle has been bothering you," or with suggestive questions: "Many kids at your school have said that your teacher has touched them, did he touch you too?"

Eventually, this method of questioning was met with overwhelming criticism, particularly by members of the legal community, who were charged with defending those individuals falsely accused of sexually abusing children in their charge. These types of questions significantly increased the likelihood of erroneous disclosures, particularly with preschool-aged children (Hewitt, 1999; Peterson & Biggs, 1997; Poole & Lindsay, 1998).

In response to such criticism, CPS agencies across the country developed pilot programs that combined the resources from several investigative branches, including CPS agencies, police departments, and district attorneys' offices. This coordinated approach not only prevents the trauma of duplicative interviews by separate enforcement agencies but also allows for the highly specialized training of investigators on forensic interviewing techniques that avoid any type of suggestive or leading questions.

Although there is a general understanding among investigators of what constitutes a forensic interview, there was still concern that many interviewers used types of questions that were somewhat leading in nature, including an interviewer's inadvertent reaction to a child's response that either encouraged or discouraged an honest disclosure. For instance, an investigator who strongly believes that a child has been abused may inadvertently respond with frustration if a child denies the abuse, which may influence the child, who wants to please the investigator, to give a false disclosure of abuse. Even an expression of sympathy on the part of the interviewer, in response to disclosures of abuse, can inadvertently encourage a child to embellish somewhat to receive more of the interviewer's compassion.

The National Institute of Child Health and Human Development (NICHD) developed a forensic interviewing protocol that teaches interviewers how to ask open-ended questions, using retrieval cues that rely on free recall. "Tell me everything you can remember" is an example of an open-ended question. "Tell me more about the room you were in" is an example of a retrieval cue (Bourg, Broderick, & Flagor, 1999; Sternberg, Lamb, & Orbach, 2001).

When to Intervene: Models for Decision Making

Many variables influence the outcome of an investigation, including the criteria with which a CPS agency uses to determine (1) whether abuse is occurring and (2) whether the abuse rises to the level of warranting intervention. In other words, it is possible for some abuse reports to be determined as *unfounded*, even though the investigator may strongly suspect that an unhealthy home environment does exist. But another reason for not substantiating an incident of child abuse relates more to poor or inconsistent decision-making policies within a CPS agency because of human errors in decision making. DePanfilis and

Scannapieco (1994) discussed the vital importance of CPS agencies developing and adhering to a consistent and realistic decision-making model when determining whether family intervention is warranted to avoid the inherent problems in making bias-free and fact-based decisions. Child abuse investigators are responsible for assessing potential abuse situations, making decisions about the types of services children need to keep them safe, and determining when a child needs to be placed in protective care.

According to the Child Welfare League of America (CWLA), there are several approaches to making risk assessments of child maltreatment in child protection. Safety assessments using structured decision making tools are either statistically based or based on consensus of experts in the field, as well as research on the area of child maltreatment. Actuarial models of risk assessment and decision making assess families based on factors and characteristics that are statistically associated with the recurrence of maltreatment. Because the inventory is based on a statistical calculation, the validity of the inventory may be considered higher than the consensus-based model risk assessments; yet, many within the child welfare field express concern that actuarial models do not allow enough for clinical assessment. An example of an actuarial model for risk assessment and decision making includes the CRC Actuarial Models for Risk Assessment (Austin, D'Andrade, Lemon, Benton, Chow, & Reyes, 2005).

Consensus-based approaches include the theoretically and empirically guided approach that ranks a series of factors that have empirical support for their association with child maltreatment and Family Assessment Scales (CWLA, 2005). Some examples of consensus-based models for risk assessment and decision making include the Washington Risk Assessment Matrix (WRAM), the California Family Assessment and Factor Analysis (CFAFA, or the "Fresno Model"), and the Child Emergency Response Assessment Protocol (CERAP) (Austin, D'Andrade, Lemon, Benton, Chow, & Reyes, 2005).

The *Child at Risk Field System* (CARF) is an example of a consensus-based risk-assessment model that has been tested in the field. The CARF provides guidelines for abuse investigators in making a determination about abuse (see Table 4.1).

As Table 4.1 reflects, despite the fact that definitions of child maltreatment are statutorily defined, child protection investigators have considerable latitude in determining whether child maltreatment is occurring and whether the extent of the abuse warrants intervention. Primarily, it is through the use of an effective

Apply Critical Thinking to Inform and Communicate Professional Judgments

Practice Behavior: Distinguish, appraise, and integrate multiple sources of knowledge, including research-based knowledge, and practice wisdom.

Critical Thinking Question: Imagine that you are a social worker employed by your county's child protective services (CPS) agency. You are currently investigating an incident of potential child abuse in the home of a Native American family. You are using a popular decision-making model that lists parents' avoidance of eye contact and parents' resistance to cooperate with an investigative caseworker as indicators for removing the child from the home. What other information and factors should you consider in making your decision, particularly in relation to the family's cultural background and historical experiences of Native Americans?

Assess your comprehension of "Overview of the Current U.S. Child Welfare System" by completing this quiz.

Social Work Application Activity

Risk Assessment and Decision Making in Child Protection

The Child Welfare League of America (CWLA) website describes how Risk Assessment and Decision making models are used in child protection. Go to the CWLA website and search for the article entitled: Child

Protective Services: A Guide for Caseworkers (Office on Child Abuse and Neglect, Children's Bureau. DePanfilis, D., Salus, M.K., 2003). After reading the article describe ways that such models can help social workers promote effective child welfare practices and also ways in which such models may potentially violate the NASW Code of Ethics.

Table 4.1   The CARF Risk Assessment Model

Maltreated and Unsafe

Parental Behavior	Caseworker Perception of Parents
• Out of Control	• Flight Risk
• Frequently Violent	• Unable to Meet Needs of Special Needs Child
• Showed No Remorse	• Life-threatening Conditions in Home
• Requests Placement of Child	• Non-offending Parent Unable to Protect
• Failed to Respond to Previous Interventions	
• Location Unknown	

Maltreated but Safe

Parent Behavior	Caseworker Perception of Parents
• Possessed Impulse Control	• Accepted Responsibility for the Situation
• Showed Concern for the Child	• Understood the Child
• Showed Remorse for Maltreatment	• Exhibited Knowledge of Good Parenting Skills
• History of Accessing Help and Services	

Pearson Education, Inc.

and well-tested decision-making model that an abuse investigator will have the greatest likelihood of making an appropriate determination in a child abuse investigation.

WORKING WITH CHILDREN IN PLACEMENT

When an abuse investigator determines that a child must be placed into protective custody, the child is removed from the home and placed in one of many environments, including relative foster care, nonrelative foster care, or an emergency shelter pending more permanent placement. The case is then transferred to a family caseworker who evaluates all the relevant dynamics of the case (i.e., reason for placement, nature of abuse, and attitude of the parents) as well as assessing the strengths and weaknesses of the biological parents and the family structure. A *permanency plan* for the child must then be determined and can include:

1. Reunification with the biological parents
2. Living with relatives
3. Guardianship with close friends
4. Short-term or long-term foster care
5. Emancipation (with older adolescents)
6. Adoption with termination of parental rights

Although reunification with the biological parents remains the most common permanency plan, recent changes in many state and federal laws have shifted the focus from protecting the biological family unit to considering the "best interest of the child." The reason for this shift can be traced to several high-profile cases in the mid-1990s where children were either seriously abused or killed after being reunified with their biological parents. Well-meaning child advocates launched campaigns in Washington, DC, appealing to Congress to do something about the horrible plight of children who were returned to their biological families only to face further abuse and sometimes even death in a failed effort to keep families together.

Although there was no documented increase of child maltreatment during this time period, newspaper and magazine articles highlighting tragic (but rare) cases of continued abuse or deaths when children were reunited with their families were passed around Congress, and articles such as "The Little Boy Who Didn't Have to Die" were utilized in an effort to make an emotional appeal to legislators to shift priorities from family reunification to parental termination and subsequent adoption (Spake, 1994). The result of this campaign was the passage of the American Adoption and Safe Family Act of 1997, which marked a clear departure away from family preservation and toward paving the way for termination of biological parents' rights, clearing the way for adoption of children in foster care placement.

> ### Engage in Policy Practice to Advance Social and Economic Well-being and to Deliver Effective Social Work Services
>
> **Practice Behavior: Analyze, formulate, and advocate for policies that advance social well-being.**
>
> Critical Thinking Question: Your agency has asked you to evaluate the *Best Interest of the Child* standard that is currently the prevailing approach in most family courts across the country in making permanency plans for children in placement. What are the pros and cons of this policy, and how would you go about advocating for change in a way that better serves your clients?

The *best interest of the child* standard may sound good on the surface, but it has been the subject of significant scrutiny, with critics questioning just how this standard is being applied. In other words, best interest of the child according to whom? According to the foster parents? The courts? The caseworker? It doesn't take much analysis to see how easily this standard can be manipulated. For instance, what if the caseworker determines that it is in the best interest of the child to be placed permanently with a two-parent financially secure family rather than to be returned to the child's poor single mother, regardless of how diligently the mother works to regain custody? The potential to make permanency plans that discriminate against biological parents who are marginalized members of society, such as parents who are poor, single, of a minority race, homosexual, and perhaps even undocumented immigrants, is significant.

Dorothy Roberts, author of *Shattered Bonds: The Color of Child Welfare* (2002), cautions that American Adoption and Safe Family Act of 1997 can lead to many problems, including a conflict created when caseworkers are required to pursue two permanency plans at the same time in order to comply with the new permanency plan time frames—reunification with the family and possible adoption. What many caseworkers do to accomplish this task is to place foster children in *preadoptive* homes while planning for reunification with the biological parents. This creates a situation where the biological parents' rights are often in conflict with the children's rights, and where foster care families, who are by definition charged with the responsibility of fostering a relationship between the children and their biological parents, are now competing for the children.

Another possible conflict according to Roberts includes the act's adoption incentive program, where states are given financial incentives of $4,000 for each child placed for adoption (above a baseline) and $6,000 for a special needs adoption. The potential for agency abuse is evident as states scramble to replace lost revenue because of the struggling economy. Roberts warns that this new legislation was not directed at effecting faster termination of parental rights in cases with severe abuse because these cases were always relatively "open-and-shut." Rather, it is the cases involving poverty-related maltreatment, most often in African American and Native American homes, that have been most affected by this new federal law, which Roberts fears has led to increased social injustice in many CPS agencies' decisions.

For this reason as well as many others, the caseworker must be careful in determining what criteria to use in making permanency determination recommendations. For instance, some experts have suggested using attachment ties as a guide in deciding a permanent placement plan (Gauthier, Fortin, & Jéliu, 2004). These researchers suggest that a child should remain with the family with whom they appear to have the greatest attachment to avoid further emotional ruptures. Yet, the potential for foster parent bias is great, particularly in light of the fact that the foster parents will have a greater advantage over the biological parents because children will, of course, have a greater likelihood of developing a stronger attachment to the family they are living with, particularly if biological parents are restricted from participating regularly in their children's lives through regular visitation. United States history is filled with reports of abuses of this sort, where parents considered unworthy have experienced unfair treatment by CPS agencies, and this legislation risks escorting in a new dawn of similar abuses. (For an example, see the discussion of Native Americans later in this chapter.)

Working With Biological Families of Children in Placement

A caseworker works with the biological parents most closely when it is determined that the most appropriate permanency plan is parent reunification. A part of any good reunification plan will involve a visitation schedule that supports and encourages the child's relationship with the biological parent(s) and provides them with applying new parenting techniques that they've learned in parenting classes and counseling (Sanchirico & Jablonka, 2000). An effective caseworker will give consistent feedback to the biological parent(s) about their progress toward meeting service plan goals, will balance constructive feedback with encouragement, will protect the parent–child relationship, and will do whatever possible to remove barriers to complying with their service plan, such as finding alternate mental health providers when waiting lists would cause unreasonable delays and resolving conflicts between goals, such as not scheduling visitation during the parents' working hours when maintaining stable employment is a service plan goal.

Once a child has been placed into foster care, the caseworker must prepare a detailed service plan, typically within 30 days, outlining goals that the biological parent(s) must accomplish before regaining custody of their child. The specific goals must be related to the identified parenting deficits. It is then the responsibility of the caseworker to facilitate the biological parents' achieving these goals. This might involve giving referrals to the parents or securing services for them, as well as monitoring their ongoing progress.

It is also important for caseworkers to be aware that biological parents who have had their children removed may be enduring emotional trauma in response to this loss, which may result in them behaving in ways that could be uncharacteristic for them. The strain of having to be accountable to external forces exerting control over their lives may render many biological parents vulnerable to feeling overwhelming shame, which may manifest in defensiveness that could be misinterpreted as indifference or a lack of remorse. An effective caseworker will understand this possible dynamic and will create an environment where biological parents will be able to overcome the barrier of defensiveness and shame and work on the issues identified in their service plan.

The intergenerational nature of child abuse has been well documented in research (Bentovim, 2002, 2004; Ehrensaft, Cohen, & Brown, 2003; Newcomb, Locke, & Thomas, 2001; Pears & Capaldi, 2001), and although the majority of individuals who have been abused in childhood do not go on to abuse their own children, parents who are abusive to their children have likely been abused in their own childhoods. Homes marked by violence, drug abuse, neglect, and sexual abuse create patterns that can be passed down to the next generation. Although it might not initially make sense that someone who endured the pain of abuse would inflict this same abuse on his or her own child, the complex nature of child abuse oftentimes renders abuse patterns beyond the control of the batterer without some form of intervention. Because of the complex dynamics associated with intergenerational abuse, it is important for caseworkers to understand the internal processes that may occur with someone who has endured physical, emotional, and sexual abuse at the hands of parents and other caregivers. Individuals who have suffered significant childhood abuse often suffer from low frustration tolerance, displaced anger, inability to delay gratification, impulse control problems, problems with emotional regulation, difficulty attaching to others, and an unstable self-identity (Bentovim, 2002, 2004). Issues such as poor parental modeling, lack of understanding about normal child development, and an individual's level of residual anger and frustration tolerance affect a person's ability to positively parent their children.

Working With Foster Children: Common Clinical Issues

Foster children obviously come in all "shapes and sizes," so it is difficult to summarize the issues and experiences of the majority of children in foster care but certain generalizations can be made, particularly with regard to the types of experiences that bring a child into substitute care, as well as the range of short-term and long-term emotional and psychological manifestations many children in foster care may experience. The clinical issues that a caseworker may deal with will vary depending on variables such as the age of the child, the length of time in placement, the reasons for placement, and the plan for permanency (i.e., adoption or family reunification). Younger children are typically easier to place and may display less oppositional behavior than adolescents, who are often placed in group homes.

Children who have been sexually abused often manifest emotional problems that require sophisticated handling on the part of the caseworkers, therapists, and foster parents. Sexually abused children may act out sexually with their foster parents as well as other children, which can create an uncomfortable situation, particularly for those who are unfamiliar with such acting out behaviors. In addition, most children who have been mistreated in some manner may behave well during the honeymoon period of placement, but then act out once they begin to feel more secure. This phenomenon can lead to disrupted placements if the foster parents are unaware of the dynamics behind this shift in behavior.

A recent national survey of approximately 4,000 foster care children, aged 2 through 14, who had been removed from their homes because of maltreatment, revealed that nearly half of these children had clinically significant psychological and/or behavioral problems. Alarmingly though, only about half of all children reporting significant problems had received any counseling in the past year. The children who were the most likely to receive mental health services were younger children who had been sexually abused. African American children were the least likely to receive mental health services, as were children who remained living in their biological homes (Burns et al., 2004). Siu and Hogan (1989) identified five clinical themes experienced by most children in foster care and made recommendations for how child welfare caseworkers should respond. These include issues related to separation; loss, grief, and mourning; identity issues; continuity of family ties; and crisis.

Separation

Children involved in the child welfare system are contending with either issues related to separation from their biological family members or the threat of separation. Siu and Hogan (1989) recommended that caseworkers be familiar with the psychological dynamics involved in such separations as they relate to each developmental stage. It is important for caseworkers to acknowledge that these children are not just being separated from their biological parents but are experiencing multiple separations, such as separation from their extended family, perhaps their siblings and their familiar surroundings, including their bedroom, house, neighborhood, and even their family pets. Caseworkers need to confront these separation issues head on with the children, resisting the temptation to avoid them in response to their own separation anxiety.

Children often go through different stages when confronted with significant separation, beginning with the *preprotest* stage, where children accept removal from their home with little protest. But this stage is ultimately followed by the *protest* stage, where children can respond with outright combative and oppositional behavior or with a more subtle uncooperative attitude. The third stage is marked by *despair*, where the child often submits to the placement with a sense of brokenness and hopelessness. The final stage involves *adjustment* to the placement but involves a sense of detachment to that which the child had been attached—namely, their biological families (Rutter, 1978).

Caseworkers can respond to children dealing with separation issues by being honest with them (in an age-appropriate manner) regarding what is happening with their families and by helping to prepare them for the upcoming changes to reduce the anxiety associated with anticipating the unknown. Younger children are far more likely to be operating in the "here and now"; thus, it is important for the caseworker to reassure the child that the separation is only temporary (if the goal is family reunification) and that the feelings of sadness and discomfort experienced after being separated will not last forever.

Children who have been removed from their homes also need to be reassured that they are not the cause of the family disruption. It is quite common for children in foster care to feel responsible for their parents "getting into trouble," and they may even be tempted to recant their disclosures of abuse in the hope that they can return home. Such children often reason that enduring the abuse is better than having their family torn apart and their parents in trouble. In fact, many abused children have been told for years that if they ever did disclose the abuse that the parents would go to jail and the children would be taken away. Thus, it is important that the caseworker anticipate the possibility of such prior conversations between children and parents and address this by encouraging the children and reassuring them that the current course of action may actually benefit and strengthen the entire family.

Loss, Grief, and Mourning

Coming alongside children who have experienced a loss and permitting them to grieve involves having a high tolerance for a wide range of emotions. Lee and Whiting (2007) discuss the concept of ambiguous loss with regard to children in foster care. Ambiguous loss is defined as loss that is unclear, undefined, and in many instances, unresolvable. Ambiguous loss in foster care situations can involve losses that are confusing for the child, such as the loss of an abusive parent. Children who are removed from an abusive home and placed in a foster home with caring, nonabusive parents may feel conflicted about the loss of the parent and entry into the child welfare system. Feelings may include confusion, ambivalence, and guilt, for instance.

Earlier research studies have found that people who endure ambivalent loss tend to experience similar feelings, such as:

- "Frozen" (unresolved) grief, including outrage and inability to "move on"
- Confusion, distress, and ambivalence
- Uncertainly leading to immobilization
- Blocked coping processes
- Experience of helplessness, and therefore, depression, anxiety, and relationship conflicts
- Response with absolutes, namely, denial of change or loss, denial of facts
- Rigidity of family roles (maintaining that the lost person will return as before) and outrage at the lost person being excluded
- Confusion in boundaries and roles (e.g., who the parent figures are)
- Guilt, if hope has been given up
- Refusal to talk about the individuals and the situation (Boss, 2004 as cited in Lee & Whiting, 2007, p. 419).

With these feelings in mind, Lee and Whiting (2007) interviewed 182 foster children, ages 2 through 10. Children were asked about each of the feelings identified in Boss's study as typical responses to ambiguous loss. The study showed that virtually all of the children interviewed exhibited these typical feelings, particularly feelings associated with confusion, ambiguity, and outrage about their situation. Several children noted confusion about their future—not knowing when they would see their parent(s) again, or how long they would be in foster care. The children also expressed feelings of uncertainty, guilt, and immobility.

Lee and Whiting (2007) recommend using the model of ambiguous loss when working with children in foster care, cautioning against pathologizing their feelings (and the consequential behaviors). In describing the application of this model of loss, Lee and Whiting state:

> Therapists, case managers, officers of the court, and foster family members need not see these externalizing and internalizing behaviors as pathology, but as active coping strategies appropriate to the children's circumstances. Attempts to squelch these behaviors in the interest of tranquil foster placements are unrealistic and may exacerbate underlying psychosocial conditions. (p. 426)

In referencing therapy goals they continue:

> The immediate goal is to make understandable those things that are disruptive to the foster placement. The diverse stakeholders, including the children, need to appreciate how unresolved grief leads to ambivalence about and fears of interdependency, relationship testing, and self-fulfilling prophecies of non-lovableness. In short, all invested members must move from deficit detecting to appreciating that many of these otherwise disturbing behaviors are signs of ego strength. (p. 426)

Siu and Hogan (1989) also cite the importance of caseworkers understanding the nature of grieving and thereby assisting foster care children to grieve the loss of their families. It is vital for caseworkers to be familiar with the possible expressions of depression among grieving children, which often manifests as irritability and can easily be mistaken for oppositional behavior. It is also quite common for children to express heartfelt grief for parents who have horribly abused them. Even children who have been sexually abused often express missing their abusive parent. Caseworkers must be careful to allow these children to grieve for their parents, despite the fact that the parents have hurt them.

Identity Issues

Identity is a multifaceted concept referring primarily to one's self-knowledge, self-appraisal, and self-assessment. Developmental theorist Erik Erikson (1963, 1968, 1975) believed that identity formation involves the integration of numerous and sometimes conflicting childhood identities. Erikson believed that this convergence of identities takes place during the adolescent stage of development, when the adolescent develops an internal continuity and consistency that integrates all the different aspects of the self, allowing one's real identity to emerge. Our individual identities are based on several factors, some involving internal traits and some involving external traits. As individuals mature, their basis for identity becomes more internally based. But children, particularly younger children, will typically base their identity more on external, rather than internal attributes. For instance, if someone were to ask you to describe yourself, you might begin by saying that you are a college student (external). You might then share that you are a soccer player (external) and on the student council (external). But, you might then describe yourself as an extrovert (internal), who is courageous (internal), loyal (internal), and kind (internal). The more internally based one's identity is, the more resilient a person will be in times of crisis and transition.

Children tend to be far more external in their self-identity, and their self-appraisal can be quite fragile, varying dramatically if their external structure is removed. Siu and Hogan (1989) suggested that caseworkers become familiar with the process of identity development and how the removal of children from their family of origin can significantly affect their sense of personal identity. The nature of this impact not only will depend, of course, on the age of the children and their stage of development but can also be affected by several other variables. Some of the factors involved in identity formation include one's gender, ethnic and cultural identity, extracurricular activities, talents, socioeconomic status, and relationships with others. Children are often unaware of how they are affected by things such as their socioeconomic status, but it affects them nonetheless.

One's positive identity is dependent on an affirming reciprocal exchange between the various aspects of identity and one's environment. Consider this reciprocity as a mirror reflecting back either a positive or a negative image of how one is perceived and valued by others. Essentially, the positive or negative nature of one's identity is based at least in part on how these various aspects of one's self are valued by others. Individuals who are extremely talented musically may only perceive this talent as a positive part of their identity if their family and community perceive musical talent as valuable. Children who are intelligent but are raised in families that value athletic prowess may not perceive their intellectual ability as a positive and valuable trait. Children who are removed from their home for maltreatment and are placed in a new environment will struggle with identity issues because despite being in a more positive environment, they are no longer the youngest sibling, no longer the owner of a small dog, no longer the funniest student in the class, and no longer the best bike rider in the neighborhood. Now they are foster children, different and set apart, perhaps living in a home much nicer than their own, leaving their feelings somewhat deficient and "less than"; they are no longer funny because they know no one in class, and they are not the youngest sibling because they are only foster children in new homes.

Because so much of children's identities reside outside the self and are dependent on external validation and encouragement, an effective caseworker must understand the various dynamics of identity development, understanding how removing children from their homes, even abusive homes, can undermine children's identity development. Any acting out behavior on the part of the child should be viewed through this lens of identity disruption, and the caseworker can then respond by providing comfort and encouragement to the child during this transition. Children who have only received praise for their ability to play good basketball are going to struggle immensely with their identity if placed in homes that value academic performance or musical ability. A caseworker can assist these children in recognizing that their worth is internal and should not be based solely on the approval and affirmation of others.

Continuity of Family Ties

Picture yourself in a boat moored to a dock on the shore of a large lake. Being anchored here provides you with a connection to the mainland and a sense of security, without fearing becoming adrift at sea. But what if you need to get to the other side of the lake? You would have to pull up your anchor and drift across the water, and it wouldn't be until you reached the other side and safely anchored yourself against that shore that you would feel secure and stable again. Many significant life transitions are like the time adrift at sea—caught between two shores, where continuity and stability are temporarily lost. Children who have been removed from their biological homes will undoubtedly lose their sense of continuity with their biological families and will feel adrift at sea during the time period when they have not yet established new bonds with their foster family.

Siu and Hogan (1989) strongly recommend that caseworkers consider the importance of continuity and stability when considering where to place a child. Ready access to the biological family and even close friends should always be a priority in placement decisions, and although this can become challenging, particularly in areas where there may be a limited number of available foster families, consideration should still be given to a placement that will facilitate ongoing parental involvement.

At times, siblings must be placed in separate foster homes, and consideration to continuity issues needs to be extended to this situation as well. Far too often, siblings in foster families do not visit with each other regularly because of the geographic constraints placed on foster families, who are often responsible for providing transportation.

Caseworkers may find themselves in double-bind situations, however, where they must make difficult choices regarding keeping siblings together by placing them in a foster home that is a significant distance away from a parent who does not have transportation, or placing the children in different foster homes that are closer to their biological parents, but precludes family visitation because of the difficulty in coordinating visits among various foster families. Caseworkers must rely on their clinical skills in deciding on the right course of action and should then recognize and acknowledge how the interruption of family continuity and stability will affect the children, particularly early in the placement.

Far too often the foster care system, with all its complications, does not do an effective job of *fostering* a relationship between children in placement and their biological families, because if children do not have ready access to their biological families, they will most likely search for continuity and connectedness with their foster families, which, although necessary and important, can pose a risk to the continuing bond with their biological parents.

Research has clearly shown that children who visit their biological parents more frequently have a stronger bond with them and have fewer behavioral problems, are less apt to take psychiatric medication, such as antidepressant medication, and are less likely to be developmentally delayed, which underscores the importance of strengthening the attachment between foster children and their biological parents through regular and consistent visitation (McWey & Mullis, 2004). Restricting visitation for any reason other than the safety of the child will have a negative effect on this attachment and might even be subsequently used against the biological parents when it is time to make reunification plans.

Crisis

Removing children from their biological homes and placing them into foster care constitutes a psychosocial crisis. Siu and Hogan (1989) referred to this crisis as a critical transition, which throws an already fragile family into complete disequilibrium. In fact, most child welfare experts put foster care placement in the category of a *catastrophic crisis*. Crises are not always bad, however, and a popular contention among mental health experts is that a crisis provides the best opportunity for personal growth and authentic change (see Box 4.2).

Box 4.2   Review: Generalist Techniques for Direct Practice

Many individuals, including children, receiving services at a social services agency will need assistance with developing better coping skills, particularly in a crisis. Regardless of whether the problems experienced by the client are pervasive or more limited, most clients can benefit from learning to manage high levels of stress, learning to prioritize the various problems in their lives, and learning how to manage the current crisis in a way that diminishes the possibility of a domino effect of crises. A crisis with one's child requiring a significant amount of time and attention can quickly result in a job loss, which can in turn result in the loss of housing. Confronting crises effectively, though, can have a positive impact on one's life, including an increase in self-esteem, the development of new and more effective coping skills, the gaining of wisdom and the development of new social skills, and the development of a better overall support system.

Most mental health experts recognize that one of the best opportunities for personal growth is a crisis, because of the possibility of shaking up long-standing and entrenched maladaptive patterns of behavior. Park and Fenster (2004) studied stress-related growth in a group of college students who experienced a stressful event and found that the struggle involved in a life crisis produced personal growth opportunities. This is true, however, only for those who expend the necessary energy to work through their struggles in a positive way. Those in the study who remain negative and avoided dealing with the problems born out of the crisis did not take advantage of the growth-producing opportunities and thus did not experience any significant personal growth. Those who worked hard to manage the stress resulting from their crisis and were able to see the crisis as an opportunity for growth often developed better personal mastery skills and developed a changed and healthier perspective. Recognizing this potential for personal growth provides the practitioner with a framework for assisting clients, including children, develop better coping skills that not only can better assist them in the management of concrete problems but can also help them to shift their entire perspective of life struggles in general. For instance, clients who once saw themselves as powerless victims can begin to see themselves as empowered survivors.

Pearson Education, Inc.

Ordinary coping skills are typically not going to be enough to help a child deal with the trauma associated with being placed in foster care. But an effective and seasoned caseworker can help a child develop more effective coping skills that can help them respond to the multiple crises of being removed from their home and placed with strangers.

Working With Foster Parents

Foster care can refer to many placement settings, including kinship care, an emergency shelter, a residential treatment center, a group home, or even an independent living situation (with older adolescents), but most frequently foster care involves placing a child with a licensed foster family (two-parent or single-parent family). Every state has certain guidelines and standards that prospective foster parents must meet to qualify to become licensed (Barth, 2001). Licensure typically requires that families participate in up to 10 training sessions focusing on topics such as the developmental needs of at-risk children, issues related to child sexual abuse, appropriate disciplining techniques for at-risk children, ways that foster parents can support the relationship between the foster children and their biological parents, and ways to manage the stress of adding new members to their family. In addition, individuals who will be foster parenting children of a different ethnicity will likely undergo training focusing on transcultural parenting issues.

Foster parents provide an invaluable service by accepting troubled children into their homes and providing love, nurturing, and security, even though they know the children may be in their homes for only a short time. In addition to good training, foster parents benefit from caseworkers who are consistently supportive and available to them, particularly during high stress times, such as when foster children are acting out. Foster placement will be far less likely to fail if the foster parents feel sufficiently well prepared and supported by their caseworker.

Because the majority of foster children return to their biological parents, foster parents must be supported in their role in the reunification process. The success of a reunification plan depends largely on the cooperation of the foster parents. A foster parent who eagerly facilitates visitation and the sharing of vital information with the biological parents will help protect and maintain the continuity between the foster children and their biological parents. The caseworker plays a pivotal role in providing support and assistance to foster parents. A foster parent who feels unsupported will be far more likely to either purposely or inadvertently undermine the relationship between the foster child and the biological parents. Most of the time, this action comes in the form of advocacy for the child. Unfortunately, though, this advocacy, as well meaning as it may be, has the potential of disrupting the process of reunification. Thus, although it is certainly understandable that the process of emotional bonding with the foster child makes foster parents vulnerable to advocating for the best interest of their foster children, foster parents who take it upon themselves to protect their foster child by discouraging the relationship with the biological parents in any way are violating their designated roles, and their effectiveness as foster parents will most likely be seriously compromised.

The PBS documentary entitled *Failure to Protect: The Taking of Logan Marr* documents the removal of five-year-old Logan and her baby sister, Baily, from their young biological mother, Christie Marr. The documentary reveals how Maine's child welfare system, the Department of Human Services (DHS), removed Logan from her mother's care on the presumption that the child might be abused at some *future* time based on some dynamics in the home. After years of jumping through hoops and getting Logan back, Christie had another child,

Read about Logan Marr on the PBS Frontline website and searching for "The Taking of Logan Marr: Failure to Protect."

but ultimately lost both of her girls after marrying someone of whom DHS did not approve. Regardless of Christie's compliance with her parenting plan, the caseworker placed her girls with another DHS worker who was also a licensed foster parent. The foster mother wanted to adopt the Marr girls and actively hindered the relationship between the girls and their mother. In this situation, as well as many others, the foster mother was responsible for providing transportation for visitation, as well as for keeping Christie informed of major events in the girls' lives. Thus, she had tremendous power to limit visitation if she so desired or to be begrudging with vital information about the girls.

Logan ultimately died in this foster mother's care, and her death led to an uproar over the treatment of Christie, the apparent "cozy" relationship between the foster mother and the DHS caseworker, as well as the caseworker's refusal to investigate Logan's earlier complaints that her foster mother had abused her. This tragic case illustrates how vital it is for foster parents to be well trained and sufficiently supported by their caseworker. An effective caseworker will be able to sense when a foster parent is either burning out or overstepping appropriate boundaries and will respond with support and limit setting as necessary.

Reunification

The decision of when or whether to reunify foster children with their biological parents is based on many factors, including the biological parents' success in meeting their service plan goals. Even if these goals are sufficiently met, the timing of reunification may depend on minimizing disruptions in the child's life, such as switching schools in the middle of the school year. If reunification is the plan from the beginning of placement, then the caseworker should be planning for this event from the initial stages of the case. Problems arise when issues such as court postponements, additional service plan goals, changes in caseworker assignments, and other factors lead to delays in reunification. A judge may deem it perfectly reasonable to postpone a reunification hearing so that a child can complete the final four months of school without disruption, but such a decision can be devastating for the biological parents who have worked diligently to reach all service plan goals and go to court expecting to leave with their biological child, only to be told they must wait an additional four months to avoid their child changing schools in the middle of the school year. The potential for a biological parent to give up attempting to regain custody and to relapse into unhealthy behaviors out of discouragement and frustration is great, and caseworkers must be sensitive to the possibility of such frustrations leading to despair or relapse.

Therefore, even though reunification with biological parents is associated with several changes in the child's life, many of which may be negative in nature (Lau, Litrownik, Newton, & Landsverk, 2003), an effective caseworker will begin preparing the child for these transitions from the beginning of placement in foster care. Simply verbalizing what

Social Work Application Activity

Logan Marr Evaluated

In what ways did child protective services fail Logan Marr? In what ways did personal bias enter into decision-making processes? How could the NASW Code of Ethics assist child protective caseworkers in making more professional and effective decisions regarding Logan's care?

is going to happen, telling the child what to expect in the future, and giving such children a voice in expressing their fears and frustrations, even if they do not have decision-making power, will go a long way in minimizing the negative effect of reunification, particularly for children who have been in placement for a significant amount of time.

Reunification is not just stressful for the child, it is stressful for the biological parents as well, and many biological parents are the most vulnerable to stress-related relapse in the weeks following reunification. The combination of increased stress and the acting out of the child due to yet another transition can create a potentially volatile situation where negative behavior patterns resurface. Any good reunification plan involves ongoing monitoring and provision of in-home services to prevent any such problems during the reunification transition. A county child welfare office can provide these services directly or through a contracted agency-based practice that specializes in providing services such as in-home case management and support. With good support services, many reunifications go quite smoothly, and in time the children and parents settle in to a regular routine where healthier communication patterns and positive parenting styles will lead to a positive response from the children.

Family Preservation

Because the number of children placed in substitute care rose consistently since the 1980s until relatively recentlys, particularly in most urban communities, there has been an increasing focus on early intervention and prevention programs since the early 1990s. Family preservation programs are designed to reduce the need for out-of-home placement by intervening in a family process before the dynamics deteriorate to the point of requiring the removal of the children. These programs are composed of a variety of short-term, intensive services designed to immediately reduce stress and teach important skills that will reduce the likelihood of out-of-home placement. Services can include family counseling, parenting training, assistance with household budgeting, stress management, child development, respite care for caregivers, and in some cases, cash assistance (Child Welfare League of America, n.d.).

Although there has been some controversy surrounding the success of these programs in reducing foster care placements, the federal government remains committed to early intervention programs, and many counties report that approximately 80 percent of families who have participated in family preservation programs remained intact in the year following the suspension of services (Child Welfare League of America, n.d.).

Relevant to any discussion on family preservation is the importance of human rights as they relate to children, particularly those who are living in environments that are fragile, thus increasing the already vulnerable nature of dependence. The United Nations Convention on the Rights of the Child (UNCRC), adopted in 1989 and enacted in 1990, is considered by most in child welfare to be one of the most significant international treaties establishing and enforcing human rights for all children. Every country in the world has signed and ratified the UNCRC except the United States and Somalia, both of which have signed but not ratified the treaty. The UNCRC consists of 41 articles setting forth basic rights of children (as well as the means for ensuring the enforcement of these rights) based on the "best interest of the child" principle, which places the needs of children, particularly in decisions relating to their care, as a primary concern above all other interests. The ultimate goal of the UNCRC is to protect the survival, health, education, and development of children, securing their well-being (UNCRC, 1989).

The UNCRC guarantees children the most basic rights, including the right to live, to develop in a healthy manner (including the right to play and enjoy a wide range of child-appropriate activities), to have a legal name and identity that is registered with the government (such as a birth certificate), to reside with parents (as long as this is in the child's best interest), to have access to appropriate healthcare, to have an education, and to have an adequate standard of living free from profound poverty. Several articles also guarantee a child's freedom of expression including having a voice in choices that affect them (as is deemed developmentally appropriate), appropriate freedom of expression, privacy, and access to information, with indigenous children even having the right to practice their own cultural traditions. Children are guaranteed the right to protection, including protection from violence, child labor, exposure to the drug trade, drug abuse, sexual exploitation, abduction, trafficking, excessive detention, and punishment. Relevant to the discussion on family preservation, several articles of the UNCRC set forth the rights of children who for whatever reason cannot reside with their families, including the right to be cared for in a manner that respects their religion, ethnic group, and cultural traditions, and the right to have all aspects of the UNCRC applied to them regardless of their residential or family status (UNCRC, 1989).

Assess your comprehension of "Working With Children in Placement" by completing this quiz.

Clearly, the international community recognizes the value of the biological family unit and supports all governmental efforts designed to support families maintain their bonds, particularly with their children. Such support can be in the form of "family-friendly" policies, financial and case management support for kinship care (increased since the passage of the Fostering Connections to Success and Increasing Adoptions Act of 2008), as well as other measures that focus on prevention and preservation rather than solely intervention.

Respond to Contexts That Shape Practice

Practice Behavior: Provide leadership in promoting sustainable changes in service delivery and practice to improve the quality of social services.

Critical Thinking Question: Research indicates that child protective caseworkers are often much less likely to refer families of color for family preservation services, and instead opt to remove the child from the home, because of perceptions that their communities lack appropriate services. This perception is based in large part on negative stereotypes that may have little basis in fact, but there is also some truth to this assumption in that often ethnic minority neighborhoods have less access to mental health and family support resources compared with neighborhoods that are more reflective of the majority population. As a social worker who has recently undergone cultural competency training, what different approaches can you take on this issue, other than excluding families of color from these early prevention service?

ETHNIC MINORITY POPULATIONS AND MULTICULTURAL CONSIDERATIONS

Children of color are overrepresented in the foster care system, comprising nearly 60 percent of all placements in the year 2004. This is nearly twice their representation in the general population. Of all children requiring child welfare intervention, the majority of African American children requiring care are placed in foster care, whereas the majority of Caucasian children receive in-home services (Child Welfare League of America, 2002). In addition, African American children remain in foster care far longer and are reunited with their families far less often. This overrepresentation of children of color in the foster care system, particularly African American children, is fueled by other long-standing factors such as social oppression, negative social conditions, racial discrimination, and economic injustice. For instance, African American children were initially excluded from the child welfare system but are now the most overrepresented of all racial groups (Smith & Devore, 2004).

Some reasons for this overrepresentation relate to complex social issues such as institutionalized racism, intergenerational poverty, and culturally based drug abuse. But other possible causes include racism within the child welfare system.

Types of racial discrimination include:

1. *Racial bias in referring families for family preservation programs versus out-of-home placement.* Certain sub-populations, including African American families, are not consistently targeted for family preservation programs. Reasons for this include caseworker bias based on the belief that the needs of the African American community may be too great to be appropriately handled by this program (Denby & Curtis, 2003).

2. *Racial partiality in assessing parent–child attachment leading to delays in returning children to their biological parents.* A 2003 study of approximately 250 black and white children in foster care placement found that racial partiality existed in assessing the parent–child attachment when the caseworker was of a different race than the biological parent. Although this result was reciprocal (i.e., black caseworkers showed partiality to black families and white caseworkers show partiality to white families), the effect of this trend has particular relevance to the African American community because the majority of caseworkers are Caucasian, and African American children are disproportionately represented among children in foster care. The results of this study revealed that Caucasian caseworkers might have erred when they concluded that African American mothers were poorly attached to their children because of the caseworker's lack of understanding of cultural differences between Caucasian and African American customs (Surbeck, 2003).

3. *Caseworkers who are poorly trained in cultural competencies.* For a caseworker to accurately assess many of the factors necessary in determining whether out-of-home placement is warranted, such as the level of violence in the home, the ability of parents to protect their children, or the level of parental remorse, a caseworker must be aware of commonly held negative stereotypes of various racial groups. It is unacceptable for a member of the majority culture to claim not to hold any negative stereotypes, and it is only through the honest admission of overt and subtle negative biases toward other cultures that a caseworker can begin to work effectively with a variety of ethnic groups.

Placing Children of Color in Caucasian Homes

Considerable controversy exists surrounding the placement of children of color in Caucasian homes. Many advocacy organizations do not support this practice, whereas others claim that it is not in the best interest of children to experience placement delays simply because there are no foster families available that are the same race as the child. From a "micro" perspective, this latter argument makes sense. If an African American child is in desperate need of a long-term foster home, how much sense would it make to have a policy in place that prevents placement in a suitable home only because the foster family is Caucasian? After all, all children deserve loving homes, and the color of their skin should not keep them from being placed in one. Right?

Yet, from a "macro" perspective, a different viewpoint is revealed. Consider the equity of a majority culture systematically destroying an entire race, as the United States has done to the African American population during the slavery and post–Civil War era or to the Native American population during colonial times and the era of early occupation of the United States. How do you think these racial groups would perceive this same majority culture then rushing in to "rescue" the children who were maltreated in great part because of this cultural genocide and the resultant social breakdown within the family and broader community?

Advocates of placing children of color in homes of the same race cite such cultural genocide in their arguments. Alternatives to transracial placement include the development of kinship care programs, where members of a child's extended family act as foster parents, often made possible through financial assistance. The National Association of Black Social Workers (NABSW) cites the long-standing tradition of informal kinship care within the African American community extending back to the Middle Ages and solidified during the slavery era, when many African Americans acted in the informal capacity of parents for children whose biological parents were sold and sent away. Such cultural traditions can serve as a precursor for federally funded programs that promote kinship care foster programs, which respect cultural identity and tradition (NABSW, 2003).

Recent studies support the concerns expressed by the NABSW and others about the difficulties faced by even the most well-meaning white adoptive parents to accurately teach their black adopted children lessons about race in a culturally appropriate manner. A recent study by Smith, Juarez, and Jacobson (2011) found that the majority of adoptive families of black adoptees were white, middle to upper-class families from primarily white communities, and despite their attempts to teach their children about matters of race and instill in them a sense of cultural pride, most of the black adoptees were often left to struggle with racial discrimination and racial enculturation on their own. The primary reason for this dynamic was that their white adoptive families more often than not experienced race quite differently than their black adopted children, viewing racial dynamics through a white Eurocentric lens (Smith, Juarez, & Jacobson, 2011).

In their study on the attempts of white parents to teach their black adopted children about race and racism in America, Smith, Juarez, and Jacobson (2011) state:

> As members of U.S. society's dominant mainstream, White adoptive parents are positioned to transmit collective understandings, interpretations, knowledge, and memories about Whiteness, not Blackness. They are well positioned to teach lessons about race that reflect and give privilege to the interests, values, experiences, and perspectives of Whites. (p. 1198)

Their study revealed that although a majority of white transracial adoptive parents cited the importance of their children developing a sense of pride in their cultural heritage, they framed "cultural pride" as an individual process, not a collective one. As the majority of transracial families interviewed in the study lived in primarily white communities, their black children did not participate or engage in communities of color; thus, any development of cultural pride was done in isolation.

Most of the white parents in this study taught their children about African American culture, including the nature of race relations in America, through books, films, and cultural events, such as attending black camps. For instance, several white adoptive parents shared that they taught their black adoptive children about overcoming racism through the telling of stories of famous black individuals who became successful despite racial barriers through personal fortitude and a lot of hard work. Yet Smith, Juarez, and Jacobson (2011) point out how this type of racial framing illustrates Western notions of individualism, rather than community efforts more reflective of African American culture and history and did not teach black adoptees about racial inequality involved in "structural relations within society that enable the hard work of some to pay off more than that of (racialized) others" (p. 1214).

This study also revealed just how committed the white adoptive parents who were interviewed were in their attempts to appropriately validate their black adoptive children's racial heritage and culture pride, but they did so in ways that were distinctly white. For instance, the white adoptive parents taught their black children to affirm and feel good about their race but not at the expense of creating conflict. According to Smith, Juarez, and Jacobson (2011), white parents also encouraged their black children to develop thick skin in response to racism, including teaching incidences of racial discrimination as opportunities to teach Caucasians about the nature of race and racial discrimination, all the while keeping their real feelings to themselves. Clearly, framing racial and cultural dynamics in such a white Eurocentric individualist way contradicted sharply with how most African American parents handle matters of race with their children. Although the white parents in this study clearly loved their black adopted children and appeared very committed to addressing matters of race, with regard to cultural pride and dealing with racial prejudice, by presuming that racism was the result of white ignorance that could be overcome only through education and hard work, the white parents were inadvertently drawing from historic white cultural narratives of racial inequality, not black ones, which are far more likely to emphasize the purposeful agenda of racial oppression and inequality within American society, and the collective struggle of African Americans to fight against it.

Although Smith, Juarez, and Jacobson (2011) do not specifically advocate against transracial adoption, they do caution white parents to be very careful about the ways in which they choose to teach lessons about race to their adopted children, to avoid even the inadvertent inculcation of white racist framing of the black experience in America. They suggest doing this by reframing race and racial issues through the experiences of the black community and not through the lens of White America. Whether this is possible, is difficult to say, but further research on ways in which race lessons can be taught to black adoptees will inform this growing area of research, particularly if informed by black adoptees themselves.

Native Americans and the U.S. Child Welfare System

The British colonization of North America involved an organized and methodical campaign to decimate the Native American population through invasion, trickery (such as trading land for alcohol), and ultimately the forced relocation of all Native Americans onto government-designated reservations, where the assimilation into the majority culture became a primary goal of the British and then U.S. governments (Brown, 2001). The few Native Americans who survived this genocide were broken physically, emotionally, and spiritually, suffering from alcoholism, rampant unemployment, and debilitating depression.

In the early part of the 19th century the U.S. government assumed full responsibility for educating Native American children. It is estimated that from the early 1800s through the early part of the 20th century, virtually all Native American children were forcibly removed from their homes on the reservations and placed in Indian boarding schools,

Male Native American students in physical education class, Carlisle Indian School, Carlisle, Pennsylvania, c 1901.

BUYENLARGE/ARCHIVE PHOTOS/GETTY IMAGES

Old Sun Residential School.

JOHNSTON, FRANCES BENJAMIN, 1864-1952/ LIBRARY OF CONGRESS PRINTS AND PHOTOGRAPHS DIVISION[LC-USZ62-72450]

where they were not allowed to speak in their native tongues, practice their cultural religion, or wear their traditional dress. During school breaks, many of these children were placed as servants in Caucasian homes rather than being allowed to return home for visits. The result of this forced assimilation amounted to cultural genocide where an entire generation of Native Americans was institutionalized, deprived of a relationship with their biological families, and robbed of their cultural heritage.

The ongoing campaign to assimilate the Native Americans into European American culture became even more aggressive between 1950 and 1970, when social workers with governmental backing removed thousands of Native American children from their homes on the reservations for alleged maltreatment, placing them in adoptive Caucasian homes. In reality, many of the problems on the reservations were the product of years of governmental oppression resulting in extreme poverty and other commonly associated social ills, and the U.S. government's response to this was to tear Native American families apart rather than intervene with mental health services.

Between 1941 and 1978, approximately 70 percent of all Native American children were removed from their homes and placed either in orphanages or with Caucasian families, many of whom later adopted them (Marr, 2002). In truth, few of these children were removed from their homes because of maltreatment as it is currently defined. Rather, approximately 99 percent of these children were removed because social workers believed that the children were victims of social deprivation due to the extreme poverty common on most Indian reservations (U.S. Senate, 1974). The result of this government action has been nothing short of devastating. Native Americans have one of the highest suicide rates in the nation, with Native American youth, particularly those who have spent time in U.S. boarding schools, having on average five to six times the rate of suicide compared to the non-Native population. When these children graduated from high school, they were adults without a culture—no longer feeling comfortable on the reservation after years of being negatively indoctrinated against their cultural heritage, yet not being accepted by the white population either. The response of many of these individuals was to turn to alcohol in an attempt to drown out the pain.

After watching *"Unseen Tears: The Native American Boarding School Experience in Western New York,"* Parts 1-3 on YouTube describe what you think about recent Supreme Court decisions that appear to be eroding the original intention of the Indian Welfare Act. (https://www.youtube.com/ watch?v=ioAzggmes8c).

In 1978, the Indian Child Welfare Act (Pub. L. No. 95-608) was passed, which prevented the unjustified removal of Native American children from their homes. The act specifies that if removal is necessary, then the children must be placed in a home that reflects their culture and preserves tribal tradition. Tribal approval must be obtained prior to placement, even when the placement is a result of a voluntary adoption proceeding (Kreisher, 2002). This act has for the most part successfully stemmed the tide of mass removal of Native American children from their homes on the reservations, but unfortunately many caseworkers still do not understand the reason why such a bill was passed in the first place, or why it is necessary, and they mistakenly believe that this act hampers placing at-risk children in loving homes.

Gaining a fuller understanding of the history between people of color and the U.S. child welfare system will make it easier to understand why some minority groups may not trust social workers in issues regarding allegations of abuse. The social worker might not be aware of the long-standing negative history between government child welfare agencies and a particular racial group, but members of that particular group are most likely aware of this history. It is vital that social workers develop cultural competencies, regardless of whether they are actively working with ethnic minority populations. It is only through a comprehensive understanding of the history of child welfare policies and abuses of power that the U.S. child welfare system will truly achieve its goal of respecting the autonomy and dignity of all people, regardless of race, gender, age, nationality, and sexual orientation.

Assess your comprehension of "Ethnic Minority Populations and Multicultural Considerations" by completing this quiz.

Summary

Social workers who work with troubled families have the opportunity to effect change that positively affects not only the present families but all future generations within that family system as well. Child welfare caseworkers often experience high caseloads and can feel overwhelmed and burned out in the face of such immensely complicated dynamics commonly involved in child welfare cases.

An increased focus on family preservation programs and other early intervention programs offer the best opportunity for reducing out-of-home placements, but these programs must be offered to all potentially appropriate families without bias. This can occur through sufficient federal and state funding of child welfare programs and the effective recruitment and training of social workers willing to work with a variety of families, from various cultures dealing with a wide range of life challenges.

Recall what you learned in this chapter by completing the Chapter Review.

Adolescent Services

My first job in social work was working for an adolescent residential facility in Colorado. I still remember my first day, which was filled with anxious anticipation. I was one of those individuals who always knew I was going to be a counselor, and it seemed as though I had waited far too long to be able to counsel professionally. I was assigned to the high-risk unit, which housed newly admitted girls, as well as girls who were at risk of suicide or self-injury. I couldn't wait to jump in and start rescuing these girls! Thus, you can imagine my surprise when the unit supervisor strapped on my own body alarm and explained that if I was physically attacked, my natural body movements would trigger the alarm and all available staff would come running to my aid. Attacked? Why would these girls attack me when all I was doing was trying to help them? I had spent four years as an undergraduate preparing to help my fellow human being, and the thought that my efforts would not only go unappreciated, but be perceived as threatening was shocking. Such was my professional introduction into the world of working with adolescents. I learned on my first day of work that the adolescent population could be a challenging one to work with and that my adolescent clients might not always express their appreciation for the work I was doing with them; but I also learned that working with adolescents was very fulfilling, dynamic and face-paced.

ADOLESCENCE: A NEW STAGE OF DEVELOPMENT?

It has been widely reported among psychologists, sociologists, and historians that the stage of adolescence is relatively new, not having been formally acknowledged until psychologist G. Stanley Hall began his study of adolescence in 1882, culminating in his groundbreaking book on adolescence published in 1904. Yet, it would be misleading to assume that because society did not formally acknowledge the stage of adolescence that it did not exist. There was little acknowledgment of childhood being a distinct stage of development prior to the late 1800s, but that does not mean that children did not throw tantrums, play, and essentially act and feel like children. Hall's earliest writing on the study of adolescence sounds strikingly similar to contemporary descriptions of adolescent behavior. Hall described adolescents as possessing a "lack of emotional steadiness, violent impulses, unreasonable conduct, lack of enthusiasm and sympathy" (as cited in Demos & Demos, 1969, p. 635).

But even if adolescents have always behaved as adolescents, there have been significant shifts in child and adolescent developmental theories, influenced by the societal changes that have occurred over the past few hundred years. These changes have influenced not only how the stages of childhood and adolescence are perceived but also the course of development itself. Lifestyles were quite different 200 years ago when the United States was a new country. The U.S. economy was different, livelihoods were different, neighborhoods were different, and families were different. An important question to consider is what kind of impact these changes have had on adolescent development and whether adolescent behavior has changed or whether society's expectations and perception of adolescents have changed.

There is no question that the mass urbanization of the past 200 years has had an impact on individual and family lives, including the lives of adolescents, who at one point in history worked alongside family members on the family farm, but who in contemporary times have far less vocational responsibility, as an increasing amount of focus is placed on the academic education of adolescents. Even the way in which many adolescents are educated has changed, likely influencing adolescent development, as teens spend significantly more time with their peers in large school environments, with increasing exposure to violence (Larsen, 2003; National Center for Education Statistics, 1999; Raywid, 1996).

Thus, although adolescents of the past acted in ways that are strikingly similar to the ways in which they act today, the many profound changes within U.S. society, including changes in family structure, the public educational system, and expectations of adolescents within these systems, have influenced the ways in which many contemporary adolescents both develop and behave.

Developmental Perspectives of Adolescence

To understand the behavior of adolescents, it is important to understand the *developmental stages* that children and adolescents progress through on their way to adulthood. Development occurs within various domains, including the intellectual, emotional, psychosocial, moral, and even spiritual spheres. Many theories of development propose that individuals progress through distinct stages of growth with earlier stages acting as foundations for successive stages. Because the course of development is influenced by many factors, both on an individual and on a broader societal level, it is important to consider both developmental theories and the course of developmental growth and maturity of children and adolescents within various contexts. For instance, in the previous section we discussed changes that have occurred in families in the United States since the mid-19th century. It is likely that what was considered "normal" behavior for adolescents in 1900 would not necessarily be considered "normal" in contemporary society.

In other words, it is important to consider the normative aspects of adolescent development within a *historical context*. What is expected of an adolescent, and what is considered adaptive and healthy behavior, depends on what is occurring in the world during the time in which the adolescent lives. A world war with a mandatory draft forces adolescents to grow up quickly, just as the Great Depression shortened childhoods across the country as adolescents were called upon to help support their families. Yet, in contemporary society, childhoods are often considered lengthened by a good economy, which reduces the need for adolescent employment, an increase in educational requirements required for professional employment, and the cessation of a mandatory draft, all of which have led to many believing that contemporary society has lower expectations of adolescents than in past eras. Adolescents who did not work during the Great Depression would likely have been considered irresponsible for not being willing to assist in the support of their families, but adolescents who do not work in contemporary society are likely presumed to be focused solely on their academic studies in preparation for college.

It is also important to consider developmental issues within a *cultural context*. What is considered normative and emotionally healthy within one culture may be considered maladaptive in another, and what is considered respectful and honorable behavior in one culture may be a sign of an emotional disorder in another. For instance, in many cultures, remaining in the family home until marriage is considered the norm. It is common in collectivist cultures, such as Asian, Latino, and even some European cultures, for single adult children as old as 30 years to live at home with their parents. In many of these cultures, it would be considered a sign of disrespect for a single adult to move from the family home to gain independence prior to getting married. The United States is, for the most part, an individualistic society that values independence and autonomy; thus, many within the U.S. culture may perceive the 30-year-old male still living with his parents as a sign of unhealthy emotional enmeshment, where the boundaries between parents and adult child are blurred.

Finally, it is important to consider development within a *regional context*. Although urbanization over the last 200 years within the United States has resulted in the majority of people living in urban or suburban communities, rural life still exists in the United States and some research suggests that there are significant differences between adolescent life in rural communities and adolescent life in urban communities. Although there is not a wide body of research comparing urban and rural adolescents, a study conducted in 2001 found that rural adolescents felt less pressure to become involved in gang activities, were confronted with less violence both on and off campus, and felt less academic pressure, from both their school and their parents, compared with adolescents residing in urban areas (Gandara, Gutierrez, & O'Hara, 2001).

Understanding the natural course of development will assist the social worker to correctly evaluate an adolescent's behavior, framing it as either adaptive or maladaptive,

Apply Knowledge of Human Behavior and the Social Environment

Practice Behavior: Critique and apply knowledge to understand person and environment.

Critical Thinking Question: What are some contextual lenses used when evaluating the feelings, beliefs, and behaviors of an adolescent? Why is it important to evaluate an adolescent contextually?

depending on the context within which the behavior is exhibited. For instance, understanding that it is normal for an adolescent to act in a self-centered and dramatic manner will aid the social worker in framing behavior that, in an adult, may be indicative of a personality disorder.

Keeping historical, cultural, and regional contexts in mind will assist the social worker in not mischaracterizing certain behaviors because their origin is either misunderstood or not valued by the majority culture. Adolescents in contemporary culture may act in a different manner than adolescents in past generations; yet, this does not necessarily mean that adolescents today are any less respectful than those of the past. It is also important for those in social work to understand that adolescents who immigrated to the United States from a Latin American country might act in a different manner than adolescents who have lived in the United States their entire lives, or that adolescents who recently moved from a farming community to a large city school might act differently than adolescents who grew up in an urban community.

Having a competent grasp of normative development can be a guide for social workers who work with adolescents and must evaluate and assess their behavior before determining the appropriate level of intervention or whether intervention is warranted at all. Most of the developmental theorists agree that adolescence is a time of searching for one's own identity and developing a sense of autonomy. Trying on different "selves" is a common mental and behavioral activity of adolescents who are in the process of developing an internally anchored sense of who they are, rather than defining themselves by what others think or expect of them (including their parents) (Erikson, 1968; Kerpelman & Pittman, 2001). Many normal and healthy adolescents can be quite dramatic and egocentric in their behavior, and although this might give many parents cause for concern, most adolescents grow out of this stage to become giving and compassionate adults.

Jean Piaget (1950), a Swiss-born biologist turned psychologist, developed a theory of cognitive development that is still the dominant theory of intellectual development today. Among Piaget's many findings is his discovery that children, adolescents, and adults each think differently. Most notably, Piaget discovered that younger children think concretely, meaning that they lack the ability to understand many adult concepts such as parables and analogies, as well as other abstract concepts. If a group of adults were asked what it meant to "let the chips fall where they may," they will most likely explain that this is an idiom meaning to let things happen naturally. But if a group of children were asked what this statement meant, they will most likely reply that it means that if chips fall on the ground, one should not pick them up.

Piaget (1950) believed that as children approached adolescence, they began to develop the ability for logical reasoning involved in abstract thought. Abstract thought or reasoning enables us to have empathy by "putting ourselves in someone else's shoes." It allows

Social Work, Social Media, and Technology

Many adolescents spend a considerable amount of time engaging with friends in the virtual world of social media on sites such as Facebook, Tumblr, and Snapchat. What kind of impact do you believe social media has had on adolescent development? Cite two positive effects and two negative effects, and explain how these interact to influence the psychosocial development of mainstream adolescents.

us to think metaphorically, to understand sarcasm, to deduce, to analyze, to synthesize, and to rationalize. It also allows us to understand, and thus internalize moral standards: not just to know that something is wrong but to understand *why* it is wrong. If children of the age of 5 are asked why it is wrong to hit another child on the playground, they might state that it is wrong because they will get in trouble. But most adults would be able to explain that this act is wrong because it violates another person's personal rights, that violence does not resolve conflict, and that they would not want to be hit, even if someone else was angry with them. This type of reasoning requires empathy, the ability to see situations from multiple perspectives, the ability to draw on other experiences, and the ability to connect the immediacy of hitting someone to the generalized concept of violence—all of which require abstract reasoning ability.

It is through the development of abstract reasoning ability that adolescents discover that their parents might not always be right, that lying can be rationalized, that breaking the rules can sometimes be fun, and that authority can be questioned. When a child asks, "Why?" the question usually relates to why the sky is blue and the grass is green. But when adolescents ask, "Why?" it often relates to asking why sex before marriage is wrong, why education must occur in a 20' × 20' classroom, why drinking alcohol is bad, and perhaps even existential questions such as the existence of a God or why they were put on this earth.

Assess your comprehension of "Adolescence: A New Stage of Development?" by completing this quiz.

Abstract reasoning is a useful and powerful intellectual tool that can at times be like a lethal weapon in the hands of an unstable and angry adolescent. Existential questions about the meaning of life can quickly spiral into questioning why one should exist at all, and questions about the concept of authority can quickly evolve into abandoning the concept of obeying authority altogether. The necessary skill of logical or abstract reasoning often enables a troubled adolescent to rationalize away reasons not to rebel.

COMMON PSYCHOSOCIAL ISSUES AND THE ROLE OF THE SOCIAL WORKER

The common stereotype of adolescents being generally rebellious and out of control is both true and untrue. Many adolescents are quite responsible and do not have mental health problems. But adolescence is a time of physical and psychological stress; of trying on different "selves" and of exploring undiscovered issues, attitudes, and behaviors. Most developmental theorists consider this time in one's life to be transitional, and typically all transitions can be both exciting and stormy. But there are other relevant issues that make adolescence unique among the various developmental stages of life, which has an impact on providing counseling services to those adolescents who are troubled.

Adolescent Rebellion

As long as there have been adolescents, one can be assured that there has been adolescent rebellion. Casually defined, adolescent rebellion can include any behavior on the part of an adolescent that is in marked opposition to standard rules, either within the family or within society in general. Determining what specifically constitutes rebellious behavior, though, can be a bit more challenging and often depends on current social mores, as well as one's own personal value system. Behaviors that involve outright destruction and the breaking of laws are easily characterized as rebellious. But whether the subtler challenging of rules is considered rebellious is certainly in the eye of the beholder, where one person's rebellion is another person's sign of autonomy and individuation. For instance, most would agree that behaviors such as taking illegal drugs, habitual lying, and engaging in chronic truancy are rebellious, but what about the occasional drinking of alcohol or the intermittent breaking of a curfew? Many mental health experts and even some parents might normalize this behavior as being typical of the majority of adolescents who are testing limits and striving for increased independence.

In general, however, any behavior in adolescents should be considered maladaptive if it is interfering with normal functioning and causing problems in the adolescent's everyday life. For instance, adolescents who skip one day of school in an entire year would not be considered rebellious, but adolescents who are truant several times per week, thereby affecting their ability to pass their classes, would likely be characterized as rebellious, or in clinical terms, struggling with conduct disorder or oppositional defiant disorder. Conduct disorder and oppositional defiant disorder are disorders included in the *Diagnostic and Statistical Manual of Mental Disorders* (*DSM-V*) and are diagnosed during adolescence. *Conduct disorder*, the more serious of these two disorders, involves a consistent pattern of behaviors in which social mores and rules are habitually broken and the rights of others are consistently violated without regard for the other person's feelings. To avoid a child being diagnosed with conduct disorder in response to uncharacteristic or minor rebellion, children cannot receive this diagnosis unless they meet at least three of the four criteria outlined by the American Psychiatric Association (APA) in the preceding 12-month period (see Box 5.1).

Again, what most often determines the difference between the adolescents who are harmlessly spreading their wings and adolescents with conduct disorder is the *frequency*, *persistence*, and *seriousness* of the maladaptive behaviors. A 12-year-old who "runs away" to the next-door neighbor's house or a 16-year-old who breaks curfew by 30 minutes on just a few occasions would certainly not be diagnosed with this disorder. But a 12-year-old who runs away for weeks at a time or a 16-year-old who comes home whenever he pleases certainly might.

Oppositional defiance disorder is another emotional disorder commonly diagnosed in adolescents and is characterized by a milder set of behavioral problems, including negative, hostile, and defiant behavior such as losing one's temper, arguing with adults, and

---

Box 5.1   Conduct Disorder Diagnostic Criteria

1. Exhibiting aggression to people and animals, such as bullying, threatening or intimidating others, initiating fights, using weapons, exhibiting physical cruelness toward people or animals, stealing from a victim (e.g., armed robbery), or forced sexual activity.

2. Destroying property, such as destructively setting a fire, or deliberately destroying another person's property, such as fire setting with the intention of causing serious damage.

3. Deceitfulness or theft, such as breaking into someone's home or car, lying to obtain something desired, or nonviolent stealing such as shoplifting.

4. Serious violations of rules, such as frequently staying out at night despite parental curfew, running away from home, and frequent truancies from school (APA, 2013).

Pearson Education, Inc.

consistently refusing to obey rules. Other criteria include blaming others for personal mistakes, being easily annoyed, frequent feelings of anger and resentment, spite, and vindictiveness.

Because social workers always evaluate the mental health of individuals *within the context of their environment*, it is vital to examine any potential environmental causes or influences of an adolescent's maladaptive behavior. For instance, socioeconomic status, gender, parenting styles, environment, genetic influences, cognitive deficits, and temperament have all been associated with juvenile delinquency (Lahey, Moffitt, & Caspi, 2003). It is important to note that although such research indicates some type of a relationship between conduct disorders and these various influences, they do not specify whether any of these variables actually *cause* conduct disorders in adolescents. Thus, it would be incorrect to assume that adolescents from lower socioeconomic backgrounds will automatically engage in juvenile delinquency. Rather there may be other explanations such as bias in diagnosing or a situation in which families that are chaotic, perhaps even abusive, are likely to be from a lower socioeconomic level because such behaviors are often not amenable to the skill sets required to be a high wage earner.

I have worked with adolescents for years—in a residential setting, in a school setting, and later in private practice, and I have found that adolescents typically act out for specific reasons. Clinically evaluating the entire picture is extremely important as many children and adolescents who meet the criteria for conduct disorder or oppositional defiance disorder come from homes where maladaptive behavior abounds (Frick, 2004). Such behaviors are often a manifestation of earlier abuse, neglect, and general chaos in the home environment. In general, if children and adolescents cannot talk out their feelings, they will likely act them out, often in a negative manner. Thus, if adolescents have neither the opportunity nor the maturity to connect behaviors with feelings, they will be at greater risk of expressing negative feelings in a destructive way.

Depression, Anxiety, and Deliberate Self-harm

Adolescents, like children and adults, do not always manifest their emotional problems in outward ways. In fact, some of the most emotionally disturbed adolescents turn their anxiety, anger, and sadness inward with behaviors that reflect forms of depression. These adolescents are often overlooked, particularly within a school system, because they are not disruptive, often sitting in the back of the class quietly, disturbing no one. Yet, internalizing behaviors can often be the most serious of all, putting these adolescents at higher risk of depression, self-abuse, and suicide.

Social Work Application Activity

Research shows that conduct disorder is disproportionately diagnosed in African American and Latino youth populations, and diagnosed teens then experienced worse outcomes, with increased risks of being involved in the juvenile justice system (see Mizock & Harkins, 2011), and that youth of color who are diagnosed with conduct disorder are more likely to be referred to the juvenile justice system than mental health interventions (see VanHook, 2012). What do you believe are some of the causes of racial disparity in diagnosing conduct disorder in the adolescent population? What are some ways that the social work profession can take the lead on addressing diagnosis bias?

Everyone experiences depression from time to time, but when feelings of sadness become so pronounced and long-standing that these emotions become barriers to normal functioning, the individual may be suffering from clinical depression, also referred to as *major depressive disorder*. The *DSM-V* lists several criteria for major depressive disorder, including abnormally depressed mood; loss of interest and pleasure; inappropriate guilt; disturbances in sleep, appetite, energy level, memory, and concentration; and, in serious cases, frequent thoughts of suicide. In children and adolescents, the melancholy can often appear as irritability, which can lead to confusion in diagnosing the appropriate disorder because an irritable teenager can look far more oppositional than a sad or melancholic one.

The term used to indicate the existence of two emotional disorders simultaneously is *comorbidity*, and the comorbidity of depression and anxiety is quite high, with approximately 80 percent of those with depression also suffering from anxiety of some type (Gorwood, 2004). Although anxiety has a completely different set of diagnostic criteria (see the *DSM-V*), if one examines the possible origin of mood disorders, then it makes sense that the emotional issues that can make someone feel depressed could likely lead to feelings of anxiety as well.

There are many treatments for depression and anxiety, ranging from counseling to drug therapy, including antidepressants and antianxiety medication. However, working with adolescents is a special challenge because adolescents can be impulsive, dramatic, and rather narcissistic as a normal part of development, but a depressed adolescent who is impulsive, dramatic, and narcissistic can be dangerous to themselves or others.

I discussed earlier how some adolescents express their negative, uncomfortable emotions by acting out in aggressive and destructive ways toward others, but another way that adolescents deal with their problems is by turning all their emotions inward. Adolescents suffering from depression and anxiety often manifest many self-destructive behaviors, the most serious being suicide. But there are many other self-abusive behaviors that emotionally disturbed adolescents may engage in that although certainly not as serious as suicide, still warrant serious clinical intervention.

Deliberate self-harm (DSH), also sometimes called self-injury, self-abuse, or self-mutilation, is defined in various ways in research studies. One definition of self-injury includes any deliberate, repetitive attempt to harm one's own bodily tissue without a conscious desire to commit suicide (Nock & Prinstein, 2005). Hicks and Hinck (2009) use a more narrow definition for DSH, which they define as "the intentional act of tissue destruction with the purpose of shifting overwhelming emotional pain to a more acceptable physical pain" (p. 409). They describe the purpose of DSH stating that the "issue damage is a visual demonstration of extreme emotional distress, and the physical act of mutilation seems to reconcile this emotion" (p. 409). DSH most often includes not only cutting the arms and legs with a razor blade or any sharp object (such as a paper clip) but can also include burning, picking at wounds, and even head-banging. People who self-mutilate using a sharp object are commonly called *cutters*.

Although self-injury occurs in the adult population (occurring in about 4 percent of the general population), adolescents are at increased risk for self-injury, with 39 percent of the adolescent population admitting to having self-injured at some point in their lives and 61 percent of adolescents in a psychiatric in-patient setting having self-injured (Nock & Prinstein, 2005). Approximately 40 percent of college students have admitted to engaging in self-injury (Whitlock, Purington, & Gershkovich, 2009).

DSH can be a difficult issue to treat because so little is known about its causes. In addition, this type of behavior tends to be resistant to treatment. What is known is that females tend to engage in DSH far more than males, with some studies indicating that of all those who self-abuse, 97 percent are women (Nock & Prinstein, 2005). One reason for this may be due at least in part to how females are socialized to internalize their negative feelings, whereas males are socialized to externalize their negative feelings.

The precise reasons why adolescents engage in DSH behaviors is unknown, but DSH has been associated with a host of emotional and psychological problems, including suicidal thoughts, eating disorders, chronic feelings of hopelessness and despair, depression and anxiety, sexual abuse, physical abuse, severe emotional abuse, perfectionism, and a pervasive sense of loneliness (Nock & Prinstein, 2005). The National Institute of Mental Health estimates that approximately 50–60 percent of cutters were sexually abused as children (Crowe & Bunclark, 2000). Many adolescents who engage in DSH cite many reasons for physically harming themselves, including the belief that the cutting or burning allows them to feel something in the midst of emotional numbness. In fact, in order for self-mutilation to be considered DSH the pain and/or the sight of blood caused by the self-mutilation must result in some relief of emotional pain, and psychological reintegration—in other words, not in pleasure as is the case with masochism. Additionally, the self-mutilation of tissue must not reflect a suicide attempt or a desire to adorn oneself, such as the case of tattooing or piercing (Clarke & Whittaker, 1998; Favazza, 1996).

Other reasons for self-injury relate to the internal expression of rage and relieving intolerable tension resulting from deep feelings of anger, frustration, despair, and loneliness. Adolescents who are survivors of sexual molestation often claim that they cut in response to the shame.

A social worker will likely encounter adolescent clients who engage in DSH in a variety of practice settings, including adolescent residential facilities, group homes, foster homes, schools, and any other settings where adolescents are served. It is important that clinicians always be on the lookout for common warning signs of self-injury, even if the adolescent or the parents deny the behavior. Adolescents who self-mutilate for attention will often flaunt their "work" by showing off what frequently amounts to superficial cuts on the forearm or thighs. But as mentioned earlier, serious self-mutilators will often hide their wounds; thus, a social worker would be wise to note suspicious behaviors, such as consistently wearing long sleeves and pants, even on warm days. More obvious signs of self-injury may include parallel scars on the forearm or thighs, burn marks in these same places or even on the fingertips, or any unexplained or suspicious wound, particularly wounds that tend not to heal (because of chronic reinjury).

The most successful treatment programs include a combination of individual, group, and family therapy with the goal of increasing the adolescent's personal insight and awareness of the dynamics underlying the compulsion to self-injure. Issues such as *impulse control* and *emotional regulation* are paramount in any successful treatment plan, as is assisting the adolescent client in learning how to understand and effectively manage intense or uncomfortable emotions in a direct manner. This approach will allow self-abusive adolescents to own their emotions, rather than deny or suppress them.

Suicide Risk in Adolescence

The ultimate internalizing behavior is, of course, the killing of one's self, and although people have been committing suicide for centuries, understanding the dynamics of suicidal behavior, or suicidal ideation, remains a relatively new area of study. Of particular interest to social scientists and mental health practitioners is discovering how to most effectively prevent suicide attempts. As with self-injury, adolescents are at particularly high risk of suicide and suicidal ideation for several reasons, including their propensity for impulsivity, as well as their frequent feelings of omnipotence.

Between 1999 and 2006 (the most recent data available), 11 percent of all deaths of adolescents between the ages of 12 and 19 were caused by suicide, making suicide the third leading cause of death, behind unintentional accidents and homicide (Miniño, 2010). *Adolescent suicidal behavior* can include suicidal gestures, suicide attempts, and serious suicide attempts and suicide completions. Each of these behaviors can result in a completed suicide, even if that is not the intention of the adolescent, but it is important to distinguish between each of these types of suicidal behavior for the purposes of intervention, as well as developing an understanding of what goes on in the mind of an adolescent who engages in any type of suicidal behavior. A *suicidal gesture* typically involves behavior on the part of an adolescent that is unlikely to result in a completed suicide but is more often a cry for help or attention. Even if a practitioner does not believe that his or her adolescent clients truly wish to kill themselves, these gestures should not be taken lightly, because it is always possible that adolescents will kill themselves even if death wasn't the intended outcome.

Certainly the most serious of all suicidal behavior involves actions that are intended to end one's life. As with the adult population, it is not necessarily the adolescents who scream their suicidal intentions from the rooftop who clinicians need to be the most concerned about, but the sad, hopeless, and depressed adolescents who quietly slink away, without drawing any attention, determined to kill themselves in a manner that precludes intervention. Fortunately, not all serious attempts are successful. Some adolescents experience a last-minute change of heart and call a family member or friend, reach out to a suicide hotline, or call 9-1-1. The types of adolescents who attempt suicide are different than those who complete suicide. For instance, research indicates that about 85 percent of "attempters" are female (Andrus et al., 1991), whereas about 80 percent of suicide completers are typically male (Arias, Anderson, Kung, Murphy, & Kochanek, 2003). Reasons for this might be related to the social acceptance of males completing suicide rather than making an attempt (Moskos, Achilles, & Gray, 2004). Other reasons may relate to gender-related methods for committed suicide, such as the male tendency to elect for far more lethal methods such as the use of firearms, whereas women tend to use less lethal methods, such as drug overdoses (Vörös, Osváth, & Fekete, 2004). Among adolescent populations, those who admitted having attempted suicide were up to 30 percent more likely to be addicted to drugs and alcohol (Vörös, Fekete, Hewitt, & Osváth, 2005).

Recognizing whether an adolescent is at real risk of attempting suicide is an important clinical skill that develops with education and experience. One of the most intimidating issues facing any social worker is knowing how to predict suicidal behavior. The answer to that question is that it is virtually impossible to definitively predict when anyone will make an attempt to end his or her life, but there are indicators and precursors that practitioners can look for, such as the psychosocial risk factors discussed in the previous section.

Although any social worker should have a "safety first" approach to treatment, there are valid concerns for not calling 9-1-1 each time an adolescent client sounds hopeless or immersed in despair, including not wanting to destroy the counseling relationship by overreacting. When adolescent clients share that they sometimes wonder what it might feel like to die, and an anxious practitioner responds by having the adolescent involuntarily hospitalized, trust can certainly be destroyed. But in light of the alarming increase in adolescent suicides since the mid-1990s, particularly within the adolescent male population, safety is of paramount importance. Thus, some sort of balance must be struck between honoring the privacy and safety of the counseling relationship and making sure that the adolescent remains safe.

Before any successful intervention strategy can be developed, the questions of why so many teenagers are killing themselves and who is most at risk must be addressed. Suicide rates among African American males are increasing dramatically, particularly among those in the higher socioeconomic status, and suicide rates in the adolescent Native American population are exceedingly high (Moskos, 2004).

Rutter and Behrendt (2004) conducted a study of 100 at-risk adolescents, focusing on psychosocial risk factors. Their research revealed that those adolescents who were plagued by feelings of *hopelessness*, had little to no *social support*, had feelings of *hostility*, and had a *negative self-concept* were at the greatest risk for committing suicide. This research is consistent with the research on self-injury, which revealed that self-mutilation was often the manifestation of rage and hostility turned inward, and as previously mentioned, suicide is the most injurious of all self-abusive behaviors.

Other risk factors for suicide include having a friend commit suicide (Hazell & Lewin, 1999), and for males having a gun available was a significant risk factor and for girls low self-esteem. Research also showed that deep involvement in school activities markedly decreased the potential for suicidal behavior (Bearman & Moody, 2004). Treatment will then emanate directly from any deficits found in these areas of functioning and will include the development of emotional insight and better coping skills to deal with all these emotions and insights.

If an adolescent is assessed to be a suicide risk, a safety plan must be developed with the parents or primary caregivers, because the desire to commit suicide can only come to fruition if there is opportunity. Thus, it is important for the adolescent's environment to be as free of risk as possible. For instance, a good home safety plan will include the removal of all pharmaceutical drugs, guns, kitchen knives, and loose razor blades. A depressed and socially isolated adolescent who is not actively suicidal but who thinks about dying from time to time may not need to be hospitalized but should be monitored at all times so that any escalation in depressive symptoms can be addressed immediately. At any time that adolescent clients acknowledge suicidal intent, admit to feeling frightened of their desire to harm themselves, or disclose having a suicide plan, the social worker may decide hospitalization is warranted, and in that case, the family will be directed to either call 9-1-1 or take their teen to their local emergency room.

> **Learn more about a suicide prevention program targeting adolescent girls, by going to the NASW website and searching for the NASW Shift Project.**

Spirito and his colleagues found that the single most powerful predictors of continued suicidal behavior are the existence of depression and family dysfunction. Therefore, any treatment plan designed to address suicidal behavior must seriously address what is most likely the interplay between negative family relations and the adolescent's feelings of depression (Spirito, Valeri, Boergers, & Donaldson, 2003).

Current treatment intervention focuses on school-based suicide prevention education programs, crisis centers including teen suicide hotlines, screening programs aimed at identifying high-risk adolescents within their community, peer support programs, and public awareness campaigns, including pleas to remove guns from homes with at-risk adolescents. Suggestions for future programs include recommendations that the juvenile justice system coordinate efforts with the school-based programs and other youth outreach agencies, because over 60 percent of adolescents who committed suicide also had a history of involvement with the justice system (Moskos, 2004).

Social workers must be prepared to deal with the growing trend of suicidal behaviors in the adolescent population. Through education, prevention, and intervention strategies, including a multidisciplinary approach that addresses depression from an emotional and social as well as a medical perspective, mental health experts are optimistic that adolescent suicide can be successfully addressed.

Eating Disorders

Another set of disorders common to adolescents is eating disorders, including anorexia nervosa and bulimia nervosa. Although individuals of all ages can suffer from eating disorders, the primary onset of eating disorders often occurs during adolescence (Ray, 2004). Females tend to suffer from eating disorders far more often than males, comprising approximately 85–90 percent of all documented cases but the incidence of eating disorders in males is increasing, particularly among male athletes (Walcott, Pratt, & Patel, 2003). Additionally, men who have eating disorders tend to overeat, whereas women tend to under-eat (Striegel-Moore, Rosselli, Perrin, DeBar, Wilson, May, & Kraemer, 2009).

Anorexia nervosa involves the intentional starving of oneself and the refusal to maintain expected body weight. The *DSM-V* criteria for anorexia includes a body weight of less than 85 percent of normal body weight, an intense fear of gaining weight, distortion of how one's body is perceived, and the absence of a menstrual cycle for at least three months (American Psychiatric Association, 2013). Among the various theories of the causes of anorexia, the most popular tend to focus on maladaptive family patterns where the adolescent's anorexia is presumed to help protect unhealthy family dynamics. These maladaptive patterns can include conflict avoidance, rigidity, and family enmeshment (Lock & le Grange, 2005).

After watching the film "Eating Disorders: Natasha: Anorexia," consider what dynamics you note in Natasha that are similar to others who struggle with anorexia nervosa.

It is for this reason that family counseling is the most commonly recommended treatment for adolescents suffering from anorexia, in addition to in-patient treatment for adolescents who are at risk of serious health complications (Fairburn, 2005).

Bulimia Nervosa involves a pattern of binge eating, indicating a lack of control followed by purging in the form of self-induced vomiting, use of laxatives, or excessive exercise in an attempt to rid oneself of the abundance of food (APA, 2013). Bulimia is far more prevalent than anorexia in the adolescent population (van Hoeken, Seidell, & Hoek, 2003). Common risk factors of adolescents suffering from bulimia include perfectionism,

Social Work Application Activity

The beauty industry is often held responsible for dramatic increase in eating disorders among the adolescent and youth population, particularly among females. The Dove® Campaign for Real Beauty—a worldwide marketing campaign launched in 2004—is designed to celebrate the real variation in physical appearance among all women and ultimately increase their self-esteem. Dove has produced several commercials that were aired nationally and are posted on their social media site on Youtube.com. Review one of the Onslaught videos located on YouTube and consider the following questions: Do you believe that the beauty industry is responsible for the staggering increase in eating disorders among the adolescent population, and if so, to what extent? What can social workers do to help confront this social problem? (https://www.youtube.com/watch?v=9zKfF40jeCA)

The body image of some struggling with an eating disorder is often distorted.

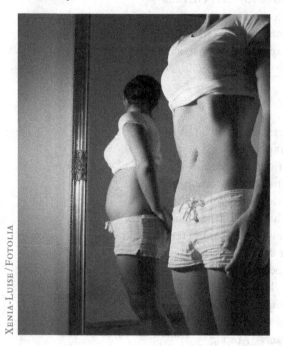

Xenia-Luise / Fotolia

body dissatisfaction, and low self-esteem (Vohs et al., 2001). Adolescents who engage in bingeing behavior often experience significant shame once the bingeing phase is over. These feelings of shame are often dealt with by purging to rid the body of the excess food. This bingeing-purging cycle often becomes a compulsion, robbing the adolescent of the ability to stop the behavior.

Treatment for bulimia often includes insight therapy, family therapy, and cognitive behavioral therapy (CBT), which focuses on the negative self-statements the adolescent thinks in response to life events, as well as negative self-appraisals (Gowers & Bryant-Waugh, 2004). Depression and anxiety are often associated with both anorexia and bulimia; thus, a course of antidepressant or antianxiety medication is often considered appropriate.

Chronic and Severe Mental Illness: Schizophrenia in Adolescence

Schizophrenia is a psychotic (or thought) disorder that is a concern to social workers working with the adolescent population because this disease is most often diagnosed in late adolescence and early adulthood, with men typically developing the first symptoms of schizophrenia in their late teens and women in their early to mid-twenties (National Institute of Mental Health, 2005). Symptoms of schizophrenia include delusions (unclear or illogical thinking); hallucinations, which may include hearing, seeing, feeling, or smelling something that is not there (with the most frequent hallucination being auditory); cognitive impairment; disorganized behavior; and an inability to express emotions or respond emotionally to typically pleasurable activities (APA, 2013; National Institute of Mental Health, 2005). Schizophrenia has several subtypes, including paranoid, catatonic, and disorganized types. The most common subtype of schizophrenia is paranoid, where the affected individuals have delusions that others are conspiring against them (Fenton, McGlashan, Victor, & Blyler, 1997).

Schizophrenia is a serious and debilitating brain disease that affects approximately 1 in 100 adults, causing dysfunction in virtually every area of life. Social workers working with the adolescent population, particularly older adolescents, must be aware of the early signs and symptoms of schizophrenia because early intervention may have a positive impact on the course of treatment. Early signs of schizophrenia onset during adolescence often include increasing social isolation, particularly from peers (Mackrell & Lavender, 2004), intellectual decline in all areas of cognitive functioning, indications of confused thought, and hallucinations (Fitzgerald, Lucas, & Redoblado, 2004).

Adolescents who are in the early stages of schizophrenia are about 30 times more likely to commit suicide than adolescents in the general population, with approximately 10 percent of all those with schizophrenia ending their lives by suicide at some point (Jarbin & von Knorring, 2004). This increased risk may be because of unclear thinking and hallucinations (particularly with those suffering from paranoid schizophrenia), but researchers found that subjects who were addicted to smoking cigarettes, had a substance abuse problem, or were depressed were at the highest risk of attempting or committing suicide (Jarbin & von Knorring, 2004). Those with paranoid schizophrenia had three times the rate of suicide than those with other subtypes of schizophrenia (Fenton et al., 1997). A strong religious belief system is one of the few variables that seemed to protect schizophrenic teens from suicidal behavior (Jarbin & von Knorring, 2004).

Treatment of schizophrenia consists primarily of antipsychotic medication, such as risperidone, which controls the hallucinations and often helps clear up delusional thinking. Social workers working with adolescents diagnosed with schizophrenia, or who are in the early stages of this psychotic disorder, can benefit from basic skill-building such as self-care and management (i.e., hygiene, medication compliance), social skills, and interventions that target the reduction of risk factors such as nicotine use, substance abuse, and social isolation.

> **Assess your comprehension of "Common Psychosocial Issues and the Role of the Social Worker" by completing this quiz.**

PRACTICE SETTINGS SPECIFIC TO ADOLESCENT SERVICES

There are many practice settings where adolescents receive direct generalist services, as well as many ways in which these services are provided. Some adolescents may receive individual counseling from therapists who are in private practice. These counseling services can be provided by anyone who has a license to provide independent counseling services such as *psychiatrists, psychologists, marriage and family therapists* (MFTs), *licensed clinical professional counselors* (LCPCs), and *licensed clinical social workers* (LCSWs). Counseling typically occurs in the counselor's office as often as the practitioner, adolescent and parents deem necessary, but once a week is the most common schedule.

Counseling also occurs in many other settings, such as in schools by school social workers; social service agencies that specialize in adolescent issues, such as runaway and homeless youth; organizations that provide therapeutic foster care; and the juvenile justice system (see Box 5.2).

Residential care is a practice setting often utilized for adolescents who are severely behaviorally disordered and at high risk of self-harm and destructive behaviors. Although institutionalized care has steadily decreased for most segments of the population, institutionalized care for the adolescent population has literally skyrocketed since the 1980s (Wells, 1991). Residential facilities for adolescents can be locked or open, private or governmental, short or long term, therapeutic or more punitive in nature, but all provide some level of mental health services in relatively large, dormitory-like settings, where the adolescent residents sleep and attend school.

Residential treatment programs vary widely in type and nature, with some residential programs offering services making them sound more like a boarding school than a treatment facility, boasting equine programs, river rafting, and "therapeutic" skiing programs, whereas others are far more sterile offering few extracurricular activities. One reason for this difference can be directly related to the range of populations served. For instance, behavior on the part of an adolescent that results in court intervention and juvenile detention in a residential facility would not necessarily be conducive to a therapeutic ski trip to Vail, Colorado.

Placement times can also vary, with some adolescents being placed in a residential facility for a few months to some who

Apply Critical Thinking to Inform and Communicate Professional Judgments

Practice Behavior: Distinguish, appraise, and integrate multiple sources of knowledge, including research-based knowledge, and practice wisdom.

Critical Thinking Question: If you were working with runaway and homeless youth in an outreach problem, what are some of the challenges you might expect in gaining the trust of this population based upon research and past experience working with this population?

Box 5.2   Review: Runaway and Homeless Youth

No one is certain just how many adolescents are homeless and living on the streets without their families, but some estimates put that number as high as 2 million in the United States alone. Runaway and homeless youth (typically considered between the ages of 12 and 24) constitute a unique population among the entire homeless population because the reasons, risk factors, and intervention needs of runaway and homeless youth are considerably different. Adolescents are far more likely to be living on the streets than in a shelter. They are also far more likely to participate in dangerous behaviors such as drug abuse (including needle sharing), panhandling, theft, and survival sex (sex for food, money, and shelter). These risky behaviors put homeless adolescents and youth at risk for HIV, hepatitis B, hepatitis C, and a range of other sexually transmitted diseases (Beech, Meyers, & Beech, 2002). These teens are also at high risk for physical and sexual violence, both by other teens as well as by adults.

Most runaway and homeless adolescents and youth are living on the streets because they have run away from an abusive home, have been kicked out of their homes by parents who no longer wish to take care of them (throw-away youth), or have aged out of the foster care system. The majority of homeless adolescents interviewed in various research studies reported a history of both physical and sexual abuse, which served as a primer for being similarly victimized on the streets (Whitbeck, Hoyt, & Ackley, 1997). One study of over 600 runaway and homeless youth found that sexual abuse was the chief reason adolescents chose to live on the streets rather than remaining in their homes (Yoder, Whitbeck, & Hoyt, 2001). The fact that many of these teens will continue to experience sexual exploitation while living on the streets, whether through outright attacks or through survival sex, is certainly a tragedy, and one that can be addressed by social workers working with this population.

Most urban cities runaway and homeless youth often operate as a somewhat cohesive group on the streets, protecting each other and helping one another survive (Auerswald & Eyre, 2002). In fact, it appears that the more seasoned adolescents would often take new homeless teens under their wings, teaching them survival tactics and welcoming them into the "fold." Newer homeless youth who were interviewed talked about what a relief it was to have someone essentially mentor them into the ways of surviving street life. But

without glamorizing this life, most teens, both boys and girls, talked of the horrors of having to participate in prostitution to survive. In fact, runaway and homeless youth living on the streets have identified the many ways in which they felt exploited, both by older teens and by adults who forced them into drug dealing and prostitution (Auerswald & Eyre, 2002).

Ironically, many runaway and homeless youth have reported a strong belief in God, who they believed watches out for them and keeps them alive. In Auerswald and Eyre's 2002 study, one teen stated that when they were not really in need, they would often get no offer of food and little money while panhandling. Yet when they were really in need, having gone without food for a few days, then whatever they needed would just come to them. This teen attributed this phenomenon to God knowing what he needed and providing for him when he needed it the most. In fact, in one study researchers found that over half of all runaway and homeless youth interviewed cited a faith in God as the primary motivation for survival (Lindsey, Kurtz, Jarvis, Williams, & Nackerud, 2000).

Yet even with this surprisingly high percentage of faith-seeking runaway and homeless youth, an estimated 40 percent of homeless youth attempt suicide (Auerswald & Eyre, 2002). They are also at high risk for post-traumatic stress disorder (PTSD), anxiety disorders, depression, substance abuse, and delinquency (Thrane, Chen, Johnson, & Whitbeck, 2008). Many runway and homeless youth report losing all contact with people in their former lives, even siblings, extended family, and those who had been supportive of them in the past. Many also talked of feeling extremely lonely and distrustful but in desperate need of love and affection. Because the majority of runaway and homeless youth have run away from abusive homes, it seems likely that many were suffering from some form of emotional disturbance even prior to entering street life (Kidd, 2003).

Unfortunately, many of the runaway and homeless youth who were interviewed reported being highly suspicious of all adults, including outreach workers with social services agencies providing assistance to the homeless adolescent population. The overall perception of these outreach agencies were negative, and adolescents who accepted assistance from these agencies were considered "sellouts" and foolish. The prevailing belief was that social workers and other

Box 5.2 *Continued*

outreach workers would force the teens to return to an abusive home environment, or they'd be turned over to the police or child protective services. Knowing these attitudes, though, can aid social service agencies in developing outreach efforts and other services designed to overcome these negative perceptions (Kidd, 2003).

Any successful intervention program is going to have to address the issue of the teens feeling like outsiders. In fact, research studies have found that homeless adolescents are acutely aware of their outsider status, and many of them manage this through incorporating this outsider status into their identity. By embracing being an outsider, through multiple piercings, for example, they take control of something that could potentially make them vulnerable (Auerswald & Eyre, 2002).

Many social workers strongly recommend that any intervention program be targeted at identifying the adolescents' strengths. But this is challenging when most intervention systems view homeless youth in a deviant manner; first, because they are "runaways," and second, because many of the behaviors they engage in while living on the streets are classified as criminal activity. Even the classification of their behavior is in pathological terms, such as diagnosing them with conduct disorder, oppositional defiant disorder, bipolar disorder, and/or ADHD. Such diagnoses can be humiliating and shaming to adolescents who are likely acting out in response to being victimized within their

family of origin. Most runaway and homeless youth have been both physically and verbally abused and degraded in their homes; thus, in many respects they are living up to their parents' negative expectations of them by dropping out of high school and living on the streets. To then enter into the juvenile justice system that continues to pathologize their behavior and responds with punitive measures rather than supportive ones only adds to their feelings of victimization.

Social workers working with this population must provide consistent encouragement, compassionate care, and understanding in a way that promotes both healthy self-esteem and self-efficacy (a sense of competence) in these emotionally broken and bruised teens. This can be accomplished while focusing on basic needs such as providing food, shelter, and good health care. Yet again the barriers that social service agencies must overcome are significant because so many runaway and homeless youth have been so horribly rejected and abandoned by their families and communities, and then further exploited and abused by adults on the streets, that to trust any adult seems far too risky. Developing one-on-one relationships where trust can grow slowly is one method of intervention that may be more successful than more traditional outreach efforts, but the ratio of outreach workers to runaway homeless youth renders this approach challenging. Regardless, any intervention must allow the teen to feel safe and empowered in seeking services.

require several years, again depending on the severity of their problems. One popular short-term residential program is Outward Bound, a wilderness therapy program that uses physical challenges to help adolescents deal more effectively with their emotional problems. These programs are offered in various locations within the United States and range from 21 to 28 days in length.

Group homes (or therapeutic foster homes) offer less-structured residential care, where various community services are often accessed and where adolescents attend the local public high school and are not isolated from the general community. More structured residential treatment programs are a bit more sterile in nature, offering services to adolescents whose conduct problems or self-destructive behaviors require a more long-term, in-depth, and controlled environment. Adolescents in these programs are isolated from the general population and even attend school within the facility where they are housed. Treatment modalities in these facilities often include a combination of behavior modification where desirable behaviors are rewarded and undesirable behaviors are punished, individual therapy, group therapy, and family therapy. Parents, public schools, or the juvenile court system may all make referrals to such programs.

The most structured and most serious of all residential treatment programs include correctional institutions for adolescents, most commonly referred to as juvenile hall or juvenile detention centers. These facilities are reserved for adolescents who have been convicted of breaking some law or are awaiting sentencing, and although there is far more of an emphasis on rehabilitation than in adult correctional facilities, there is a far greater emphasis on corrections and punishment than in a therapeutic treatment center.

A creative version of the juvenile correctional institution that has received mixed reviews is "boot camp" programs, which offer rehabilitation (as well as restraint) in the form of a military-like, highly structured environment. The philosophy behind boot camps is that adolescents or young adults who suffer from poor impulse control, low self-esteem, and high rates of acting out behavior can benefit from a military-like structured setting that pushes them to their limit (both physical and emotional). The high emphasis on structure and self-discipline, coupled with the push to achieve, is believed to have a positive impact on both self-esteem and self-respect, which is hoped to generalize into more respectful behavior in society. Many parents and participants commonly claim dramatic changes in the behavior of participants after a boot camp experience, but research appears to indicate that boot camps do not necessarily reduce recidivism rates in young offenders (Peters, Thomas, & Zamberlan, 1997).

> **Read more about juvenile boot camps by going to the Office of Juvenile Justice and Delinquency Prevention website and searching for the article entitled: "Juvenile Boot Camps: Lessons Learned."**

Another type of treatment facility for adolescents experiencing mental health problems is in-patient psychiatric hospitals. These programs tend to be acute (short term), focusing on stabilizing the adolescent's high-risk behaviors, such as suicidal behavior, self-abuse, substance abuse, and eating disorders. Some in-patient programs specialize in one or more of these disorders or are more general in nature, offering short-term acute services to any adolescent who cannot be maintained safely outside a hospital setting. Many of the same type of therapies are available in an in-patient setting as in a residential treatment center, with the exception that drug therapies may be more prevalent in a psychiatric hospital. In-patient hospitals also rely heavily on discharge planning, a task that typically falls to a hospital social worker or other social worker who works with the family and community resources to ensure that the adolescent will transition back to home and school with enough outpatient support to minimize the need for re-hospitalization.

> **Assess your comprehension of "Practice Settings Specific to Adolescent Treatment" by completing this quiz.**

MULTICULTURAL CONSIDERATIONS

It would be naïve to assume that race and ethnicity did not have a significant effect on adolescent development, including the types of problems adolescents of various races experience as well as the various responses to those problems, both within the family and within the community. Social workers must be aware of the way in which race and ethnicity affect adolescent development and behavior, as well as any negative stereotypes that might affect the types of diagnoses adolescents receive.

A 2001 study found that African American adolescents were more commonly diagnosed with conduct disorders, whereas Caucasian adolescents more often received a diagnosis of depression (DelBello, Lopez-Larson, & Soutullo, 2001). But is this because more African American adolescents actually have conduct disorders? Or is it because the negative stereotype that African American males are typically more violent influenced the practitioner rendering the diagnosis? DelBello, (2001) doubted that the difference in diagnosing reflected any real variation in disorders among adolescents of different races but was more likely attributable to variables such as misdiagnosing based on cultural differences and misperceptions.

Other research studies indicate that Latino adolescents, specifically Mexican Americans, are at higher risk for delinquency, depression, and suicide than Caucasians (Roberts, 2000). African American youth tend to show the greatest need for mental health services, yet were severely underserved, and although most mentally ill African American adolescents had a long history of diagnosable mental health problems, often their first exposure to treatment was within the juvenile justice system. One reason for this might be that there is a negative stigma associated with mental health disorders in certain ethnic minority groups. But another equally significant reason is likely the lack of affordable mental health services among ethnically diverse neighborhoods, as well as issues such as poor or no insurance coverage for mental health services among ethnically diverse populations.

A recent study showed that very little has changed in this trend in the last few decades, despite considerable research in this area and policy recommendations. For instance, a 2011 study revealed that African American, Latino, and Asian adolescents with major depression were significantly less likely to receive mental health treatment, including prescription medication, than non-Hispanic white adolescents, regardless of income levels and health insurance (Cummings & Druss, 2011). It is interesting to note that Latino adolescents were rated as the most underserved of all racial groups, despite the fact that they had significant needs, and Caucasians were reported to have the highest rate of mental health utilization, although they have less serious mental health diagnoses compared to other racially diverse groups (Rawal, Romansky, & Jenuwine, 2004).

Certainly not all differences in adolescent diagnoses can be attributed to cultural misperceptions, misdiagnoses, and underutilization of services. Social conditions, such as poverty, high crime neighborhoods, and unemployment likely contribute to a significant proportion of mental health problems in some racially diverse youth populations. Rawal (2004) noted that African American adolescents are far more likely to be raised in single-parent households, be placed in foster care, and experience significantly higher rates of familial abuse and neglect, all of which can be expected to have a negative impact on their mental health. Latino adolescents also exhibited higher incidences of acting out and antisocial behaviors, such as juvenile delinquency, compared to Caucasians; yet, they also had greater familial support, with their caregivers exhibiting greater understanding and involvement in their mental health issues, which might act as an intervention negating the necessity of more serious intervention.

Regardless of the reasons for the differences in mental health issues among adolescents of different ethnic groups, it is imperative that social workers be trained to deliver culturally competent counseling and case management services. Education that addresses all these issues, including institutionalized racism, both within the community and within the juvenile justice system; culturally based stigmas associated with mental health issues; social conditions affecting adolescents of all races; and the relevant histories of various racially ethic minority groups within the United States (e.g., the history of slavery among African Americans or the history of forced institutionalized care among Native American youth) will assist the social worker render a bias-free mental health evaluation and provide the most appropriate treatment for the adolescent client.

Engage Diversity and Difference in Practice

Practice Behavior: Recognize and communicate their understanding of the importance of difference in shaping life experiences.

Critical Thinking Question: What are some ways in which African American youth experience disparity in diagnoses and treatment compared to their Caucasian cohorts, and what are some ways that social workers can respond?

Assess your comprehension of "Multicultural Considerations" by completing this quiz.

Summary

Clearly, our society will continue to change and evolve, affecting all its members, including adolescents. As our society becomes more technologically based, it will become more complex as well, which will no doubt mandate increasing levels of education—a trend that the United States has seen steadily increase in the last 50 years at least. This does not mean that juvenile violence will continue to rise. Most mental health experts refuse to adopt such a fatalistic attitude. History reveals that adolescence has always been a difficult stage to navigate, long before it was even recognized as an official stage of development. The greatest hope one can offer parents and educators alike is that adolescents who often seem destined for a lifetime of narcissistic obsession most often evolve into loving, caring, and responsible adults. Social workers can help families ensure that this is the path for as many adolescents as possible through effective program development and supportive services on all levels.

Recall what you learned in
this chapter by completing the
Chapter Review.

6

Social Work and Older Adults

Glenn was shocked as he walked down La Salle Avenue, in the heart of the business district in Chicago. He was used to seeing homeless people, either standing or sitting along the side of the road with signs asking for money, but he had never seen an old couple begging for money before. What was unique about this couple was that they looked as though they could be his own mother and father.

He began to walk by them, avoiding their stare as he usually did when people begged for money, but this time was different, and he could not resist approaching this couple. "Hi, my name is Glenn, and I'd love to give you some money." The couple looked at him sheepishly, and he noticed the shame in their eyes. "Thank you," the woman said quietly, diverting her glance downward. Glenn handed them $10 and started to walk away, but curiosity got the better of him. He turned around and asked them if he could talk to them about their situation. The husband and wife looked at each other, and Glenn did not know if it was with suspicion or simple caution, but they eventually agreed once he offered to buy them lunch.

Over their meals of hot soup and sandwiches, Rosemary and Donald shared about their all-American lives. They raised two children in a suburb of Chicago, owned a home, and even had a family dog. They were like anyone else in the neighborhood or their church, until Donald was laid off two years before his scheduled retirement when his company downsized. He had worked for the same company for 40 years. Donald was unable to find a job because of his age, and eventually they had to let their health insurance lapse because they could no longer financially handle the extremely high monthly premiums.

Unfortunately, Rosemary became ill the following month with a bout of influenza that ultimately developed into pneumonia. The hospital bill for her two-week stay was almost $10,000. With no retirement plans and only Social Security benefits to count on, and with their two adult children serving overseas in the military, Donald and Rosemary began a downhill financial descent that didn't stop until they depleted their life savings and ultimately lost their house. Thus, although most couples like Donald and Rosemary spend their golden years playing golf in Florida, Donald and Rosemary spend their days sitting outside the train station, begging for money.

Carrie looked at the sea of faces before her. They looked empty— almost as if they had no souls. The only sounds in the camp were the incessant, never ceasing buzzing of hungry flies. Even the children were quiet. Carrie reasoned that the calm was because of hunger—people were often subdued when they hadn't eaten well in days, but she knew this calm was related to something far removed from hunger.

Just three days ago the people in this camp were victims of an Arab militia known as the Janjaweed. These bands of marauding fighters combed the countryside, indiscriminately killing black Africans. As the villagers looked on in horror, Janjaweed militia began to systematically slaughter the innocent villagers one by one. Not even infants were spared; some militia tossed babies and toddlers into the air, calling them future enemies, as they shot them with machine guns. The few villagers who managed to escape joined other escaping villagers running through the desert and were eventually picked up by the American Red Cross.

Carrie is a missionary with an organization that specializes in sending retirees abroad. When Carrie became a widow at the age of 71, she thought her life was over. However, the pastor at her church approached her, and after months of talking, he finally convinced her that her years of nursing experience need not go to waste. Carrie was initially skeptical when her pastor shared the stories of other retirees, many of whom were widows, who served in clinics and refugee camps overseas in countries like Guatemala, Burma, and Sudan, but it wasn't until she met some older adult missionaries at home on sabbatical that she finally realized that this was something she could do.

Of course, Carrie's adult children thought she'd lost her mind, they even questioned whether her decision to become a missionary was a sign of early Alzheimer's, but they eventually grew to understand her decision and even respect it, although she was certain that they never felt truly comfortable with the thought of their old mother living in a refugee camp in the middle of a war-torn country. Carrie's contemplative thoughts were interrupted with the announcement of the most recent influx of shell-shocked and injured refugees, and she ventured out of the makeshift hospital to meet the new arrivals.

THE AGING OF AMERICA: CHANGING DEMOGRAPHICS

The opening vignettes illustrate the vast range of experiences of those considered "older adults" in the United States. Today's older adults experience a broader range of lifestyles than ever before, but they experience a greater range of challenges as well. There are several reasons for this vast array of lifestyle choices and options, including the increase in the human life span, changes in the perception of old age in general, changes in the economy, and finally changes in the nature and definition of the American family, including a dramatic increase in divorce and two-parent working families.

Read more about the transformative power of the aging baby boomer generation by going to the Huffington Post website and searching for the article entitled "Baby Boomers Will Transform Aging in America, Panel Says."

The term *Graying of America* refers to the increase in the older adult population in the United States (as well as in most parts of the world). This dramatic increase, as well as the projected increase in the U.S. older adult population between now and 2050, is related to the aging of a cohort of individuals referred to as the *baby boomers* as well as other factors. Google these terms and you will likely get thousands of hits about recent population trends in the United States (globally as well) and their impact on society, including in the areas of health care, family constellation, and education.

The baby boomers are popularly defined as those having been born between 1946 and 1964. The name refers to the *boom* of births after World War II, which caused an unusual spike in the U.S. population. Approximately 76 million individuals (roughly 29 percent of the U.S. population) fall into the cohort of baby boomers, and thus it is obvious why this cohort has been the focus of particular interest to social scientists, the media, politicians, and others. For one thing, despite the somewhat broad range of ages within this cohort, similarities between members are numerous, including their socioeconomic status, which tends to be higher than earlier cohorts, consumer habits, and political concerns. As the boomers age, their tastes and concerns transition, and in recent years this collective focus has included discussions regarding the consequences of this large cohort heading into their retirement years. The Graying of America, then, refers to the projected increase in the older adult population in large part because of the aging boomers.

The aging of the baby boomers is not the only variable leading to the increase in the older adult population. In the 20th century, the United States has experienced a 50 percent increase in human life expectancy. In 1900, the average human life span in the United States was about 47 years. But by 1999 it had increased to about 77 years, which is where it stands today, although it is expected to increase at least another 15 years by the year 2100 (Arias, 2004). This life expectancy increase is due to many variables, including improved medical technology, medical discoveries such as antibiotics and immunizations for various life-threatening diseases, and generally safer lifestyles.

Currently there are approximately 40 million people over the age of 65 living in the United States (NHSTA, 2009), but that number is projected to double by the year 2050, growing to more than 88 million (Passel & Cohn, 2010). Additionally, the U.S. Census Bureau projects that the population of those aged 85 and older is expected grow from 5.8 million in 2009 to approximately 20 million by the year 2050 (Department of Health and Human Services, 2010). When one considers that from 1900 to 2050 the over-65 population in the United States will grow from about 3 million to almost 90 million, it is not difficult to understand why the field of gerontology has received so much attention in recent years!

So far this all sounds pretty good—we're living longer, and in the next 10 or 20 years a third of the population will be classified as older adults, which will no doubt increase the attention paid to social and political issues important to those in their retirement years. However, the landscape for older adults in the United States is not completely rosy; quite the opposite, in fact. Some will no doubt enjoy their longer life span, but for many, their extra years on this earth may be spent in a long-term care facility with chronic health problems far too complex to make remaining in their home a possibility. Increases in rates of dementia, depression, and alcohol abuse are valid concerns for older adults and their family members, as they face a multitude of challenges in a rapidly changing world.

The most recent economic crisis starting in 2007 and 2008, also called the *Great Recession*, resulted in the forced retirement and unanticipated layoff of many aging individuals within the workforce, like Donald, from the Chapter Opening Vignette. In addition, changes in the U.S. and global economies risk leaving many individuals approaching retirement in economically vulnerable positions as companies shift away from offering employees lifelong careers with permanent and secure retirement plans. Sharp increases in the cost of medical care and possible changes in Social Security benefits are also putting some older adults at risk of financial vulnerability. Thus, an increasingly older population will no doubt have an impact on the financial, housing, medical, mental health, and even transportation needs of the older adult population. Adding to that, changes in the U.S. family structure, such as the significant increase in divorce rates, have put some older adults in the position of having to provide day care for their grandchildren and, in some cases, even parenting their grandchildren. Thus, although some older adults will be able to take advantage of the many medical advances, healthier lifestyles, and increased opportunities for enjoying life, many others will not.

Assess your comprehension of "The Aging of America: Changing Demographics" by completing this quiz.

OLD AND OLD-OLD: A DEVELOPMENTAL PERSPECTIVE

Many theorists have argued that adults do not go through systematic and uniform developmental stages in the same way that children do; thus, earlier developmental theories typically stop at early adulthood or lump all adult development into one category stretching from post-adolescence and beyond. One reason for this approach is that if development consists of the combined impact of physical, cognitive, and emotional maturity, then certainly one can see that children who are spurred on to extend their social boundaries will be motivated to push themselves from a crawl to a walk in their quest to explore their social worlds. Yet, once one has reached physical and cognitive maturity, this interplay between physical ability and emotional desire (where one dynamic acts as the incentive for the other) subsides, and the motivation to pursue a particular life course becomes based more on personal choice and internal motivation, making adult maturity anything but systematic and universal. Thus, before beginning any real discussion about clinical issues affecting older adults or the role of the social worker, it is important to understand the various aspects of physical, social, and emotional development common to individuals in the last quarter or so of their lives.

Most of us have heard about the infamous "midlife crisis" marking the entry into middle age, or "empty nesting," the universal life crisis some women experience in response to their adult children leaving home. Regardless of the validity of the universality of such life events, it does seem reasonable to assume that individuals within a particular society will respond and adapt to both internal and external demands and expectations placed on them by cultural mores and norms. It would also be reasonable to assume that there would be some interplay between their physical development or decline and their emotional and cognitive development, influenced by their social worlds, which give meaning to their experiences. For example, cultural expectations in the United States, such as marriage, child rearing, employment, and home ownership, certainly have an impact on those in early and middle adulthood, just as retirement, increased physical problems, and widowhood will have an impact on those in later adulthood. Yet, because the options and choices available to adults are so broad, any developmental theory must be considered in somewhat broad and descriptive terms, rather than the narrower and more prescriptive terms often used to evaluate and consider child developmental.

Erik Erikson (1959, 1966), a psychodynamic theorist who studied under Sigmund Freud (the father of psychoanalysis), developed a theory of psychosocial development, beginning with birth and ending with death. According to Erikson, each stage of development presented a unique challenge or crisis brought about by the combining forces of both physiological changes and psychosocial need. Successfully resolving the developmental crisis resulted in being better prepared for the next stage. The eighth stage of Erikson's model is *integrity versus despair* and spans from age 65 to death. Erikson believed that individuals in this age range needed to reflect back on their lives, taking stock of their choices and the value of their various achievements. If this reflection resulted in a sense of contentment with one's choices and life experiences, then the individual will be able to accept death with a sense of integrity, but if he or she does not like the choices made, the relationships developed, and the wisdom gained, then he or she will face death with a sense of despair.

A ninth stage was added posthumously by Erikson's wife, Joan Erikson, based on discussions they had in recognition of the lengthening lifespan, as well as Erikson's notes from interviews (Erikson & Erikson, 1997). The ninth stage, *Very Old Age* (Despair and Disgust vs. Integrity) pertains to those in their 80s and 90s, who are dealing with the reality of death in a way not previously experienced. Joan Erikson cites the increasing isolation of the *old-old adult* as they deal with loss in numerous realms. She cites cultural implications common in many western countries, noting that "aged individuals are often ostracized, neglected, and overlooked; elders are seen no longer as bearers of wisdom but as embodiments of shame" (Erikson & Erikson, 1997, p. 144). This is an extremely challenging time, according to Joan Erikson, where the old-old adult must in some respects rework or confront earlier stages, with the negative outcome at times becoming more dominant. She argues that such cultural determinants are destructive forces, negating the "grand-generative" contributions adults in their 80s and 90s (and older) can make.

Similar to Joan Erikson's conceptualization of grand-generativity is Tornstam's theory of gerotranscendence, which posits that the *old-old* transcend above their everyday realities toward a more cosmic connection with the universe. Tornstam (1994) describes the changes individuals experience from middle to older adulthood on emotional, cognitive, and physical levels is called *gerotranscendence* (Tornstam, 1994). This theory explores how an individual moves from a strong connection to the material world to transcending above the material aspects of the world into a more existential approach to the world. In a similar way to Levinson, Tornstam describes how individuals progressing from midlife onward transition from an externalizing perspective, where they are focusing outward toward the world, to a more internally focused approach in life.

Tornstam (2003) describes three dimensions of transcendence, including the "cosmic level" where individuals change their notions of time and space, such as reorienting themselves with regard to how they view life and death, ultimately accepting death with a sense of peace. The second realm relates to "the self," where individuals increasingly move away from self-centeredness, transcending above a focus on the physical, and move toward more altruism. The third level of transcendence is a realm involving social and individual relationships, where the relationships are viewed in a new light with new meaning, including developing new insights into the differences between "the self" (who they really are), the roles they play in life (mother/father, son/daughter, friend, etc.), and the ability to rise above black-and-white thinking, embracing the gray in life (Degges-White, 2005).

Degges-White (2005) discusses implications of Tornstam's theory of gerotranscendence for counselors working with the older adult population, highlighting key issues involved in the process of personal transcendence across the three dimensions (cosmic, self, and relationships with others). For instance, Degges-White cites the importance of counselors becoming comfortable with the concept of death within themselves, so that they can help their aging clients accept the inevitability of death without fear and anxiety. With regard to transcendence in the "self" domain, Degges-White describes how counselors can help their older clients conduct a "life review" where they seek to better understand and accept their life choices, thus finding a level of peace and self-acceptance about their choices and experiences, particularly the challenging and painful ones. The ultimate focus of counseling older adults using a gerotranscendence model is to assist older adults move toward increased self- and other-acceptance and wisdom in various dimensions and domains in life, and in a sense, giving them permission to drawn intrinsically inward as they let go of the more transitory dimensions of life, and toward a more existential framework.

Daniel Levinson (1978, 1996) is probably one of the most well-known adult developmental theorists, having developed a life span theory extending from birth through death. Levinson wrote two books explaining his theory, *The Seasons of a Man's Life* (1978) and *The Seasons of a Woman's Life* (1996), where he focused on middle adulthood, but what was revolutionary about his theory was his argument that adults do continue to grow and develop on an age-related timetable. Levinson noticed that adults in the latter half of their lives are more reflective, and as they approached a point in their lives where they had more time behind them than ahead of them, this reflection intensified. Levinson also believed that individuals progress through periods of stability that are followed by shorter stages of transition. The themes in his theory most relevant to social workers include this notion of *life reflection*—the taking stock of one's life choices and accomplishments, the need to be able to give back to society, which encompasses an acknowledgment that at some point the goal in life is not solely to focus on one's own driving needs, but to give back to others and the community through the sharing of gained wisdom and mentoring.

Finally, Levinson's belief that as people age they need to become more intrinsically focused rather than externally based is equally relevant. Consider the man who in his 30s gains self-esteem and a sense of identity through working 80 hours per week and running marathons. How will this same man define himself when he is 70 and no longer has the physical stamina or agility to perform these activities? Levinson believed that a developmental task for aging adults was to become more internally anchored, more intrinsic in their self-identify, lest they develop a sense of despair and depression later in life when they are no longer able to live up to their own youthful expectations.

Essentially, these more contemporary theories point to the need to reconsider traditional notions of "old age," with a deeper and more nuanced

Assess your comprehension of "Old and Old-Old: A Developmental Perspective" by completing this quiz.

understanding of aging, in all of its complexity. Attempts at better understanding the aging process in a contemporary context are increasingly focusing on the concept of successful aging.

SUCCESSFUL AGING

A relatively recent concept that has become popular in relation to the study of geriatrics is the concept of *successful aging*, which is used to describe the process of getting the most out of one's life in later years. Successful aging literally means to add years to one's life and to get the most out of living (Havighurst, 1961). Researchers have examined individuals who age better than others to determine what differences might account for their success and some of the variables at play include maintaining a moderately high physical and social activity level, including keeping active with hobbies, social events, and regular exercise (Warr, Butcher, & Robertson, 2004). A study in 2007 found that when older adults participated in some type of social activity, such as paid or unpaid work, religious activities, and political involvement, mortality and cognitive function impairment were reduced, yet disparity in opportunities for meaningful social activities left some older adult groups more vulnerable to physical and cognitive decline (Hsu, 2007).

The natural aging process, though, seems to discourage high activity levels in virtually all domains. Physical limitations also contribute to disengagement. For example, few older adults play on intramural softball teams and even something like poor night vision can keep an older adult from being able to hop in the car and visit family. Employment provides most people with the greatest opportunities for social interaction, and when individuals retire, a significant portion of their social life is lost along with their career. Thus, many older people naturally begin withdrawing from the world, both physically and socially, in response to diminished capability and opportunity, and with such disengagement comes an increase in physical and emotional problems, such as depression and even alcohol abuse to combat loneliness.

A recent study seems to indicate that good psychological health is the most important factor of all in ensuring good quality of life in later years (Bowling & Iliffe, 2011). For instance, the ability of older adults to rely on their psychological resources, such as a good *self-efficacy* (one's perception of personal competency) and *resilience* were more strongly linked to successful aging than

Apply Knowledge of Human Behavior and the Social Environment

Practice Behavior: Utilize conceptual frameworks to guide the processes of assessment, intervention, and evaluation.

Critical Thinking Question: Describe how transcendence can help older adults move beyond physical limitations often inherent in aging.

Social Work Application Activity

Take a moment to reflect on the experiences of Carrie, depicted in the opening vignette at the beginning of this chapter. Would you characterize her as someone who is aging successfully? If so, why? How have her experiences differed from the stereotypical older adults? If Carrie's adult children expressed concern to Carrie's counselor, a licensed social worker, about their mother's activities and life choices, asking her to take action to prevent their mother from continuing in her volunteer activities, do you believe that the NASW Ethical Standard 1.02—Self-Determination would be sufficient in guiding the social worker's response? What other ethical standards would help the social worker in responding to Carrie's children's concerns?

were biological and social factors. This does not mean that good physical health and an active social life aren't important, but as Tornstam (2005) and Degges-White (2005) suggest, older adults who can mentally and emotionally transcend beyond the physical and social limitations inherent in the aging process seem to age more successfully and have a better quality of life compared with older adults who lack these psychological resources.

Consider an individual's level of psychological resilience, which encompasses one's coping strategies that can be relied upon during challenging times. Many older adults must not only face increased health problems and physical limitations but also deal with the loss of friends, siblings, and even their spouse to death. Many older adults must move from their longtime home into residential care or the home of a family member, and even the loss of independence can create a situation where their mental health is determined by the veracity of their coping mechanisms. Psychological resilience enables older adults to manage these multiple losses in a healthier manner, even perhaps finding some existential meaning in facing these losses with a sense of wisdom and acceptance, despite the deep pain and sense of powerlessness many older adults may feel.

Assess your comprehension of "Successful Aging" by completing this quiz.

CURRENT ISSUES AFFECTING OLDER ADULTS AND THE ROLE OF THE SOCIAL WORKER

In anticipation of the increase in the older adult population as well as an increase in the needs and complex nature of the issues facing many older adults, the *Older Americans Act* was signed into federal law in 1965. This act led to the creation of the Administration on Aging, and it funded grants to the states for various community and social service programs and provided money for age-related research and the development of social service agencies called Area Agencies on Aging (AAA) operating at the local level. The Administration on Aging also acts as a clearinghouse, disseminating information about a number of issues affecting the older adult population in the United States.

Numerous issues affect today's older adult population, including ageism, housing and homelessness, retirement, increased responsibility for parenting grandchildren, depression, dementia, and elder abuse. Social workers are often included in the group of professionals most likely to come into contact with the older adult population, either through direct service, case management services, or through providing counseling services to a family member of an older adult, and therefore they must be familiar with these key issues, knowing how they affect older adults and their family.

Social Work Application Activity

Before reading any further, write down or type three descriptions of a typical 70-year old man in the United States. What types of clothes is he likely wearing? What does he spend most of his time doing and talking about? Did you conceptualize an old man with graying or no hair, sitting in a rocker complaining about today's clothing styles, the state of the country, and the failure of his adult children to visit more often? Would it surprise you to know that the typical description of older adults is a myth based on deeply entrenched negative stereotypes and can serve as a foundation of a form of prejudice and discrimination of older adults called *ageism*? How would NASW Ethical Standard 1.05— Cultural Competence and Social Diversity assist social workers in both recognizing and avoiding internalizing negative stereotypes of older adults?

Ageism

The term *ageism* was first coined by Robert Butler (1969), chair of a congressional committee on aging in 1968. He defined ageism as "a systematic stereotyping of and discrimination against people simply because they are old, just as racism and sexism accomplish this with skin color and gender." Butler theorized that the basis of this negative stereotype is a fear of growing old. This fear and the resultant negative stereotyping can often result in the discrimination of the older adult population in all areas of life and is the basis of many forms of elder abuse.

Ageism typically involves any attitude or behavior that negatively categorizes older adults based either on partial truth (often taken out of context) or on outright myths of the aging process. Such myths often describe old age as involving (1) poor health, illness, and disability; (2) lack of mental sharpness and acuity, senility, and dementia; (3) sadness, depression, and loneliness; (4) an irritable demeanor; (5) a sexless life; (6) routine boredom; (7) a lack of vitality and continual decline; (8) an inability to learn new things; and (9) loss of productivity (Thornton, 2002).

> Learn more about ageism by watching the film "Cut Back: Facing Ageism" on YouTube. (http:// www .youtube.com/playlist?list =PL744F7B492A19B976)

Gerontologists caution that the promotion of such negative stereotypes of old age and older adults not only trivializes older individuals but also risks displacing the older adult population as communities undervalue them based on the perception that older adults are a drain on society. A further risk of ageism is that older adults may internalize this negative stereotype, creating a self-fulfilling prophecy of sorts (Palmore, 2009; Thornton, 2002). This is similar to what happens with other vulnerable populations, such as ethnic minority groups, who internalize the negative perceptions of them held by many in the majority population (Snyder, 2001).

Old age has not always been something those in the United States have viewed negatively. In fact, earlier in the 20th century, societal attitudes reflected a relatively positive view of older adults and of the aging experience. Older adults were respected for their wisdom and valued for their experience. They were not typically perceived as being a drain on society or as a burden to the community. Yet, sometime around the mid-1900s, as life expectancy began to grow and medical technology improved dramatically, professionals such as physicians, psychologists, and gerontologists began discussing older adults in terms of the *problems* they posed (Hirshbein, 2001).

Many social psychologists and gerontologists cite the media as a major source of negative stereotypes of older adults. These critics claim that the consistent negative portrayal of older adults in both television shows and commercials, for example, portraying them as dimwitted, foolish individuals living in the past, has a dehumanizing effect on the entire older adult population and has a negative effect on the self-concept of many older adults. Yet, the results of a study conducted in 2004, which reviewed television commercials from the 1950s to the 1990s, did not support this critical view of the media (Miller, Leyell, & Mazacheck, 2004). In fact, Miller and his colleagues found that the media's depiction of older adults has been relatively positive, particularly in the latter two decades.

It is vital that social workers make certain that they do not hold any negative misconceptions of old age. For instance, assuming that someone over the age of 70 is incapable of being productive and of learning something new, of gaining a new insight, whether in the counseling office or in life in general, would undoubtedly affect the dynamic between the counselor and the older adult client. In fact, research shows that negative stereotypes about aging are often internalized by older adults and can actually increase feelings of loneliness and dependency (Coudin & Alexopoulos, 2010). Practitioners then must address any misconceptions they have of old age and of the older adult population in general. Practices such as talking down to older adult clients and not directly addressing difficult issues for fear that they lack the capacity to understand them will undoubtedly affect the level of investment the client makes in the counseling relationship. This type of behavior on the part of the practitioner can also encourage a self-fulfilling prophecy within older adult clients, where they begin to act the part of the incapable, unproductive, and cognitively dull individual. Making positive assumptions about older adult clients will increase the possibility of bringing out the most authentic and dynamic aspects of older adult clients.

Housing

The majority of older adults remain in their homes until death and are cared for by family members (Bergeron & Gray, 2003). However, as medical technology allows people to live longer, albeit not necessarily healthier lives, many older adults find themselves needing to move out of their homes once they reach a certain level of physical and/or cognitive decline. They might move into the home of a family member, which was far more prevalent when the United States was an agricultural society, and both men and women were home based in their work. Today, with more women than ever in the workforce, many families are unavailable to care for their older and chronically ill relatives. Instead, some older adults opt to move into a *retirement community*, where they can still enjoy their independence while enjoying many facility-offered services to meet their needs, such as shuttle service, handicapped-accessible facilities, and child-free living.

Engage Diversity and Difference in Practice

Practice Behavior: Recognize and communicate their understanding of the importance of difference in shaping life experiences.

Critical Thinking Question: What are some ways in which poverty impacts the older adult population, particularly in relation to housing and life satisfaction?

Government-subsidized older adult housing can make housing costs more affordable for the older adult population, whether in the form of a subsidy provided directly to older adults in the form of tax credits, loans, or rental vouchers or subsidies provided to the housing community, which then passes on this discount to the renter. One problem with many of these programs, however, is that they require older adults to find their own housing in the community, much of which is older and not appropriate for older adult residents who often need special age-related accommodations. Another concern relates to government-subsidized communities that are designed for older adult populations but tend to be fraught with problems related to safety, including problems with poor physical upkeep of the property.

A 2003 longitudinal study that followed 1,200 older adults in their transition from independent living to age-restricted housing in 1995 found that those older adults who transitioned to more expensive communities fared the best with regard to physical health and overall life satisfaction. In contrast, those who transitioned to government-subsidized housing programs fared the worse. Although the study investigators acknowledged that levels of life satisfaction might be related to a cumulative effect of a lifetime of poverty, they concluded that overall quality of housing has a direct relationship to life satisfaction (Krout, 2003).

Older adults needing more consistent care with their *activities of daily living* (ADL) sometimes enter *long-term care facilities*, also sometimes called *assisted-living facilities*. These facilities offer apartment-like living in a more structured environment. In many respects, assisted-living facilities act as a bridge between independent living and nursing home care. Assisted-living facilities offer assistance with eating, bathing, dressing, house-keeping, and medication, and some even have fully functioning medical centers. Many assisted-living apartments have alarm systems in every unit, offer a restaurant-style cafeteria, a club for social activities, a hairdresser, a medical staff, home healthcare, and a relatively full array of social services. The services are far more intensive than in a retirement community, as residents in assisted-living facilities are there because they cannot manage their ADL without daily assistance.

Social workers working in long-term care facilities with older adults provide pre-admission services, such as conducting biopsychosocial assessments; identify needs and coordinate services; work on multidisciplinary teams to develop individualized social service plans; provide outreach services to residents' families to keep them updated on their family member's status; provide case management and counseling services to residents and their family members, which may include locating additional services within the community, and grief and bereavement counseling when a resident or resident spouse dies; provide financial counseling to the residents and their family members; serve as a resource for behavioral health matters for staff; and act as a liaison to the community on behalf of the facility.

For more comprehensive information on the role of social workers in long-term care facilities, go to the NASW website and search for the NASW Standards statement.

Homelessness and the Older Adult Population

The story of Rosemary and Donald in the opening vignette highlights the issue of homelessness in the older adult population. Although older adults are at a lower risk for homelessness than other age groups, homelessness in the older adult population is a growing concern because the percentage of older adults experiencing housing insecurity is expected to grow as the baby boomer generation ages (Gonyea, Mills-Dick, & Bachman, 2010). Additionally, for years the problem of homelessness among the older population has been essentially ignored by policy makers and legislators, rendering this population relatively invisible (Gonyea, Mills-Dick, & Bachman, 2010).

The common causes of homelessness in the general population apply to older adult subgroups as well, such as a lack of affordable housing, too few jobs for unskilled workers, and a reduction in social services support (Hecht & Coyle, 2001; Kutza & Keigher, 1991), but the older adult population in general has additional risk factors such as being too old to sufficiently recover from a job loss, enter a new career, or reenter the workforce, as well as chronic illnesses that either are costly or bar older adults from being self-supporting (Kutza & Keigher, 1991).

An older homeless woman living in a public park.

For statistical purposes, individuals above the age of 50–55 are usually considered in the older adult category, but generally the lower threshold for what is considered "older" is increasing as human life expectancy increases. Homeless older adults are a particularly vulnerable subgroup because of age-related physical vulnerability, which is often exacerbated by poor nutrition and difficult living conditions either on the streets or in a homeless shelter. Older adults are also at a much higher risk of becoming victims of crime while living on the streets (Hecht & Coyle, 2001).

JOSEPH SOHM/VISIONS OF AMERICA/CORBIS

Check out more information on older adult homelessness by going to the National Coalition for the Homeless website and searching for the fact sheet called: "Homelessness Among Elderly Persons" (2009).

A research study based in Los Angeles found that unlike the homeless in the general population, 85 percent of the older adult population was white (versus 61 percent in the younger homeless population), and 59 percent were veterans (versus 27 percent in the younger homeless population). Older homeless adults were far more likely to be socially isolated and suffer from a physical illness but less likely to suffer from substance abuse, mental illness, or domestic violence (Linn & Mayer-Oakes, 1990). Older homeless adults between the ages of 50 and 65 are often the most vulnerable group because they are frequently the target of ageism when attempting to reenter the workforce but too young to qualify for Medicare and Social Security benefits (Hecht & Coyle, 2001).

The differences between younger homeless and older homeless populations become important when considering programs designed to assist the older adult homeless population (see Box 6.1).

Box 6.1   Differences Between Homelessness in Younger and Older Adult Homelessness

Differences exist between homelessness among younger and older persons, both in terms of the root causes of homelessness and effective responses. Younger homeless individuals report domestic violence and previous incarceration as reasons for becoming homeless far more frequently than older populations. Both groups report equal difficulty in finding affordable housing, and both groups report equivalent rates of alcohol and substance abuse as reasons for homelessness, with 4 percent of younger individuals reporting this as a reason and just over 6 percent of older adults reporting substance abuse as the primary reason for their homelessness. Yet in light of the nature of substance abuse and the tendency for alcoholics and drug addicts to minimize or deny the impact of their addiction, these percentages might be underreported.

Older adult homeless persons report being without shelter for far longer periods than younger individuals, with older adult men reporting an average homeless episode lasting over 60 days, and younger homeless men averaging about 14 days. Older men also reported far longer episodes without a permanent shelter, some reporting homeless episodes of over two years, whereas younger men reported being homeless an average of 11 months (Hecht & Coyle, 2001). This is likely because of fewer social supports and the difficulty in either moving in with a roommate or living with family, often because of caretaking issues related to common age-related physical problems.

Even though there are more similarities than differences between older and younger homeless persons, the response to older adults who are homeless must be vastly different because of all the variables associated with their advanced age. One variable mentioned in the previous paragraph relates to the diminished capacity of older people in getting back on their feet by finding new employment opportunities or entering a reeducation program to enter a new career; thus, the possibility of regaining financial independence is greatly diminished in the older adult population.

Other issues affecting older adults include their increased vulnerability—both physically and psychologically, leaving them open to physical and financial victimization. Physical disability and illness are also complicating factors in meeting the needs of the older adult homeless population.

Although there is increased funding for services for older adults, most economic support is not available until the age of 65. Self-sufficiency models designed for the general homeless population do not work with the older adult population for the reasons mentioned earlier; thus, some experts suggest responding to the older adult homeless population by developing aid-assisted low-cost housing with social services to assist with financial, physical, and psychological support to deal with the trauma of becoming homeless. As referenced earlier, homeless advocates and policy experts have expressed concern that the recent financial crisis that began in about 2007 involving the crash of the stock market, loss of retirement funds, mass layoffs, and dramatic increases in foreclosures will have a significantly negative impact on the older adult population because of decreased possibilities to rebound financially.

Many homeless assistance programs focus on the root causes of homelessness that are more common in younger populations, such as providing assistance with substance abuse and domestic violence. Social services programs designed to assist the older adult subgroups with housing issues need to focus more on issues related to insufficient income, health concerns, and low-income housing, offering supportive services to the older adult population with declining health.

Adjustment to Retirement

The concept of retirement is so common to the 21st century that it rarely needs explanation. When an individual comments on his or her upcoming retirement, others seem to instinctually understand that what is being discussed is the practice of leaving one's employment to permanently enter a phase of chosen nonemployment. Even though some might choose to dabble in part-time employment from time to time, the most common conceptualization of retirement involves an employee permanently surrendering his or her position, at approximately age 65, and drawing on a pension or retirement account that has likely been accruing for years. Of course, there are numerous variations on this theme—some people don't ever formally retire, and some people work in fields that have mandatory retirement ages, such as the airline industry, which requires that all commercial airline pilots retire at the age of 65, and for some, retirement is a luxury they cannot afford. Also, it would be incorrect to assume that everyone in the workforce has accrued a pension sizeable enough to permit them to live on it for years. But despite the range of retirement experiences, certain generalizations can be made about the retirement experience for the majority of those living in the United States during the 21st century.

Robert Atchley (1976) was one of the first researchers who attempted to describe the retirement experience for men and women. He identified five distinct, yet overlapping, stages that most retirees progress through on formal retirement (see Table 6.1). There has been some controversy about whether retirees actually progress through such distinct phases or whether there is just too much of a range of experiences among retirees in the United States to categorize experiences in a stage theory. Yet, a study by Reitzes and Mutran (2004) appears to support Atchley's stage theory, finding that retirees experience

Table 6.1   Robert Atchley's Stages of Retirement

Stage	Description	
1	The Honeymoon Phase:	Retirees embrace retirement and all their newfound freedom in an optimistic but unrealistic manner.
2	Disenchantment:	Retirees become disillusioned with what they thought retirement was going to be like and get discouraged with what they often feel, as though there is too much time on their hands.
3	Reorientation:	Retirees develop a more realistic view of retirement, with regard to both increased opportunities and increased constraints.
4	Stability:	Retirees adjust to retirement.
5	Termination:	Retirees eventually lose independence because of physical and cognitive decline.

Pearson Education, Inc.

a temporary lift right after retiring (for about 6 months), but then develop an increasingly negative attitude after about the 12-month mark, with some retirees rebounding with increased optimism after about two years. The study also found that an individual's level of self-esteem preretirement seemed to have an effect on their overall mental health after retirement, with those who had higher levels of self-esteem faring better. A more recent study on postretirement dynamics seems to support some of Atchley, and Reitzes and Mutran's findings, while refuting others.

One study, which was funded by the National Institute on Aging, found that men and women who continued to work for a period of time after retirement, on a part-time or temporary basis (called *bridge employment*) had much better physical and psychological quality during their elder years, indicating that sudden and complete retirement, without any transition, may have negative side effects for an older adult's physical and mental health. Interestingly, the positive effects gained from bridge employment existed regardless of the retiree's preretirement mental and physical health (Zhan, Wang, Liu, & Shultz, 2009).

Finally, race and gender have a significant effect on retirement experiences. Research has shown that women and minority workers often have different attitudes and experiences surrounding retirement issues because of disparity in income and education levels (McNamara & Williamson, 2004). Thus, the social worker must understand that most factors affecting a client's retirement experience are going to be influenced by the client's gender and racial background.

Because nearly 50 percent of the U.S. population is now over the age of 50, the implications of retirement preparation and adjustment to retirement for the social work field obviously cannot be ignored. Social workers will likely come into contact with retired or retiring adults in many different settings, and thus it is important to realize that impending retirement can become an issue for someone even in middle adulthood.

Grandparents Parenting

The practice of grandparents raising grandchildren has increased dramatically over the past several years, signaling many problems within U.S. society that have emerged since the 1970s. The U.S. Congress became interested in this issue in the mid-1990s, and in 1996, passed a legislation that required the 2000 U.S. Census to include questions regarding whether grandparents were residing with grandchildren, whether they had primary responsibility for them, and what length of time they had acted in a parental role (i.e., revealing whether the situation was temporary or permanent).

Current figures (as of 2010, the most recent statistics available) estimate that approximately 7 million U.S. households (about 5 percent of the population) are composed of grandparents co-residing with grandchildren under the age of 18, 2.7 million of which had primary caregiving responsibility. The majority of grandparent families were female headed households (see Table 6.2) (U.S. Census Bureau, 2012). These statistics represents a significant increase over past years and means that 28 percent of grandparents in the United States are responsible for raising their grandchildren. About two-thirds of these grandparents are between the

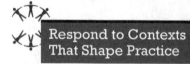

Respond to Contexts That Shape Practice

Practice Behavior: Provide leadership in promoting sustainable changes in service delivery and practice to improve the quality of social services.

Critical Thinking Question: What are some ways in which social workers can take the lead in advocating for better service delivery for grandparents who are parenting their children?

Table 6.2   Major Reasons Why Grandparents Become Surrogate Parents

1. The high divorce rate, leaving many women facing potential poverty, resulting in them returning home to live with parents

2. The sharp rise in teen pregnancies, resulting in the mother residing with her parents for economic (and oftentimes emotional) reasons

3. The increase in relative foster care in response to a sharp increase in child welfare intervention due to child abuse

4. The increase in parents serving time in prison, primarily for drug abuse and drug-related offenses punishable by high prison sentences due to the U.S. government's War on Drugs

5. The sharp increase of drug use, particularly among women of color whose use of crack cocaine has literally exploded over the past 10 years

6. The AIDS crisis, which has devastated many communities, leaving children orphaned and in need of permanent homes. These cases are complicated when the children have contracted HIV, particularly when one considers their complex medical needs (de Toledo & Brown, 1995)

Pearson Education, Inc.

ages of 50 and 59, and about a third are over 60. Some of these households included at least one of the parents, but many of them included one or both grandparents acting in the role of surrogate parent(s).

Although the demographics of grandparent-headed households vary considerably, ethnic minority children are far more likely to be raised by a grandparent than Caucasian children. African American children in the Southeastern portion of the United States have a significantly higher rate of living with custodial grandparents than children in other regions in the United States. Households led by only a grandmother are far more likely to face economic hardship. Grandparent caregivers in the Southeast and in urban areas have the highest levels of poverty and the lowest levels of education (Simmons & Dye, 2003; Whitley & Kelley, 2007). African American grandparents are far likelier to experience poverty, despite the fact that the majority are in the labor force. They are also far likelier to not have sufficient health insurance and they experience greater physical and emotional stressors (Whitley & Kelley, 2007). Interestingly, a recent research study indicates that, in general, older grandparents may experience less emotional strain related to their primary parenting role than do younger grandparents, likely related to their increased ability to manage stressful life situations (Conway, Jones, & Speakes-Lewis, 2011).

Take a look at articles on grandparents raising grandchildren on the AARP website in the Home & Family section.

The issues facing grandparents raising grandchildren are complex involving emotional as well as financial, legal, and physical challenges. Many grandparent caregivers are often forced to live in a type of limbo, not knowing how long they will remain responsible for their grandchildren, particularly when the biological parents are either in jail or suffering from drug addiction that prevents them from resuming their primary parenting role.

The choice to act as a surrogate parent is in many instances made in a time of crisis; thus, older adults who may have been planning their retirement for years may find themselves in a position where they either take on this parenting role in the face of the situation that rendered the biological parents unable to continue parenting or allow their grandchildren to enter the county foster care system. Parenting younger children has its unique challenges but often comes with some level of social support, at least within the elementary school system, but this is often not the case with older children, particularly adolescents.

Parenting adolescents can often present significant challenges for grandparents, particularly those who are very old. Parenting adolescents can be an exhausting endeavor for the young or middle-aged parent, but imagine the demands placed on someone who is an older adult, has limited physical capacity, and even more limited financial means. Adolescents who have endured significant loss through death or abandonment, have been raised in abusive homes, or have been raised by parents who abuse drugs or are serving time in prison are likely to act out emotionally and even physically, putting even greater stress on an already vulnerable family system.

Social workers may enter a grandparent-led family system in numerous ways—they could be the school social worker working with the children, they might be the child welfare caseworker assigned to assist the grandparents who are serving as relative foster care parents, or they might work for a social services agency offering outreach services to grandparent caregivers.

Depression

Another significant concern affecting the older adult population is the increased incidence of depression. In fact, the *National Institute of Mental Health* (NIMH) estimates that approximately 2 million individuals over the age of 65 suffer from some form of depression, and as many as 5 million more suffer from some form of depressive symptoms, although they may not meet all the criteria for clinical depression. Although prevalence rates can vary rather widely within the population, due in part to how depression is defined, these statistics indicate that at any given time anywhere from 5 to 30 percent of the older adult population may suffer from some form of depression, compared with a 1 percent prevalence rate in the general population (Birrer & Vemuri, 2004).

Read more on depression among older women by going to the NIMH website and searching on depression in older women.

Depression rates in nursing homes are even higher, with some studies finding up to 50 percent of the residents meeting the criteria for clinical depression. Older adults are also disproportionately at risk for suicide. Although individuals aged 65 years and older make up about 12 percent of the U.S. population, they account for nearly 16 percent of all those who committed suicide in the year 2004, which is the highest rates of all age groups. Surprisingly, older adults at the highest risk for suicide are white males over the age of 85, many of whom are widowed (Birrer & Vemuri, 2004; Kraaij & de Wilde, 2001; McIntosh, 2004; NIMH, 2007).

Many believe that depression is just a normal part of the aging process caused by the natural course of cognitive and physical decline and the multiple losses associated with growing old. But depression is not a natural part of growing older and can be avoided. Unfortunately, many in the medical and mental health fields, even older adults themselves, believe that it is, and thus many in the older adult population who are suffering from depression remain undiagnosed and untreated. Misdiagnosis is also relatively common, with depression often being mistaken for dementia or some other form of cognitive impairment (Birrer & Vemuri, 2004).

Social workers working with the older adult community must be observant of the signs of depression. They must also be aware of the many risk factors for depression, including anxiety; chronic medical conditions such as heart disease, stroke, and diabetes;

dementia; being unmarried; alcohol abuse; stressful life events; and minimal social support (Birrer & Vemuri, 2004; Lynch, Compton, Mendelson, Robins, & Krishnan, 2000; Waite, Bebbington, Skelton-Robinson, & Orrell, 2004).

Dementia

The American Psychiatric Association defines *dementia* as a progressive, degenerative illnesses experienced during old age that impairs brain function and cognitive ability. Dementia is an umbrella term likely encompassing numerous disorders. Two of the most common forms of dementia are Alzheimer's disease and multi-infarct dementia (small strokes in the brain).

The general symptoms of dementia include a comprehensive shutting down of all bodily systems indicative by progressive memory loss, increased difficulty concentrating, a steady decrease in problem-solving skills and judgment capability, confusion, hallucinations and delusions, altered sensations or perceptions, impaired recognition of everyday objects and familiar people, altered sleep patterns, motor system impairment, inability to maintain ADL (such as dressing oneself), agitation, anxiety, and depression. Ultimately, the dementia sufferer enters a complete vegetative state prior to death.

According to the NIMH, multi-infarct dementia accounts for nearly 20 percent of all dementias, affecting about 4 in 10,000 people. Even more individuals suffer from some form of mild cognitive impairment but do not yet meet the criteria for full-blown dementia (Palmer, Winblad, & Fratiglioni, 2003). Alzheimer's disease affects approximately 4.5 million Americans, or about 5 percent of the population between the ages of 65 and 74 years, and the incident rate increases to 50 percent for those over 85 years of age. Diagnosis is based on symptoms, and it is only through an autopsy that a definitive diagnosis of

> Take a look at HBO's series of documentaries on Alzheimer's disease by going to the HBO website and searching for "The Alzheimer's Project."

Social Work, Social Media, and Technology

How has the Internet impacted the older adult population? According to a Pew Research Internet Report published in August of 2013, almost half of all adults over the age of 65 use social media, such as Facebook, compared with only 1% in 2006, driven in large part by an increase in older adults using tablets (compared to laptops or desktop computers). Another new study suggests that retired older adults who use the Internet are about one-third less likely to experience depression. Recent research also indicates that Facebook can help older adults' cognitive functioning, evaluated through a series of neuropsychological tests for such social variables as loneliness and levels of social support. The study showed that adults between the ages of 65 and 91 years of age improved their cognitive functioning by about 25% if they used Facebook on a daily basis in an interactive manner by creating online social connections, compared with older adults who posted daily on a private diary (with no social networking) and a control group of older adults who did not engage in any online activity, suggesting a possible link between online social interaction and cognitive functioning. Check out ProjectGoal, an online social justice advocacy effort to get older adults online in a safe and effective manner (conduct an Internet search for ProjectGoal Get Older Adults Online). What are some ways that social workers can use this information to develop programs for older adults designed to combat depression and cognitive impairment?

dementia can be made. The United States has experienced a dramatic increase in the incidence of dementia in the latter part of the 20th century, primarily due to the increased human life span. It is theorized that dementia did not have an opportunity to develop prior to the 1900s, when the average life span was about 47 years. There is no known cure for dementia, and thus treatment is focused on delaying and relieving symptoms.

Social workers may work directly with the sufferer of dementia or with the caregiver (typically a spouse or adult child) if they work in a practice setting that serves the older adult community. However, dealing with dementia as a clinical issue can occur in any practice setting because any client may have a relative suffering from dementia and will therefore need counseling and perhaps even case management in that regard. Consider the practitioner who assists clients in managing an ailing parent, questioning dealing whether their parent is suffering from cognitive impairment, grieving the slow loss of the parent they love, and needing support in making difficult decisions such as determining when their parent can no longer live alone. Or, consider the school social worker who is counseling a student whose grandfather was recently diagnosed with Alzheimer's disease. The pressure that dealing with a family member with dementia on the entire family system will affect the student in numerous ways—academically, emotionally, perhaps even physically—and will frequently magnify any existing issues with which the student is currently struggling.

Elder Abuse

Older adults are a vulnerable population because of factors such as their physical frailty, dependence, social isolation, and the existence of cognitive impairment, and as such are at risk of various forms of abuse and exploitation. The National Center on Elder Abuse (NCEA) defines elder abuse as any "knowing, intentional, or negligent act by a caregiver or any other person that causes harm or a serious risk of harm to a vulnerable adult." The specific definition of elder abuse varies from state to state, but in general can include physical, emotional, or sexual abuse; neglect and abandonment; or financial exploitation.

Although elder abuse is presumed to have always occurred, just as other forms of abuse (such as child abuse and spousal abuse), it was not legally defined until addressed within a 1987 amendment of the Older Americans Act. Reports of elder abuse have increased significantly over the last several years because of not only an increase in reporting requirements but also societal changes that are putting more older adults at risk. In 1986, there were 117,000 reports of elder abuse nationwide, and by 1996 the number of abuse reports increased to 293,000 (Tatara, 1997). By the year 2000 (the most recent reported data), the number of elder abuse reports had risen to an alarming 472,813 among all 50 states, Guam, and Washington, DC. One reason for the rise in abuse reports is that the newest figures include not only abuse in domestic settings, but abuse in institutional settings as well, but despite the more comprehensive data collection methods, there is no escaping the fact that elder abuse is increasing within the United States (Teaster, 2000). Elder abuse is projected to continue to rise in the coming years because of the increased life span and the resultant increase in chronic illnesses, changing family patterns, and the complexity involved with contemporary caregiving.

Sixty percent of all reported abuse victims are women, 65 percent of all abuse victims are white, more than 60 percent of abuse incidences occurred in domestic settings, and about 8 percent of abuse incidences occurred in institutionalized settings. Family members were the most commonly cited perpetrators, including both spouses and adult children (Teaster, 2000). After years of failed attempts, in March 2010, the *Elder Justice Act of 2009* (EJA) was passed and signed into law by President Obama as part of the Patient Protection and Affordable Care Act (PPACA). The EJA sets forth numerous provisions for addressing the abuse, neglect, and exploitation of older adults, both in the form of preventative and responsive measures. For instance, the legislation provides grants for a number of training programs focusing on prevention of abuse and exploitation of older adults; provides measures for expanding long-term care services, including a long-term care ombudsman program; establishes mandatory reporting requirements for abuse against older adults occurring in long-term care facilities; and includes provisions for creating national advisory councils (National Health Policy Forum, 2010).

Visit the White House website and search for the article entitled "The White House Takes a Stand Against Elder Abuse."

Despite the fact that there remain relatively limited mechanisms on a national level regulating how elder abuse is to be handled (primarily because of a lack of funding), every state in the United States has an adult protective services (APS) agency. Where there had been significant variation in reporting requirements between states, the EJA now requires that mandated reporters notify the government Health and Human Services (HHS) and at least one law enforcement entity with reasonable suspicions of elder abuse.

Elder abuse tends to be grossly underreported for several reasons, but many cite a lack of knowledge and awareness of new reporting requirements as a primary reason. It is therefore essential that social workers become aware of the requirements stipulated in the EJA, as well as related policies in their state.

Caregiver burnout is one of the primary risk factors of elder abuse. The most common scenario involves a loving family member who becomes intensely frustrated by the seemingly impossible task of caring for a spouse or parent with a chronic illness such as dementia. Providing the continuous care of someone with Alzheimer's disease, for example, can be frustrating, provoking an abusive response from someone with no history of abusive behavior. One of the most effective intervention strategies is *caregiver support groups*. These groups are typically facilitated by a social worker or other helping professional and focus on providing caregivers, many of whom are older adults themselves, a safe place to express their frustrations, sadness, and other feelings related to caring for their dependent older adult loved one.

Assess your comprehension of "Current Issues Affecting Older Adults and the Role of the Social Worker" by completing this quiz.

LEGISLATION AFFECTING OLDER ADULTS

Several new federal bills have been passed in recent years that have or will likely have a significant impact on the older adult population. The American Tax Relief Act of 2012 (PL 112-240), signed by President Obama on January 2, 2013, mandates the creation of a 15-member commission to examine the issue of long-term care on a national level. The goal of the commission is to develop a plan for the implementation and funding of a high-quality and coordinated national long-term care system serving older adults and people with disabilities. Older adult advocates hail the passing of this legislation as a significant accomplishment but express caution about the accelerated timeline for the commission to complete its work (they have six months from formation), and the law does not require Congress to vote on the commission's plan.

Another new federal law that has the potential of significantly affecting the older adult population is the *Patient Protection and Affordable Care Act* (PL 111-148), which President Obama signed into law on March 23, 2010. This broad-based legislation is the first federal law designed to overhaul the U.S. healthcare system. The legislation was phased in beginning in 2010 with full implementation in 2014. Benefits for seniors include automatic discounts of up to 50 percent on prescription drugs covered by Medicare Part D, an end to insurance carrier imposed limits on lifetime care, access to no-cost prevention and wellness services, protection of Medicare benefits prohibiting future cuts, better coordination between different Medicare programs, and legislative efforts to prohibit Medicare fraud and waste (The White House, 2010). The law also provides for grants to educational institutions providing training for direct care workers through the *Direct Care Training Grants Program*, as well as grant programs providing incentives for entering the field of geriatrics, including clinical social workers (Lewis-Burke, 2011).

Assess your comprehension of "Legislation Affecting Older Adults" by completing this quiz.

PRACTICE SETTINGS SERVING OLDER ADULTS

Unfortunately, Up until recently, working with older adults was a rather unpopular choice for social workers in the United States and across the globe (Weiss, 2005). Yet, a commitment on the part of several educational accreditation agencies to increase infusion of gerontology issues in the educational curriculum, as well as financial incentives, such as scholarships and stipends for students in gerontological field placements, is making a difference in the number of students who select gerontology as their career focus.

For social workers wishing to provide direct service to the older adult population, a wide array of choices in practice settings awaits them. Virtually all practice settings delivering services to older adults have certain treatment and intervention goals, including the promotion of the health and well-being of older adults, special attention to the needs of special populations such as women and ethnic minority groups, providing effective services at an affordable price, identifying the common needs of all older adults, and removing existing social barriers so that elders can be empowered to seek assistance in meeting those needs.

AAAs, discussed earlier in this chapter, often serve as social service agencies offering direct service to the older adult community on a local level. Generally, these agencies offer a multitude of services for older adults, such as nutrition programs, services for homebound older adults, and low-income ethnic minority older adults, and other programs focusing on the needs of older adults within the local community. Many AAAs also act as a referral source for other services within the local community. For instance, the Mid-Florida AAAs offer programs for those suffering from Alzheimer's disease (including caregiver respite), a toll-free hotline that links older adults with local resources, an emergency home energy assistance program, paralegal services, home care for older adults, Medicaid waivers, and practitioners who work with older adults in helping them make informed decisions. Most AAAs offer both in-home services, many of which are facilitated by social workers, as well as an array of off-site programs. Social workers working at an AAA-funded center might facilitate caregiver respite programs, or they might provide case management services for an agency that provides employment services for clients over 60 years of age. Even at centers where services are primarily medical in nature, social workers often provide adjunct counseling and case management services as a support service.

Other practice settings include adult day cares, geriatric assessment units, nursing home facilities, veterans' services, elder abuse programs, adult protective services, bereavement services, senior centers, and hospices. A social worker will likely perform similar types of direct service, consultation, and educational services focused on assisting older clients maintain or improve their quality of life, independence, and level of self-determination. Tasks are typically performed using a multidisciplinary team approach and can include conducting psychosocial assessments, providing case management, developing treatment plans, providing referrals for appropriate services, and providing counseling to older adult clients and their families. Services are also provided to family caregivers offering support and respite care.

Learn more about working with the older adult population by going to the CSWE website and searching for the pamphlet called "Exciting Careers in Social Work and Aging."

Assess your comprehension of "Practice Settings Serving Older Adults" by completing this quiz.

SPECIAL POPULATIONS

As the older adult population has increased in numbers, the government has shifted its priorities and developed programs aimed at long-term healthcare needs, with a particular focus on vulnerable populations such as women, ethnic minorities, and older adults living in rural communities. It is difficult to define who is particularly vulnerable within the older adult population because in many senses, *all* older adults could conceivably be considered vulnerable to social, economic, physical, and psychological harm or exploitation simply by virtue of their advancing age and corresponding dependency needs. But many gerontologists classify various subpopulations as more vulnerable for various reasons. For instance, successful aging has been linked to good economic status, good healthcare, relatively low stress levels, and high levels of social connections. A 2004 study also showed a link between good health and financial stability, finding that Caucasians tend to have greater economic wealth and better health than African American and Latino populations (Lum, 2004).

Women are often considered a special population because as a group they are more prone to depression and typically have a worse response to antidepressant medication (Kessler, 2003). Women often experience greater financial vulnerability, particularly if divorced or widowed, and are often in lower wage jobs, undereducated, and underinsured. Widowhood is a common occurrence for women because they live an average of seven years longer than men, and although the majority of women in the United States marry, 75 percent of women are unmarried by the age of 65. Widowhood puts women at increased risk for lower morale and other mental health problems, even though these often symptoms often abate with time and intervention (Bennett, 1997).

Research has also shown a link between stress and racism that often affects quality of life. A study conducted in 2002 found that racism, and particularly institutionalized racism (such as government-sanctioned racism through discrimination in housing, employment, and healthcare), had a detrimental effect on older African

Americans, particularly men, who tend to experience worse racial discrimination than women (Utsey, Payne, Jackson, & Jones, 2002). Other research has shown how institutionalized racism can lead to feelings of being invisible, stress, depression, and ultimately despair as the person experiences a sense of futility in combating a lifetime of discrimination and white privilege (Franklin, Boyd-Franklin, & Kelly, 2006).

Other special populations could conceivably include any subgroup that is vulnerable at any point across the life span because of physical and/or mental disability, veteran status, and those individuals living in isolated rural areas. Identifying special populations within the older adult population will allow the social worker to explore issues that can potentially render older adult clients at increased risk and vulnerability during old age. For example, research has shown that veterans are at special risk for depression, post-traumatic stress disorder (PTSD), and alcohol abuse. Thus, older adult veterans will be at particular risk for these conditions. An older adult client who is developmentally disabled will also face increased vulnerability compared with those in the older adult population who have intelligence in the normal range. A social worker who is well versed on common risk factors for older adults in the United States, as well as for the increased risk factors facing special populations, will be far more effective in protecting and advocating for their older adult clients.

Assess your comprehension of "Special Populations" by completing this quiz.

Summary

The older adult population is increasing at a dramatic rate in the United States, rendering this one of the fastest growing target populations of social service agencies. As the baby boomers continue to age and as life continues to become more complex, many within the older adult population will rely on social workers to meet many of their basic needs. Many social work educational programs are adding the field of gerontology, as an area of specialization in response to the growing need for practitioners committed to work with this population in a variety of capacities. In fact in 2004 the CSWE created the National Center for Gerontological Social Work Education, also referred to as the Gero-Ed Center. The Gero-Ed Center exists to promote competencies in the field of gerontology in BSW and MSW programs. The center provides resources such as curricular materials and teaching tools for social work educational programs to enhance their "gero" specializations, certifications, and, in general, to assist with the gero-infusion into social work curriculum. The Gero-Ed Center is funded by the John A. Hartford Foundation, which enables the center to provide grants to social work programs wanting to start gero programs.

Future considerations include the continued effort to identify vulnerable populations, as well as addressing ongoing concerns such as the shortage of available affordable housing, the availability of long-term care and healthcare services directed to the older adult population, and the increased role of parenting responsibilities placed on many older adults. Social workers can make a significant positive impact on the lives of older adults and their family members by addressing both ongoing and anticipated needs of this population. This is an exciting time to enter the gero social work field, and in a time when jobs are sometimes hard to come by, this field should be a serious consideration for any social worker who wants to make a significant contribution to the health and wellness of this growing segment of the population. In fact, according to the U.S. Department of Health and Human Services (2006) study approximately 55,000 social workers will be needed in the older adult long-term care area, and by 2050 this number is expected to rise to about 109,000!

Recall what you learned in this chapter by completing the Chapter Review.

Mental Health and Mental Illness

Kimberly was very charming when I first met her. She exuded charisma, had comic timing, and she lit up a room when she walked in. When she came to me for counseling she was convincing in her assertions that she wasn't concerned about her own functioning, but rather she was concerned about a number of people in her life who she was having trouble with. She described conflict with her brother, challenges with her father, and difficulty with her partner's teenage children. What was creating the most difficulty with her, however, were her relationships with colleagues. Over the course of the next several weeks Kim told story after story of problems she had with her coworkers, who she complained were not as smart as she was, received preferential treatment, and stole her glory time and time again. Interspersed throughout these stories were other stories, rather dramatically delivered, about her own accomplishments, along with assertions that given the chance she could take over the department and lead it to greatness. Within each story, Kimberly shared how she was the best at what she did, how she accomplished more than her coworkers, and how funny and smart people thought she was, and how much she was liked. She appeared to overvalue her own accomplishments and contributions and undervalued the contributions of others. During the psychosocial assessment, Kimberly shared that she was raised by an overbearing father and an indulgent mother, who passed away when she was a teenager. Kimberly shared that throughout her childhood, particularly after her mother's death, she was quite rebellious. She used drugs, drank alcohol, and shoplifted consistently. When asked how she felt when she shoplifted, Kimberly stated that it was "thrilling." At no point did Kimberly appear to consider the negative consequences of her behavior or the impact her delinquency had on others. Rather, it appeared as though she felt entitled to take what she wanted, and responded with anger when she was punished, justifying her behavior by asserting that "others did it all the time." These feelings that she was received unfair treatment impacted her ability to develop deep and authentic friendships and created significant challenges in her relationship with her partner, whom she felt didn't pay enough attention to her and didn't recognize her special worth. What was clinically remarkable about Kimberly's case was that she experienced difficulty in virtually all domains of her life—within family, friends, and work domains. Additionally, she experienced challenges to such an extent that she had difficulty managing her daily relationships and responsibilities.

THE HISTORY OF MENTAL HEALTH TREATMENT IN THE UNITED STATES

Every society has mentally ill members whose behaviors are considered outside what is normal and appropriate. Each society has also developed ways to manage such individuals so that healthy societal functioning is not disrupted. But because the criteria for what is considered *normal behavior* changes from era to era, as well as from culture to culture, it is important to keep cultural mores and generational issues in mind when characterizing someone's behavior as abnormal or unhealthy.

It is important to have some understanding of the historic treatment of the severely mentally ill in order to understand the current climate with regard to perceptions of mental illness, as well as treatment paradigms commonly used in the United States. It has been said that the measure of a truly civil, ethical, and compassionate society is reflected in how it treats its most vulnerable members. The mentally ill, particularly the severely and chronically mentally ill, certainly fall into this category, and if this statement is in fact true, then U.S. society has undoubtedly gone through some periods that were uncivilized, unethical, and compassionless.

Early in human history, mental illness, or *madness* as it was often called, was commonly believed to be caused by demonic possession. Skulls dating back to at least 5000 BCE were found with small drilled holes, assumed to allow the indwelling demons to escape. Demonic possession and witchcraft were still thought to be the cause of insanity and "lunacy" throughout the Middle Ages and well into the 17th and 18th centuries. A common cure for madness in the Middle Ages involved capturing those suspected of being witches or demon-possessed and tying them up with a rope and lowering them into freezing cold water. If they floated, they were believed to be witches and were then killed in some horrible way. If they sunk, they were not deemed witches, but the cold water was believed to be a cure for madness, so either way the problem of insanity was resolved (Porter, 2002).

During colonial times, the problem of the insane and "feebleminded" was considered a family matter, but as populations in the cities grew, those suffering from some form of mental illness increasingly became a problem for the community. Almshouses, typically used as poorhouses or workhouses for those unable or unwilling to find work on their own, were often used to house the mentally ill as well. By the mid-1700s many towns in Colonial America were following the trend in Europe of building separate almshouses and even specialized hospitals for those deemed insane (Torrey & Miller, 2002). Yet, reports of mistreatment were common. In fact, the trend of abuse of the mentally ill noted in the Middle Ages continued throughout the 19th century, where members of society whose behavior was not in line with social mores and the general expectations of society were subjected to public beatings, incarceration, and sometimes death, particularly if their strange behavior was perceived as threatening. Typical "treatment" in asylums, in almshouses, and even in the new state hospital system included, among other things, beatings with chains and rods. Chains were also used to contain patients in insane asylums—some for most of their lives (Torrey & Miller, 2002).

By the early 18th century, mental health reform had begun, led in part by Philippe Pinel of France, who when appointed chief physician at a hospital for the incurably mentally insane was appalled at the barbaric conditions of the hospital. He found patients chained to walls, some for up to 40 years, and a system where community residents could pay an admission fee to see the "insane" patients as if they were animals in a zoo. Pinel is most remembered for his decision in 1792 to unchain up to 5,000 patients when he was chief physician at a Paris asylum for "incurably insane men." His decision marked the beginning of the era of "moral treatment" of the mentally ill. Pinel later became chief of another hospital in Paris, where he consistently pushed for reform for more compassionate care.

Social work's involvement in the practice of caring for the mentally ill was formally marked by the *aftercare movement* of the late 1800s and early 1900s. Aftercare, a social reform issue of the time, involved the short-term care of the formerly "insane" and "lunatics" (Vourlekis, Edinburg, & Knee, 1998). Aftercare was typically managed by private charitable societies that offered temporary assistance and housing for those coming out of the state asylum system. Social workers were on the forefront of this helping model, which was really before its time because this type of "continuum of care" was not a part of the psychological mainstream during that era. It wasn't long before aftercare programs were considered the sole domain of social workers, who were paid by the state, and ultimately by public or private hospitals. This program served as the foundation for the contemporary role of those in the social work field who provide both advocacy and direct service to those who suffer from mental illness.

Dorothea Dix, a U.S. social activist, was a leader in advocating for more compassionate treatment of the mentally ill in asylums. Her plea to the Massachusetts state legislature in 1843 poignantly described the deplorable conditions those with mental illness were forced to endure, including being held in cages by chains, often naked, beaten with rods, and whipped to ensure obedience. Dix pleaded for the legislators to intercede on behalf of society's most vulnerable members. Dix's efforts resulted in an improvement in the conditions of both hospitals and asylums (Torrey & Miller, 2002).

By the beginning of the 20th century, most of the almshouses and insane asylums had closed, and state mental institutions became the primary facilities housing the seriously mentally ill. Yet although institutionalized care was considered revolutionary, compassionate, and far better than the plight of the mentally ill in former generations, rampant abuses involving cruel treatment, neglect, and physical and emotional abuse were increasingly reported throughout the early 1900s.

The Deinstitutionalization of the Mentally Ill

Although horrible abuses in state and private mental hospitals were well documented through the mid-1900s, institutionalized care remained the primary method of treatment for the seriously mentally ill for another 50 years. The U.S. government's first legislative involvement in the care of the mentally ill occurred in 1946, when former president Harry Truman signed the National Mental Health Act. The signing of this act allowed for the creation of the National Institute of Mental Health (NIMH) (one of the first four institutes under the National Institutes of Health) in 1949.

In 1955 the Mental Health Study Act was passed, which directed the convening of the Joint Commission on Mental Health and Illness (under the auspices of the NIMH), charged with the responsibility of analyzing and assessing the needs of the country's mentally ill, as well as making recommendations for a more effective and comprehensive national approach to their treatment. The committee was composed of professionals in the mental health field, such as psychiatrists, psychologists, therapists, educators, and representatives from various professional agencies, including the American Academy of Neurology, American Academy of Pediatrics, American Psychological Association, National Association of Social Workers (NASW), and National Association for Mental Health.

In general, in addition to making recommendations for increasing funding for both research and training of professionals, the committee recommended transitioning from an institutionalized treatment model to an outpatient community mental health model, where patients were treated in the *least restricted environment* within the community. This report led to the creation of the Community Mental Health Centers (CMHC) Act of 1963, which was passed under the Kennedy administration. This act enabled funding of a new national mental healthcare system focusing on prevention and community-based care, rather than on institutionalized custodial care (Feldman, 2003). The passage of the CMHC Act set the deinstitutionalization movement into motion, prompted by an overall dissatisfaction with public mental hospitals in general, the development of new psychotropic medications, and a new focus on the brain–behavior connection that fostered a sense of hope and optimism among those in the mental health field (Mowbray & Holter, 2002).

Several decades after President Kennedy described the CMHC program as a "bold new approach" to dealing with mental illness, many in the mental health field cite frustration and discouragement with what many perceive as numerous failures of the program. The replacement of hope with discouragement is in part

The mentally ill were often housed in inhumane conditions, sometimes restrained for extended periods of time.

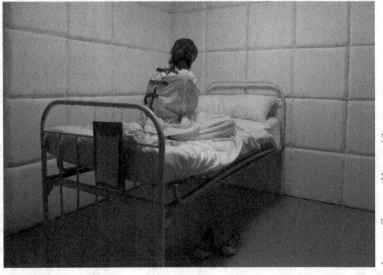

ALVARO GERMAN VILELA/SHUTTERSTOCK

due to the reality that mental illness has been a far more worthy opponent than early advocates suspected. Early proponents of deinstitutionalization had hoped that through early detection, increased research, psychotropic medication, and better intervention strategies, mental illness could be greatly reduced and perhaps even eliminated. Yet, mental illness remains a pervasive problem in today's society regardless of significant efforts to curb its devastating impact on individuals, families, and society. The most serious criticisms the deinstitutionalization movement are leveled at the federal government, which many claim fell short of funding commitments, resulting in far fewer community mental health centers being opened across the United States than was originally planned, which in turn resulted in the burden of care for the country's mentally ill shifting from the public mental hospital system to nursing homes, the streets, and the prison system (Sullivan, 1992).

Assess your comprehension of "The History of Mental Health Treatment in the United States" by completing this quiz.

COMMON MENTAL ILLNESSES AND PSYCHOSOCIAL ISSUES

It would be difficult to imagine social workers who do not at some point in their career come into contact with clients suffering from some form of mental illness. *Mental illness* is a term that, in its broadest sense, refers to a wide range of mental and emotional disorders, such as depression and anxiety disorders and, in its most narrow sense, refers to those individuals who suffer from severe and chronic mental illness, requiring at least intermittent custodial care. Because of the broadness of this term, it can be challenging to reach a consensus on just how many people suffer from mental illness in the United States at any one time.

A recently published report found that close to 27 percent of the U.S. adult population suffer from some diagnosable mental disorder, about 40 percent suffered from a mental illness of a moderate severity, and about 25 percent suffered from mental illness that was considered severe (SAMHSA, 2010). The term *severely mentally ill* typically refers to those individuals who suffer from schizophrenia, bipolar disorder, severe and recurrent depression, and other mental disorders that prevent normal functioning such as maintaining employment or performing activities of daily living. Individuals suffering from severe mental illness are often unable to consistently provide self-care, think clearly, reason, relate to others, and cope with the demands of daily life. Research has also shown that there is a correlation between poverty and mental illness (SAMHSA, 2010), which is important to remember when considering the complexity of mental illness, and how the mentally ill are treated within the United States and other places around the globe.

Social workers may encounter mental illness directly when clients seek therapy for previously diagnosed disorders, or they may encounter mental illness indirectly when clients seek services from a social service agency for reasons unrelated to their mental health and symptoms of mental illness begin to surface in the midst of the counseling relationship. Whether clients present with prior diagnoses or have no previously identified mental health issues, practitioners must be able to recognize the common signs and symptoms of mental illness in their clients.

In the United States, individuals are diagnosed using the *Diagnostic and Statistical Manual of Mental Disorders*, fourth edition, text revision (*DSM-V*), which categorizes mental disorders in a manner similar to physical disorders. Certain criteria must be met to diagnose someone with a particular mental or emotional disorder. It is important to remember, however, that mental and emotional disorders are diagnosed based on symptoms, not causes or etiology, as with medical illness.

Serious Mental Disorders Diagnosed on Axis I

Clinical or mental disorders are diagnosed on Axis I in 14 different categories. For instance, disorders such as anxiety disorders, eating disorders, mood disorders (depression and bipolar disorder), and substance-related disorders are all diagnosed on Axis I. Many clinical disorders are amenable to treatment through psychotherapy and psychotropic medication, but they are diagnosed on the first axis because they are serious enough to warrant clinical attention. Depending on the severity of their illness, these individuals might be in and out of inpatient psychiatric facilities, referred through the court system, or even living on the streets. It is important, then, that even entry-level social workers be generally familiar with these disorders so that their cases can be as effectively managed as possible and referred for appropriate services.

Psychotic Disorders

Psychotic disorders include a number of illnesses where contact with reality is severely impaired. Common symptoms of a psychotic disorder include hallucinations, delusions, and generally bizarre and eccentric behavior.

The most common psychotic disorder is *schizophrenia*, which is actually an umbrella term referencing what is theorized to be a number of disorders with similar symptoms, but with many different causes, such as genetic anomalies, brain chemistry disturbances, and brain damage. Recent research has even suggested that some forms of schizophrenia may be caused by exposure to the Borna virus (Terayama et al., 2003). Schizophrenia usually manifests during the teen and early adulthood years. It is important to note that schizophrenia is *not* a split personality, and that a diagnosis of schizophrenia does not automatically mean that someone will become violent (despite sensationalized media reports). Schizophrenia is not caused by a bad childhood, although stress and trauma can trigger a psychotic episode.

For more details, view the DSM-5 Schizophrenia Fact Sheet by going to the DSM website and searching in the "What's New" section.

The historic treatment methods used for schizophrenia consisted primarily of custodial care and heavy tranquilizers to minimize symptoms, particularly destructive ones. Antipsychotic medication has been available since the mid-1950s, but negative side effects of the medication, such as sexual impotence, tardive dyskinesia (involuntary jerking spasms of the muscles), and tranquilizing effects, kept many individuals with schizophrenia from taking their medication consistently. Yet new "atypical" antipsychotic drugs, such as risperidone, have shown great promise in significantly reducing schizophrenic symptoms such as hallucinations and delusions without nearly the number of side effects.

Affective Disorders

Affective disorders include disorders of one's mood and emotions and include depression and bipolar disorder. People who suffer from clinical depression, referred to in the *DSM-V* as major depressive disorder, often feel sad, anxious, empty, hopeless, irritable, guilty, worthless, helpless, and feeling chronically tired. Major depression also often involves sleep and eating disturbances, difficulty concentrating and remembering things, various somatic symptoms such as head and body aches, and may also include thoughts of suicide. Someone with clinical depression may experience all of these feelings or a combination of them (e.g., they may be feeling sad and guilty but not anxious, or they may be eating relatively normally but they can't sleep at night). In order for a diagnosis of clinical depression to be given, the *DSM-V* stipulates that the individual experience five or more of these symptoms for at least a two-week period (APA, 2013). Depression is quickly becoming one of the most significant disorders affecting the population, and it tends to co-occur with many other disorders and social conditions, such as poverty (SAMHSA, 2010). In fact, the World Health Organization has projected that depression will continue to be widespread globally, becoming a leading cause of disability by 2020 (Michaud, Murray, & Bloom, 2001).

References to depression date back to the beginning of recorded time. Hippocrates wrote about melancholy in the 4th century, citing an imbalance in the body's "humors" or liquids (blood, bile, phlegm, and black bile) as the cause of melancholy. Everyone feels sad at times, and grieving over a loss is perfectly normal and in fact healthy, despite the pain and discomfort involved. A productive depression can motivate people to change both themselves and their circumstances, where complacency might otherwise keep someone in an unhealthy situation. But debilitating depression is rarely productive and can leave people feeling ashamed, particularly in a productivity-oriented society such as the United States. Such shame and guilt just serves to add an increased burden to the depressed person, exacerbating depressive symptoms and often leading to a downward emotional spiral.

A popular theory of depression is Aaron Beck's cognitive theory of depression, which hypothesizes that depression is related to negative or irrational thinking. Thoughts such as "I'm a horrible person" or "Nothing good will ever happen to me," "I will always fail" if thought consistently enough can ultimately lead to feelings of sadness, despair, and hopelessness (Beck, 1964). Another popular theory, particularly with social workers, is a social-contextual model of depression in which environmental conditions such as negative life events, racial discrimination, and poverty impacting an individual is believed to contribute to depression, particularly if the depressed individual does not have the coping skills to deal with them in a positive manner (Swindle, Cronkite, & Moos, 1989).

In the last several decades, a biological model of depression has emerged in which a predisposition to depression is believed to be genetically related, and depressive symptoms are believed to be caused by neurohormonal irregularities, such as problems with neurotransmitter functioning. Most social workers embrace a biopsychosocial model of depression that recognizes the biological basis of depression, the emotional nature of depression, and the impact that one's environment, including factors such as an abusive childhood, and even social oppression, can have on depression.

Because depression often co-occurs with other disorders, such as anxiety, eating disorders, substance abuse disorders, and even psychotic disorders, it is essential that all social workers involved in direct service, including case management be able to screen for depression, even if a client is not seeking services for this purpose.

Serious Mental Disorders Diagnosed on Axis II

Axis II is reserved for personality disorders and mental retardation. Personality disorders differ from clinical disorders in many respects, but most notably, many clinicians believe that personality disorders can be resistant to treatment because many of the problems that individuals with personality disorders experience are, by definition, ingrained in their personalities, and thus authentic change is challenging because changing one's personality requires pervasive transformation and high personal motivation. Examples of personality disorders include antisocial personality disorder (sociopathy), borderline personality disorder, and narcissistic personality disorder. Kimberly, featured in the opening vignette at the beginning of this chapter exhibited many of the symptoms consistent with narcissistic personality disorder—including a grandiose sense of self-importance, a preoccupation with fantasies of unlimited success, a need of excessive admiration, a belief that she is unique and special, a tendency to exploit others, a lack of empathy, envy of others, and arrogant and haughty behavior.

Personality disorders include generally rigid and inflexible patterns of inner experience and outward behavior. Personality disorders often involve unhealthy and maladaptive patterns of perceiving things, difficulty controlling or regulating emotions, and difficulty controlling emotional impulses. Someone with a personality disorder will often perceive things differently than others and often misperceive another's behavior and intentions. Up to 30 percent of all individuals seeking mental health services have at least one personality disorder (Dingfelder, 2004).

But just because someone has personality traits that are irritating or somewhat eccentric, it does not mean that they have a personality disorder. One of my friends can be defensive if someone is criticizing her children. She often misperceives innocent comments as slights or criticism of her parenting. But does this mean that she has a personality disorder? Of course not. But what if her defensiveness was so intense that she started arguments constantly with friends and family members? What if she could not enjoy going out socially because all she could think about was protecting her children? What if she perceived insults everywhere and could not get along with anyone, including her children's teachers? This behavior might then push her in the direction of a personality disorder—a collection of maladaptive and rigid personality traits that are exhibited across different contexts and interfere with one's ability to function effectively in life, including interfering with one's ability to enjoy reasonably healthy relationships with others.

For instance, it might be perfectly normal for a woman to feel emotionally attacked whenever she gets into an argument with her husband if he has an attacking way of expressing his needs and frustrations. But it is not necessarily healthy or normative for a woman to feel emotionally attacked whenever she receives constructive feedback that she perceives as criticism from her husband, friends, family, coworkers, supervisor, teachers, and children. It also might be perfectly healthy for a man to consistently focus on himself in certain situations where perhaps he feels somewhat insecure, such as in large social environments. But it might not be considered healthy if he excessively focused on himself in virtually all areas of his life—at home, at work, with family, in social situations large and small, often at the expense of others.

The relative level of health or adaptive aspects of one's personality traits are evaluated on a continuum, like so many other mental and emotional conditions. If someone is a bit on the rigid side with certain issues, it wouldn't necessarily be appropriate to diagnose this person with a personality disorder. Yet, if someone gets far enough out on the continuum with regard to rigidity, for example, so that it interferes with an ability to function at work, with family, or with social situations, then this person might have what is considered a disordered personality. The key difference according to the *DSM-V* is that a personality disorder must cause distress and impairment of functioning in several important areas of functioning (APA, 2013).

The *DSM-V* categorizes personality disorders into three groups or clusters with three to four personality disorders in each cluster. Although all personality disorders share some factors in common, such as misperception, rigidity, pervasive problems in inter-personal relationships, and emotional regulation, each cluster of personality disorders varies considerably with both symptoms and cause. For instance, many of the Cluster A personality disorders, such as schizoid personality disorder, are strongly believed to be precursors of psychotic disorders. Obsessive compulsive personality disorder is also theorized to be at times obsessive compulsive disorder (a clinical disorder) in the early stages. Yet the Cluster B and C personality disorders such as borderline personality disor-der and dependent personality disorder are theorized to have strong biological influences but are believed to be related to abuse in childhood, particularly sexual and physical abuse (Bandelow et al., 2005).

Counseling individuals with personality disorders is often frustrating for practi-tioners because progress is slow, and clients are often resistant to change. Yet many new and promising counseling techniques are being developed, but progress is always slow because authentic change requires that clients actually alter the entire way they perceive

Assess your comprehension of "Common Mental Illnesses and Psychosocial Issues" by completing this quiz.

the world, and themselves within it. They must also learn how to *sit with their emotions* rather than act on them and to control their impulses rather than indulg-ing them. Thus, teaching self-discipline and restraint is a significant component of counseling most individuals with personality disorders. Antidepressant and antianxiety medication can help with the co-occurring depression and anxiety common with many personality disorders.

MENTAL HEALTH COUNSELING INTERVENTIONS

According to the NASW, social workers provide the majority of the mental health ser-vices in the United States, whether providing case management, counseling services, or advocacy on either a micro, mezzo or a macro level. Social workers work in a variety of practice settings including social service agencies; military and veterans services agen-cies; psychiatric inpatient or day treatment programs; police departments and criminal justice agencies, such as police departments, probation departments, and county pros-ecutor offices; hospitals and skilled nursing facilities; private practices; and community mental health centers.

Historically, social workers and other mental healthcare providers had somewhat of a love–hate relationship with providing direct service to the mentally ill. A century ago, social workers and other professionals in the mental health field tended to opt for practice settings with more functional clients so they could actually use their advanced

Engage, Assess, Intervene, and Evaluate With Individuals, Families, Groups, Organizations, and Communities

training, often not required with those needing only custodial care. Unfortunately, a survey conducted in 1985 revealed that social workers had similarly negative attitudes about working with the chronically mentally ill population (Mirabi, Weinman, & Magnetti, 1985).

Practice Behavior: Assess client strengths and limitations.

Critical Thinking Question: How does the strengths perspective influence how social workers might perceive their clients struggling with mental illness?

This trend might be changing, though, indicated by a more recent survey revealing more positive attitudes among students regarding working with the seriously mentally ill population. Also, a 2004 study of NASW members found that attitudes about working with the seriously mentally ill, among social workers with master's level training was improving, and a great majority of those queried expressed a strong commitment to working with a range of vulnerable populations, including the severely mentally ill. In fact, the primary frustration among social workers was not working with high-need clients, but rather working within a system that is fraught with treatment barriers and inconsistencies barring practitioners from providing the best service possible for their clients (Newhill & Korr, 2004).

A chief complaint of many in the social work field is the mental health community's general tendency to approach mental illness from a pathological perspective. This inclination to see human behavior in what often amounts to polarized terms of good and bad, acceptable and unacceptable, desirable and undesirable has only served to promote the social stigma of mental illness. Viewing mental illness through the lens of biology solely can also contribute to the tendency to pathologize the mentally ill where individuals are seen as sick and defective. So although the discovery that many forms of mental illness have biological roots can relieve the mentally ill and their family of unnecessary guilt, it also suggests limited potential on the part of the mentally ill, increasing the potential of both social stigma and social rejection (Sullivan, 1992).

An alternative approach to viewing mental illness is to use a *strengths perspective*, a model commonly used in the social work field. This theoretical perspective encourages the practitioner to recognize and promote a client's strengths, rather than focusing on deficits. A strengths perspective also presumes clients' ability to solve their own problems through the development of self-sufficiency and self-determination. Although there are several contributors to strengths-perspective research in the social work field, Saleebey (1996) has developed several principles for practitioners to follow that can help clients experience a sense of empowerment in their lives (see Box 7.1).

Sullivan (1992) was one of the first theorists to apply the strengths perspective to the area of chronic mental illness where clients suffering from mental illness are encouraged to recognize and develop their own personal strengths and abilities. Sullivan compared this approach to one often used when working with the physically challenged, where focusing on physical disabilities is replaced with focusing on and developing one's physical abilities. Sullivan claimed that by redefining the problem (rather than continuing to search for new solutions), by fully integrating the mentally challenged into society, and by focusing on strengths and abilities rather than solely on deficits, an environment can then be created that is more consistent with the early goals of mental health reformers who sought to remove treatment barriers by promoting respectful, compassionate, and comprehensive care of the mentally ill. Operating from a strengths

---

Box 7.1   Assumptions of the Strengths Perspective

According to saleebey, practitioners must recognize that all clients:

1. Have resources available to them, both within themselves and their communities;

2. Are members of the community and as such are entitled to respect and dignity;

3. Are resilient by nature and have the potential to grow and heal in the face of crisis and adversity;

4. Need to be in relationship with others to self-actualize; and

5. Have the right to their own perception of their problems, even if this perception isn't held by the practitioner.

Source: Saleebey, D. (1996). The strengths perspective in social work practice: Extensions and cautions. *Social work*, *41*(3), 296–305.

Pearson Education, Inc.

perspective is important, regardless of what intervention strategies a social worker uses in direct practice.

Social workers utilize many tools and interventions when working with clients struggling with mental illness. Some of these intervention strategies include *insight counseling*, where clients develop self-awareness skills intended to help them cope more effectively with their various mental health–related challenges. *Group counseling* assists mentally ill individuals with gaining strength and support from others in similar situations—some a few steps ahead of them and some a few steps behind. *Psychotropic medication*, based on recent brain research, offers many clients hope of controlling the often debilitating symptoms common to many serious mental illnesses.

Psychiatric rehabilitation focuses on skill building, where social workers help seriously mentally ill clients function to the best of their abilities within the community (Stromwall & Hurdle, 2003). Clients are empowered, as they develop skills giving them a sense of competence as they learn important skills enabling them to work and live within the community, interact appropriately with others, and provide necessary self-care. Skills development focuses on areas related to budgeting, parenting, social skills, stress management, time management, and symptom management. The skill level targeted is dependent on the functioning level of the client. Clients functioning at a higher level will develop higher level skills, such as learning effective parenting techniques, whereas clients functioning at a lower level might focus on more rudimentary skills, such as the importance of daily personal hygiene, including showering and brushing one's teeth. The guiding principles of psychiatric rehabilitation of personal empowerment and competence use the strengths perspective previously discussed by assisting clients to achieve their highest level of functioning on both a personal and social level.

> **Assess your comprehension of "Mental Health Counseling Interventions" by completing this quiz.**

These are just a few of the wide range of intervention strategies that social workers use, and successful programs often utilize all these strategies in combination with case management services. Providing a variety of services for mentally ill clients addresses not only the wide range of issues often confronted by such clients but also effectively manages the cyclical nature of serious mental illness because the continuum of services can be adapted to fit the needs of the client at any given time.

Social Work, Social Media, and Technology

The Internet has changed the way that social work is practiced. For instance, electronic therapy, frequently referred to as e-therapy, has increased in popularity, particularly in the last several years, as discussed in a recent CNN article entitled "Therapy Online? Good as Face to Face?" In response to this growing trend, the NASW in partnership with the Association of Social Work Boards (ASWB) published Standards for Technology and Social Work Practice with the goal of addressing the quality of technology-related social work services, including providing guidance to social workers who incorporate technology into their practice. The standards include important topics such as ethical practice (e.g.,

Can confidentiality be assured on the Internet?) and technical competencies. An organization referenced in the standards is the International Society for Mental Health Online (ISMHO), which promotes responsible and ethical "mental health in a digital age" for students, educators, and practitioners who are interested in integrating the Internet into their practice. After reviewing these articles and online documents, identify ways in which you believe the Internet could enhance your own social work practice working with a particular target population and social problem, identifying possible benefits and risks.

CLINICAL DIAGNOSES

Most licensed social workers use the *Diagnostic and Statistical Manual of Mental Disorders*, (*DSM-V*), to diagnose the mental and emotional disorders of their clients. The *DSM-V* is a classification system developed by the American Psychiatric Association (2013) and is in its fifth edition. As mentioned previously in this chapter, the DSM-V includes criteria for mental and emotional disorders, such as schizophrenia, depressive disorders, and anxiety disorders, and personality disorders, such as narcissistic personality disorder and antisocial personality disorder (sociopathy). The *DSM-V* is a multiaxial diagnostic system, which means that individuals are diagnosed on five axes or five different areas of functioning.

Box 7.2   Explore: Criticisms of the DSM

Although the diagnostic criteria of the *DSM-IV-TR* and its predecessors relies significantly on professional peer consensus and review and is backed by a large body of research, many professionals in the social work field have concerns about the *DSM* because it applies the medical model to emotional disorders. This paradigm in many respects pathologizes what might just be a broader range of human thoughts and behaviors, which, in turn, tends to create a stigma for those who are experiencing emotional struggles. Consider someone who has recently been the victim of a violent crime. If he experiences mental flashbacks of the traumatic event, is he exhibiting behaviors that are adaptive and expected? Or, in the alternative, is he suffering from post-traumatic stress disorder (PTSD)? Is the angry adolescent whose parents were just divorced exhibiting a normal grief response to this loss? Or does he have oppositional defiant disorder? Even if social workers do not naturally view human behavior from a disease perspective, using the *DSM* can influence practitioners to view their clients from a pathological perspective (Duffy, Gillig, Tureen, & Ybarra, 2002). Yet, even if one believes that the medical or disease model is appropriate to use when evaluating psychological disorders, an important distinction between the diagnostic system used to diagnose medical conditions and the system used to diagnose mental disorders is that the *DSM* uses criteria based on symptoms, whereas medical conditions are diagnosed based on the etiology (cause or origin) of the disorder. Thus, rather than diagnosing a patient with a stomachache, which could potentially have many causes, the medical diagnosis would be a virus, an ulcer, or cancer. Yet, when considering mental disorders, one is not diagnosed with a neurotransmitter disorder, negative thinking, or an abusive childhood but is diagnosed with major depressive disorder based on the symptoms the client is experiencing, not on etiology.

Other criticisms of the *DSM* include questioning the process that determines what behaviors are deemed abnormal enough to be included in the *DSM* and what behaviors are not, and whether it is appropriate to categorize human behavior at all, pathologizing alternative understandings of human behavior (Duffy et al., 2002). Consider how sexual orientation was at one time included in the DSM until societal attitudes shifted. Many practitioners have also expressed concerns about health insurance companies' reliance on the *DSM* for the diagnoses of mental disorders required for reimbursement, which can put both practitioner and client in a precarious position—the practitioner might feel compelled to diagnose a client to get paid and the client may have difficulty obtaining insurance coverage in the future if diagnosed with a serious mental health disorder. Yet, despite the criticisms of the *DSM*, it remains the most well-researched, collaborative classification system for mental pathology currently in existence and does provide a means for organizing various emotional problems and mental disorders.

Many social workers use the *DSM* but in general rely on it less than other mental health disciplines because the social work profession is based on empowerment theory, where clients are encouraged to recognize that they have more control over their lives than they may have previously thought. Self-determination is a related concept and refers to the rights of all individuals to make choices that they believe are in their own best interest. Self-determination can be empowering as clients realize that they have learned to have good judgment, which increases their sense of competency and self-reliance.

Pearson Education, Inc.

Clinical disorders requiring clinical attention, such as schizophrenia or depression, are diagnosed on Axis I. Personality disorders, such as borderline personality disorder and mental retardation, are diagnosed on Axis II. General medical conditions that might have an impact on one's mental health are diagnosed on Axis III. Psychosocial and environmental problems, such as problems with housing and employment, are diagnosed on Axis IV. Axis V is reserved for the client's global assessment of functioning (GAF). The GAF scale ranges from 0 to 100, with 0 indicating someone at a homicidal or suicidal level and 100 indicating a functioning level far higher than any of us will likely ever achieve. Although the assessment of one's GAF is somewhat subjective and arbitrary, the *DSM-V* contains a guide that assists practitioners in determining where their clients might fall in their overall functioning level. In general, individuals who are struggling in most areas of their lives and are in need of clinical intervention will be functioning somewhere in the range of 0–50 (see Box 7.2 for a different perspective on the DSM, including common criticisms).

Social workers working with the chronic and seriously mentally ill must manage several ethical considerations. Although most entry-level social workers will not be formally diagnosing clients using the *DSM-V*, unless they are licensed to engage in professional counseling, it is still important to be aware of the ethical challenges facing those social workers who do, as often social workers will be working within a multidisciplinary team, as well as with clients who have received one or more *DSM-V* diagnoses. Challenges in diagnosing clients abound, but many relate to conducting a thorough assessment of clients and diagnosing them accurately without "upcoding" (rendering a more serious diagnosis for insurance reimbursement purposes) (Kress, Hoffman, & Eriksen, 2010), diagnosing based upon the "trendy" disorders (e.g., not allowing pharmaceutical companies to drive diagnoses), or diagnosing based on a client's ability to pay. For instance, a recent research study found that counselors were more likely to render a *DSM-V* diagnosis to managed care clients than those who pay out of pocket (Lowe, Pomerantz, & Pettibone, 2007) reflecting a possible tendency to allow reimbursement for services to influence diagnosing patterns. Other ethical considerations include avoiding reductionist approaches to clients based on a client's diagnoses (e.g., "my borderline client," "my OCD client"), and avoiding assessing, diagnosing, and treating clients in ways that emanate from personal bias related to gender, income level, education level, sexual orientation, ethnicity, or immigration status.

Assess your comprehension of "Clinical Diagnoses" by completing this quiz.

COMMON MENTAL HEALTH PRACTICE SETTINGS

Social workers working with the mentally ill population do so in a variety of practice settings, including outpatient mental health clinics, not-for-profit agencies, outreach programs, job training agencies, housing assistance programs, prisoner assistance programs, government agencies—such as departments of mental health and human services—and probation programs. Social workers might work as case managers responsible for conducting needs assessments and coordinating the mental health care of clients, they might be providing psychotherapy services on an individual and/or group basis, or they may provide more concrete services such as job training. In truth, a social worker will likely encounter clients with serious mental illnesses in just about any practice setting, but in this section I will focus on those settings where the seriously and chronically mentally ill is the target population.

Community mental health centers provide direct services to the seriously and chronically mentally ill population. They are typically licensed by the state and designated to serve a certain catchment area within the community. Services offered often include out-patient services for adults and children, 24-hour crisis intervention, case management services, community support, psychiatric services, alcohol and drug treatment, psycho-logical evaluations, and various educational workshops. They might also offer partial hospitalization and day treatment programs. Although most community mental health centers operate on a sliding scale, they cannot turn away clients who have no ability to pay, and thus they are highly reliant on public funding.

Another practice setting that often encounters the seriously and chronically mentally ill is the *full-service social service agency*. It is difficult to define *social service agencies* because there exists such a range in nature and type, but a full-service social service agency essen-tially is a not-for-profit organization, meaning that the agency is tax-exempt, any financial profits must be reinvested in the agency. This distinction also means that the agency is exempt from paying state and federal taxes, allowing more money to be directed back into the agency. Social service agencies typically offer an array of services aimed at var-ious target populations, including the seriously mentally ill. The agency might provide general counseling services or might target more specific services, such as providing job skills training, housing assistance, or substance abuse counseling.

A social worker might work in a number of capacities within a social service agency, depending in large part on what types of programs the agency offers. For instance, a social worker might offer general case management services coordinating all the care the client is receiving and act as the point person for the psychologist, psychiatrist, and any other service providers involved. They might provide direct counseling services or run support groups focusing on a number of psychosocial and daily life issues. If the agency provides outreach services, the social worker might be out in the community providing emergency crisis intervention services for the local police department or other emer-gency personnel. Obviously, the list of program services is almost endless, particularly because a part of the role of the social worker and agency is to identify needs within a community and fulfill those needs if not otherwise met.

An alternative to inpatient hospitalization is *partial hospitalization* or *day treatment programs*. These programs, often operated within a hospital setting, are intensive and offer services for individuals who are having difficulty coping in their daily lives but are not at a point where inpatient hospitalization is a necessity. Clients attend the pro-gram five days a week, for approximately seven hours a day, and typically work with a multidisciplinary team of professionals, including a psychiatrist, psychologist, and social worker. Family involvement is highly encouraged.

Certain partial hospitalization programs narrowly focus on specific issues, such as eating disorders, self-abuse, or substance abuse, whereas others focus on a wider range of clinical issues such as severe depression, anger management, and past abuse issues. The nature of the program will also vary depending on whether the target population is adults, adolescents, or children. These structured programs can either serve as an alterna-tive intervention to inpatient hospitalization or they can be utilized in the transition from inpatient hospitalization.

Although the deinstitutionalization of the mentally ill has resulted in a dramatic reduction in long-term hospitalization of the severely mentally ill, some individuals who are acutely disturbed or suicidal are hospitalized on a short-term basis for diagnostic assess-ment and stabilizing in inpatient or *acute psychiatric hospitals*. Psychiatric units are typically locked for the safety of the patients who are often either actively psychotic or a danger to themselves or others. Again, services are focused on assessment and stabilization with a focus on discharge planning. Licensed clinical social workers, counselors, and psychologists often provide counseling, case management and discharge planning services in inpatient settings providing adult services and will likely provide more intensive counseling services such as facilitating individual and group counseling, as well as behavioral management if the program is focused on children and adolescents.

Another successful practice setting based on a social work model of empowerment is called the *clubhouse model program*. Clubhouses were first developed in the mid-1950s but have gained in popularity since deinstitutionalization. This model of service delivery has been compared with the settlement house model of a century ago, where clients struggling with mental illness are called members, not patients, and meeting the needs of the whole person is seen as the key to recovery. At the foundation of the clubhouse model is a philosophy based on the tenets of mutual respect and personal empowerment, as well as a focus on accepting responsibility, and a recognition of the members' strengths and abilities.

Read more about the Clubhouse Model by searching on the Internet for "Clubhouse Model— Clubhouse International"

Clubhouses are designed to provide a sense of community to mentally ill members who are valued for their personhood and are not defined by their mental illness. Services are coordinated through clubhouse staff, and members are responsible for contributing to the overall function of the clubhouse. Clubhouses are open at least five days a week, during normal business hours, and members who are not working outside the clubhouse are given transitional employment within the clubhouse, and thus they feel both productive and valued because they have a place to go every day, where they have valuable work waiting for them. Other services include basic tutoring, including high school equivalency courses, counseling referrals, general advocacy, employment placement, and transitional housing. Members and staff prepare meals together, clean together, and work as a team in ensuring that all clubhouse services and activities run smoothly, including reaching out to new members.

One of the most important values members gain at a clubhouse setting is a sense of social connectedness and cohesion. Each member has assigned responsibilities, which allows them to feel valued and needed. Clubhouses also have reciprocal agreements with various organizations and businesses in the community to assist members in obtaining work, shelter, and other needed services and activities (Jackson, Purnell, Anderson, & Sheafor, 1996).

The clubhouse model is used as an alternative to day treatment programs and partial hospitalization programs, which became popular once long-term hospitalization was phased out after deinstitutionalization. Social workers make ideal staff members in clubhouses because of the emphasis on generalist skills, client participation and empowerment, and a philosophy that embraces the ecological perspective, attending to the individual, the community, and the larger society, and understanding how all these levels work together to affect the client. Social workers working in a clubhouse setting are able to consistently engage client members, promoting their strengths and values, both within the clubhouse and within the community, providing both counseling and case management by acting as a liaison with community partners and clients, and most importantly, creating a homelike atmosphere for individuals who often have little or no other family or place to call home.

Assess your comprehension of "Common Mental Health Practice Settings" by completing this quiz.

MENTAL ILLNESS AND SPECIAL POPULATIONS

Certain populations are at increased risk of mental illness, either because of biological predisposition or because they are a member of an at-risk group. For instance, certain populations are at increased risk because of chronic and intergenerational stress related to poverty and homelessness. Some of these populations warranting special attention are explored in this section, including ethnic minority populations, the military, the homeless and prisoners.

Ethnic Minority Populations

Early studies have shown that ethnic minority populations are often poorly served in mental health centers because of a lack of culturally competent counselors and bilingual counselors, as well as other factors (Sue, 1977). Other early studies showed that whereas those in the Latino and Asian populations were underrepresented in community mental health center settings, those within the African American and Native American populations were overrepresented (Sue & McKinney, 1975; Diala, Muntaner, Walrath, Nickerson, LaVeist, & Leaf, 2001). This pattern may be partly due to cultural acceptance or rejection of psychotherapy within different cultural groups, and it might also be related to the relative complexity of issues facing the populations served, particularly Native Americans, who traditionally have high rates of substance abuse and depression and often reside in remote areas.

A 1997 study found that African American caregivers of mentally ill individuals face a number of barriers, making it difficult for them to be involved in their family member's treatment, including a failure on the part of practitioners to recognize them as an integral part of the treatment team. Mental health practitioners need to partner with the family members of mentally ill clients and keep an open line of communication so that family caregivers do not feel marginalized in the treatment process. The authors of the study suggested that by working hard to engage family caregivers in treatment, common negative assumptions of family members of African American clients can be countered and overcome (Biegel, Johnsen, & Shafran, 1997).

Mental health providers and social justice advocates have increasingly expressed concerns about the impact of anti-immigration policies on the Latino community, particularly with regard to the additional stress such as legislation and the associated *xenophobia* (an irrational fear of immigrants or those presumed to be foreigners) that can affect the immigrant community (Ayon, Marsiglia, & Bermudez-Parsai, 2010). A recent study of Latino youth and their families in the Southwest, which has higher levels of anti-immigrant policies and attitudes, showed that the majority of the Latino youth and parents surveyed had experienced significant discrimination related to their ethnic backgrounds, and immigrant status, even if they were born in the United States. Yet, their strong ties to family (immediate and extended) and their communities (referred to as *familismo*) seemed to counter some of the effects of discrimination (Ayon, Marsiglia, & Bermudez-Parsai, 2010). Mental health providers, including social workers who embrace Euro-American values of individualism, could potentially view the cultural tradition of *familismo* as something negative rather than as a cultural strength that can serve as protection from the negative effects of discrimination and xenophobia.

It is important that social workers be aware of their negative biases, whether they are toward people of color, sexual orientation, or socioeconomic status. Most people, particularly within the majority culture, deny having negative or stereotypical biases against cultures different than their own, because few want to be characterized as racist, homophobic, or elitist, but all individuals possess some negative biases, and if not directly confronted both through personal awareness and in clinical supervision within their agency, even subtle biases will unfold within the counseling relationship. Racial bias can influence many factors associated with mental healthcare and counseling. For instance, a relatively recent study found that African Americans were far more likely to be diagnosed with disruptive behavioral disorders in mental health counseling compared with Caucasians who were far more likely to be diagnosed with less serious clinical disorders, such as adjustment disorder (Feisthamel & Schwartz, 2009). Racially disproportionate clinical diagnostic assessment not only may be due to personal racial biases on the part of social workers but may also be due to counselors not taking into consideration the disproportionate challenges facing many ethnic minorities, such as increased levels of poverty, racial oppression, and higher rates of unemployment compared with Caucasians in America (Feisthamel & Schwartz, 2009).

Other types of bias can enter the counseling relationship as well. Consider the bias that many in the United States (particularly Euro-Americans) have about time. The U.S. culture tends to highly value time and promptness. When someone is punctual, they are often considered to be respectful, considerate of others, and organized. Conversely, those who are consistently late are often presumed to be disrespectful, inconsiderate of others, disorganized, and perhaps even lazy. Yet not all cultures value time in the same manner, and a stereotyped bias is that individuals from certain cultures (e.g., Latino and East Indian cultures) are lazy, disrespectful, and disorganized. Social workers who have been acculturated in U.S. values might not even realize that they hold this stereotype and might unconsciously attribute negative traits to clients who consistently show up late to their appointments. Thus, although it might be worth exploring whether this pattern is related to lacking motivation, it may be racist to make negative assumptions about a client's character based solely on the fact that the client is from a culture that does not value time in the same manner as those embracing U.S. values.

Hence, although rarely is someone eager to admit holding negative stereotypes about certain races, cultures, or lifestyles, it is imperative, particularly when working with the seriously mentally ill population, that these negative stereotypes are explored, challenged, and discarded. Otherwise they will remain powerful forces in how social workers subtly or overtly evaluate and assess client actions and motivations, strengths, and deficits, including assessing accountability and causation for a client's life circumstances.

Military Personnel

A relatively recent phenomenon within the armed services involves a dramatic spike in mental health disorders, including suicide, among military personnel—both within service members who have been deployed to combat zones, as well as those deployed within the United States. Suicides among military personnel (active duty and post-enlistment) have skyrocketed in recent years, particularly between 2007 through 2009 (during the Iraqi and Afghanistan conflicts). In fact, despite efforts to confront this epidemic, in 2012 the number of military suicides outpaced the number of soldiers killed in combat (Briggs, 2013), and the mental health community is scrambling to figure out why, and also to find viable and enduring solutions to this mental health crisis. Not only have these wars been protracted, they have been extremely violent, involving unprecedented re-deployments and longer-than-average deployment times. Soldiers are returning home with a range of mental, physical, and psychosocial challenges, including traumatic brain injuries, stress-related disorders, such as PTSD and

Engage, Assess, Intervene, and Evaluate With Individuals, Families, Groups, Organizations, and Communities

Practice Behavior: Implement prevention interventions that enhance client capacities.

Critical Thinking Question: What are some ideas you have on prevention programs targeting military and veteran populations?

Social Work Application Activity

On March 11, 2012, U.S. Army Staff Sgt. Robert Bales, staff sergeant who was serving his fourth combat deployment since enlisting in the Army in November 2001, shortly after the 9/11 terrorist attacks, opened fire on 17 innocent Afghani civilians, primarily women and children. The Kandahar Province massacres were committed in the middle of the night, solely by Sgt. Bales, following a night of drinking with his buddies. The married father of two from Washington described in court how he brutally attacked victims in two villages by gunning them down and then stacking some like firewood and setting them on fire. This incident is certainly disturbing (to say the least), but what is almost equally disturbing is what Sgt. Bales's defense attorney described as a normal family man turned homicidal maniac, because of the horrific stress endured on the battle field—four combat deployments in high violence combat zones; two injuries, one including traumatic brain injury (TBI); exposure to high levels of violence and trauma, including numerous roadside bombings and carrying dead bodies, some burned beyond recognition, off the battle field; coupled with excessive drinking to relieve stress and the regular consumption Valium

and steroids allegedly supplied by his superiors. Fellow soldiers described Sgt. Bales as "competent and positive." His wife described him as a wonderful husband and father. But when he returned from each of his tours, he described how his depression and anger worsened, how his drinking and misuse of sleeping pills increased, and how ineffective counseling caused him to withdraw from family and friends even more. In court Sgt. Bales stated that while he could not explain the murders, he believed he just snapped because he could no longer manage his mounting anger and stress resulting from the trauma he had endured from multiple deployments. Brown, his defense attorney, described Sgt. Bales as "crazed and broken" the night of the attack—"He's broken, and we broke him" (Johnson, 2013).

The NASW Standards for Social Work Practice with Service Members, Veterans & Their Family Members (available on the NASW website) is a resource for social workers working with this population in direct service or engaging in policy and/or advocacy practice. After reviewing the Standards, list at least three ways that the Standards could have guided a social worker working with Sgt. Bales that could have potentially prevented this crisis.

"combat stress," intimate partner violence, substance abuse, trauma resulting from sexual abuse and assault, and readjustment issues, and often return to face lacking support, including insufficient (and stigmatized) mental health services, financial difficulties and challenges finding employment.

Mental health problems, such as PTSD, depression, explosive disorders, and substance abuse have long been associated with military service and are prevalent among the veteran population. There has been increased attention on the mental health of military personnel recently because of several high profile cases involving homicide, suicide, and domestic violence. Research on the impact of trauma on military personnel and their families focuses on answering important questions about the causes, nature, and extent of mental illness in military personnel. For instance, was Sgt. Bales's murderous rampage (see Social Work Application Activity above) a result of long-standing homicidal tendencies rooted in childhood or adolescence? Or was it brought on solely by the stress of multiple deployments and untreated PTDS and a TBI? What were the warning signs, if any that Bales was struggling beyond his ability to cope? What structures did the Army have in place to deal with Bales's deteriorating mental health status?

In response to the recent spike in mental health disorders and suicides among service members, the Army, in cooperation with the National Institutes of Mental Health, has initiated the largest research study of military service members and veterans ever commissioned. The study is called the Army Study to Assess Risk and Resilience in Service members (STARRS).

After watching the film "Update on Virtual Patient Avatar for Military Social Work" located on YouTube, describe whether you believe that this type of technology would be helpful to you as a social work student, particularly if you were entering the field of military social work. (https://www.youtube.com/watch?v=20lE7PeAYoc)

Learn more about the STARRS – a series of longitudinal studies exploring the mental health, risk, and resilience of U.S. military personnel – by visiting the Army STARRS website.

STARRS consists of a series of studies categorized into five types, including:

- The Historical Administrative Data Study—Involves the examination of the administrative and health records of 1.6 million active duty soldiers between 2004 and 2009 looking for "risk and protective factors related to psychological resilience, mental health, risky behaviors, and suicide."
- The New Soldier Study—Involves the assessment of the "health, personal characteristics, and prior experiences of new Soldiers as they begin their Army service" through surveys, and health examinations, such as neurocognitive testing.
- The All Army Study—Involves the assessment of soldiers' psychological and physical health, by examining various events encountered by service members during "training, combat, and noncombat operations; and life and work experiences across all phases of Army service."
- The Soldier Health Outcomes Study—Involves two studies that compare service personnel who have experienced suicidal behavior with those who haven't. SHOS-A focuses on soldiers who attempted suicide and were admitted to a medical treatment facility. The goal of these studies is to "identify characteristics, events, experiences and exposures that predict negative (or positive) health and behavior outcomes"
- Special Studies—Involves the *Pre/Post Deployment Study*, which examines the effects of deployment to a combat zone with the goal of identifying risk factors for suicide and factors relating to psychological resiliency among service members who have faced combat.

According to three recently released STARR studies published in March of 2014, suicide rates more than doubled for soldiers who served in Iraq and Afghanistan between 2004 and 2009, but almost even more alarming was that soldiers who were not deployed, but remained in the United States nearly tripled (Schoenbaum et al, 2014). Additionally, most subjects who were diagnosed with post-deployment mental disorders (e.g., PTSD, anxiety, depression, attention-deficit-hyperactivity disorder [ADHD], anger management, and substance abuse), as well as those who experienced suicide ideation and suicide attempts, had a history of pre-enlistment mental disorders, most often rooted in childhood and adolescence (Kessler, Heeringa, & Stein, 2014; Nock, et al., 2014). These findings are vitally important because not only do they highlight the nature of the problems experienced by many current and former service members, (active duty, deployed, and veterans) but they also provide insights into ways in which the mental health community can better support recruits, soldiers, and veterans through better mental health screening, the development of prevention programs and treatment programs.

Social workers have long been members of multidisciplinary teams serving on military bases as both officers and civilian employees dating back to World War I, and are currently on the front lines (so to speak) in the development and facilitation of effective treatment programs to address contemporary issues facing soldiers and their family members. Social workers work within all branches of the armed forces (the Department of Defense, or DoD), as well as the U.S. Department of Veteran's Affairs (more commonly called the VA), and serve on emergency response teams that are deployed in times of crisis, such as violence on a base, or humanitarian and disaster relief. They also serve on military bases throughout the world working with soldiers and their families, as well as within VA hospitals and mental health facilities.

The NASW acknowledged the importance of social workers specializing in military social work through the recent development of advanced competencies for social work practice in military social work (NASW, 2010). These advanced competencies stipulate the nature of specialized course work and field experience, as well as defining military social work and its parameters. According to the NASW

> Military social work involves direct practice; policy and administrative activities; and advocacy including providing prevention, treatment, and rehabilitative services to service members, veterans, their families, and their communities (NASW, 2010).

There are approximately 22 MSW programs that now offer advanced course work, including certificates in military social work, focusing on training social workers in the areas of clinical practice with military personnel, veterans and their families, and understanding military culture. Fieldwork occurs on military bases, social service agencies serving the armed forces and veterans, and with branches of the DoD and VA. Probably one of the most innovative teaching tools is one used in University of Southern California's (USC) military social work training program called the Virtual Patient and Motivational Interviewing Learning Environment and Simulation (MILES). MILES uses avatars with voice recognition technology and human voice recordings to accurately portray real-life symptoms experienced by many military personnel, including PTSD and depression. Social work students can engage in simulated role-playing exercises using a therapy technique called *Motivational Interviewing* with an avatar in a way that is similar to working with a range of military-related dynamics, allowing social work students to practice their clinical skills.

Check out an article and a short video on the MILES avatar, by going to USC's website and searching for the article entitled: "Virtual Teaching Tool Schools Students in Helping Veterans."

Through innovations such as MILES, social workers can better learn how to be effective advocates and counselors as they provide much needed assistance to an underserved population struggling with a range of mental health issues.

The Homeless Population

Another special population among those disproportionately suffering from mental disorders are members of the homeless population (many of whom happen to be veterans). One unanticipated consequence of the deinstitutionalization of the mentally ill was the shifting of literally thousands of mentally ill patients from institutions to the streets. In fact, a 2005 study found that nearly one in six mentally ill individuals are homeless (Folsom, Hawthorne, & Lindamer, 2005). Such individuals would have previously been hospitalized, but with the closing of the majority of public mental hospitals and the transitioning of most psychiatric units to a focus on short-term stays, the severely mentally ill who do not have a network of supportive and able family members are often left with no place to live. Even individuals who do have supportive families will often live on the streets because of the nature of psychosis, which clouds judgment and impairs the ability to think without distortion, leading some individuals to disappear for literally years at a time.

This link between homelessness and mental illness is not solely related to deinstitutionalization. Certainly, warehousing the mentally ill kept them off the streets, but the nature of this connection is far more complex and likely reciprocal in nature, meaning that severe mental illness leaves many incapable of providing

Engage in Research-Informed Practice and Practice-Informed Research

Practice Behavior: Use research evidence to inform practice.

Critical Thinking Question: How would researching the relationship between mental illness and homelessness impact your approach if you were working with the homeless population?

for their basic needs, and the stressful nature of living on the streets, not knowing where one will lay their head at night, dealing with exposure to violence as well as inclement weather, and not knowing where their next meal will come from would put the healthiest of individuals at risk for developing some mental illness.

Government sources estimate that approximately 26 percent of the homeless population is severely mentally ill (U.S. Conference of Mayors, 2011), and if mental illness is broadened to include clinical depression and substance abuse disorders (often used to self-medicate), that percentage jumps to an astounding 50–80 percent, and this number is continuing to rise (North, Eyrich, Pollio, & Spitznagel, 2004; Shern et al., 2000). The mentally ill homeless population is a somewhat diverse group, but African American single men and veterans are most likely to be homeless and suffering from mental illness (Folsom et al., 2005; Koerber, 2005; Shern et al., 2000). Although deinstitutionalization is credited for being the primary cause of this increase in the homeless population, the increase in homelessness did not occur until the 1980s, and thus other issues are at play as well, including a shortage in affordable housing and again a lack of funding of housing assistance programs targeted to middle-aged men and veterans.

One of the biggest challenges in getting individuals with severe mental illness off the streets is engaging them in treatment. One of the problems noted after deinstitutionalization was the common difficulty of mentally ill individuals exercising their newly won right to refuse treatment. But a deeper look into this issue reveals that it may not be as simple as individuals in need not wanting help, but rather may be far more related to the difficulty and complexity of *accessing* needed services (Shern et al., 2000).

Barriers to accessing services often include difficulties in applying for government assistance such as Medicaid and Medicare to pay for both treatment and medication. Another barrier involves the actual service delivery model most popular in counseling and mental health centers, where the client comes into an office for services. History clearly reveals that this model simply does not work with seriously mentally ill individuals, particularly those living on the streets. Such individuals are often confused, disoriented, and frequently distrustful of others, particularly if they are suffering from some sort of paranoid disorder. To expect a person who is homeless and suffering from some mental illness to remember a weekly appointment and somehow figure out how to navigate transportation is clearly unrealistic.

Another barrier to seeking treatment involves the many stipulations and requirements common in standard treatment models used by many community mental health centers. Most standard mental health programs have strict participation requirements, particularly related to behavioral issues such as maintaining sobriety to remain in a housing assistance program, or program requirements such as requiring clients to participate in weekly counseling support groups to qualify for other services. In fact, most standard programs are directive with seriously mentally ill clients, often determining treatment goals and interventions for the client, rather than empowering clients to assist in determining their own treatment goals and interventions (Shern et al., 2000).

The treatment models commonly used within social work are far more successful in engaging the seriously mentally ill homeless population. This model involves the social worker going out into the community to meet the client in the client's environment. Thus, rather than sessions occurring in the comfort of the provider's office, they occur on park benches, or on curbs, or in homeless shelters. The value of this model lies not only in its practical approach to reaching psychologically unstable and marginalized clients, but in addition, clients are not as likely to be intimidated by entering an environment where they likely may feel they do not belong. Finally, social workers will undoubtedly learn more about the lives of their seriously mentally ill clients by spending time with them where they live.

A study conducted in 2000 tested a pilot program that differed significantly from standard mental health programs targeting the homeless mentally ill population. The experimental program called *Choices* offered comprehensive mental health services including (1) outreach and engagement of "street-dwelling" mentally ill individuals; (2) a Choices center that offered desirable services such as food and showers, as well as more structured services such as case management, mental health services, and rehabilitation services; (3) respite housing; and (4) in-community and on-site assistance in locating community-based housing.

The key differences between the experimental program and standard mental health programs were an extensive focus on outreach and community engagement, low-demand program requirements that increased client self-determination, and increased integration and streamlining of services because all programs were offered under the umbrella of the Choices program. The results of this study clearly indicate that participants in the Choices program were better served in all areas compared with the participants in traditional mental health programs. These results support the theory that rejection of services is likely not the primary reason why the homeless mentally ill population is underserved, but rather, issues related to barriers to accessing services, such as complicated coordination of services and programs with mandatory participation requirements and stipulations that might be unrealistic for the target population, are more likely to blame (Shern et al., 2000).

It is clear, then, that any program designed to engage the seriously mentally ill must include intensive case management that effectively engages clients and keeps them engaged, regardless of where they are in the cycle of their mental illness (e.g., stable, unstable, or actively psychotic). The issue of homelessness is always a relevant concern because the majority of seriously mentally ill individuals are at a high risk for homelessness. Empowering the client to feel they are an active part of treatment is also essential, as is making sure that all levels of service, particularly those offered by networking agencies, are sufficiently integrated so clients do not lose touch with service providers when transitioning from one level of treatment to another. For instance, close coordination between social workers from inpatient hospitals and outpatient programs will ensure that discharged patients are closely tracked and seen at a community-based outpatient center within days of being released from an inpatient setting.

The problem of homelessness among the mentally ill population will not be resolved until sufficient long-term housing assistance can be provided. Housing assistance programs typically have long waiting lists and often allow only women with children accelerated access to the program. Because African American men and veterans are overrepresented in the mentally ill homeless population, more programs need to be developed that target these populations most at risk for homelessness. Such programs must also be designed to address issues related to alcohol and substance abuse problems as well because many within the mentally ill homeless population have co-occurring substance abuse problems.

Prisoner Populations: The Criminalization of the Mentally Ill

Another unintended by-product of deinstitutionalization is what has effectively amounted to the inadvertent shifting of chronically mentally ill patients from public hospitals to jails and prisons. In fact, many mental health advocates have argued that prisons have now become one of the primary institutions warehousing the United States' most severely mentally ill individuals (Palermo, Smith, & Liska, 1991; Torrey, 1995). Thus, although this was never the intention of policy changers and proponents of deinstitutionalization, it appears that the United States has in many respects returned to the era where the mentally ill were locked away in almshouses.

Human Rights Watch (2006) reports that the number of imprisoned mentally ill in the United States has quadrupled in the last six years, from 283,000 prisoners in 1998 to over 1.25 million in 2006. In fact, it has recently been reported that there are more mentally ill individuals in prisons and jails than in hospitals. Further, approximately 40 percent of the mentally ill population will come into contact with the criminal justice system at some point in their lives (Torrey, Kennard, Eslinger, Lamb, & Pavle, 2010).

Women are particularly overrepresented in the prison population with approximately 31 percent of women in state prisons suffering from some form of serious mental illness (compared with about 14 percent for men) (Torrey, Kennard, Eslinger, Lamb, & Pavle, 2010). Most mentally ill prisoners are poor and were either undiagnosed prior to their incarceration or untreated in the months prior to entering the prison system. Mentally ill inmates were twice as likely to have a history of physical abuse and four times as likely to have been the victim of sexual abuse. In fact, almost 65 percent of mentally ill female inmates reported having been physically and/or sexually abused prior to going to prison (Ditton, 1999).

But what does this really mean? Could it simply mean that some mentally ill individuals break the law more than mentally healthy individuals? Couldn't it be argued that one must certainly be mentally ill to kill a string of women or one's entire family? After all, what sane person would do such a thing? Depending on how mental illness is defined, it could be argued that those who commit heinous crimes are by definition mentally ill, but their mental illness does not and should not negate the appropriateness of sending them to prison for their crimes. But even in situations where offenders clearly should be incarcerated, a retrospective look at their mental health histories might reveal a history of poor service utilization, treatment refusal, or an outright inability to access much needed mental health treatment.

While prisons have always held mentally ill prisoners, the number of incarcerated mentally ill has increased sharply, in large part because of a decrease in treatment options available for the mentally ill population in the general population. The reasons for this decrease include a reduction in funding of community mental health centers, barriers to accessing treatment for certain segments of the population, and increasing difficulty in involuntary hospitalization of the severely mentally ill (King, 2008).

The majority of incarcerated mentally ill have been convicted of nonviolent petty crimes related to their mental illness. In fact mentally ill individuals in prisons and jail are targets for violence, such as assault, robbery, and sexual assault (Marley & Buila, 2001). Far too often mentally ill prisoners, particularly those in the general prison population, are consistent targets of victimization, particularly sex-related crimes, many of which go unreported.

The incarceration of the mentally ill is not a simple problem, and thus it has no simple answers. Mental health and prison advocates cite barriers to accessing mental health services and problems with early intervention as direct causes of seriously mentally ill individuals ending up in the penal system, rather than in psychiatric facilities. Once again the controversial issue of an individual's right to refuse treatment is relevant in this matter as well evidenced by the many family members of the mentally ill who consistently complain that the courts have refused to order involuntary treatment, only to have their mentally ill family member commit a crime some time later. What is so unfortunate in these incidences is that the majority of mentally ill defendants are amenable to treatment, but many were not receiving any treatment at the time of their incarceration (Marley & Buila, 2001).

Mental Health Courts

Many steps are currently being taken by those in the criminal justice system and mental health and social work fields to address the issue of the incarceration of the mentally ill. The development of Mental Health Courts Program (MHCP) is an example of a significant step in the right direction. The MHCP was developed pursuant to the America's Law Enforcement and Mental Health Project (Pub. L. No. 106-515 passed in November 2000) and is administered under the Bureau of Justice Assistance (BJA), a component of the U.S. Department of Justice, in cooperation with the Substance Abuse & Mental Health Services Administration (SAMHSA).

The goal of the BJA is to encourage, lead, and fund the development of comprehensive programs run by criminal justice systems across the country that offer alternatives to incarceration as well as helping to avoid future court involvement.

MHCP goals include the following:

- Increased public safety for communities—by reducing criminal activity and lowering the high recidivism rates for people with mental illnesses who become involved in the criminal justice system
- Increased treatment engagement by participants—by brokering comprehensive services and supports, rewarding adherence to treatment plans, and sanctioning nonadherence
- Improved quality of life for participants—by ensuring that program participants are connected to needed community-based treatments, housing, and other services that encourage recovery
- More effective use of resources for sponsoring jurisdictions—by reducing repeated contacts between people with mental illnesses and the criminal justice system and by providing treatment in the community when appropriate, where it is more effective and less costly than in correctional institutions

Even though the goal is for all court jurisdictions to have a mental health court, as of 2007, only 175 mental health courts were in existence across the United States (Council of State Governments, 2008). But their numbers are growing, from only a handful in the 1990s, and preliminary research indicates that they are successfully diverting the mentally ill from jail to programs offering much needed services. One study researching one of the first mental health courts (located in Broward County, Florida) found that participants spent 75 percent less time in jail, received needed mental health services on a more frequent basis, and were less likely to commit a new crime, compared with mentally ill defendants who proceeded through the traditional court process (Christy, Poythress, Boothroyd, Petrila, & Mehra, 2005).

> Learn more about the Mental Health Courts Program by going online and searching the Internet for Bureau of Justice Affairs, and then going to the Programs section.

> Assess your comprehension of "Mental Illness and Special Populations" by completing this quiz.

CURRENT LEGISLATION AFFECTING ACCESS TO MENTAL HEALTH SERVICES AND MENTAL HEALTH PARITY

Some mental illnesses take a lifetime to develop. Others seem to hit out of nowhere, such as schizophrenia. Mental illness cuts across all socioeconomic, racial, and gender lines; in fact, one could say that mental illness is an "equal opportunity" affliction. I have worked with both the lower-income and undereducated population and the upper-income and highly educated population, and my only observation about the difference regarding these two groups is that oftentimes those on the upper end of the income/education continuums do a better job of hiding their mental illnesses and emotional disorders, at least for a time. For this reason, as well as the increasing evidence of the biological basis of many mental illnesses formerly believed to be solely psychological in nature, most mental health advocates argued the importance of requiring health insurance companies to cover mental health conditions in the same manner as they cover general medical conditions. Yet in the 1980s, when managed care became the norm in health insurance coverage, many advocates complained that managing costs became synonymous with limiting much-needed benefits, particularly in the area of mental health coverage.

Through bipartisan efforts, the Mental Health Parity Act was passed in 1996, which bars employee-sponsored group health insurance plans from limiting coverage for mental health benefits on a greater basis than for general medical or surgical benefits. This initial bill removed annual and lifetime dollar limits commonly used by insurance companies to limit mental health benefits. Unfortunately, the majority of health insurance companies found loopholes, allowing them to avoid complying with this legislation.

The Mental Health Parity and Addiction Equity Act of 2008 (sponsored by President Obama when he was a senator), which was attached to the 2008 federal bail-out legislation, promised significant reform of mental health parity in the United States. The act went into effect January 1, 2010, and required group health plans (covering 50 or more employees) that already provided medical and mental health coverage to provide mental health and substance abuse benefits at the same level as medical benefits are provided (i.e., it does not require employers to provide mental health and substance abuse coverage). Thus, if an employer-sponsored insurance plan offered mental health benefits, the benefits must be consistent with what is offered in the medical plan with regard to deductibles, co-pays, number of visits allowable per year, and so on. Although some exemptions existed in this act, it went a long way in securing parity of mental health and substance abuse benefit coverage (mental health parity was ultimately attached to the ACA of 2010, as referenced later in this section).

Former president George W. Bush announced the establishment of the *New Freedom Initiative*, designed to identify and remove barriers to community living for all individuals with mental disabilities and long-term mental illness. This initiative led to the formation of the Commission on Mental Health on April 29, 2002. The commission was charged with the responsibility of studying the mental health delivery system and making recommendations on ways for adults and children with serious mental illnesses to integrate into their communities as fully and as effectively as possible. Referring to the current system as offering a "piecemeal" approach to mental healthcare, the commission made recommendations for change based on the contention that people can recover from mental illness and are not destined to accept a life of long-term disability. The commission promised to transform mental healthcare in America by promoting access to educational and employment opportunities to individuals with mental disabilities, as well as promoting full access to community life (New Freedom Commission on Mental Health, 2003).

One of the chief complaints of the commission's report was that the current system did not offer much hope of recovery to those suffering from a mental illness. In addition, the commission noted that it sometimes took years for new treatment strategies discovered at research institutes to be used in clinical settings. Thus, although thousands of government dollars were being spent identifying new treatment modalities, those suffering from mental illness often did not benefit from these discoveries, because of many factors, including poor communication between research facilities and clinical settings. The commission then made several recommendations for removing barriers to treatment and lifting the stigma often associated with mental illness.

Ironically, the final report for the committee studying the CMHC program in 1963 had goals that were very similar in nature and just as admirable as the newer commission's goals, and the implementation of either commissions' goals did not unfold as anyone had hoped or planned. Former president Bush's administration did move forward on some of his commission's goals, including providing some assistance to states in developing a more effective mental health delivery system, as well as increasing the number of screening programs designed to increase early detection and treatment of serious mental illness. Yet, in the midst of these ambitious goals and promises of sweeping reforms, federal funding for mental health programs under former president Bush was significantly cut by billions of dollars over several years.

Perhaps one of the most significant federal laws to be passed in years is the Affordable Care Act (ACA), a comprehensive health care reform bill signed into law by President Obama in March of 2010. The ACA took effect incrementally between 2010 to 2014, and as referenced earlier, has and will continue to have an impact on behavioral and mental healthcare coverage. Overall this legislation is designed to make it easier for individuals and families to obtain quality health insurance, despite pre-existing conditions, and will make it more difficult for health insurance companies to deny coverage. It also incorporated mental health parity legislation, and expanded Medicare in a variety of ways, including bolstering community- and home-based services, as well as providing incentives for preventive, holistic, and wellness care. With respect to behavioral and mental healthcare, the ACA provides increased incentives for coordinated care, school-based care including mental healthcare and substance abuse treatment. Additionally, it includes provisions that require the inclusion of mental health and substance abuse coverage in benefits packages, including prescription drug coverage, and wellness and prevention services, incorporating earlier mental health parity legislation.

One of the most powerful ways that the federal government can influence policy and program development is through sufficient funding, and a chief complaint about the many failures of community-based mental healthcare programs is the lack of sufficient federal funding. Thus, the success or failure of any new federal legislation or program focusing on mental healthcare reform is dependent on broad-based government financial commitment. Some of the funding that was cut under the George W. Bush administration was reinstated under President Obama, and while the success of the ACA in many respects remains to be seen, advocates are hopeful that it will address many of the challenges faced by those struggling with mental illness, including attempts to get their holistic needs met.

Mental illness devastates the lives of individuals and their families, particularly those suffering with chronic and severe mental illness. Not only does it rob people of their dreams, their potential, and their ability to earn an income, but mental illness also devastates the families of those afflicted both emotionally and economically. Although current federal legislation requires health insurance companies to offer mental health coverage at comparable levels as physical health coverage, and although the ACA addresses mental illness, families are often faced with devastating financial challenges as they attempt to care for their loved ones. But families aren't the only entities that must endure the economic cost of mental illness. While it is challenging to pin down the economic impact of mental illness on society, the Agency for Health Care Research and Quality has estimated that in 2006 alone, the cost of providing mental healthcare in the United States approached $57.5 billion, about the same economic cost as treating cancer (Soni, 2009).

According to the Centers for Disease Control (CDC) (Reeves et al., 2011), public health experts are increasingly recognizing the significant impact of mental illness on society, including its economic impact. The cost of mental health treatment (which may require frequent hospitalizations and long-term residential care) is often quite high, and because of the debilitating nature of most mental illnesses, which often impacts an individual's ability to maintain consistent employment, a disproportionate number of the mentally ill do not have private healthcare insurance, and thus are dependent on the woefully inadequate U.S. public healthcare system. The ACA addresses some of these issues by significantly reducing uninsured rates and expanding Medicaid coverage for low-income adults, as well as requiring compliance with mental health parity (as of January 2014).

Some social workers might question the importance of understanding federal trends in funding programs designed to meet the needs of the mentally ill, yet virtually all social workers will be affected one way or another if state and federal budget cuts continue to be implemented. Attempting to facilitate much-needed mental health–related programs without proper funding can involve everything from understaffing and high caseloads to inadequate office space and the general inability to meet the comprehensive needs of the chronically mentally ill. Thus, although social workers involved in direct practice may prefer to steer clear from administrative and policy concerns, such involvement particularly on an advocacy level is important because the effective facilitation of vital mental health programs is dependent on effective legislation and appropriate funding.

> **Assess your comprehension of "Current Legislation Affecting Access to Mental Health Services and Mental Health Parity" by completing this quiz.**

Summary

Evaluating the full impact of mental illness on individuals as well as society is difficult, primarily because many mental illnesses are highly correlated with other conditions and dynamics, such as substance abuse and poverty. Consider that approximately 25 percent of the U.S. population suffers from some form of mental illness, and about half of the U.S. population will develop a mental illness at some point in their lifetime. This means that most families in the United States will be impacted by mental illness at some point in their lives. Mental illness is a significant public health concern, not only because of the debilitating nature of most mental illnesses, but also because of the economic cost of mental illness that amounts to almost $300 billion per year in the United States alone, due not only to the cost of healthcare, but also due to lost revenue of both the mentally ill, as well as those of family members who attempt to care for them (Reeves et al, 2011). Social and economic implications of mental illness are significant, particularly as many mental illnesses exacerbate existing physical health conditions, including the high rate of dual diagnosis—individuals struggling with substance abuse and coexisting mental illness—within the mentally ill population (estimated to be about 50 percent) (Drake, Mueser, & Brunette, 2007).

The field of mental health is a dynamic practice area for the social worker for many reasons. Social workers have the ability to make a significant impact while working with some of society's most vulnerable members. Because the concept of mental illness is so broad, encompassing such a wide array of psychological, emotional, and behavioral issues, the social worker works as a true generalist whether in a direct service capacity or whether providing advocacy within the community. The United States has experienced dramatic shifts in its mental health delivery system during the past 50 years and will no doubt continue to experience future changes, some intended and some unintended. Social workers are often on the front lines of these intended changes lobbying for increased funding, and developing new programs to meet the complex needs of the severely and chronically mentally ill population.

> **Recall what you learned in this chapter by completing the Chapter Review.**

Homelessness

I met Kendall when she was homeless and looking for permanent housing and attempting to put the pieces of her life together. Kendall was raised in an unstable and abusive home environment where she had been told repeatedly throughout her childhood that she was worthless and that no one would ever love her. Her every move was criticized and served as proof that she was no good. She had the natural need and desire to be loved and accepted, and by the time she was 17 this need peaked to a point that she could not resist the affections of an older man who promised her the world. Although she initially resisted his attempts to become sexually involved with her, he eventually convinced her that the only way he would know she loved him was if they had sex, and if she refused he would leave her. Kendall's immense insecurities and her deep need to be cared for made her vulnerable to his manipulative threats, and so she relented and agreed to become sexually involved with him, believing that she had finally found someone who truly loved and accepted her. Yet when she became pregnant, he became abusive and used many of the same abusive statements she had confided that her father had used to manipulate and control her. She believed that her father must have been right all along, because how else could she explain yet another man seeing such ugliness in her? Ultimately, he abandoned her and her unborn child, and when her father learned of her pregnancy he kicked her out of the house and refused to allow her to return.

For the next four years, she was intermittently homeless, finding temporary stability through various transitional housing programs that helped her secure employment and an apartment, but any crisis put her on the streets again, such as the time her son got chicken pox, resulting in her needing to stay home with him for two weeks. Kendall was fired even though she had medical verification of her son's illness. This led to yet another financial downward spiral and another episode of homelessness. By the time her son was five, he was acting out, considerably adding to her sense of frustration and burden. So when she met a new man who showered her with attention and compliments, all she could think of was that she had finally met the man of her dreams. He said all the right things, offered to let her and her son move in with him, and offered to manage every part of her life. He even told her that she would not have to work and could stay home with her son, and so she gladly quit her job and embraced being a stay-at-home mom at last—something she had wanted to do for years.

Kendall wanted desperately to believe this was real and accepted his seemingly generous offers because she believed that to do otherwise would mean robbing her son of his only opportunity for a real home and family. When her new boyfriend told her that she was the first woman he ever wanted to have a baby with, she was so flattered she agreed immediately to get pregnant. She believed with all her heart that she finally had it all, and that all the years of suffering were behind her.

Kendall became pregnant quickly and dreamed of her new life with her new boyfriend. Although she would have preferred they get married, he claimed to not be ready yet, and because she did not want to create waves in the relationship, she did not push the subject. She talked endlessly to her son about their good fortune in finding this man who was going to take care of them forever. When her new boyfriend hit her for the first time, she convinced herself that it was a one-time incident caused by the stress of having a new family. When she noticed that he drank too much alcohol and seemed impatient with her son, she convinced herself that he needed time to adjust to having an instant family. Then one day he did not come home from work, and when a few days had gone by and he still did not return with her car, she came to the agency where I worked asking for financial assistance because she had no money to pay for the rent due in a few short days.

Unfortunately, we learned that this man had a pattern of treating women in this way, and this was not the first time he had encouraged a single mom to depend on him only to flee when the good feelings ended. Equally unfortunate was the fact that she had absolutely no recourse against him, even for taking her car, because to make insurance matters easier, she had agreed to put his name on the title, a decision that seemed foolish now, but in light of all that he was offering her it seemed the least that she could do. Now she had no money; no job; no car; a devastated, hurt, and angry child; and a baby on the way; and she would be homeless again within the month.

Adding to her burden was the intense sense of humiliation she felt when she realized that she had once again been taken advantage of. She firmly believed that she deserved this treatment and argued that there must be something terribly defective about her because these things kept happening to her. She was devastated that she was so horribly abandoned in the wake of breathing her first sigh of relief in years. She was extremely depressed, which made her at risk for either inadvertently abusing her child or neglecting him in some way, particularly when he expressed anger at her for driving his new daddy away. And, her additional loss of self-esteem left her in no shape to problem solve by gaining employment, finding low-cost housing, and searching out assistance programs, most of which would require her to disclose her reasons for becoming homeless, forcing her to repeat her failures and leaving her vulnerable to the criticisms of others. Although she should have been hospitalized for severe depression and risk of suicide, she refused because it would mean placing her son in temporary foster care.

Ultimately, she managed to piece her life back together, and it was the security of an authentic counseling relationship that enabled her to resist getting into another whirlwind romance and allowed her to see that saying no to a man was not saying no to a secure future, but likely saying no to another abusive and exploitative relationship. Virtually all my guidance meant her acting in a counterintuitive manner. She was desperate for love and companionship, yet I cautioned her to resist getting into a relationship until she was out of crisis. She desperately wanted to avoid revisiting old wounds from her childhood, yet I encouraged her to delve into her early experiences drawing parallels with relationships in her adult life and helping her to see the patterns she seemed helpless to escape. It would be difficult to imagine my client developing the wisdom to respond to her psychological issues and her current life crisis without the benefit of the objective and unconditional support of a social worker trained to understand and respond to suffering from a social systems perspective—embracing, encouraging, supporting, and guiding in a nonjudgmental manner.

Although Kendall's life is complicated, it is not at all unique. Understanding the dynamics involved in intergenerational abuse and poverty helps one to understand how and why people repeatedly make what often turns out to be unhealthy choices that when combined with social and structural factors leave them vulnerable and at risk for severe poverty and homelessness. Thus, although it might be easy to sit in the comfort of one's stable and healthy home environment and criticize the immoral lifestyle of single mothers who jump from relationship to relationship getting pregnant along the way, once all the situational factors are known and someone takes the time to truly look at the world through the eyes of someone suffering and alone, it becomes far easier to understand how someone could make the choices my client did. One of the saddest assessments of humankind is that it seems as though for every vulnerable and hurting person, there is someone waiting to exploit him or her. Fortunately, there are just as many people waiting to lend them an accepting, nonjudgmental, and helping hand as well.

HISTORY OF HOMELESSNESS IN THE UNITED STATES

The types of people who have experienced homelessness and the reasons for their homelessness have changed significantly throughout the years. Prior to the Middle Ages (from about the 14th to the 17th century), the Catholic Church was primarily responsible for the care of the poor, including those without stable shelter. Most monasteries embraced this responsibility as one given by God. Thus, at least the "deserving poor" (those who were perceived to be poor through no fault of their own) were considered blessed, and it was considered a blessing to care for them (Duncan & Moore, 2003).

The Great Depression resulted in extremely high unemployment and homelessness.

ARCHIVE HOLDINGS INC. / ARCHIVE PHOTOS / GETTY IMAGES

Throughout the Middle Ages, the homeless population consisted primarily of the wandering poor—those individuals, most commonly men, who migrated for employment, either working someone's land or selling goods. The English poor laws (discussed in Chapter 2), which were adopted by many of the American colonies, included harsh measures for dealing with the poor and destitute, adding to the overall negative social stigma associated with poverty. For example, most communities enforced strict residency requirements designed to discourage the wandering poor from settling in more affluent districts to collect social welfare intended to serve longtime residents who had contributed to the community before falling on hard times. Policies against vagrancy, and even unemployment, are reflective of the overall negative sentiment held of the homeless and transient population in general, particularly when it could be assumed that one was homeless either through choice or some personal and moral failing.

Making distinctions between the deserving and undeserving poor was practiced throughout the Middle Ages (in fact, many argue that U.S. policy continues this practice even today). Under English poor laws, many of the undeserving poor and homeless were sent to work camps or almshouses, where they were forced to perform demeaning work for excessively long hours in what amounted to slave labor. This practice also continued to play into the overall stigma of poverty and homelessness by stripping the poor and destitute of their self-determination, their family, and their freedom. Even the "deserving poor" who received public assistance were often forced to wear badges or some marking signifying that they were receiving public assistance (Phelan, Link, Moore, & Stueve, 1997).

Throughout the 19th and early 20th centuries, the homeless population consisted primarily of men—either vagrants (men who were unemployed for a variety of reasons, including mental illness or alcoholism) or migrant workers, such as men who were making their way out West to work in the gold mines, the railroads, or the fields. Hobos, migrating laborers of European descent, were also counted among the homeless population and were treated with mistrust and contempt despite the fact that they were an integral part of the labor force throughout the 19th century (Axelson & Dail, 1988).

It was not until the Great Depression in the mid-1930s that families began to appear on the homeless scene in significant numbers. The failure of the financial markets, the closings of many banks, and rampant unemployment resulted in many families losing their homes and wandering the streets in search of sustenance and shelter. Because the Great Depression hit just about everyone in the United States, there was increased compassion for the homeless population and for those suffering from poverty in general. The Great Depression brought most people back to a time where people recognized and acknowledged that poverty and homelessness could be caused by circumstances beyond one's control. Thus, although the Protestant ethic, with its focus on hard work and frugality, and Social Darwinism, the philosophy that poorer members of society were weaker and must be selected out of the population, might have had many people believing that falling on hard times was a result of laziness, the Great Depression reminded everyone that sometimes, no matter how hard one works or is willing to work, circumstances could occur that may render someone destitute and impoverished. Unfortunately, this spirit of empathy and compassion for society's poor and homeless did not last much past the next economic boom.

Assess your comprehension of "History of Homelessness in the United States" by completing this quiz.

Apparently, a by-product of personal good fortune may be a reduction in one's ability to empathize with those less fortunate.

A SNAPSHOT OF HOMELESSNESS

To confront the problem of homelessness, it must first be determined who is homeless, and determining who is homeless begins with defining "homelessness," which is far more challenging than one might expect because of its complex and transient nature. For instance, is someone homeless only if they reside in a homeless shelter or live on the streets? What about people who live in their cars? Or people who "couch surf," "double up," or live in motels? What about those people who are at risk of becoming homeless, such as those who live with friends or relatives on a temporary basis?

Homeless definitions are important because they determine funding for service provision, as well as eligibility requirements. For instance, the McKinney-Vento Homeless Assistance Act of 1987—comprehensive federal legislation that provides funding for a range of shelter services (as well as stipulating provisions for educating homeless children)—defined homelessness in a rather narrow manner, prior to being reauthorized in 2009. In the older legislation, homelessness was defined as individuals or families who did not have a fixed, regular, or adequate nighttime residence and lived somewhere that was not designed for sleeping (such as a car or abandoned building), or lived in a supervised temporary shelter (including motels and hotels if paid for by local government programs) (42 U.S.C. § 11302, et seq., 1994). The problem with this definition according to homeless advocates is that it was outdated and did not reflect the changing nature of homelessness, including trends away from using traditional transitional shelters for fixed periods of times, and toward a more cyclical pattern of housing instability, where individuals and families experience bouts of homelessness, often residing with friends and relatives, outside of the formal housing assistance system. In fact, any contemporary definition of homelessness must include those individuals who experience homelessness on an intermittent basis, in an ongoing cycle of temporary or tenuous housing (joblessness, foreclosure, or renting a foreclosed on property), leading to eventual homelessness because of chronic economic instability, as well as highlighting the dramatic increase in homeless families and runaway and homeless youth.

More narrow definitions of homelessness result in an underestimation of the homeless population, which in turn results in lower federal and state spending on homeless services and the targeting of a narrower segment of the homeless population (e.g., those struggling with chronic homelessness seeking services in traditional shelters, or living on the streets). When homelessness is defined using the older federal definition, there were on average 610,042 individuals who experienced homelessness (sheltered and unsheltered) on any given night in the United States. (U.S. Department of Housing and Urban Development, 2013). If the definition is broadened to include the *hidden homeless*—those experiencing cyclical homelessness and living in nontraditional housing situations, such as with family with friends, national estimates of homelessness jump to between 2.5 and 3.5 million (National Alliance to End Homelessness, 2009; Urban Institute, 2010).

Under the Obama administration, the McKinney-Vento Act was reauthorized as the Homeless Emergency Assistance and Rapid Transition to Housing (HEARTH) Act, under the No Child Left Behind Act. Among many significant

After watching the film "Employed But Still Homeless, Working Poor Say 'Homelessness Can Happen to Anybody'" on YouTube, describe what surprised you about the film, particularly about the struggles those called "the working poor" experience. (https://www.youtube.com/watch?v=MdbHEZpoWPA)

changes to the act, the definition of homeless underwent a much-needed expansion to reflect changing demographics and dynamics, some of which were related to the 2007 housing foreclosure crisis (e.g., renters who were evicted when the homes they were renting went into foreclosure). The updated definition also includes those who are on the verge of losing their homes (whether rented or owned), those who live in homes without paying rent, live in shared homes because they were evicted and forced by court order to move out within 14 days, and those living in a hotel or motel but who cannot remain there for more than 14 days because of lack of resources (42 U.S.C. § 11302, et seq., 2009). In tenuous housing situations where an individual or family is outside of the formal housing assistance system, such as those cases where someone is living in another's house temporarily, the HEARTH Act requires "credible evidence" that they are only being housed for 14 days (or less) and has no means for obtaining permanent housing. The HEARTH Act also has an expanded focus on runaway and homeless youth (referred to as "unaccompanied youth") and homeless families with children and youth, defined as those who have experienced a "long-term period without living independently in permanent housing, a long-term period without living independently in permanent housing, persistent instability as measured by frequent moves over such period, and can be expected to continue in such status for an extended period of time because of chronic disabilities, chronic physical health or mental health conditions, substance addiction, histories of domestic violence or childhood abuse" (42 U.S.C. § 11302, et seq., 2009).

The HEARTH Act goes a long way in addressing deficits in the previous version of the act by now including many of the hidden homeless previously excluded under the former legislation, as well as capturing the tenuous housing situations experienced by individuals and families during times of economic recession. The Act also specifically addresses the growing problem of homelessness among families with children and unaccompanied youth. It also increases the focus on prevention of homelessness, by identifying risk factors that often lead to housing insecurity, such as domestic violence and child abuse. This is very important as according to recent research about half of all homeless single mothers surveyed had experienced child abuse, including child sexual abuse, during their childhoods, and almost all had experienced domestic violence at some point in their lives (National Law Center on Homelessness & Poverty, 2006). Thus, effective prevention programs need to focus on these risk factors as one way of addressing the underlying causes of homelessness and housing instability, and cutting mental health programs, including programs focusing on family violence, will likely lead to a continued increase in the number of homeless families.

Gauging the Scope of the Problem

Rates of homelessness in the United States have leveled off somewhat recently but continue to increase overall, particularly within larger urban communities. In fact, in the annual U.S. Conference of Mayors report (2013), 52 percent of cities reported an increase in the number of homeless people of about 3 percent. Although this is an improvement compared with prior years (homelessness increased almost 20 percent in 2012) (U.S. Conference of Mayors, 2013), homelessness remains a significant and complex problem with limited viable solutions on the horizon. Despite an overall improvement in the U.S. economy, the job market remains tight, which is significantly impacting people's ability to maintain adequate shelter. In fact, for the first time in years, unemployment leads the list of causes of homelessness, ahead of a lack of affordable housing and poverty (U.S. Conference of Mayors, 2013).

The rate of homelessness began to increase between 1970 and 1980 due in large part to a decrease in affordable housing and an increase in poverty (National Coalition for the Homeless, 2006; U.S. Conference of Mayors, 2013). The Great Recession of 2007 (also referred to as the global financial crisis) has exacerbated this trend of financial vulnerability (particularly in urban communities), when the bottom fell out of the mortgage market, the job market essentially collapsed, and many people lost their homes in a mass of foreclosures. As an indication of how hard families were hit financially in the wake of the Great Recession, cities across the country reported marked increases in requests for emergency shelter and food assistance (Supplemental Nutrition Assistance Program, or SNAP benefits) between 2008 through 2013. This is a particularly disconcerting trend in light of significant cuts in SNAP benefits currently being considered by Congress. The majority of U.S. city mayors expect the trend of homelessness to continue to increase and yet do not expect funding for services to keep pace.

Because of the methodological challenges involved in attempting to accurately count the homeless population, demographic studies often estimated homelessness using a methodology that relied on indirect counts obtained by surveying professionals working with the homeless population, rather than a direct headcount, which often resulted in underreporting. Just as a narrow definition of homelessness can lead to underfunding, poor demographic methodology that fails to capture the extent of the homeless problem also leads to underreporting, and as government grant money is often directly linked to census numbers, underreporting leads to less money, which in turn leads to fewer services. This is one reason why in 2004 Congress directed the Department of Housing and Urban Development (HUD) for the first time to collect comprehensive data on the homeless population in the United States using direct headcount methods. HUD responded to this mandate by developing the Housing Management Information System (HMIS), which provides a computerized method for collecting data on the use of shelter and transitional housing programs within each state. The annual reports, called *The Annual Homeless Assessment Report (AHAR) to Congress* include "point-in-time" counts of homeless persons as well as demographic characteristics of homeless individuals and homeless families. This reporting method still omits the hidden homeless, but direct head counts are a step forward in more accurately determining the extent of the homeless problem.

The 2013 AHAR revealed that on a single night 610,042 individuals were homeless nationwide (living both in shelters and on the streets) (again, it's important to note that as reflected earlier in this chapter, this number still reflects significant underreporting). The 2013 homeless estimate reflects a slight decline in the number of homeless compared with prior years, with a decrease in the people living on the streets (about 35 percent of all homeless people) compared with those living in shelters (about 65 percent). The report also revealed that approximately 64 percent of the homeless population consisted of individuals, and about one-third consisted of families (this is not surprising as families tend not to utilize traditional homeless shelters and tend to opt more for "couch surfing," "doubling up," or living in motels). The report also revealed that about one-quarter of all homeless people in 2013 were children, under the age of 18, and about 13 percent were unaccompanied and runaway youth, mostly between the ages of 18 and 24, who were unsheltered. About 50 percent of individuals were sheltered and about 48 percent were unsheltered, while most families (78 percent) were living in some type of other living arrangement on any given night. Overall, homelessness among families has declined about 11 percent since 2007.

The typical homeless person in 2013 was a solitary middle-aged man who was a member of an ethnic minority group. Over two-thirds of the homeless population has some type of disability, and about one-third suffer from chronic mental illness. There has also been a consistent increase in the overall age of the homeless population, which may be due to the aging cohort of homeless individuals who became vulnerable to homelessness when they were younger (veterans, for example).

At any given night in 2013 there were approximately 109,132 chronically homeless adults living in shelters. Of these, 30 percent were severely mentally ill, 17 percent were physically disabled, 16 percent were survivors of domestic violence, 13 percent were veterans, 3 percent were HIV positive, and 34 percent had a chronic substance abuse problem (down from 39 percent in 2007) (U.S. Mayor's Conference, 2013). The average length of stay in an emergency shelter was anywhere from a week to a month, with most staying about two weeks. The average length of stay in a transitional housing program was just under 100 days. Among homeless families, the majority consist of younger single mothers with two children who enter transitional housing programs, are members of an ethnic minority group (e.g., African American, Latin American, and Native American), and who became homeless after leaving someone else's home.

With a dramatic increase in housing foreclosures, the tightening of the credit market, and mass layoffs following the 2007 recession, the picture of homelessness in the United States will likely change for the worse, particularly if funding cannot keep pace with financial need. Although it is still too soon to capture specific statistics reflecting future changes, a 2009 study conducted by the Urban Institute exploring the impact of the foreclosure crisis on U.S. families showed that many families that experienced foreclosure found it difficult to rent because of damaged credit ratings and instead were forced to live with family members or friends. This trend is troublesome because the typical path toward homelessness often involves a pattern of moving from self-sufficiency in one's own home (owned or rented), to living in someone else's home, to ultimately moving into an emergency shelter. Older adults appear to be particularly vulnerable to the potential of future housing instability because of unstable retirement accounts and physical health problems that often create barriers to finding employment in a very tight job market (Kingsley, Smith, & Price, 2009).

The Many Causes of Homelessness

Determining the root causes of homelessness is as challenging as is determining who is homeless, but it is essential to understand causes and risk factors, particularly for social workers. Equally important is the task of identifying common biases against and negative stereotypes of poverty and homelessness that may influence the general perception of the poor and homeless, which in turn often influences support for assistance programs by state and federal policy makers as well as the voting public.

In general, underlying causes and risk factors of homelessness often lead to negative stigma associated with poverty and homelessness. One reason for this negative stigma relates to the very public nature of homelessness, where those without permanent homes are forced to live out in the open, such as on the streets or alleyways, or in parks or automobiles, where good hygiene is virtually impossible and begging for money and food is often the only means of survival (Phelan, Link, Moore, & Stueve, 1997). Additionally, the links between mental illness, substance abuse, poverty, and homelessness also contribute to this negative stigma. Research has repeatedly shown that the homeless in the United

States (particularly those living on the streets) are portrayed and perceived in terms highlighting individual character deficits, including being portrayed (in the media and otherwise) as mentally ill substance abusers, who engage in criminal activities, have poor hygiene and who aggressively beg for money (to buy drugs and alcohol). Research also shows that overall, the general public does not feel overly compassionate about the homeless population, which may very well be rooted in a lack of understanding (Belcher & DeForge, 2012; Frye, 2011; Lind & Danowski, 1999). Regardless, such perceptions reflect the ongoing negative stigmatization associated with homelessness.

Despite ample research that problems in society lead most often to chronic poverty and homelessness, it appears that most people in the United States blame the poor for their bad lot in life. For instance, in an older national survey conducted in 1975 the majority of those questioned attributed poverty and homelessness to personal failures, such as having a poor work ethic, poor money management skills, a lack of any special talent that might translate into a positive contribution to society, and low personal moral values. Respondents ranked social causes, such as poverty, racism, poor schools, and the lack of sufficient employment, the lowest of all possible causes of poverty (Feagin, 1975).

More recent surveys conducted in the mid-1990s revealed an increase in the tendency to blame the poor for their lot in life (Weaver, Shapiro, & Jacobs, 1995), even though a considerable body of research points to social and structural dynamics as the primary causes of poverty, such as shortages in affordable housing, recent shifts to a technologically based society requiring a significant increase in educational requirements, long-standing institutionalized oppression and discrimination of certain racial and ethnic groups, and a general increase in the complexity of life (Wright, 2000). A 2007 study comparing attitudes toward homelessness among respondents in seven countries—the United States, the United Kingdom, Belgium, Germany, and Italy—found that respondents in the United States and the United Kingdom had far higher rates of lifetime homelessness and fewer social programs compared to the other countries, as well as lower levels of compassion for the homeless population (Toro et al., 2007).

In general, compassion for poverty-related homelessness tends to be greater during difficult economic times and lower during economic booms, and general compassion for homeless individuals such as families, who are unlike the stereotypical "skid row" alcoholic, tends to be greater as well. The general public also has greater compassion for individual situations but do not tend to be particularly sympathetic toward the homeless population as a whole. Recent studies reflecting attitudes about poverty during the most recent economic crisis in 2007 reveal this same sense of increased compassion, but they also show an increase in class conflict, with lower income individuals expressing resentment toward the wealthy for maintaining an unfair grip on the country's economic wealth, and the wealthy expressing resentment toward the poor for expecting "handouts." This dynamic has been popularly coined as "class warfare" and was reflected clearly in the *Occupy Wall Street* movement—a series of staged demonstrations across the United States beginning September 17, 2011, in Manhattan's Financial District, and spreading to over 100 cities nationwide. Reflecting this notion of class conflict, the Occupy Wall Street (2011) movement website states that it they are an organization powered by people who are fighting to restructure current global financial markets, including Wall Street, that cater to the powerful 1% of the world's wealthiest, at the expense of the other 99%.

Engage Diversity and Difference in Practice

Practice Behavior: Gain sufficient self-awareness to eliminate the influence of personal biases and values in working with diverse groups.

Critical Thinking Question: What are some ways in which social workers who are uncomfortable working with the homeless population can increase their self-awareness to become more at ease?

Social Work, Social Media, and Technology

Lee Jeffries has dedicated his life to capturing the true images of the homeless. His public Facebook page called *The Lee Jeffries Homeless Project* and his website, feature photographs of people who are homeless and living on the streets. In his biography included on his website, Jeffries discusses how he initially "stole" a photo of a young homeless girl huddled in a sleeping bag on the streets of London, but rather than following his initial instinct and walking away once the girl noticed him, he approached her and they had a conversation. From that point forward he made a commitment to learn everything he could about the people he photographed, and rather than merely photographing homeless people living on the streets without their permission, he spends time getting to know his subjects before asking for permission to photograph them. After reviewing Jeffries' public Facebook page and website and reading his biography, answer the following questions. What do you think about Jeffries's decision to learn about the subjects in his photographs prior to taking their picture? Do you believe that Jeffries's work has a positive impact on society's perceptions of homelessness, and if so, how? In what ways (if any) do you believe Jeffries's work is a form of social justice advocacy?

This popular social movement reflects the findings of a 2012 study conducted by the Pew Center, which found that negative perceptions of each class—the poor of the rich, and the rich of the poor—has significantly increased in recent years. In fact, an interesting shift in attitude is that more white people than ever before are noticing a conflict between the classes, whereas the majority of African Americans and Latinos have always perceived a conflict between the rich and the poor. Attitudes toward the wealthy, something not explored in earlier attitudinal surveys about income levels, reveal that almost half of all respondents (about 46 percent) believe that the majority of the rich are wealthy because of social contacts and inheritance (Taylor, Parker, Morin, & Motel, 2012).

Based on these studies it appears as though the stigmatization of the poor and homeless is enduring, and there remains considerable confusion about the causes of poverty and wealth (whether poverty and homelessness are caused by behavioral factors or social conditions, and whether wealth is a result of privilege and inheritance or hard work). Despite intermittent increases in compassion toward the poor and homeless, the general public does not appear to understand the underlying causes of poverty and homelessness, which may make it easier to jump to incorrect conclusions based on negative stereotypes. Also perceptions of certain subgroups within the homeless population tend to be particularly negative, such as single men, certain ethnic minority groups, substance abusers, and undocumented immigrants.

Possible reasons for the overall negative perception of the homeless population may relate to the *fundamental attribution error*, where people tend to attribute their own personal struggles or the struggles of people they know well and like to situational factors but attribute the struggles of those they do not know or do not like to personal or dispositional factors. Thus, according to the fundamental attribution error, the average person would assume that those homeless whom they did not know were so because of their own personal shortcomings. Yet, if someone they knew became homeless, they would be more likely to attribute the homelessness to situational causes, such as being laid off or abruptly leaving an abusive relationship. Again, it's easy to assume the worst of people when we don't know the intimate details of their lives, and it's easier to show compassion for people when we know them well and to understand the complexity of their situations. Social workers must understand the stigma associated with poverty and homelessness because unless these negative attitudes are acknowledged and challenged,

Social Work, Social Media, and Technology

Social media is often used for advocacy purposes, Including fund-raising through one of the many online fund-raising websites or online videos that challenge common negative stereotypes of the homeless population, such as this time-lapse video of a homeless veteran on YouTube that recently went viral. What are some other ways that social workers can use social media to advocate for the homeless population? (https://www.youtube.com/watch?v=6a6VVncgHcY)

they may influence social workers' attitudes, significantly impacting their perceptions and treatment of their homeless clients. In fact, studies have shown that when service providers—the gatekeepers of much needed services—hold stigmatizing views of those struggling with chronic poverty and homelessness, feelings of dehumanization increase and service provision decreases, which significantly impact the outcomes for this very vulnerable population (Frye, 2011).

Assess your comprehension of "A Snapshot of Homelessness" by completing this quiz.

THE RISE OF HOMELESSNESS IN SINGLE-MOTHER FAMILIES

The number of homeless families—primarily single mothers with children—rose dramatically in the 1970s and 1980s (U.S. Conference of Mayors, 2013). The great majority of homeless single parents are single mothers, approximately 25 years of age, with two to three children in the preschool to 6 years of age range. The majority of these single mothers are U.S. citizens, native born, and fluent English speakers. Families of color are at greatest risk of becoming homeless, although single parent homelessness among Caucasians is significant as well.

Most single mothers and their children become homeless as a result of a complex set of circumstances, as illustrated in the Chapter Opening Vignette. Most have never been married, and although many are high school graduates, a significant number of single mothers never established a solid work history. Most cite either never having had stability in their housing situations or having experienced unstable housing for several years prior to becoming homeless. Most have experienced homelessness chronically on a cyclical basis, securing housing for a short time only to experience a financial crisis, such as a job loss, which results in a domino effect of negative life events and ultimately another incident of homelessness. Many homeless single mothers are either underemployed or unemployed, with the majority citing the inability to pay for child care as the primary barrier to finding employment, but others cited being undereducated (often because of an early history of running away) and an inability to secure employment that would pay for market rent (Dashora, Slesnick, & Erdem, 2012; Fothergill, Doherty, Robertson, & Ensminger, 2012).

The Great Recession of 2007 has resulted in an increase in single-mother unemployment. For instance, the percentage of single mothers employed in an average month between 2000 and 2009 decreased by about 8 percent, from 76 percent in 2000 to only 68 percent in 2009 (U.S. Department of Labor, 2010). This trend has led to increases in food and housing insecurity among single-mother households as well (Legal Momentum, 2010). Despite these trends, the U.S. Conference of Mayor's report (2013) notes a slight decrease in family homelessness, but the reason for this decline remains unknown, and it

Children are at increasing risk of becoming homeless.

BRUCE AYRES/STONE/GETTY IMAGES

is impossible to determine whether single mothers and their children are finding secure housing or are just becoming increasingly invisible.

Unfortunately, the safety net in the form of public assistance programs has significantly shrunk since the passage of federal welfare reform legislation in 1996. Welfare reform effectively ended the Aid to Families with Dependent Children (AFDC) program and initiated the Temporary Assistance for Needy Families (TANF), a program that provides assistance at about one-third of those within the federal poverty level (Nickelson, 2004). Historically, only about 20 percent of homeless individuals have been on any form of public assistance, even though the majority would have qualified for some form of assistance (Shlay & Rossi, 1992). Although single mothers qualify for more aid than single homeless men and single homeless women, as a group they still tend to underutilize public assistance programs. In fact, according to a report evaluating how single mothers and their children have fared between 2000 and 2009, unemployment has increased and welfare utilization has decreased, which has resulted in an increase in extreme poverty among single mothers as most employment is part time and often does not include benefits, such as subsidized healthcare insurance.

What may surprise many is that despite the increases in single-mother unemployment and overall poverty levels in single-mother families between 2007 through 2009, the percentage of these families receiving welfare benefits decreased from 16 percent in 2001 to only about 10 percent in 2010 (Legal Momentum, 2010). To add to the dilemma of shrinking public assistance programs, aid that is provided in the form of block grants or aid packages may have long waiting lists for certain types of assistance, such as child care, which creates a challenge for those single mothers seeking increased economic opportunities for self-sufficiency.

Another contributing factor to homelessness of single-mother families may relate to the bad childhoods many homeless women experienced. Many single mothers have reported unstable childhoods filled with physical and sexual abuse (Bassuk et al., 1997; Green et al., 2012). In fact, it appears as though many of these women proceeded to recreate these patterns of abuse in their adult lives because approximately three-quarters of all homeless single mothers who were partnered prior to becoming homeless cited domestic violence as the primary reason for leaving their marital home and moving into a shelter with their children. Other reasons include having a baby early, either during adolescence or early adulthood, which interrupts the development of educational and career goals (Ruedinger & Cox, 2012; Núñez & Fox, 1999). Other personal vulnerabilities include having a substance abuse disorder or mental illness. In fact, a recent study found that over half of homeless single mothers struggle with one or more diagnosable mental illnesses (Chambers et al., 2013). Other risk factors include having grown up in the state foster care system and having a poor or absent social support system (Bassuk et al., 1997; Chambers et al., 2013; Green et al., 2012).

Some structural causes of the dramatic increase in homeless single-parent families in the last 40 or so years include the failure of many courts to enforce child support orders, dramatic cutbacks in federal housing programs starting in the 1980s, the failure of public welfare to keep pace with inflation and increases in the cost of living, and cuts in mental health programs, particularly for adolescents. Further increases in homeless families are expected, particularly now that welfare benefits are limited to only two to five years (depending on the state), rather than providing long-term benefits on a case-by-case basis.

It is important to discuss the strengths that many of these single mothers exhibit, particularly because social workers will need to work with the single-parent client to enhance and build on existing strengths. A 1994 study found that single mothers living in shelters had an impressive (and unexpected) amount of determination, a sense of personal pride, and an ability to confront their problems directly. Many of the homeless single mothers interviewed exhibited a strong commitment to the welfare of their children (particularly those who chose homelessness over remaining in an abusive relationship), had strong moral values that acted as a guide in decision making, and had deep religious convictions that provided them with a sense of purpose and meaning. Despite being homeless, many of these single mothers maintained a commitment to helping others in need (Montgomery, 1994). Many also overcame what seemed to be insurmountable odds to keep their children with them rather than have them placed within the state foster care system, despite harsh living conditions. A more recent study evaluating the resiliency of single mothers in general (not solely the homeless) found that respondents were quite resilient, despite all of the challenges they faced. Most stated that they disagreed with the negative stereotypes of single mothers as inadequate and believed that they had personally grown through the challenges they faced in raising their children alone. Many found the experience of single parenting transformative and confidence building (Levine, 2009). Research has also identified some unique coping mechanisms many homeless single mothers use to reduce stress and increase resiliency, such as volunteering to help other low-income families (Broussard, Joseph, & Thompson, 2012). Social workers can tap into these strengths when assisting single parents' access to resources to gain self-sufficiency in the face of multiple challenges.

Homeless Shelter Living: Families With Children

The increase in single-mother family homelessness has resulted in the need for significant changes in social welfare policies regarding how homelessness is managed on local, state, and federal levels. When the homeless population was more homogeneous, consisting primarily of single men living in single-room occupancy (SRO) or on "skid row," the community response was less complex, focusing on low-cost housing and substance-abuse counseling. But this newer homeless population presents more complex problems requiring a more multifaceted approach. For instance, the traditional homeless person typically resided on the streets, whereas families often avoid street dwelling opting for shelter living instead. Yet, many emergency shelters are not equipped to serve families.

Elizabeth Lindsey (1998) interviewed single mothers who had lived in homeless shelters with their children and asked them about their experiences in shelters and the impact it had on their family life. The results of her study revealed just how woefully inadequate traditional shelters are in meeting the needs of single mothers and their children. For example, many shelters would not allow boys as young as eight years to sleep in the same area as their mothers, requiring them to stay on the men's side of the shelter alone, stay with relatives, or in some cases, even enter the foster care system. Other shelters

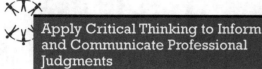

Apply Critical Thinking to Inform and Communicate Professional Judgments

Practice Behavior: Demonstrate effective oral and written communication in working with individuals, families, groups, organizations, communities, and colleagues.

Critical Thinking Question: When writing a court assessment about the nature of a mother's relationship with her child currently residing in a homeless shelter, what types of contextual factors would be important to consider?

applied the same rules to families as they did to singles, forcing single mothers to leave the shelter at 7:00 a.m., even if they had infants or preschool-aged children, and not allowing them to return to the shelter until 5:00 or 6:00 p.m., regardless of weather conditions or the safety of the community where the shelter was located. Many single mothers complained that there was no way to look for a job when they had to stay out of the shelter with their kids for so many hours a day. Other complaints included staff who seemed insensitive to children's needs, such as enforcing rules against children running around and playing, which created difficult situations for parents who were mandated to keep their children quiet at all times, with no distractions, such as television or toys, to assist them.

But by far the most difficult aspect of shelter life according to these women involved staff who would override their parenting decisions, such as correcting a parent in front of the child and other shelter residents for how a mother was disciplining her child. Mothers complained that shelter rules and interfering shelter staff often diminished their authority as a parent. Other shelter rules that made parenting difficult included rules prohibiting anyone eating in the shelter at any time other than designated meal times, including prohibiting mothers from bringing snacks into the shelter for their young children.

Research studies have shown that such shelter rules and policies, often not created with families in mind, have a powerfully devastating effect on the parent–child relationship, as mothers find themselves no longer the "head of household" with the power to make parenting decisions in the best interest of their children—even basic decisions such as when to bathe and feed their children. Instead, their children are cared for on the shelter's time frame. These issues might seem like minor inconveniences and relatively innocuous in light of the other major crises going on in the lives of homeless mothers, but researchers noted that the disintegration of the mother–child relationship is not just temporarily disruptive, rather, this disruption essentially further degrades and disempowers parents who were already feeling shamed and powerless by their homeless status, leading to an increase in parental distress and depression, which in turn often leads to an increase in child misbehavior and acting out, among a host of other negative consequences for the family (Lindsey, 1998).

More recent research on single mothers living in homeless shelters with their children showed similar dynamics. In a 2009 study of single mothers' attitudes about the effect of living in a shelter on child-rearing, the mothers cited several challenges to their parenting, such as the loss of privacy, the lack of financial resources, and the lack of child care. They also cited several personal strengths that helped them cope with these challenges, such as their ability to persevere their faith and their optimism. The authors of the study recommended that those working with single-mother homeless families maintain a humble attitude and avoid acting like an expert, as well as avoiding negative stereotyping of single mothers (Swick & Williams, 2010).

Homeless Children: School Attendance and Academic Performance

Children are the fastest-growing segment of the homeless population, which creates new challenges for shelters and other social welfare responses, particularly when these children are school aged. Developing effective programs designed to keep homeless children in school and succeeding academically is essential; otherwise homeless children will be at risk for continuing the cycle of homelessness in the next generation, having never experienced physical or emotional security in their own childhoods.

Between the chronic and cyclical nature of homelessness and the fact that most emergency shelters limit the amount of time residents can stay, ranging anywhere from 1 to 30 days, a significant problem for school-aged children was switching schools every time their families were forced to move to a new shelter. I recall when I was working as a school social worker in the inner city of Los Angeles having several school-aged children who were homeless on my caseload. Often these children would get settled and acclimated to their classroom and start the long process of building a trusting relationship with me and others in the school and then they would literally disappear one day. I would typically learn at some later point that the family was forced to move to a different shelter, and even if remaining at their school of origin was a legal possibility, it was not a realistic one because there was no guarantee that the next shelter would be anywhere close to the children's current school.

A 2000 report to Congress stated that only 87 percent of homeless children were enrolled in school, and of these only 77 percent attended school regularly (U.S. Department of Education, 2001). Many school districts attempted to resolve this issue by creating special schools or programs for homeless children, but these programs have been criticized because they segregate homeless children, increasing their social stigma and sense of rejection. Federal legislation, discussed later in this chapter, was designed to address this issue and reduce poor school attendance, and poor academic performance related to homelessness.

The McKinney-Vento's Education for the Homeless Children and Youth (EHCY) Program is designed to address many of the problems experienced by homeless students with regard to successfully completing their education. Through this act, states can apply for funding to assist in managing the many academic challenges associated with a student being homeless. Problems related to enrollment, attendance, and academic achievement are all addressed in this program, and states applying for grant funds must abide by certain standards and meet various criteria in meeting the complex needs of homeless students. For instance, according to the EHCY program, schools must offer the same educational experiences and opportunities for homeless children as for mainstream children and youth. Also, schools are not permitted to segregate homeless children solely because they are homeless (in other words, as school cannot have a special class just for homeless kids even if school personnel believe it is in the best interest of the children and school). Homeless children cannot be educated off-site, but rather must be educated alongside mainstream students in a regular classroom. Homeless children must be allowed to remain in their home school, even if they are forced to move out of the district because of shelter requirements. In light of the fact that most homeless parents would not be able to provide transportation for their children if they move to a shelter a considerable distance away from the home school, the school is required to make the necessary accommodations to ensure that the child has transportation to and from the school. Schools are also required to identify a homeless student liaison who provides case management assistance and helps families overcome the many barriers to school enrollment, regular attendance, and academic achievement. Schools are also legally required to enroll homeless students even if they lack the appropriate records, such as birth certificates, mandatory health records, and proof of residency. The program also requires that schools admit unaccompanied youth without requiring authorization by a legal guardian.

Assess your comprehension of "The Rise of Homelessness in Single-mother Families" by completing this quiz.

The EHCY program goes a long way in addressing the many challenges facing homeless families with school-aged children, yet much more must be done. School social workers, for instance, can be utilized to assist in the identification of homeless youth because a great number of families are too overwhelmed and embarrassed to come forward and report their homeless status. In addition, many homeless parents are simply unaware of their children's educational rights, and even though the McKinney-Vento Act requires that school liaisons inform students and their families of these rights, school social workers are often the link between the families, students, liaison, and school administration and can therefore be quite instrumental in ensuring that these kids remain in school, without disruption, despite the immense level of instability homelessness causes.

RUNAWAY AND HOMELESS YOUTH

No one is certain just how many adolescents and young adults are homeless and living on the streets without their families, but some estimates put that number as high as 2 million in the United States alone. Runaway and homeless youth (typically considered between the ages of 12 and 24) constitute a unique population among the entire homeless population because the reasons, risk factors, and intervention needs of runaway and homeless youth are considerably different. Adolescents are far more likely to be living on the streets than in a shelter. They are also far more likely to participate in dangerous behaviors such as drug abuse (including needle sharing), panhandling, theft, and survival sex (sex for food, money, and shelter). These risky behaviors put homeless youth at risk for HIV, hepatitis B, hepatitis C, and a range of other sexually transmitted diseases (Beech, Meyers, & Beech, 2002). These youth are also at high risk for physical and sexual violence, both by other teens as well as by adults.

Most runaway and homeless youth live on the streets because they have run away from an abusive home, have been kicked out of their homes by parents who no longer wish to take care of them (throwaway youth), or have aged out of the foster care system. The majority of homeless adolescents interviewed in various research studies reported a history of both physical and sexual abuse, which served as a primer for being similarly victimized on the streets (Whitbeck, Hoyt, & Ackley, 1997). One study of over 600 runaway and homeless youth found that sexual abuse was the chief reason adolescents chose to live on the streets rather than remaining in their homes (Yoder, Whitbeck, & Hoyt, 2001). The fact that many of these teens will continue to experience sexual exploitation while living on the streets, whether through outright attacks or through survival sex, is certainly a tragedy, and one that can be addressed by social workers working with this population.

Most urban cities' runaway and homeless youth often operate as a somewhat cohesive group on the streets, protecting each other and helping one another survive (Auerswalk & Eyre, 2002). In fact, it appears that the more seasoned adolescents would often take new homeless teens under their wings, teaching them survival tactics and welcoming them into the "fold." Newer homeless youth who were interviewed talked about what a relief it was to have someone essentially mentor them into the ways of surviving street life. But without glamorizing this life, most teens, both boys and girls, talked of the horrors of having to participate in prostitution to survive. In fact, runaway and homeless youth living on the streets have identified the many ways in which they felt exploited, both by older teens and by adults who forced them into drug dealing and prostitution (Auerswalk & Eyre, 2002).

Ironically, many runaway and homeless youth have reported a strong belief in God, who they believed watches out for them and keeps them alive. In Auerswalk and Eyre's 2002 study, one teen stated that when they were not really in need, they would often get no offer of food and little money while panhandling. Yet when they were really in need, having gone without food for a few days, then whatever they needed would just come to them. This teen attributed this phenomenon to God knowing what he needed and providing for him when he needed it the most. In fact, in one study researchers found that over half of all runaway and homeless youth interviewed cited a faith in God as the primary motivation for survival (Lindsey, Kurtz, Jarvis, Williams, & Nackerud, 2000).

Yet even with this surprisingly high percentage of faith-seeking runaway and homeless youth, an estimated 40 percent of homeless youth attempt suicide (Auerswalk & Eyre, 2002). They are also at high risk for post-traumatic stress disorder (PTSD), anxiety disorders, depression, substance abuse, and delinquency (Thrane, Chen, Johnson, & Whitbeck, 2008). Many runway and homeless youth report losing all contact with people in their former lives, even siblings, extended family, and those who had been supportive of them in the past. Many also talked of feeling extremely lonely and distrustful but in desperate need of love and affection. Because the majority of runaway and homeless youth have run away from abusive homes, it seems likely that many were suffering from some form of emotional disturbance even prior to entering street life (Kidd, 2003).

Unfortunately, many of the runaway and homeless youth who were interviewed reported being highly suspicious of all adults, including outreach workers with social services agencies providing assistance to the homeless adolescent and youth population. The overall perception of these outreach agencies were negative, and adolescents who accepted assistance from these agencies were considered "sellouts" and foolish. The prevailing belief was that social workers and other outreach workers would force the teens to return to an abusive home environment or they'd be turned over to the police or child protective services. Knowing these attitudes, however, can aid social service agencies in developing outreach efforts and other services designed to overcome these negative perceptions (Kidd, 2003).

Any successful intervention program is going to have to address the issue of runaway and homeless youth feeling like outsiders. In fact, research studies have found that homeless adolescents are acutely aware of their outsider status, and many of them manage this through incorporating this outsider status into their identity. By embracing being an outsider, through multiple piercings, for example, they take control of something that could potentially make them vulnerable (Auerswalk & Eyre, 2002).

Many social workers strongly recommend that any intervention program be targeted at identifying the adolescents' strengths. But this is challenging when most intervention systems view homeless youth in a deviant manner; first, because they are "runaways," and second, because many of the behaviors they engage in while living on the streets are classified as criminal activity. Even the classification of their behavior is in pathological terms, such as diagnosing them with conduct disorder, oppositional defiant disorder, bipolar disorder, and/or ADHD. Such diagnoses can be humiliating and shaming to adolescents who are likely acting out in response to being victimized within their families of origin. Most runaway and homeless youth have been both physically and verbally abused and degraded in their homes; thus, in many respects, they are living up to their parents' negative expectations of them by dropping out of high school and living on the streets.

To then enter into the juvenile justice system that continues to pathologize their behavior and that responds with punitive measures rather than supportive ones only adds to their feelings of victimization.

Social workers working with this population must provide consistent encouragement, compassionate care, and understanding in a way that promotes both healthy self-esteem and self-efficacy (a sense of competence) in these emotionally broken and bruised youth. This can be accomplished while focusing on basic needs such as providing food, shelter, and good healthcare. Yet again the barriers that social service agencies must overcome are significant because so many runaway and homeless youth have been so horribly rejected and abandoned by their families and communities, and then further exploited and abused by adults on the streets, thus trusting any adult may seem far too risky. Developing one-on-one relationships where trust can grow slowly is one method of intervention that may be more successful than more traditional outreach efforts, but the ratio of outreach workers to runaway and homeless youth renders this approach challenging. Regardless, any intervention must allow the youth to feel safe and empowered in seeking services.

Assess your comprehension of "Runaway and Homeless Youth" by completing this quiz.

SINGLE HOMELESS MEN: MENTAL ILLNESS AND SUBSTANCE ABUSE

Although single-parent families now comprise a large proportion of the homeless population, just less than 50 percent of the homeless population consists of men, many of whom are single, some of who are mentally ill, some of whom have substance abuse issues, and many of whom are veterans (U.S. Conference of Mayors, 2013). Of course these are overlapping categories in many instances. Among single homeless adults, 67 percent are male (U.S. Conference of Mayors, 2013) and while the reasons for their homelessness often vary, some are similar to the causes noted in single-parent families—childhood histories of abuse, growing up in the foster care system, having little or no family or social support, being undereducated and stuck in minimum wage jobs, substance abuse, and mental illness. Social causes include institutionalized racism and oppression, suffering from PTSD after having served in the military during wartime, and changes in the economic infrastructure resulting in fewer well-paying jobs.

Assess your comprehension of "Single Homeless Men: Mental Illness and Substance Abuse" by completing this quiz.

Veterans' services address many of these issues in programs designed to meet the complex needs of the homeless population who were at one time enrolled in the armed services. Social workers working for the Department of Veterans Affairs (VA) provide both in-house and outreach services and are trained on PTSD recovery and the unique needs of this special population.

OLDER ADULT HOMELESS POPULATION

The federal budget for fiscal year 2009 allotted $2.62 billion of funding for 10 different programs spread across several federal agencies, including the Department of Housing and Urban Development (HUD), the Department of Health and Human Services (HHS), the VA, and the Department of Education (ED), just to name a few. Initially, the increase in homelessness funding did not result in a decrease in homelessness, including a $1.5 billion grant to be spent on homeless prevention. Unfortunately, in response to the 2007 economic crisis, spending cuts were made essentially across the board in the federal budgets through 2014, affecting virtually all social welfare programs, but particularly those focusing on housing security. Cuts to housing programs, such as housing for older adults and for people with disabilities, averaged about 70 percent in 2011 from prior years. Rates of homelessness among older adults are significantly lower than younger individuals, but recent research suggests they are on the rise, particularly after the 2007 recession. In fact, the National Alliance to End Homelessness projects a 33 percent increase in homelessness among the older adult population between 2010 and 2010, and double by 2050 (Sermons & Henry, 2010).

Learn more about the older adult homelessness by going to the National Alliance to End Homelessness website and searching for the article entitled "Demographics of Homelessness Series: The Rising Elderly Population."

Differences exist between homelessness among younger and older persons, both in terms of the root causes of homelessness and effective responses. Younger homeless individuals report domestic violence and previous incarceration as reasons for becoming homeless far more frequently than older populations. Both groups report equal difficulty in finding affordable housing, and both groups report equivalent rates of alcohol and substance abuse as reasons for homelessness, with 4 percent of younger individuals reporting this as a reason and just over 6 percent of older adults reporting substance abuse as the primary reason for their homelessness. Yet in light of the nature of substance abuse and the tendency for alcoholics and drug addicts to minimize or deny the impact of their addiction, these percentages might be underreported.

Older adult homeless persons report being without shelter for far longer periods than younger individuals, with older adult men reporting an average homeless episode lasting over 60 days, and younger homeless men averaging about 14 days. Older men also reported far longer episodes without a permanent shelter, some reporting homeless episodes of over two years, whereas younger men reported being homeless an average of 11 months (Hecht & Coyle, 2001). This is likely because of fewer social supports and the difficulty in either moving in with a roommate or living with family, often because of caretaking issues related to common age-related physical problems.

Even though there are more similarities than differences between older and younger homeless persons, the response to older adults who are homeless must be vastly different because of all the variables associated with their advanced age. One variable mentioned in the previous paragraph relates to the diminished capacity of older people in getting back on their feet by finding new employment opportunities or entering a reeducation program to enter a new career; thus, the possibility of regaining financial independence is greatly diminished in the older adult population.

Other issues affecting older adults include their increased vulnerability—both physically and psychologically, leaving them open to physical and financial victimization. Physical disability and illness are also complicating factors in meeting the needs of the older adult homeless population.

Although there is increased funding for services for older adults, most economic support is not available until the age of 65. Self-sufficiency models designed for the general homeless population do not work with the older adult population for the reasons mentioned earlier; thus, some experts suggest responding to the older adult homeless population by developing aid-assisted low-cost housing with social services to assist with financial, physical, and psychological support to deal with the trauma of becoming homeless. As referenced earlier, homeless advocates and policy experts

Assess your comprehension of "Older Adult Homeless Population" by completing this quiz.

have expressed concern that the recent financial crisis that began in about 2007 involving the crash of the stock market, loss of retirement funds, mass layoffs, and dramatic increases in foreclosures will have a significantly negative impact on the older adult population because of decreased possibilities to rebound financially.

HOMELESSNESS DUE TO NATURAL DISASTERS

In 2005, Hurricane Katrina hit the Gulf Coast of the United States, resulting in 1800 deaths, and one million people being displaced, and causing over $123 billion in damage. Williams (2008) recalls how the millions of individuals displaced after Hurricane Katrina created a modern-day diaspora with a significant portion of Gulf Coast residents being forced to relocate throughout the country, resulting in the largest forced migration in the history of the United States. In 2012, Hurricane Sandy hit the Atlantic basin, including New Jersey, resulting in 109 dead, 100,000 people being displaced, and causing over $60 billion in damage to infrastructure and homes (Kaleem & Wallace, 2012).

Situations involving extreme weather and non-weather related events, such as floods, tornados, hurricanes, wildfires, and earthquakes, have resulted in a significant number of deaths and millions of people being displaced, sometimes permanently. A "natural disaster" is defined most commonly as an unexpected event that is contained in time and space (Fritz, 1961) that affects the majority of people in an affected community (Hossain, 2011), putting its members at extreme danger, causing significant loss (personal and environmental), and the disruption in essential societal functioning (Fritz, 1961), at a level beyond the affected communities' capacity to respond (Hossain, 2011). Natural disasters can cause millions of dollars in destroyed property and infrastructure (Martin, 2015; Williams, 2008). They also cause extreme collective stress because of the crisis nature of the event, often leading to significant psychological harm and life disruption among those affected by the disaster (Hossain, 2011; Quarantelli, 1998). While disaster relief and emergency management will be explored in more detail within an international context in (Chapter 13), in this section I will be exploring disaster work within a domestic context, with a particular focus on post-disaster displacement of natural disaster survivors.

Disaster response and management has been defined in a variety of ways, but one of the most commonly accepted definitions is one offered by the International Federation of Red Cross Red Crescent Societies [IFRC] (2011), which defines disaster management as the facilitation and organization of all humanitarian-related activities involved in preparedness, response, and recovery, to reduce the devastating impact of disasters. According to the Federal Emergency Management Agency (FEMA), there are four phases of emergency relief: *mitigation* (which involves prevention efforts), *preparedness* (which involves the development of disaster relief plans), *response* (which includes emergency actions taken during the disaster designed to save lives and protect individuals), and *recovery* (which includes actions taken to return life to normal) (FEMA, 2007). FEMA also notes the importance of all phases of emergency response efforts occurring within a framework that is comprehensive, progressive, integrated, collaborative, well coordinated, flexible, and professional (FEMA, 2007).

According to the NASW (2003), social workers are "uniquely suited to interpret the disaster context, to advocate for effective services, and to provide leadership in essential collaboration among institutions and organizations." Social work's core mission involves helping members of vulnerable communities with necessary social services, which becomes particularly important in disaster situations (Zakour & Harrell, 2004). Social workers engage in a variety of case management tasks when responding to a natural disaster, including building up a professional network; creating awareness about the disaster; transmitting important information about a disaster zone; participating in rescue operations in coordination with other agencies and serve as a liaison between survivors and the government by conducting rapid surveys on losses and needs (Hossain, 2011). Social workers can also assist in all phases of disaster relief, coordinating with other professionals and paraprofessionals. In fact, social workers play a key role in all stages of natural disaster relief, including crisis response, emergency management, and case management, such as coordination of services, and trauma services (Williams, 2008).

It's important to note that it is often the most vulnerable members of affected communities—those struggling with chronic poverty and members of historically marginalized groups based on race and gender—who are the most profoundly affected by natural disasters. Bell (2008) describes how in New Orleans, one of communities hit hardest by Hurricane Katrina, many members of the African American community struggled with poverty prior to the hurricane at significantly higher rates than the rest of the population, were congregated in "pockets of poverty," and were more isolated from outside support networks. Consequently, the African American community was disproportionately affected by the hurricane since not only did many not have the means to evacuate but also their post-hurricane displacement resulted in the loss of a highly supportive community.

As many natural disasters result in large numbers of people being displaced–either temporarily or permanently–social workers often provide services centered on housing assistance, including finding temporary and long-term housing for those displaced, as well as providing case management services focused on plugging displaced populations into services in their new communities. For instance, in the wake of Hurricane Katrina, approximately 92,000 individuals and families moved into temporary housing units called FEMA trailers, often located quite far from hurricane victims' original homes (Muskal, 2012).

Recovery work for survivors of natural disasters is a long-term prospect, reflected not only in the personal testimonies of impacted populations but also in research studies on survivor and community recovery (Bell, 2008; Cunningham, 2009; Dewan & Pugh, 2008; Laska & Morrow, 2006; Mills, Edmondson & Park, 2007). For instance, a study conducted by the Texas Health and Human Services Commission on Hurricane Katrina survivors living in Texas found that two years after the hurricane, almost 60 percent of survivors were still unemployed, almost 50 percent relied on housing subsidies, and between 37 and 40 percent of those surveyed reported that they had significant physical and mental health needs (Texas Health and Human Services Commission, 2006; as cited in Bell, 2008). Six years later New Orleans reported a 70 percent rise in homelessness compared with before Katrina (Reckdahl, 2011).

Social workers were on the front lines of relief efforts in the aftermath of Hurricane Katrina providing disaster relief and emergency management services on micro, mezzo, and macro levels, including trauma and grief counseling, and case management services for survivors, including providing services to survivors living in FEMA trailer communities. What is unique to the social work profession is the training students receive in dealing with crisis situations on a micro and macro level. In fact, many social workers begin their careers as crisis workers, and trauma work remains a key element of many

Assess your comprehension of "Homelessness Due to Natural Disasters" by completing this quiz.

social work jobs. Whether engaging in emergency response or working with survivors months after a crisis to connect them with valuable resources as they strive to get their lives back on track, social workers engaging in disaster relief and emergency services provide invaluable services, particularly to those survivors experiencing short- and long-term displacement.

WORKING WITH HOMELESS POPULATIONS: THE ROLE OF THE SOCIAL WORKER

Apply Social Work Ethical Principles to Guide Professional Practice

Practice Behavior: Make ethical decisions by applying standards of the National Association of Social Workers Code of Ethics and, as applicable, of the International Federation of Social Workers/International Association of Schools of Social Work Ethics in Social Work, Statement of Principles.

Critical Thinking Question: What NASW ethical codes could guide a social worker working with a client who is homeless and refuses to go to a shelter, even during the winter?

Working with the homeless population is as challenging as it is meaningful. Whether a homeless client is a middle-aged man or woman, an older adult, a child, or an entire family, being homeless is traumatic, degrading. It is a terrifying experience to have one's foundation crumble without any sort of safety net to stop the fall. For many people, homelessness is not an isolated incident, but rather, a way of life, and even when employed and residing in a permanent home, for many people homelessness is only one unexpected financial crisis away.

Many believe that there is a reciprocal relationship between many mental and emotional disorders and homelessness. The process of becoming homeless, which typically comes on the heels of months or even years of financial and residential instability, is extremely stressful and often leads to anxiety disorders, depression, loss of self-esteem, substance abuse, and even personality disorders as individuals respond to the harshness of life in various maladaptive and defensive ways. For example, research indicates that children who have experienced extreme poverty and homelessness are at risk for higher rates of physical illnesses, depression, anxiety, behavioral problems, learning problems, and low self-esteem (Davey, 2004). Children who live in shelters are often negatively affected as they watch their parent's caretaking roles and responsibilities taken over by shelter staff and social workers. Thus, working with the homeless population, whether directly at an emergency or domestic violence shelter, in a transitional housing program, at a school as a homeless liaison, or in some other capacity where homeless clients might seek services, will involve working with an extremely wide range of clients experiencing an equally wide range of psychosocial issues.

Social workers provide counseling services to homeless adults and children and facilitate support groups. Social workers also supervise shelter residents and provide case management services for adult and child residents, assisting them in connecting to an array of social services that will help them obtain economic and housing stability. But one of the most significant roles that social workers play is advocating for the homeless population, both on a personal level, as well as on a macro level, by influencing policy and the development of legislation designed to assist those experiencing chronic housing insecurity.

One of the underlying values of social work is to empower clients by plugging them into a variety of social support systems, and moving them toward a state of self-sufficiency. This is particularly important when working with the homeless population and those suffering, thus, networking with other social service agencies and professionals to provide a comprehensive continuum of care is a powerful intervention tool. The effective social worker will not attempt to meet all of a homeless client's needs alone but will work in coordination with a network of services provided by governmental, not-for-profit, and faith-based organizations in the local community that provide related services, such as respite care for parents, job training and networking, and financial assistance.

Many clients facing or experiencing homelessness tend to have multiple problems, which the social worker might find challenging to address. Single-parent families that are either homeless or on the verge of homelessness are particularly challenging because the social worker must address the needs of the children as well as the parent, and these needs might conflict with one another. For instance, consider the young, overwhelmed single mother with two young children who has absolutely no one to help her with her child care responsibilities. Life in the shelter is depressing and difficult, her children are acting out more than ever because they miss their home and do not understand why they have to live in a shelter with so many strangers and with so many odd and confusing rules. It is perfectly understandable for this mother to desperately need some time alone without her children, yet the tremendous amount of instability and the trauma associated with being homeless will likely result in the children needing her more than ever. This dynamic can result in increased frustration on the part of the mother, which in turn creates increased fear and insecurity in the children. In fact, children in such situations often respond with physical and emotional clinginess. The social worker can work with the mother to help her recognize this relationship dynamic and take steps to resolve it through intermittent child care respite and counseling, so that each member better understands the impact homelessness has on each other as well as themselves.

In light of the burden and stress placed on the single mother, who rarely enjoys a break from the frightening stressors and responsibilities she experiences living on the streets and in shelters with her children, it is no wonder that many women rush into romantic relationships believing promises of never-ending love and caregiving from the men they may meet. And although it would be tempting for anyone so completely overwhelmed with life to accept a man's offer to take over the control of her life and the lives of her children, a relationship that moves too quickly will often result in dysfunction, and in some cases, domestic violence.

Some single mothers make decisions to proceed too quickly into relationships with men, believing that such a relationship will provide the stability of an intact family for their children, only to find out a short time later that they have entered into yet another dysfunctional, and even abusive relationship with someone who wants to control them emotionally and physically. The shame these women feel is often immense and sometimes results in their choice to remain in the abusive relationship because it seems a better choice than facing homelessness again and having to admit that they made another devastating mistake. In light of the fact that so many homeless single mothers experienced physical and verbal abuse in their childhoods and then repeated this pattern in their adult relationships, it is no surprise that many will eventually believe the horrible things being said to them, causing them to further doubt whether they have the ability to make good choices for themselves and their children. This kind of negative thinking only serves to lower self-esteem and forestall self-sufficiency.

Many people, including social workers, may become frustrated with single mothers who enter into a string of relationships with abusive men, sometimes becoming pregnant, but it is important to consider how these critics might respond if they had no one in the world to help and support them, had no one to share the burdens and difficulties of

Social Work Application Activity

Research clearly indicates the complex nature of homelessness. Reflecting on the opening vignette, what are some risk factors Kendall experienced that increased her risk of homelessness, and how do these various risk factors relate specifically to her chronic housing instability? For a social worker working with someone like Kendall, how can the NASW Code of Ethics provide necessary guidance? When answering this question make sure to review the NASW Ethical Principles—specifically, the value of social justice, as well as Social Workers' Ethical Responsibilities to Clients, and Social Workers' Ethical Responsibilities to the Broader Society.

Assess your comprehension of "Working with the Homeless Population: The Role of the Social Worker" by completing this quiz.

life with, and did not have the luxury of taking their time to build a truly loving and healthy relationship because they had never enjoyed a solid foundation of love and security in their childhoods, causing them to enter into an adult world desperate for someone to love them and provide them with the security they so desperately seek. This dynamic has the potential to lead anyone to impulsively jump into a relationship that looks good at first glance, because when you are desperately alone in the world anything looks good—in fact, it is a little like living in a desert with no water and thinking seawater tastes absolutely wonderful, only to find out later that rather than saving you, it will poison you.

COMMON HOUSING ASSISTANCE PRACTICE SETTINGS

Programs designed to aid the homeless population are often categorized into three levels of provision, each focusing on increasing levels of assistance. The first level of provision includes *emergency shelters* and *daytime drop-in centers*. Both offer short-term solutions to a long-term problem. Although emergency services are definitely needed, particularly when dealing with a population that might experience a crisis resulting in sudden homelessness, some emergency shelters are criticized for their often unsafe and inflexible environment where residents can stay for as short as one night to as many as 30 days. Another area of criticism is that historically, far greater amounts of funding are appropriated for emergency services rather than for long-term programs and services (Shlay & Rossi, 1992).

The second level of provision includes *transitional housing programs*. These programs offer temporary housing for anywhere from six months to two years, with most programs offering a one-year program. Housing is only one part of the program package, however, and residents are typically required to participate in a wide range of adjunct social services such as job training, budgeting workshops, adult literacy courses, substance abuse treatment, and parenting training. Other support services may include child care, job placement, and medical care. Most transitional housing programs focus on a specific target population, such as survivors of domestic violence, single-mother families, single men suffering from substance abuse, runaway and homeless youth, veterans, or older adults. These programs tend to be more successful because they provide a wide range of intensive services aimed at addressing the root causes of chronic poverty and homelessness, but they are also challenging to facilitate because of the complexity of the psychosocial issues being addressed, as well as the cost associated with administering

Social Work Application Activity

Mercy Housing of Chicago is a national nonprofit organization that offers affordable housing options and supportive programs for those struggling with poverty and housing instability. Mercy Housing provides assistance to families, older adults, and individuals with special needs but does so in a unique way. Approximately 60 percent of those whom Mercy Housing helps are women, many of whom are single parents. Not only does Mercy Housing offer affordable housing options for women experiencing housing instability but it also offers several supportive programs offered on-site in community rooms in the apartment buildings, such as the Woman of Worth Program, focusing on nutrition and exercise, and Courageous Women, Fierce Times, focusing on careers, time management, and budgeting. Locate Mercy Housing in Chicago, Illinois by conducting an Internet search and then answer the following question: What role do you believe social workers could play in programs such as these?

programs offering comprehensive services, particularly because one of the primary root causes of homelessness is the lack of low-cost housing. Unfortunately, transitional housing programs have not garnered the majority of governmental funding, which has had a significant impact on the homeless population, particularly single head-of-household families.

A type of homeless service that combines levels one and two are domestic violence shelters. Because domestic violence is such a significant issue in the prevalence of single-mothers and child homelessness, shelters specialize in meeting the needs of individuals (most commonly women and children) who are fleeing dangerous intimate family partner relationships. Although there variations do exist, the most common scenario involves a woman with children fleeing from a boyfriend or husband who is physically, emotionally, and/or verbally abusive. Domestic violence shelters operate on a 24-hour emergency basis, providing confidential safe houses for women and/or children escaping abusive situations.

Most domestic violence shelters operate homes and apartments spread throughout the community, each shared by a few women and children. Shelter stays range from one month to several months, and residents and their children participate in a broad range of services and activities, including support groups for the mothers and the children. Social workers provide counseling, case management, and advocacy services, including assisting clients in obtaining orders of protection through the court system and advocating for them during any criminal or civil court hearings. Support groups often focus on empowerment issues and educating the women on the nature of domestic violence, parenting from a perspective of strength, and developing more healthy boundaries in relationships. Services may also include providing job training skills and job networking, securing child care, referrals for substance abuse treatment, and assistance in locating permanent housing.

Issues related to domestic violence will be explored in greater depth in Chapter 12, but it is important to understand that working with domestic violence victims who are homeless can be challenging for a variety of reasons, one of which relates to the cyclical nature of domestic violence where many victims repeatedly return to their batterers when promises of authentic change are made. Such a pattern often disrupts efforts made toward self-sufficiency and housing security.

The third level of provision involves services on a longer-term basis in the form of low-cost housing assistance, often called *public housing assistance* provided by the federal government's housing agency, Housing and Urban Development (HUD). HUD has been providing long-term solutions for decades but has faced numerous challenges along the way. For instance, many of the traditional public housing units, primarily built in the 1950s and 1960s were developed as high-rise units in low-income urban neighborhoods, essentially creating segregated societies of the poor, which were often plagued with high crime. Not only did this contribute to the development of dangerous neighborhoods, but it also contributed to the already existing negative stigma associated with poverty. Gang activity, drug dealing, and other crimes often associated with the urban inner city were common in what is often casually referred to as the "projects." Once government policy makers realized that housing projects of this type were likely causing more harm than good, an organized attempt was initiated to close the projects down, particularly in large cities such as Chicago and Philadelphia, and to transition residents to new low-rise housing units scattered throughout the city. Yet squatting became a significant problem in the former high-rises that remained partially open (during transition periods that often took years), with some squatters even using the empty units as drug labs or gang hideouts.

A more current form of permanent low-cost housing includes governmental voucher programs facilitated by HUD. HUD's Section 8 housing voucher program is designed for the general population, and Section 811 is designed for individuals with disabilities (including mental illness). These programs require eligible individuals or families to apply for the housing voucher benefit during open application periods (often only a few short periods throughout the year). Once their eligibility and benefit amount is determined, they then receive a voucher indicating the amount of monthly rent they are eligible to receive, and it is then up to the beneficiary to find a landlord willing to accept the voucher.

Theoretically the voucher can be used with any rental within a particular geographic area, but either through bias or because of a competitive rental market, many landlords in more expensive communities will not accept Section 8 or 811 rental vouchers. Thus, even though one intention of this program was to avoid the isolation and segregation created by high-rise congregated public housing projects, in many communities the result is still much the same because it is not the individual landlord of units scattered throughout the city that is most likely to accept a HUD rental voucher, but the owners of large apartment complexes in low-income areas where occupancy rates of low-income individuals and families run high, who are the most likely to accept rental vouchers, creating the same sort of isolated high-crime environment experienced with public housing high rises.

The stigmatization of poverty contributes to problems in securing permanent solutions to homelessness. Not only is poverty stigmatized, but many populations that are at increased risk of poverty (and as such homelessness) are stigmatized. Intersectionality refers to how areas of vulnerability intersect within an individual (and population) to create increased levels of vulnerability. For instance, an individual who is a member of the majority Caucasian population and is struggling with poverty and homelessness will experience some stigmatization. But a person of color will likely experience more stigmatization. Further, if this same person was struggling with a physical and/or mental illness, then the level of stigmatization would be compounded further. Certain groups are protected legally against discrimination in the housing market, and thus landlords who reject a potential renter based solely on their race, for instance, can be legally prosecuted. But there are numerous historically marginalized groups in the United States that are not protected under federal law, including members of the lesbian, gay, bisexual, and transgendered (LGBT) population (Shankle, Maxwell, Katzman, & Landers, 2003).

Assess your comprehension of "Common Housing Assistance Practice Settings" by completing this quiz.

Summary

Effectively addressing the problem of homelessness requires a comprehensive understanding of the nature of this social condition, including the extent of the homeless problem, determining who is most vulnerable to becoming homeless, as well as discovering the root causes of homelessness. It is only through having a better understanding of the demographic nature of and common reasons for homelessness that social programs can be developed to assist people in obtaining permanent, stable housing, as well as developing preventative measures to protect against homelessness in the future. Many homeless advocates believe that significantly reducing the homeless population is a reasonable goal, and in fact it truly does seem plausible to assume that one of the wealthiest countries in the world would have enough resources to wipe out homelessness all together, and yet it remains a persistent problem within society, particularly among certain subpopulations.

Homelessness is a complex social problem with multifaceted causes, including several root causes that lie in the personal domain (such as domestic violence, substance abuse, mental illness, and teen pregnancy), as well as causes within broader societal domains, such as institutionalized racism and oppression, stigmatization and discrimination, and structural causes related to the changing U.S. economy, including a difficulty economy and a lack of affordable and low-cost housing.

Structural issues related to an industrialized and capitalistic society include declining salaries, particularly for the poor, and escalating housing prices, which when combined creates an abundance of low-income renters competing for fewer affordable housing units. The development of affordable housing, although a good idea in theory, is challenging because of the high cost of land and housing in safer areas. In addition, most people who are at risk of homelessness often cannot afford to pay a significant portion of their own rent and many cannot afford to pay any rent at all. Thus, regardless of how the rental subsidies are structured, focusing on affordable subsidized housing as the primary resolution to the homeless problem essentially requires permanent governmental support, and unless adjunct services are provided, some argue that permanent subsidized housing programs may encourage dependency rather than fostering independence (Wright, 2000).

It appears, then, that programs offering a wide array of social services focusing on the personal root causes of homelessness, while at the same time addressing structural causes such as declining incomes and escalating housing costs, will have the greatest likelihood of successfully addressing the homeless problem with long-term solutions in mind. Social service agencies are on the front lines of developing such programs designed to promote self-sufficiency and personal security. In light of continued cuts to much-needed housing assistance programs, social workers are not only in positions of providing direct service to those struggling with homelessness and housing insecurity but can also advocate on a policy level for the restoration, and even increase of government benefits for members of the homeless population. One way social workers can do this is by raising awareness of the complexities of homelessness, so that policy makers recognize that complex solutions are necessary to decrease the growing problem of homelessness among a wide range of populations.

Recall what you learned in this chapter by completing the Chapter Review.

9

Healthcare and Hospice

LEARNING OBJECTIVES

- Describe the skills necessary for the rapid assessment of patients in an acute medical situation.

- Identify populations most at risk of contracting the HIV virus, including ways that social workers can most effectively work with at-risk populations.

- Analyze key aspects of the Affordable Care Act, including the current and potential impact of this federal legislation on the consumer and society.

- Describe ways that social workers can advocate for marginalized and at-risk populations when seeking care in a healthcare setting.

- Compare and contrast the hospice philosophy of palliative care with traditional curative models of medical treatment.

- Compare and contrast various theoretical models of grief and mourning, including traditional stage models as well as more contemporary task model approaches.

- Analyze common ethical dilemmas involved in the care of the sick and dying, including euthanasia, and the inadvertent omission of those individuals who are economically disadvantaged.

CHAPTER OUTLINE

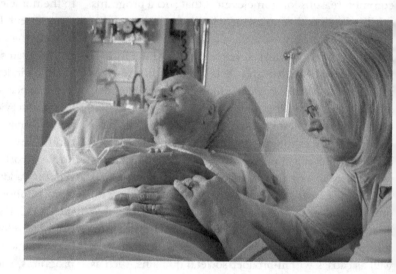

At 9 a.m. Glenn is called to the labor and delivery department of a large hospital where he tries to talk with a teenage girl who just had a baby. The young girl holds her new infant as Glenn initiates a conversation with her. He explains that he is visiting her because it is hospital policy for the social worker to visit with all adolescents who have just given birth. He asks the young mother a few basic questions, such as whether she has a place to live once she and her infant leave the hospital, whether her parents knew about her pregnancy, whether the father of the baby is involved, and whether she has a plan for raising her child. The young mother admits that her parents knew nothing of her pregnancy, as she managed to hide it by wearing large clothing and spending a lot of time in her room. She admits she is frightened that if she shares the news with them, they will force her to leave their home. And she admits that the father is no longer in her life and that she has no ability, nor any real desire, to raise a child. Glenn understands that this mother's ambivalence about raising her child is far more related to her age than her character. After some further discussion, Glenn asks her if she'd be interested in talking with a counselor who can assist her in sorting through all the options available to her. After learning that her parents are generally supportive and loving people, he offers to call them for her so that they can help her decide how to best manage this unplanned pregnancy. The young mother appears relieved and admits that she considered just leaving the hospital without her baby because she was so desperately frightened and didn't know what else to do. When Glenn returns to his office, he makes the call to the parents; after a 20-minute emotional phone call, he makes plans to meet them in 30 minutes in their daughter's hospital room. After meeting with the entire family, he supplies them with several names of counseling agencies that can assist the young mom in either parenting or placing her infant for adoption.

While walking out of the hospital room, Glenn is paged to the emergency room. When he arrives, he finds the entire unit in chaos. Three cars had collided, and many people were injured. After talking to the emergency room nurses and physicians, Glenn learns that one of the cars had several children in it, many of whom were seriously injured. Glenn gets to work right away collecting and identifying information, making sure that each child's parent is accounted for, and obtaining numbers of parents who need to be notified of the accident and their child's condition. After obtaining all necessary information, Glenn makes himself available to the parents who had children in surgery— parents who were not in the accident whom he recently called to the hospital—and the children who are not seriously injured but had parents who were. He offers to contact friends and family for support. After contacting spouses and two family pastors, Glenn sat with one family who had two seriously injured children and provided crisis counseling so that they could be calm enough to understand all that was going on with their children. Glenn also offers to be the conduit between the waiting families and the medical team, and so for over an hour he goes back and forth between the medical personnel working on the injured and delivering any new information to the family members. Two hours later, all parties were out of crisis and had support systems by their sides, and Glenn was cleared to return to his office.

Next, Glenn began working on several discharge planning cases for various patients who were scheduled to be released from the hospital within the next two days. One was an older patient who was not healthy enough to return home, and it was Glenn's responsibility to assist the family in finding either appropriate alternate housing or in-house services that would enable the patient to remain in his home. Another case involved a survivor of a serious car accident who needed continued therapy but could no longer remain in the hospital. Glenn's job was to locate a rehabilitation center close to the family that would be covered under his insurance plan.

As Glenn's day was coming to a close, he was paged again to the emergency room, where he learned there was a potential victim of sexual assault. Glenn asked the victim if she was comfortable talking to him, but she stated that she was not—she preferred a female counselor. Glenn then called the local county rape crisis center and asked for a volunteer to come to the hospital immediately to counsel and support a sexual assault victim.

On his way out of the emergency room, he was asked to consult on a potential child abuse case. Glenn interviewed the parents of a six-year-old boy who suffered a spiral fracture of the arm. Glenn became concerned when he interviewed each parent separately and their stories differed significantly. Because of this and the child's inability to describe in detail how he injured his arm, Glenn felt the case warranted a call to child protective services (CPS). He explained to the parents that he would be making an abuse allegation report and that the child would not be released until a CPS caseworker came to the hospital and interviewed everyone in the family.

Prior to Glenn leaving for the day, he was asked to visit with a patient and her adult son who just learned of her terminal diagnosis. Glenn provided both with some crisis counseling and made a referral to a local hospice agency. He offered to meet with them again tomorrow and to meet with them and the hospice team if they wished. Glenn's last case for the day was to provide counseling to a 60-year-old man who had recently undergone a liver transplant and was about to be released from the hospital. Research indicates that transplant patients often experience depression after being released from the hospital, and thus Glenn's focus was to help this patient adjust to the realities of being a transplant patient, as well as preparing him for experiencing some depression in the coming weeks. He made sure this patient left armed with names of counselors who had experience working with transplant patients.

SOCIAL WORK IN HOSPITALS AND OTHER HEALTHCARE SETTINGS

Glenn's day, depicted in the vignette, represents a typical day of a social worker working in a healthcare setting, and although this description is realistic, it is probably more realistic to state that there is no such thing as a "typical" day for a social worker in a healthcare setting! In fact, someone interested in a career in the social work field looking for structure and predictability would probably not fare well in a healthcare setting, where the broad range of patient issues determines the range of issues dealt with by social workers working in this practice setting, whereas social workers who embrace change and unpredictability, and the chance to be creative and novel, will likely thrive in a typical healthcare setting.

Social workers working in healthcare settings are true generalists: They must be flexible and able to deal with a variety of issues, often in a setting fraught with crisis and trauma. But despite their broad generalist duties, the scope of social worker functions in healthcare and medical settings can be quite specific. These functions and responsibilities may include

- Conducting psychosocial assessments on patients as needed
- Providing information and referrals for patients
- Preadmission planning
- Discharge planning
- Psychosocial counseling
- Financial counseling
- Health education
- Postdischarge follow-up
- Consultation with colleagues
- Outpatient continuity of care
- Patient and family conferences regarding health status, care, and future planning
- Case management for patients
- Facilitation of and referral to self-help and emotional support groups for patients and families

- Patient and family advocacy
- Trauma response
- Assistance in exploring bioethical issues
- Outcome evaluations on best practice committees

In addition to performing these various functions, social workers working in healthcare settings also address patient problems related to activities of daily living (ADL), assisting patients and their families in dealing with illness adjustment, assessing possible physical and sexual crimes, including child abuse, sexual assault and domestic violence, as well as assessing patients with potential mental health problems. Chief among all of these functions is the ability of social workers working in healthcare settings to contribute to a multidisciplinary team providing a continuum of care, particularly for chronically ill patients in need of a wide range of services (NASW, 1990; 2005).

Crisis and Trauma Counseling

A large part of a social worker's role in a healthcare setting is to provide crisis and trauma counseling to patients and their families. In fact, when the hospital has notified the family of a patient who has been seriously injured either through illness or accident, it is often someone from the social work department who meets the family at the emergency room doors.

When individuals are facing a significant crisis, they often feel compelled to focus on their most basic needs before exploring higher functions, such as making meaning of

Social Work Application Activity

Maslow (1954) created a model focusing on needs motivation to help explain the process of how people are motivated to get their needs met (Figure 9.1). According to Maslow, people are motivated to get their most basic physiological needs met first (such as the need for food and oxygen) before they attempt to meet their safety needs (such as the security we find in the stability of our relationships with family and friends). Based on this theory, most people would find it difficult to focus on higher level needs related to self-esteem or self-actualization when their most basic needs are not being met. Consider anyone you know who suffers from low self-esteem and then consider how he might react if they were diagnosed with a debilitating disease, such as cancer. Maslow's theory suggests that thoughts of low self-esteem would quickly take a backseat as worries about mere survival took hold Maslow's model can assist social workers working with individuals and families in crisis by better understanding how to priorities client needs.

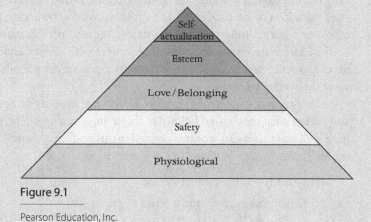

Figure 9.1

Pearson Education, Inc.

the crisis, which is where many social workers want to start! In situations where family members or close friends have been called to the hospital in response to a loved one having been in a serious accident or suffering from some life-threatening illness, their first priority is often to obtain information about the medical status of the patient. It is very important for the social worker to avoid escalating panic or anxiety. In fact, it is vital that professionalism be maintained amidst crying, screaming, and perhaps even misplaced anger, so that the social worker can serve as a calming influence the family can rely on as they attempt to regain their composure.

Each family handles crises differently; thus, it is important for the social worker to quickly recognize the family's coping style. Some families will focus on mundane details, such as asking how long their loved one will be in the hospital when the patient has not even emerged from emergency surgery, and some families will focus directly on important issues, such as repeatedly asking whether the patient will survive the surgery, even though there might be no way to answer such a question until the patient is out of surgery. Regardless of these individual coping styles, the social worker must be able to read between the lines, recognizing that a family confronted with the shocking news of a loved one having a life-threatening condition often leaves them feeling dazed and powerless, and many of the questions or actions are rational or irrational attempts to recover some sense of control over the situation. By understanding this dynamic, the social worker can take concrete steps to assist the individual family members in gaining as much control as possible by acting as the conduit between the medical staff and the family, by helping the family focus on the most important issues, and by assisting them in developing a plan of action that might include finding child care for younger children, having someone go to the patient's house to care for pets, and notifying friends and employers on behalf of the patient.

The social worker's role continues with the family as the situation progresses but takes on a different role, including assisting the patient and family adjust to any limitations posed by the patient's condition or injury, finding necessary resources, and conducting discharge planning when the patient is well enough to leave the hospital. The social worker will even follow up with the patient and family after discharge to check on their progress.

Single Visits and Rapid Assessment

Most social workers assume that they will be able to work with their clients over an extended period of time regardless of their role in the helping process. Yet, this is typically not the case in a healthcare setting because of the trend toward significantly shortened durations of hospital stays. In fact, social workers working in a hospital setting will often see patients only one or two times. Because of this pattern, there is a growing body of literature on single-session encounters with clients, and how social workers can develop a set of skills that allows for rapidly assessing the patient and their situation, and assist them effectively.

Gibbons and Plath (2009) explored this very issue by interviewing several patients and asking what they found helpful in these single sessions. The patients identified seven basic skill sets that social workers needed to utilize during a single session. These included the ability to:

1. Quickly put the patient at ease
2. Establish a rapport and a sense of trust quickly

3. Exhibit a sense of competence

4. Engage in active listening and exhibit empathy

5. Be nonjudgmental

6. Provide needed information quickly

7. Organize support services

Because lengths of stay in hospitals are decreasing, the reality for most social workers is that they will have very brief access to the majority of their patients in a hospital setting. To maximize the time they do have, it's important for social workers to make sure that they are listening with a tolerant ear, practicing empathy, are nonjudgmental and provide practical assistance to be truly effective, and have some impact on the lives of their patients.

Assess your comprehension of "Social Work in Hospitals and Other Healthcare Settings" by completing this quiz.

WORKING WITH PATIENTS WITH HIV/AIDS

Social workers working in healthcare settings, particularly in public health, commonly encounter health-related epidemics or pandemics like HIV, which causes AIDS. HIV/AIDS was first discussed in the medical literature in 1981 (Gottlieb et al., 1981). Medical treatment during these early years typically occurred in a crisis setting when patients presented in the emergency room with advanced or end-stage AIDS infections, such as *Pneumocystis carinii* pneumonia (PCP) and Kaposi's sarcoma, both opportunistic infections common in end-stage AIDS patients.

In August 1981, 108 AIDS cases were reported in the United States by the Centers for Disease Control and Prevention (CDC) and by 1988 the CDC estimates that approximately 1.1–1.5 million people were living with the HIV infection, indicating just how quickly HIV/AIDS has spread throughout the United States (CDC, 1988). The World Health Organization (WHO) estimates that 36 million people have died from AIDS worldwide since 1981, with 1.6 million people dying worldwide in 2012 (WHO, 2013). Overall, 60 million people in the world have been infected with the HIV virus and an estimated total of 25 million people have died from the disease and related complications (WHO, 2013).

Identify as a Professional Social Worker and Conduct Oneself Accordingly

Practice Behavior: Use supervision and consultation.

Critical Thinking Question: How would supervision assist a social worker who was uncomfortable working with patients with HIV because of fear and lack of information?

When HIV/AIDS first emerged in the United States, there were no medical treatments available to address the actual disease process (other than symptomatic relief), but through grassroots efforts (that led to significant fund-raising efforts for medical research) significant medical advances were gained throughout the 1990s resulting in HIV/AIDS now being considered more of a chronic disease, rather than a terminal one—for those individuals fortunate enough to have access to expensive antiviral therapy. Despite these medical advances, however, the treatment of HIV/AIDS remains a serious public health concern, particularly for those individuals who have no access to advanced medical treatment or who do not respond positively to the most aggressive antiviral therapies, commonly referred to as the *AIDS cocktail*.

During the early years of the AIDS crisis, the role of the social worker focused almost exclusively on the crisis of receiving a terminal diagnosis and involved conducting emergency discharge planning, death preparation, arranging for acute care, and initiating hospice services. By the 1990s, education efforts led to earlier diagnoses and better medical treatment for those who could afford it. Clinical intervention focused more on the psychosocial issues involved with having a chronic, debilitating, and sometimes terminal disease that carried a stigma with it. These psychosocial issues experienced by those with HIV/AIDS typically included a fear of discrimination, concerns about receiving quality medical care, job accommodations and securing other income sources in the event of a job loss, and housing accommodations in response to declining health (Kaplan, Tomaszewski, & Gorin, 2004).

According to the HIV Surveillance Report published by the Centers for Disease Control and Prevention (CDC, 2011) estimated that by the end of 2011, about 1.1 million people in the United States were living with HIV/AIDS (both diagnosed and undiagnosed). The CDC also estimates that annual rates of new infections are remaining stable at about 50,000 per year. According to the CDC, the population at greatest risk remains what the CDC refers to as "men who have sex with men" or the MSM group, followed by intravenous drug users. The MSM group is overrepresented in the HIV/AIDS infected population, as it represents about 2 percent of the population but consists of 62 percent of all new HIV cases diagnosed in 2011, as well as about half of all people currently living

> **Check out the latest information on HIV/AIDS in the United States by going to the CDC website and searching for HIV/AIDS under "Diseases and Conditions" in the online menu.**

with HIV/AIDS. White MSM and black MSM accounted for the majority of new diagnoses in 2011 (11,810 and 10,8375 cases, respectively), followed by Latino MSM (7,266 cases). Heterosexuals consisted of approximately 28 percent of all new diagnoses in 2011. Women consisted of about 23 percent of all new diagnoses in 2009, with black women consisting of about 65 percent of those cases. With regard to trends in newly diagnosed cases of HIV infection, young MSM experienced an increase in diagnoses, up 22 percent (8800 new cases) in 2010, compared with prior years, while women experienced a decrease in diagnoses of about 21 percent (6100 new cases) (CDC, 2011).

The ongoing trend in the demographics of AIDS that disproportionately affects people of color, particularly young black men, and black women, has led to many changes in the psychosocial needs of the HIV/AIDS population, which has had an impact on the roles and functions of social workers working with this population. There is still considerable social stigma associated with an HIV/AIDS diagnosis, particularly in light of the uninformed belief that it is a disease affecting only the homosexual population. But because HIV/AIDS was a disease that affected primarily Caucasians when it first surfaced in the United States, racial discrimination was not a central psychosocial issue. But now that this disease is affecting many minority communities, racial discrimination has been coupled with the existing social stigmas that often presume immoral behavior,

> **View the documentary "Endgame: AIDS in Black America" on YouTube. (https://www.youtube.com/watch?v=eIOJWkPFx-g)**

such as sexual promiscuity and drug abuse. Despite aggressive public awareness campaigns in both the general public and the professional community designed to increase general awareness and remove stigma, many individuals with the HIV/AIDS virus are forced to endure numerous barriers to getting basic needs met—some of which are related to the stigma, some related to institutionalized racial discrimination, and some related to a combination of both (Kaplan, Tomaszewski, & Gorin, 2004).

For instance, quality medical care is lacking on most Native American reservations, and native advocates argue that the reason for this relates to racial disparity and historic mistreatment and oppression. When reservations were first confronted with a rapidly increasing incidence of HIV/AIDS in the 1990s, elders complained that the medical neglect experienced on most reservations was yet another form of racial discrimination and oppression, evidenced by the fact that the federal government was not allocating sufficient funding to address this issue on the reservations (Weaver, 1999). Social workers working within the medical field must be aware of the various ways that racial prejudice plays out within the community, whether such discrimination is direct and overt or institutionalized (e.g., governmental resource allocation). This awareness can then translate into advocacy and outreach as well as increased sensitivity as practitioners challenge their own perception of the HIV/AIDS crisis, including their attitudes about those populations that are currently the most significantly affected by this disease.

HIV/AIDS and the Latino Population

According to the CDC (2011), the Latino population is disproportionately affected by the HIV/AIDS virus (even though the white MSM population still accounts for the majority of those in the United States diagnosed with HIV/AIDS). While Latinos represent approximately 16 percent of the population, they constituted about 20 percent of all new HIV diagnoses in 2009, an incidence rate three times that of Caucasians (relative to their representation in the population). The largest group among Latinos diagnosed with HIV in 2011 is Latino MSM.

Among the U.S. Latina/o population, those living in the southern United States, where the Latina/o population has grown by over 200 percent since 1990, are particularly vulnerable for a variety of reasons. A report focusing on a two-year fact-finding and cooperation program facilitated by the *Latino Commission on AIDS* explored the extent and nature of the HIV/AIDS problem within the Latina/o population living in the Deep South, which includes Alabama, Georgia, Louisiana, Mississippi, North Carolina, South Carolina, and Tennessee (Frasca, 2008).

The program, also referred to as the *Deep South Project*, found evidence that Latinas/os are being infected with HIV at disproportionate rates in the South, and yet are often excluded from the healthcare system, as well as HIV/AIDS-related services, (such as prevention and educational programs) because of their immigration status, fear related to an increase in anti-immigrant hostility, and the stigmatization of the disease within the Latina/o community. They also often lack access to HIV/AIDS-related services because of geographic isolation. In general, there are insufficient HIV/AIDS-related programs in the Deep South that target the Latina/o population, and an insufficient number of bilingual service providers. The report found that because of a lack of awareness of the nature of the disease and lack of access to quality healthcare, many within the Latina/o population are diagnosed in the later stages of the disease, which limits the success rate of the antiviral therapy (ART) protocol (Frasca, 2008).

Many Latina/o relationships tend to reflect more traditional gender roles consistent with machismo culture, which increases the risk of contraction and transmission of the HIV/AIDS virus. For instance, within the machismo culture, men commonly engage in high-risk sexual behaviors to prove their manhood, such as having multiple sex partners, despite being married, and not wearing a condom. Latina women often cite an awareness that their male partner's sexual behavior places them at greater risk for contracting the HIV/AIDS virus, but they do not believe they have enough power in the relationship to make demands for safe-sex practices, such as fidelity and/or wearing a condom (Acevedo, 2008).

Social workers working within the Latina/o population must develop a level of cultural competence in working with this population, becoming aware of the many culturally related risk factors affecting this population. They must also be aware of how racial prejudice, social exclusion based upon immigration status (or perceived status), and various stigmas impact the Latina/o's access to educational and prevention services, as well as access to quality and timely healthcare (Acevedo, 2008).

The Deep South Project report makes several recommendations, including public health departments conducting needs assessment of the Latina/o population, increasing outreach efforts in high Latina/o communities, increasing the number of bilingual service providers, increasing the cultural competency of service providers working with the Latina/o population, and increasing HIV/AIDS research on Latina/o populations so that the literature more accurately reflects the nature and needs of the Latina/o population (Frasca, 2008).

Three-pronged Approach to Working With the HIV/AIDS Population

When confronting the HIV/AIDS crisis, social workers engage in a three-pronged approach to psychosocial care, including prevention and educational awareness (such as the practice of safe sex), client advocacy, and case management/counseling. Social workers are actively involved in both practice and policy aspects of the HIV/AIDS crisis, including meeting the psychosocial needs of those diagnosed with HIV/AIDS, as well as being on the front lines of prevention efforts, community and patient educational and awareness campaigns, advocacy for increased funding of intervention and treatment programs, and participating in lobbying efforts advocating for the passage of laws designed to protect the privacy and legal rights of those diagnosed with HIV/AIDS.

Social workers working in hospitals and other healthcare settings assist those with HIV/AIDS in obtaining necessary medical services and providing counseling and case management for those affected by this disease. The nature of the counseling will change depending on the progression of the virus. Clients newly diagnosed will need counseling focusing on acceptance of a potentially terminal disease, whereas other clients will need counseling focusing on living with a chronic illness, accepting a life of potential disability, accepting a life that includes multiple medications taken on a daily basis, and learning to live with the consequences of stigmatized disease.

Assess your comprehension of "Working with Patients With HIV/AIDS" by completing this quiz.

Depending on the unique needs of the patient, the social worker may help secure child care; help the patient apply for financial assistance; obtain home healthcare; maintain or obtain employment, housing, and medical care, including care for other health-related issues, such as substance abuse; and finally help the patient and family contend with the various stressors involved with having a stigmatized illness (Galambos, 2004).

THE U.S. HEALTHCARE CRISIS: A LEGISLATIVE RESPONSE

In 2007, Michael Moore, American film director, writer, and social advocate released his documentary called *Sicko*, highlighting a range of serious problems with the U.S. healthcare system. Throughout the film, Moore featured everyday Americans who faced insurmountable challenges in attempting to pay for and receive quality healthcare. In some cases, patients did not have sufficient healthcare insurance, either because it was unaffordable or because they were denied coverage. In his film, Moore cited a range of insurance industry policies designed to avoid providing coverage to many mainstream Americans–policies that Moore alleged were designed to benefit the for-profit insurance industry, not the consumer. The crux of Moore's film was that the United States was the only industrialized country where an individual could potentially face financial ruin and in some cases death because of increasingly unaffordable healthcare and unsavory

Check out an analysis of the accuracy of Michael Moore's film *Sicko*, by going to the CNN website and searching for an article entitled: "Analysis: Sicko' numbers mostly accurate; more context needed"

practices by a for-profit insurance industry that, according to Moore, was more concerned about its financial bottom line than the healthcare of its consumers.

Advance Human Rights and Social and Economic Justice?

Practice Behavior: Engage in practices that advance social and economic justice.

Critical Thinking Question: Many social justice advocates believe that healthcare is a human right. How can social workers help advocate for equal access to quality healthcare in the United States?

After a contentious partisan battle over the role of government in ensuring that all Americans have access to quality and affordable healthcare, the Patient Protection and Affordable Care Act (ACA) was signed into law by President Obama on March 23, 2010. Proponents of the ACA (also referred to as "Obamacare" and the PPACA) framed the healthcare crisis in the United States as a human rights issue, often relying on arguments that all individuals deserve affordable healthcare. Advocates of the ACA have cited the recent trend of reductions in employer-provided healthcare benefits to employees, including increases in employee contributions, making it nearly impossible for many lower and middle-class individuals to afford healthcare insurance, despite many being employed full-time.

Linking compulsory healthcare insurance coverage to employment dates back to the early 1900s, when Congress passed legislation limiting wage increases, and employers responded by offering employees "fringe benefits" to increase/quality workers (Scofea, 1994). Employment-provided insurance benefits were also thought to guarantee a full-time workforce, as people would be required to work to receive much-needed benefits. Yet government incentives for employers that provided employee healthcare benefits have not been able to keep pace with skyrocketing costs of healthcare, and thus generous benefit packages became less commonly offered to the average full-time employee. Further, the nature of healthcare provision has changed dramatically in the last 100 years, due in large part to technological advances, which has increased the cost of medical care, as well as the expected human lifespan.

The concept of a single-payer government-sponsored healthcare program is not new. In fact, President Truman attempted to introduce such a program for all Americans, and had considerable public support, but universal healthcare program was vehemently opposed by the American Medical Association (Corning, 1969). In response to strong opposition to a government-sponsored single payer system, no such program was successfully implemented in the United States (despite several attempts), until that is, when the ACA was voted into law in 2010. The ACA isn't a true universal healthcare program, but rather is a complex network of policies and requirements that place limitations on third-party payers (e.g., private insurance companies) and employers with regard to the nature of the benefits they provide and how such benefits are to be facilitated. Implementation of the ACA was incremental, with most aspects of the law being implemented by January 1, 2014.

The goal of the ACA is to reform the healthcare system in the United States by expanding insurance coverage, making healthcare more affordable, and increasing

Social Work, Social Media, and Technology

In the months preceding the final roll out of the ACA the government used the Internet and social media to provide information about the new legislation to the American public and also to counteract misinformation. The government's social media campaign includes a website, a Twitter account, and a Facebook page.

Conduct an Internet search and find at least two other ways that the social media is currently being used to provide advocacy and/or educational services in the healthcare realm. Do you think these campaigns are effective? Why or why not?

consumer protections. The ACA includes an emphasis on prevention and wellness and taking steps to limit rising healthcare costs. According to the NASW (2014), key provisions of the legislation as of January 1, 2014, include the following:

- Employers must provide health insurance for their employees (citizens and legal residents), or pay penalties, with exceptions for small employers.
- Tax credits are provided for certain small businesses that reimburse certain costs of health insurance for their employees (began 2010).
- Citizens and legal residents must sign up for health insurance by April 1, 2014, with some exceptions such as financial hardship or religious belief.
- Policies must provide what is called "Essential Health Benefits," at varying rates of coverage, starting at the bronze level (covers 60 percent of healthcare costs) or the platinum level (covers 90 percent of healthcare cost) (Note: the minimum benefit level is referred to as Essential Health Benefits.)
- The creation of state-based insurance exchanges to help individuals and small businesses purchase insurance. Federal subsidies are provided for individuals and families to 2 percent of income for those with incomes at 133 percent of federal poverty guidelines, and 9.5 percent of income for those who earn between 300 percent and 400 percent of the poverty guidelines.
- Medicaid is expanded to cover people with incomes below 138 percent of federal poverty guidelines.
- Creation of temporary high-risk pools for those who cannot purchase insurance on the private market because of preexisting health conditions (began 2010).
- Young adults covered under parents' policies until age 26 (began 2010).
- National, voluntary long-term care insurance program for "community living assistance services and supports" (CLASS) established in 2012.
- The enactment of a range of consumer protections to enable people to retain their insurance coverage (beginning 2010), such as no lifetime monetary caps, no exclusions for preexisting conditions, prohibits insurance plans from rescinding coverage (unless fraud is involved) if consumers become ill, limits on insurance premium increases due to illness and/or gender, etc.

The NASW estimates that the ACA will result in the coverage of at least 32 million people. Gorin (2013), editor-and-chief of NASW's journal *Health & Social Worker*, asserts that social workers play a key role in the debate about healthcare by being advocates for the ACA and assisting in the process of educating consumers about the real nature of this revolutionary healthcare legislation (to confront misinformation and fear of the unknown) and advocate for individual's rights to quality and affordable healthcare. Social workers also serve an important role in providing assistance to clients as they navigate their way through what can be a confusing process of obtaining health insurance through the marketplace exchange and understanding the nature of their benefits.

For an unbiased review of many arguments for and against the ACA, check out the FactCheck website, a nonpartisan project by the Annenberg Foundation.

The ACA is not without its critics, however, from both sides of the political fence. Some common criticisms include compelling millions of uninsured (or underinsured) individuals to purchase healthcare insurance or face financial penalties. Critics are also concerned about the high cost of implementing the ACA, particularly in the first several years. There are also concerns about the impact the ACA will have on small businesses, as well as on the medical community, particularly in terms of whether physicians will accept policies generated through the Health Insurance Marketplace. The reality is that it is simply too early to determine the short- and long-range impact of the ACA on consumers as well as the U.S. economy.

Assess your comprehension of "The U.S. Healthcare Crisis: A Legislative Response" by completing this quiz.

ETHICAL CONSIDERATIONS FOR SOCIAL WORKERS IN HEALTHCARE SETTINGS

In 2005, the NASW published a set of standards for social workers working in domestic or international healthcare settings. The standards set forth 20 expectations for social work behavior and commitments while working in a healthcare setting. Standard 1 focuses on Ethics and Values and emphasizes the importance of social workers supporting clients seeking healthcare services in making ethical decisions, particularly in light of recent technological advances that can lead to challenges in making ethical and moral healthcare decisions, such as those involved in end-of-life care. Standard 2 focuses on healthcare disparities, citing the importance of social workers' ethical obligation to act as "brokers, advocates and mediators, for the healthcare needs of members historically disenfranchised populations," many of whom do not have equal access to healthcare services. Social workers working in a healthcare setting must also become competent in working with a diverse population, as many ethical dilemmas can emerge when diverse populations, particularly those from underrepresented and historically marginalized populations, receive disparate care within the U.S. healthcare system.

Assess your comprehension of "Ethical Considerations for Social Workers in Healthcare Settings" by completing this quiz.

THE HOSPICE MOVEMENT

Hospice care is a service provided to the terminally ill that focuses on comprehensive care addressing their physical, emotional, social, and spiritual needs. Although hospices have existed since about the 4th century, the biblical and Roman concepts of hospice involved providing refuge for the poor, sick, travelers, and soldiers returning from war. Hospice as a refuge or service for the terminally ill was not developed until the mid-1960s.

The modern hospice movement emerged from the general dissatisfaction with how dying individuals were being treated by the established medical community. Western medicine is curative by design with a focus on restoring individuals back to a state of healthy functioning. This model left the majority of the traditional medical community at a loss as to how to treat those who were beyond the hope of recovery. Dying patients often felt neglected and isolated in depersonalized hospital settings where they were typically subjected to needless and futile medical interventions. The hospice movement challenged the treatment provided by the traditional medical community that often failed to address pain management effectively and often neglected the psychosocial and spiritual needs of the dying patient.

The History of Hospice: The Neglect of the Dying

Dame Cicely Saunders, the founder of the modern hospice movement, recognized this lack of appropriate care for the dying and set about to make significant changes that would affect how the world viewed the dying process. Originally trained as a nurse,

Saunders eventually earned her degree in medicine and quickly challenged what she saw as the medical community's failure to address the comprehensive needs of terminally ill patients. Saunders was passionate about the care of the terminally ill and in 1958 wrote her first paper, entitled "Dying of Cancer," addressing the need to approach dying as a natural stage of life (Saunders, 1958). Through her work with the terminally ill, Saunders recognized that dying patients required a far different approach to treatment than the traditional one that tended to see death as a personal and medical failure.

In Saunders's personal letters, she describes in detail her discussions with terminally ill patients in the hospice where she worked, as well as her dedication to the prospects of developing a system of care committed to a dying process without pain, while enabling terminally diagnosed patients to maintain their sense of dignity throughout the dying process (Clark, 2002). Saunders founded St. Christopher's Hospice of London in 1967. Her model of care used a multifaceted approach, where dying patients were treated with compassion so that their final days were spent in peace rather than undergoing invasive and futile medical treatments; thus they were free to attend to the business of dying, such as saying good-bye to their loved ones.

The Connecticut Hospice, Inc. was the first hospice opened in the United States in 1974 in New Haven, Connecticut, funded by the National Cancer Institute (NCI). The hospice was created for many of the same reasons noted by Saunders—the belief that good end-of-life care was severely lacking within the U.S. hospital system and the belief that the dying process was a meaningful one worthy of honor and respect (Stein, 2004). When the HIV/AIDS crisis first began in the 1980s, and prior to the development of antiviral treatment, hospices took on a significant role in the end-of-life care of those dying of the AIDS virus. Although there are some freestanding hospices remaining today, hospice is not a "place," but rather it is a concept of care and can be provided anywhere a patient resides (Paradis & Cummings, 1986).

The hospice movement has grown immensely in a relatively short period of time. What began as a grassroots effort of trained volunteers supported by philanthropic agencies, such as the United Way, has become a highly regulated and profitable industry staffed by a team of professional service providers. Although the core goals and philosophy of hospice remain the same, the professionalization and governmental regulation of this field has influenced its service delivery model. For instance, although hospice care was originally developed as an alternative to hospital care, many hospices in the United States are now in some way affiliated with a hospital or other healthcare organization, most are accredited, and almost all are Medicare certified (National Hospice and Palliative Care Organization, 2003; Paradis & Cummings, 1986).

The Hospice Philosophy

The hospice philosophy employed today is similar to the one envisioned by Saunders. Dying is seen not as a failure, but as a natural part of life, where every human being has the right to die with dignity. Hospice care involves a team approach to the care and support of the terminally ill and their family members. A core value of the hospice philosophy is that each person has the right to die without pain and that the dying process should be a meaningful experience. Because Western culture often perceives accepting death as synonymous with giving up, individuals battling illness are often inadvertently encouraged to fight for their survival to the end; thus, the hospice philosophy is counterintuitive to Western cultural wisdom.

Hospice treatment involves palliative care rather than curative care, thus many hospice agencies require that patients agree to cease all curative medical treatments before hospice services are initiated. The hospice movement is highly supportive of patients remaining in their homes, but when that is not possible, hospice service is provided in hospitals, nursing homes, and long-term care facilities and can be an adjunct to other palliative medical services provided. Additionally, hospice agencies require that patients have received a terminal diagnosis of six months or less.

The Hospice Team and the Role of the Hospice Social Worker

The hospice team is interdisciplinary by design, and although there is considerable overlap in many of the roles of the various service providers, the hospice social worker serves a unique purpose on the team, emanating from the distinct values underlying the social work discipline (MacDonald, 1991).

The hospice team typically consists of a *hospice physician* who makes periodic visits and monitors each case through weekly reports from other team members; a *nurse* who visits patients wherever they reside at least three times per week; a *social worker* who provides case management services, counseling to the patient and family, including helping the patient say good-bye to friends and family, help resolve any past conflict, and assistance with end-of-life issues such as preparation of legal documents such as wills, and advance directives (which will be explored in the next section); a *chaplain* who provides spiritual support; a *home health aide* who provides daily care such as personal hygiene; a *trained volunteer* who provides companionship including reading to patients or taking them for strolls in a wheelchair; and a *bereavement counselor* who provides counseling and support to surviving family members after the death of the patient. One might question whether the interdisciplinary team model works, when so many varied professions are involved; yet, research indicates that this model

> After watching the film "Walking with You: A Dialogue of a Hospice Social Worker" on YouTube, consider the particular and unique role of hospice social workers. Why do you think that the hospice social worker in the film found working in hospice less sad than she anticipated? (https://www.youtube.com/watch?v=R8kY8CtKCiM)

Social Work Application Activity

Review the *NASW Standards for Palliative and End of Life Care* brochure on the NASW website, and then consider the following case study, and answer the related questions.

You are a hospice social worker and have just conducted a psychosocial assessment on a new hospice client. Your client is older and has an aging spouse and no adult children in the immediate area. The assessment reveals that you need to make plans about the patient's eventual placement into a facility for full-time care once the illness has progressed to a point beyond the spouse's caregiving ability. Thus, even though the patient's spouse might currently be managing the daily rigors of caring for the patient, plans will need to be made for the patient's full-time care once care requirements become more complex. The psychosocial assessment reveals a history of depression in the patient and conflict within the family. The patient reports a considerable amount of pain, but several family members are concerned about pain medication reducing the patient's level of awareness, thus impacting quality of life. The family has asked that the patient not be consulted on medical care issues, including being told about the terminal diagnoses, because they are afraid it will cause him to lose hope. What kind of intervention strategy might you develop that is consistent with the Standards for Palliative and End of Life Care that will help the family work out their issues, so that they might move toward a place of resolution before the patient dies? What is a priority in hospice care, pain management or mental acuity, or a balance of both? Do you honor the family's request to not discuss with the patient his medical condition? Why or why not?

Assess your comprehension of "The Hospice Movement" by completing this quiz.

is effective as long as there is good communication, trust, and mutual respect among team members, as well as administrative support (Oliver & Peck, 2006).

The hospice social worker provides numerous services to hospice patients and their families, including providing *advocacy* for patients, particularly with regard to obtaining services and financial assistance; *crisis intervention* when emergencies arise; *case management* and *coordination of services* for the comprehensive care of patients and their family members; *case consultation* services among hospice and other healthcare staff; assisting the patient and family in *planning* for the patient's eventual death; and *bereavement counseling* to assist patients in accepting their terminal illness and in saying good-bye to loved ones, as well as counseling surviving family members after the patient's death.

INTERVENTION STRATEGIES: COUNSELING THE TERMINALLY ILL AND THEIR FAMILY MEMBERS

Prior to engaging in any intervention strategies with hospice patients, the social worker must complete a thorough psychosocial assessment to evaluate the patient's current situation, as well the strengths and deficits of the patient and family members. How are the client and family accepting the reality of the terminal illness? What are the family's resources? Is there a history of mental illness? Can the family realistically provide for current and future needs of the patient? Family members who are still reeling from the news that their loved one is dying are often unrealistic in their expectations of the rigors involved with caring for a terminally ill person and will need help to recognize their limitations and need for outside assistance.

Conducting a thorough psychosocial assessment is the first step in making these clinical determinations and ascertaining what services are needed. Although there are basic criteria of a psychosocial assessment, the information sought and the focus of the assessment change depending on the issues at hand. Thus, a psychosocial assessment of a hospice patient will focus more on the patient's current living conditions, and whether they are appropriate in relation to the patient's declining health, as well as end-of-life issues. Other dynamics explored may include the state of the patient's current relationships and whether there are any unresolved issues that need to be resolved before the patient's passing.

Once a thorough psychosocial assessment has been conducted, the social worker can determine the nature and level of intervention necessary to meet the needs of the patient and family members. In fact, the psychosocial assessment in many respects acts as the blueprint for the social worker, determining the course of case management and counseling intervention strategies for the patient and family.

One of the most common roles for hospice social workers includes providing case management and counseling services to patients and their family members that address the issues noted in the psychosocial assessment. For instance, issues related to how the patient and family are dealing with the terminal illness, any loss of control due to increasing debilitation, and the impending

Apply Social Work Ethical Principles to Guide Professional Practice

Practice Behavior: Apply strategies of ethical reasoning to arrive at principled decisions.

Critical Thinking Question: Imagine that you are a hospice social worker working with a terminally ill patient and his family. The family informs you that you are not allowed to talk about the impending death with the dying patient because they do not want him to lose hope. You understand their perspective but also believe that the patient has a right to know about his diagnoses and have someone to talk to about his feelings. What NASW ethical principles would help you navigate this ethical dilemma?

death are all explored and counseling can then be provided as necessary. Yet, because each family is different, the counseling will vary dramatically from patient to patient. For instance, if the patient is a five-year-old child dying of cancer, the social worker will need to assess the needs of the parents and siblings involved. Yet, if the patient is 85 years old with an ailing spouse and adult children in their sixties, the clinical issues will be different, and although it would be incorrect to automatically assume that the level of grief is lessened simply because this death is expected in the natural course of life, the needs of the different parties involved are obviously going to vary significantly. Thus, the actual nature of the illness or condition, the age of the patient, and the specific demographics and characteristics of the family members all combine to determine the nature of the intervention.

I recall working with one client who was dying of amyotrophic lateral sclerosis (ALS), also known as *Lou Gehrig's disease*. She was suffering from almost complete paralysis and was unable to communicate thus I worked primarily with her husband. This couple was in their early eighties and had been married for over 50 years. The surviving spouse was heartbroken at the prospect of losing his wife, who was also his best friend. Our counseling relationship lasted for months and consisted primarily of him talking about his wife, their relationship, and how agonizing it was for him to watch his once capable, articulate wife, who was a leader both in the community and within their family, become slowly imprisoned and paralyzed by ALS. During our initial sessions he shared some wonderful memories of their life together and of his wife's strengths and accomplishments (attending seminary after raising their children) but would then become emotionally upset when sharing the pain and powerlessness he felt as he watched her struggle to communicate, at that point by blinking. My role was not to put a "happy face" on his suffering nor was it to reframe this tragedy in some positive light, as might be appropriate in another type of counseling in another practice setting. Rather, my role was to remain comfortable when in the presence of his emotional expressions of grief and sadness, which in some sense gave him permission to experience these necessary feelings. I did my best to provide comfort and a forum for his sadness, but I never gave him the impression that his feelings were in any way wrong or in need of being fixed.

Well-meaning but misguided social workers are often uncomfortable when confronted with a client's intense emotions of sadness, grief and anger and, in an attempt to alleviate the client's pain and their own discomfort, try to make the client feel better by pointing out the positive side of a crisis or by encouraging the client to not dwell on feelings of sadness and anger. This approach often leaves grieving clients feeling as though their intense feelings are somehow unacceptable, or at the least burdensome, which in turn may result in the client withdrawing and ultimately suffering in isolation.

Hence, one of the greatest challenges hospice social workers face is their ability to increase their comfort level for intense and unpleasant emotions. Those who are grieving can intuitively sense when those around them are comfortable with their emotions, and many hospice clients report that hospice counselors are the only people with whom they feel safe and comfortable sharing their deepest and most painful feelings of loss, sadness, anger, and mourning.

There are several common issues that a hospice social worker may encounter when working with terminally ill patients and their family members. Ways in which patients and family members manage the impending death on an emotional and practice level often determines the nature of the intervention strategies used in the counseling process. For instance, do the patient and family accept the diagnosis and grieve openly and collectively? Or do they perceive such acceptance as a sign of lost hope? Are they prepared to deal with the more practical aspects of dying, such as getting the affairs of the patient in order? What coping mechanisms do they possess to help them through this difficult journey? Most likely social workers will encounter a broad range of attitudes, approaches, and coping strategies, with some families presenting a unified approach, and others presenting a complex system of contradictory perspectives and approaches to death. An effective social worker helps terminally ill patients and their families navigate this difficult path, using a range of client-centered and culturally sensitive strategies.

Resisting the Reality of Death

Hospice patients and their family members often struggle with the realities associated with a terminal diagnosis. As mentioned earlier, embracing death often feels all too much like letting go of life, and North American culture is far more comfortable embracing life, even if that means engaging in a futile fight. Many people are fearful that if they accept the reality of the terminal diagnosis, they are essentially letting go of their loved one, which not only risks sending the wrong message, but also feels far too much like giving up. This attitude has contributed to the creation of a sort of taboo surrounding death where many people are resistant to even think about their own deaths, let alone the impending death of a loved one.

In some families, to accept the reality of the terminal diagnosis is synonymous with losing hope, and thus resisting the acceptance of a terminal diagnosis can feel like fighting for life. A hospice social worker might be seen as someone who will attempt to rob the patient and family of their hope by forcing them to deal with the reality of the impending death of a loved one. Many times families make the decision to either reject social work services when first signing up for hospice care or accept social work services but prohibit the social worker from talking about the terminal diagnosis in front of the patient. Yet, because many of the issues addressed by hospice social workers are designed to also deal with problems that will confront the family at some point in the future—perhaps even years after their loved one has died when social work services are not available to assist them, it is important that the social worker be able to confront the family's denial with empathy and compassion and assist them in understanding that to accept the impending death of their loved one is not synonymous with hastening the death or with losing hope.

Counseling can be particularly challenging when the patient is asking for information and the family does not want the information about the terminal diagnosis to be shared. In this situation, the social worker must be sensitive but clear that the patient is the identified client, and what is in the best interest of the patient will also eventually be in the best interest of the family, even if they do not initially recognize this as such. A social worker must delicately assist the family with the task of accepting the terminal illness, facing this approaching loss, and addressing each emotional complication that arises.

Hospice social workers must be comfortable confronting the realities of death within themselves before they can ever hope to be comfortable dealing with the emotional minefield of the death and dying process with patients and families. Knowing how to respond effectively and compassionately when a family accepts social work services but prohibits any discussion of the terminal illness, requires advanced clinical skills based not only on good training and education but also on the social worker's self-awareness and comfort level in dealing with these difficult issues.

Planning for the Death

A hospice social worker also assists the patient and family with the practical aspects of planning for increased disability and eventual death. Such practical planning may include something as specific as assisting the patient and family prepare *advanced directives* or as broad as helping the patient and family sort through their feelings of sadness and even anger in response to the reality of the impending death. Generally, advanced directives include the spelling out of one's end-of-life wishes. Legal documents such as do-not-resuscitate (DNR) orders, living wills, and medical powers of attorney are designed to clearly define hospice patients' wishes regarding the nature of their medical care if and when they reach a point where they are no longer able to make decisions for themselves. Preparing advanced directives is an emotional process, however. Imagine sitting with a patient who recently learned he is terminally ill and will likely die in less than six months and discussing whether or not the patient and his family want extraordinary measures taken to save his life when a point is reached in his disease process where he is unresponsive and stops breathing. Making a decision that essentially will mean allowing a family member to die without intervention, either through the removal of a feeding tube or not using cardiopulmonary resuscitation (CPR) to revive their loved one, often generates feelings of immense guilt. Such emotional turmoil has the potential to create significant conflict and rifts within a family system that may already be buckling under the emotional strain of their impending loss. A social worker's role then is not simply to assist the patient and family with the practical matters involved with preparing advanced directives but to help the family navigate this rocky path on an emotional level as well.

Another role of the social worker is to assist the patient with the preparation of *funeral arrangements*. The thought of planning one's own funeral might seem rather morbid to some, but it can actually be rather therapeutic for someone who is facing a terminal illness or other life-limiting condition. Consider experiencing a life event that stripped you of all control—you can no longer plan for your future because you have only six months to live, you can no longer bound out of the door for a morning jog or even to run errands whenever the mood strikes. A terminal illness not only robs its victims of their hopes for the future but it also robs them of their control in all respects, particularly in their everyday lives. Patients—even aging patients—often struggle with the reality of their increasing dependence on others. Planning their funeral gives patients a sense of control in the midst of their increasing powerlessness.

The hospice social worker can utilize what might initially appear to be a practical matter (making funeral arrangements) to facilitate discussions and elicit feelings about the patient's increasing debilitation and resultant confinement and dependence. I recall working with a hospice patient who, at the age of 93, shared heartfelt grief at the thought that he could no longer take his dog for a walk or run to catch up with a friend. In his confinement to a bed, he recalled how he had taken his physical freedom for granted and felt powerless and hopeless in response to the realization that his body could no longer cooperate with what his mind wanted to do. Planning his funeral was the one thing he felt he still had control over in the midst of the powerlessness he felt in every other aspect of his life.

The Spiritual Component of Dying

Hospice care has its roots in the caring of the dying by religious orders, because religious leaders recognized the spiritual component of facing one's mortality and eventual death. Even though religious issues and spiritual concerns may technically fall under the purview of the hospice chaplain, every professional on the hospice team will likely be asked by a patient or family member to pray with them, and social workers, including bereavement counselors, must be comfortable in doing so, even if they do not happen to share the same faith as the patient. Facing one's mortality can be a frightening experience for many, and relying on or reconnecting to the faith of one's youth is a common experience for those dying of a terminal illness.

Counseling commonly takes on a spiritual tone as hospice patients attempt to make sense out of their terminal diagnosis. Patients might experience anger, confusion, and a loss of hope and may seek answers from God, yet pose these questions to the social worker. Although no one expects someone in social work to be an expert in theology, it is important that the social worker feel comfortable enough to help the patient sort through these questions, and even if questions cannot be answered, the social worker can then direct a pastor or other religious leader to the patient.

Effective Bereavement Counseling

Several research surveys have noted that whereas about 60 percent of social work programs at both a bachelor's and a master's level offered courses related to death and dying, these courses were primarily offered as electives, and only about 25 percent of students actually took them. Related studies found that over 60 percent of new social workers felt as though their educational program did not adequately prepare them for counseling clients dealing with end-of-life issues (for a complete discussion of these surveys, see Kramer, Hovland-Scafe, & Pacourek, 2003). This is unfortunate because many social workers work directly or indirectly with death and dying issues, including loss and bereavement. In light of this, it is essential that those in the social work obtain the necessary education and training so that they feel competent in providing services to clients dealing with death and dying.

Several theoretical models are available for dealing with bereavement related to death and dying. Traditional grief models, including Elisabeth Kübler-Ross's (1969) model of grief, depict grieving in terms of distinct, but overlapping, stages where a mourner meets a loss with a sense of *denial* and disbelief, then moves on to the *anger* stage, where the mourner often feels a sense of injustice and even rage in response to the loss. The object of the anger varies depending on the circumstances surrounding the loss but might include being angry with God, the loved one who died, or everyone in general. The next stage is marked by the mourner *bargaining* to avoid the loss. Individuals whose loss is due to a death will often bargain with God—perhaps promising a sinless life if their loved one can be returned to them. The stage of *depression* follows the bargaining stage. During this stage, mourners experience deep melancholy, often citing a sense of hopelessness and despair. The final stage of grieving involves the mourner's *acceptance* of the loss. Although Kübler-Ross's stage theory has dominated the field of grief and loss for many years, there has been a recent shift away from perceiving the mourning process as one where the bereaved progress through distinct and linear emotional stages.

Many contemporary theorists have recently focused more on task theories, which suggest that mourners are confronted with tasks or challenges they need to master as they make their way on their grief journey. Alan Wolfelt, a *thanatologist* (an expert on death and grieving), has developed a task-based theory of grief and loss. Wolfelt (1996) cites seven reconciliation needs that both adults and children need to progress through toward healing. It is interesting to note that Wolfelt does not discuss healing in terms of acceptance, which he believes may put too much pressure on the bereaved, particularly those mourning a significant loss, such as the death of a child. Wolfelt's seven reconciliation needs include acknowledging the reality of the death, embracing the pain of the loss, remembering the person who died through memories, developing a new self-identity in the absence of the loved one, searching for some meaning in the loss, receiving ongoing support from others, and reconciling the grief (reconciling is different than acceptance).

Bereavement counseling can be facilitated by a social worker, a counselor, or depending upon state licensing requirements, even hospice volunteers. In fact, it is typically a volunteer who follows up with family members after the death of the patient to explore how the surviving family members are faring, as well as to determine the need for ongoing bereavement counseling. Social workers who conduct bereavement counseling may do so on an individual basis but will commonly facilitate support groups focusing on a particular loss. Groups for children surviving the loss of a parent or groups for widows or widowers are examples of grief-specific bereavement support groups. Most hospices offer free bereavement counseling for up to one year after the death of the patient as a part of the full continuum of care. Knowing that their loved ones will be cared for after their death often provides a sense of comfort for dying hospice patients; thus, bereavement counseling is an important aspect of hospice care.

Assess your comprehension of "Intervention Strategies: Counseling the Terminally Ill and Their Family Members" by completing this quiz.

MULTICULTURAL CONSIDERATIONS

In general, individuals from many ethnic minority and migrant groups tend to underutilize hospice care. The reasons for this underutilization appear to relate to numerous factors, including lack of awareness of hospice care; Medicare regulations, which create barriers for immigrant, low-income, and minority groups; a lack of diversity within the hospice staff leading to a general mistrust and discomfort with hospice services; and a lack of knowledge of hospice care on the part of many physicians who serve ethnic minority and migrant populations. Many ethnic groups maintain values that are inconsistent with hospice values and perceive acceptance of a death negatively, and although this attitude is not significantly different from Western values in general, many within the majority culture have slowly adopted new cultural values that espouse acceptance of death as an important part of life.

A 1999 study that examined barriers to hospice service for African Americans found that many African Americans held religious beliefs that conflicted with the hospice philosophy. Subjects stated that they did not feel it was appropriate to talk about, plan for, or accept their own deaths. In addition, a majority of the subjects interviewed stated that they felt more comfortable turning to those within their own community, particularly their church, for support during times of crisis, rather than to strangers within the healthcare system (Reese, Ahern, Nair, O'Faire, & Warren, 1999).

Researchers involved in this study acknowledge the importance of not pushing a service on the African American culture if it is truly unwanted and perhaps even unneeded, but they cite leaders within the African American community who argue that members

Social Work, Social Media, and Technology

Online communities are increasingly being used for the purposes of bereavement and grieving. Many people who may not wish to attend a support group in person may feel more comfortable attending a support group online because of the ease of access and the increased anonymity. Compassionate Friends is a nonprofit organization that has been providing psychosocial support and advocacy for the bereaved for years, and they now offer online community support groups targeting specific populations (e.g., parents, grandparents, children, etc.). What do you believe are the pros and cons of online community support groups for the bereaved? Do you believe this type of support can be a stand-alone service, or an adjunct to more comprehensive services? Do you believe that online community support groups violate confidentiality as described in the NASW Code of Ethics? Why or why not?

within their community would in fact benefit from hospice care, stating that a chief reason why hospice care is often rejected lies more in the lack of knowledge about the services provided. Thus, rather than accepting these differences in philosophy, the study authors suggest that hospice agencies adapt their services to meet the needs of the African American community (Greiner, Perera, & Ahluwalia, 2003; Reese et al., 1999).

No research has been conducted to date on usage patterns or barriers to service for Asian Americans, Latina/o Americans, or Native Americans, but similar issues are likely to emerge within these communities as well. It is imperative that hospice agencies remain flexible enough to meet the needs of all cultural groups and that policies that either directly or inadvertently discriminate against ethnic minority groups and migrant communities, such as various admittance requirements, be challenged and if possible changed so that all individuals who desire hospice care can benefit from this service. Although there may be multiple barriers facing some populations in receiving hospice care services—some financial and some cultural—one of the foundational values of the hospice philosophy is that hospice care will be available to every dying individual.

Assess your comprehension of "Multicultural Considerations" by completing this quiz.

Certainly hospice administrators are responsible for developing admittance policies that do not directly or inadvertently discriminate against low-income patients while protecting the financial status of the hospice. But social workers who are professionally committed to advocating for low-income and underserved populations are in the unique position of securing financial assistance in the form of private and government assistance through effective case management.

ETHICAL CONSIDERATIONS FOR SOCIAL WORKERS WORKING IN HOSPICE SETTINGS

A key ethical dilemma faced by hospice staff involves the issue of euthanasia, or physician-assisted suicide. Dr. Jack Kevorkian made national headlines in the 1990s for assisting numerous terminally ill patients in the ending of their lives and served time in prison as a result of his activities. Because euthanasia is illegal in most states, patient requests for physician-assisted suicide create an ethical dilemma complicated by the illegal nature of such an act. Requests for physician-assisted suicide present a particularly challenging ethical dilemma for faith-based hospice agencies that believe that issues related to death and dying fall under the sole dominion of God (Burdette, Hill, & Moulton, 2005).

Those who believe that euthanasia should be legalized typically cite an argument based on the inalienable human right to choose death when pain and suffering rob them of a meaningful life. Although a counterargument could be based on the meaningful nature of suffering, a better argument might be based on the hospice philosophy that dying persons have a right to die without physical, emotional, and spiritual pain. In fact, several studies examining similarities among terminally ill patients expressing a desire to hasten their deaths found that the chief reasons cited included (1) depression and a sense of hopelessness, (2) poor symptom management, (3) poor social support, (4) fear of becoming a burden on family members, and (5) a poor physician–patient relationship (Kelly et al., 2002; Leman, 2005). Thus, the question is: If these issues could be addressed effectively, would these same patients still seek physician-assisted suicide?

Although the hospice philosophy advocates for neither hastening nor postponing death, hospice agencies have more in common with supporters of physician-assisted suicide than one might initially think. In fact, the leading reasons among terminally ill patients for requesting a quicker end to their lives listed previously include the very issues hospice care is designed to manage. Hospice social workers can respond to this ethical dilemma by advocating for the meaningful nature of the dying process from spiritual, psychological, and social perspectives, made possible when patients are helped to confront feelings of sadness and hopelessness, when symptoms are well managed, when social support is bolstered, when families are assisted with the care of the patient, and when the hospice physician maintains a close relationship with patients based on a palliative care model. In fact, one social worker working in hospice explained that if a choice is made to cut the dying process short, then many opportunities for growth and even last-minute resolution may be lost, as it is often the last weeks, days, hours, or even minutes of a person's life that many lifelong problems are resolved. Hospice advocates cite the value of every life experience and remind us how these types of end-of-life realizations and resolutions also benefit surviving family members and friends (Mesler & Miller, 2000).

Assess your comprehension of "Ethical Considerations for Social Workers Working in Hospice Settings" by completing this quiz.

Summary

Hospital social workers provide crisis counseling, case management, discharge planning, and a range of other generalist services focused on the care of clients receiving services in relation to a medical issue. Some examples include providing counseling and case management services to patients and their family members experiencing a medical emergency, and providing psychosocial support to those struggling with HIV/AIDS. Hospital social workers commonly work on interdisciplinary teams and possess an array of skills that equip them to manage a wide range of issues within a client population seeking medical services. The passage of the ACA health care delivery, management and reimbursement models have changed dramatically the healthcare model in the United States, impacting both patients receiving medical care, and social workers.

Hospice care grew out of a general discontent with Western curative treatment models, which often involves subjecting the terminally ill to unnecessary, futile and often painful treatment, as well as a loss of dignity in their final months of life. The hospice philosophy is based upon a palliative model, which involves a patient and family-centered approach that allows patients to die with dignity with the least amount of pain possible. Although hospice care has been around for over four decades, many patients and their families are resistant to accepting hospice services, because they believe that doing so is tantamount to accepting defeat and losing hope. Social workers play a key role in helping families perceive hospice care in a different light, where embracing the dying process recognized as an important and meaningful part of living.

Finally, the authors challenge the common notion that social service involvement increases and strains budgets, suggesting that although budgets might increase initially with social work involvement, consistent social work intervention from case inception reduces financial outgo in the long run as expensive and time-consuming crises are avoided. This contention is based on the well-researched connection between many psychosocial and physical crises, where many medical emergencies requiring costly intervention have their origin at least in part in the psychosocial realm, such as patient depression and anxiety (Reese & Raymer, 2004).

Another challenge facing hospice agencies is the well-established pattern of patients being referred for hospice far too late for any of the meaningful work to be effectively accomplished. Despite the immense growth of the hospice movement and the general assumption that hospice care is a wonderful concept, only 22 percent of dying individuals are actually referred for hospice services, and of these about three-quarters are referred within three weeks of their death (Stein, 2004). Lorenz, Asch, Rosenfeld, Lui, and Ettner (2004) cited numerous barriers to hospice admission including patients being rejected for hospice admittance because they were still seeking curative medical treatment such as chemotherapy. Lorenz et al. recommended that hospices reexamine their enrollment policies that might inadvertently exclude appropriate patients from receiving services. They suggested that there might be a link between the general knowledge that the majority of hospices deny enrollment to patients still undergoing curative treatment and the fact that the majority of dying patients are either not referred at all to hospice or are referred too late in their disease process to benefit from hospice services.

It seems clear that hospices must be more proactive in developing educational programs focusing on the nature of hospice care and the importance of early referral. As experts in the psychosocial dynamics commonly at play in end-of-life care, social workers can lead these educational efforts both with the hospice administrators who determine enrollment policies and within the medical community and general public. A family's willingness to forgo curative treatment immediately on learning of the terminal diagnosis (necessary for hospice referral) is likely an unrealistic expectation on the part of hospice administrators. Deciding to pull a feeding tube or stop chemotherapy are psychosocial issues that evoke considerable emotional turmoil within families and could be considered a psychosocial goal of hospice counseling. Thus, although continuing to actively seek a medical cure is contrary to the hospice philosophy, perhaps the transition from curative to palliative care could be one that occurs as a part of hospice care, not as a condition of it.

Social workers must continue to be an integral part of the hospice team for hospice care to remain true to its original goals and philosophy. But social workers must also be on the front lines of effecting change within the hospice field, which will ensure that hospice care is flexible in meeting the needs of a changing society.

Recall what you learned in this chapter by completing the Chapter Review.

10

School Social Work

Mario is a junior at a public high school in a large urban school in a state bordering Mexico. He does not have a behavior problem and does relatively well in his academic studies but has come to the attention of school social workers because of excessive absences. His teachers also report that he seems particularly "stressed out" lately, and not himself. There is concern that he may be withdrawing emotionally and socially because of an increase in anti-immigrant sentiment exhibited among some students and school personnel. A psychosocial evaluation reveals that Mario is the oldest of four children. Mario's parents are undocumented immigrants from Mexico who have been living in the United States for approximately 15 years, having been recruited to the United States by a large agri-cultural company. Mario's parents do not speak English, and Mario disclosed that he often misses school so that he can translate for his parents or intercede on behalf of his parents who are often scared to seek out services themselves in light of anti-immigration legislation recently passed in the state. Mario also disclosed that he has in fact been the target of anti-immigrant sentiment in the form of deroga-tory statements and scapegoating. For instance, on several occa-sions while walking down the halls in school he has heard random students shout out to him asking for proof of his legal status. He has also experienced negative statements directed toward all Latina/o immigrants, including a few teachers and some office assistants making statements appearing to scapegoat this population for everything from escalating violence in the drug war, to scapegoating Latina/os for high regional unemployment rates. The school social worker, Kate, responds to Mario and his parents reassuringly and explains that Mario can receive supportive services—both from government social services and from programs within the school without fear of his parents' immigration status being disclosed. At this point in the session, Mario admits that he just learned that he does not in fact have legal status. Mario grew up believing that he was born in the United States, but after a recent meeting with a state social service agency, he was informed that his Social Security number was not valid. His parents then told him that he was six months old when they emigrated from Mexico, and they used false papers provided to them by men from the U.S. agricultural company that recruited them. Mario became extremely distraught when sharing this secret, expressing discouragement and fear that he would not be able to attend college and receive financial aid, despite having lived in the United States almost his entire life and working so hard to do well in school, or worse, that he could be legally deported to a country he has never visited, and where he knows no one.

Before Kate can competently provide guidance, services, and referrals for Mario and his family, she must be aware of several areas of law that impact the migrant population—both those who have legal immigration status and those who do not. These overlapping areas include federal and state immigration laws (much of which has? changed significantly post-9/11), changes in public assistance policies in response to 1996 welfare reform (that barred the majority of legal residents, documented and undocumented, from receiving any public assistance), differences in legislation and policies on various levels (federal, state, county, and school), as well as having an awareness of any pending legislation that may have an impact on Mario and his family, such as the DREAM Act (Development, Relief, and Education for Alien Minors), pending bipartisan, federal legislation that would make it possible for students like Mario to attend college, under certain circumstances. Gaining this level of awareness of macro issues affecting Latina/o students at Kate's school is a vital part of providing culturally competent social work services. One way to learn more about current issues affecting students like Mario is to attend workshops and conferences focusing on immigration issue, as well as seeking out resources identifying key issues and dynamics published by advocacy organizations or other authoritative sources. For instance, the National School Boards Association and the National Education Association jointly published an online report in 2009 in cooperation with several professional organizations, including School Social Work Association of America, entitled "Legal Issues for School Districts Related to the Education of Undocumented Immigrants" (Borkowski & Sorensen, 2009). This publication would be a great place for Kate to start in learning about a public school's obligations and responsibilities regarding the education of students with a range of immigration situations.

THE HISTORY OF SOCIAL WORK
IN THE PUBLIC SCHOOL SYSTEM

The field of social work has had a strong presence in the U.S. public school system for over 100 years and has roots in the settlement house movement. Settlement house workers in the late 1800s and early 1900s, all of whom were women, recognized the poor job urban schools were doing establishing and maintaining connections with the parents of many of their students, thus served as liaisons between migrant school children and their families, and school personnel. Because settlement houses were designed to provide services and relief primarily to low-income immigrant populations in large urban areas, using Settlement house workers in this capacity (as pioneer school social workers) was ideal since most of the children who were the original focus on these early efforts to connect school with home were from families who had recently emigrated from non-English-speaking countries, and were already receiving services at Settlement houses. (McCullagh, 1993, 1998). Thus, these early school social workers served an important support function of supporting mandatory school attendance policies, enabling teachers to focus on the task of teaching academics (Allen-Meares, 2006).

Migrant children were not the only focus of early school social workers though. Mass urbanization meant that scores of families were moving from agricultural lifestyles to the city in search of factory jobs. With them came children, many of whom were not adjusting well to city life, particularly when it involved living in cramped quarters with parents who worked long hours. Of chief concern among school districts that were the first to use school social workers was child "maladjustment," child "handicaps," and erratic school attendance. It was the school social worker's primary goal to address these concerns by ensuring that children's adjustment needs were met, children with handicaps received necessary services, and children attended school regularly (Allen-Meares, 2006; McCullagh, 1993).

These school social work pioneers had many different titles: visiting teachers, home visitors, special visitors, and visiting social counselors, and they often lived in the settlement houses acting as a liaison between the school, child, and home. This early work, often referred to as the *Visiting Teacher's Movement*, tended to focus on school-related matters such as irregular attendance issues, various health problems, searching the city for children who were not attending schools (such as deaf children and orphans living on the streets), and various other home-centered matters affecting students. The guiding philosophy of home and school visiting committees was that the child was to be viewed from a holistic perspective—not solely as a student causing problems for the school (McCullagh, 1993).

Through the development of numerous committees, and the creation of a governing and organizing association called the Public Education Association (PEA), visiting teachers or counselors grew in popularity and quickly became an integral part of many school districts throughout New York, Boston, and Philadelphia over the next several decades. By the early part of the 20th century, teachers in low-income, high-need, urban neighborhoods had begun to look to these home visitors for advice and assistance on several issues related to their students, including those concerning inappropriate behaviors, potential problems at home, lack of attendance, and general issues related to school functioning. This reliance on and general appreciation of the services provided by these early school social workers reflected the teachers' and school administrators' increasing respect for this support service. In fact, by about 1910, many larger school districts were lobbying to have school social workers become paid members of the school district and board of education, rather than being contracted volunteers of the settlement houses supported by philanthropic organizations.

Schools were also seen as the chief means for "Americanizing" foreign children (and, it was hoped, their families), and thus government interest remained high in social work efforts to connect schools with families because it was believed that through such connections more effective assimilation of immigrant families would occur. The increasing focus on expanding the purpose of schools to include both the education and the social needs of the child is still widely reflected in today's public school systems that not only offer academic education and services but also counseling, case management, food programs, and on-campus health services. But even if the goal of government was social control, the focus of the school social worker remained on the individual child and his or her family members; in fact, the commonly cited goal of these early social workers involved making certain that the individuality of each child did not get lost in the chaos of the overcrowded classroom (McCullagh, 1993).

School social work continued to expand and professionalize over the next 40 years, along with social work in general, and although originally more aligned with teachers and the field of education, by the 1940s visiting teachers and counselors were wholly aligned with the social work profession, and the PEA officially changed its name to the American Association of School Social Workers; and later in the decade the name was again changed to the National Association of School Social Workers (NASSW). By 1955, several different social work-related committees merged to create the National Association of Social Workers (NASW), and although the NASSW still exists, it is now under the auspices of the NASW. The role of the school social worker continued to grow and expand through the 1960s, fueled by the social turbulence that marked this era. This awareness led to many universities developing school social work degree programs (McCullagh, 2001). Finally, in 1975, Congress passed the Individuals with Disabilities Education Act (Pub. L. No. 94-142), requiring that public schools provide "free and appropriate" public education to all school-aged children between the ages of 3 and 21 years, regardless of their disability. This law has required school districts to provide increased funding for social work services for students with special needs, when deemed appropriate.

In recent years, despite significant cuts to public school budgets, which have resulted in significant cuts in mental health services in many schools across the country (Johnson, Oliff, & Williams, 2011), the need for mental health services in school settings is greater than ever (Foster, Rollefson, Doksum, Noonan, Robinson, & Teich, 2005), particularly in urban areas, where crime and poverty continue to flourish. Teachers are increasingly reporting that children with behavioral problems fare worse in their academic performance and overall school adjustment (Baker, Kamphaus, Home, & Winsor, 2006). Poverty is known to increase psychosocial problems in children (Smith, Stagman, Blank, Ong, & McDow, 2011), and child poverty has increased markedly, particularly between 2000 and 2009 (Wight, Chau, & Aratani, 2011). Thus, despite consistently shrinking budgets in public schools across the nation, resulting in cuts in mental health services in a majority of U.S. public schools, schools remain an ideal setting to meet the psychosocial needs of children, particularly because it is psychosocial challenges that often create the most profound barriers to learning and academic success. Recognizing the vital role public schools play in addressing children's mental and emotional well-being is particularly important in light of the fact that mental health services for children in community-based social services programs have been subject to considerable cuts as well.

Currently, school social work remains a growing field that offers excellent practice opportunities for those wanting to work with school-aged children. Issues such as international academic competition, concerns about increasing violence in schools, and continued reliance on social work services for regular as well as special education students have continued to propel school social work forward into the 21st century and helped to offset periodic reductions in education budgets because of cyclical economic downturns. During difficult economic times, however, it is not uncommon for school districts to consider cutting back social work services. This is unfortunate because research consistently shows that school social workers have a positive impact on the lives of students, including improving their academic success. When school social workers self-advocate, by sharing their success stories with school administrators, research shows that cut backs in social work (including lay-offs) significantly decline (Bye, Shepard, Partridge, & Alvarez, 2009; Garrett, 2006).

> **Assess your comprehension of "The History of Social Work in the Public School System" by completing this quiz.**

SCHOOL SOCIAL WORK: THE TRADITIONAL MODEL, ROLES, FUNCTIONS, AND CORE COMPETENCIES

The traditional model of school social work involves the social worker providing school-based social work services as an employee of the school district and as a part of a multidisciplinary team. Although some districts utilize school-based social workers employed by outside agencies (primarily as a cost-saving measure), most school districts in the United States still utilize the traditional model. Regardless of the school social worker's actual employer, the roles and functions of the school social worker are typically generalist in nature but have become increasingly specialized as managed care has forced many school districts to seek government reimbursement for services (such as Medicaid or Medicare), which in turn has prompted an increase in specialized credentials beyond licensing (Lewis, 1998). Essentially, school social workers serve as important liaisons between the school system, a student's family system, and the community, in order to remove barriers to a student's optimum academic performance (Constable, 2009).

Most states require that school social workers have an MSW with a specialization in school social work, have accrued several hundred hours in an internship at a public school, and have passed a state content-area test. Some states still require only a bachelor's degree from an accredited social work program, but there is a national push toward master's level education.

School social workers perform a variety of tasks, serve numerous functions, and operate within several different roles depending on the demographics of the school population, the type of children served, and the capacity in which the social worker is functioning. In general, school social workers assist children in managing any psychosocial issues that are creating a barrier to learning. These could include physical barriers in the form of a disability, cognitive barriers such as intellectual or learning disabilities, or behavioral barriers such as students who are depressed, anxious, or acting out. School social workers also work to develop, enhance, and maintain a close working relationship between student families and the school, advocating for the family in a variety of situations.

> **After viewing the film "A Day in the Life of a School Social Worker" on YouTube, consider whether the field of school social work is an area you would consider. Were there any activities referenced in the film that surprised you? (https://www.youtube.com/watch?v=Ggsz7qtPcoY)**

According to the National Association of Social Workers (NASW), school social workers should be competent in providing individual, group, and family counseling; should be well versed in theories of human behavior and development; and should

Social Work Application Activity

Conduct an Internet search for the School Social Work Association website. Once found, click on the Resources link, and then navigate to the Promoting School Social Work link in the drop down box. Read some of the articles available in the public section and then answer the following questions. How do standard models used in school social work address the academic and behavioral needs of students? What are some of the roles and common functions of a school social worker? How are these roles and functions unique to school social workers compared with other helping professions working within the public school system? What services do school social workers provide that are unique compared with other practice settings?

have knowledge of and be sensitive to the demographic makeup of the school population with which they work, including relevant issues related to socioeconomic status (SES), gender, race, sexual orientation, and any community stressors that might affect a student's ability to perform academically (such as a high crime rate or gang infiltration). School social workers must also have competencies in the areas of assessment, must be familiar with local referring agencies, and must be committed to the values and ethics of the social work profession, including those relating to social justice, equity, and diversity (NASW, 2003).

School social workers may work with the general school population or may be hired to work within the special education department either with physically or mentally disabled children or with students who are deemed behavior disordered. Direct practice will often include individual and group counseling, as well as some family counseling, if necessary. The nature and duration of social work services is often determined by a student's Individualized Education Plan (IEP), which serves as a sort of contract between the school and family for students identified for special education services, including social work services. Thus, students experiencing depression, with unaffected academic performance might not be appropriate candidates for social work services and would likely be referred for mental health services within the community.

Individual counseling might include insight counseling with a high school student, or it might involve play therapy, including drawing, therapeutic games, or doll play, for an elementary school–aged student. *Group counseling* might involve gathering six or eight students together whose parents recently divorced, or who recently moved from another school, and providing them with an opportunity to talk about their struggles and feelings. Yet group counseling might also have a structured and specific curriculum focusing on issues such as anger management or social skills training. School social workers may also conduct home visits to obtain vital information about the student's life outside school as well as to ensure a strong link between home and school.

Case management is also provided by school social workers, and can include the organization and coordination of numerous services received by a student. For instance, a student's case might involve an outside therapist who is providing psychological counseling, a psychiatrist who supervises medication such as antidepressants, a truancy officer, the police department, a child welfare agency, the family, all the student's teachers, and the school administrators. Thus, depending on the actual issues of the student receiving services, the social worker will likely be involved in the coordination of services and the appropriate dissemination of information of a number of involved parties. For instance, new medications or medication changes in students who are suffering from clinical depression would be vital information for school social workers to share with other concerned parties (depending upon confidentiality restrictions, of course).

Crisis intervention is also an important function of a school social worker. Whether the crisis involves a natural tragedy, such as a tornado or earthquake, a student's suicide, or the crisis of on-campus violence such as student-on-student assaults, school social workers provide crisis counseling to the entire student population, families, and even the school staff. Crisis counseling might include helping students face the initial shock of some tragedy, but it also often involves implementing a safety plan, providing ongoing services, and developing changes in policies, often incorporated into prevention programs. For instance, the suicide of a student often elicits emotional distress in other students and can lead to an increased chance of other students committing suicide. A school social worker will be involved in creating awareness (through classroom presentations or staff meetings), maintaining a visible presence on campus, conducting outreach services to vulnerable students, and working on a multidisciplinary team to examine existing school policy, and develop or improve prevention programs.

School social workers may also facilitate *conflict resolution* and *violence prevention* programs. For instance, a school social worker might conduct a structured violence prevention workshop or presentation in a classroom or manage a peer-led conflict resolution program, training students to conduct conflict resolution sessions with students who are engaged in some type of conflict.

Most social workers are assigned to more than one school, and thus they might spend only a few days per week at any one school site. They typically have a caseload of students they must see on a weekly or biweekly basis either on an individual basis or in a group setting, and then perform these various other tasks on an as-needed basis. Because the range of issues school social workers deal with is so broad, it is difficult to describe precisely what they do on a daily basis, but in general school social workers must be generalists to effectively manage the variety of issues with which they are confronted. The Chapter Opening Vignette provides a realistic example of some of the issues a school social worker might encounter, but again the specific nature of the work depends in great part on the demographics of the student population, the age of the students, and the capacity in which the social worker was hired.

Assess your comprehension of "School Social Work: The Traditional Model, Roles, Functions, and Core Competencies" by completing this quiz.

INTERPROFESSIONAL COLLABORATION: WORKING WITH OTHER MENTAL HEALTH PROFESSIONALS WITHIN THE PUBLIC SCHOOL SETTING

Counseling on public school campuses is primarily conducted by three types of professionals: school social workers, who are typically trained professionals with a Master of Social Work (MSW) degree; school counselors, who have a master's degree in school counseling and often have a background in teaching; and school psychologists, who have a master's degree or doctorate in school psychology and, in addition to instruction in educational counseling, are trained to conduct specialized educational and psychological testing of students. Together, these support professionals comprise what is often called *student services* or *pupil support services*. It is with the complexity of student psychosocial challenges in mind then that there has been an increased focus on ways in which school

Apply Critical Thinking to Inform and Communicate Professional Judgments.

Practice Behavior: Demonstrate effective oral and written communication in working with individuals, families, groups, organizations, communities, and colleagues.

Critical Thinking Question: Why is it important for social workers to be able to work in interdisciplinary teams within the public school system?

social workers, school counselors, and school psychologists can move beyond mere cooperation, toward real collaboration (Kim, 2012). Collaboration within a public school context is defined as a process where professionals within each discipline (school social work, school counseling, and school psychology) provide reciprocal information, informing mutual understanding of the client(s) while acknowledging the expertise and roles played by each respective profession (Axelsson & Axelsson, 2009). There is increased need for interprofessional collaboration not only because of the shrinking budgets (requiring the pooling of resources) but also because of a national movement toward school-based mental health programs that are dependent on professionals from each helping discipline working together more effectively (Kim, 2012).

An example is the Expanded School Mental Health (ESMH) program, a three-tiered framework incorporating prevention, early intervention, and treatment. The ESMH framework expands on existing core mental health services provided in the public school system and emphasizes shared responsibility among all school service professionals, as well as community mental health providers.

While school social workers, school counselors, and school psychologists provide psychosocial services in some respect, they use somewhat different approaches to counseling and student support provision and have different standards of practice, and even have different service and treatment goals. Social workers tend to focus more on the psychosocial aspects of students' lives, providing counseling and case management that focus on traditional social work concerns such as the students' overall mental health, violence on campus and at home, the risk of suicide among the student population, poverty and its effect on school performance, as well as the need for advocacy on behalf of vulnerable students, including the homeless student, students of color, and a range of other students who fall into various at-risk groups. School counselors tend to focus more on academic counseling and career guidance, while focusing on emotional or psychological issues that directly pertain to student achievement, and school psychologists focus primarily on testing, particularly in response to numerous federal and state mandates that require the academic testing of students to place them in the proper educational setting but may also provide counseling for students who are experiencing emotional difficulties affecting their academic achievement.

The school counseling profession often has roles and professional identities that overlap with the school social workers, but they typically focuses on academic concerns and career rather than psychosocial issues. School counseling also has a history reaching back to the late 1880s and early 1900s, with roots in the vocational guidance counseling movement (Schmidt & Ciechalski, 2001). In fact, early school counselors focused primarily on matching male high school graduates with an appropriate vocational or job placement. In the 1920s, theories of intelligence and cognitive development became popular, influencing the work of school guidance counselors who, with the advent of intelligence and aptitude testing, now had new tools with which to do their jobs. The 1930s saw advancements in the areas of personality development and motivation psychology, which directly influenced the field of school counseling, enabling counselors to further assist students in identifying areas of aptitude, as well as developing motivational techniques to move students from the academic realm into professional ones. Social trends and political movements were chief among various influences that led to a gradual shift from a primary focus on the vocational needs of students to a more comprehensive and holistic focus where school counselors proactively could meet various developmental needs of students (Schmidt & Ciechalski, 2001).

As with school social work, the Education for All Handicapped Children Act of 1975 (Pub. L. No. 94-142)—which required, among other things, that children with special needs receive all support services necessary for their academic success—led to school counselors becoming involved in special education programs. In addition, government committee reports, such as "A Nation at Risk" (1983), and federal legislation, such as the No Child Left Behind Act of 2001 (now referred to as the *Elementary and Secondary Education Act* [ESEA]) (U.S. Department of Education, 2001), have meant an increase in funding in many school districts' budgets for school counseling, because concerns for academic achievement (or, in some districts, concerns about academic decline) have in many senses outweighed budgetary concerns.

School counseling programs generally focus on three basic areas: *academic counseling, career development,* and *personal–social development* (Dahir, 2001). What form this counseling takes depends in large part on whether the counselor is working at an elementary school, middle school, or high school (secondary school). Other issues influencing the nature of the counseling include the size of the student population, whether the school is in an urban or rural area, and the nature of surrounding community. For instance, a school counselor who works in a high-crime, overcrowded high school in inner-city Chicago will certainly have a different role and perform different functions than a school counselor working in a high-income suburban elementary school.

In general, school counselors provide individual student guidance, such as helping students develop good study skills, engage in preliminary career planning, develop effective coping strategies, and foster good peer relationships through the development of pro-social skills, such as exhibiting empathy, showing kindness to others, and managing anger appropriately. School counselors also develop and facilitate programs on substance abuse awareness and multicultural awareness, for instance. School counselors assist students with goal setting, academic planning, and planning for college. They facilitate crisis intervention with individual students, the student body, families, and the school as a whole. They collaborate with parents, teachers, and school administrators and provide community referrals as necessary. They may also facilitate programs focusing on making the transition to the next level in school or to work. School counselors identify and work with at-risk students, managing behavioral and mental health issues such as substance abuse, suicide threats, classroom disruptions, student–teacher conflicts, and other issues as they arise. Additional school counseling competencies include cultural competence, the ability to advocate for students in an attempt to remove barriers to academic success, a willingness to be leaders in educational reform, and the ability to effectively communicate and collaborate with other educational professionals.

For more information and a list of the activities that school counselors may engage in visit the ASCA website.

The school counseling profession has evolved considerably in the last few decades, and along with that evolution has come professional role redefinition and some role confusion. In fact, a review of the literature relating to the school counseling field clearly reveals a long-standing struggle to define the role and function of school counselors. This is perhaps because of the professional overlap—and even at times, territorial "turf war"—with school social workers and school psychologists, all of whom are concerned with psychosocial counseling and interventions with students who are struggling academically.

School psychologists work alongside both social workers and school counselors. According to the National Association of School Psychologists (NASP, n.d.) "school psychologists help children and youth succeed academically, socially, and emotionally. They collaborate with educators, parents, and other professionals to create safe, healthy, and supportive learning environments for all students that strengthen connections between home and school." If you think this explanation is similar to the description of school social workers and school counselors, you are correct! New paragraph with the other two student services disciplines discussed in this chapter, school psychologists have a broad range of responsibilities and functions that depend in large part on the school environment within which the school psychologist is working. But one significant difference between a school psychologist and a school social worker and/or school counselor is that a school psychologist conducts academic testing on students to evaluate and assess their academic abilities and deficits.

Regardless of a mental health professional's designated role, when one works with human beings experiencing strife, one immediately becomes a generalist having to deal with a broad range of issues while serving in several different roles. Thus, although a school counselor might initiate a counseling session with a student regarding academic performance, study skills, or career planning, the session can take a quick detour focusing on the student's recent breakup, a bullying incident, a friend's suicide,

> **Assess your comprehension of "Inter-professional Collaboration: Working With other Mental Health Professionals Within the Public School Setting" by completing this quiz.**

or a parent's alcohol abuse. School psychologists charged with the responsibility of facilitating all the school district's educational testing might easily find themselves spending extra time with a student who breaks down during testing because she or he is living in a homeless shelter and knows no one at school. In a similar vein, school social workers whose goal is to focus on students' psychological and emotional issues that are creating a barrier to learning might find themselves conducting a study skills workshop or helping students explore where they want to attend college or what they want to do for a career.

THE PLIGHT OF URBAN SCHOOLS

Problems plaguing urban or "inner-city" schools have received considerable attention in recent years from many concerned individuals and groups, including educators, scholars, law enforcement, and even the federal government. In response to these concerns, the Education Trust, a not-for-profit agency committed to working for high academic achievement among all children, has made numerous recommendations regarding school mental health programs, including developing systematic programs designed to address many of the issues currently confronting urban schools, such as gang activity, poverty, homelessness, child abuse, violence on and off campus, increasing rates of clinical depression, unplanned pregnancy, and low academic performance (Baggerly & Borkowski, 2004; Holcomb-McCoy, 2005; Lee, 2005). In addition, many urban schools face what is referred to as an achievement gap when compared with suburban youth. Urban youth are far more likely to drop out of high school and are less likely to meet the minimum standard on national standardized tests. Urban schools have far greater difficulty retaining quality teachers, must contend with political issues often not confronting suburban schools, and are often located in high-crime areas of concentrated poverty (Goldmann, et al., 2011; Jacob, 2007 Olson & Jerald, 1998).

Other issues facing urban schools and thus school social workers working in these settings include dealing with high student absenteeism and unstable family systems, including a high percentage of students living in foster care, and high student transience, where students transfer in and out of school frequently (Green, Conley, & Barnett, 2005; Lee, 2005). Each of these issues is far more complex than one might think. For instance, consider the issue of high student mobility. One might think that this issue would not necessarily affect the school the student is leaving, yet students who leave schools suddenly because of family instability often fail to return their textbooks, which can lead to significant financial losses for schools, many of which are already suffering serious budgetary shortfalls. California is one state that has a significantly higher incidence of student mobility than many other states, due in part to the immigrant population. In a 1999 study of the impact of student transience on school districts, researchers made several suggestions including utilizing school social workers to reach out to departing and incoming students to coordinate transfers and minimize disruptions (Rumberger, Larson, Ream, & Palardy, 1999). Unfortunately with increasingly drastic school budget cuts, far too often those school personnel who are deemed less essential, such as school social workers, are the first ones to be cut despite the important and often cost-saving services they provide (Johnson-Reid, 2011).

WILL HART/PHOTOEDIT, INC

Urban schools are often overcrowded and located in high-crime neighborhoods.

Assess your comprehension of "The Plight of Urban Schools" by completing this quiz.

DIVERSITY IN THE SCHOOLS: DEVELOPING CULTURAL COMPETENCE

In virtually every school, some students fit into the mainstream and others do not. It is often the student who does not fit in who is most likely to be vulnerable to scapegoating, bullying, and violence. Students who do not feel safe at school, who are subject to bullying, and who are made to feel like outcasts because of their gender, race, sexual orientation, religion, body type, family constellation, or any other factor that seems to set them apart from the mainstream will be at risk for academic failure or at least academic difficulty if their differences place them at increased risk of negative targeting. Although the responsibility for keeping students safe rests with all adults associated with the student—teachers, all school personnel, and even parents—social workers are in a unique position to identify potential problems related to diversity and difference and intervene by advocating for at-risk students.

Working With Racial and Ethnic Minority Groups

Racial and ethnic diversity can be a wonderful asset to any school environment leading to a richness in experiences for students and teachers alike. But in some school environments, racial prejudice and discrimination can lead to violence and conflict among many within the student population. Students who comprise a \part of a racial group, and ethnic minority either within the school or within the broader society, are at risk for academic failure for many reasons including social, economic, and political conditions. For example, a school environment that is hostile to racial and ethnic minorities contributes to an environment where students feel unwelcome and possibly where school policies either directly or indirectly discriminate against students of color.

School social workers can assist teachers and school administrators in recognizing and addressing racial and ethnic discrimination and prejudice on campus. They can also assist in the development of cultural diversity training focusing on racial and ethnic sensitivity and respect for diversity. Equally important is the cultural competence of the social workers themselves. It is vital that school social workers undergo additional diversity training, focusing on the nature of counseling from a multicultural perspective (Holcomb-McCoy, 2004). This type of training is particularly important as research shows that traditional counseling theories and interventions are often biased against racial and ethnic minorities, particularly African Americans, Latina/os, and Native Americans. For instance, many traditional Euro-American theories tend to pathologize racial and ethnic minorities rather than recognizing the social oppression that contributes to violence, gang activity, and juvenile delinquency (Fusick & Charkow, 2004). Any theory (or theorist) that disregards the power of long-standing racism and the effect that intergenerational oppression has on a population would be hard pressed to explain why these groups experience significantly higher rates of poverty and violence than other groups that haven't experienced intergenerational racism and oppression. Are the former merely more innately violent? Are they just lazy? Less moral as a whole? If not, then credence must be given to the possibility that behavior deemed maladaptive is not solely a result of individual psychopathology but must be the result of social causes as well.

In addition to the lack of cultural competency reflected in many psychological theories, another area cultural competency can address is helping school social workers to better understand the reasons why certain racial and ethnic minority groups are wary of many government agencies established to provide assistance, such as child protective services. Government child welfare agencies in the United States either historically excluded certain racial and ethnic minority groups from services, or negatively targeted them, leading many groups to hold such agencies in general mistrust (Horejsi, Craig, & Pablo, 1992; Surbeck, 2003). Cultural competency training can assist school social workers in considering alternate explanations for what may appear to be a reticence on the part of some parents to cooperate with social work services, particularly if government child welfare agencies are involved. Social workers should not jump to the conclusion that a student's or family's wariness of social work services is a sign of deception, but should recognize and understand the root causes of such mistrust—and assist the student and family in overcoming mistrust through the development of an authentic helping relationship and student-centered advocacy.

Many of the psychosocial assessment tools used in the public school system (and within the mental health field in general) are biased against racial and ethnic minority groups, having been developed for the assessment and evaluation of the majority culture, based on Caucasian middle-class values and mores (Fusick & Charkow, 2004). Cultural competency training can aid school social workers in assessing the appropriateness of using standard assessment tools and adapting them when possible for racial and ethnic minority populations. This practice will contribute to alleviating the broad-based problem of overidentifying racial and ethnic minority students for social work services because of behavioral problems.

Because of the specialized training school social workers undergo related to cultural competency, they are in a great position to address discrimination and prejudice against racial and ethnic minority groups, whether overt, as with the use of racial slurs, or covert, as in the case of biased assessment tools and intervention methods.

Lesbian, Gay, Bisexual, Transgendered, and Questioning Youth

Students who are in the sexual minority, such as lesbian, gay, bisexual, transgendered youth, and those students who are questioning their sexuality in some way (LGBTQ), are often the victims of violence, both verbal and physical. Many of these children spend a considerable amount of time feeling different and isolated, often believing that no one will understand their feelings and accept them unconditionally. Such individuals have an alarmingly high rate of suicide attempts, with over 30 percent of LGBTQ youth admitting to having attempted suicide at some point in their lives. Approximately 75 percent of gay and lesbian students admit to having been verbally abused at school, and over 15 percent have been physically abused (Pope, 2003).

Most of the youth in Pope's study reported that the violence they experienced was a direct result of their sexual orientation, with boys being abused more often than girls. Pope discussed this type of abuse in terms of the pressure on most high school students to conform to the norms of their peer group. When faced with the overwhelming demands to be just like everyone else, students who stand out, either because they look different or, as is the case of LGBTQ student when their sexual orientation is different, they can quickly become outcasts.

In 2009, the advocacy organization Gay, Lesbian and Straight Educational Network (GLSEN) conducted a national survey of LGBTQ students on their experiences with the following issues:

- Hearing biased and homophobic remarks in school
- Feeling unsafe in school because of personal characteristics, such as sexual orientation, gender expression, or race/ethnicity
- Missing classes or days of school because of safety reasons
- Experiences of harassment and assault in school

The results of the study found that a significant majority of LGBTQ students experience verbal and physical harassment on a daily basis in school, with little to no intervention or advocacy on the part of school personnel. For instance, between 75 percent and 90 percent of LGBTQ students surveyed heard homophobic terms used in a derogatory manner, such as "gay," "dyke," and "faggot," in school, and most respondents reported feeling distress in response. Almost 85 percent reported that they had been verbally harassed at school because of their sexual orientation, and almost as many reported that they'd been verbally harassed because of their gender expression (not being feminine or masculine enough). About 40 percent of respondents reported that they had been victims of physical harassment at school because of their sexual orientation, and about 20 percent were physically assaulted. Over 50 percent of respondents were victims of cyberbullying and harassment through text messaging, emails, and social media. In most of these cases, there was little to no response on the part of school personnel, leaving the majority of these students feeling very unsafe in their respective school environments.

The report details the most frequent consequences of these various types of bullying related to a student's sexual orientation and gender expression, including higher-than-average absenteeism, lower educational achievement, and a negative impact on

Engage in Diversity and Difference in Practice

Practice Behavior: View themselves as learners and engage those with whom they work as informants.

Critical Thinking Question: Imagine that you are working as a school social worker in a public high school. You hear rumors that members of the LGBTQ population are experiencing harassment and bullying. You haven't witnessed this yourself, but you've heard of this type of thing happening in other schools. What steps can you take to educate yourself and your colleague on the problem of harassment and bullying of sexual minorities in public school settings?

their psychological well-being (higher rates of depression, anxiety, and lower levels of self-esteem). The authors of the report recommend the following solutions: gay-straight alliance clubs (GSAs), inclusive curriculum (course curriculum that includes positive representations of LGBTQ people and events, currently and historically), supportive educators (training educators in LGBTQ awareness and advocacy), and incorporation of strict bullying and harassment legislation and policies. Schools that had incorporated these remedies experienced marked reductions in LGBTQ bias–based bullying (Kosciw, Greytak, Diaz, & Barkiewicz, 2010).

It is vital that school social workers address the harassment that LGBTQ students experience on a daily basis in the public school system and help to develop programs to combat poor treatment of students in the sexual minority. The first step in this effort is to establish a *zero-tolerance policy*, where teachers, school administrators, and student services professionals make it clear to the student population through policy and action that harassment will not be tolerated in any respect. Developing a plan for making school safe for all vulnerable students begins with the education of school personnel.

School social workers are the ideal candidates to educate both school staff and students on the importance of tolerating diversity. Such a program must begin with the school staff, particularly the teachers, who are most likely to be present when the abuse of gay and lesbian students occurs. What needs to be emphasized is that regardless of one's personal beliefs about the issue of sexual orientation and same-sex partnerships, no human being should be subjected to verbal and physical harassment and abuse. Nor should sexual orientation or any other singular aspect of one's personhood solely define an individual. Advocacy and educational programs should focus on teaching students to respect human dignity and everyone's basic right to self-determination.

A particularly effective program facilitated by school social workers across the nation is called the *Making Schools Safe Project* (Otto, Middleton, & Freker, 2002). This program was developed by the American Civil Liberties Union (ACLU) and was designed to combat antigay harassment on school campuses. The ACLU recommends that all teachers and administrators use this curriculum, which focuses on the vital importance of creating a safe learning environment for all children. Despite such programs, as well as a general increase in societal tolerance of the LGBT population, harassment of LGBT students (as well as students with gay and/or lesbian parents) continues. School social workers must challenge the status quo that exists on many school campuses, ranging from overt bullying to more subtle forms of harassment, such as the generalized use of the word "gay."

The Terrorist Threat and "Islamophobia"

Many school districts scrambled to develop programs to address students' feelings and concerns in the wake of the September 11, 2001 terrorist attacks. The events of September 11, 2001, were difficult for adults but were particularly hard on children, many of whom lacked the maturity to effectively communicate their feelings. A 2004 study found that 65 percent of respondents reported that students experienced moderate to high levels of distress in the weeks following the attacks (Auger, Seymour, Roberts, & Waiter, 2004). The most frequently reported symptoms included fear, worry, anxiety, sadness, anger, and aggression. Students who were personally affected by terrorist attacks or who were already suffering from some mental health issues, such as depression, were the most at risk for developing symptoms of post-traumatic stress disorder (PTSD).

Auger et al. (2004) also noted that although most schools surveyed took appropriate action in responding to the attacks, with regard to the students the majority of the schools surveyed took no action to assist school personnel in dealing with their own feelings. Over one-third of school counselors stated that they did not feel prepared to respond to a serious trauma, suggesting that ongoing training of all school personnel is essential.

There have been many longer term consequences of the terrorist attacks but one particularly troubling reaction is a marked increase in what is called "Islamophobia," the irrational fear and hatred of Muslims (or those perceived to be Muslims). A 2011 policy brief published by the Institute for Social Policy and Understanding found that bullying of Muslim children in school environments was on the rise since the September 11, 2001, terrorist attacks (Britto, 2011). While the increase in bias-based bullying is on the rise in general, the report identified the chief reason why Muslim children were being bullied was because of "American mainstream's limited knowledge, pervasive misperceptions, and negative stereotypes about Muslims" (p. 1). Britto cites the influence of media on the attitudes of non-Muslim youth, which frequently depict Muslims as potential terrorists and ideological extremists. She recommends using the media to counteract these negative and incorrect stereotypes, such as creating YouTube videos depicting accurate reflections of Muslim culture.

Conduct an Internet search for Runnymede Trust, and then search within the website for a report entitled "Islamophobia: A Challenge for Us All". Review this report for a comprehensive definition of Islamophobia.

The Learning Channel (TLC) attempted to do just that with a series called *All-American Muslims*—a reality-based show featuring Muslim families in their everyday lives. The show featured the lives of several families living in Michigan, including a high school football coach and his family and a young newlywed couple expecting their first child. The purpose of the show, according to TLC and its producers, was to educate the non-Muslim American population about the diversity within Muslim culture by illustrating how Muslim-Americans are often concerned about the same ordinary issues as everyone else. Yet, despite the positive intention of the show's producers, significant controversy ensued, leading to most of the show's advertisers pulling their ads during the show, and the show was ultimately canceled. The majority of the criticism came from a conservative Christian organization called Florida Family Association (FFA), founded by fundamentalist David Caton, (Freedman, 2011). Caton claimed that *All-American Muslims* had an "Islamic agenda" that was a threat to American traditional values.

Go to the Pew Research Center website and conduct a search on Islamophobia, and review the recent research studies and surveys on the discrimination that many Muslims face living in the United States.

This is just one example of what many fear is becoming mainstream Islamophobia. Other examples of Islamophobia, particularly those affecting school children, include references to Muslim children as being terrorists and jokes about Muslim children and their families making bombs (Abdelkader, 2011). Such bias-based bullying should not be tolerated, and school social workers, in coordination with school counselors, school psychologists, teachers, school administrators, parents, and other students, can counteract Islamophobia through the implementation of educational programs designed to increase awareness of the range of moderate belief systems embraced by the mainstream Muslims, both in the United States and abroad. Yet, as TLC found, social workers would be wise to expect controversy on some level, particularly by those in the community who may be threatened by attempts of any marginalized group to assert its collective right to enter the mainstream of America.

Assess your comprehension of "Diversity in the Schools: Developing Cultural Competence" by completing this quiz.

DEPRESSION AND OTHER PSYCHOSOCIAL CONCERNS

Major depression involves feelings of hopelessness, hopelessness, melancholy, loss of interest in pleasurable activities, difficulty sleeping, loss of appetite, and general feelings of unworthiness (APA, 2013). In 2011 approximately 8 percent of youth between the ages of 12 and 17 experienced at least one episode of major depression in the past year, with female youth experiencing almost double the rate of depression as male youth (SAMHSA, 2012). Also, close to three-quarters of youth with major depression reported that their depression caused significant problems with regard to functioning in one or more areas of their lives, including in school (SAMHSA, 2012). Symptoms of depression in children and adolescents are similar to that of adults, except that oftentimes children exhibit symptoms of irritability rather than melancholy (APA, 2000). Another important consideration is that it is often the quiet children, sitting in the back of the classroom bothering no one, suffering silently, who are the most in need of help yet are likely to be overlooked by school personnel because they are not acting out in any visible way.

Abrams, Theberge, and Karan (2005) recommend that school mental health professionals, including social workers, use an ecological model as a lens for evaluating students struggling with major depression (see Box 10.1). For instance, in assessing and evaluating a potentially depressed student, the school social worker would evaluate the relationship the student has with peers, family members, and even teachers. Is the student experiencing conflict with one or both parents? Has the student recently experienced fights with peers? The counselor will then evaluate the relationship the student has with the broader community. Is the student involved with the legal system? Does the student have involvement with a truancy officer? Finally, the school social worker would evaluate whether anything in the broader society might be affecting the student.

Consider Hurricane Katrina in August of 2005, and the devastating impact this natural disaster had on those in the affected areas, particularly New Orleans. The evaluation of any student for depression who was directly impacted by the hurricane, was likely assessed in the context of this devastating disaster. Did the student have any friends or family members

---

Box 10.1   Review Bronfenbrenner's Ecological Systems Theory

Urie Bronfenbrenner (1979) developed the Ecological Systems Theory. In his theory, Bronfenbrenner categorized an individual's environment into four expanding spheres, all with increasing levels of intimate interaction with the individual. The Microsystem includes the individual and his family, the Mesosystem (or Mezzosystem) includes entities such as one's neighborhood and school, the Exosystem includes entities such as the state government, and the Macrosystem would include the culture at large. Figure 10.1 illustrates the most basic systems that most individual interact with, including one's family, friends and school. Again, it is important to remember that the primary principle of Bronfenbrenner's theory is that individuals can best be understood when seen in the context of their relationship with the various systems in their lives. Understanding the nature of these reciprocal relationships will aid in better understanding the individual.

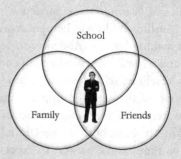

Figure 10.1
A simple conceptualization of the "Person-in-Environment" model.

who were directly affected by Hurricane Katrina? Does the student have a parent or close family member who was displaced, injured or killed? Similarly, any significant changes in governmental social policy relating to providing provisions for hurricane survivors have the potential to affect students, particularly those who were living in government-subsidized housing and who had parents who living in subsidized by public assistance due to being displaced by the hurricane. Do these changes in policy affect the student's family in a way that consequently puts pressure on the student because of increased stress within the household?

In general, school social workers not only evaluate anything that might be a contributing factor to the student's current mental health status but also evaluates strengths and support within the student's world (Abrams et al., 2005). Does the student belong to a church body or faith community that offers or has the potential of offering support? Does the student have any extended family members who might come forward and offer to support the student during a difficult time? Students experiencing depression might have an untapped support system, and by using an ecological model, the school social worker can assist the student in expanding his or her existing support system, thus helping to not only address existing depression but also to potentially stem the tide of future psychosocial problems that may evolve if the core issues were left unaddressed.

The value of the ecological model is that it is complementary with the overall model of social work, which relies on a "person-in-environment" approach to nearly all psychosocial issues. The ecological model also enables the social worker to provide more effective case management once contributing factors and support systems are identified. This model also encourages inter-professional collaboration on a variety of levels.

Parental involvement is a key factor in the treatment of students experiencing major depression. One of the first things that a social worker can do to ensure parental involvement in a student's counseling is to identify any potential barriers to their engagement. Barriers might be cultural in nature, such as a less-than-welcoming environment for non–English-speaking parents or environments where parents do not feel well treated by school personnel (Vanderbleek, 2004). Barriers can also be more concrete, such as a parents' lack of transportation or a work schedule that makes meeting with school personnel during prescribed times impossible. Flexibility on the part of schools, particularly school social workers, is important and may include a willingness to conduct home visits—after school hours, if necessary.

Auger (2005) is in favor of a multifaceted approach to depression intervention within the school system and suggested an approach that relies on interprofessional and family engagement to help students address pessimistic or negative thinking, develop greater insights into the connection between feelings and behavior, develop better social skills, and create opportunities for the student to succeed in the school environment. Auger also advocated for encouraging the student to increase physical activity because there appears to be a relationship between physical activity and positive mental health.

There is, of course, a limit to the amount of mental health services a school can provide to its students, but the current trends clearly reveal that the school system can be an optimal environment to address many of the psychosocial problems students experience, including depression, particularly those issues that have the greatest potential to create barriers to academic achievement.

Substance Abuse in the Schools

Substance abuse both on and off campus continues to be a growing problem across the United States, primarily in high schools and also in some middle schools. School social workers (in coordination with school counselors and school psychologists) must be able to identify the signs of substance abuse, as well as be prepared for the various ways of intervening when substance abuse is suspected. Although many graduate programs in social work and related fields are addressing this issue by including more courses on substance abuse, the majority of programs still only offer substance abuse courses as electives. Many school social workers are unprepared to deal with substance abuse issues or the complexity of adolescent substance abuse, particularly with regard to complicated family systems (Lambie & Rokutani, 2002). The reality is that 74 percent of high school seniors in suburban high schools have reported using alcohol, and 40 percent of high school seniors in suburban high schools have reported using illegal drugs (Greene & Forster, 2004), making substance abuse one of the most significant issues confronting school personnel (SAMHSA, 2012).

School social workers need to be able to identify adolescent substance abuse and respond with an effective intervention strategy, which includes school engagement, as well as involvement with outside referral sources that will engage the entire family system, whenever possible. The model most often used to describe the nature of adolescent substance abuse is similar to an adult model but often does not take into consideration factors related to adolescent development. Adolescents tend to be developmentally "egocentric" in the sense that they often act in more self-focused manners than adults. They also tend to display behavior that is impulsive, appearing to lack a consistent sense of the consequences of their use of alcohol and drug use and abuse. This seeming sense of omnipotence, coupled with normative developmental egocentrism, often complicates the application of traditional models of substance abuse within the adolescent population.

Lambie and Rokutani (2002) suggest using a "systems perspective" in evaluating substance abuse in the adolescent population. Rather than viewing substance abuse in the adolescent as an individual problem, a systems perspective views the substance abuse as a sign of something amiss within the family system. The substance-abusing adolescent often serves some purpose within the family system, such as enabling the parents to focus on the adolescent's dysfunctional behavior rather than on problems in the marriage. The substance-abusing adolescent sometimes serves as an apparent symptom of deeper problems within the family system that are purposely hidden from view. For instance, the family who works hard to appear "normal" and healthy will be compelled to deal with underlying dysfunction when one or more of the children begin acting out in ways that require outside attention and intervention, such as abusing drugs and alcohol.

Another issue to consider when using a systems perspective is whether the adolescent's substance abuse is mirroring a parent's substance abuse. A parent's abuse of alcohol or drugs has been shown to influence an adolescent's decision to begin drinking (Lambie & Sias, 2005; Piercy, Volk, Trepper, Sprenkle, & Lewis, 1991). In general, families that have system problems such as parental substance abuse and other forms of maladaptive behavior are sometimes rigid and closed-family systems and lack the ability or capacity to handle the increased stressors associated with children entering the adolescent years. Adolescents demanding changes to long-standing rules, pushing for more privileges, developing a far wider circle of peers, and questioning family rules can often leave a family that is wary of outsiders and rigidly adheres to rules and discipline with few effective coping skills to adapt to these changes. In addition, problems that have their roots in early childhood most often manifest during adolescence.

A school social worker working with substance-abusing adolescents must first be able to identify the common signs of abuse, including erratic behavior, mood swings, red eyes, and slurred speech. They must then be able to provide support to both the student and the family, acting as a liaison between student, family, school, and community-based treatment programs. On a broader level, school social workers can help institute prevention programs in the school, such as the Drug Abuse Resistance Education (DARE) program, which involves police and other community agencies educating students about the dangers of drug abuse through the use of plays, dance and songs.

Child Abuse and Neglect: Protecting Students

School social workers, counselors, and school psychologists are often in the position of having to report child abuse to their local child welfare agency. School social workers, counselors, and psychologists are often in the precarious position of having to decide what should constitute a "hotline" call. For instance, a child showing up to school with bruises who discloses she has been physically abused by her mother clearly mandates a call to child protective services, but frequently a clear indication of abuse may not exist and a social worker must make a determination based on clinical instinct. It is important for student services personnel to understand that they do not need to be certain of abuse; if there are indicators of any type of abuse, it is their legal obligation to file a report and allow child protective services to conduct an investigation.

It is important that the school social worker, counselor, or school psychologist remain composed when a student discloses abuse, while expressing compassion, support, and encouragement. It is equally important that promises are not made that cannot be kept. For instance, the counselor should not promise not to tell anyone, because the student will feel betrayed when a report of child abuse is made (Lambie, 2005). There might also be reticence on the part of some social workers to make a report of child abuse if they know the parents and are suspicious of the student's disclosure, but the social worker must adhere to the law, which requires that any abuse disclosure be reported as required.

Bullying

Bullying within the public school system is gaining increasing attention among the general U.S. population, as well as among school administrators and policymakers on a local and national level. The increased attention is at least in part due to what appears to be a vast increase in bullying incidents, particularly involving cyber-bullying (bullying via social media sites, such as Facebook and Twitter). In fact, a recent study suggests that over a quarter of all U.S. students reported being victims of bullying while at school (over 7 million students), and about 6 percent of U.S. students reported being a victim of cyber-bullying on or off campus (just over 1.5 million students) (DeVoe & Murphy, 2011). Whether bullying incidences is actually increasing, or whether reporting rates have increased remains unclear, but this is an important issue that directly affects social work, particularly school social work.

Bullying can include name-calling and insults, being the object of rumors, threats of harm, physical assaults (shoving, hitting, tripping, and spitting), being purposely excluded from activities and property destruction. Cyber bullying can include posting hurtful, harassing, and threatening information on the Internet, as well as unwanted contact via email, text, online gaming site, or other online community, or purposeful exclusion from an online community (DeVoe & Murphy, 2011). Bullying of males and females tends to be relatively equal, with slightly more girls than boys being victims of bullying (DeVoe & Murphy, 2011). Students who are perceived as different are at the greatest risk of bullying, particularly those from racial and ethnic minority groups, students of lower socio-economic status, and students who are perceived to deviate from expected gender norms (whether or not they actually identify of gay or lesbian) (DeVoe & Murphy, 2011; Kosciw, Greytak, Diaz, & Barkiewicz, 2010), and students who are overweight (Biggs, Simpson, & Gaus, 2009).

Bullying in school is an important issue for many reasons, but chief among them include evidence that victims of bullying experience both short- and long-term consequences, including poor school performance, depression, and increased health problems (Rigby, 2003). And while research is not conclusive in this area, there is growing concern that extreme bullying may cause retaliation with devastating consequences. For instance, the U.S. government's bullying website notes that in 12 out of 15 student-initiated campus shootings in the 1990s, the shooters disclosed histories of being bullied, some severely. Research also suggests that many incidents of bullying go unreported to parents and to schools, which hinders a school's ability determine the scope of bullying within a school system, as well as to effectively address the problem (Petrosino, Guckenburg, DeVoe, & Hanson, 2010).

Although to date there is no federal legislation mandating how schools must respond to bullying, there is considerable encouragement from the White House, as well the Department of Education, for schools to adopt proactive measures to address bullying on campus as well as online. For instance, in March of 2011, President Barack and Michelle Obama reached out to students, parents, educators, and education advocates across the country, as well as other concerned parties at the White House Conference on Bullying Prevention, acknowledging the very serious nature of school bullying and announcing several programs designed to assist schools, nonprofit organizations, and other advocates in putting a stop to bullying, both on campus as well as in cyberspace. The StopBullying website was launched as a part of this conference, providing information from numerous government agencies on the nature of bullying and bullying prevention and treatment strategies.

School social workers are aptly placed to be leaders in the fight against bullying, but far too often they lack the training and resources to effectively address bullying on a macro and micro level. For instance, in a recent study on cyberbullying about half of social workers surveyed reported that they felt ambivalent about their role in addressing cyberbullying, despite the majority reporting that they recognize the seriousness of this form of bullying (Slovak & Singer, 2011). Other research indicates that a part of the

Social Work, Social Media, and Technology

Cyberbullying involves bullying through any electronic format, such as texting, and social media, such as Facebook and Twitter. There are several recent examples of cyberbullying, particularly incidences targeting certain groups, such as teens, members of the LGBT population, and women. For instance, in 2010 Rutgers University freshman Tyler Clementi committed suicide after he was cyberbullied by his dorm roommate and hallmate who secretly videotaped him having a sexual encounter with another man. When the video clip was circulated via Twitter, Tyler, who had not yet come out as gay, jumped to his death from the George Washington Bridge. #Gamegate is another example of cyberbullying, but involving cybermobs, rather than individual bullies. #Gamergate began in August of 2014 when a news story about a female online game developer resulted in hoards of mysogenistic men using Reddit and other social media sites to disseminate sexual harassing comments and even death threats. When cyberbullying is perpetrated by a large group, it is often referred to as cybermobbing. The Internet and social media specifically, can also be used to help prevent cyberbullying. For instance, the federal government uses a Stop Bullying website, Facebook page and Twitter account to disseminate anti-bullying messages and information for those who are targets of cyberbullying. The Stop Bullying campaign is a joint program of the Department of Education (ED), Department of Health and Human Services (HHS), Centers for Disease Control and Prevention (CDC), Health Resources and Services Administration (HRSA), and Substance Abuse and Medical Health Services Administration (SAMHSA).

challenge involves a lack of clear school policies and a general lack of training in managing all aspects of the school bullying problem (Mason, 2008).

Biggs, Simpson, and Gaus (2009) recommend that social workers develop a strategy to address school bullying that involves a multidisciplinary team approach, using a strengths-based perspective. The team approach allows each professional distinction to provide support for the others on the team, as well as serving as inter-disciplinary consultants "sharing feedback, and disseminating valuable resources and information among the various disciplines" (p. 41).

Teenage Pregnancy

A newspaper article in 2005 reported that 13 percent of the female students at an Ohio high school were pregnant, causing serious concern about why this high school's pregnancy rate was nearly double the national average (Garvey, 2005). Although teenage pregnancy has been on the decline in recent years (Karraker, 2004), it remains a serious concern, with over 60 percent of high school seniors reporting they were sexually active (Greene & Forster, 2004). Various research studies have pointed to many factors that might influence pregnancy rates within the adolescent population. Beyond sexual activity in the adolescent population, other factors include early alcohol use (Stueve & O'Donnell, 2005) and poverty (Young, Turner, Denny, & Young, 2004).

Research on prevention points to religiosity (Rostosky, Regnerus, & Wright, 2003), peer influence, appropriate parental supervision, good and direct parental communication, SES, race (Corcoran, Franklin, & Bennett, 2000), and involvement in sports that is correlated with remaining abstinent in high school or at least becoming sexually active later in adolescence.

Sex and pregnancy prevention programs have been included in school curriculums for several decades with mixed reviews. *Abstinence-only* programs, although somewhat controversial, have shown to be surprisingly successful (Toups & Holmes, 2002). In fact, Toups and Holmes reviewed several studies that revealed marked reductions in teenage pregnancy after experiencing a school-based abstinence-only program. In fact, one study evaluated all 5,000 teenagers who participated in an abstinence program in one year. Not only did few of these teenagers become sexually active but also over 50 percent of the students who had been sexually active stopped having sex. Proponents of abstinence-only sex education cite the decrease in adolescent sexual activity as evidence that these programs work. Yet others have questioned whether these programs are as successful as some of these studies indicate, citing poor study designs and a wide range of abstinence programs with some defining abstinence as postponing sex until early adulthood and some more religiously based programs sending the message that premarital sex should always be avoided. Without a clear definition of "abstinence," critics claim that it's impossible to determine the success of these programs (Kirby, 2002).

Some educators are concerned, however, that abstinence-only programs will not work for all teenagers, particularly those who have any of the complicating factors mentioned earlier. Teenagers living in poverty, who have poor communication with their parents, and who are not supervised well by their parents may not respond positively to abstinence-only programs because of the other forces pushing them in the direction of sexual activity. Based on the belief that some adolescents will have sex no matter who tells them not to, many education programs focus on safe sex practices, such as using condoms during sexual intercourse. Many of these programs also focus on HIV/AIDS education, which is often later cited as a chief reason among adolescents for using condoms.

Although there has been some concern that educating teenagers to use contraception and even making contraception available is sending a mixed message (i.e., "You should not have sex during adolescence, but just in case you do, use a condom!"), which in essence promotes sexual activity during adolescence. A review of 28 studies examining this issue clearly indicates that such programs do not increase sexual activity among teenage participants, nor do they lead to sexual activity at an earlier age. In fact, many studies indicated that safe sex programs increase the usage of contraception (Kirby, 2002).

One of the most popular programs currently used in high schools across the country is called the Baby Think It Over (BTIO) program, which uses a computerized doll programmed to cry and fuss intermittently throughout the day and night to educate teenagers on the realities of having a baby. This program has been successful in educating teenagers about the hardship and burden of having a child at such an early age (Somers, Johnson, & Sawilowsky, 2002).

Another issue commonly noted by school social workers who work with female high school students is a pervasive tendency for girls who are sexually active to report that they had not considered the possibility that they could have said no to a boyfriend's sexual advances. Developing "empowerment" support groups where girls can have a safe place to talk about their feelings about sex, support each other in their right to say no, and consider the positive consequences of doing so can be a successful tool in encouraging better boundary setting, which is likely to result in a reduction of sexual activity.

Assess your comprehension of "Depression and Other Psychosocial Concerns" by completing this quiz.

COMMON ETHICAL DILEMMAS FACING SCHOOL SOCIAL WORKERS

Advance Human Rights and Social and Economic Justice

Practice Behavior: Engage in practices that advance social and economic justice.

Critical Thinking Question: What steps can social workers take to ensure that they are advocating for all students equally and not merely the ones that they can best relate to?

As in many other social work settings, social workers working in a school setting face many ethical dilemmas on a daily basis that require them to not only be acutely aware of the ethical standards of the school social work profession but also be aware of common dynamics they may face that could result in an ethical dilemma, or potentially, the violation of an NASW ethical standard. Some of these challenges are pretty straightforward, such as maintaining confidentiality of student counseling and related records or reporting child abuse in accordance with mandatory child abuse laws. But there are other areas of ethical concern that are not so clear cut and involve far more of an ethical "slippery slope," where appropriate responses to complex situations are very much in the gray area.

For instance, consider the Latina school social worker who is passionate about advocating for Latina students because of what she endured in school with racially biased teachers. Her motivation to advocate for Latina students is good, but if she doesn't thoroughly evaluate the circumstances surrounding situations involving seemingly similar dynamics, she might be biased toward Latina students and against students and staff from other ethnic groups. Or, consider the Caucasian school social worker who, without awareness, seems to automatically show bias toward other Caucasian students, and against students of color, because he relates better to someone from his own race. At what point does passionate advocacy become excessive single-minded bias toward one subpopulation, and directly or indirectly, against another? School

The School Social Work Association of America website is an excellent source for information about the school social work profession.

Social Work Application Activity

Imagine that you are a school social worker working in a middle school in an urban community with a high percentage of children in foster care. Approximately 50 percent of the students in your school are in either kinship care or in a group home. You are seeing a 12-year-old boy who is experiencing significant grief after having lost his mother to cancer the prior year. His father abandoned him when he was only three years old, thus he was placed in kinship care with his aunt. You've been asked to provide grief counseling to him, particularly because his homeroom teacher has reported suspicions that he is being physically abused and neglected in his new home. What are the ethical dilemmas you may face in counseling this boy, particularly if he does in fact disclose that he is being abused in his foster home? In its Resolution Statement, the SSWAA recommends that school social workers adopt an ethical decision-making model to help resolve ethical dilemmas involving minors. Conduct an Internet search and locate such a model that is appropriate for use in a school social work environment.

social workers deal with very complex situations on a daily basis, and make decisions about how to handle these situations based not solely upon their professional training but also on their own personal experiences—often those very experiences that led them to this career to begin with. Thus, it is important for a school social worker to be aware of how easy it is for unethical behavior to be rooted in a sincere desire to show care and concern for students, particularly those students who are especially vulnerable.

School social workers are bound by the NASW Code of Ethics but can benefit from additional training in ethical management from a variety of sources. School social workers can also seek additional guidance from the specialty practice section of the NASW website that focuses on school social work, where articles on issues related to confidentiality and boundary setting, for example, are posted, as well as on the School Social Work Association of America (SSWAA) website, which has several articles and professional statements regarding ethical dilemmas faced by school social workers.

Assess your comprehension of "Common Ethical Dilemmas Facing School Social Workers" by completing this quiz.

Summary

School social workers are an integral part of the public school system, providing psychosocial and case management support to students to remove barriers that negatively impact their academic success. School social workers work on a multidisciplinary team along with other mental health professionals, including school counselors and school psychologists, as well as educators, school administrators, families, and the broader community to meet the student's holistic needs. The role of the school social worker is expected to expand in the future in response to a projected increase in many of the social trends experienced today, including an increase in poverty, homelessness, and single-parent families. To remain relevant in an era of increasing budget cuts across all aspects of public school education, school social workers must remain current in areas most likely to impact students in the future, such as the effect of social media on student emotional and academic development, issues related to migration, such as xenophobia (the irrational fear of immigrants), and other dynamics related to the increasing reach of globalization.

Recall what you learned in this chapter by completing the Chapter Review.

11

Religion, Spirituality, and Faith-based Agencies

Maya is a 42-year-old Muslim woman who was referred to an Islamic women's center for advocacy and counseling. She has been married to Asad, a 44-year-old physician, for 18 years. Maya is the stay-at-home mother of their three children, aged 10, 12, and 14. Both Maya and Asad are originally from Egypt, having immigrated to the United States shortly after getting married. Maya reports that she and her husband have always been devout Muslims, being very involved in their local mosque. They have had what she considers a traditional Muslim marriage, where her husband is the leader of the home and provides for the family financially, and Maya takes care of the home and the children. For the majority of their marriage, Maya believes that their marriage has been a good one. She believes that her husband was always very respectful of her and relied on her wisdom and input in making decisions impacting the family, particularly with regard to the children. Because Maya was an accountant prior to getting married, Asad has relied on her to help with financial matters related to his medical practice. Maya reported that about five years ago Asad began to "bring his work home with him," which led to an increase in his general irritability and frustration. In the last two years Maya noted that he began to become more controlling of her whereabouts, getting angry with her if he could not reach her at a moment's notice. She did not reach out then because she believed Asad when he said that it was his right to control her in this manner. Although Maya's father did not behave in this manner, she began to believe that perhaps she needed to endure Asad's behavior to be a good Muslim wife. Maya shared that in the past few months his aggression had escalated to the point of screaming at her, both at home and in public, and backing her into corners.

His drinking has escalated as well. The incident that prompted Maya to finally reach out for help occurred after she refused to sleep with Asad because he was extremely intoxicated and verbally abusing her. Asad became irate and began beating her, citing his right per the Qur'an (4:34–35). Maya initially went to the Imam at her mosque, who supported her completely and also explained that her husband's use of the Qur'an was a misinterpretation. He explained that Islam did not in any way condone abuse. He provided her with a considerable amount of information regarding the "cycle of violence" and services in the community for victims of domestic violence, including support groups for both adults and children. Maya contacted the Muslim women's center that day and saw a counselor later in the week. At Maya's first counseling appointment she expressed relief that her community was so supportive of her, but she expressed sadness as well because the information and resources she received seemed so fatalistic and hopeless. Her counselor explained that her husband was acting in a manner inconsistent with the will of Allah, and if he was truly committed to following Islam and being a good Muslim husband and father, then perhaps he would be open to receiving counseling as well. Domestic violence, the counselor explained, not only destroyed everyone in the family but also affected the entire community, thus the Muslim community was as concerned about Asad as it was about Maya. During counseling Maya began to understand the underlying dynamics of her husband's behavior and gained wisdom regarding the difference between a husband who led his family with respect, as described by Muhammad, and the controlling and abusive behavior exhibited by her husband. As Maya gained confidence in herself and her decisions, she felt strongly that Allah was leading her to be strong for the sake of her family. Strength, according to her counselor, meant that she could not tolerate abuse. Asad met with the Imam for several weeks and then reluctantly agreed to attend a one-year anger management program that was led by an Imam at the community Islamic center, and Maya agreed not to make any decisions about whether to consider a divorce until after Asad had finished his program. Both the Imam and the counselor agreed that family counseling should not occur until after Asad had received enough counseling to recognize that the root of the family and marital problems lay within him. As Maya continued counseling, she began to realize the intergenerational cycle of abuse that existed in her husband's family and how important it was, particularly for the sake of her children, that she become strong enough to break the cycle. The most difficult aspect of this process for Maya was maintaining good boundaries with Asad and realizing that he had the choice not to change, which would force her hand in a sense, compelling her to leave the marriage to avoid repeating the patterns of abuse.

THE HISTORICAL ROLE OF RELIGION IN CARING FOR THE POOR AND DISADVANTAGED

Despite the common belief that social service provision is the sole responsibility of government, religious institutions have a long history of caring for the poor and disadvantaged. The perception that religious institutions have an obligation to care for those in need has been influenced by religious teachings, particularly teachings within the Judeo-Christian tradition, and was reinforced by church authorities, who historically shouldered the primary responsibility, within a governmental capacity, of administering relief to those unable to support themselves. Almost in the same way that evil was perceived as a necessity to highlight good, poverty was likewise perceived as necessary to highlight charity and goodwill as required by God.

A policy of charity is not limited to Judeo-Christian faiths; in fact, most religions include charity as requirements of faith. Followers of Islam are required to contribute a fifth of their income to the poor (Qur'an 8: 41), and believers also practice regular charity (Qur'an 2: 43) and care for the orphans (Qur'an 2: 177). In the tradition of Buddhism (more correctly referred to as a philosophy than a religion because of the lack of a deity), suffering and giving are foundational to understanding the meaning of life.

Because social work practice is highly influenced by social welfare policy, which in turn is highly influenced by prevailing attitudes about the poor, it is important to understand how major religions and key social philosophies framed poverty over the course of history. In the mid-19th century, several philosophical movements existed that attempted to address problems in the social world, particularly problems of social inequity and poverty. In his book *The Protestant Ethic and the Spirit of Capitalism*, Max Weber describes the vast influence of John Calvin's concept of *predestination*, an integral aspect of the Protestant Reformation and Puritan theology, and the Protestant ethic, on European and American society. According to Weber, Calvin asserted that God perceived all humans as sinful and wholly undeserving of salvation, yet God in his infinite wisdom and providence determined who would go to heaven and who would be condemned to hell, based solely upon his all-knowing determination of what action would best glorify himself. Human action in an attempt to secure salvation thus was futile as one's eternal fate rested not upon human goodness (which according to Calvin would always fall short of the perfection of God) but solely upon God's mysterious desire (Weber, 1958).

Although Calvin rejected the notion that one could determine the state of one's salvation from any outward signs, Weber noted that determining the "state of grace" of oneself and others became an integral part of Reformed doctrine in part because a considerable amount of social functioning depended on society's ability to separate the "elect" from the condemned. For instance, only God's faithful were allowed to become members of the church, receive communion, and enjoy other benefits of salvation (such as societal respect).

In time, particular behaviors and conditions became certain indicators—or signs—of one's eternal fate. Most notably among these behaviors were hard work and good moral conduct. The high value placed upon hard work, commonly referred to as the Protestant ethic, is reflective of Calvin's belief that one was called to a particular vocation and should work tirelessly as a sign of faithfulness. Thus, according to Weber, individuals did not need to endure a lifetime of questioning their salvation; rather, the commitment to a strong work ethic was "the best possible means of attaining this self-assurance. This and this alone would drive away religious doubt and give assurance of one's state of grace" (Weber, 1905/1958, pp. 77–78).

A life lived in pursuit of purity and denial of worldly pleasures, what Weber referred to as *Puritan asceticism*, also became an indicator of one's "state of grace" because, according to Calvin and Reformed theology, only members of the elect were capable of manifesting such a state of sanctified holiness. Thus, material success in response to hard work and high moral conduct became the universally accepted signs among mainstream, so-called respectable society of those predestined for eternal salvation (Hudson & Coukos, 2005; Weber, 1905/1958).

The influence of the Protestant ethic and Calvin's doctrine of predestination on society as a whole, and specifically upon society's cultural mores related to poverty and the poor were significant, extending beyond that of the religious community (Kim, 1977). With hard work, good moral conduct, and material success serving as the best signs of election to salvation, it did not take long for poverty and presumed immoral behavior (because it was presumed that only the elect had the spiritual fortitude to behave morally) to become a clear indication of one's condemnation (Chunn & Gavigan, 2004; Gettleman, 1963; Hudson & Coukos, 2005; Kim, 1977; Schram, Fordingy, & Sossz, 2008; Tropman, 1986; Weber, 1905/1958).

Social Darwinism was another social philosophy that significantly influenced how poverty and the poor were perceived and treated within the American social welfare system. Social Darwinism involved the application of Charles Darwin's theory of natural selection to the human social world. Darwin's theory, developed in the mid-19th century, was based on the belief that environmental competition—a process called *natural selection*—ensured that only the strongest and most fit organisms would survive (allowing the biologically fragile to perish), thus guaranteeing successful survival of a species (Darwin, 1859/2009). Darwin's theory was focused primarily on the biological fitness of animals and plant life; yet he did apply his theory to humans as well, providing naturalistic explanations for various phenomena in human social life. Weikart (1998) describes written discussions with contemporaries where Darwin espoused a belief that humans were subject to natural law and that economic competition was a necessary component of natural selection in the human species. In fact, Darwin even went so far as to argue that socioeconomic inequality was primarily because of biological inequality, and thus it could not be avoided intimating that those in society who suffered from poverty and other forms of misfortune were merely victims of their own biological inferiority; therefore, their demise was necessary in order for the survival of society as a whole (Weikart, 1998).

Thiel, another social Darwinist, argued that not only was the struggle for survival within society unavoidable, it was desirable, asserting that competition for economic resources should be maximized to weed out the weaker members of society, thus allowing the biologically (and mentally) superior to prevail. Thiel (1868, as cited in Weikart, 1998) cautioned against most forms of government intervention designed to lift individuals out of poverty and misfortune, or create social equality, asserting that giving the weak an opportunity to survive could actually pose a threat to society.

One of the most influential social Darwinists was Herbert Spencer, an English philosopher who actually preceded Darwin in applying concepts of natural selection to the social world. Spencer coined the term *survival of the fittest* (a term often incorrectly attributed to Darwin) in reference to the importance of human competitiveness for limited resources in securing the survival of the "fittest" members of society. Spencer was a fierce opponent of any form of government intervention or charity on behalf of the poor and disadvantaged, arguing that such interventions would interfere with the natural order, thus threatening society as a whole (Hofstadter, 1992). Although Spencer's theory of social superiority was developed in advance of Darwin's theory, his followers relied upon Darwin's theory of natural selection for scientific validity of social Darwinism.

The fatalistic nature of social Darwinism, predestination and the Protestant ethic became deeply imbedded in both American religious and secular culture and were used to justify a laissez-faire approach to charity and social welfare throughout most of the 19th and 20th centuries (Duncan & Moore, 2003; Hofstadter, 1992). Although the specific tenets of these ideologies may have softened over the years, the significance of hard work, good fortune, material success, and living a socially acceptable life have remained associated with a collective sense of entitlement to special favor and privilege in life, whereas poverty and disadvantage have remained associated with weak character, laziness, and questionable behavior. Standing back then and leaving the poor and disadvantaged to their own devices was perceived as nothing more than complying with God's (or nature's) grand plan (Duncan & Moore, 2003).

The popularity of social Darwinism and the Protestant ethic in American culture was related, at least in part, to the American cultural more of rugged individualism and self-sufficiency. Whereas traditional Catholicism focused on the transformation of the community and the giver by being blessed through the act of giving, the Protestant ethic and social Darwinism focused on the individual who was transformed (behaviorally) by the act of receiving (Duncan & Moore, 2003). With the focus of charity placed on the one in need, the dilemma faced by the state and charity providers was determining who deserved help and who did not (Chunn & Gavigan, 2004; Duncan & Moore, 2003; Gettleman, 1963; Hudson & Coukos, 2005; Kim, 1977; Schram et al., 2008; Tropman, 1986; Weber, 1905/1958). This dilemma led to the practice of categorizing the poor as "worthy" or "unworthy" based on the perceived cause of their impoverishment and misfortune and presumed likelihood of behavioral change in response to charity. Yet, with many asserting that providing charity to the poor would only serve to increase their immorality and dependence, even the worthy poor experienced difficulty in obtaining material assistance (Chunn & Gavigan, 2004; Gettleman, 1963; Weber, 1905/1958).

Assess your comprehension of "The Historical Role of Religion in Caring for the Poor and Disadvantaged" by completing this quiz.

These ideological themes of moral deficiency of the poor and the belief that giving material support to the poor would only serve to increase their immoral nature, laziness, and dependency have been reflected in the policy perspectives of the American social welfare system at some level throughout U.S. history (Chunn & Gavigan, 2004; Duncan & Moore, 2003; Gettleman, 1963; Hudson & Coukos, 2005; Kim, 1977; Schram et al., 2008; Tropman, 1986).

THE ROLE OF SPIRITUALITY IN SOCIAL WORK

Despite the historic role of religious institutions providing social services, many in the helping professions, particularly social workers, have been reticent about incorporating faith or spirituality into practice, often out of a fear that such services will be delivered in a manner that is dogmatic and directive, thus robbing clients of their right to self-determination. Integrating Christianity into social work practice has been a particular concern as Christianity is the dominant faith tradition in the United States. Yet, not all faith-based agencies provide services that are religious and/or spiritual in nature, nor do all mental health practitioners who provide spiritual or faith-based counseling work with

faith-based agencies. In fact, in many instances, it would be difficult to determine any substantive difference between the services
provided by a secular agency and those provided by a faith-based
agency.

It's also important to clarify distinctions in the terms *religious*
and *spirituality*, since despite often being used interchangeably,
they are quite different constructs. Religiousness is often defined
as a social or cultural experience grounded in a religious tradition,
whereas spirituality is often defined as the experience of having
an independent relationship with a deity, involving a search for
the sacred—a process that involves seeking out that which is considered holy or the divine (Miller & Thoresen, 2003; Pargament & Mahoney, 2009). Of
course, people can be religious and spiritual (searching for the divine within the context
of a particular religious tradition), religious without being particularly spiritual (a cultural or secular involvement in a religious faith), or spiritual without being grounded in a
particular religious tradition (searching for the divine within the context of various spiritual practices, such as New Age or Eastern philosophies). When clients use these terms,
it's important for social workers to explore what religiousness and spirituality mean to
them, so that incorrect assumptions are not made.

> ### Engage Diversity and Difference in Practice
>
> **Practice Behavior: Gain sufficient self-awareness to eliminate the influence of personal biases and values in working with diverse groups.**
>
> Critical Thinking Question: Why is it important for social workers to gain a comfort level integrating spirituality and practice?

Although social workers may have historically been reticent about integrating spirituality into the counseling relationship, recent studies have revealed the dramatic ways
in which religion or personal spirituality affect people's physical and mental health and
psychosocial functioning. In fact, several research studies in the last two decades have
focused on the mind–body–soul connection in an attempt to understand the reciprocal
relationship of each, with a specific focus on how spirituality affects an individual's overall
physical and mental well-being (Idler & Kasl, 1992; Koenig et al., 1998; Koenig, Larson, &
Weaver, 1998; McLaughlin, 2004; Powell, Shahabi, & Thoresen, 2003). For instance, many
of these studies have shown that personal spirituality has been linked to a decrease
in depression, an increase in greater social support, an increase in cognitive functioning (Koenig, George, & Titus, 2004), an improvement in the ability to cope with crises
(McLaughlin, 2004), and better ability to cope with substance abuse problems (Fallot &
Heckman, 2005).

The issue of faith within the context of social service provision is an area in need
of increased attention, particularly in light of the various studies that have revealed that
the majority of U.S. Americans (between 80 and 90 percent) identify themselves as being
either religious or spiritual, stating that their faith is an important aspect of their daily
lives (Gallup & Lindsey, 1999; Grossman, 2002). In fact, several research studies suggest
that counselors should acknowledge and address the religious and spiritual dimensions
of mental and emotional disorders within the counseling relationship, particularly if
clients identify themselves as being "spiritually grounded" (Fallot, 2001; Kliewer, 2004;
Miller, Korinek, & Ivey, 2004). Social workers must also realize that as much as incorporating spirituality into the counseling relationship may be helpful for some clients, there
is also the potential for harm, particularly when the religion of a provider is pushed onto
a client in a directive or aggressive manner.

The question pertinent to all social workers then is to how to remain client-centered
while incorporating spirituality into practice. This process will undoubtedly involve
engaging in some conceptual or paradigm shifts, from a Western model to a more holistic one. Traditionally, the mental health and medical communities in societies in the

Global North (often referred to a 'Western' society) have had a tendency to divide human beings into biological, intellectual, social, emotional, and spiritual parts, with minimal recognition of how each of these dimensions interacts with the other. But in recent years there has been a growing interest, both within professional circles and within the general public, in moving away from such a compartmentalized view of the human experience, and toward regarding humans more holistically, where one is considered as a whole with each part or dimension of the person being inextricably linked with the other.

Essentially, a holistic approach to psychosocial health involves the process of acknowledging, addressing, and evaluating the mind, the body, and the spirit (or soul) when considering any potential issue affecting one's psychosocial functioning. In other words, rather than attempting to determine whether depression is a biological disorder with psychological manifestations or a psychological disorder with biological implications, depression would be considered a condition having a reciprocal impact on the whole person: mind, body, and soul.

> **Learn more about the CSWE Religion and Spirituality work group by going to the CSWE website and navigating to "Curriculum Resources" under the Centers & Initiatives link.**

In response to the recognized need for increased competence in the area of faith-based practice, in 2011 the Council on Social Work Education (CSWE) created the Religion and Spirituality Work Group to promote social work practice in a way that illustrates acknowledgement of and respect for the diverse range of religious expression. In 2012, the NASW joined the CSWE Work Group, which includes a range of members reflecting the group's commitment to interfaith cooperation.

It is important to have a basic working understanding of the values held by these different religious faiths in the event that a social worker has a client who practices a different faith tradition or coordinates services with a faith-based agency of a different faith. Possessing interfaith competency will enhance the social worker's ability to provide faith-based or spiritual counseling by enabling them to move beyond common negative stereotypes and see the value of diversity within a service delivery context. Incorporating spirituality into a counseling relationship requires skills reflecting cultural competence because many religious traditions are rooted in cultural tradition.

A social worker who does not possess cultural competence risks inflicting harm onto the client, even if the harm is unintentional. For instance, the social worker may feel unprepared to address the client's spiritual needs, and in response, may simply ignore the client's references to spiritual matters, which may result in the client feeling ashamed or trivialized. Prior to the recent surge of interest in holistic health, practitioners in the Global North were often dismissive of Eastern philosophy, which acknowledged the mind–body–soul connection for centuries (Tseng, 2004), rendering many in the social work profession ill-equipped to provide effective services to Asian clients from Buddhist or Hindu traditions (for instance) (Hodge, 2004). A more overt form of cultural

Social Work Application Activity

Religion is often considered to be a component of cultural expression, which is why the NASW references religion as a component of cultural competence. Could you effectively counsel someone who practiced a different faith tradition than you? Go onto the NASW website and search for the "NASW Standards for Cultural Competence." Once you review these standards describe how you might handle a situation where you were providing case management services to a client who practiced a different faith tradition than your own.

incompetence is when social workers are inappropriately directive in pushing their religious beliefs onto their client. This can be particularly egregious if the social worker is a member of the dominant culture and practices the dominant religion and is providing social work services to members of a minority religious tradition. Cultural competence in religion and spirituality requires that social workers practice religious humility, sensitivity, and receptivity, integrating spirituality into their practice in a way that is client-driven and client-centered (Hall, Dixon, & Mauzey, 2004).

Assess your comprehension of "The Role of Spirituality in Social Work" by completing this quiz.

FAITH-BASED AGENCIES: SOCIAL SERVICE DELIVERY FROM DIFFERENT FAITH TRADITIONS

Social workers can incorporate matters of spirituality in virtually any practice setting in response to their clients' disclosure that faith is an integral part of their lives or something they wish to explore within the context of their current challenges. Thus, it is important that social workers receive inter-faith training on various religious traditions, particularly those they might have an opportunity to encounter in their practice. But there are also numerous faith-based social services agencies operating within and outside of their particular religious tradition.

There is some confusion surrounding what constitutes a faith-based agency, and how it is different from a secular agency. It's easy to identify a faith-based organization when it's a synagogue, church, or mosque filled with religious symbols and a mission statement that identifies serving God or deity as a primary function and purpose of the organization. But what about agencies that might be considered parachurch organizations that do not function as churches, but more as social services agencies? Or social service agencies that have their roots in a particular religious tradition but don't integrate religion or faith into practice? Would those agencies be considered faith based?

These are more challenging questions than they might initially appear. Even the U.S. judicial system is not particularly clear on what makes an organization religious in nature (Ebaugh, Pipes, Chafetz, & Daniels, 2003). The difficulty lies in the fact that many secular agencies provide almost identical services as faith-based agencies, and there is often no distinguishable difference between the two, and yet being able to distinguish differences is important for a variety of reasons relating to legal distinctions and funding considerations. Ebaugh et al. (2003) discussed the various ways in which policymakers, social scientists, and historians have defined faith-based organizations, explaining that a social service agency will likely be deemed faith based if it is *dependent* on religious entities or denominations for support, if its *mission statement* identifies agency goals that reflect *core values* that are religious in nature, and if the employees of the organization are religious and adhere to a *statement of faith*.

However a faith-based agency is defined, it is important to remember that being "faith based" does not necessarily mean *Christian*, as might be presumed in some countries in the Global North, such as the United States. In fact, a number of religiously oriented organizations provide faith-based social services grounded in faiths other than Christianity. Thus, although it is true that the majority of faith-based organizations in the United States are Christian in nature, many are not. Faith-based agencies may be Jewish, Muslim, Mormon, or Buddhist, serving communities broadly or more narrowly serving individuals predominantly from their own identified faith tradition.

Faith-based social services can be facilitated as a ministry of a house of worship, or they can be facilitated as a program within a religious organization that functions as a social service agency, such as the Salvation Army. Such organizations may have the goal of converting clients to that particular faith tradition, believing that conversion is the first step toward wholeness, or they might deliver social services in a manner similar to secular agencies but operating in a manner consistent with the values of its religious roots. It's important to be aware of the church or agency's mission statement because the agency's foundational values will likely have a significant impact on how social services are delivered.

Legislation and Policy Affecting Faith-based Agencies

Historically, it has been quite challenging for a faith-based organization to receive federal funding. The Fourth Amendment to the U.S. Constitution, which guaranteed freedom of worship, has frequently been interpreted by the courts to require separation between religion and the government. The federal government remains sensitive to those members of society who do not share the same faith as the majority culture and, as such, has attempted to protect members of minority religious traditions, as well as individuals who practice no faith tradition. One way of accomplishing this is through legislation that ensures such individuals will not be subject to direct or indirect coercion into praying to a God in which they do not believe.

Out of concern that some faith-based agencies were being excluded from federal funding inappropriately, in 2001 former president George W. Bush passed the Faith-Based Community Initiatives Act, also known as Charitable Choice, or Care Services Act (CSA), which made it easier for faith-based organizations to receive federal funding as long as religious worship, instruction, or proselytization was not a part of service provision (at least within the aspect of the organization seeking federal funding). Many people saw this as a positive step toward reengaging religious organizations in the care of those in need, many of which had been providing valuable services to people in need for generations. Yet others expressed concern that this new legislation not replace the federal government as being chiefly responsible for social service provision. While acknowledging the important role faith-based organizations have played in social service provision, the NASW has expressed concern that historically marginalized populations not be excluded from services by federally funded faith-based agencies with a moral imperative. This sentiment was articulated in a 2001 NASW press release, which expressed support for public-private partnerships, as long as they upheld the values of *open access to services* that prohibits exclusion based upon "gender, marital status, sexual orientation, disability, religion, political views, race, ethnic or national origin"; *accountability*, where agencies receiving federal funding are subject to accountability measures to ensure they are providing appropriate and effective social services; *separation of Church and State*, where organized religion is not promoted through federal policy; *appropriate staffing*, where all agencies providing social service agencies are staffed with professionals who have the recommended levels of education and training, equipping them to be able to manage clients' often complex needs; and, *maintaining government*

Engage in Policy Practice to Advance Social and Economic Well-Being and to Deliver Effective Social Work Services

Practice Behavior: Collaborate with colleagues and clients for effective policy action.

Critical Thinking Question: What roles do social workers play in advocating for policy that supports a client's right to seek services from faith providers, while at the same time ensuring that religious minorities' rights are also respected?

responsibility for ensuring equal opportunities for all members of society, based on the government's mandated commitment to a public service ethos (NASW, 2001).

Essentially, the NASW's concerns about Charitable Choice relate primarily to issues of forced morality, the value of self-determination, and the importance of keeping services voluntary for all members of society regardless of their race, gender, religion, and sexual orientation. All one needs to do is conduct a cursory review of history to recognize how easy it is to confuse faith with cultural values. For example, slavery was once considered a practice sanctioned by God, and scriptural support was even offered in support of a Christian man's right to have a slave. In fact, a host of issues once considered sinful (e.g., divorce, same sex relationships, women in the ministry, single parenting) are now considered relatively mainstream within many mainstream religious denominations, indicating that the interpretation of biblical scripture—and thus God's intent—is influenced by the current moral climate of society.

Most critics of former president Bush's faith-based initiative are not necessarily critical of faith-based agencies' ability to provide effective social services; rather, they assert that faith-based agencies should not become the primary social service provider in the United States (NASW, 2001).

Potentially in response to these concerns, on February 5, 2009, President Obama signed Executive Order 13199, which established the White House Office of Faith-Based and Neighborhood Partnerships. After signing the order, President Obama pledged to avoid favoring one religious group over another—and to change how decisions on funding practices are made. According to a February 2009 White House press release, the Office of Faith-Based and Neighborhood Partnerships stated the following regarding the order's four key priorities:

1. The Office's top priority will be making community groups an integral part of our economic recovery and poverty a burden fewer have to bear when recovery is complete.

2. It will be one voice among several in the administration that will look at how we support women and children, address teenage pregnancy, and reduce the need for abortion.

3. The Office will strive to support fathers who stand by their families, which involves working to get young men off the streets and into well-paying jobs and encouraging responsible fatherhood.

4. Finally, beyond American shores, this Office will work with the National Security Council to foster interfaith dialogue with leaders and scholars around the world. (White House, 2009, para. 5–6).

The shift in priorities has alleviated many of the concerns expressed by the NASW, and other social workers who recognized the value and long-term contributions of faith-based organizations but advocated for distribution of funding to agencies from a wide range of religious traditions, views and perspectives. Many agree that the arbitrary exclusion of all religious organizations from federal funding is neither fair nor in the best interest of clients, and social workers must advocate for fairness, equity, and objectivity in the dissemination of federal funding, avoiding the politicization of this issue so that clients of *all faith traditions* have similar opportunities to seek assistance from agencies that share their religious views.

Learn more about President Obama's faith initiative program by going to the White House website, clicking on The Administration link, and then navigating to the "Office of Faith-based and Neighborhood Partnerships" section under the Domestic Policy Council link.

The Benefits of Faith-based Services

The majority of Americans identify religion and spirituality as being an important part of their lives, and also identify themselves as being members of specific faith communities (groups of individuals who share similar religious beliefs and come together for a time of worship and fellowship). Many members of faith communities rely on their churches or houses of worship when going through a difficult time. Faith communities provide individuals with a valuable support system during difficult times, providing guidance, emotional support, and concrete services, such as financial assistance to clients in need. One goal of social work is to connect people to a support system, and a healthy faith community can usually provide this type of support for its active members, as well as others within the broader community. Coping methods that rely on spirituality and faith communities has also been found to provide increased benefits over other coping methods, such as general social support and even counseling, in some contexts (Pargament, Tarakeshwar, Ellison, & Wulff, 2001). For instance, a recent study questioned individuals within a church congregation who had recently experienced a crisis. The subjects were asked to rank various resources that they found to be helpful during their crisis. Factors included family, friends, religious beliefs, prayer, reading scripture, and professional services, including counseling, legal services, and psychological services. The researchers were surprised to learn that most people ranked professional services last as far as helpfulness and ranked religious beliefs and praying the highest (Stone, Cross, Purvis, & Young, 2003).

Examples of positive religion include seeing God (or higher power) as a source of strength and support a faith community as supportive rather than a source of judgment (Meisenhelder & Marcum, 2004). These studies suggest that in times of crisis, many people draw strength and support from their faith communities, which provide them with comfort and familiarity while also providing them with a sense of belonging, reminding them that they are not alone.

Religious Diversity in Faith-based Organizations

Faith-based organizations provide social services in similar ways as secular agencies, but there are also differences. Some of these differences relate to variations in the underlying theology practiced by the faith tradition offering the services, but there are surprising similarities in service provision practices among faith-based agencies operating from vastly different theological and ideological bases. For instance, many faith-based organizations from non-Christian traditions provide many of the same services in a similar manner as many Christian-based services. Jewish Family Services (JFS), which serves as an umbrella agency for Jewish Community Centers, offers comprehensive social services to Jewish and non-Jewish clients on a national basis. Islamic social service agencies focus primarily on Muslim communities, both within the United States and abroad, such as Bosnians and Palestinians, but also support people and communities outside the Muslim community, such as providing international and national disaster relief. In fact, a recent Associated Press article discussed the outpouring of Muslim support for victims of Hurricane Katrina, the devastating natural disaster that hit New Orleans and surrounding states in August 2005, leaving thousands of people homeless and destitute. Faith-based organizations such as the Muslim American Society, the Council on American-Islamic Relations, and the Islamic Relief USA all participated in the Muslim Hurricane Relief Task Force, which took turns facilitating relief shelters and feeding those in need (Associated Press, 2005). These examples illustrate how divergent faith traditions come together to offer similar types of assistance to those in need.

Assess your comprehension of "Faith-Based Agencies: Social Service Delivery From Different Faith Traditions" by completing this quiz.

THE ROLE OF THE SOCIAL WORKER: SOCIAL SERVICES AND INTERVENTION STRATEGIES

In this section, I will explore examples of social service provision through mainstream faith-based agencies within Abrahamic religious traditions (Jewish, Christian, and Islamic) as they tend to be the major providers of social services, both on a local and global level, as well as spiritually-centered traditions that do not tend to be associated with traditional religious organizations. I will also explore the role of the social worker working in these faith-based organizations, and spiritual orientations. Most of the agencies featured in this section operate separately from any church or religious entity but are either supported by or are a component of particular religious or spiritual traditions or philosophies. I will also explore ways in which social workers can use common spiritually based intervention strategies based in more Eastern philosophies, as oftentimes clients are seeking a spiritual awakening, but outside of a traditional mainstream religious framework.

Jewish Social Service Agencies

> If one of your countrymen becomes poor and is unable to support himself among you, help him as you would an alien or a temporary resident, so he can continue to live among you. (Leviticus 25: 35)

The Jewish faith is rich in instructions and examples of charity and general provision of the poor. The Torah, the Jewish holy book called the *Tanakh*. The Talmud is the transcribed collection of oral tradition handed down from generation to generation, guiding the interpretation of the Tanakh. Charity, as referenced in both the Tanakh and the Talmud, is defined as giving to the poor and is a requirement for the Jewish people. According to Jewish law, forgiveness of sins is granted with prayer, repentance, and charity.

The Jewish faith has different denominations called *movements*, including Orthodox, Conservative, Hasidic, Humanist, Reform, Sephardic, Ashkenazi, and Reconstructionist. Some of these movements evolved through geographic divisions and some through philosophical divisions. Nevertheless, all Jewish movements hold that charity and benevolence (kindness and compassion) are an integral part of righteousness. Good financial stewardship is highly valued in many faith traditions, and the Jewish faith is no exception, where giving 5 to 10 percent of one's income to charity is considered an obligation among all Jewish denominations. Charity is not solely related to duty, however, but also reflects the value of community and the commitment to remain connected to all Jews worldwide. This sense of community is based on shared experiences of both current and historical persecution, which binds the Jewish community together in a collective determination of self-sufficiency and survival. The Talmud specifies different levels of giving, with the lowest level involving giving begrudgingly and the highest levels including giving anonymously to a stranger and helping someone attain self-sufficiency by giving them work (Babylonian Talmud, Chagigah 5a; Maimonides, Hilchos Matnos Aniyim 10: 7–14).

Jewish social service agencies are coordinated through a national umbrella organization that serves as a network of support for smaller social service agencies that provide direct service. Social services are directed toward Jewish and non-Jewish communities and target domestic and international causes.

The Jewish Federations of North America

The Jewish Federations of North America (JFNA) is an international umbrella humanitarian organization that represents over 100 Jewish federations in North America alone. The JFNA provides humanitarian relief and social services worldwide to those in need. The goals of social justice and strengthening the Jewish community are a reflection of the scriptures in the Talmud that command giving to the poor, sick, widows, and orphans. The JFNA exists to provide financial support and educational services to Jewish federations and Jewish community centers; it also funds the rescue and resettlement of Jews living in high-conflict or unsafe areas worldwide.

A component of the JFNA is the Human Services and Social Policy Pillar (HSSP), which is responsible for social lobbying action on local and national levels in an attempt to influence social policy. Whether it's lobbying for increased funding for geriatric services, homeless resources, or refugee programs, the HSSP, or *the pillar* as it is commonly called, relies on social workers and volunteers to coordinate services within and outside of the Jewish community.

Association of Jewish Family and Children's Agencies

The Association of Jewish Family and Children's Agencies (AJFCA) acts as the umbrella organization for JFS and Jewish community centers across the United States and Canada. The AJFCA also acts as an information clearing house for local JFS agencies, which provide comprehensive social services. AJFCAs also provide funding for local federations of Jewish social service agencies, advocate for social justice, and provide information on education and training opportunities.

Local JFS agencies offer a number of different services including individual and family counseling, marital counseling, substance abuse counseling, AIDS counseling and awareness programs, anger management courses, employment services, parenting workshops, children's camps, teen programs, and geriatric programs including Kosher Meals on Wheels and hospice. No one is denied services because of an inability to pay, and payment for services is typically on a sliding scale.

One program that is relatively unique to this organization includes refugee resettlement programs, which assist individuals and families who have legally entered the United States having fled from persecution. Refugees of either Jewish or non-Jewish descent come from various countries, including Russia and other former Soviet-bloc countries, the Middle East, and Africa. Services typically include providing short-term housing on arrival, emergency financial support, case management, medical care, assistance with school enrollment, job placement, and language courses. These agencies have excellent reputations in assisting refugees to gain financial independence rapidly, particularly in light of the often tragic circumstances the refugees have faced prior to coming to the United States.

Services focused exclusively on the Jewish community include Holocaust survivor services to Jews who lived in European countries under Nazi rule between 1933 and 1945. In addition to providing counseling services related to post-traumatic stress disorder (PTSD), in-home services related to geriatric care are also provided. Other Jewish-related services offered include counseling and case management services for Jewish armed services personnel, Jewish chaplaincy services, family services, and outreach focusing on assisting families reconnect with their Jewish roots by learning how to incorporate Jewish traditions and values into their family systems. Premarital and marriage services are also offered to Jewish couples and interfaith couples, focusing on marriage and parenting in a Jewish context.

Social workers within these agencies provide a wide range of services because JFS agencies typically offer comprehensive social services similar to those discussed through this entire text. In fact, many of the JFS agencies offer just about every type of social services one could imagine! The primary difference between the manner in which social services professionals deliver services at a JFS agency versus a secular agency is the focus on connecting Jewish clients to the broader Jewish community, both domestically and worldwide, as well as the incorporation of Jewish values throughout the various programs. Counselors and case managers are also primarily Jewish and well connected to the Jewish community, including being familiar with local synagogues and other Jewish services within the local community. There are exceptions though as some JFSs do hire non-Jewish social workers, and again, these agencies serve clients outside of the Jewish community.

> Check out AJFCA on Facebook by going to the Facebook website and searching for "Association of Jewish Family & Children's Agencies."

Virtually all JFS programs are eligible for federal funding as long as proselytizing does not occur as a function of any program receiving funding. Even synagogues offering social services are eligible to receive government funding as long as the programs are operated separately from any religious functions.

The Jewish social service agencies provide a network of comprehensive services designed to address human needs on all levels. They provide invaluable services to the Jewish community, as well as those outside of the Jewish faith, both within the United States and abroad.

Christian Social Services Agencies

> For I was hungry and you gave me something to eat, I was thirsty and you gave me something to drink, I was a stranger and you invited me in, I needed clothes and you clothed me, I was sick and you looked after me, I was in prison, and you came to visit me . . . I tell you the truth, whatever you did for one of the least of these brothers of mine, you did for me. (Matthew 25: 35–36, 40)

Because a fair amount of faith-based organizations in the United States are Christian in nature, it is valuable to have an understanding of the range of theologies and ideologies within the Christian church. The historic role of the Catholic Church discussed earlier in the chapter reflects Catholicism's strong commitment to caring for the poor. This commitment is reflected in today's Catholic Church in ministries such as Catholic Charities, which facilitates numerous social service programs throughout the United States, and abroad.

Mainstream Protestant denominations such as Methodist, Presbyterian, and Lutheran often embraced the "social gospel," the Old Testament mandate to provide for those in society in need, but these denominations do not necessarily link charity to evangelism. Rather, the predominant view among many mainstream denominations is to show the love of Christ through giving as well as through addressing social concerns for the poor and the oppressed.

Conservative Christians, such as evangelicals, fundamentalists, and Pentecostals, tend to focus on evangelism as the initial priority, addressing social causes and the needs of the poor through "winning souls for Christ". This approach makes sense if one truly believes that the only path toward wholeness is by surrendering one's life to Christ, repenting of one's sins, and becoming a new creation through a personal relationship with God. An ethical dilemma arises though when such evangelism occurs in the counseling office or anywhere else where social services are being provided, without the client understanding that this is the goal of the service provider. As mentioned earlier in this chapter, professional standards of the social work profession, discourage proselytizing to clients. Critics of evangelical practitioners who do attempt to evangelize clients might suggest that as worthy as this act may be perceived, it is more appropriately conducted in the vein of pastoral counseling or ministry efforts (Belcher, Fandetti, & Cole, 2004).

This ethical dilemma is worth exploring in both secular and religious circles and can be addressed in a variety of ways. For instance, there is nothing inherently unethical in talking about matters of faith and spirituality as long as it is client driven. In fact, it is the social worker's comfort level in talking about such issues and willingness to allow the client to determine the depth and direction of the discussion that is important. For instance, consider the client who enters a counseling session utilizing negative religious coping strategies such as perceiving God as punishing, abandoning, and distant, particularly when in the midst of a crisis. A social worker in a faith-based agency can reframe the client's punitive view of God by teaching the client to use positive religious coping methods where God is perceived as a source of guidance, strength, and support. Because research supports the mental health benefits of positive religious coping strategies, this intervention strategy can be used with the understanding that it is in the best interest of clients who are being hurt by their negative views of God.

Although evangelizing clients is not appropriate in a secular setting or even in a faith-based organization receiving federal funding, it may be appropriate if the social worker works for a religious organization that makes clear its goal to evangelize the client so that the client enters the counseling relationship with full disclosure and equal participation. For instance, many outreach ministries provide emergency services such as food pantries or homeless shelters but do not hide the fact that the ultimate goal of the agency is to lead one down the path of greater religious commitment, which may involve a deepening relationship with a client's existing faith or may involve a complete conversion to a new faith.

Rural Communities and the Black Church

Rural communities, typically those with high racial or ethnic minority populations, tend to be significantly underserved with regard to mental health and social services. Yet research in the last 10 to 15 years has revealed that African American churches, particularly those within rural communities, have picked up the slack by offering significantly more social services than traditionally white churches (Blank, Mahmood, Fox, & Guterbock, 2002).

For many generations the African American church has been the center and backbone of the African American community, and thus these clergy might be more willing to engage deeply in the lives of their parishioners and those within their community, particularly since African Americans have been historically excluded from many mainstream social services—both facilitated by private organizations, as well as those facilitated by the federal government. It appears that in many respects African American churches, particularly those in rural communities, have acted in some respects as the Catholic Church in the Middle Ages, taking responsibility for the mental health concerns and basic needs of those within the community, providing a much needed safety net for the community, in a range of ways (Blank, Mahmood, Fox & Gutervock, 2002; Thomas, Quinn, Bilingsley, & Caldwell, 1994).

Catholic Charities

Catholic Charities USA is a network of Christian social service agencies that has a long tradition of caring for those in need. Services are provided to all individuals seeking assistance regardless of religious affiliation. Currently, there are approximately 1,600 local Catholic Charities agencies across the United States offering a wide variety of social services designed to meet the needs within the particular community served. According to the Catholic Charities website, services provided at most of its local agencies focus on advocacy and direct services related to reducing poverty, supporting families, and empowering communities. They do this by facilitating programs that focus on adoption, disaster relief, housing counseling, disaster case management, racism and diversity, human trafficking, and climate change (Catholic Charities USA, 2010).

Catholic Charities USA claims to have provided services to over 10 million individuals in the year 2010 alone, making it one of the largest networks of social service agencies in the world, similar in nature to the Jewish federations. The majority of funding comes from federal and state sources, with only a small percentage coming from the Catholic Church. Catholic Charities has not had significant problems obtaining federal funding because providing services directly linked to religious ministry is not typically an aspect of service provision and thus Catholic Charities has not been particularly affected by various faith-based initiatives.

In many respects, Catholic Charities provides similar services to secular agencies except that most local Catholic Charities agencies also provide support to archdiocesan schools and parishes. Adoption and children's services remain consistent with the values of the Catholic faith, and thus option counseling for women experiencing an unplanned pregnancy would not typically include referrals to abortion services. Most agencies also provide Catholic Youth Organizations (CYO), an after-school and weekend athletic program focusing on the development of sportsmanship-like behavior and ethical values consistent with the Catholic faith.

Learn more about the work of Catholic Charities by conducting an Internet search on "Catholic Charities USA."

Other services include child care, domestic and international adoption, domestic violence prevention and intervention, employment and job training, gang intervention, healthcare, HIV/AIDS services, immigration and naturalization services, nutrition counseling, refugee resettlement services, senior services, homeless assistance and emergency housing, senior housing, and substance abuse counseling. Most local Catholic Charities agencies also offer community centers that focus on providing comprehensive social services for those who are homeless or at risk of becoming homeless.

Social workers are not required to be Catholic, but many of those in leadership positions are due to the close and supportive relationship with local Catholic parishes. Services provided tend to be generalist in nature, depending on the actual services being provided. Social workers working at Catholic Charities have the benefit of working within a broad network of agencies that provide extensive support and educational opportunities.

Prison Fellowship Ministries

The late Chuck Colson reached the peak of his political career as President Richard Nixon's aide, or as many referred to him, President Nixon's "hatchet man." In 1973, Colson became a Christian, and in 1974 he pleaded guilty to obstruction of justice charges in association with the Watergate scandal. Colson served seven months of a three-year sentence and on his release founded Prison Fellowship Ministries (PFM) in 1976, based on his own dramatic religious conversion and his belief that no one is beyond hope. His ministry is now one of the largest prison ministries in the world, reaching out to prisoners, ex-prisoners, their families, and victims. PFM is also involved in criminal justice reform through a PFM affiliate, Justice Fellowship, which focuses on numerous social justice issues including prison safety and eliminating prison rape.

Such social advocacy is particularly important for groups of individuals who do not evoke sympathy in the average person, and prisoners certainly fall into this category. Yet, it is essential for people to realize that prisoners are not a uniform group who deserve whatever hardship the prison system can dish out. Most prisoners have had childhoods marked by poverty and abuse, many serve longer sentences because they could not afford adequate legal defenses, and some prisoners are innocent. PFM is committed to stopping the intergenerational cycle of crime and poverty by offering prisoners hope for a second chance through the Christian faith.

Citing the difference that this ministry can make in the lives of prisoners as well as in society in general, Colson referenced the dramatic shift in climate experienced at Angola Prison in Louisiana, once touted as the most dangerous prison in the United States, but now considered the most peaceful under the leadership of Burl Cain, a Christian who invoked the services of local seminaries to minister to inmates. In a similar vein, PFM trains volunteers to counsel and minister to prisoners in virtually every prison across the country.

PFM facilitates a number of ministries including training volunteers to visit prisoners, many of whom receive no other visits. The ministry does not receive federal funding because PFM volunteers focus extensively on the evangelism of prisoners and their family members. The goal of PFM is to bring the gospel of Christ to every prisoner incarcerated in the United States. PFM also facilitates a "pen pal" program linking prisoners with volunteers who are willing to minister to them in writing. PFM provides services to the family members of prisoners, particularly those with children. An example of such services includes the Angel Tree program, which collects Christmas presents for these children and also facilitates a camp and a mentoring program.

Social workers, who are primarily volunteers, working with PFM provide markedly different services than those working in secular agencies. Because evangelism is the primary intervention tool, volunteers facilitate Bible studies and in-prison seminars, mentor at-risk youth, counsel prisoners and crime victims, serve in youth camps, organize Angel Tree programs, visit prisoners regularly, counsel ex-prisoners and crime victims, and write letters to prisoners in the pen pal program. Social workers also hold paid positions with PFM, including field director positions, which manage and provide support of ministry teams, including recruiting and training volunteers and reaching out to local churches for assistance and financial support.

Islamic Social Services Agencies

It is not righteousness that you turn your faces toward East or West; but it is righteousness to believe in Allah and the Last Day and the Angels and the Book and the Messengers; to spend of your substance out of love for Him, for your kin, for orphans, for the needy, for the wayfarer, for those who ask; and for the ransom of slaves; to be steadfast in prayers and practice regular charity; to fulfill the contracts that you made; and to be firm and patient in pain (or suffering) and adversity and throughout all periods of panic. Such are the people of truth, the God fearing. (Qur'an 2: 177)

And those in whose wealth is a recognized right; for the needy who asks and those who are deprived. (Qur'an 70: 24–25)

Islam is a religion that is often misunderstood and mischaracterized, both by the general public and by the media. This mischaracterization is due in part to the differences between more liberal values in the Global North and more conservative values held by many in the Islamic community. The terrorist acts of September 11, 2001 and after, and the subsequent increase in xenophobia (an unreasonable fear, dislike, or hatred of foreigners, or people who are different) and Islamophobia have further exacerbated the tendency to view the entire Muslim world as one that endorses violence, extremist dogma, and female oppression. In truth, every culture and every religious faction has its peaceful members and its violent ones. A domestic batterer who uses the Christian concept of submission to justify the oppression and abuse of his wife does not define Christianity any more than does a terrorist bent on destruction define the Muslim religion.

The word *Islam* means submission, and followers of Islam submit themselves to the monotheistic God, Allah. The Islamic holy book is called the Qur'an (sometimes referred to as Koran, but because this is the Anglicized spelling, most Muslims prefer the spelling included previously because it most accurately reflects the correct pronunciation in Arabic). The Qur'an is considered by Muslims to be the recited words of God revealed to the Prophet Muhammad in the 7th century. Islam recognizes and relies on the holy books of Judaism and Christianity (the Old and New Testaments), but Muslims consider the Qur'an to be God's final revelation to humankind.

There are approximately one billion followers of Islam, which makes it the second-largest religion in the world. The majority of Muslims live in Southeast Asia, Northern Africa, and the Middle East. There are two primary sects within Islam because of an early dispute over who should have been Muhammad's successor. The Sunnis tend to be more religiously and politically liberal (for instance, they believe that Islamic leaders should always be elected). Approximately 90 percent of all Muslims are Sunnis. Shiites, on the other hand, tend to be more orthodox in their religious beliefs and political philosophies, having developed a more strictly academic application of the Qur'an. They believe that all successors to Muhammad (Imams) are infallible and sinless. They appoint their clergy and hold them in high regard.

Apply Social Work Ethical Principles to Guide Professional Practice

Practice Behavior: Recognize and manage personal values in a way that allows professional values to guide practice.

Critical Thinking Question: There are some tensions that exist between social work values and those embraced by many within the Muslim faith. How can social workers manage any personal feelings they may have about the Muslim faith to ensure they are guided solely by professional values?

The majority of Muslims who live in the United States are Sunnis, 75 percent of whom are foreign born. The Islamic community tends to be both college educated and middle class, and thus Muslims tend not to rely on government-sponsored social services to meet basic needs, and much of the focus of charity is directed toward Muslims in other parts of the world who are suffering, either because of war or some other form of oppression, or is focused on concerns related to marriage and family.

Because Muslims hail from many different countries, there is considerable diversity within the Muslim community, particularly in the United States. Yet despite the variability of cultural beliefs and practices, the House of Islam shares five basic pillars of faith:

- *Shahada*: Faith in one God
- *Salat*: Ritual prayer five times a day while facing Mecca
- *Zakat*: Charitable giving to the poor with the understanding that all wealth belongs to God
- *Sawm*: Fasting from sunrise to sunset during the month of Ramadan
- *Hajj*: Pilgrimage to Mecca

According to the Qur'an (9:60), there are eight categories of people who qualify to receive zakat. These include the poor, the needy, those who collect zakat, those who are being converted, captives, debtors, and travelers. The three foundational values within the Islamic community include community, family, and the sovereignty of God. Family is often defined as the joining of two extended families, thus what might be considered *enmeshment* in North American society is often seen as a sign of respect as extended families are drawn close and remain an active part of the immediate family's life. Men and women typically adopt traditional roles with men working outside of the home and women caring for the home and children, although this trend is changing, just as it is in other cultures within U.S. society, and abroad. Modesty is seen as an important ingredient necessary for keeping order within society, and women often wear clothing (*hijab*) that covers at a minimum their hair, the greater percentage of their bodies within some Muslim sects (Hodge, 2005).

Hodge (2005) notes the areas of obvious conflict between Islamic values and liberal North American values. For instance, Western culture values individualism, self-expression, and self-determination, whereas Islamic culture values community, self-control, and consensus. Thus, whether working with an Islamic social services agency, coordinating services, or directly serving the Islamic community, Hodge cautions social services workers not to view Islamic values through the eyes of North American culture.

For example, it is common for Westerners to view the Islamic tenet of modesty as primitive and oppressive to women, which for some in the United States (and other countries in the Global North) is a "hop, skip, and a jump" away from endorsing domestic violence. Yet the Qur'an states that husbands and wives must express respect and compassion toward one another, and domestic violence is not endorsed. To truly understand the values of modesty and traditional roles embraced within the Islamic culture, one must take the time to understand what these values mean to Muslim men and women. Hence, although a social worker might not share the traditional values held within the Islamic community, working in association with Islamic social service agencies provides social workers with an opportunity to display their respect for cultural diversity.

There has been a recent surge in interest in developing social service programs within mosques and Islamic centers across the United States in response to growing concerns about social issues and demonstrated needs within the community, particularly related to marriage and family. The profession of social work is relatively new to the Islamic community, and the opening vignette exploring the experiences of Maya and Asad provide an example of how social workers can effectively work within Islamic communities. Islamic social service providers include social workers, counselors, and psychologists, but these services can also be offered by an Imam (a Muslim religious leader). Islamic social service agencies provide services to both Muslims and non-Muslims and are increasingly relied upon to serve as a liaison for Western aid agencies in Islamic communities experiencing a crisis (De Cordier, 2009).

Islamic charities have suffered since the 9/11 terrorist attacks, though, because many Muslims in the United States are afraid that monies they donate in good faith to Islamic charities may be frozen by the U.S. government and not directed to humanitarian causes as planned. Muslims are also giving less because they are afraid that they might be held in suspicion if a charity they donate money to is later investigated for diverting funds to terrorist causes. Mosques and Islamic centers across the nation are reaching out to legislators in a campaign called Charity without Fear, asking them to establish a list of Islamic charities in good standing, so that Muslims can give to a charity without fear of being accused of supporting terrorist organizations (Council of Islamic Organizations, 2005).

Although there are not as many Muslim social service agencies as there are agencies from other faith traditions, there are several that make valuable contributions to the social services field on a national and international level. The following agencies are a few of these:

Islamic Social Services Association

The Islamic Social Services Association (ISSA) acts as an umbrella organization for all Muslim social service agencies in the United States and Canada. The ISSA provides training and educational services, acting as a network linking and equipping Muslim communities.

Inner-City Muslim Action Network

One group of agencies is called The Inner-City Muslim Action Network (IMAN) focuses on meeting the needs of those in the inner city in Chicago by operating food pantries, health clinics, and prayer services. The agency's offices, which are located in a storefront on Chicago's South Side, offer a free computer lab with free Internet service, General Educational Development (GED) courses, and computer training classes. IMAN is also involved in community activism such as lobbying against the granting of liquor licenses in high-crime areas, community development, and coordination of outreach events with other community agencies both Muslim and non-Muslim.

Check out "Inner-City Muslim Action Network" on Facebook.

Muslim Family Services

There is considerable concern within the Islamic faith community that Muslim marriages are being negatively affected by the casual nature of divorce in the United States. Muslim Family Services (MFS), located throughout the United States, attempts to address these concerns through programs focusing on divorce prevention. MFS is a division of the Islamic Circle of North America (ICNA), an organization designed to assist Muslims live a more devout life. MFS offers social services to families and couples, teaching them how to have a marriage according to Islamic principles.

MFS provides education, such as workshops for married couples and training for Imams; premarriage, marriage, and parenting counseling; emergency services; foster care; and advocacy in court and with social services. Islamic values are stressed, including the belief that marriage is the foundation of society and the pillar on which family is built. Social workers working for MFS understand that Muslim couples living in the United States are often caught between two cultures, which has led to increased divorce rates and also many parenting challenges as adolescents in particular challenge traditional Islamic values such as modesty and patriarchal male–female relationships.

Islamic Relief USA

Islamic Relief USA engages in poverty alleviation, disaster relief, and development work throughout the United States and throughout the world. A similar organization that coordinates services with Islamic Relief USA is Islamic Relief Worldwide, which provides services on a worldwide basis, including disaster relief and recovery services, including the protection of vulnerable and marginalized populations through confronting poverty. Islamic Relief Worldwide and Islamic Relief USA both engage in six types of aid work, including poverty alleviation in the form of sustainable livelihoods, education, health and nutrition, child welfare, water and sanitation, and emergency relief and disaster preparedness.

Social service providers working within these agencies are Muslim and must be familiar with Islamic family values and the Qur'an, particularly in matters related to marriage and raising children. Many social service providers use similar counseling methods as do providers in secular agencies, but case management and generalist services are not as widely practiced because a social services network is not as well developed within the Islamic community.

The Islamic community within the United States will continue to be confronted with issues related to acculturation, modernization, and the eroding of traditional values, and problems within the family will no doubt continue to rise. Competing marital roles, adolescent rebellion, and at times social isolation, including the internalization of the majority culture's often negative views of the Islamic faith, will continue to add stress to many Muslim families. Social service agencies can assist Muslim families feel less isolated, can provide much-needed education and support, and a sense of connectedness among Muslims who are feeling unsupported within their broader communities.

The Mindfulness Movement

Spiritual counseling need not be facilitated within a traditional religious framework but can also involve general spirituality, where the social worker provides resources, counseling and other interactive services focusing on a belief that all people are interconnected on some level, and are guided by a divine presence. Many clients who wish to seek a deeper connection with a higher power but are not comfortable doing so within a particular theological framework can greatly benefit from exposure to a more general spirituality. Thus it is important for social workers to be aware of a wide range of spiritual resources, which include traditions rooted

Social Work, Social Media, and Technology

Shira Vardi, a Chicago area social worker, recently began her own mindfulness organization called "Encounters in Motion." Vardi uses her social work skills and training in a unique way that incorporates all aspects of the mind and body, with a particular focus on movement. Encounters in Motion is not psychotherapy in that problems aren't approached from the framework of mental illness and its healing or management. Rather, Vardi views the source of suffering as a society as rooted in disconnection: from ourselves (mind/body/spirit) and from those around us (see the research on vulnerability by Brene Brown, and on happiness through connection by Barbara Fredrickson). Vardi therefore shares tools and facilitates experiences—for individuals, groups, and organizations—that support connection in the moment. Using her Feldenkrais®

practitioner training, she uses gentle touch to guide individual client movement and attention toward their physical structural support in relation to gravity. This enables clients to move through life with greater support, lightness, and ease. Using meditation and internal family systems training with individuals and groups, she helps clients relate to their thoughts and feelings with leadership and good will. This process enables a client's whole self to work in harmony, rather than the internal chatter and infighting that often uses up so much of our energy. Using West African dance and expressive movement, Vardi helps clients sense, feel, and move their bodies and their spirits to music, from a place of connection, pleasure, and ease. Check out Shira Vardi's work by going to the Facebook website and searching for "Encounters in Motion."

in what would be considered more "Eastern," or New Age philosophies. Examples include yoga traditions and the mindfulness movement. New Age traditions approach the person holistically, focusing on making connections between the person and the divine, and often rely on using all of the senses, as well as meditation practices, with the goal of helping individuals gain increased awareness and connectedness. The Mindfulness movement (also called Contemplative practice), rooted in the Buddhist tradition, helps individuals develop a sense of awareness and presence in one's daily life. Mindfulness traditions focus on cultivating an accepting awareness and enhanced attention to present moment experiences, and a belief that with this experience, a sense of interconnectedness to everything else emerges on its own. Practicing living each moment with this awareness promotes resilience in relating to life's obstacles as well as healing, love, and compassion. Those practicing mindfulness believe that if one seeks wisdom and balance in life and a connection with that which is bigger than oneself, then conditions such as depression, anxiety, substance abuse, and unresolved grief can be overcome, and ultimately replaced with living mindfully with greater compassion, appreciation, and joy.

Learn more about mindfulness and contemplative practices by searching the Internet for "The Center for Contemplative Practices," and exploring this organization's website for informational articles and Webinars.

Assess your comprehension of "The Role of the Social Worker: Social Services and Intervention Strategies" by completing this quiz.

Summary

Far too many of the world's conflicts center on religion, and religious dogma has far too often been at the heart of marginalization and the justification of oppression

of members of the "out-group" population. Yet religion can also be a source of peace, faith, optimism, and hope. Despite the misuse and misapplication of religion by some, religion, particularly personal spirituality, is often key to the self-actualization of many, and social workers must be comfortable engaging in this process to be effectively client centered. Further, faith-based agencies from a range of religious traditions have had a long history of providing assistance to underserved and at-risk populations and are often working in partner-ship with secular and government agencies providing valuable services to clients throughout the country, and many current movements based in historic traditions, such as mindfulness and contemplative practices can help a range of clients tap into their internal resources in a way that reflects greater connectedness and holistic functioning.

Recall what you learned in this chapter by completing the Chapter Review.

12

Violence, Victim Advocacy, and Corrections

BlueSkyImage/Shutterstock

Rick grew up in a home marked by domestic violence, which oftentimes extended to the children. Rick's mother was chronically depressed and often resorted to using alcohol to avoid dealing with her feelings. Rick recalls days and sometimes weeks where his mother refused to get out of bed, and he was responsible for caring for his younger siblings. His father also had an alcohol problem and would fly into nightly rages where he would physically abuse Rick's mother. When Rick got older, he attempted to intervene and protect his mother, which only resulted in his father physically abusing him. In addition to physical abuse, Rick was also the victim of emotional abuse and neglect. Rick's father would often call him derogatory names and humiliate him by telling him that he would amount to nothing in life and that he was worthless. It seemed as though Rick could do nothing right, and when he was about 12 years old, he promised himself that he would never allow anyone to hurt or humiliate him again. Rick married when he was 21 and was hopeful that his life of being victimized was over. He loved his wife Sarah very much and was determined to be the best husband

263

and father he could possibly be. He vowed not to repeat the mistakes of his parents, but deep inside he was plagued with fears that he wasn't good enough for his wife and that she would eventually leave him. He became increasingly jealous and accused his wife constantly of plotting behind his back to leave him, likely with another man. If Rick's wife tried to convince him otherwise, he accused her of lying. When she became pregnant he was thrilled, but after the baby was born he became upset because his wife seemed to want to spend all her time with the baby, leaving him to fend for himself. One day Rick's boss called him into his office and pointed out a mistake that Rick made. All Rick could think of was the promise he had made to himself years ago to never allow anyone to hurt or ridicule him again. Even though his boss's comments would have seemed reasonable to most people, to Rick they were a recreation of the abuse he endured as a child. He lost control of his temper, slammed his fist into the wall, and quit his job. When he got home he told Sarah and fully expected her to sympathize with him and support his decision to not tolerate such abuse, but instead she complained that his act was selfish, particularly in light of his responsibilities as a father. Rick completely lost his temper and in a blind rage accused Sarah of betraying him. In the blur that followed, Rick accused her of cheating on him, of caring about the baby more than him, and of even getting pregnant by another man. In the midst of his angry outburst, he shoved Sarah against the wall and knocked her down, and then began kicking her in the stomach and head. All he could think of was how this woman, whom he thought was his "savior" was really his enemy, and at that moment he hated her for allowing him to lower his guard and trust her. All the pain of his childhood, with all the hurt and humiliation, came rushing back, and he began to choke her. When his baby interrupted his rage, he screamed at his son to shut up. When his baby's crying got louder, he picked him up and shook him violently. Rick was arrested on charges of felony domestic violence, unlawful restraint, and child endangerment. After Sarah was released from the hospital, she listened to her voicemail and listened to several frantic and pleading voicemail messages from Rick crying and profusely apologizing and expressing intense fear about being in jail. The next call was from a social worker at the Victim-Witness Assistance program with the local prosecutor's office asking her to return the call so that she could provide Sarah with information about the court case, her order of protection, and resources for counseling. Sarah then received a call from the local domestic violence shelter. The social worker at the shelter asked her several questions about her safety and whether she needed shelter. She also offered Sarah court advocacy and resources to help with her baby's medical care. Sarah was hesitant to say too much. Mostly she was overwhelmed and felt a flood of emotions—fear, sadness, confusion, and guilt. She felt sorry for Rick. She knew he was a good person, and she couldn't stand the thought of him being in jail, alone and scared. The sound of Rick's voice on the voicemail rang in her ears, and she began going over what happened in her mind again and again, questioning her original version of the events that night—did Rick mean to knock her down? Did he really shake the baby? Why wasn't she more sympathetic? She really had been neglecting him lately . . . was she a bad wife? During Sarah's first meeting with the prosecutor and court advocate about Rick's case, she became immediately uncomfortable about the prospect of testifying against her husband. In fact, she couldn't imagine it! She felt sorry for Rick—he'd had a horrible childhood, and she felt like she was the only one he could confide in, and that made her feel good. She believed in her heart that good people forgave easily, especially their husbands. As soon as Rick was released on bond, and even though he was not allowed to contact her, she had been receiving almost nightly calls from him, begging for her forgiveness. This Rick was the Rick she fell in love with—the soft Rick, the vulnerable Rick, the sweet Rick, and the kind Rick. She reasoned that as awful as this incident had been, maybe it was the wake-up call their family needed to get back on track. When the prosecutor informed Sarah that she did not have the power to drop the charges or the order of protection she became enraged. She did not want nor ask for their involvement. She was certain that she could handle this matter on her own, as a family, and she wanted no part of the free advocacy from Victim-Witness Assistance or from the local shelter. She found their perception of her as a "battered wife" embarrassing and humiliating. Despite her numerous attempts to play down what happened, even blaming herself denying that it was "that bad" and explaining that Rick had never kicked her and was actually trying to soothe the baby, not shake him, the prosecutor refused to budge, and in fact warned Sarah that if she allowed Rick back into the house, she too could be facing charges of child maltreatment for putting her baby at risk. Sarah left the courthouse in a rage, feeling misunderstood, scared, embarrassed, and completely alone. She knew none of her friends and family members would understand because no one understood Rick like she did, and they didn't like him. In fact, the only person she believed she could rely on was the one person who was forbidden to see her—her husband Rick.

FORENSIC SOCIAL WORK: WORKING WITH SURVIVORS AND PERPETRATORS OF VIOLENCE

The field of forensic social work, sometimes called corrections social work, is a multidisciplinary practice area focusing broadly on any area that relates to the legal and justice system, including juvenile and adult justice services, corrections, intimate partner violence (IVP), and mandated treatment (among other areas). The National Organization of Forensic Social Work (NOFSW) is a professional organization committed to the education and training of forensic social workers engaging in policy practice and program development.

Learn more about the field of forensic social work by conducting an Internet search for the National Organization of Forensic Social Work.

Forensic social workers may work in practice settings dealing with inter-partner violence, sexual assault, and gang activity. Or may work at police departments, probation departments, state, county prosecutors, and correctional facilities, such as jails and prisons. The role and function of forensic social workers will vary dramatically depending on the legal or criminal justice issues involved. Forensic social workers require specialized training beyond their social work education, in areas such as crime victimization and trauma, forensic interviewing, crisis counseling, and grief counseling. They must also develop a thorough understanding of the legal and criminal justice systems pertinent to the target client or client systems with which they are working.

Violence has always been a part of human history and exists in virtually all segments of life among living creatures. Although some may argue that violence is a natural aspect of survival in the animal kingdom, controversy abounds when this theory is applied to humankind. Does a review of history reveal that war is necessary? Certainly war has always existed, but is our existence dependent on competition for resources won through violent means? At what point does the act of war become an atrocity involving crimes against humanity, or worse, genocide? How can ordinary people live side-by-side peacefully for years and then suddenly commit heinous acts, such as were the case during the Holocaust or the more recent genocide in Rwanda, and somehow justify their actions?

Determining the answer to these questions lies at the heart of violence research within the domain of social scientists such as sociologists, social psychologists, anthropologists, and criminologists, as well as those who work in the applied fields such as social work and criminal justice. In this chapter, the various types of violence will be explored, such as IPV, sexual assault, battery, and murder. Ways in which society and those within the social work field most often intervene to reduce violence that affects not only its survivors but also society as a whole will also be explored.

> **Assess your comprehension of "Forensic Social Work: Working With Survivors and Perpetrators of Violence" by completing this quiz.**

INTIMATE PARTNER VIOLENCE

Intimate partner violence (IPV) (a more inclusive term than the traditionally used term domestic violence) involves physical, sexual, and emotional abuse acted out between intimates. This may include violence between husbands and wives, violence between boyfriends and girlfriends, violence within lesbian, gay, bisexual, and transgendered (LGBT) populations, and violence between family members (such as siblings, parents, etc.). IPV can include hitting, punching, slapping, pinching, shoving, and throwing objects at or near the victim, or threatening to do so. IPV also includes verbal and emotional abuse including name-calling, harassment, taunting, put-downs, ridiculing, and sexual violence, such as forcing an intimate partner to engage in a sexual act without his or her consent.

The Centers for Disease Control and Prevention (CDC) estimates that one in three women (36 percent) and one in four men (29 percent) in the U.S. population report having been a victim of some form of IPV in the prior year, with one in four women (24 percent) and one in seven men (14 percent) have experienced severe IPV. Both men and women who were survivors of IPV reported significantly higher rates of physical and mental health problems than the general population. According to a CDC recent survey conducted, although both men and women are survivors of IPV, women are survivors far more often of multiple forms of violence, such as physical, sexual, and emotional violence, than men, who are far more often survivors of solely physical violence. IPV has resulted in 1.3 million injuries each year, and 2,340 deaths in 2007, with the majority of victims being women (Black et al., 2011).

Nearly 325,000 women are survivors of IPV while pregnant, and research suggests that pregnancy can actually make women more vulnerable to abuse. Once considered a personal family matter, IPV in recent generations affects entire communities, both fiscally and socially. Women who have a history of IPV report having significantly higher rates of physical health problems. For instance, physical problems from assaults, partner rape, and stress from living in a violent environment can lead to chronic pain, gynecological problems, HIV/AIDS, other sexually transmitted diseases, gastrointestinal problems, unwanted pregnancy, miscarriage, and premature births.

IPV does not just affect the abused partner. The children living in the home are impacted as well, even if the violence is not aimed directly toward them. For instance, boys who witness IPV are twice as likely to commit violence against their partners as adults (NCADV, 2007). IPV costs the U.S. economy about $8.3 billion per year in health costs and another 727 million in lost productivity and lost revenue, with survivors of IPV missing collectively about 8 million days from work (CDC, 2003; Rice, Finkelstein, Bardwell, & Leadbetter, 2004). Clearly, IPV is not a private family matter. The cost to society, both in injured members, lost revenue, and psychologically impacted survivors, is far too high to ever allow this issue to be ignored as it has been in the past.

The Nature of IPV: The Cycle of Violence

Lenore Walker (1979) was the first to coin the phrase the *cycle of violence* to describe the pattern of interpersonal violence in intimate relationships. Most abusive relationships often begin in a *honeymoon-like state* with the abusers often telling their new partners that they are the only people in the world they can trust—the only ones who understand them. New partners are usually swept off their feet with compliments and many promises for a wonderful future. Once the abusers feel comfortable in the relationship, a dual process typically occurs. The abusers begin to feel vulnerable by recognizing their partner's power to hurt them deeply, and as familiarity in the relationship increases, the abusers often increase their sense of entitlement to have all their needs met.

Plagued with fears that they will be abandoned, taken advantage of, and humiliated (as many were in their childhoods), jealousy, possessiveness, and accusations begin. Emotional immaturity often prevents abusers from being able to separate their feelings from possible causes, and thus a common assumption among batterers is that if they feel badly, their partners must be doing something to cause it.

In response to these threatening feelings of vulnerability and entitlement, and poised to be hurt once again, innocent partners often become the focus of the batterer's mistrust, fear, and ultimate rage. Batterers often misinterpret the intentions of their partners, mentally ticking off injustice after injustice. These types of negative misperceptions and misassumptions are prevalent and are rarely checked against fact.

Most partners of batterers will sense the increasing *tension* brought about by their abusive partner's underlying anger that is bubbling to the surface. Batterers might ask more questions about their partner's whereabouts, and make sarcastic comments to their partners. They will typically have a shorter fuse, becoming easily frustrated often without provocation. In response, most survivors do their best to walk on eggshells to avoid an explosion. But no amount of running interference or offered reassurances will help because the process is an internal one, occurring within the mind of the batterer. In fact, most batterers have an actual *need* to be proven correct in their fear of being hurt and humiliated again because to a batterer, being too trusting is often synonymous with being an unsuspecting fool.

Eventually the *explosion* occurs despite all peacemaking efforts. Abusive rages can take on several forms including frightening bouts of screaming and yelling; intimidation; and physical abuse such as hitting, kicking, scratching, grabbing, slapping, and shoving. Attacks might also include throwing objects at or near the victim, punching walls, and making threats to harm either the person or the personal property of the victim.

Once batterers have perpetrated violence, they are often temporarily relieved of their internal feelings of rage and in many respects take on the persona of a remorseful child seeking reassurance and approval. Batterers often circle back around to the *honeymoon phase* again, promising never to repeat the abusive behavior. There is commonly a manipulative aspect to the batterer's professions of regret and apologies, to the extent that authentic remorse is often somewhat questionable. One reason for this is that the batterer's apologies are often riddled with a series of "buts": "I'm sorry I hit you, *but* you know how I hate to be awakened early in the morning." "I'm sorry I shoved you, *but* you know I don't like you talking to other men." "I'm sorry I slapped you, *but* you know how stressed I get when work is so busy."

Rarely is the batterer's focus authentically placed on the pain and trauma caused to the partner or other family members. Rather, the honeymoon phase involves more of a panicked pleading, begging the victim not to leave, to forgive and forget, to move on quickly by minimizing the extent of the abuse. Statements intended to reframe the abuse, such as "I can't believe you think I shoved you! I clearly remember me reaching out to you and you jerking away and tripping," are common.

This can be an immensely confusing time for the victim, who usually knows instinctively that the batterer needs help, but any attempt to point out a pattern of abuse or to hold the batterer accountable (particularly after the batterer gets comfortable once again and stops apologizing) will hasten the tension-building phase, something the victim desperately wants to avoid. Attempts to demand authentic change in the batterer often result in the batterer accusing the victim of holding a grudge, being unforgiving, and punishing. Comments such as, "How dare you rub my face in this when I've already apologized . . . What do you want me to do? I've already said I'm sorry 100 times. Let's move on!" are common.

With the hope that the honeymoon phase might just last forever, victims often comply with the dangerous demands of the batterer to relinquish their own sense of reality and accept the reality of the batterer that the abuse was not that bad, that it will never happen again, and that it was a one-time event. Living in the here and now allows both the batterer and the victim to avoid seeing the pattern of abuse, which in some respects allows them both to avoid their fear of facing the truth and seriousness of the situation. But no matter how many promises the abusive partner makes or how desperately the victim wants to believe the abuse will never occur again, without intervention the cycle is destined to repeat itself.

Engage, Assess, Intervene, and Evaluate With Individuals, Families, Groups, Organizations, and Communities

Practice Behavior: Social workers critically analyze, monitor, and evaluate interventions.

Critical Thinking Question: Why is it important for social workers to carefully monitor and evaluate intervention strategies when working with survivors of IPV?

Working With Survivors of IPV

There is power in words, which is why I have chosen to use the term *survivor*, rather than *victim* from this point forward, when describing those individuals who are or were in relationships with intimates who battered them. While using the term *victim* is not incorrect, the term *survivor* is often preferred within the advocacy community because it reflects the personal agency and strength that many survivors have that enables them to escape their abusive relationships and live lives free of violence.

Working with survivors of IPV requires specialized training that focuses on the unique dynamics commonly at play in abusive relationships. One significant element of counseling survivors of

IPV is assisting them in making decisions about their future that will not compromise their safety. Thus, although social workers may not actually tell the clients to leave an abusive relationship, they will often lead abused clients down this path, particularly if it is the only way to secure their safety and if the batterer has refused to enter into a structured treatment program.

Many survivors of IPV have a *locus of control* that is far too internal. This means that they have a tendency to see themselves as responsible for more than they actually are, and they do not necessarily recognize when their personal responsibility ends and when someone else's begins. They also experience guilt unnecessarily that can quite often be framed as toxic. In an unhealthy respect, this makes them a good match for a partner with an *external locus of control*. Those with an external locus of control have a tendency to see outside factors as responsible for the events in their lives. Batterers commonly have an external locus of control and blame their partners (as well as a host of other people and things) for their mistakes and failures. Those with a healthy locus of control will be able to recognize when something lies inside or outside their domain of responsibility. A healthy locus of control indicates that one has good personal boundaries and will likely refuse to accept responsibility for something she knew was not her fault. But many survivors of IPV do not have healthy personal boundaries and readily accept responsibility for virtually everything that is wrong in their relationship or with their partners. So, the batterer externalizes blame, and the survivor of abuse internalizes blame.

Attribution theory attempts to explain a core issue in IPV relationships by exploring how some victims attribute the partner's abusive behavior. Some research indicates that if victims of battering hold their partners at fault for the abusive behavior, attributing the abuse to personality factors such as an inability to manage anger, a refusal to take responsibility for their behavior, or a lack of empathy, then they will be more likely to leave the abusive relationship (Pape & Arias, 2000; Truman-Schram, Cann, Calhoun, & Vanwallendael, 2000), but if victims attribute their partners' abusive behavior to situational or outside sources such as work stressors, family problems, or even alcoholism they will have a greater likelihood of forgiving the batterer quickly and returning to the abusive relationship (Gordon, Burton, & Porter, 2004).

Social workers can assist survivors of IPV in learning how to attribute causality of the abusive behavior to the batterer, incorporating an "even if" attitude: even if work is stressful, your mother is ill, you've had too much to drink, you've lost your job, money is tight, the kids are acting up, or you've injured your knee, it's never okay to behave in an abusive manner. Survivors of IPV also commonly need to develop more healthy personal boundaries so that they can understand what they are responsible for and not responsible for in their relationships and with their abusive partners. For instance, the client might be responsible for responding to her husband's question in an irritable tone, but she is not responsible for her husband's choice to hit her in response; that was his choice, and it was unwarranted and an unreasonable response, one for which he was completely responsible.

A common clinical issue in helping someone develop new boundaries is the experience of unreasonable guilt. Many survivors of IPV feel toxic guilt in response to setting limits with others, often believing that saying no to someone or upsetting another person is equivalent to being unkind. An emotionally healthy individual with good personal boundaries might feel badly when saying no to a request or when firmly telling a partner that she is not responsible for his behavior, but she will not allow these bad feelings to influence what she knows to be true. In other words, she knows that despite feeling some guilt, she must honor her personal boundaries because to neglect them will negatively affect her self-esteem and self-respect. Yet survivors of IPV will often allow their irratio-nal guilt to determine their actions. If an action makes them feel guilty, they commonly assume that this action must be wrong.

Social workers can help clients who are in a self-reflective process and express a desire to leave an abusive relationship see the irrational nature of this way of thinking. Cognitive behavioral therapy (CBT) is a counseling technique commonly used to help survivors of IPV recognize and change unhealthy thinking that influences their relationship styles. Helping survivors of IPV realize that feelings are not always the best indicators of appro-priate action will assist them in setting better boundaries in their relationships and more efficiently recognizing the signs that a partner or potential partner is merely looking for a life scapegoat, rather than a life partner.

Does S/He Stay or Does S/He Go?

One of the most frustrating aspects of counseling survivors of IPV is the pattern of the client returning to the abusive relationship despite a client's stated desire to leave due to the risk of continued abuse, and ongoing intervention efforts to support the client in her deci-sion-making process. It is important that social workers not directly or covertly blame the victim for the abuse, which will just add to feelings of shame and powerlessness such clients are likely already experiencing. Thus gaining greater understanding into the dynamics of IVP from the victim's perspective, will assist the social worker in supporting IVP clients in a way that empowers them and does not infantize them, or blame them for the abuse they are enduring. One theory that attempts to explain the multitude of complex challenges many victims of violence face when exploring a decision to leave an abusive relationship is called the *social-exchange theory*. This theory posits that many victims of IPV enter into a kind of cost-benefit analysis when attempting to make a decision about whether to stay or leave the abusive relationship. Is the cost more if the survivors stay in the abusive rela-tionship where they will be forced to endure more abuse? Or will the cost be higher if they leave, possibly facing economic insecurity, navigating the court system if a divorce is immi-nent, and managing work and family responsibilities alone? The *investment model of decision making* can be used when attempting to realistically weigh these pros and cons. This model involves the victim evaluating factors such as her resources with and without the batterer, her ability to manage risk, and the risk involved in leaving, as well as estimating what will be gained or lost if she leaves the relationship (Rusbult & Martz, 1995).

For the objective observer, the cost of staying means enduring abuse of increasing escalation and the cost of leaving may mean enduring financial hardship and other strug-gles relating to managing work and family alone. While the first option often results in worsening conditions, the latter option typically promises to improve with time. But survivors of abuse often have a somewhat skewed perception of the risks of staying or leaving, using a positive bias when evaluating the cost-benefit analysis of staying—idealistically assuming that their partner will really change "this time," assuming that the abuse was "really not that bad," and overestimating their ability to rescue and compel change in their abusive partner. They may consider the difficulties they are bound to face the first few months on their own and assume that this transitional stage will last forever. They may use negative thinking, assuming that they will never get a job, will never be able to balance work and family, partly based on years of emotional abuse and partly based on the fear and low self-esteem that may have even been the prime motivators for getting into the unhealthy relationship in the first place.

Social workers can help survivors of IPV more effectively process the pros and cons of leaving by helping them evaluate realistic risk factors and accurate scenarios. Counseling can also assist survivors in learning how to manage risk more effectively without lapsing into negative thinking. In addition, practitioners can help the client "think outside of the box" exploring all alternatives and avoiding all-or-nothing thinking (I will be either financially secure or living on the streets; I will either be a part of an intact family or be constantly lonely and a social outcast). Encouraging the client to consider possibilities not previously acknowledged can help the client realize that she has far more control over her destiny than she might have previously thought. For instance, obtaining *factual* information about her financial situation, including learning laws related to an equitable division of property and the likely levels of child support and spousal maintenance, will assist survivors of IPV in making good decisions that are based on fact, not fear.

Despite the specialized nature of working with survivors of IPV, a generalist approach is most effective, often involving case management, court advocacy, individual counseling, group support using an empowerment model, counseling children and adolescents, providing housing assistance, job coaching, and assistance with life skills. The social worker working with survivors of IPV must be familiar with contemporary theories of abuse, effective intervention strategies, common clinical disorders associated with being a survivor of IPV such as post-traumatic stress disorder (PTSD), domestic violence laws, the criminal justice process, and resources designed to meet the needs of survivors and their children.

IPV Practice Settings

One of the most common practice settings where social workers work with survivors of IPV is a *battered women's shelter* (see Box 12.1). Although such shelters often have a physical site where counseling and case management occur, the actual shelters are usually sprinkled throughout the community in confidential locations to ensure the safety of the survivors utilizing shelter services. Shelters may include houses converted into shelters or even rented apartments located throughout a community. Survivors of IPV and their children usually remain in a shelter for a time determined by their primary counselor. The goal of shelter services focus on self-sufficiency, and thus job placement, child care assistance, and transportation needs are also addressed.

Most shelters involve communal living, where residents share their living space with other survivors. Residents are often required to participate in group counseling sessions with other residents as well as assisting with the general functioning and maintenance of the shelter. Social workers are often assigned to each shelter living space and facilitate in-house programs to maintain smooth functioning within the home, as well as among the residents. Social workers will also likely engage in individual counseling, case management, and court advocacy. The focus of counseling will likely vary depending

---

Box 12.1   Common Services Offered at Many Battered Women's Shelters

Battered women's shelters typically offer numerous services, including the following:

- A 24-hour hotline for immediate access to information and services
- Immediate safety shelters for IPV survivors and their children
- Individual counseling for all survivors
- Survivor support groups
- Court advocacy

- Children's programs
- Teen programs
- Information referral
- Medical advocates who provide on-site support at hospitals
- Immigrant programs (depending on the ethnic makeup of the community)

Pearson Education, Inc.

Social Work, Social Media, and Technology

Technology can help in the fight against domestic violence through online awareness campaigns, such as the No More campaign, which includes actors providing YouTube public service announcements. Facebook is also being used to provide an online space for virtual support groups, such as the community Facebook group "Domestic Violence Support Group." Consider that you are working with a client who is experiencing domestic violence in her home. Conduct an Internet search for "NCADV," and navigate to the section on Internet safety. Once you have reviewed this section, develop a safety plan for your client.

on the needs of the residents but most often be on educational awareness, life skills and self-sufficiency, learning about healthy relationships, including healthy parenting, and how to be safe. It is particularly important for social workers to be familiar with the Internet and social media, as perpetrators can now easily track a survivor's whereabouts online and may even use social media to harass and intimidate their partners (sometimes called "digital abuse," cyberbullying or cyberstalking). The growing awareness of ways in which perpetrators can track the online activity of their partners is the primary reason why many domestic violence websites now have "quick escape" buttons and hyperlinks, allowing survivors to quickly close out a website if their abusive partners enter the room.

The Prosecution of IPV

In 1993, the federal government passed the Violence Against Women Act of 1994 (reauthorized in 2005 as the Violent Crime Control and Law Enforcement Act [Pub. L. No. 103-322]). The Violence Against Women Act established policies and mandates for how states were to handle IPV cases, such as encouraging mandatory arrests of alleged batterers, encouraging interstate enforcement of IPV laws, and maintaining state databases on incidences of IPV. This act also provides for numerous grants for educational purposes (e.g., the education of police officers and judges), an IPV hotline, battered women's shelters, and safety improvements of public areas such as public transportation and parks. Since the passage of the Violence Against Women Act, incidents of IPV have been cut in half. Social workers are working alongside other advocates and pushing for more protection for immigrant women, as well as increased safety measures in the work place.

The Violence Against Women Act spurred several states to pass similar legislation, which continues to change the nature of IPV prosecutions. With regard to current policies regarding the prosecution of IPV, it is important to note that unlike a civil case, where a plaintiff brings an action and thus has the right to subsequently drop the case, in criminal cases the plaintiff is the state and the survivors are witnesses. But in the past, prosecutors have allowed survivors to 'drop' a case (typically at the urgings of the batterer) by refusing to cooperate. IPV legislation has for the most part put a stop to this practice. Instead, IPV is typically treated as any other crime where the victim is called as a witness and must appear at the trial to testify on behalf of the state.

This can create emotional tension for survivors, who may initially want court involvement immediately after experiencing violence, but resists any intervention when the honeymoon phase begins and renewed hope for authentic change seems possible, a dynamic explored in the opening vignette of Rick and Sarah. Counseling for the survivor of abuse often focuses on developing healthier strategies for responding to abusive dynamics in the relationship (often in counterintuitive ways) that will have the greatest likelihood of moving the survivor toward real change, including greater self-sufficiency and higher self-esteem. As long as survivors relinquish their own reality of the events and yield to the batterers' demands to forgive and forget without any real accountability, no real change will occur. Any effective counseling program must address the *denial, wishful thinking, indiscriminate forgiveness* (without accountability), and a desire to *protect* the batterer, as well as the *fear* of the future that many survivors of IPV experience, which can prevent an honest and realistic appraisal of their abusive relationship. As reflected in the case of Rick and Sarah, even finding that initial foothold into the life of the nonoffending partner can be challenging. Counseling victims and survivors of IPV is a long process, in a kind of "one step forward, two steps back" type of way, and requires significant patience and understanding on the part of the social worker working with this population.

Batterer Intervention Programs

It might be tempting to focus intervention efforts solely on the survivors of abuse, leaving the perpetrators of abuse to fend for themselves. But if those who committed abuse were treated effectively, then IPV would no longer be a pressing social problem. It is also important to be aware that not all "batterers" are alike. In fact, although there are many batterers who are narcissistic with antisocial tendencies (sociopathy) who abuse their intimates with no remorse, there are also those who act out in anger but are truly remorseful, some who have never committed violence before but a combination of circumstances lowered their impulse control, some who are in reciprocally abusive relationships, and some who have been falsely accused.

It is vital that social workers take the time to understand the dynamics involved and not assume that if an accusation is made, it must be true. I have worked in IPV for years and worked with many survivors who had quite abusive partners. Yet I will never forget the case involving a woman who presented with plausible stories of abuse at the hands of her husband, who was recently arrested for IPV. I was sold before having even met her husband because my client's stories were convincing, and I consider myself an avid advocate of women rights. Yet the criminal trial revealed that *she* had been emotionally abusive for years, and when her husband sought a divorce she threatened to seek revenge. She did so by causing self-injury and going upstairs privately to call the police. The tape of the 9-1-1 call was chilling as she screamed and cried while reporting the alleged abuse. If it had not been for the friend she told, who bravely testified at trial on behalf of the husband, her husband might have been convicted of a crime he did not commit, and she might have unfairly gained sole custody of their children because everyone, including me, was so quick to believe her at least in part because of her gender.

In the past, the criminal justice system sought traditional forms of justice for those convicted of IPV, such as incarceration, but this approach was often unsuccessful because judges were sometimes reluctant to break apart families, and more often survivors of IPV were reluctant to testify against their partners or spouses, particularly if it meant a possibility of jail time. Thus, several years ago IPV courts started mandating batterers to attend treatment programs often in lieu of incarceration.

Most batterer intervention programs are based on the Duluth Model—a psychoeducational program drawn from feminist theory of IPV, which posits that IPV is caused by patriarchal ideology, and men's perception that they have the right to control their female partners. Many batterer intervention programs consist of group treatment using CBT and anger management training. Many newer programs combine these models, based on the premise that IPV is a complex problem, thus a combination of psychoeducation, CBT, and anger management in a group setting will be most successful.

Learn more about Domestic Abuse Intervention Programs by conducting an Internet search for the Duluth Model website.

Batterer programs range in duration from six weeks to one year and are often mandated by the court as a part of sentencing. Batterers are taught to respect personal boundaries, the difference between feelings and actions, the concept of personal rights and egalitarian relationships, and the dynamics of social learning theory including modeling so that they can discover how their violent behavior is likely patterned after their parent(s) or some other influential person in their lives. They also learn how to identify their personal triggers and learn strategies for managing their anger, including how to control impulses, and how to use "I" statements to avoid getting caught up in making accusations.

Most batterer treatment programs have similar goals, including *increasing awareness of violent behavior* and *encouraging the batterer to take responsibility for violent behavior*. Common program philosophies include the following beliefs:

- Violence is an intentional act.
- IPV uses physical force and intimidation as coercive methods to obtain and maintain control in the relationship.
- Using violence is a learned behavior and as such can be unlearned.

Many participants make authentic changes in group treatment not only because of the curriculum but also because of the built-in accountability that a group setting provides. Ironically it is the other group members who have been charged with domestic battery who often challenge those who refuse to engage or who consistently blame the victim. Unfortunately, at least an equal number of participants do not authentically change while in the program. Some batterers fail to complete the program, and others are reluctant to change because they actually love the rush and power they get from feeling intense anger (Pandya & Gingerich, 2002).

Whether batterer intervention programs actually work is a question that remains unanswered for the most part. A 2003 study commissioned by the U.S. Department of Justice (DOJ) found little support for the success of batterer intervention programs with regard to recidivism rates, or attitudes toward IPV. The only significant difference found was in the re-offense rates of men who completed programs 26 weeks or longer. Yet, while these men had significantly lower recidivism rates, their attitudes about IPV did not appear to change much. For instance, men in the experimental group (the batterer intervention program) viewed their partners only slightly less responsible for the battering incident, than men in the control group. The study's authors cited numerous limitations of the study, which may have been at least partly responsible for the results, including a high dropout rate in the batterer intervention programs and questionable validity of the attitudinal surveys. Based on these

Assess your comprehension of "Intimate Partner Violence" by completing this quiz.

limitations, the authors recommended that batterer intervention programs be allowed to continue to evolve (as they are a relatively new tool in the fight against IPV), but in a manner that was responsive to the increased knowledge that is being gained about the nature of IPV, including common risk factors for becoming a batterer so that the focus of intervention could be as much on prevention as response.

SEXUAL ASSAULT

Another form of personal violence is the act of rape or sexual assault. Sexual assault involves forcing some form of sexual act on another person without his or her consent. Determining the rate of sexual assault in the United States is difficult because of dramatic variations in the way sexual assault is defined, as well as underreporting. Although both men and women can be raped, women are raped more often than men. Approximately one in five women in the United States have been raped sometime during her lifetime, and more than half of them were raped by intimate partners (Black et al., 2011).

Hundreds of people take part in a candlelight march to call attention to violence against women and children during a "Take Back the Night" event.

BETTYE LANE/PHOTO RESEARCHERS/GETTY IMAGES

In 2012, the FBI changed its legal definition of forcible rape, which is the first time the definition had been updated since 1927. The previous definition reflected in the Uniform Crime Reports (UCR) was: "the carnal knowledge of a female, forcibly and against her will." That definition was far too narrow, limiting rape to penile penetration of a female vagina. Thus, not only did the former definition exclude the wide range of ways that sexual assaults can occur, but it also excluded the rape of males. The new UCR definition of rape is: "[t]he penetration, no matter how slight, of the vagina or anus with any body part or object, or oral penetration by a sex organ of another person, without the consent of the victim." Expanding the definition of rape to include a range of assault types, as well as including male victims, is an important victory for advocates because it provides law enforcement more tools to fight sexual assault, as they can now report sexual assaults more accurately (U.S. Department of Justice, 2012).

Approximately 170,000 women, 12 years and older, and 15,000 men were raped or sexually assaulted in 2010. About 75 percent of all women who were raped were assaulted by a perpetrator they knew, and about 25 percent were assaulted by strangers. Of these, the Federal Bureau of Investigation reports that 83,425 cases of forcible rape were reported. Black women are raped at a higher rate (relative to the population) than white or Hispanic women. The actual incidence of forcible rape is presumed to be much higher though because of underreporting. In fact, only half of all rapes and sexual assaults in 2010 were reported to police (Federal Bureau of Investigation, 2011). According to the CDC, rape and sexual assaults typically fall into four categories (Basile & Saltzman, 2002):

1. *Completed sexual acts* such as sexual penetration but may also include any act of a sexual nature attempted or otherwise such as contact between a sexual organ and another part of the body
2. *Attempted sexual assault*
3. *Abusive sexual contact* such as intentional touching even through clothing
4. *Noncontact sexual abuse* such as intentional exposure and exhibitionism ("flashing") and voyeurism ("Peeping Tom")

Why People Commit Rape

Social workers who work with survivors of sexual assault must understand the psychological dynamics of rape. One of the more common myths of why rape occurs involves blaming the victim by asserting that victims wanted it, liked it, or in some way deserved the sexual assault because they provoked the assailant (by dressing or acting provocatively, etc.). Myths about rapists include assertions that only truly evil or insane men rape or that men rape because they just cannot control their sexual desires and thus are not responsible for sexually assaulting women (Burt, 1991). The damage done by the proliferation of these rape myths is plentiful because they blame the victim while exonerating the perpetrator, which undermines societal prohibition against sexual violence.

In fact, a 1998 study at University of Mannheim in Germany found that such myths might actually encourage sexual assault by giving rapists a way of rationalizing their anti-social behavior (Bohner et al., 1998). In other words, although Western social customs may claim to abhor rape, popular rape myths provide rapists a way around such social mores by convincing themselves that the women in some way *asked for it* and that men simply *cannot control themselves*, thus they really haven't done anything wrong, or at least nothing that many other men don't do.

The Psychological Impact of Sexual Assault

The physical and psychological impact of sexual assault is serious and long lasting and may include post-traumatic stress syndrome (PTSD), depression, increased anxiety, fear of risk taking, development of trust issues, increased physical problems including exposure to sexually transmitted diseases such as HIV / AIDS, chronic pelvic pain, gastrointestinal disorders, and unwanted pregnancy (CDC, 2005).

In 1975, Lynda Holmstrom and Ann Burgess coined the term *rape trauma syndrome* (RTS), a collection of emotions similar to PTSD, commonly experienced in response to being a survivor of a violent sexual assault. RTS includes an immediate phase where the survivor experiences both psychological and physical symptoms such as feeling extreme fear, consistent crying and sleep disturbances, and other reactions to the actual assault as well as the common fear of being killed during the assault. Survivors in subsequent phases of recovery experienced a variety of symptoms, including avoidance of social interaction, experiencing a loss of self-esteem, inappropriate guilt, and clinical depression. Many survivors deny the effects of the sexual assault because they do not want to be subject to the negative stigma associated with being a rape victim. In fact, one of the primary reasons most rape crisis advocates refer to clients as *survivors* rather than as *victims* is to reduce this stigma by focusing on the strength it takes to survive a sexual assault.

Male-on-Male Sexual Assault

Men are also survivors of sexual assault, in the form of child sexual abuse, same-sex date rape, and male-on-male stranger rape. Research on male-on-male sexual assault is sparse with the exception of some early efforts to identify the nature and dynamics of male rape. The reason for the lack of studies in this area may be related to the belief that male rape is rare, at least outside prison walls.

Because of the stigma associated with being a victim of male-on-male sexual assault, most incidences of rape go unreported, and thus it is impossible to know just how common this crime is. Even rapes that occur in prisons are often unreported not only because of the fear of retaliation but also because of the shame men feel in response to being victimized in this manner.

Treating men who have been sexually assaulted is similar in some respects to serving the female survivor population except that the shame men feel, although equal in intensity, tends to be more focused on their gender identity as males. For instance, heterosexual men who were survivors of rape reported questioning their sexual orientation because they were unable to fight off their attackers. Men also have a greater tendency to turn toward alcohol and drugs in response to the rape. Men who have been raped by another man tend to experience sexual dysfunction, problems getting close to people, particularly in intimate relationships, and as is the case with female survivors, additionally, some male survivors become sexually promiscuous after being raped (Mezey & King, 1989).

More studies need to be conducted on both female and male rape, particularly on the differing dynamics of sexual assault in ethnic minority populations. What research there is on this population seems to indicate that survivors of sexual assault who are Caucasian and have higher levels of academic education tend to seek mental health counseling more often than survivors of color or those with less education (Ullman & Brecklin, 2002; Vearnals & Campbell, 2001). This certainly has practical implications for social workers who through assessment or advocacy have the opportunity to reach out to survivors or potential survivors of sexual assault.

Common Practice Settings: Rape Crisis Centers

Social workers working in any practice setting will likely encounter a survivor of sexual assault at some point in their careers. This might involve a recent survivor seeking support services on the heels of an assault, but it is far more likely that rape survivors will present for counseling at some point long after an assault, perhaps even years later, and might not even connect that the problems they are currently experiencing are connected to a past sexual assault.

Social workers who work directly with survivors of sexual assault usually do so at a rape crisis center or sexual assault advocacy organization. Many states require that each county have at least one rape crisis center that offers a wide range of services including a 24-hour hotline, around-the-clock on-site advocacy during medical examinations and investigative interviews, and crisis counseling, as well as long-term individual and group counseling.

Many social workers who work with sexual assault survivors receive between 40 to 50 hours of specialized training focusing on the history of the rape crisis movement, the nature of crisis counseling, the dynamics of RTS, rape myths, and the dangers of gender oppression and patriarchy. Training also includes information on normal child and adult developmental stages and how these stages are affected by sexual violence and trauma.

Assess your comprehension of "Sexual Assault" by completing this quiz.

WORKING WITH SURVIVORS OF VIOLENT CRIME

IPV and sexual assault are two types of violent crime that receive considerable attention within the social work field as well as within the public arena. There are other types of victimization that do not garner as much attention but are also important for social workers to be familiar with. Every year millions of people in the United States become victims of a crime, many of which are violent in nature. According to the FBI's UCR, there were just over 1.2 million violent crimes reported in 2011, which represents a decrease of almost four percent from 2010 (Federal Bureau of Investigation, 2012). Although violent crime has been declining in recent years, the issue of victimization and the recognition and enforcement of survivors' rights remains a relevant issue for social workers.

The victims' rights movement is a relatively new phenomenon having gained momentum in the 1980s when survivors of crime came together along with social justice advocates to secure both a voice within the criminal justice community and some basic rights in the criminal justice system. Historically, survivors of crime had virtually no rights in criminal proceedings because the U.S. criminal justice system is based on the presumption of innocence. Because defendants charged with a criminal offense are innocent until proven guilty, legally there can be no survivors. If there are no victims prior to a defendant being convicted, then there are no rights to enforce. In addition, in criminal proceedings the case is considered an action committed against the state, thus other than being a witness, historically, survivors of crime have had no special status. This logic, which is consistent with the U.S. criminal justice system, is completely backward according to most survivors of violent crime and victim advocates.

Advance Human Rights and Social and Economic Justice

Practice Behavior: Advocate for human rights and social and economic justice.

Critical Thinking Question: In what ways can social workers engage in advocacy for male and female survivors of IPV that will lead to increased mechanisms on a policy level?

The Victims' Bill of Rights and Victim-Witness Assistance

The victims' movement is based not on the desire to lessen the rights of criminal defendants, but rather on the desire to increase the rights of crime victims including being notified of court hearings, to appear at all legal proceedings, to make a statement at sentencing, and to be kept apprised of the incarceration status of perpetrators.

Most crime victims and victim advocates state that a primary goal of the survivors' movement is to ensure that crime victims have a voice within the community, specifically within the criminal justice system (Mika, Achilles, Halbert, Amstutz, & Zehr, 2004). How that voice gets heard is certainly up for debate. Whether through direct face-to-face meetings with criminal justice officials or through an active involvement in victim-sensitive training of police personnel, prosecutors, and judges, victims advocacy groups continue to work toward a system that views survivors as a central aspect of the criminal justice process (Quinn, 1998).

In response to the victims' movement and subsequent federal legislation (42 U.S.C. § 10606[b]), all states now have a Victims' Bill of Rights ensuring certain basic rights as well as protection. Although there is some variation from state to state, most states ensure that survivors of violent crime be afforded several rights.

In response to federal legislation and Victims' Bill of Rights state prosecution units within prosecutors' offices (state's attorney, district attorney, and attorney general offices) developed specialized units called Victim–Witness Assistance, designed to enforce survivors' rights. Social workers work within these departments offering the following services:

Learn more about the Victims' Bill of Rights by conducting an Internet search for the Office for Victims of Crime website, and then clicking on the Crime Victims' Rights link.

- Crisis intervention counseling
- Referrals to coordinating social services agencies, such as rape crisis centers, battered women's shelters, and crime victim support groups
- Referrals to advocacy organizations such as Mothers against Drunk Driving (MADD), who have a presence in court to ensure enforcement of survivors' rights
- Advocacy and accompaniment in court proceedings
- Special services or units for survivors of IPV, child survivors, older adults, and survivors with disabilities
- Case status updates including notification of all public court proceedings

- Foreign language translation
- Assistance with obtaining compensation such as reimbursement for counseling and medical costs
- Assistance in preparation and writing of victim impact statements to be read by the victim at the sentencing hearing

Victim–witness advocates may have a master's degree in any of the applied social science disciplines (e.g., social work, psychology, or human services), but often work at the bachelor's level with some specialized training in the dynamics involved in violent crime victimization. Advocates must also be familiar with the inner workings of the criminal justice system because survivors of violent crime often feel revictimized when they must endure the often-confusing labyrinth of the prosecution system. The average person may not be familiar with the differing duties of a local police department and a state prosecuting office, nor may the average person know how a criminal case proceeds toward prosecution. Those individuals who have become victims of a crime learn about the criminal justice system quickly so that they can be prepared for what is going to happen next. Victim–witness advocates can help crime victims understand the process of a criminal trial and the importance and value of each step within the prosecution process.

If a case goes to trial the victim–witness advocate will work closely with the crime victims to help prepare them for testifying, if that is required. The psychosocial issues involved depend on the nature of the crime and victimization. For instance, if the defendant who is charged with domestic battery is the victim's spouse, the psychosocial issues will likely involve fear of retaliation and guilt in response to testifying against a spouse, particularly if there is a possibility that the defendant might have to serve time in jail or prison. If the defendant was charged with sexual assault, the victim will likely experience feelings of shame, embarrassment, and fear. A victim of home invasion might experience intense fear of retaliation once the defendant becomes aware of the victim's cooperation and testimony. In each instance the victim–witness advocate will work with community social service agencies and community advocates to provide support and assistance to the victim in preparation for trial and to ensure that the victim receives the appropriate follow-up care within the community.

Once a defendant is found guilty, through either trial or a plea arrangement, a sentencing hearing is scheduled. In a sentencing hearing, both sides have an opportunity to advocate for a sentence believed to be appropriate. It is the responsibility of the victim–witness advocate to assist crime victims in writing a victim impact statement, which will often be read in open court before the judge, jury, and defendant. Although the statements are written in the words of the victim, they have a dual purpose—giving survivors a voice in court and assisting the prosecutor obtain the desired sentence—and thus it is important that victims receive guidance in the preparation for writing their statement. This also serves as another opportunity for survivors to express and work through their pain, and thus it is often an effective clinical tool.

Survivors of Homicide

Some of the most emotionally intense and difficult cases for victim–witness advocates are homicide cases, particularly when the primary victim is a child. The victim–witness advocate must develop a high threshold for dealing with another's emotional pain because the pain of losing a loved one through violence is often unlike any other loss. Revictimization through the criminal justice process is almost a certainty as survivors of homicide are forced to balance their desire to represent their loved one in court by being present at all hearings with the trauma inherently involved in having to hear the gruesome details of the crime.

Research strongly suggests the importance of providing supportive counseling services and advocacy in the weeks immediately following the homicide. Surviving survivors of intra-familial homicides, where one family member kills another, are particularly prone to psychologically complex reactions involving both internal and external stressors. Most experts suggest the use of crisis counseling immediately following the crime that focuses on the concrete needs of the surviving survivors. This approach is important in light of research, which suggests that surviving victims of homicide are mostly likely to utilize advocacy services during the initial crisis phase (Horne, 2003).

The needs of surviving victims of homicide are complex, particularly in the weeks and months after the murder. Surviving victims of homicide must cooperate with various law enforcement agencies and attend court proceedings at the same time that they must plan a funeral and contend with the effects and belongings of the murdered victim (which may include pets or even children in addition to physical belongings). This can be significantly overwhelming during a time when they are dealing with the paralyzing shock of losing a loved one in a sudden and violent manner.

Common Psychosocial Issues Among Survivors of Violent Crime

Regardless of the nature of the crime committed, victims of violent crime all have basic needs that need to be addressed by the social workers working with them in treatment (Courtois, 2004). These issues often framed as treatment goals include the following:

1. Building formal and informal social support systems
2. Reinforcing ways to regain a sense of safety
3. Teaching survivors of crime how to manage their emotions, such as anger, sadness, and fear
4. Achieving physical and psychological stability
5. Building skills that will help survivors regain a sense of personal power and control over their lives
6. Educating the client on the nature of the crime victimization so they know what to expect
7. Reconditioning victims to minimize negative triggering of the traumatic incident
8. Helping victims through the mourning process
9. Seeking resolution and closure, which leads to personal growth and allows the victim to regain the confidence and strength to trust people once again

Assess your comprehension of "Working With Survivors of Violent Crime" by completing this quiz.

By focusing on these core issues, as well as addressing the factors and needs specific to each type of crime victimization, the social worker will be instrumental in fostering healing and growth in victims of crime so they can begin the process of seeing themselves no longer as victims but as survivors.

WORKING WITH PERPETRATORS OF CRIME

Forensic social workers working in the criminal justice arena often work with survivors of crime, but they may also work with offenders or perpetrators of crime. Direct practice with offenders might occur in an agency setting that offers mandated programs, such as batterer programs discussed earlier in this chapter, programs for alcoholics with drunken driving convictions, or group therapy for pedophiles. Many work within the criminal justice system in probation departments or juvenile justice programs, and many work in programs that facilitate outreach efforts focusing on gang members, recently released prisoners, or individuals who are at risk for continued criminal activity.

Gang Activity

Gangs consist of groups of individuals who actively participate in criminal activities on an organized or coordinated basis. Gang activity has become an increasingly severe problem in recent years, not only with regard to the number of gangs in operation within the United States, but also with regard to the type of violent activities in which many gang members participate. A survey conducted by the National Youth Gang Survey in 2010 revealed that there are approximately 29,400 gangs and 756,000 gang members in the United State (Egley & Howell, 2012). Despite comprehensive efforts to combat gang activity and violence, gang activity is on the rise. For instance, gang-related homicides have increased over 10 percent since 2009 in urban areas (cities with populations of more than 100,000) (Egley & Howell, 2012). Gang activity remains primarily a big-city phenomenon, with some of the larger cities having more than 30 gangs operating at one time. Smaller towns and rural communities also experience gang problems, but these tend to be relatively sporadic with gangs that are loosely organized (Howell & Egley, 2005).

Gang members not only commit crimes such as theft and drug trafficking to support gang activity, but some of the most serious crimes committed by gang members involve turf wars where one gang is in conflict with another, leading to gang fights that often include both assaults and homicides. In some inner-city communities, drive-by shootings are a way of life, and parents respond by keeping their young children off the streets and away from windows (Egley & Howell, 2012).

Most gang members are between the ages of 13 and 25, but some studies found gangs that have members as young as 10. Generally, there are more adult gang members than youth, with the number of juvenile gang members declining slightly since 1996 (National Gang Center, 2012). Most gang members come from backgrounds of poverty and racial oppression, live in high-crime urban communities, and live in neighborhoods with high gang activity (Vigil, 2003). Although there has been a slight increase in female gang activity, most gangs are still primarily comprised of males, with female membership remaining steady at just under 10 percent (National Gang Center, 2012).

There are several theories focusing on the reasons why adolescents join gangs. Most sociological and anthropological theories focus on the sense of solidarity and feelings of belonging that gangs can provide disenfranchised youth. Identifying risk factors is important so that effective intervention strategies can be developed and put into action. A comprehensive study facilitated by the DOJ evaluated the gang membership and backgrounds of over 800 gang members from 1985 to 2001 in an attempt to identify some of the reasons why adolescents join gangs. This study, referred to as the Seattle Social Development Project, confirmed that the majority of gang members are men (90 percent) and that gang members came from diverse ethnic backgrounds including Caucasian (European American), Asian, Latino, Native American, and African American, with African Americans having the highest rates of gang membership. Interestingly, the study found that the majority of gang members joined for only a short time, with 70 percent of youths belonging to a gang for less than a year (Hawkins et al., 2003).

Social Work, Social Media, and Technology

The National Gang Center, a part of the Bureau of Justice Assistance and the Office of Juvenile Justice and Delinquency Prevention, offers communities an online interactive strategic planning tool to assist in designing gang prevention and intervention programs tailored to the unique needs of particular communities.

Consider the gang problems in your own community, or the closest urban center to you, then access the website by going to the National Gang Center website, navigating to the "Research & Tools" area, and then clicking on the OJJDP Strategic Planning Tool. Follow the instructions to learn more about best practice models for program planning and implementation, risk factors, and program matrix components that would be helpful in designing a community social service agency.

The study identified multiple risk factors for gang membership, including living in high-crime neighborhoods, coming from a single-parent household, poverty, parents who approved of violence, poor academic performance, learning disabilities, little or no commitment to school, early drug and alcohol abuse, and associating with friends who commit delinquent acts. The study's authors recommended early prevention efforts that target youth with multiple risk factors. Programs need to focus on all aspects of the adolescent's life, including family dynamics, school involvement, peer group, and behavioral issues such as drug and alcohol abuse as well as any antisocial and delinquent behaviors.

What this study seems to underscore is that for youth with multiple risk factors gang membership may be less a choice and more a way of life. Adolescents who are fortunate enough to have cohesive families, where high-functioning parents work hard to maintain structure, provide accountability, and keep teens engaged in positive activities, can often help adolescents avoid the temptation to join a gang. This is particularly true for African American youth living in large urban areas (Walker-Barnes & Mason, 2001). Adolescents without the benefit of such positive influences, including those who have neglectful and uninvolved parents, often face a reciprocal pull into gang life where they are targeted by existing gang members who recognize the existence of these risk.

Forensic Social Work Practice Settings Focusing on Gang Involvement

Social workers who work with gang populations may do so on school campuses, in agencies that target at-risk youth, in faith-based outreach agencies, at police departments, or within the juvenile justice system. Most outreach programs target adolescents who live in large urban communities where gang activity is prevalent and violent behavior a fact of life, especially those who come from single-parent homes, have poor academic histories, and have shown early signs of delinquent behaviors. Social workers also target social conditions on a macro level such as poverty, racism, and the lack of opportunities in urban communities, because these factors contribute to the development of gang activity.

Many social service programs that target at-risk adolescents operate after-school programs or evening community programs that give adolescents a place to go to socialize other than the streets. This is particularly important for youth who are in search of a sense of cohesion, security, and social belongingness, elements that might be missing from their home life. In light of the research indicating that most gang members have relatively loose, short-term affiliation with gangs, these types of programs have the potential of being successful in steering even active gang members away from gang life.

Finally, social service programs committed to reducing the gang problem must be willing to engage in active and aggressive outreach efforts, maintain a highly visible presence in the community, coordinate services with other gang intervention programs, and be willing to engage at-risk adolescents and their family on multiple levels.

Social Workers in the Corrections System

The social work profession has a long history of working within the criminal justice system, most notably working in jails, prisons, government probation departments, police departments, and agencies offering services to recently released offenders. Social workers working within the criminal justice system may provide counseling and facilitate support groups focusing on various treatment issues designed to reduce rates of *recidivism* (the process of relapsing into criminal behavior), or they may work within probation departments charged with the responsibility of assisting in the preparation of pre-sentencing reports, or coordinating treatment plans, supervising the offender's compliance with the conditions of probation (e.g., entering a drug treatment program, obtaining counseling, attending an anger management program, or completing community service), or they may be bachelor's level correctional treatment specialists or case managers who provide general counseling to the prison population, assisting them in preparing for release and reentry into society. Social workers may also work on a community level advocating for prison reform such as the development of mental health courts, substance abuse treatment programs in prisons, or increased mental health services for mentally ill prisoners. Thus, although this field of service is broad, the clinical issues are specialized, requiring training focusing on the common issues facing offenders both within prison and on release.

The U.S. prison system is plagued with violence including sexual assaults, drug problems, and mental illness. Social workers working within the area of corrections will likely encounter a wide range of issues that vary with the level of incarceration security, the gender and race of the prisoners, and the culture and climate of the specific prison. One of the chief problems affecting prisons across the country relates to the problem of overcrowding, with most state and federal prisons operating at either full or over capacity (Salins, & Simpson, 2013). In an environment already fraught with tension, overcrowding can be the ingredient that leads to increased violence against both inmates and correctional staff.

Disparity in Sentencing: The Incarceration of Ethnic Minorities

Many people might be surprised to learn that violent crime in the United States has steadily declined since the early 1990s. Rates of homicide, forcible rape, assault, robbery, firearms-related crimes, and even violent juvenile crimes have all dropped in the last two decades in response to various crime prevention efforts, yet the population in prisons and jails across the country has continued to skyrocket. In fact, the United States has the highest incarceration rate in the world (Guerino, Harrison, & Sabol, 2011), with the U.S. prison population quadrupling from 1980 to 2008 (NAACp, 2009).

So what is to account for this seeming contradiction? Why, when virtually all forms of violent crime are on a downhill slide for many years, is the nation's prison system experiencing such a dramatic increase in population? Many social scientists and prison advocates agree that the primary reason for prison overcrowding

Apply Knowledge of Human Behavior and the Social Environment

Practice Behavior: Critique and apply knowledge to understand person and environment.

Critical Thinking Question: In what ways have drug sentencing laws impacted male youth ethnic minority populations? Do you believe that their treatment in the U.S. criminal justice system promotes disparity in treatment? If so, how?

Social Work Application Activity

Learn more about disparity in sentencing by conducting an Internet search for the Sentencing Project, an
advocacy and research organization focusing on racial
disparity and practices in U.S. sentencing policy. Did the
materials on this website change your opinion about the
U.S. War on Drugs? If so, how?

relates to the U.S. "War on Drugs," a set of federal policies initiated in 1971 during the Nixon administration, designed to combat the growing drug problem in the United States. In fact, about half (51 percent) of all federal prisoners are incarcerated for non-violent drug-related offenses (Guerino, Harrison, & Sabol, 2011), and 80 percent of the increase in prisoners in the federal prison system between 1985 and 1995 is related to increased convictions of drug-related offenses (James, 2013).

The U.S. war on drugs might seem like a good policy on the surface. Certainly no one would argue that the using and selling of illicit drugs is good for the American public. But many argue that the federal government's aggressive policies related to the prosecution and punishment of drug offenders unfairly targets poor, young ethnic minorities (particularly African American males), many of whom are serving extremely long prison sentences because of minimum federal sentencing guidelines (sometimes 20 years to life), despite not committing any violent crimes (Human Rights Watch, 2000a). In fact, recent reports indicate that black males account for over a third of all state and federal prison inmates, and combined with Latinos, comprised about 58 percent of the U.S. prison population. In fact, according to the Sentencing Project (2010), five times as many Caucasians use drugs as African Americans, and yet African Americans are sentenced to prison 10 times the rate of Caucasians. To put this another way, African Americans represent 12 percent of the total drug user population, 32 percent of those arrested for drug offenses, and almost 60 percent of those serving time in prison for a drug offense. Although recent reports indicate that the incarceration rate for African Americans are dropping (particularly for black women), the racial disparity in the "War on Drugs" warrants concern.

There are several reasons for this disparity, including federal and state policies that target ethnic minority communities, and mandatory sentencing laws that treat crack cocaine (used more often by ethnic minorities) than powder cocaine (used more often by Caucasians). Additionally, "urban blight," poverty, and social exclusion are contributing factors to drug problems within some ethnic minority populations. Social workers should be concerned about social conditions and governmental policy that either directly or indirectly targets a certain segment of the population. Many advocates claim that the war on drugs appears to do just this, evidenced by the significant overrepresentation of ethnic minorities, particularly African American men, within the federal and state prison system (Human Rights Watch, 2000b). Whether by design or not, one must ask why the U.S. government has not waged a "War on Domestic Violence" or a "War on Child Sexual Abuse," two social ills that have seriously negative consequences for U.S. society that would target offenders across all socioeconomic levels and racial groups.

Social workers working within the U.S. criminal justice system must be aware of potentially unfair political policies so that they can develop a truly objective perspective of social conditions leading to the overrepresentation of minorities in correctional facilities, the reasoning behind sentencing guidelines for various criminal offenses, even identifying social influences that tend to hold one behavior in a particular era as socially acceptable, only to criminalize it several decades later. For instance, determining which drugs are socially acceptable and which ones are not is influenced by constantly shifting social mores. During the Prohibition era the use and sale of alcohol was considered criminal, yet today it is considered perfectly socially acceptable. Thus, there is a temporal aspect to the criminalization of certain behaviors, and it is vital that social workers recognize this dynamic.

Assess your comprehension of "Working With Perpetrators of Crime" by completing this quiz.

PSYCHOSOCIAL ISSUES IN THE PRISON POPULATION: THE ROLE OF THE SOCIAL WORKER

The issues confronting social workers working within the criminal justice system, particularly within a correctional facility, will vary depending on the gender, race, and type of crime committed by the defendant. A key goal of the criminal justice system is to reduce recidivism, and thus "success" in terms of treatment is often focused on whether a prisoner, once released, reoffends and returns to prison.

Mental Health Programs in Correctional Facilities

Behavioral programs within prisons can focus on many clinical issues, some related to criminal behavior and some related to other issues the inmates might be experiencing. Programs related to criminal behavior typically focus on issues such as drug abuse, sexual violence, IPV, anger management, and the development of social skills. Programs designed to address psychosocial issues not directly related to criminal behavior typically focus on grief and separation issues, sexual abuse victimization (particularly for female inmates because a large proportion of the female inmate population have been victims of sexual violence at some point in their lives), self-esteem, and issues related to the impact of being incarcerated.

Prison and Pregnancy

Female inmates are often incarcerated for offenses related to drug addictions (writing bad checks, petty theft, prostitution, etc.), and those who are pregnant or parenting often have to rely on the county foster care system for the care of their children during their incarceration (Siefert & Pimlott, 2001). Social workers working in a correctional facility will likely encounter women (particularly women of color) who are grieving over the loss of their children or are anticipating their loss once they give birth. One of the roles of social workers is to work with outside agencies that can arrange to transport children to see their incarcerated mothers to maintain the mother–child bond. Parenting issues are often explored as well as the impact of drug abuse during pregnancy, with the goal of maintaining close family ties and reducing the incidence of prenatal damage and infant mortality related to drug use during pregnancy.

Watch a few video clips of "Pregnant and Behind Bars" on the Discovery Fit and Health website, then, describe the role that you believe social workers can take in a prison setting, and why or why not you believe having social workers in prison is important.

Some prisons have grant-funded programs that provide intensive prenatal care, nutrition counseling, substance abuse treatment, and individual and group counseling. One such program is called the Women and Infants at Risk (WIAR), developed by social work students, which helps mothers break intergenerational cycles of abuse, giving infants the best start in life possible. This is particularly important in light of how the odds are already against infants who are born behind prison walls (Siefert & Pimlott, 2001). Another program focusing on the plight of women in prison is called the Women in Prison Project, which, according to its website, exists to bring awareness to and confront the social injustice that exists within the U.S. prison system against women and their families. The project is framed as a resistance movement and includes the real life stories of current and former female prisoners. The website focuses on the interconnections between women and prison, including poverty, substance abuse, sexual orientation, prostitution, violence, racism, poor healthcare, and homelessness. The website features artwork and poetry of women in prison (and former prisoners) as well as interviews.

> **Conduct an Internet search for the Women and Prison Project to learn about its various advocacy efforts and programs.**

Sexually Transmitted Diseases and AIDS

Another significant issue often confronting both inmates and social workers involves the high rate of infectious diseases that exists within the prison population, made worse by the ongoing problem of sexual assaults. Diseases such as hepatitis B and hepatitis C are prevalent in some prisons, and HIV/AIDS remains a serious concern among prisoners and correctional staff. A 2002 report by the National Commission on Correctional (NCCHC) indicated that the incidence of AIDS in the U.S. prison population is five times that of the general population, and the primary method of transmission is sexual assault (Robertson, 2003).

The fear of being raped is the number one fear among men serving time in prison, and although no one is certain of the exact number of male-on-male sexual assaults within the prison system, it is estimated that between 7 and 12 percent of the male prison population have been victims of sexual assault while incarcerated, although the actual number is presumed to be much higher (Human Rights Watch, 2001), with many prisoners suffering multiple rapes throughout their incarceration. This issue is of such significant concern that in 2003, President George W. Bush signed an act appropriating $13 million in funding for rape prevention programs within the prison system (Robertson, 2003).

Barriers to Treatment

One complaint among mental health providers in correctional settings is the underfunding and understaffing of mental health programs often experienced in many jails and prisons across the country. Developing effective and comprehensive mental health services within correctional facilities is an important aspect of efforts to reduce recidivism rates among the prison population, but the U.S. criminal justice system is punitive in nature and not based on a rehabilitation model; thus mental health programs are often not a priority evidenced by a consistent lack of funding, understaffing, and limited outreach.

Yet even in prisons that have sufficient mental health services, barriers still exist that often prevent prisoners from accessing these services. A 2004 study surveying prisoner attitudes about mental health services identified several perceived barriers to service, including being uncertain how or when to access counseling, a belief that mental health services are for "crazy" people, the lack of confidentiality involved in the counseling relationship with a fear that the information shared would later be used against them, a fear that other prisoners would believe they were a snitch, a belief that people should deal with their own problems, a preference for talking with friends and family rather than a professional counselor, and having had a past bad experience with counseling (Morgan, Rozycki, & Wilson, 2004).

Social workers need to be aware of these common perceptions held by prisoners so that strategies can be designed to overcome both real and perceived barriers to seeking mental health counseling. Although many of these negative perceptions held are common among the mainstream (non-incarcerated) population as well, many are related to being in custodial care where prisoners' personal rights are extremely limited by necessity.

Assess your comprehension of "Psychosocial Issues in the Prison Population: The Role of the Social Worker" by completing this quiz.

Summary

Working within the legal and criminal justice systems offer rich opportunities for social workers to work with a wide range of individuals experiencing a variety of challenges. The opportunity to interact with several other advocacy organizations and to coordinate services with agencies offering complementary services provides social workers with a broad range of professional experiences. Social workers provide counseling, case management, and advocacy to both survivors and offenders, thus making a difference in the lives of the members of society most in need.

Survivors of crimes such as IPV, sexual assault, and other violent crimes need advocacy and counseling to turn tragedy into triumph and powerlessness into empowerment. Social workers are on the front lines of bringing issues out into the open that had been formerly hidden, removing stigmas, and creating changes in policies and legislation. Criminal activity and subsequent incarceration leaves long-lasting scars on the families of offenders, often plunging them into a cycle of poverty and social isolation. This process significantly increases the likelihood of creating an intergenerational pattern of incarceration, and thus some of the most important work that forensic social workers do involves working with the family members of prisoners, particularly children who not only feel abandoned by their incarcerated parents but often are forced to enter the foster care system if no family members are available to care for them.

Rehabilitation offers the most hope of lowering recidivism rates among the prison population, yet a correctional philosophy that incorporates rehabilitation is controversial because in the eyes of many in the general public, counseling and other mental health programs may seem too much like a luxury, not deserved by those who have committed crimes. Yet prisoners are not a homogeneous group (i.e., many prisoners have been incarcerated for relatively minor offenses), and even those prisoners who have committed the most serious offenses are in many cases the ones who need mental health services the most. Unfortunately, mental health programs are often the first to be cut from state and federal budgets because on the whole the prisoner population does not garner much sympathy within the general public. For this reason, it is imperative that social workers advocate for the basic rights and needs of prisoners, as they do with all vulnerable populations.

Recall what you learned in this chapter by completing the Chapter Review.

13

International Social Work

NLPHOTOS/FOTOLIA

LEARNING OBJECTIVES

- Describe how the forces of globalization are changing the world order and how the discipline of social work is responding.

- Identify the impact of the AIDS pandemic on vulnerable populations in sub-Saharan Africa.

- Describe key responses to major human rights violations against women and girls occurring on a global scale.

- Identify ways in which indigenous people have been marginalized globally and ways in which social workers can respond.

- Describe the role of service providers in responding to emergency international disaster situations.

- Identify advocacy responses to global patterns of human rights violations against members of the LGBT community.

- Describe the long-lasting consequences of genocide and rape as a weapon of war on surviving victims and their families.

Since when do you have to agree with people to defend them from injustice?

—*Lillian Hellman*

Rwanda, a country in Eastern Africa, experienced genocide in 1994 against the Tutsi ethnic group, after a four-year civil war. The Rwandan genocide against the Tutsi resulted in the slaughter of approximately 800,000 Tutsis and about 30,000 moderate Hutus. The genocide was the culmination of years of social exclusion of and propaganda against the Tutsi population, an ethnic minority. After the genocide, about 2 million ethnic Hutus fled into exile in fear of retaliation by the new Tutsi-dominated government. Many Tutsis went into exile as well during the genocide—with many members from both groups ultimately migrating to Western countries. Imaculee is 20 years old and was recently granted political asylum in the United States. She arrived in the country alone, leaving what remains of her family behind in Rwanda. Imaculee was five years old when the genocide started and she recalls much of what she and her family endured. She recalls her parent's decision to take her, her three-year-old brother, and sisters ages 7, 9, 14, and 15 to stay with her grandparents out in the countryside, believing they would be safer there. She recalls her grandparents' neighbors, mostly ethnic Hutu, surrounding the house with machetes and everyone running into the night. She recalls realizing that she could not keep up with her mother and older sisters and staying behind with her grandfather, younger brother, aunt, and two young cousins. She recalls a group of angry neighbors demanding to know where the rest of her family was, pulling her cousin away from her aunt, and killing her in punishment for not revealing where the rest of the family had gone. She remembers the attackers saying that they didn't have time to kill each of them with machetes because they needed to find the rest of the Tutsis. She remembers them pushing her and her family into a barn and lighting it on fire. She remembers being pushed out a window with her younger brother and her aunt following shortly thereafter, and then the screams—she remembers the screams as the barn collapsed killing her aunt's remaining child and her grandfather. It was three months before she would learn that her mother and oldest siblings survived and that her seven- and nine-year-old sisters were murdered along with the rest of her extended family when they discovered by the genocidaires seeking shelter in a Catholic church. Imaculee lived her life under a cloud. She learned to laugh again and had times when she thinks her family felt normal, but in retrospect she realizes that they were all just surviving. The consequences of the genocide continued to affect Imaculee and her family. She learned later that her surviving aunts were all raped during the genocide, and two of them contracted HIV, which ultimately progressed to AIDS. One aunt died recently leaving her young children in the care of an aging relative. When Imaculee arrived in the United States she described her father as very old and unable to protect her. Although he was only 53, Imaculee explained that this is old when one has endured a genocide. Imaculee's father had the responsibility of raising his remaining children as well as 13 of his nieces and nephews who were orphaned during the genocide. She explained that he is tired and is ready to die. Imaculee has never received counseling and takes her history in stride. She cries when she tells her story, especially the part where her six-year-old cousin was pulled away from her mother and cut down with a machete. She remembers that event vividly and it haunts her, as well as the gut-wrenching sobs of her aunt—her cousin's mother. Imaculee is alone in a foreign country and fears she will never see anyone in her family again. She experienced significant loss as a child and continues to experience loss as a consequence of a genocide over two decades years ago. Although she is high functioning, she has multiple needs, including concrete needs such as housing, financial support, and educational support, as well as emotional needs such as culturally appropriate trauma and grief counseling.

THE GLOBAL COMMUNITY

The world is getting smaller, not in terms of population, of course, but in terms of globalization—the increase in inter-connectedness among all countries and, consequently, all people. Countries are no longer isolated in either their financial economy or political

Identify as a Professional Social Worker and Conduct Oneself Accordingly

Practice Behavior: Demonstrate professional demeanor in behavior, appearance, and communication.

Critical Thinking Question: Imagine that you are an international social worker and someone asks you why you are working with people abroad when there are so many problems in the United States. What might you say in response?

You can obtain detailed information on the types of abuses currently occurring throughout the world, as well as instructions on how to take steps to assist in the global campaign to stop such oppression and abuse by visiting Amnesty International's website.

Learn more about the IFSW by conducting an Internet search for the "International Federation of Social Workers."

The ICSW mission (available on its website) captures the way in which macro practice occurs on a global level through a comprehensive network of agencies and organizations on all levels of society to achieve the global mission of eliminating social injustice (refer to paragraph 3).

climate. In the world's new era of globalization, each country is connected to every other country through increased ease in communication, the development of a global economy (international financial interdependence, mutual trade, and financial influence), and increased international migration, combining to create a situation where the political state of one country influences the economic and political climate of another (Ahmadi, 2003).

Although many consider the term *globalization* to refer solely to matters of economics where businesses can sell goods and trade services without much concern for geographic borders, it also reflects the increased awareness, communication, and cooperation among social advocates. In fact, social reform on a global level is more possible now than ever before. Consider the impact the Internet has had on the exchange of information between relatively remote communities, including regions wrought with oppression. Although limits can be placed on information exchange, the Internet has made global awareness of social issues as easy as pressing a few buttons. Of course that is a somewhat simplistic statement, but the importance of the Internet cannot be understated with regard to direct communication and global awareness of social issues.

The increased ease in global communication has meant that social workers in one part of the world can quickly communicate with social workers in another part of the world, sharing valuable information, coordinating efforts and services. In fact, there are several international organizations that exist for this very purpose. The International Federation of Social Workers (IFSW) is an international organization founded in 1956 that works with other international social work and human rights organizations to encourage international cooperation and communication among social workers around the globe. The IFSW has members from 80 countries, including countries in Africa, Asia, Europe, Latin America, and North America.

The International Association of Schools of Social Work (IASSW) is a support organization and information clearinghouse that works to "develop and promote excellence in social work education, research and scholarship globally in order to enhance human well being" (IASSW, n.d.). The IASSW also supports an exchange of information and expertise between social work educational programs.

The International Council on Social Welfare (ICSW) is an independent organization founded in 1928 in Paris, which is committed to social development and works with the United Nations (UN) on matters related to social development, social welfare, and social justice throughout the world. The work of the ICSW is an excellent example of community development at work using networking and international liaisons with other organizations to achieve its goals.

Even mental health professionals whose training has traditionally leaned more in the direction of clinical practice have recently been encouraged to venture into global matters by advocating for social justice. Chi-Ying Chung (2005) made several recommendations to mental health professionals to get involved in international human rights work, suggesting that they apply their training in multicultural counseling and competencies to the international arena to combat global human rights abuses.

Although the social work profession exists worldwide, the nature of the social issues and the function and role of the social worker will vary depending on the political and economic conditions unique to each region. Social workers around the globe have many shared values but have differences in values as well. For instance, in the United States, a client's right to self-determination is very highly valued, but not only is self-determination not considered a core value of the profession in other countries, in Asia, Africa, and even Denmark, the concept of client self-determination is considered either unimportant or dangerous as it detracts from the value of community and cooperation (Weiss, 2005).

Overall, though, social workers in virtually every country place a high value on optimal well-being and the protection of human rights, social justice, and the end to human oppression in whatever form it might be taking within that particular region. For instance, a primary concern of social workers in South Africa relates to issues of race emanating from the country's former system of apartheid. School social workers are commonly relied upon to teach positive race relations among the students in South African public schools. Race issues take on a different form in the United States related to its history of slavery and mass immigration.

Assess your comprehension of "The Global Community" by completing this quiz.

HIV/AIDS PANDEMIC

AIDS, a life-threatening disease found disproportionately in sub-Saharan Africa, has had a devastating effect on families, particularly children, with the life expectancy in many African countries dropping from 61 to 35 years of age. AIDS has had a profound effect on children and the quality of their childhoods. For instance, as of 2007, of the approximately 17 million children estimated to have been orphaned by the AIDS epidemic, approximately 15 million live in sub-Saharan Africa (UNAIDS, 2008). This represents an increase over prior years despite the fact that adult HIV-infection rates have declined in recent years, and use of antiviral medications has become increasingly available, particularly in several sub-Saharan African countries (UNAIDS, 2008). In Zimbabwe alone, United Nations Children's Fund (UNICEF) estimates that 30 percent of all children have been orphaned because of AIDS (UNICEF, 2004). AIDS is then not only a major public health problem, but is also an economic one, since many developing countries have neither the funding nor the capacity to place child welfare issues as a priority (Dhlembeu & Mayanga, 2006). Women bear the primary burden of this disease with regard to both the stigma and the brunt of caregiving, despite the fact that women are being infected at far higher rates than men (Joint United Nations Programme on HIV/AIDS, 2004).

Social workers working in the highest risk countries in sub-Saharan Africa, including Ethiopia, Nigeria, South Africa, Zambia, and Zimbabwe, must contend with the devastating impact of HIV/AIDS, including the complicated and far-reaching implications of so many children being orphaned as a result of the death of one or both of their parents due to AIDS. This situation is further complicated by the fact that many of the child welfare agencies in these countries (if they even exist) are ill equipped to handle the vast number of orphans, many of whom are not being well cared for and may be infected with the HIV virus as well.

In many countries in Africa as well as other regions, traditional beliefs and stigmas exist that are counterproductive to HIV/AIDS treatment protocol compliance. But even in situations where a country is highly compliant with international healthcare protocols, such as Rwanda, the management of the AIDS pandemic is extremely complex and presents numerous challenges to social workers. For instance, in Rwanda, thousands of women were infected with HIV/AIDS by the genocidal government's Interahamwe Hutu militia who raped the majority of women during the genocide. Those women who were not cut down by machetes, learned months or years later that they were infected with HIV (Des Forges, 1999). Thus in the Rwandan context, an entirely new generation of orphans was created because of conditions directly linked to the 1994 genocide against the Tutsi. Further, many of these orphans are HIV-positive as well. The agency WeActx in Kigali works with HIV-infected women and their children, providing them with healthcare and trauma services. The director of this agency recently shared that a significant concern among the youth population being served by this agency relates not only to their daily provision and educational needs but also to the resistance among many of the youth to adhere to the AIDS treatment protocol because they are in "denial" about having this disease. Their HIV status is yet another ongoing reminder of the genocide, which has affected and will continue to affect the Rwandan population, particularly Tutsi survivors, for generations to come (it is important to note that many Hutu women were raped during the genocide as well, and were also infected with HIV, which is why the WeActx agency does not restrict its services to solely Tutsi genocide survivors but to Hutu women as well).

Assess your comprehension of "HIV/AIDS Pandemic" by completing this quiz.

Several social service agencies exist solely to care for these orphaned children. Other agencies focus their efforts on education and testing. The global AIDS pandemic has far-reaching implications that must be addressed on a global basis, since the implications extend worldwide.

CRIMES AGAINST WOMEN AND CHILDREN

Crimes against women and children are of concern to social workers throughout the world, as well as other professionals, involved in advocacy, counseling, and political activism. Social workers work with other professionals to create international awareness effecting social action to put a stop to atrocities such as honor killings, sexual assaults, exploitation and harassment, and discrimination that strips women and children of their basic human rights.

Female Genital Mutilation

One issue often confronting social workers in many countries around the globe, including countries in Africa and the Middle East involves female genital mutilation (FGM), or "female circumcision." In many countries historical tradition and tribal culture prescribe that a girl's external genitalia, typically including her labia and clitoris, be cut away in a rite of passage ceremony celebrating her entry into her womanhood. The most serious type of FGM is Type 3, which includes the cutting away of the labia minora and sewing

Social Work, Social Media, and Technology

Social media is increasingly being used for advocacy campaigns with great success. Here is an example of a very successful social media campaign implemented after 230 Nigerian school girls were kidnapped by Boko Haram terrorists. Social media was successful in creating an international movement called "Take Back Our Girls." Check out the Facebook page for this social movement.

together the labia majora (the outer vaginal lips), which then creates a seal with only a small opening for the passage of menstrual blood and urine. The vaginal seal is intended to keep the women in the tribe from having sexual relations before marriage. The artificial seal is literally torn open during the woman's first sexual encounter with her husband, which not only causes extreme pain, but also has serious health consequences such as bleeding and possible infection. In some cultures the torn pieces of labia are then sewn back together if the woman becomes pregnant and are then torn open again during childbirth.

Young girl endures female genital mutilation in Somalia.

It is estimated that nearly 100 to 130 million girls have undergone FGM, which carries serious health risks including lifelong pain, infertility, and sometimes death (World Health Organization, 1998). FGM is frequently conducted by a village leader often with unsterile medical tools and no pain medication. There has been a recent backlash among women in some African countries who are discouraging FGM in their communities, although this practice is still quite prevalent in many rural regions. Social workers are conducting educational campaigns to influence local leaders who have the power to discourage this practice. Social workers also work to influence many countries in the Global North to provide humanitarian aid to organizations working to change long-held cultural beliefs about FGM, and have even worked to grant refugee status for at-risk women and girls who are seeking political asylum in another country.

Human Sex Trafficking

Social workers in many countries in south Asia (for instance) must contend with numerous human rights violations, the most prevalent and disturbing of which includes the trafficking of women and children for the purposes of slavery, forced marriage, and the sex trade. For instance, according to Human Rights Watch (HRW) (2002), approximately 10,000 women and girls are "recruited" from Burma to brothels in Thailand each year. A recent U.S. Department of State (2012) Trafficking in Persons report states that government corruption and the involvement of public officials in the human trafficking trade makes matters even more challenging for human rights workers who are attempting to achieve social justice for these women and girls.

As of 2011, there were approximately 12.3 million individuals who were victims of human trafficking worldwide, the majority of whom were young females trafficked for sexual purposes (U.S. Department of State, 2012). In fact, young girls are the most sought after targets of large criminal organizations that are in the business of trafficking human beings. Although people can be sold for various reasons, including forced servitude and child labor, the majority of human trafficking involves forced sexual slavery, where young women and girls are forced to become prostitutes. Girls are sold into sex slavery by family members in need of money, are kidnapped, or are lured into the sex trade with promises of modeling contracts or domestic work in other countries. Many of these

As of 2011, there were approximately 12.3 million individuals who were victims of human trafficking worldwide, the majority of whom were young females, the majority of whom were trafficked for sexual purposes (U.S. Department of State, 2012). In fact, young girls are the most sought after targets of large criminal organizations that are in the business of trafficking human beings. After watching the film "CNN: Child Sex Slaves in America," consider what kind of intervention plan you might develop if you were working with girls who had been trafficked, either domestically or internationally, and were in a support group focusing on trauma and recovery. (https://www.youtube.com/watch?v=7PLAPvxbYTM)

Social Work Application Activity

Go to the Polaris Project website, by conducting an
Internet search, and then clicking on the Resources link.
Navigate to the Tools for Service Providers and then
to the Service Provider Resources and download and
review the Comprehensive Trafficking Assessment form.

How is this assessment different than other
assessment forms you've worked with? Why do you

think it's important to avoid certain terminology, such
as identifying the client as a victim of "human sex
trafficking"? What is your overall impression of this
assessment form? Can you envision yourself as a social
worker evaluating a potential victim of trafficking using
this model?

girls are kept in inhumane environments where they are forced to have sex with up to 10 men a day. Many contract HIV/AIDS and are cast out onto the street once they become too sick to be useful (U.S. Department of State, 2012).

Much of the effort of social workers in countries with high rates of human trafficking, such as India, Burma, Thailand, and Sri Lanka, is focused on rescuing these women and children and ensuring that they are delivered to safe communities where they will not be exploited again. Complicating intervention strategies is the fact that many government officials in these countries either look the other way when confronted with the illegal sex trade or openly contribute to it by protecting criminal organizations responsible for human trafficking. Human rights organizations have reported that many police officers, members of the military, and other government officials in Thailand, for instance, often arrest victims who attempt to escape, putting them in prison on charges of prostitution, a clear act of retaliation, rather than helping them to escape (Human Rights Watch, 2004).

Orphans and Vulnerable Youth: Street Children

Social workers in Central and South American as well as Eastern European countries must contend with the significant problem of thousands of homeless children roaming the streets in search of food and shelter. The problem of street children is growing worldwide, leading several human rights organizations to call social workers and other advocates to action. Street children are sometimes orphans but are often children who have one or both parents but have left home because of poverty and/or lack of supervision. In many Eastern European countries, including Romania, the problem of street children is a direct result of political policies resulting in families having a large number of children with the promise of government provisions, only to be left in terribly vulnerable positions when these governments failed, leaving parents with no means of providing for their exceptionally large families.

Street children are at risk of abuses by older children as well as police and government officials who often physically abuse children as young as five years old (Human Rights Watch, 2002). In some countries, children have even been murdered by the police with no official response. Drug abuse is also rampant within the street children population, many of who often sniff glue to keep warm and to abate hunger pains.

Social workers have organized outreach efforts helping street children by finding homes for them, either with religious organizations or through international adoption. International social service agencies also work with local agencies to bolster aid efforts, including lobbying government officials to address the issue of orphaned and vulnerable youth by funding child welfare efforts.

Child Labor and Economic Injustice

Child labor is a social justice issue across the globe but is a particular concern in Asian, African, and Latin American countries, where children as young as four years are required to work up to 12 hours per day in jobs that put them in both physical and psychological danger. Child labor abuses include children in India who plunge their hands into boiling water while making silk thread, children as young as four years throughout Asia who are tied to rug looms for many hours a day and forced to make rugs, and children as young as seven who work in U.S. tobacco fields in North Carolina, Kentucky, Tennessee, and Virginia.

Of the 120 million children forced into full-time labor, the majority reside in Asia, followed by Africa, Latin America, and (as referenced earlier), the United States (Human Rights Watch, 2004). International human rights organizations such as HRW, Amnesty International, and UNICEF work diligently to protect children's rights, including lobbying of international policies and legislation that protect children as well as funding human rights efforts in specific countries allowing for intervention at the local level. But the problem of child labor, particularly in sweatshops in the Global South (Central and South America, Southeast Asia, India, and certain countries in Africa), remain a serious problem impacting the entire world both socially and economically.

> **Apply Social Work Ethical Principles to Guide Professional Practice**
>
> **Practice Behavior: Recognize and manage personal values in a way that allows professional values to guide practice.**
>
> **Critical Thinking Question:** Is it unethical for social workers to advocate for child labor laws while at the same time shopping at stores that sell products produced with child labor in other countries? Why or why not?

For instance, Polack (2004) discussed the impact of hundreds of billions of dollars in loans made to countries in the Global South by countries in the Global North (England, Spain, France, the United States, etc.). Polack argued that the cumulative impact of these loans to some of the poorest countries in the world has been devastating, particularly for the most vulnerable members of these countries because these loans (1) financed large-scale projects, such as hydroelectric plants, that benefited the Global North while displacing millions of indigenous peoples, pushing them even further into poverty, (2) financed military armaments for government regimes in the Global South that oppressed the countries' most vulnerable and poorest residents, and (3) lined the pockets of corrupt leaders of many countries in the Global South, resulting in increased oppression of the country's least-privileged members.

According to Polack very little if any of this loan money benefited the majority of the citizens of these countries; rather, it harmed them and in fact continues to harm them by increasing the poverty within these already devastatingly poor regions. In an attempt to repay this debt, many countries in the Global South exploit their own workers to make loan payments. For example, countries in South America have sold sections of rain forest formerly farmed by local residents to Northern timber companies. Other countries have been forced to privatize government services such as selling utility services formerly provided by the government, resulting in dramatic increases in the cost of utilities. Polack cites how these developments have resulted in many Northern companies making millions of dollars at the expense of the poorest residents of these debt-ridden countries.

One of the most devastating impacts of what has now evolved into trillions of dollars of debt for many countries in the Global South is the evolution of the sweatshop industry- large-scale factories that develop goods exported to the Global North. Some of the poorest people in the world, including children, work in sweatshops throughout Asia, India, and Latin America, where horrific abuses abound. Labor abuses occur legally in many countries because in a desperate attempt to attract export contracts, many countries in the Global South established "free-trade" agreements or free-trade zones for corporations in the Global North, allowing them to circumvent local trade regulations, such as minimum wage, working hour limits, and child labor laws.

Almost every major retail supplier in the United States benefits from these sweatshop conditions in the form of extremely low wages, extremely poor working conditions, physical and sexual exploitation without retribution, excessively long working hours (sometimes in excess of 12 hours per day with no days off for weeks at a time), and severe retribution such as immediate termination for complaints or requests for better working conditions (Institute for Global Labor and Human Rights, n.d.; Polack, 2004). Child labor is the norm in these sweatshops with most sweatshop owners preferring adolescent girls as employees because they tend to be more compliant and are more easily exploited (Institute for Global Labor and Human Rights, n.d.).

Although local and international human rights advocates work diligently to change these working conditions, at the root of the problem of child exploitation is economic injustice rooted in generations of intercountry exploitation. Thus, there is significant complexity not easily confronted without government involvement, which is often slow in coming when large corporations are making billions of dollars with the system as it currently operates. For instance, as labor unions have become the norm in the United States, many companies such as Nike and Wal-Mart moved their factories to Asia and Central and South America, where millions of dollars can be saved in wages and benefits cuts (Institute for Global Labor and Human Rights, n.d.). Addressing the issue of child labor and economic injustice will take the lobbying efforts of many international human rights organizations working with other organizations, as well as the media to create public awareness where buying power is often the only tool powerful enough to influence sweatshop owners and large retail establishments.

Learn more about labor abuses around the world by visiting the website for the "Institute for Global Labor and Human Rights."

Assess your comprehension of "Crimes Against Women and Children" by completing this quiz.

INDIGENOUS PEOPLE

Protecting the rights of indigenous people is a common concern of social workers practicing in countries such as the United States, Australia, and many Central and South American countries. Indigenous populations are often forced to engage in harsh and dangerous labor practices, such as working in fields sprayed with insecticides, transporting supplies on their person, or begging, to survive.

The human rights issues pertaining to indigenous peoples of Australia, primarily comprising of Aborigines, are similar in nature to those of Native Americans in the United States, where the historic immigration of Europeans displaced the indigenous tribal communities. In addition, both countries engaged in an official campaign of discrimination and cultural annihilation as indigenous tribes were forced off their historic lands and onto restricted areas, where they were unable to practice traditional methods of self-support. Both Native Americans in the United States and Aborigines in Australia were subject to the mass forced removal of children, who were mandated to attend schools where they were forced to abandon their cultural heritage and native language.

The 36-year civil war in Guatemala, which ended in 1996, involved what many human rights organizations cite as the genocide of indigenous populations, or what is commonly referred to as the "disappearances" or the invisible war. The UN Truth and Reconciliation

Committee estimates that up to 200,000 people were killed by government forces in the Guatemalan Civil War (Human Rights Watch, 2008).

In response to the intergenerational trauma that has resulted from physical and cultural genocide, many indigenous people have experienced a decimation of their population as well as extreme poverty, forced migration, and marginalization often manifesting in physical and mental health problems. Social workers work with indigenous people in reconciliation efforts to restore them to a level of self-sufficiency and cultural pride. Several movements are underway within indigenous tribal communities intended to move them toward wholeness and a life without substance abuse, depression, and brokenness in families.

The Healing Forest Model is a program within a Native American community that was developed by a tribal member who suffered from alcoholism for years and who received inspiration and input from tribal elders who shared their wisdom regarding traditional cultural laws for authentic change. The *Healing Forest Model* is based on the philosophy of the Medicine Wheel, a Native American concept that addresses the interconnectedness of everything in life. According to the teachings of the Medicine Wheel, the pain of one person creates pain for the entire community, thus there are no individual issues or concerns. This community concept of healing is very consistent with a model of macro practice, which posits that there is no such thing as individual problems but instead, all individual problems become community problems. This philosophy may be counterintuitive to North Americans, who as a society place an high value on individuality, oftentimes at the cost of community. Yet many believe that the key to reclaiming physical and mental health in indigenous culture is through such a community practice approach (Coyhis & Simonelli, 2005).

> **Assess your comprehension of "Indigenous People" by completing this quiz.**

REFUGEES

According to the Office of the United Nations High Commissioner for Refugees (UNHCR), there are approximately 42 million displaced people who have been forcibly removed from their homes and communities because of civil war, conflict, political and cultural persecution, natural disaster, ethnic cleansing, and genocide.

The Immigration and Nationality Act defines "refugee" as:

(A) any person who is outside any country of such person's nationality or, in the case of a person having no nationality, is outside any country in which such person last habitually resided, and who is unable or unwilling to return to, and is unable or unwilling to avail himself or herself of the protection of, that country because of persecution or a well-founded fear of persecution on account of race, religion, nationality, membership in a particular social group, or political opinion, or (B) in such circumstances as the President after appropriate consultation (as defined in section 207(e) of this Act) may specify, any person who is within the country of such person's nationality or, in the case of a person having no nationality, within the country in which such person is habitually residing, and who is persecuted or who has a well-founded fear of persecution on account of race, religion, nationality, membership in a particular social group, or political opinion. (Sec. 101(a)(42))

Engage Diversity and Difference in Practice

Practice Behavior: Recognize the extent to which a culture's structures and values may oppress, marginalize, alienate, or create or enhance privilege and power.

Critical Thinking Question: Currently, the United States accepts the most refugees of any other country in the Global North, but there is no federal legislation that requires mental healthcare for refugees once they've been resettled. What role can social workers play in advocating for more effective policies with regard to refugee resettlement?

> **Check out UNHCR on Twitter by going to the Twitter website and searching for @unhcr.**

Individuals may become refugees through a variety of circumstances. In the last two decades, there have been between 17 and 33 armed civil conflicts at any one time, leading to civil unrest and instability in several developing countries. In the midst of a civil war, innocent civilians are often forced to flee in search of safety, a phenomenon referred to as *forced migration*. If civilians flee but do not cross international boundaries, they are referred to as internally displaced persons (IDPs), but if they are forced to flee across international boundaries, to another country, then they often receive the legal designation of refugee. Some refugees may live in secret, in a country with closed borders, and thus are considered by the host country to be illegal immigrants. Life as an illegal immigrant is lived on the fringes, in constant fear of detection, detainment, and repatriation. In other situations, refugees are warehoused in refugee settlements or camps. Most refugee camps are managed by the UNHCR, but despite such management, many refugee camps are places of great risk and despair. In many refugee camps, refugees are not allowed to leave the camp as they are considered a serious risk to the host country. Most refugee camps are established in "border regions" and may remain in close proximity to the war that caused the displacement in the first place. The majority of refugees in protracted situations develop a sense of significant despair as their situation lingers on for generations, as with the Burundi, who have been in refugee camps in Tanzania since the early 1970s. Those refugees fortunate enough to be selected for resettlement in the United States often face years of challenges as they struggle to survive in a complex society, often underemployed and socially isolated (Hollenbach, 2008; Loescher, Milner, & Troeller, 2008). Social workers often work with refugees in a variety of practice settings, including refugee resettlement agencies (contracted with the U.S. Department of State), schools, and mental health agencies. International social work practice involves advocacy and policy practice effecting changes in policies that create additional challenges to an often immensely vulnerable and traumatized population.

Refugee communities, also referred to as *diaspora communities*, should not be considered powerless victims without personal agency though as many come together to form quite powerful lobbying groups advocating for their agendas both within their host countries as well as in home country affairs. In fact, recent research has shown that a country in post-conflict is at a significantly higher risk of renewed conflict if there is a related diaspora that is politically active and advocating against the home country government (Collier & Hoeffler, 2000; Lyons, 2007). Thus, it is vital that social workers working with diaspora groups be aware of the sociopolitical dynamics related to the history of conflict in the refugees' country of origin so that they can assist the diaspora members to engage in ways that will support peace processes and not exacerbate old and existing conflicts.

Assess your comprehension of "Refugees" by completing this quiz.

Social Work Application Activity

Conduct an Internet search for the UNHCR website and click on "News and Views," and then on the "Human Stories." Select one story about refugees under the care of the UNHCR and consider the following questions: What is the role of the UNHCR in meeting the needs of the refugees in the story? How do policy and practice intersect in the sociopolitical circumstances surrounding the refugees featured in the story? How can you see social workers engaging in this work?

INTERNATIONAL DISASTER RELIEF

When natural disasters occur in countries in the Global South, particularly those countries that experience chronic poverty, the consequences are often devastating. Because many countries in the Global South are plagued with absolute and chronic poverty they often do not have the infrastructure necessary to rebound from disasters, such as earthquakes, typhoons, and tsunamis. In many developing countries, a large percentage of the population reside in the countryside far from urban centers, making it difficult for humanitarian aid and other assistance to reach people in need. Social conditions such as chronic poverty, high crime, and poor infrastructure (insufficient or no law enforcement and emergency response, poor or no roads, insufficient or no healthcare facilities and social services), dramatically increases vulnerability, extending the negative consequences of a natural disaster for years, contributing to significant human and economic loss.

The need for international relief work is increasing as the occurrence of global natural disasters is increasing, in large part because of changing weather patterns caused by global climate change (Jennings, 2011). For instance, in December of 2004 one of the world's largest recorded earthquakes, the Sumatra–Andaman earthquake, caused a series of tsunamis along the Indian Ocean resulting in a death toll of almost 280,000 people across several countries, including Indonesia and Sri Lanka. These tsunamis were also responsible for approximately 1.8 million people being displaced and billions of dollars in damage and loss (resulting in over $14 billion dollars pledged in humanitarian aid) (Jayasuriya & McCawley, 2010). According to the United Nations, more than 260,000 people died between 2010 and 2012 in the Somali famine, almost half of whom were children (UN, 2013). The famine has also resulted in over 1.5 million IDPs, as well as millions of dollars lost in cattle and lost productivity. In December 2012, Typhoon Bopha hit the Philippines over a several-day period, resulting in over 2,000 deaths (some people are still reported as missing), over six million people being displaced, and over $584 million in damage to crops and infrastructure, including over 200,000 homes that were completely destroyed. As of March 2013, almost 850,000 people remained displaced (see Box 13.1).

The Effectiveness of International Disaster Relief and the Role of the Social Worker

Pawar's (2008) case study on the Krishna River Flood in Maharashtra, India, highlighted several deficiencies in disaster relief and management, including politicized and disorganized

Box 13.1 Categories of Disaster Relief

United Methodist Committee on Relief (UMCOR), an agency that responds to numerous natural disasters worldwide, categorizes the phases of disaster relief:

- Readiness: being prepared for disasters, including developing a plan for response
- Rescue: includes search and rescue efforts in the hours and days following the disaster
- Relief: providing for the basic needs of those effected on an emergency basis, such as food, water, medicine, and shelter in the weeks and months following the disaster

- Recovery: helping survivors find short, medium, and long-term solutions to the devastation they've endured in the months and years following a disaster, which includes community development efforts
- Review: evaluating the disaster response to make improvements for the next disaster, including disaster risk reduction (Crutchfield, 2013)

Pearson Education, Inc.

dissemination of humanitarian aid (food, kerosene, clothing, etc.); inadequacy of relief aid, including frequent distribution of aid to those who were not in need, and the failure to provide aid to many who were; and likely the most damaging of all deficiencies was a significant shortage of post-disaster relief programs, including case management and trauma counseling. Pawar asserted that social workers can make significant contributions in these areas of deficiencies. In particular, Pawar recommends that social workers engage in:

- Coordination of better communication and coordination, including community education and awareness programs;
- Development of more efficient methods for accurately assessing affected community members' needs;
- Coordination of equitable and timely aid distribution that reflects appropriate prioritizing based on need;
- Serving as a liaison between community and political leaders and community members, encouraging a moral, rather than partisan response;
- Fostering existing informal community support networks;
- Development and facilitation of post-disaster relief programs focusing on longer term social welfare provision, including post-trauma counseling.

Social workers possess skills that can meet many of the needs disaster survivors experience (Pawar, 2008). The challenge, however, is determining what these needs are as well as the best way to meet identified needs. One of the first tasks facing international disaster relief workers is *assessing the needs of survivors* (Bell, 2008). This can be especially challenging since as Williams (2008) noted, those with the greatest needs are often those who were in need prior to the natural disaster.

An empirical review of 160 studies exploring the impact of natural disasters on 60,000 survivors revealed that survivors of natural disasters experienced a wide range of psychosocial and physical problems, including chronic problems with daily living; the loss of psychosocial resources (coping mechanisms), such as optimism, resiliency, perceived control, and self-efficacy; and a range of somatic complaints. Thus, determining the needs of those impacted by a natural disaster and developing a case management plan that acknowledges previous vulnerability, while remaining focused on the survivor's present needs related to the disaster is often a tangled process wrought with complicating factors and unforeseen challenges.

Learn more about the UN-Habitat assessment tools by conducting an Internet search for "Disaster Assessment Portal."

Several disaster organizations have developed *rapid assessment tools* for service providers to aid in the process of assessing the needs of disaster survivors and affected communities. The United Nations Habitat agency (UN-Habitat) facilitates a website called the Disaster Assessment Portal designed for those involved in humanitarian disaster relief. The website provides information on current humanitarian disasters, assessment tools for disaster response and early recovery, and more comprehensive disaster risk assessment tools. The International Red Cross and Red Crescent Societies (IFRC), the world's largest humanitarian network, also provides information on emergency response, including conducting emergency (rapid) assessments and other resources for responders on its website.

Providing Psychosocial Support for Disaster Survivors

According to Flynn and Norwood (2004), when providing psychosocial support for survivors of a natural disaster, social workers should focus on three factors: their psychosocial history; their personality characteristics, including their coping mechanisms (such as resiliency and attitude); and the nature and availability of their social supports. They also note that the goal of all psychosocial intervention should be to reduce individual suffering and increase functioning and resiliency. Psychological problems appeared to be the most frequently experienced and enduring consequence of a natural disaster, the most significant of which was post-traumatic stress disorder (PTSD), followed by depression, anxiety, and loss of self-esteem (Norris, Friedman, Watson, Byrne, Diaz, & Kaniasty, 2002). Additional responses to enduring a natural disaster include fear, anger, distress, sadness, and grief, all of which can increase the risk of psychiatric and psychological disorders, depending on an individual's past psychological history, current coping mechanisms, personal resiliency, and level of social support (Flynn & Norwood, 2004).

> Learn more about providing psychosocial support to international disaster survivors by going to the IRFC website, clicking on "What we do," and then "Health," and then "Psychosocial support."

The area of international disaster relief, particularly with regard to the role of social work, is a relatively new area. Currently, the body of research in the area of disaster relief and emergency management beyond descriptive studies is not very large, and thus we are just beginning to learn more about the short and long-term impact of disasters on the needs of survivors and communities. As we learn more about the impact of natural disasters on survivors and their communities, social workers will be better able to engage in disaster relief and emergency management in an international context.

> Assess your comprehension of "International Disaster Relief" by completing this quiz.

CRIMES AGAINST LESBIAN, GAY, BISEXUAL, AND TRANSGENDERED POPULATIONS

Individuals who have nontraditional sexual orientations, including lesbians, gays, bisexual men and women, and transgendered individuals have long been the victims of abuse, discrimination, and at the very least a tremendous amount of misunderstanding. *Homophobia* is defined as an irrational fear of members of the gay and lesbian population. Lesbian, gay, bisexual, and transgendered (LGBT) individuals are subjected to homophobic sentiments and outright discrimination and violence in all parts of the world. Until recently, the majority opinion of those in the United States was that LGBT individuals were either morally perverse or mentally ill. In fact, it wasn't until 1987 that all references to homosexuality were completely removed from the American Psychiatric Association's *Diagnostic and Statistical Manual of Mental Disorders*.

Acts of harassment and violence against individuals based on their perceived sexual orientation are prevalent all over the world, causing significant distress, depression, and even suicidal ideation (Huebner, Rebchook, & Kegeles, 2004). LGBT youth are at risk of discrimination in school and community settings even in more tolerant countries, such as the United States and the United Kingdom, although many school districts now use policies designed to protect at-risk adolescents (Ryan & Rivers, 2003). LGBT individuals are commonly the victims of direct or subtle discriminatory practices, verbally abused and harassed, and the victims of violence, sometimes even murdered, solely because of their sexual orientation.

Although abuse and discrimination against LGBT individuals is assumed to be far worse in developing countries, this is not always the case. In many regions of the world, sexual orientation is expressed on a continuum, particularly compared with Western cultural norms, and the focus of scrutiny is far more on behavioral norms rather than sexual behavior. For instance, in some parts of the world as long as men behave in ways that are consistent with gendered expectations of men, they can engage in sex with other men, but not experience discrimination, because culturally, they are not considered gay. An example of this phenomenon can be found in Bangladesh where married men often frequent male prostitutes but do not necessarily consider themselves gay. They are rarely victims of harassment or abuse because they do not violate gender stereotypes, which essentially means that these men continue to act like "men" (Dowsett, 2003). The relevance of this is that in many parts of the world violence is based more on non-traditional gender expression contrary to traditional gender role expectations than it is on sexual behavior.

In many regions of the world same-gender sexual behavior is considered a criminal act punishable by anything from a prison sentence to death. Same-gender sexual behavior is considered illegal in South Africa, and LGBT individuals are often the victims of human rights abuses, including punitive rapes on women who either identify as lesbian or who do not behave in ways that are consistent with traditional female gender expression. In addition, they are often unjustly blamed for the HIV/AIDS crisis currently occurring in South Africa (Graziano, 2004). Members of the gay and lesbian community (or those perceived to be gay or lesbian) in Saudi Arabia are subject to public floggings and imprisonment. In Egypt, vice officers travel through towns in vans arresting in excess of 100 men at a time who are suspected of being gay. Many of these men were arrested because they knew what the word *gay* meant, a North American word assumed to be known only by gay men. Men arrested on suspicion of being gay are then subject to severe beatings until they agree to sign arrest papers admitting that they are gay. Signing these papers means a lifetime of certain harassment and refusing to sign them means certain death. In Jamaica, LGBT individuals are often the target of horrible human rights abuses, oftentimes fueled by the police who have been known to invite bystanders to attack men suspected of being gay. One incident reported to a human rights organization involved a man suspected of being gay who was attacked by police and ultimately beaten and stabbed to death in the middle of the street by bystanders who joined in the beating. Police in Jamaica also commonly stop individuals suspected of being gay on the streets, searching them looking for any sign of same-gender sexual behavior such as condoms or lubricants. If these items are found, the men are often beaten and arrested (Human Rights Watch, 2005).

Several countries in Africa, including Uganda and Nigeria, are currently considering "anti-homosexuality" laws that would make same-gender sexual behavior illegal and punishable by brutal penalties, including death. What is particularly disturbing about this recent antigay and lesbian trend in Eastern Africa are reports that some U.S. Evangelical leaders may be behind the effort to criminalize same-gender behavior, based on a belief that the "homosexual agenda" threatens the traditional family (Gettleman, 2010). Human rights organizations have expressed outrage in response to the reported link between antigay and lesbian legislation in Africa and certain factions of the U.S. Evangelical church for a variety of reasons. Chief among these concerns is the potential for dictatorships with poor human rights records to use such legislation to silence (either through long-term incarceration or death) anyone who opposes their autocratic rule (Human Rights Watch, 2009). Hence, such misplaced advocacy has a great possibility of significantly increasing human rights abuses against an already marginalized population.

Many social workers and human rights workers around the globe are working tirelessly to reduce crimes against LGBT individuals through the passage of policies and legislation designed not only to protect individuals whose sexual orientation is not traditional but also to decriminalize same-gender sexual behavior in all countries. The recent passage of the Matthew Shepard & James Byrd Jr. Hate Crimes Prevention Act (P.L. 111-84) in the United States, signed into law in October 2009 by President Obama, makes it a federal crime to assault individuals because of their sexual orientation, gender, or gender identity. The passage of this legislation has been lauded by civil rights organizations as a significant step forward in the fight for equality and protection of the LGBT population (Human Rights Campaign, 2009).

What might be one of the most important issues to consider is that regardless of one's personal opinion violence against anyone based on their sexual behavior, sexual orientation or gender expression should never be permissible under any circumstances, thus social workers should be called to action to ensure that *all* individuals are treated with compassion and dignity.

Assess your comprehension of "Crimes Against Lesbian, Gay, Bisexual, and Transgendered Populations" by completing this quiz.

GOVERNMENT-SANCTIONED TORTURE AND ABUSE

Countries in Eastern Europe, as well as several countries in Africa, are overwhelmed with the repercussions of war and genocide. Social workers and human rights workers working in these regions deal with numerous human atrocities such as torture, war crimes, and the crisis of thousands of refugees. Countries in the midst of war are particularly vulnerable to human rights abuses involving torture because war seems to have a diminishing effect on human compassion and empathy. Human torture and abuse can include anything from random physical abuse to the systematic abuse and even murder of groups of people common in genocide, prisoner of war camps, and refugee camps. Many of the abuses documented in Taliban-ruled Afghanistan included government-sanctioned gang rapes of women who were accused of bringing disgrace on their countrymen, and physical torture such as the cutting off of limbs for minor infractions (U.S. Department of State, 2001).

Most, if not all, victims of wartime atrocities such as rape and torture suffer from post-traumatic stress disorder (PTSD) and other psychiatric conditions related to trauma, grief and loss. Social workers work with victims of torture on all fronts—some within refugee camps, and some in other countries who that have accepted survivors of war on refugee status. The psychological issues involved with working with survivors of war are vast and in addition to the issues mentioned earlier include depression, anxiety, and adjustment disorders. Many social workers in developing countries and former Soviet bloc countries are employed by the government and deliver broad-ranging services on a community level, focusing on the manifestation of a history of war. For instance, a relatively significant portion of social work in Croatia is focused on postwar issues, including the care of Bosnian refugees and other war victims, focusing on trauma recovery and helping victims to manage the comprehensive impact of war on the individual and families (Knežević & Butler, 2003).

Torture and other human rights abuses are not just perpetrated by evil and fallen dictatorships. Several advocacy organizations, including Amnesty International, Human Rights Watch (HRW), and the International Red Cross, have cited numerous egregious examples of the U.S. government torturing prisoners suspected of involvement in the

September 11, 2001, terrorist attacks, or of being a supporter of "enemy combatants." Both former president George W. Bush and former vice president Cheney defended their administration's policy of using "enhanced" interrogation techniques, denying that such practices constituted a violation of the Geneva Convention, (a collection of international humanitarian laws that among other remedies provides parameters on how prisoners of war are to be treated).

In 2006, the HRW submitted a report to the U.N. Human Rights Committee detailing numerous human rights violations occurring under the Bush/Cheney administration in violation of International Covenant on Civil and Political Rights (ICCPR), including the secret and indefinite detention of prisoners at Guantanamo Bay and at undisclosed locations abroad. According to the report, most of these prisoners had not been charged with any crime and had thus been denied due process. Other human rights violations included the use of torture as an interrogation technique, such as sleep deprivation, isolation, sexual humiliation, and waterboarding (which gives the subject the sensation of drowning).

Federal legislation that was enacted in 2005, entitled the Detainee Treatment Act, permitted the use of information obtained from torture and also prevents Guantanamo Bay detainees from ever bringing action against the U.S. government, even if the detainment was unwarranted, and even in cases where a detainee was abused, tortured, and the victim of cruel and inhumane treatment. The 2006 HRW report described the cases of Kahled el-Masri, a German citizen and Maher Arar, a Canadian citizen, as examples of how U.S. treatment of those deemed "enemy combatants" violated international humanitarian law. Both El-Masri and Arar were picked up and detained without being provided an opportunity to challenge their detention. Both were flown to third-party countries likely to torture them (El-Masri was flown from Macedonia to a CIA-run prison in Afghanistan for five months, where he was beaten and tortured repeatedly, including being tortured with electric cords). El-Masri contends that one of the officials admitted that he was detained in error; he was ultimately flown to Albania and abandoned on a deserted road. Arar was detained in the United States, held for two weeks incommunicado, was flown to Jordan and then driven across the border to Syria where he was held in a Syrian prison for 10 months, and beaten and tortured repeatedly. He too was ultimately released. Both men sued the U.S. government and in both situations their cases

Social Work Application Activity

Access the HRW report referenced above online by conducting an Internet search for "Human Rights Watch Supplemental Submission to the Human Rights Committee During its Consideration of the Second and Third Periodic Reports of the United States," and read more about cases of torture of international detainees by the U.S. government. After reading the report, review the IFSW Statement of Ethical Principles on the IFSW website. What IFSW ethical principles were violated in the cases of Kahled el-Masri and Maher Arar? Is it permissible to torture detainees suspected of terrorist acts against the United States, even in cases where lives are at stake and torturing detainees may be the only way to obtain the information? Why or why not? If you answered that torture is acceptable under certain circumstances, what would those circumstances be? When exceptions of humanitarian law are made for certain groups of people, how can limits on mistreatment be set? What roles can social workers play in advocating against abuse and torture of any population perceived as a potential threat to national sovereignty and safety?

were dismissed by U.S. District courts based on the U.S. government's claim to national security privilege.

Some of the most egregious security policies have been passed during times of crisis when people are scared and willing to sacrifice civil and human rights for the sake of security. Social workers must advocate for human rights in all situations and resist the temptation to dehumanize any group, an act that tends to make it far easier to justify such horrendous mistreatment.

Assess your comprehension of "Government-Sanctioned Torture and Abuse" by completing this quiz.

GENOCIDE AND RAPE AS A WEAPON OF WAR

The 1948 UN Convention on the Prevention and Punishment of Genocide defines genocide as any act committed with the intention to destroy, in whole or in part, a national ethnic, racial, or religious group: killing members of the group; causing serious bodily or mental harm to members of the group; deliberately inflicting on the group conditions of life calculated to bring about its physical destruction in whole or in part, imposing measures intended to prevent births within the group, and forcibly transferring children of the group to another group (UN General Assembly, 1948).

Genocides most typically occur within a broader armed civil or international conflict, thus determining whether civilian deaths as a result of a conflict rise to the level of genocide can be political in nature. Such a determination can be made by any country that is a signatory of the Genocide Convention, as well as by the General Assembly of the United Nations. There may be political reasons why the United Nations, or a member country, does not level charges of genocide against a particular government, such as the lack of political will to engage in humanitarian intervention.

There have been several genocides in the world's recent history, each one seemingly more gruesome than the next. The American genocide against Native Americans during the 1700s through the 1800s and Turkey's genocide of the Armenians in 1917 are examples of genocides that have never been officially recognized by the international community. More recent genocides include the Nazi Holocaust against the Jews in Europe during World War II, and the Serbian genocide against the Bosnians in 1992 through 1994 in former Yugoslavia. The opening vignette focused on the aftermath of the 1994 Rwanda genocide against the Tutsi where approximately 800,000 Tutsis were macheted to death by government-sponsored Hutu militia (Buss, 2009; Cohen et al., 2009; Des Forges, 1999; Human Rights Watch, 1996).

Rape as a weapon of war is a systematic tactic used in armed conflict and genocide targeting the civilian population (primarily women and girls) involving sexual violence in an orchestrated manner and as a purposeful policy to humiliate, intimidate, and instill fear in a community or ethnic group (Buss, 2009; Human Rights Watch, 1996). Thus, rape during wartime is not a by-product of armed conflict, but an instrument of it (Buss, 2009). Rape was used as a weapon of war in both the Bosnian genocide and the Rwandan genocide against the Tutsi. In June 2008, the United Nations Security Council passed Resolution 1820, which recognizes rape as a weapon of war and establishes a commitment to addressing sexual violence in conflict, including punishing perpetrators (UN Security Council, 2008). This resolution became an important part of convictions by international criminal tribunals in response to genocides in former Yugoslavia (the ICTY), Rwanda (the ICTR), and in the United Nations–backed Special Court for Sierra Leone (SCSL) (UNDPKO, 2010).

Assess your comprehension of "Genocide and Rape as a Weapon of War" by completing this quiz.

INTERNATIONAL SOCIAL WORK PRACTICE IN ACTION

The passage of one domestic violence law can protect thousands of women in Mexico. One press release can lead to a boycott that can increase wages for thousands of young women in sweatshops in India. Global social work practice can change the lives of an entire community or a whole country. International social work offers significant rewards to those social workers willing to develop multidisciplinary expertise through education and experience that when combined with the networking power of other organizations and the Internet can create positive change for all members of society around the globe.

Much of international social work is facilitated through non-governmental organizations (NGOs), which often involves the collaboration and coordination with local grassroots organizations working directly with the local community. An example of a grassroots organization is Stop FGM in Kenya, a project of the Loreto Sisters of Eastern Africa Province, that is working to end FGM in Eastern Africa. The project was started by Sr. Dr. Ephigenia Gachiri, a member of the Kikuyu tribe, who lives in a convent in Nairobi, Kenya. Sr. Ephigenia grew up with FGM as a part of her culture and didn't realize the very serious ramifications of the ritual until she had the opportunity to attend a UN convention on women's rights and heard a presentation on the grave consequences of FGM. She states that she made a decision after this conference to spend the rest of her career fighting FGM in her native country of Kenya. Sr. Ephigenia conducts educational seminars with village elders, tribal leaders, as well as school-aged children to confront dangerous long-standing myths that serve as the basis for FGM, such as the belief that women who are not circumcised will become promiscuous, even potentially entering the life of prostitution. Sr. Ephigenia has developed alternate rites of passage based on Christian beliefs, which she advocates should replace FGM as a rite of passage into adulthood. To facilitate the replacement rite of passage, Sr. Ephigenia and her colleagues conduct training seminars in schools across Kenya where girls and boys engage in educational activities culminating in the alternate rite of passage ceremony where they and their families commit to not allowing the girls in the family to undergo FGM. Sr. Ephigenia describes the serious ramifications of this choice in many tribes, including the Maasai tribe, where a girl who is uncircumcised is unable to marry and will often be completely shunned from her community—barred from engaging in communal meals and even barred from collecting water at the same time as the other women. Sr. Ephigenia credits her success to the fact that she is not perceived as an outsider among her neighboring villages, and thus she has greater legitimacy and credibility than outsiders from Western countries would likely have. Stop FGM Kenya serves as an example of a grassroots organization that can benefit from collaboration with international NGOs, which often have access to greater funding sources, as well as research, and technology that can benefit local and indigenous efforts.

Learn more about the work of Sr. Ephigenia and her organization by conducting an Internet search for "Stop FGM Kenya."

Assess your comprehension of "International Social Work Practice in Action" by completing this quiz.

Summary

It is sometimes easy to see all of the problems in our world and respond with a feeling of futility. Yet what many social workers soon realize is that making the world a better place is possible, particularly for those with a passion for meeting the needs of the most vulnerable members of society in a way that reflects empathy, compassion, justice, and respect for human dignity. Also, while some people in the United States (or in the Global North) might challenge a social worker's desire to work in the field of international social work because there are so many people who need help in our own backyards, it is important to recognize that because of globalization, our impact on one another (despite geographic distance), and our global awareness, we have a practical obligation to extend our reach to help those who have the greatest need. And finally, it is important to recognize that policies and practices in the Global North have contributed to (if not caused) many of the problems experienced by the world's most vulnerable populations, particularly those in the Global South, which increases our ethical obligation to work for justice on behalf of everyone, despite their geographic location.

Recall what you learned in this chapter by completing the Chapter Review.

Epilogue: The Future of Social Work in an Ever-Changing World

The social work profession exists to assist people, particularly disenfranchised populations, meet their basic needs and function to their optimum level while expanding their support networks. Unlike many other helping disciplines, generalist social worker practice is less often focused on particular psychological disorders and more often focused on social problems, such as domestic violence, mental health and well-being, child welfare, and homelessness.

The passion to create meaningful change in the lives of others creates a drive in many social workers that may compensate for the relatively low pay and often less-than-ideal working conditions (although it would be incorrect to assume that just because one wants to enter the social work field, he or she cannot earn a decent living). Nonetheless, it is this drive and passion that pushes so many individuals forward in a career that does not always have particularly high status but affords the unique experience of making a significant difference in the lives of others by reminding people of their worth. Holding the hand of the dying, reminding a grieving child that there is still hope, or standing with victims of violence who are facing their attackers in court are all examples of ways that social workers make an impact on the lives of those in need. This is an empowering career, one that changes with every new client.

Social work is a unique career in that it can often lead to other opportunities including a career in academia, writing, public speaking, policy analysis, or international human rights work. Even a career track that leads to clinical private practice can remain exciting and varied if the social worker remains committed to social justice and advocacy on behalf of clients and their communities.

AVOIDING PROFESSIONAL BURNOUT

As wonderful as this career is, it is also wrought with stress, crises, and a significant potential to "burn out" quickly. There are many ways to avoid burnout, and several of these ways involve developing mental paradigms that help social workers avoid becoming over-involved in the lives of their clients. One paradigm that benefits many social workers is to recognize that their clients are on a journey—on *their own* journey—and the role of the social worker is to assist the client on a small portion of this journey. Many social workers experience professional burnout because they take too much responsibility for the lives of their clients. Understanding that clients are on their own journey and trusting that the social worker is one of many mentors, counselors, or guides who will come along in their clients' lives puts the clinician–client relationship into healthy perspective.

A common side effect of social work practice is vicarious trauma, where a social worker absorbs his or her client's trauma and in many respects is impacted in a similar way. Consider the earlier discussion about working with survivors of homicide. Imagine spending hours listening to clients share the gruesome details of how their loved one was murdered. To empathize effectively, a social worker in many senses "goes along on the ride" with clients, and when clients experience significant exhaustion social workers can experience it too. Mary Jo Barrett, social worker and author refers to this condition as "compassion fatigue," which she defines as "physical, emotional, spiritual and intellectual exhaustion brought on by being a caregiver." Barrett believes that the primary way that social workers can avoid and address vicarious trauma and compassion fatigue is by ensuring that they have balance in their lives within five realms: physical, emotional, spiritual, intellectual, and sexual. Barrett suggests achieving balance through not overworking and taking time to engage in self-care, such as eating well, exercising, and meditating.

SOCIAL WORK AND TECHNOLOGY

Technology has changed (and continues to change) the world, but social workers have been somewhat slow in making use of technological changes. The reasons for this may include the lack of security in email communication, which has an impact on confidentiality. Email communication between practitioners discussing clients, or email communication between practitioner and client, may expose a social service agency to legal liability if privacy cannot be guaranteed. Another reason for social service agencies' general reluctance to become more technologically based relates to the costs associated with purchasing and maintaining computer systems. Additionally, some social workers may believe that technology will replace the human-to-human contact that has served as the foundation of social work practice since its inception.

Despite these concerns, the Internet can be a wonderful resource for social workers, such as searching for appropriate referrals for clients. Most counties have websites that include comprehensive information about available services. Many social services organizations, government assistance programs, and various grant-giving agencies not only have invaluable information on their websites but also allow applicants to apply for services online, expediting the application process.

The Internet can be tremendously useful for social workers who want to coordinate services with other professionals or obtain information on a particular issue. Technology is also being used to facilitate various types of testing, including personality and career assessments, attention deficit/hyperactivity disorder (ADHD) evaluations, and adaptive functioning evaluations. Advocacy efforts have been made easier through the Internet. For instance, legislation can be researched online and a virtual letter-writing campaign can be conducted in minutes, potentially involving thousands of people.

Thus, despite concerns about privacy and confidentially, technology can serve both social workers and their clients. The Internet can be empowering for clients, enabling them to be more self-sufficient in finding resources, including housing, job opportunities, and child care. In addition, there are resources for homebound individuals who might not be able to benefit from an on-site support group but can garner some of the same benefits from online support groups or chat rooms.

Another important factor to consider is how technology is changing the lives of our clients. Use of social media has dramatically increased in the last five years, among all age groups. Social media sites such as Facebook and Twitter can alleviate feelings of isolation and loneliness, but it can also create fractures in relationships. Cyberbullying is a social problem impacting children and adults alike. In order for social workers to remain relevant and helpful to their clients, they must have an awareness of current trends and ways that technology impacts the lives of their clients.

THE EFFECT OF RECENT ECONOMIC CRISES AND CHANGES IN THE POLITICAL LANDSCAPE

The social work field is expected to continue to grow in the coming decades. There are various reasons for this, including the increasing complexity of society, which tend to create numerous challenges for families, particularly those who struggle with a range of vulnerabilities. As the challenges facing societies increase, social services agencies will continue to serve as valuable resources for individuals, families, and communities, providing services for a broad range of clients dealing with a broad range of social problems. Whether working in schools, hospitals, criminal justice agencies, mental health facilities, or the government, social workers serve those who often do not have the resources to meet their most basic needs or are experiencing some type of challenge or crisis that exceeds their ability to manage. Additionally, social workers engage on a macro level as well and thus serve communities in much the same way. Unfortunately, this increased need exists in the face of significant fiscal cuts on local and national levels, most of which affect the funding of social service programs. The long-term effect of recent economic crises on the social work field remains to be seen, but those in social work do have a lot to be optimistic about in light of the federal government's stated commitment to social justice in policies affecting the country's most vulnerable members.

GLOBALIZATION

Our world is shrinking because of a variety of domains becoming "globalized," which is having a dramatic impact on the world and how it functions. The globalization of market economies means that if one country sinks into a recession, it will likely take the rest of the world with it. If civil war rages in a far-off country, the ripple effect will be felt worldwide, whether through forced migration and refugee flow, or through the spreading of ideologically-based conflict, such as we have seen in recent global terror plots targeting Westerners, and their allies. The globalization of communication technologies means that we can switch on our televisions, or our laptops, and know instantly what is happening thousands of miles away. We can Skype friends and family across the globe, text for free using our smartphones attached to a wireless connection, and make connections with old friends from elementary school and new friends in foreign countries using social media sites such as Facebook, Tumblr, or Twitter. These are exciting times for communication, but such rapid technological developments create both positive and negative consequences. Migrants can remain connected to home on a daily basis (good), and wage "virtual war" against their homeland governments using the Internet (bad). Child pornography is rampant online (bad), but law enforcement can use virtual online stings to catch perpetrators and consumers (good). The social work profession has no doubt been affected by the globalization of communication technologies because our clients have, and, as previously mentioned, social workers must become proficient technologically to remain current and effective.

Those in the social work field are committed to addressing problems in society, often before those within society are prepared to admit that such problems even exist. Social workers are consistently on the frontlines of social problems, creating change in the lives of individuals and communities, and while the trajectory of the profession is difficult to determine, what is certain is that social work will become increasingly globalized. Society is constantly evolving, which creates the sometimes-negative by-products of conflict, complexity, and challenges for many. It is for this reason that social workers will always be needed to recognize and confront human problems, helping society's most vulnerable members meet their basic needs and function at the most optimal level possible so that they can be fully integrated into their respective societies and enjoy equal access to all that society has to offer.

References

Abdelkader, E. (2011, October 24). Islamophobic bullying in our schools. *Huffington Post: Religion*. Retrieved July 2, 2013, from http://www.huffingtonpost.com/engy-abdelkader/islamophobia-in-schools_b_1002293.html

Abrams, K., Theberge, S. K., & Karan, O. C. (2005). Children and adolescents who are depressed: An ecological approach. *Professional School Counseling, 8*(3), 284–292.

Acevedo, V. (2008). Cultural competence in a group intervention designed for Latinos living with HIV/AIDS. *Health & Social Work, 33*(2), 111–120.

Acheson, A. W., Thompson, A. C., Kristal, M. B., & Baizer, J. S. (2001). Methylphenidate induces c-fos expression in juvenile rats. *Society of Neuroscience Abstracts, 27*, 223–224.

Addams, J. (1912). *Twenty Years at Hull House; with autobiographical notes* [Kindle Edition]. New York: MacMillan.

Ahmadi, N. (2003). Globalisation of consciousness and new challenges for international social work. *International Journal of Social Welfare, 12*, 14–23.

Alderman, C. L. (1975). *Colonists for sale: The story of indentured servants in America*. New York: Macmillan.

Allen-Meares, P. (2006). One hundred years: A historical analysis of social work services in Schools [Special Issue]. *School Social Work Journal*, 24–43.

American Counseling Association. (2005). *ACA code of ethics*. Alexandria, VA.

American Psychiatric Association. (2000). *Diagnostic and statistical manual of mental disorders* (4th ed., text rev.). Washington, DC.

American Psychiatric Association. (2013). *Diagnostic and statistical manual of mental disorders* (5th ed.). Washington, DC.

American Psychological Association. (2002). *Ethical principles of psychologists and code of conduct*. Washington, DC.

American School Counselor Association. (2005). *The ASCA national model: A framework for School Counseling Programs* (2nded.). Alexandria, VA. Retrieved January 27, 2012, from http://www.schoolcounselor.org/files/appropriate.pdf

Andersen, S. L., Arvanitogiannis, A., Pliakas, A. M., LeBlanc, C., & Carlezon, W. A. (2002). Altered responsiveness to cocaine in rats exposed to methylphenidate during development. *Nature Neuroscience, 5*(1), 13–14.

Andrus, J. K., Fleming, D. W., Heumann, M. A., Wassell, J. T., Hopkins, D. D. Y., & Gordan, S. (1991). Surveillance of attempted suicide among adolescents in Oregon, 1988. *American Journal of Public Health, 81*, 1067–1069.

Arias, B. (2004). United States life tables, 2002. *National Vital Statistics Reports, 53*(6). Hyattsville, MD: National Center for Health Statistics.

Arias, E., Anderson, R. N., Kung, H. C., Murphy, S., & Kochanek, K. D. (2003). Deaths: Final data for 2001. *National Vital Statistics Reports, 52*(3). Hyattsville, MD: National Center for Health Statistics.

Associated Press. (2005). *Muslim groups help Katrina victims on 9/11 anniversary*. Retrieved December 31, 2009, from http://www.amvoice-two.amuslimvoice.org/html/body_katrina_relief.html

Atchley, R. C. (1976). *The sociology of retirement*. New York: John Wiley.

Auerswalk, C. L., & Eyre, S. L. (2002). Youth homelessness in San Francisco: A life cycle approach. *Social Science and Medicine, 54*, 1497–1512.

Auger, R. W. (2005). School-based interventions for students with depressive disorders. *Professional School Counseling, 8*(4), 344–352.

Auger, R. W., Seymour, J. W., Roberts, W. B., & Waiter, B. (2004). Responding to terror: The impact of September 11 on K–12 schools and schools' responses. *Professional School Counseling, 7*(4), 222–230.

Austin, M. J., D'Andrade, A., Lemon, K., Benton, A., Chow, B., & Reyes, C. (2005). *Risk and safety assessment in child welfare: Instrument comparisons*. University of California, Berkeley, School of Social Welfare (BASSC), Number 2, 1–16. Retrieved January 1, 2012, from http://cssr.berkeley.edu/bassc/public/risk_summ.pdf

Austin, S. (2005). Community-building principles: Implications for professional development. *Child Welfare, 84*(2), 105–122.

Axelson, L. H., & Dail, P. W. (1988). The changing character of homelessness in the U.S. *Family Relations, 37*(4), 463–469.

Axelsson, S. B., & Axelsson, R. (2009). From territoriality to altruism in interprofessional collaboration and leadership. *Journal of Interprofessional Care, 23*(4), 320–330. doi:10.1080/13561820902921811

Ayon, C., Marsiglia, F. F., & Bermudez-Parsai, M. (2010). Latino family mental health: Exploring the role of discrimination and familismo. *Journal of Community Psychology, 38*(6), 742–756.

Baggerly, J. N., & Borkowski, T. (2004). Applying the ASCA national model to elementary school students who are homeless: A case study. *Professional School Counseling, 8*(2), 116–124.

Baggerly, J. N., & Rank, M. G. (2005). Bioterrorism preparedness: What school counselors need to know. *Professional School Counseling, 8*(5), 458–465.

Bandelow, B., Krause, J., Wedekind, D., Broocks, A., Hajak, G., & Rüther, E. (2005). Early traumatic life events, parental attitudes, family history, and birth risk factors in patients with borderline personality disorder and healthy controls. *Psychiatry Research*, 134(2), 169–179.

Barth, R. P. (2001). Policy implications of foster family characteristics. *Family Relations*, 50(1), 16–19.

Basile, K. C., & Saltzman, L. E. (2002). *Sexual violence surveillance: Uniform definitions and recommended data elements* (Version 1.0). Atlanta, GA: Centers for Disease Control and Prevention, National Center for Injury Prevention and Control. Retrieved September 14, 2005, from http://www.cdc.gov/ncipc/pub-res/sv_surveillance/sv.htm

Bassuk, E. L., Buckner, J. C., Weinreb, L. F., Browne, A., Bassuk, S. S., Dawson, R., et al. (1997). Homelessness in female-headed families: Childhood and adult risk and protective factors. *American Journal of Public Health*, 87(2), 241–248.

Bearman, P. S., & Moody, J. (2004). Suicide and friends among American adolescents. *American Journal of Public Health*, 94(1), 89–95.

Beaucar, K. O. (2000). Licensing a mixed bag in '99. *NASW News*, 45(2), 9.

Beck, A. T. (1964). Thinking and depression: 2. Theory and therapy. *Archives of General Psychiatric*, 10, 561–571.

Beech, M., Meyers, L., & Beech, D. J. (2002). Hepatitis B and C infections among homeless adolescents. *Family Community Health*, 25(2), 28–36.

Beier, A. L. (1974). Vagrants and the social order in Elizabethan England. *The New England Quarterly*, 43(1), 59–78.

Belcher, J. R., & DeForge, B. R. (2012). Social stigma and homelessness: The limits of social change. *Journal of Human Behavior in the Social Environment*, 22(8), 929–946.

Belcher, J. R., Fandetti, D., & Cole, D. (2004). Is Christian religious conservatism compatible with the liberal social welfare state? *Social Work*, 49(2), 269–276.

Bell, H. (2008). Case management with displaced survivors of Hurricane Katrina: A case study of one Host Community Holly Bell. *Journal of social service research*, 34(3), 15–27.

Bellingham, B. (1984). *Little wanderers: A socio-historical study of the nineteenth century origins of child fostering and adoption reform, based on early records of the New York Children's Aid Society.* Unpublished doctoral dissertation, University of Pennsylvania. (Available from University Microfilm Incorporated (UMI), Ann Arbor, MI.)

Belzberg, E. (Director). (2001). *The forgotten children underground* [Docudrama]. Childhope International. Red Horse Productions, Cinemax, Reel Life.

Bender, T. (1975). *Toward an urban vision: Ideas and institutions in Nineteenth century America.* Baltimore, MD: The John Hopkins University Press.

Bennett, K. M. (1997). Widowhood in elderly women: The medium- and long-term effects on mental and physical health. *Mortality*, 2, 137–148.

Bentovim, A. (2002). Preventing sexually abused young people from becoming batterers, and treating the victimization experiences of young people who offend sexually. *Child Abuse & Neglect*, 26(6–7), 661–678.

Bentovim, A. (2004). Working with abusing families: General issues and a systemic perspective. *Journal of Family Psychotherapy*, 15(1–2), 119–135.

Bergeron, R. L., & Gray, B. (2003). Ethical dilemmas of reporting suspected elder abuse. *Social Work*, 48(1), 96–106.

Biegel, D. E., Johnsen, J. E., & Shafran, R. (1997). Overcoming barriers faced by African-American families with a family member with mental illness. *Family Relations*, 46(2), 163–178.

Biggs, M., Simpson, C. G., & Gaus, M. D. (2009). A case of bullying: Bringing together the disciplines. *Children & Schools*, 31(1), 39–42.

Birrer, R. B., & Vemuri, S. P. (2004). Depression in later life: A diagnostic and therapeutic challenge. *American Family Physician*, 69(10), 2375–2382.

Birtles, S. (1999). Common land, poor relief and enclosure. *Past & Present [Great Britain]*, 165, 74–106.

Black, M. C., Basile, K. C., Breiding, M. J., Smith, S. G., Walters, M. L., Merrick, M. T., et al. (2011). *The National Intimate Partner and Sexual Violence Survey (NISVS): 2010 Summary Report.* Atlanta, GA: National Center for Injury Prevention and Control, Centers for Disease Control and Prevention.

Blank, M. B., Mahmood, M., Fox, J. C., & Guterbock, T. (2002). Alternative mental health services: The role of the Black church in the South. *American Journal of Public Health*, 92(10), 1668–1672.

Bohner, G., Reinhard, M., Rutz, S., Sturm, S., Kerschbaum, B., & Effler, B. (1998). Rape myths as neutralizing cognitions: Evidence for a causal impact of anti-victim attitudes on men's self-reported likelihood of raping. *European Journal Social Psychology*, 28, 257–268.

Borkowski, J. W., & Sorensen, L. E. (2009). *Legal issues for school districts related to the education of undocumented students.* Alexandria, VA: National School Boards Association. Retrieved January 29, 2012 from http://www.nsba.org/SchoolLaw/COSA/Search/AllCOSAdocuments/Undocumented-Children.pdf

Bourg, W., Broderick, R., & Flagor, R. (1999). *A child interviewer's guidebook.* Thousand Oaks, CA: Sage Publications.

Bowen, M. (1978). *Family therapy in clinical practice.* New York: Jason Aronson.

Bowling, A., & Iliffe, S. (2011). Psychological approach to successful ageing predicts future quality of life in older adults. *Health & Quality of Life Outcomes*, 9(1), 13–22. doi:10.1186/1477-7525-9-13

Brace, C. L. (1967). *The dangerous classes of New York and twenty years work among them.* Montclair, NJ: Patterson Smith.

Brandon, C. L., & Steiner, H. (2003). Repeated methylphenidate treatment in adolescent rats alters gene regulation in the striatum. *European Journal of Neuroscience*, 18(6), 1584–1592.

Briggs, B. (2013). One every 18 hours: Military suicide rate still high despite hard fight to stem deaths. *NBC News.* Retrieved March 9, 2014, from http://usnews.nbcnews.com/_news/2013/05/23/18447439-one-every-18-hours-military-suicide-rate-still-high-despite-hard-fight-to-stem-deaths?lite

Britto, R. (2011). *Global battleground or school playground: The bullying of America's Muslim children* (Policy Brief #49).

Washington, DC: Institute for Social Policy and Understanding. Retrieved January 29, 2012, from http://ispu.org/pdfs/ISPU_Policy%20Brief_Britto_WEB.pdf

Bronfenbrenner, U. (1979). *The ecology of human development: Experiments by nature and design*. Cambridge, MA: Harvard University Press.

Broussard, C. A., Joseph, A. L., & Thompson, M. (2012). Stressors and coping strategies used by single mothers living in poverty. *Affilia, 27*(2), 190–204.

Brown, D. (2001). *Bury my heart at wounded knee: An Indian history of the American west*. New York: Henry Holt.

Brown, T. E., & Modestino, E. J. (2000). Attention-deficit disorders with sleep/arousal disturbances. In T. E. Brown (Ed.), *Attention-deficit disorders and comorbidities in children, adolescents, and adults* (pp. 341–362). Washington, DC: American Psychiatric Association.

Brownridge, D. (2009). *Violence against women: Vulnerable Populations*. New York: Routledge.

Burdette, A. M., Hill, T. D., & Moulton, D. E. (2005). Religion and attitudes toward physician-assisted suicide and terminal palliative care. *Journal for the Scientific Study of Religion, 44*(1), 79–93.

Burns, B. J., Phillips, S. D., Wagner, H. R., Barth, R. P., Kolko, D. J., Campbell, Y., et al. (2004). Mental health need and access to mental health services by youths involved with child welfare: A national survey. *Journal of the American Academy of Child & Adolescent Psychiatry, 43*(8), 960–970.

Burt, M. R. (1991). *Rape myths and acquaintance rape*. In A. Parrot & L. Bechhofer (Eds.), *Acquaintance rape: The hidden crime* (pp. 26–40). New York: Wiley.

Buss, D. E. (2009). Rethinking "Rape as a Weapon of War". *Feminist Legal Studies, 17*(2), 145–163.

Butler, R. N. (1969). Ageism: Another form of bigotry. *Gerontologist, 9*, 243–246.

Bye, L., Shepard, M., Partridge, J., & Alvarez, M. (2009, April). School social work outcomes: Perspectives of school social worker and school administrators. *Children & Schools, 31*(2), 97. Retrieved September 15, 2009, from MasterFILE Premier database.

Calkin, C. (2000, June). Welfare reform. *Peace and Social Justice: A Newsletter of the NASW Committee for Peace and Social Justice, 1*(1). Retrieved September 17, 2005, from http://www.naswdc.org/practice/peace/psj0101.pdf

CAPTA Reauthorization Act of 2010, Pub. L No. 111-320 (1974). Retrieved September 9, 2012, from http://www.govtrack.us/congress/bills/111/s3817/text

Catalano, S., Smith, E., Snyder, H., & Rand, M. (2009, September). *Female survivors of violence* (NCJ 228356). Bureau of Justice Statistics Selected Findings. Retrieved from http://www.ojp.usdoj.gov/bjs/pub/pdf/fvv.pdf

Catholic Charities USA. (2010). *Catholic Charities at a glance*. Retrieved from http://www.catholiccharitiesusa.org/document.doc?id=2853

Centers for Disease Control and Prevention (CDC). (1988). Quarterly report to the domestic policy council on the prevalence and rate of spread of HIV and AIDS—United States. *Morbidity and Mortality Weekly Report, 37*(36), 551–554.

Centers for Disease Control and Prevention (CDC). (2002, July). Infant mortality and low birth weight among black and white infants—United States, 1980–2000. *Morbidity and Mortality Weekly Report (MMWR), 51*, 589–592.

Centers for Disease Control and Prevention (CDC). (2003). *Costs of intimate partner violence against women in the United States*. Atlanta (GA): CDC, National Center for Injury Prevention and Control.

Centers for Disease Control and Prevention (CDC). (2005). *Sexual violence: Fact sheet*. Atlanta, GA: National Center for Injury Prevention and Control. Retrieved September 15, 2006, from http://www.cdc.gov/ncipc/factsheets/svfacts.htm

Centers for Disease Control and Prevention (CDC). (2011). *HIV surveillance report, 2011* (Vol. 22). Retrieved January 15, 2014, from http://www.cdc.gov/hiv/topics/surveillance/resources/reports/

Centers for Disease Control and Prevention (CDC). (2004). HIV Surveillance Report. *Table 5a. Estimated numbers of cases and rates (per 100,000 population) of AIDS, by race/ethnicity, age category, and sex, 2004—50 states and the District of Columbia*. Retrieved July 12, 2012, from http://www.cdc.gov/hiv/surveillance/resources/reports/2004report/pdf/table5.pdf

Child Welfare League of America. (2002). Minorities as majority: Disproportionality in child welfare and juvenile justice. *Children's Voice*. Retrieved March 4, 2005, from http://www.cwla.org/articles/cv0211minorities.htm

Child Welfare League of America. (2005). *A comparison of approaches to risk assessment in child protection and brief summary of issues identified from research on assessment in related fields*. Retrieved online January 1, 2012, http://www.childwelfare.gov/responding/iia/safety_risk/

Child Welfare League of America. (n.d.). *Family preservation and permanency planning: About this area of focus*. Retrieved March 2, 2004, from http://www.cwla.org/programs/familypractice/fampractabout.htm

Chi-Ying Chung, R. (2005). Women, human rights & counseling: Crossing international borders. *Journal of Counseling and Development, 83*, 262–268.

Christy, A., Poythress, N. G., Boothroyd, R. A., Petrila, J., & Mehra, S. (2005). Evaluating the efficiency and community safety goals of the Broward county mental health court. *Behavioral Sciences and the Law, 23*, 227–243.

Chunn, D. E., & Gavigan, S. A. M. (2004). Welfare saw, welfare fraud, and the moral regulation of the 'Never Deserving' poor. *Social & Legal Studies, 13*(2), 219–243.

Clarke, L., & Whittaker, M. (1998). Self-mutilation: Culture, contexts and nursing responses. *Journal of Clinical Nursing, 7*, 129–137.

Cloud, H. C., & Townsend, J. (1992). *Boundaries*. Grand Rapids, MI: Zondervan.

Cohen, M. H., Fabri, M., Cai, X., Shi, Q., Hoover, D. R., Binagwaho, A., et al. (2009). Prevalence and predictors of posttraumatic stress disorder and depression in HIV-infected and at-risk Rwandan women. *Journal of Women's Health (15409996), 18*(11), 1783–1791. doi:10.1089/jwh.2009.1367

Collier, P., & Hoeffler, A. (2000). Economic causes of civil conflict and their implications on policy. In C. Crocker,

F. Hampson, and P. Aall (Eds.), *Leashing the dogs of civil war: conflict management in a divided world* (pp. 197–218). Washington, DC: United States Institute of Peace.

Condran, G. A., & Cheney, R. A. (1982). Mortality trends in Philadelphia: Age and cause-specific death rates 1870–1930. *Demography, 19*(1), 97–123.

Conner, K., & Grote, N. (2008, October). Enhancing the cultural relevance of empirically-supported mental health interventions. *Families in Society, 89*(4), 587–595. Retrieved September 14, 2009, from Academic Search Premier database

Constable, R. (2009). The role of the school social worker. In C. Massat, R. Constable, S. McDonald, & J. P. Flynn (Eds.), *School social work: Practice, policy, and research* (7th ed., pp. 3–29). Chicago, IL: Lyceum Books.

Convention on the Rights of the Child, Resolution adopted by the U.N. General Assembly, 44th Session, November 20, A/RESZ (1989).

Conway, F., Jones, S., & Speakes-Lewis, A. (2011). Emotional strain in caregiving among African American grandmothers raising their grandchildren. *Journal of Women & Aging, 23*(2), 113–128. doi:10.1080/08952841.2011.561142

Conway, G. (1997). *Islamophobia: A challenge for us all.* London: Runnymede Trust.

Corcoran, J., Franklin, C., & Bennett, P. (2000). Ecological factors associated with adolescent pregnancy and parenting. *Social Work Research, 24*(1), 29–39.

Corning, P. A. (1969). *The evolution of Medicare: From idea to law* [Research Report No. 29, U.S. Social Security Administration, Office of Research and Statistics]. Washington, DC: Government Printing Office.

Coudin, G., & Alexopoulos, T. (2010). "Help me! I'm old!" How negative aging stereotypes create dependency among older adults. *Aging & Mental Health, 14*(5), 516–523. doi:10.1080/13607861003713182

Council of Islamic Organizations. (2005). *Charity without Fear.* Retrieved December 31, 2009, from http://www.ciogc.org/Go.aspx?link=7654625

The Council of State Governments. (2008). *Mental health courts: A primer for policymakers and practitioners.* Retrieved January 2, 2013, http://consensusproject.org/mhcp/mhc-primer.pdf

Courtois, C. (2004). Complex trauma, complex reactions: Assessment and treatment. *Psychotherapy: Theory, Research, Practice, Training, 41*(4), 412–445.

Coyhis, D., & Simonelli, R. (2005). Rebuilding Native American communities. *Child Welfare, 84*(2), 323–336.

Crowe, M., & Bunclark, J. (2000). Repeated self-injury and its management. *International Review of Psychiatry, 12*(1), 48–53.

Crutchfield, M. (2013). Phases of disaster recovery: Emergency response to the long term. United Methodist Church on Relief [UMCOR]. Retrieved from http://www.umcmission.org/Find-Resources/New-World-Outlook-Magazine/2013/March-April-2013/0430-Phases-of-Disaster-Recovery-Emergency-Response-for-the-Long-Term

Cummings, J. R., & Druss, B. G. (2011). Racial/ethnic differences in mental health service use among adolescents with major depression. *Journal of the American Academy of Child & Adolescent Psychiatry, 50*(2), 160–170.

Cunningham, M. (2009). *Preventing and ending homelessness: Next steps.* Washington, DC: Urban Institute.

Cunningham, P., Foster, S., & Henggeler, S. (2002, July). The elusive concept of cultural competence. *Children's Services: Social Policy, Research & Practice, 5*(3), 231–243. Retrieved September 14, 2009, from Academic Search Premier database

Dahir, C. A. (2001). The national standards for school counseling programs: Development and implementation. *Professional School Counseling, 4*(5), 320–327.

Darwin, C. (2009). *The origin of species: By means of natural selection, or the preservation of favoured races in the struggle for life.* Boston: Cambridge University Press. (Original work published 1859.)

Davey, T. L. (2004). A multiple-family group intervention for homeless families: The weekend retreat. *Health & Social Work, 29*(4), 326–329.

Davidson, J.W. (2008). *They say, Ida B. Wells and the reconstruction of race.* New York: Oxford University Press.

De Cordier, B. (2009). Faith-based aid, globalisation and the humanitarian frontline: An analysis of Western-based Muslim aid organisations. *Disasters, 33*(4), 608–628. doi:10.1111/j.1467-7717.2008.01090.x

Degges-White, S. (2005). Understanding gerotranscendence in older adults: A new perspective for counselors. *Adultspan: Theory Research & Practice, 4*(1), 36–48.

DelBello, M., Lopez-Larson, M. P., & Soutullo, C. A. (2001). Effects of race on psychiatric diagnosis of hospitalized adolescents: A retrospective chart review. *Journal of Child and Adolescent Psychopharmacology, 11*(1), 95–103.

Demos, J., & Demos, V. (1969). Adolescence in a historical perspective. *Journal of Marriage and the Family, 31*(4), 632–638.

Denby, R. W., & Curtis, C. M. (2003). Why special populations are not the target of family preservation services: A case for program reform. *Journal of Sociology & Social Welfare, 30*(2), 149–173.

DePanfilis, D., & Scannapieco, M. (1994). Assessing the safety of children at risk of maltreatment: Decision-making models. *Child Welfare, 73*(3), 229–246.

Department of Health and Human Services: Administration on Aging (2010). *Projected future grown of the older adult population.* Retrieved January 20, 2012, http://www.aoa.gov/AoARoot/Aging_Statistics/future_growth/future_growth.aspx#age

Des Forges, A. (1999). *Leave none to tell the story.* New York: Human Rights Watch. Retrieved from http://www.hrw.org/legacy/reports/1999/rwanda/rwanda0399.htm

de Toledo, S., & Brown, D. E. (1995). *Grandparents as parents: A survival guide for raising a second family.* New York: Guilford Press.

DeVoe, J., & Murphy, C. (2011). *Student reports of bullying and cyber-bullying: Results from the 2009 school crime supplement to the national crime victimization survey* [Web Tables. NCES 2011-336]. Washington, DC: National Center for Education Statistics.

Dewan, S., & Pugh, P. (2008). Resources scarce, homelessness persists in New Orleans. *New York Times.* Retrieved January 22, 2013, from http://www.nytimes.com/2008/05/28/us/28tent.html?pagewanted=all&_r=0

Dhlembeu, N., & Mayanga, N. (2006). Responding to orphans and other vulnerable children's crisis: Development of Zimbabwe's national plan of action. *Journal of Social Development in Africa, 21*(1), 5–49.

Diala, C. C., Muntaner, C., Walrath, C., Nickerson, K., LaVeist, T., & Leaf, P. (2001). Racial/ethnic differences in attitudes toward seeking professional mental health services. *American Journal of Public Health, 91*(5), 805–807.

Dingfelder, S. (2004). Treatment for the untreatable. *Monitor in Psychology, 35*(11), 48–49.

Ditton, P. M. (1999). *Mental health and treatment of inmates and probationers* (Special report NCJ 174463). Washington, DC: U.S. Department of Justice, Office of Justice Programs, Bureau of Justice Statistics.

Doogan, K. (2009). *New capitalism? The transformation of work.* Cambridge: Polity Press.

Dover, E. (2011, December 1). Gingrich says poor children have no work habits. *ABC News.* Retrieved December 23, 2011, from http://abcnews.go.com/blogs/politics/2011/12/gingrich-says-poor-children-have-no-work-ethic/

Dowsett, G. W. (2003). HIV/AIDS and homophobia: Subtle hatreds, severe consequences and the question of origins. *Culture, Health & Sexuality, 5*(2), 121–136.

Drake, R. E., Mueser, K. T., & Brunette, M. F. (2007). Management of persons with co-occurring severe mental illness and substance use disorder: program implications. *World Psychiatry, 6*(3), 131.

Duffy, M., Gillig, S. E., Tureen, R. M., & Ybarra, M. A. (2002). A critical look at the DSM-V. *The Journal of Individual Psychology, 58*(4), 362–373.

Duncan, C. M., & Moore, D. B. (2003). Catholic and Protestant social discourse and the American Welfare State. *Journal of Poverty, 7*(3), 57–83.

Ebaugh, H. R., Pipes, P. F., Chafetz, J. S., & Daniels, M. (2003). Where's the religion? Distinguishing faith-based from secular social service agencies. *Journal for the Scientific Study of Religion, 42*(3), 411–426.

Edwards, C. E., & Williams, C. L. (2000). Adopting change: Birth mothers in maternity homes today. *Gender and Society, 14*(1), 160–183.

Egley, A., & Howell, J. C. (2012). *Highlights of the 2010 National Youth Gang Survey.* Washington, DC: U.S. Department of Justice, Office of Juvenile Justice and Delinquency Prevention [OJJDP]. Retrieved from http://www.ojjdp.gov/pubs/237542.pdf

Ehrensaft, M. K., Cohen, P., & Brown, J. (2003). Intergenerational transmission of partner violence: A 20-year prospective study. *Journal of Consulting & Clinical Psychology, 71*(4), 741–753.

El-Bassel, N., Caldeira, N. A., Ruglass, L. M., & Gilbert, L. (2009). Addressing the unique needs of African American women in HIV prevention. *American Journal of Public Health, 99*(6), 996–1001.

Erikson, E. H. (1959). Identity and the life cycle. *Psychological Issues, 1*, 1–171.

Erikson, E. H. (1963). *Childhood and society* (2nd ed.). New York: W. W. Norton.

Erikson, E. H. (1966). Eight ages of man. *International Journal of Psychiatry, 2*, 281–300.

Erikson, E. H. (1968). *Identity: Youth and crisis.* London: Faber & Faber.

Erikson, E. H. (1975). *Life history and the historical moment.* New York: Norton.

Erikson, E. H., & Erikson, J. (1997). *The life cycle completed.* New York: W. W. Norton.

Escalas, J. E., & Stern, B. B. (2003). Sympathy and empathy: Emotional responses to advertising dramas. *Journal of Consumer Research, 29*, 566–578.

Fairburn, C. G. (2005). Evidence-based treatment of anorexia nervosa. *International Journal of Eating Disorders, 37*(Suppl.), S26–S30.

Fallot, R. D. (2001). Spirituality and religion in psychiatric rehabilitation and recovery from mental illness. *International Review of Psychiatry, 13*, 110–116.

Fallot, R. D., & Heckman, J. D. (2005). Religious/spiritual coping among women trauma survivors with mental health and substance use disorders. *Journal of Behavioral Health Services and Research, 32*(2), 215–226.

Favazza, A. R. (1996). *Bodies under siege: Self-mutilation and body modification in culture and psychiatry* (2nd ed.). Baltimore: Johns Hopkins University Press.

Feagin, J. R. (1975). *Subordinating the poor: Welfare and American beliefs.* Englewood Cliffs, NJ: Prentice Hall.

FEANTSA. (2007). *ETHOS—European typology on homelessness and housing exclusion.* Retrieved September 14, 2009, from http://www.feantsa.org/code/EN/pg.asp?Page=484

Federal Bureau of Investigation. (2011). *National crime victimization survey.* Washington, DC: U.S. Department of Justice, Office of Justice Programs, Bureau of Justice Statistics. Retrieved from http://bjs.ojp.usdoj.gov/content/pub/pdf/cv10.pdf

Federal Bureau of Investigation. (2012, September). *Crime in the United States 2011.* Washington, DC: U.S. Department of Justice. Retrieved from http://www.fbi.gov/about-us/cjis/ucr/crime-in-the-u.s/2011/crime-in-the-u.s.-2011/overviews/table-1-overview

Feisthamel, K. P., & Schwartz, R. C. (2009). Differences in mental health counselors' diagnoses based on client race: An investigation of adjustment, childhood, and substance-related disorders. *Journal of Mental Health Counseling, 31*(1), 47–59.

Feldman, S. (2003). Reflections on the 40th anniversary of the U.S. Community Mental Health Centers Act. *Australian and New Zealand Journal of Psychiatry, 3*, 662–667.

First Nations Orphan Association. (n.d.). Retrieved March 28, 2006, from http://www.angelfire.com/falcon/fnoa

Flango, V., & Flango, C. (1994). *The flow of adoption information from the States.* Williamsburg, VA: National Center for State Courts.

Florida Family Association. (2012). *Emails to all-American Muslim advertisers made a difference. 101 out 112 companies did not return to the show.* Retrieved January 29, 2012, from http://floridafamily.org/full_article.php?article_no=108

Flynn, B. W., & Norwood, A. E. (2004). Defining normal psychological reactions to disaster. *Psychiatric Annals, 34*(8), 597–603.

Folsom, D. P., Hawthorne, W., & Lindamer, L. (2005). Prevalence and risk factors for homelessness and utilization of mental health services among 10,340 patients with serious mental illness in a large public mental health system. *American Journal of Psychiatry, 162*(2), 370–376.

Fortier, J. P., & Shaw-Taylor, Y. (2000). *Assuring cultural competence in healthcare: Recommendations for national standards and an outcomes-focused research agenda.* Resources for Cross-Cultural HealthCare and the Center for the Advancement of Health. Rockville, MD: U.S. Department of Health and Human Services, Office of Minority Health.

Fostering Connections to Success and Increasing Adoptions Act of 2008, Pub. L. No. 110-351, 122 Stat. 3949 (2008).

Fothergill, K. E., Doherty, E. E., Robertson, J. A., & Ensminger, M. E. (2012). A prospective study of childhood and adolescent antecedents of homelessness among a community population of African Americans. *Journal of Urban Health, 89*(3), 432–446.

Franklin, A., Boyd-Franklin, N., & Kelly, S. (2006, June). Racism and invisibility: Race-related stress, emotional abuse and psychological trauma for people of color. *Journal of Emotional Abuse, 6*(2–3), 9–30. doi:10.1300/J135v06n02-02

Frasca, T. (2008). *Shaping the new response: HIV/AIDS and Latinos in the Deep South.* New York: Latino Commission on AIDS. Retrieved January 28, 2012, from http://img.thebody.com/press/2008/DeepSouthReportWeb.pdf

Freedman, S. (2011, December 16). Waging a one man war against Muslims. *New York Times.* Retrieved from http://www.nytimes.com/2011/12/17/us/on-religion-a-one-man-war-on-american-muslims.html?_r=0

Frick, P. (2004). Developmental pathways to conduct disorder: Implications for serving youth who show severe aggressive and antisocial behavior. *Psychology in the Schools, 41*(8), 823–834.

Frye, L. E. A. (2011). *Crazy, dirty, and lazy? Stigmatization of homeless mentally ill people by providers of homeless services.* Doctoral dissertation, Emory University, Atlanta, GA.

Fulero, S. M. (1988). Tarasoff: 10 years later. *Professional Psychology: Research and Practice, 19,* 184–190.

Fusick, L., & Charkow, B. (2004). Counseling at-risk Afro-American youth: An examination of contemporary issues and effective school-based strategies. *Professional School Counseling, 8*(2), 102–116.

Galambos, C. M. (2004). The changing face of AIDS. *Health & Social Work, 29*(2), 83–85.

Gallup, G., & Lindsey, D. M. (1999). *Surveying the religious landscape: Trends in U.S. beliefs.* Harrisburg, PA: Morehouse.

Gandara, P., Gutierrez, D., & O'Hara, S. (2001). Planning for the future in rural and urban high schools. *Journal of Education for Students Placed at Risk, 6*(1–2), 73–93. (ERIC Document Reproduction Service No. UD522844)

Garcia, J. G., Cartwright, B., Winston, S. M., & Borzuchowska, B. (2003). A transcultural integrative model for ethical decision making in counseling. *Journal of Counseling & Development, 81*(3), 268–277.

Gardener, J. W. (1994). *Building community for leadership training programs.* Washington, DC: Independent Sector.

Gardner, A., & Thompson, K. (2010). Tea Party group battles perceptions of racism. *Washington Post-ABC News Poll.* Retrieved June 12, 2012, from http://www.washingtonpost.com/wp-dyn/content/article/2010/05/04/AR2010050405168.html?hpid=moreheadlines

Garrett, K. (2006, April). Making the case for school social work. *Children & Schools, 28*(2), 115. Retrieved September 15, 2009, from MasterFILE Premier database

Garvey, M. (2005, September). Preggo high school; kids are readin', writin' & reproducin'. *New York Post,* p. 19.

Gauthier, Y., Fortin, G., & Jéliu, G. (2004). Clinical application of attachment theory in permanency planning for children in foster care: The importance of continuity of care. *Infant Mental Health Journal, 25*(4), 379–396.

Geithner, T. F. (2009). *Regulatory perspectives on the Obama administration's financial regulatory reform proposals-part two.* House Financial Services Committee. Retrieved November 18, 2009, from http://www.house.gov/apps/list/hearing/financialsvcs_dem/geithner_-_treasury.pdf

Gettleman, J. (2010, January 4). *Americans' role seen in Uganda anti-gay push.New York Times.* Retrieved January 11, 2010, from http://www.nytimes.com/2010/01/04/world/africa/04uganda.html

Gettleman, M. E. (1963). Charity and social classes in the United States, 1874–1900. *American Journal of Economics & Sociology, 22*(2), 313–329.

Gibbs, J. (2003). *Moral development and reality: Beyond the theories of Kohlberg and Hoffman.* London: Sage Publications Ltd.

GLAAD. (2010). GLAAD's media reference guide—In focus: Marriage. Retrieved November 12, 2011, from http://www.glaad.org/reference/marriage.

Goldmann, E., Aiello, A., Uddin, M., Delva, J., Koenen, K., Gant, L. M., & Galea, S. (2011). Pervasive exposure to violence and posttraumatic stress disorder in a predominantly African American Urban Community: the Detroit Neighborhood Health Study. *Journal of Traumatic Stress, 24*(6), 747–751.

Goldman, J., & Salus, M. (2003). *A coordinated response to child abuse and neglect: The foundation for practice.* Washington, DC: U.S. Department of Health and Human Services, National Center on Child Abuse and Neglect.

Gonyea, J. G., Mills-Dick, K., & Bachman, S. S. (2010). The complexities of elder homelessness, a shifting political landscape and emerging community responses. *Journal of Gerontological Social Work, 53*(7), 575–590. doi:10.1080/01634372.2010.510169

Gordon, K. C., Burton, S., & Porter, L. (2004). Predicting the intentions of women in IVP shelters to return to partners: Does forgiveness play a role? *Journal of Family Psychology, 18*(2), 331–338.

Gordon, L. (1991). Black and white visions of welfare: Women's welfare activism, 1890–1945. *Journal of American History, 78*(2), 559–590.

Gorwood, P. (2004). Generalized anxiety disorder and major depressive disorder comorbidity: An example of genetic pleiotrophy? *European Psychiatry, 19*(1), 27–33.

Gottlieb, M. S., Schroff, R., Schanker, H. M., Weisman, J. D., Fan, P. T., Wolf, R. A., et al. (1981). *Pneumocystis carnii* pneumonia and mucosal candidiasis in previously homosexual men: Evidence of a new acquired cellular immunodeficiency. *New England Journal of Medicine, 305*(24), 1425–1431.

Gowers, S., & Bryant-Waugh, R. (2004). Management of child and adolescent eating disorders: The current evidence base and future directions. *Journal of Child Psychology & Psychiatry, 45*(1), 63–83.

Graziano, K. J. (2004). Oppression and resiliency in a post-apartheid South Africa: Unheard voices of black gay men and lesbians. *Cultural Diversity and Ethnic Minority Psychology, 10*(3), 302–316.

Green, A. G., Conley, J. A., & Barnett, K. (2005). Urban school counseling: Implications for practice and training. *Professional School Counseling, 8*(3), 189–195.

Green, H. D., Jr., Tucker, J. S., Wenzel, S. L., Golinelli, D., Kennedy, D. P., Ryan, G. W., et al. (2012). Association of childhood abuse with homeless women's social networks. *Child Abuse & Neglect, 36*(1), 21–31.

Green, J. C., Rozell, M. J., & Wilcox, C. (2003). *The Christian right in American politics: Marching to the millennium*. Washington, DC: Georgetown University Press.

Greenberg, L. S., Elliot, R., Watson, J. C., & Bohart, A. C. (2001). Empathy. *Psychotherapy: Theory, Research, Practice, Training, 38*(4), 380–384.

Greene, J. P., & Forster, G. (2004). *Sex, drugs, and delinquency in urban and suburban public schools* (Education Working Paper 4). New York: Center for Civic Innovation, Manhattan Institute. (ERIC Document Reproduction Service No. ED483335)

Greiner, K. A., Perera, S., & Ahluwalia, J. S. (2003). Hospice usage by minorities in the last year of life: Results from the National Mortality Follow Back Survey. *Journal of the American Geriatrics Society, 51*, 970–978.

Grossman, C. L. (2002, March 7). Charting the unchurched in America. *USA Today*, p. D01.

Guardiola, A., Fuchs, F. D., & Rotta, N. T. (2000). Prevalence of attention-deficit hyperactivity disorders in students: Comparison between *Diagnostic and Statistical Manual of Mental Disorders-IV* (*DSM-IV-TR*) and neuropsychological criteria. *Arquivos de Neuro-Psiquiatria, 58*(2b), 401–407.

Guerino, P., Harrison, P. M., & Sabol, W. (2011). *Prisoners in 2010* (Revised). Washington, DC: Bureau of Justice Statistics. Retrieved from http://bjs.ojp.usdoj.gov/content/pub/pdf/p10.pdf

Gumpert, J., & Saltman, J. E. (1998). Social group work practice in rural areas: The practitioners speak. *Social Work with Groups, 21*(3), 19–34.

Guth, J., & Green, J. C. (1986). Faith and politics: Religion and ideology among political contributors. *American Politics Quarterly, 14*(3), 186–199.

H.R. 8—112th Congress: American Taxpayer Relief Act of 2012. (2012). *www.GovTrack.us*. Retrieved February 9, 2013, from http://www.govtrack.us/congress/bills/112/hr8

Hacker, J. S. (2002). *The divided welfare state: the battle over public and private social benefits in the United States*. New York: Cambridge University Press.

Hall, C. R., Dixon, W. A., & Mauzey, E. D. (2004). Spirituality and religion: Implications for counseling. *Journal of Counseling & Development, 82*, 504–507.

Hausman, D. M., & McPherson, M. S. (2006). *Economic analysis, moral philosophy, and public policy*. New York: Cambridge University Press.

Havighurst, R. J. (1961). Successful aging. *Gerontologist, 1*(1), 8–13.

Hawkins, J. D., Smith, B. H., Hill, K. G., Kosterman, R., Catalano, R. F., & Abbott, R. D. (2003). Understanding and preventing crime and violence: Findings from the Seattle Social Development Project. In T. P. Thornberry & M. D. Krohn (Eds.), *Taking stock of delinquency: An overview of findings from contemporary longitudinal studies* (pp. 255–312). New York: Plenum.

Hazell, P., & Lewin, T. (1999). Friends of adolescent suicide attempters and completers. *Journal of American Academy of Child & Adolescent Psychiatry, 32*(11), 76–81.

Hecht, L., & Coyle, B. (2001). Elderly homeless: A comparison of older and younger adult emergency shelter seekers in Bakersfield, California. *American Behavioral Scientist, 45*(1), 66–79.

Henry, M., Cartes, A., Morris, S., & Abt Associates. (2013). *The 2013 Annual Homeless Assessment Report (AHAR) to Congress*. The U.S. Department of Housing and Urban Development. Retrieved from https://www.onecpd.info/resources/documents/AHAR-2013-Part1.pdf

Hewitt, S. K. (1999). *Assessing allegations of sexual abuse in preschool children: Understanding small voices*. Thousand Oaks, CA: Sage Publications.

Hicks, K., & Hinck, S. M. (2009). Best-practice intervention for care of clients who self-mutilate. *Journal of the American Academy of Nurse Practitioners, 21*(8), 430–436. doi:10.1111/j.1745-7599.2009.00426.x

Hirshbein, L. D. (2001). Popular views of old age in America, 1900–1950. *Journal of American Geriatrics Society, 49*, 1555–1560.

Hodge, D. R. (2004). Working with Hindu clients in a spiritually sensitive manner. *Social Work, 29*(1), 27–38.

Hodge, D. R. (2005). Social work in the house of Islam: Orienting practitioners to the beliefs and values of Muslims in the U.S. *Social Work, 50*(2), 162–173.

Hofstadter, R. (1992). *Social Darwinism in American thought*. Boston: Beacon Press.

Holcomb-McCoy, C. C. (2004). Assessing the multicultural competence of school counselors: A checklist. *Professional School Counseling, 7*(3), 178–186.

Holcomb-McCoy, C. C. (2005). Investigating school counselors' perceived multicultural competence. *Professional School Counseling, 8*(5), 414–423.

Hollenbach, D. (2008). *Refugee rights: Ethics, advocacy and Africa*. Washington, DC: Georgetown University Press.

Holmstrom, L. L., & Burgess, A. W. (1975). Assessing trauma in the rape victim. *American Journal of Nursing, 75*(8), 1288–1291.

Holt, M. (1992). *The Orphan Trains: Placing out in America*. Lincoln: University of Nebraska Press.

Horejsi, C., Craig, B. H., & Pablo, J. (1992). Reactions by Native American parents to child protection agencies: Cultural and community factors. *Child Welfare, 71*(4), 329–343.

Horne, C. (2003). Families of homicide survivors: Service utilization patterns of extra- and intrafamilial homicide survivors. *Journal of Family Violence, 18*(2), 75–81.

Howell, J. C., & Egley, A. (2005). *Gangs in small towns and rural counties* (NYGC Bulletin, 1). Office of Juvenile Justice and Delinquency Prevention [OJJPD]. Retrieved from http://www.nationalgangcenter.gov/Content/Documents/Gangs-in-Small-Towns-and-Rural-Counties.pdf

Hsu, H. (2007, November). Does social participation by the elderly reduce mortality and cognitive impairment? *Aging & Mental Health, 11*(6), 699–707. Retrieved September 14, 2009, from doi:10.1080/13607860701366335

Hudson, K., & Coukos, A. (2005, March). The dark side of the Protestant Ethic: A comparative analysis of welfare reform. *Sociological Theory, 23*(1), 1–24.

Huebner, D. M., Rebchook, M., & Kegeles, S. M. (2004). Experiences of harassment, discrimination, and physical violence among young gay and bisexual men human rights watch. *American Journal of Public Health, 94*(7), 1200–1203.

Human Rights Campaign. (2009). *President Obama signs hate crimes legislation into law.* Retrieved January 11, 2010, from http://www.hrc.org/13699.htm

Human Rights Watch. (1996). *Shattered lives: Sexual violence during the Rwandan genocide and its aftermath.* New York.

Human Rights Watch. (2000a). *Key recommendations from punishment and prejudice: Racial disparities in the war on drugs.* Retrieved November 4, 2005, from http://www.hrw.org/campaigns/drugs/war/key-reco.htm

Human Rights Watch. (2000b). *Punishment and prejudice: Racial disparities in the war on drugs, 12*(2). Retrieved November 4, 2005, from http://hrw.org/reports/2000/usa/index.htm#TopOfPage

Human Rights Watch. (2001). *No escape: Male rape in U.S. prisons.* Retrieved September 27, 2005, from http://www.hrw.org/reports/2001/prison/report.html

Human Rights Watch. (2002). *Burmese women and girls trafficked to Thailand.* The Human Rights Watch Report on Women's Human Rights. Retrieved September 30, 2005, from http://www.hrw.org/about/projects/womrep/General-123.htm#P1937_535306

Human Rights Watch. (2004). *All Jamaicans are threatened by a culture of homophobia.* Retrieved September 30, 2005, from http://hrw.org/english/docs/2004/11/23/jamaic9716.htm

Human Rights Watch. (2005). *Saudi Arabia: Men "behaving like women" face flogging: Sentences imposed for alleged homosexual conduct violate basic rights.* Retrieved September 30, 2005, from http://hrw.org/english/docs/2005/04/07/saudia10434.htm

Human Rights Watch. (2006). *U.S.: Number of mentally ill in prisons quadrupled: Prisoners ill equipped to cope.* Retrieved from http://www.hrw.org/news/2006/09/05/us-number-mentally-ill-prisons-quadrupled

Human Rights Watch. (2008). *Guatemala: World Report 2009.* Retrieved January 10, 2009, from http://www.hrw.org/en/node/79213

Human Rights Watch. (2009). *Uganda: "anti-homosexuality" bill threatens liberties and human rights defenders proposed provisions illegal, ominous, and unnecessary.* Retrieved January 10, 2009, from http://www.hrw.org/en/news/2009/10/15/uganda-anti-homosexuality-bill-threatens-liberties-and-human-rights-defenders

Iatridis, D. (1995). Policy practice. In R. L. Edwards (Ed.), *Encyclopedia of social work* (19th ed., pp. 1855–1866). Washington, DC: NASW Press.

Idler, E. L., & Kasl, S. (1992). Religion, disability, depression and the timing of death. *American Journal of Sociology, 97*, 1052–1079.

International Council on Social Welfare. (n.d.). *What is our mission?* Retrieved from http://www.icsw.org/intro/missione.htm

Isadora, H. (2004), Defining Social Work for the 21st Century: The International Federation of Social Workers' Revised Definition of Social Work. *International Social Work; 47*; 407.

Jackson, R. L., Purnell, D., Anderson, S. B., & Sheafor, B. W. (1996). The clubhouse model of community support for adults with mental illness: An emerging opportunity for social work education. *Journal of Social Work Education, 32*(2), 172–180.

Jacob, B. A. (2007). The challenges of staffing urban schools with effective teachers. *The Future of Children, 17*(1), 129–153.

Jayasuriya, S., & McCawley, P. (2010). *The Asian tsunami: Aid and reconstruction after a disaster.* Northampton, MA: Edward Elgare Publishers.

Jennings, S. (2011). Time's Bitter Flood: Trends in the number of reported natural disasters. *Oxfam Policy and Practice: Climate Change and Resilience, 7*(1), 115–147.

Johnson, A. (2004). Social work is standing on the legacy of Jane Addams: But are we sitting on the sidelines? *Social Work, 49*(2), 319–322.

Johnson, G. (2013). Soldier to admit Afghan massacre. *Associated Press.* Retrieved March 9, 2014, from http://www.military.com/daily-news/2013/05/30/soldier-to-admit-afghan-massacre.html

Johnson-Reid, M. M. (2011). Looking toward the future. *Children & Schools, 33*(1), 1–4.

Joint United Nations Programme on HIV/AIDS. (2004). *Report on the global AIDS epidemic.* Geneva: UNAIDS.

Joint United Nations Programme on HIV/AIDS, & World Health Organization. (2009). *AIDS epidemic update, December 2006.* Geneva: UNAIDS.

Kaplan, L. E., Tomaszewski, E. S., & Gorin, S. (2004). Current trends and the future of HIV/AIDS services: A social work perspectives. *Health & Social Work, 29*(2), 153–159.

Karraker, M. W. (2004). Adolescent pregnancy: Policy and prevention services. *Family Relations: Interdisciplinary Journal of Applied Family Studies, 53*(1), 115.

Katz, M. B. (1996). *In the shadow of the poorhouse: A social history of welfare in America.* New York: Basic Books.

Kelly, B., Burnett, P., Pelusi, D., Badger, S., Varghese, F., & Robertson, M. (2002). Terminally ill cancer patients' wish to hasten death. *Palliative Medicine, 16*, 335–339.

Kerpelman, J. L., & Pittman, J. F. (2001). The instability of possible selves: Identity processes within late adolescents' close peer relationships. *Journal of Adolescence, 24*(4), 491–512.

Kessler, R. C. (2003). Epidemiology of women and depression. *Journal of Affective Disorders, 74*(1), 5–13.

Kessler, R. C., Heeringa, S. G., & Stein, M. B. (2014). Army STARRS Collaborators. Thirty-day prevalence of DSM-IV mental disorders among nondeployed soldiers in the US Army: Results from the Army Study to Assess Risk and Resilience in Service members (Army STARRS). *JAMA Psychiatry, 71*(5), 504–513.

Kidd, S. A. (2003). Street youth: Coping and interventions. *Child and Adolescent Social Work Journal, 20*(4), 235–261.

Kim, A. J. (2012). *Interdisciplinary collaboration in school social work: building relationships for ecological change.* Doctoral dissertation.

Kim, H. C. (1977). The relationship of Protestant Ethic beliefs and values to achievement. *Journal for the Scientific Study of Religion, 16*(3), 252–262.

Kingsley, G. T., Smith, R., & Price, D. (2009, May). *The impacts of foreclosures on families and communities: A report prepared for the Open Society Institute.* Washington, DC: The Urban Institute. Retrieved August 4, 2009, from http://www.urban.org/UploadedPDF/411909_impact_of_forclosures.pdf

Kirby, D. (2002). Effective approaches to reducing adolescent unprotected sex, pregnancy and childbearing. *Journal of Sex Research, 39*(1), 51–57.

Kitchener, K. S. (1984). Intuition, critical evaluation, and ethical principles: The foundation for ethical decisions in counseling psychology. *The Counseling Psychologist, 12*, 43–55.

Kliewer, S. (2004). Allowing spirituality into the healing process. *Journal of Family Practice, 53*(8), 616–624.

Kluegal, J. R. (1987). Macro-economic problems, beliefs about the poor and attitudes toward welfare spending. *Social Problems, 34*(1), 82–99.

Knežević, M., & Butler, L. (2003). Public perceptions of social workers and social work in the Republic of Croatia. *International Journal of Social Welfare, 12*, 50–60.

Knuckey, J. (2005). A new front in the culture war? Moral traditionalism and voting behavior in U.S. House elections. *American Politics Research, 33*, 645–671.

Knudsen, S. (2005, October 26–29). *Intersectionality: A theoretical inspiration in the analysis of minority cultures and identities in textbooks.* Presented at the Eighth International Conference on Learning and Educational Media "Caught in the Web or Lost in the Textbook?" *IUFM DE CAEN (France).* Retrieved March 25, 2008, from http://www.caen.iufm.fr/colloque_iartem/pdf/knudsen.pdf

Koenig, H. G., George, L. K., Hays, J. C., Larson, D. B., Cohen, H. J., & Blazer, D. G. (1998). The relationships between religious activities and blood pressure in older adults. *International Journal of Psychiatry Medicine, 28*, 189–213.

Koenig, H. G., George, L. K., & Titus, P. (2004). Religion, spirituality, and health in medically ill hospitalized elderly patients. *Journal of American Geriatrics Society, 52*(4), 554–562.

Koenig, H. G., Larson, D. B., & Weaver, A. J. (1998). Research on religion and serious mental illness. *New Directions in Mental Health Surveys, 80*, 81–95.

Koerber, G. (2005). *Veterans: One-third of all homeless people.* National Alliance on Mental Illness, Issue Spotlight. Retrieved June 1, 2005, from http://www.nami.org/Template.cfm?Section=Issue_Spotlights&template=/ContentManagement/ContentDisplay.cfm&ContentID=26958

Kopel, S., Charlton, T., & Well, S. J. (2003). Investigation laws and practices in child protective services. *Child Welfare, 82*(6), 661–684.

Kos, J. M., Richdale, A. L., & Jackson, M. S. (2004). Knowledge about attention-deficit/hyperactivity disorder: A comparison of in-service and preservice teachers. *Psychology in the Schools, 41*(5), 517–526.

Kosciw, J. G., Greytak, E. A., Diaz, E. M., and Bartkiewicz, M. J. (2010). *The 2009 national school climate survey: The experiences of lesbian, gay, bisexual, and transgender youth in our nation's schools.* New York: GLSEN.

Kraaij, V., & de Wilde, J. (2001). Negative life events and depressive symptoms in the elderly life: A life span perspective. *Aging & Mental Health, 5*(1), 84–91.

Kramer, B. J., Hovland-Scafe, C., & Pacourek, L. (2003). Analysis of end-of-life content in social work textbooks. *Journal of Social Work Education, 39*(2), 299–320.

Kreisher, K. (2002, March). Coming home: The lingering effects of the Indian adoption project. *Children's Voice.* Child Welfare League of America. Retrieved July 10, 2004, from http://www.cwla.org/articles/cv0203indianadopt.htm

Kress, V. E., Hoffman, R. M., & Eriksen, K. (2010). Ethical dimensions of diagnosing: Considerations for clinical mental health counselors. *Counseling & Values, 55*(1), 101–112.

Krout, J. A. (2003). *Residential choices and experiences of older adults: Pathways for life quality.* New York: Spring.

Krugman, P. (2007). *Conscience of a Liberal.* New York: W.W. Norton.

Kübler-Ross, E. (1969). *Living with death and dying.* New York: Macmillan.

Kusmer, K. (1973). The functions of organized charities in the progressive era: Chicago as a case study. *Journal of American History, 60*(3), 657–678.

Kutza, E. A., & Keigher, S. M. (1991). The elderly "new homeless": An emergency population at risk. *Social Work, 36*(4), 283–293.

Lahey, B. B., Moffitt, T. E., & Caspi, A. (Eds.). (2003). *Causes of conduct disorder and juvenile delinquency.* New York: Guilford Press.

Lambie, G. W. (2005). Child abuse and neglect: A practical guide for professional school counselors. *Professional School Counseling, 8*(3), 249–258.

Lambie, G. W., & Rokutani, L. J. (2002). A systems approach to substance abuse identification and intervention for school counselors. *Professional School Counseling, 5*(5), 353–359.

Lambie, G. W., & Sias, S. (2005). Children of alcoholics: Implications for professional school counseling. *Professional School Counseling, 8*(3), 266–273.

Lambie, G. W., & Williamson, L. L. (2004). The challenge to change from guidance counseling to professional school counseling: A historical proposition. *Professional School Counseling, 8*(2), 124–131.

Larsen, M. (2003). *Violence in U.S. public schools: A summary of findings.* New York: ERIC Digest. (ERIC Document Reproduction Service No. ED482921)

Laska, S., & Morrow, B. H. (2006). Social vulnerabilities and Hurricane Katrina: An unnatural disaster in New Orleans. *Marine Technology Society Journal, 40*(4), 16–26.

Lau, A. S., Litrownik, A. J., Newton, R. R., & Landsverk, J. (2003). Going home: The complex effects of reunification on internalizing problems among children in foster care. *Journal of Abnormal Child Psychology, 31*(4), 345–358.

Lee, C. C. (2005). Urban school counseling: Context, characteristics, and competencies. *Professional School Counseling, 8*(3), 184–188.

Lee, R. E., & Whiting, J. B. (2007). Foster children's expressions of ambiguous loss. *American Journal of Family Therapy, 35*, 417–428.

Legal Momentum. (2010). *Single mothers since 2000: Falling farther down.* Retrieved from http://www.legalmomentum.org/our-work/women-and-poverty/resources—publications/singlemothers-since-2000.pdf

Leman, R. (2005). *Seventh annual report on Oregon's death with dignity act*. State of Oregon, Department of Human Services, Office of Disease Prevention and Epidemiology. Retrieved March 2, 2004, from http://oregon.gov/DHS/ph/pas/docs/year7.pdf

Levine, K. A. (2009). Against all odds: resilience in single mothers of children with disabilities. *Social Work Health Care, 48*(4) 402–419.

Levinson, D. (1978). *The seasons of a man's life*. New York: Knopf.

Levinson, D. (1996). *The seasons of a woman's life*. New York: Knopf.

Lewis, M. R. (1998). The many faces of school social work practice: Results from a research partnership. *Social Work in Education, 20*(3), 177–190.

Lewis-Burke Associates. (2011). *CSWE Patient Protection and Affordable Care Act of 2010: A resource guide for social workers*. Retrieved from http://www.cswe.org/File.aspx?id=48334

Lind, R. A., & Danowski, J. A. (1999). The representation of the homeless in U.S. electronic media: A computational linguistic analysis. In E. Min (Ed.), *Reading the homeless: The media's image of homeless culture* (pp. 109–120). Westport, CT: Praeger.

Lindsey, E. W. (1998). The impact of homelessness on family relationships. *Family Relations, 47*(3), 243–252.

Lindsey, E. W., Kurtz, D. P., Jarvis, S., Williams, N. R., & Nackerud, L. (2000). How runaway and homeless youth navigate troubled waters: Personal strengths and resources. *Child and Adolescent Social Work Journal, 17*(2), 115–140.

Linn, G. L., & Mayer-Oakes, S. A. (1990). Differences in health status between older and younger homeless adults. *Journal of American Geriatric Society, 38*(11), 1220–1229.

Lock, J., & le Grange, D. (2005). Family-based treatment of eating disorders. *International Journal of Eating Disorders, 37*(Suppl.), S64–S67.

Loescher, L., Milner, J., & Troeller, G. (2008). *Protracted refugee situations: Political, human rights and security implications*. New York: United Nations University Press.

Lorenz, K. A., Asch, S. M., Rosenfeld, K. E., Lui, H., & Ettner, S. L. (2004). Hospice admission practices: Where does hospice fit in the continuum of care? *Journal of Geriatrics Society, 52*, 725–730.

Lowe, J., Pomerantz, A. M., & Pettibone, J. C. (2007). The influence of payment method on psychologists' diagnostic decisions: Expanding the range of presenting problems. *Ethics & Behavior, 17*, 83–95. doi:10.1080/10508420701310141

Lum, Y. (2004). Health-wealth association among older Americans: Racial and ethnic differences. *Social Work Research, 28*(2), 106–116.

Lundblad, K. (1995, September). Jane Addams and social reform: A role model for the 1990s. *Social Work, 40*(5), 661–669.

Lynch, T. R., Compton, J. S., Mendelson, T., Robins, C. J., & Krishnan, K. R. R. (2000). Anxious depression among the elderly: Clinical and phenomenological correlates. *Aging and Mental Health, 4*(3), 268–274.

Lyons, T. (2007). Conflict-generated diasporas and transnational politics in Ethiopia. *Conflict, Security, and Development, 7*(4), 529–549.

MacDonald, D. (1991). Hospice social work: A search for identity. *Health & Social Work, 16*(4), 274–280.

Marley, J. A., & Buila, S. (2001). Crimes against people with mental illness: Types, perpetrators, and influencing factors. *Social Work, 46*(2), 115–124.

Marr, C. (2002). *Assimilation through education: Indian boarding schools in the Pacific Northwest*. Seattle, WA: University of Washington Libraries Digital Collections. Retrieved February 22, 2002, from http://content.lib.washington.edu/aipnw/marr/marr.html

Martin, M. (2012, January). Philosophical and religious influences on social welfare policy in the United States: The ongoing effect of Reformed theology and social Darwinism on attitudes toward the poor and social welfare policy and practice. *Journal of Social Work, 12*(1), 51–64. doi:10.1177/1468017310380088

Martin, M.E. (2014). *Advocacy for social justice: A global perspective*. Upper Saddle, NJ: Pearson Publishing.

Maslow, A. (1954). *Motivation and personality*. New York: Harper.

Mason, K. L. (2008). Cyberbullying: A preliminary assessment for school personnel. *Psychology in the schools, 45*(4), 323–348.

McCullagh, J. G. (1993). The roots of school social work in New York City. *Iowa Journal of School Social Work, 6*, 49–74.

McCullagh, J. G. (1998). Early school social work leaders: Women forgotten by the profession. *Social Work in Education, 20*(1), 55–64.

McCullagh, J. G. (2001). NASW and school social work: Selected events, developments and publications, 1947–2001. *Journal of School Social Work, 12*(1–2), 5–35. (ERIC Document Reproduction Service No. ED467859)

McIntosh, J. L. (2004). *U.S.A. suicide: 2004 official final data*. Retrieved December 21, 2009, from http://www.ct.gov/dmhas/lib/dmhas/prevention/cyspi/AAS2004data.pdf

McKinney Homeless Assistance Act, Pub. L No. 100-77, § 103(2)(1), 101 Stat. 485 (1987).

McLaughlin, D. (2004). Incorporating individual spiritual beliefs in treatment of in-patient mental health consumers. *Perspectives in Psychiatric Care, 40*(3), 114–119.

McNamara, T. K., & Williamson, J. B. (2004). Race, gender, and the retirement decisions of people ages 60 to 80: Prospects for age integration in employment. *International Journal of Aging and Human Development, 59*(3), 255–286.

McWey, L., & Mullis, A. K. (2004). Improving the lives of children in foster care: The impact of supervised visitation. *Family Relations: Interdisciplinary Journal of Applied Family Studies, 53*(3), 293–300.

Meisenhelder, J. B., & Marcum, J. P. (2004). Responses of clergy to 9/11: Post-traumatic stress, coping and religious stress. *Journal for the Scientific Study of Religion, 43*(4), 547–554.

Mesler, M. A., & Miller, P. J. (2000). Hospice and assisted suicide: The structure and process of an inherent dilemma. *Death Studies, 24*, 135–155.

Meyer, B. (2002). Extraordinary stories: Disability, queerness, and feminism. *NORA, 3*, 168–173.

Meyer, C. H. (1988). The eco-systems perspective. In R. A. Dorfman (Ed.), *Paradigms of clinical social work* (pp. 275–294). Philadelphia: Brunner/Mazel, Inc.

Mezey, G., & King, M. (1989). The effects of sexual assault on men: A survey of 22 survivors. *Psychological Medicine, 19*, 205–209.

Michaud, C. M., Murray, C. J., & Bloom, B. R. (2001). Burden of disease—implications for future research. *Journal of the American Medical Association, 285*(5), 535–539.

Mika, H., Achilles, M., Halbert, E., Amstutz, L., & Zehr, H. (2004). Listening to survivors—a critique of restorative justice policy and practice in the United States. *Federal Probation, 68*(1), 32–39.

Miller, D., Leyell, T., & Mazacheck, J. (2004). Stereotypes of the elderly in U.S. television commercials from the 1950s to the 1990s. *International Journal of Aging and Human Development, 58*(4), 315–340.

Miller, M. M., Korinek, A., & Ivey, D. C. (2004). Spirituality in MFT training: Development of the spiritual issues in supervision scale. *Contemporary Family Therapy, 26*(1), 71–81.

Miller, W. R., & Thoresen, C. E. (2003). Spirituality, religion, and health: An emerging research field. *American Psychologist, 58*, 24–35.

Mills, M. A., Edmondson, D., & Park, C. L. (2007). Trauma and stress response among Hurricane Katrina evacuees. *American Journal of Public Health, 97*(Suppl. 1), S116–S123.

Miniño, A. M. (2010). *Mortality among teenagers aged 12–19 years: United States, 1999–2006* (NCHS data brief no. 37). Hyattsville, MD: National Center for Health Statistics.

Mizock, L., & Harkins, D. (2011). Diagnostic bias and conduct disorder: Improving culturally sensitive diagnosis. *Child & Youth Services, 32*(3), 243–253.

Mizrahi, T. (2001). The status of community organization in 2001: Community practice context, complexities, contradictions, and contributions. *Research on Social Work Practice, 11*, 176–189.

Montgomery, C. (1994). Swimming upstream: The strength of women who survive homelessness. *Advances in Nursing, 16*(3), 34–45.

Morgan, R. D., Rozycki, A. T., & Wilson, S. (2004). Inmate perceptions of mental health services. *Professional Psychology: Research and Practice, 35*, 389–396.

Moskos, M. A., Achilles, J., & Gray, D. (2004). Adolescent suicide myths in the U.S. *Journal of Crisis Intervention & Suicide Prevention, 25*(4), 176–182.

Mowbray, C. T., & Holter, M. C. (2002). Mental health & mental illness: Out of the closet? *Social Service Review, 76*(1), 135–179.

Muskal, M. (2012). Last FEMA trailer leaves Louisiana 6 years after Katrina. *Los Angeles Times.* Retrieved from http://latimesblogs.latimes.com/nationnow/2012/02/last-fema-trailer-leaves-new-orleans-six-years-after-hurricane-katrina.html

National Alliance to End Homelessness. (2009). What we know about housing and homelessness. In *2009 Policy Guide* (pp. 3–6). Retrieved August 10, 2009, from http://www.endhomelessness.org/content/article/detail/2462

National Association of Black Social Workers. (2003). *Kinship care.* Retrieved October 23, 2005, from http://www.nabsw.org/mserver/KimshipCare.aspx?menuContext=760

National Association of School Psychologists. (n.d.). *What is a school psychologist?* Retrieved January 5, 2005, from http://www.nasponline.org/about_sp/whatis.aspx

National Association of Social Workers [NASW]. (1990). *Clinical indicators for social work and psychosocial services in the acute care medical hospital.* Washington, DC.

National Association of Social Workers [NASW]. (1999). *Code of ethics of the National Association of Social Workers.* Washington, DC.

National Association of Social Workers [NASW]. (2000). Cultural competence in the social work profession. In *Social work speaks: NASW policy statements* (pp. 59–62). Washington, DC: NASW Press.

National Association of Social Workers [NASW]. (2001, January). *NASW cautions about Bush's Faith-based initiative.* Retrieved March 5, 2013, from http://www.naswdc.org/pressroom/2001/021401.asp

National Association of Social Workers [NASW]. (2002). *NASW standards for social work case management.* Retrieved May 25, 2004, from http://www.naswdc.org/practice/standards/sw_case_mgmt.asp#intro

National Association of Social Workers [NASW]. (2003). *NASW standards for school social work services.* Washington, DC.

National Association of Social Workers [NASW]. (2010). *Advanced social work practice in military social work.* Retrieved March 9, 2014, from http://www.cswe.org/File.aspx?id=42466

National Association of Social Workers [NASW]. (2014). *Fact sheet: What consumers should know about health reform.* Retrieved March 5, 2014, from http://www.socialworkers.org/assets/secured/documents/practice/health/hcronsumerfactsheet.pdf

National Center for Education Statistics. (1999). *Digest of education statistics.* Washington, DC: National Research Council Panel on High Risk Youth, National Academy of Sciences.

National Clearinghouse on Child Abuse and Neglect. (2005). *Definition of child abuse and neglect state statutes.* Series 2005. U.S. Department of Health and Human Services, Administration for Children & Families. Retrieved May 30, 2013, from http://www.childwelfare.gov/systemwide/laws_policies/statutes/define.cfm

National Coalition against IVP [NCADV]. (2007). *IVP facts.* Retrieved August 17, 2012, from http://www.ncadv.org/files/DomesticViolenceFactSheet(National).pdf

National Coalition for the Homeless. (2006). *How many people experience homelessness?* (NCH Fact Sheet 2). Washington, DC. Retrieved October 7, 2005, from http://www.ncchca.org/files/Homeless/NCH_How%20Many%20are%20Homeless_06.pdf

National Gang Center. (2012). *National youth gang survey analysis: Demographics.* Washington, DC: U.S. Department of Justice, Office of Justice Programs, Office of Juvenile Justice and Delinquency Prevention. Retrieved from http://www.nationalgangcenter.gov/Survey-Analysis/Demographics

National Health Forum Policy. (2010, November). *The Elder Abuse Act: Addressing elder abuse, neglect and exploitation.* Retrieved January 20, 2012, http://www.nhpf.org/library/the-basics/Basics_ElderJustice_11-30-10.pdf

National Highway Safety and Traffic Administration [NHSTA]. (2009). *Traffic safety facts 2009 data: Older population.* Retrieved January 20, 2012, http://www-nrd.nhtsa.dot.gov/Pubs/811391.pdf

National Institute of Mental Health. (1999). *Depression research at the National Institute of Mental Health* (NIH Publication No. 00-4501). Bethesda, MD.

National Institute of Mental Health. (2005). *Schizophrenia.* Bethesda, MD. Retrieved November 15, 2005, from http://www.nimh.nih.gov/publicat/schizoph.cfm#definition

National Institute of Mental Health. (2007). *Older adults: Depression and suicide facts* (NIH Publication No. QF 11-7697). Bethesda, MD.

National Labor Committee. (n.d.). *Working conditions in China.* Retrieved December 21, 2005, from http://www.nlcnet.org/campaigns/archive/report00/introduction.shtml

National Law Center on Homelessness & Poverty. (2006). *Some facts on homelessness, housing and violence against women.* Retrieved January 20, 2012, from http://www.nlchp.org/content/pubs/Some%20Facts%20on%20Homeless%20and%20DV.pdf

National Organization for Human Services. (n.d.). *What is human services?* Retrieved from http://www.nationalhumanservices.org/what-is-human-services

National Youth Gang Center. (2005). *Highlights of the 2002–2003 national youth gang surveys.* Washington, DC: U.S. Department of Justice, Office of Justice Programs, Office of Juvenile Justice and Delinquency Prevention.

Nelson, J. I. (1992). Social welfare and the market economy. *Social Science Quarterly, 73*(4), 815–828.

Netting, E., Kettner, P., & McMurtry, S. (2009). *Social work macro practice.* Boston: Pearson Education.

Neville, H., Worthington, R., & Spanierman, L. (2001). Race, power, and multicultural counseling psychology: Understanding White privilege and color blind racial attitudes. In J. Ponterotto, M. Casas, L. Suzuki, & C. Alexander (Eds.), *Handbook of multicultural counseling* (pp. 257–288). Thousand Oaks, CA: SAGE.

New Freedom Commission on Mental Health. (2003). *Achieving the promise: Transforming mental health care in America* (DHHS Publication No. SMA 03-3832). Rockville, MD.

Newcomb, M., Locke, D., & Thomas F. (2001). Intergenerational cycle of maltreatment: A popular concept obscured by methodological limitations. *Child Abuse & Neglect, 25*(9), 1219–1240.

Nickelson, I. (2004). *The district should use its upcoming TANF bonus to increase cash assistance and remove barriers to work.* Washington, DC: DC Fiscal Policy Institute. Retrieved December 22, 2005, from http://dcfpi.org/?p=69

Nock, M. K., & Prinstein, M. J. (2005). Contextual features and behavioral functions of self-mutilation among adolescents. *Journal of Abnormal Psychology, 114*(1), 140–146.

Nock, M. K., Stein, M. B., Heeringa, S. G., Ursano, R. J., Colpe, L. J., Fullerton, C. S., & Kessler, R. C. (2014). Prevalence and correlates of suicidal behavior among soldiers: Results from the Army Study to Assess Risk and Resilience in Service members (Army STARRS). *JAMA Psychiatry, 71*(5), 514–522.

Norris, F. H., Friedman, M. J., Watson, P. J., Byrne, C. M., Diaz, E., & Kaniasty, K. (2002). 60,000 disaster victims speak: Part I. An empirical review of the empirical literature, 1981–2001. *Psychiatry: Interpersonal and Biological Processes, 65*(3), 207–239.

North, C. S., Eyrich, K. M., Pollio, D. E., & Spitznagel, E. L. (2004). Are rates of psychiatric disorders in the homeless population changing? *American Journal of Public Health, 94*(1), 103–108.

Nunez, R., & Fox, C. (1999). A snapshot of family homelessness across America. *Political Science Quarterly, 114*(2), 289–307.

Occupy Wallstreet. (n.d.). *About.* Retrieved July 4, 2012, from http://occupywallst.org/about/

Office of the High Commissioner for Human Rights [OHCHR]. (2006). *Human Rights Watch supplemental submission to the Human Rights Committee during its consideration of the second and third periodic reports of the United States.* Retrieved December 9, 2010, from http://www2.ohchr.org/english/bodies/hrc/docs/ngos/HRW.pdf

Oliver, D., & Peck, M. (2006, September). Inside the interdisciplinary team experiences of hospice social workers. *Journal of Social Work in End-of-Life & Palliative Care, 2*(3), 7–21.

Olson, L., & Jerald, C. D. (1998). *Quality counts '98: The urban picture.* Retrieved June 18, 2004, from http://rc-archive.edweek.org/sreports/qc98/challenges/tables/ta-n.htm

Otto, N., Middleton, J., & Freker, J. (2002). *Making schools safe: An anti-harassment program from the Lesbian & Gay Rights Project of the American Civil Liberties Union.* New York: Lesbian & Gay Rights Project, American Civil Liberties Union. (ERIC Document Reproduction Service No. ED475274)

Palermo, G. B., Smith, M. B., & Liska, F. J. (1991). Jails versus mental hospitals: A social dilemma. *International Journal of Offender Therapy and Comparative Criminology, 35*(2), 97–106.

Palmer, K., Winblad, B., & Fratiglioni, L. (2003). Detection of Alzheimer's disease and dementia in the preclinical phase: Population based cohort study. *BMJ: British Medical Journal, 326*(7383), 245.

Palmore, E. (2009). Reducing ageism. *Journal of Aging Humanities and the Arts, 3*(2), 144–146.

Pandya, V., & Gingerich, W. J. (2002). Group therapy intervention for male batterers: A microethnographic study. *Health & Social Work, 27*(1), 47–55.

Pape, K. T., & Arias, I. (2000). The role of attributions in battered women's intentions to permanently end their violent relationships. *Cognitive Therapy and Research, 24*, 201–214.

Paradis, L., & Cummings, S. (1986). The evolution of hospice in America toward organizational homogeneity. *Journal of Health and Social Behavior, 27*(4), 370–386.

Pargament, K. I., & Mahoney, A. (2009). Spirituality: The search for the sacred. In C. R. Snyder & S. J. Lopez (Eds.), *Oxford handbook of positive psychology* (2nd ed., pp. 611–620). New York: Oxford University Press.

Pargament, K. I., Tarakeshwar, N., Ellison, C. G., & Wulff, K. M. (2001). The relationships between religious coping and well-being in a national sample of Presbyterian clergy, elders, and members. *Journal for the Scientific Study of Religion, 40*(3), 497–513.

Park, C. L., & Fenster, J. R. (2004). Stress-related growth: Predictors of occurrence and correlates with psychological adjustment. *Journal of Social and Clinical Psychology, 23*(2), 195–215.

Passel, J. S., & Cohn, D. (2008). U.S. population projections: 2005–2050. *Pew Research Center: Social & Demographic Trends.* Retrieved June, 11, 2010, from www.pewhispanic.org/files/reports/85.pdf

Patient Protection and Affordable Care Act, Pub. L. No. 111-148, §2702, 124 Stat. 119, 318–319 (2010).

Patrick, M., Sheets, E., & Trickel, E. (1990). *We are a part of history: The Orphan Trains.* Virginia Beach, VA: Donning.

Pawar, M. (2008). The flood of Krishna River and the flood of politics: Dynamics of rescue and relief operations in a village in India. *Asia Pacific Journal of Social Work Development, 18*(2), 19–35.

Pears, K. C., & Capaldi, D. M. (2001). Intergenerational transmission of abuse: A two-generational prospective study of an at-risk sample. *Child Abuse & Neglect, 25*(11), 1439–1461.

Peters, M., Thomas, D., & Zamberlan, C. (1997). *Boot camps for juvenile offenders.* Office of Juvenile Justice and Delinquency Prevention, U.S. Department of Justice. Washington, DC: U.S. Government Printing Office.

Peterson, C., & Biggs, M. (1997). Interviewing children about trauma: Problems with "specific" questions. *Journal of Traumatic Stress, 10*(2), 279–290.

Petrosino, A., Guckenburg, S., DeVoe, J., & Hanson, T. (2010). What characteristics of bullying, bullying victims, and schools are associated with increased reporting of bullying to school officials? Issues & answers. (National Center for Education Evaluation and Regional Assistance, 2010-No. 092). Waltham, MA: Regional Educational Laboratory Northeast & Islands.

Phelan, J., Link, B. J., Moore, R. E., & Stueve, A. (1997). The stigma of homelessness: The impact of the label "homeless" on attitudes toward poor persons. *Social Psychology Quarterly, 60*(4), 323–337.

Piaget, J. (1950). *The psychology of intelligence.* London: Routledge & Kegan Paul.

Piercy, F. P., Volk, R. J., Trepper, T., Sprenkle, D. H., & Lewis, R. (1991). The relationship of family factors to patterns of adolescent substance abuse. *Family Dynamics of Addiction Quarterly, 1*(1), 41–54.

Pinterits, E. J., Poteat, V. P., & Spanierman, L. B. (2009). The White Privilege Attitude Scale: Development and initial validation. *Journal of Counseling Psychology, 56*(3), 417–429.

Planty, M., & Truman, J. L. (2012). *Criminal victimization, 2011.* Bureau of Justice Statistics Bulletin. Washington, DC: Bureau of Justice Statistics. Retrieved October 2012, from http://www.bjs.gov/content/pub/pdf/cv11.pdf

Polack, R. (2004). Social justice and the global economy: New challenges for social work in the 21st century. *Social Work, 49*(2), 281–290.

Poole, D. A., & Lindsay, D. S. (1998). Assessing the accuracy of young children's reports: Lessons from the investigation of child sexual abuse. *Applied & Preventive Psychology, 7*(1), 1–26.

Pope, M. (2003). *Sexual minority youth in the schools: Issues and desirable counselor responses.* Information Analysis. (ERIC Document Reproduction Service No. ED480481)

Porter, R. (2002). *Madness: A brief history.* New York: Oxford University Press.

Powell, J. (2003). Letter to the editor. *Issues in Mental Health Nursing, 24*(5), 463.

Powell, L., Shahabi, L., & Thoresen, C. E. (2003). Religion and spirituality: Linkage to physical health. *American Psychologist, 58,* 36–52.

Prest, L. A., & Protinsky, H. (1993). Family systems theory: A unifying framework for codependency. *American Journal of Family Therapy, 21*(4), 352–360.

Quinn, T. (1998). *An interview with former visiting fellow of NIJ, Thomas Quinn.* Washington, DC: The National Institute of Justice Journal, Office of Justice Programs, U.S. Department of Justice.

Rawal, P., Romansky, J., & Jenuwine, M. (2004). Racial differences in the mental health needs and service utilization of youth in the juvenile justice system. *Journal of Behavioral Health Services & Research, 31*(3), 242–254.

Ray, S. L. (2004). Eating disorders in adolescent males. *Professional School Counseling, 8*(1), 98–102.

Raywid, M. (1996). *Downsizing schools in big cities.* New York: ERIC Clearinghouse on Urban Education. (ERIC Document Reproduction Service No. ED393958)

Reckdahl, K. (2011). Homeless population in New Orleans rises 70 percent since Hurricane Katrina. *The Times-Picayuna.* Retrieved from http://www.nola.com/politics/index.ssf/2011/06/homeless_population_in_new_orl.html

Reese, D. J., Ahern, R. E., Nair, S., O'Faire, J. D., & Warren, C. (1999). Hospice access and use by African Americans: Addressing cultural and institutional barriers through participatory action research. *Social Work, 44*(6), 449–559.

Reese, D. J., & Raymer, M. (2004). Relationships between social work involvement and hospice outcomes: Results of the National Hospice Social Work Survey. *Social Work, 49*(3), 415–422.

Reese, E. (2007). The causes and consequences of U.S. welfare retrenchment. *Journal of Poverty, 11*(3), 47–63.

Reeves, W. C., Strine, T. W., Pratt, L. A., Thompson, W., Ahluwalia, I., Dhingra, S. S., & Safran, M. A. (2011). Mental illness surveillance among adults in the United States. *MMWR Surveillance Summary, 60*(Suppl. 3), 1–29.

Reid, W. J. (1975). A test of a task-centered approach. *Social Work, 20*(1), 3–9.

Reitzes, D. C., & Mutran, E. J. (2004). The transition to retirement: Stages and factors that influence retirement adjustment. *International Journal of Aging and Human Development, 59*(1), 63–84.

Rice, M. W., Finkelstein, E., Bardwell, R. A., & Leadbetter, S. (2004). The economic toll of intimate partner violence against women in the United States. *Violence and Survivors, 19*(3), 259–272.

Rigby, K. (2003). Consequences of bullying in schools. *Canadian Journal of Psychiatry, 48*(9), 583–590.

Rittner, B., & Wodarski, J. S. (1999). Differential uses for BSW and MSW educated social workers in child welfare services. *Children & Youth Services Review, 21*(3), 217–238.

Roberts, D. (2002). *Shattered bonds: The color of child welfare*. New York: Basic Civitas Books.

Roberts, R. E. (2000). Depression and suicidal behaviors among adolescents: The role of ethnicity. In I. Cuéllar & F. A. Paniagua (Eds.), *Handbook of multicultural mental health* (pp. 360–389). San Diego, CA: Academic Press.

Robertson, J. E. (2003). Rape among incarcerated men: Sex, coercion and STDs. *AIDS Patient Care and STDs, 17*(8), 423–430.

Rocha, C., & Johnson, A. (1997). Teaching family policy through a policy framework. *Journal of Social Work Education, 33*(3), 433–444.

Ross, B., Schwartz, R., Most, M., & Chuchman, M. (2011, May). Michele Bachmann Clinic: Where you can pray away the gay? *ABC News the Blotter*. Retrieved May, 2, 2012, from http://abcnews.go.com/Blotter/michele-bachmann-exclusive-pray-gay-candidates-clinic/story?id=14048691#. UIWryGnuW18

Rostosky, S. S., Regnerus, M. D., & Wright, M. L. C. (2003). Coital debut: The role of religiosity and sex attitudes in the add health survey. *Journal of Sex Research, 40*(4), 358–367.

Rullo, D. (2001). The profession of social work. *Research on Social Work Practice, 11*(2), 210–216.

Rumberger, R. W., Larson, K. A., Ream, R. K., & Palardy, G. J. (1999). *The educational consequences of mobility for California students and schools*. Berkeley, CA: Policy Analysis for California Education. (ERIC Document Reproduction Service No. ED441040)

Rusbult, C. E., & Martz, J. M. (1995). Remaining in an abusive relationship: An investment model analysis of nonvoluntary dependence. *Personality and Social Psychology Bulletin, 21*, 558–571.

Rutter, B. (1978). *The parents' guide to foster family care*. New York: Child Family League of America.

Rutter, P. A., & Behrendt, A. E. (2004). Adolescent suicide risk: Four psychosocial factors. *Adolescence, 39*(154), 295–302.

Ryan, C., & Rivers, I. (2003). Lesbian, gay, bisexual and transgender youth: Victimization and its correlates in the U.S. and U.K. *Culture, Health and Sexuality, 5*(2), 103–119.

Saleebey, D. (1996). The strengths perspective in social work practice: Extensions and cautions. *Social Work, 41*(3), 296–305.

Samuels, G. M., & Ross–Sheriff, F. (2008). Identity, oppression, and power: Feminisms and intersectionality theory. *Affilia, 23*, 5–9.

Sanchirico, A., & Jablonka, K. (2000). Keeping foster children connected to their biological parents: The impact of foster parent training and support. *Child and Adolescent Social Work Journal, 17*(3), 185–203.

Saunders, C. (1958). Dying of cancer. *St Thomas's Hospital Gazette, 56*(2), 37–47.

Schatz, M., Jenkins, L., & Sheafor, B. (1990, Fall). Milford redefined: A model of initial and advanced generalist social work. *Journal of Social Work Education, 26*(3), 217–231. Retrieved June 24, 2009, from Professional Development Collection database

Schlabach, T. (1969). *Rationality & welfare: Public discussion of poverty and social insurance in the United States 1875–1935*. Social Security Commission, Research Notes and Special Studies.

Retrieved September 18, 2005, from http://www.ssa.gov/history/reports/schlabachpreface.html

Schmidt, J. J., & Ciechalski, J. C. (2001). School counseling standards: A summary and comparison with other student services' standards. *Professional School Counseling, 4*(5), 328–333.

Schneiderhan, E. (2008, July). *Jane Addams and the rise and fall of pragmatist social provision at Hull-House, 1871–1896*. Paper presented at the annual meeting of the American Sociological Association, Sheraton Boston, and the Boston Marriott Copley Place, Boston.

Schoenbaum, M., Kessler, R. C., Gilman, S. E., Colpe, L. J., Heeringa, S. G., Stein, M. B., & Cox, K. L. (2014). Predictors of suicide and accident death in the Army Study to Assess Risk and Resilience in Servicemembers (Army STARRS): Results from the Army Study to Assess Risk and Resilience in Servicemembers (Army STARRS). *JAMA Psychiatry, 71*(5), 493–503.

Schram, S. F., Fordingy, R. C., & Sossz, J. (2008). Neo-liberal poverty governance: Race, place and the punitive turn in U.S. welfare policy. *Cambridge Journal of Regions, Economy and Society, 1*, 17–36.

Schultz, C. B. (1985). Children and childhood in Eighteenth Century. In Joseph M. Hawes & N. Ray Hiner (Eds.), *American Childhood: A Research Guide and Historical Handbook* (pp. 70, 79–80). Westport: CT: Greenwood Press.

Scofea, L. A. (1994). The development and growth of employer-provided health insurance. *Monthly Labor Review, 117*, 3–10.

Sentencing Project. (2010). *Racial disparity*. Retrieved from http://www.sentencingproject.org/template/page.cfm?id=122

Sermons, M. W., & Henry, M. (2010). *Demographics of homelessness series: The rising elderly population*. Washington, DC: National Alliance to End Homelessness.

Shankle, M. D., Maxwell, C. A., Katzman, E. S., & Landers, S. (2003). An invisible population: Older lesbian, gay, bisexual, and transgender individuals. *Clinical Research and Regulatory Affairs, 20*(2), 159–182.

Shern, D. L., Tsemberis, S., Anthony, W., Lovell, A. M., Richmond, L., Felton, C. J., et al. (2000). Serving street-dwelling individuals with psychiatric disabilities: Outcome of a psychiatric rehabilitation clinical trial. *American Journal of Public Health, 90*(12), 1873–1878.

Shlay, A. B., & Rossi, P. H. (1992). Social science research and contemporary studies of homelessness. *Annual Review of Sociology, 18*, 129–160.

Shughart, W. F., & Chappell, W. F. (1999). Fostering the demand for adoptions: An empirical analysis of the impact of orphanages and foster care on adoptions in the U.S. In R. D. McKenzie (Ed.), *Rethinking orphanages for the 21st century* (pp. 151–171). Thousand Oaks, CA: Sage Publishers.

Siefert, K., & Pimlott, S. (2001). Involving pregnancy outcome during imprisonment: A model residential care program. *Social Work, 42*(2), 125–134.

Siegel, J., & Williams, L. (2003). The relationship between child sexual abuse and female delinquency and crime: A prospective study. *Journal of Research in Crime and Delinquency, 40*(1), 71–94.

Simmons, T., & Dye, J. L. (2003, October). *Grandparents living with grandchildren: 2000*. Washington DC: U.S. Bureau of the Census.

Siu, S., & Hogan, P. T. (1989). Common clinical themes in child welfare. *Social Work, 34*(4), 229–345.

Slovak, K., & Singer, J. B. (2011). School social workers' perceptions of cyberbullying. *Children & Schools, 33*(1), 5–16.

Smith, C. J., & Devore, W. (2004). African American children in the child welfare and kinship system: From exclusion to over inclusion. *Children & Youth Services Review, 26*(5), 427–446.

Smith, D. T., Juarez, B. G., & Jacobson, C. K. (2011). White on Black: Can White parents teach Black adoptive children how to understand and cope with racism? *Journal of Black Studies, 42*(8), 1195–1230. doi:10.1177/0021934711404237

Snyder, M. (2001). *Self and society*. Malden, MA: Blackwell Publishers.

Somers, C. L., Johnson, S. A., & Sawilowsky, S. S. (2002). A measure for evaluating the effectiveness of teen pregnancy prevention programs. *Psychology in the Schools, 39*(3), 337–342.

Soni, A. (2009). *The five most costly conditions, 1996 and 2006: Estimates for the U.S. civilian noninstitutionalized population* (Statistical Brief 248). Rockville, MD: Agency for Health care Research and Quality. Retrieved from http://www.meps.ahrq.gov/mepsweb/data_files/publications/st248/stat248.pdf

Spake, A. (1994, November). The little boy who didn't have to die. *McCall's*, 142.

Spirito, A., Valeri, S., Boergers, J., & Donaldson, D. (2003). Predictors of continued suicidal behavior in adolescents following a suicide attempt. *Journal of Clinical Child and Adolescent Psychology, 32*(2), 284–289.

Stacks, J. (1995, April 10). 100 days of attitude. *Time Magazine*. Retrieved December 23, 2011, from: http://www.time.com/time/magazine/article/0,9171,982782,00.html

Stein, G. (2004). Improving our care at life's end: Making a difference. *Health & Social Work, 29*(1), 77–79.

Stephenson, C. (1943). Feudalism and its antecedents in England. *The American Historical Review, 48*(2), 245–265.

Sternberg, K. J., Lamb, M. E., & Orbach, Y. (2001). Use of a structured investigative protocol enhances young children's responses to free-recall prompts in the course of forensic interviews. *Journal of Applied Psychology, 86*(5), 997–1005.

Stone, C. (2011, July). Boundary crossing: The slippery slope. *ACSA School Counselor*. Retrieved January 27, 2012, from http://www.ascaschoolcounselor.org/article_content.asp?edition=91&section=140&article=1221

Stone, H. W., Cross, D. R., Purvis, K. B., & Young, M. J. (2003). A study of the benefit of social and religious support on church members during times of crisis. *Pastoral Psychology, 51*(4), 327–340.

Striegel-Moore, R. H., Rosselli, F., Perrin, N., DeBar, L., Wilson, G., May, A., & Kraemer, H. C. (2009). Gender difference in the prevalence of eating disorder symptoms. *International Journal of Eating Disorders, 42*(5), 471–474. doi:10.1002/eat.20625

Stueve, A., & O'Donnell, L. N. (2005). Early alcohol initiation and subsequent sexual and alcohol risk behaviors among urban youths. *American Journal of Public Health, 95*(5), 887–893.

Substance Abuse and Mental Health Services Administration. (2010). *Mental Health, United States, 2008* (HHS Publication No. (SMA) 10-4590). Rockville, MD: Center for Mental Health Services, Substance Abuse and Mental Health Services Administration.

Substance Abuse and Mental Health Services Administration. (2012). *Results from the 2011 national survey on drug use and health: Summary of national findings* (NSDUH Series H-44, HHS Publication No. (SMA) 12-4713). Rockville, MD.

Substance Abuse and Mental Health Services Administration (SAMHSA). (2011). *Center for behavioral health statistics and quality, national survey on drug use and health, 2010 and 2011* (2010 Data – Revised March 2012). Retrieved from http://www.samhsa.gov/data/NSDUH/2k11State/NSDUHsaeTables2011.pdf

Sue, S. (1977). Community mental health services to minority groups: Some optimism, some pessimism. *American Psychologist, 32*, 616–624.

Sue, S., & McKinney, H. (1975). Asian Americans in the community mental health system. *American Journal, 45*, 111–118.

Sullivan, W. P. (1992). Reclaiming the community: The strengths perspective and deinstitutionalization. *Social Work, 37*(3), 204–209.

Surbeck, B. C. (2003). An investigation of racial partiality in child welfare assessments of attachment. *American Journal of Orthopsychiatry, 73*(1), 13–23.

Swick, K. J., & Williams, R. H. (2010). The voices of single parent mothers who are homeless: Implications for early child education professionals. *Early Child Education Journal, 38*(1), 49–55. doi:10.1007/s10643-010-0378-0

Swindle, R. W., Cronkite, R. C., & Moos, R. H. (1989). Life stressors, social resources, coping, and the 4-year course of unipolar depression. *Journal of Abnormal Psychology, 98*(4), 468–477.

Tatara, T. (1997). *Summaries of the statistical data on elder abuse in domestic settings*. Washington, DC: National Center on Elder Abuse.

Taylor, P., Parker, K., Morin, R., & Motel, S. (2012). *Rising share of Americans see conflict between rich and poor*. Washington, DC: Pew Research Center. Social and Demographic Trends. Retrieved October 23, 2012, from http://www.pewsocialtrends.org/files/2012/01/Rich-vs-Poor.pdf

Teaster, P. B. (2000). *A response to the abuse of vulnerable adults: A 2000 survey of state adult protective services*. Washington, DC: National Center on Elder Abuse.

ten Boom, C., Sherrill, J., & Sherrill, S. (1974). *The hiding place*. New York: Bantam Books.

Terayama, H., Nishino, Y., Kishi, M., Ikuta, K., Itoh, M., & Iwahashi, K. (2003). Detection of anti-Borna Disease Virus (BDV) antibodies from patients with schizophrenia and mood disorders in Japan. *Psychiatry Research, 120*(2), 201–206.

Thomas, S. B., Quinn, S. C., Billingsley, A., & Caldwell, C. (1994). The characteristics of Northern Black churches with community health outreach program. *American Journal of Public Health, 84*(4), 575–579.

Thornton, J. E. (2002). Myths of aging or ageist stereotypes. *Educational Gerontology, 28*, 301–312.

Thrane, L., Chen, X., Johnson, K., & Whitbeck, L. (2008). Predictors of post-runaway contact with police among homeless adolescents. *Youth Violence and Juvenile Justice, 6*(3), 227–239.

Tornstam, L. (1994). Gerotranscendence—a theoretical and empirical exploration. In L. E. Thomas, & S. A. Eisenhandler (Eds.), *Aging and the Religious Dimension.* Westport: Greenwood Publishing Group.

Tornstam, L. (2003). *Gerotranscendence from young old age to old old age.* Retrieved January 20, 2012, from www.soc.uu.se/ Download.aspx?id=SpeY85XbP%2Bg%3DShare

Tornstam, L. (2005). *Gerotranscendence: A developmental theory of positive aging.* New York: Springer Publishing.

Toro, P. A., Tompsett, C. J., Lombardo, S., Philippot, P., Nachtergael, H., Galand, B., et al. (2007). Homelessness in Europe and the United States: A comparison of prevalence and public opinion. *Journal of Social Issues, 63*(3), 505–542.

Torrey, E. F. (1995). *Surviving schizophrenia (3rd ed.).* New York: Harper-Perennial.

Torrey, E. F., & Miller, J. (2002). *The invisible plague: The rise of mental illness from 1750 to present.* Piscataway Township, NJ: Rutgers University Press.

Torrey, E. F., Kennard, A. D., Eslinger, D., Lamb, R., & Pavle, J. (2010). *More mentally ill persons are in jails and prisons than hospitals: A survey of the states.* Report for the Nation al Sheriff's Association and the Treatment Advocacy Center. Arlington, VA: Treatment Advocacy Center.

Toups, M. L., & Holmes, W. R. (2002). Effectiveness of abstinence-based sex education curricula: A review. *Counseling and Values, 46*(3), 237–240.

Trattner, W. (1998). *From poor law to welfare state (6th ed.).* New York: Free Press.

Tropman, J. E. (1986). The "Catholic ethic" versus the "Protestant ethic": Catholic social service and the welfare state. *Social Thought, 12*(1), 13–22.

Truman-Schram, D. M., Cann, A., Calhoun, L., & Vanwallendael, L. (2000). Leaving an abusive dating relationship: An investment model comparison of women who stay versus women who leave. *Journal of Social and Clinical Psychology, 19*, 161–183.

Tseng, W. S. (2004). Culture and psychotherapy: Asian perspectives. *Journal of Mental Health, 13*(2), 151–161.

U.S. Code, Title 42, Chapter 119, Subchapter I, § 11302. General Definition of Homeless Individuals. (2005). Retrieved from http://uscode.house.gov/download/pls/42C119.txt

U.S. Conference of Mayors. (2011). *Hunger and homelessness survey: A status report on hunger and homelessness in America's cities.* Washington, DC.

U.S. Conference of Mayors. (2013, June). *The United States Conference of Mayors Hunger and Homelessness Survey: A status of report of hunger and homelessness in America's cities.* Retrieved from http://usmayors.org/pressreleases/uploads/2013/1210-report-HH.pdf

U.S. Department of Education. (2001a). *No Child Left Behind Act of 2001 (H.R.1).* Washington, DC.

U.S. Department of Education. (2001b). *Report to Congress fiscal year 2000.* Washington, DC.

U.S. Department of Education. (2008). *A nation accountable: Twenty-five years after a nation at risk.* Washington, DC.

U.S. Department of Health and Human Services (DHHS). (2006). *The supply and demand of professional social workers providing long-term care services. Report to Congress.* Retrieved from http://aspe.hhs.gov/daltcp/reports/2006/SWsupply.htm

U.S. Department of Health and Human Services, Administration for Children & Families, Administration on Children, Youth and Families, Children's Bureau. (2008). *The AFCARS report.* Retrieved June 22, 2009, from http://www.acf.hhs.gov/ programs/cb/stats_research/afcars/tar/report14.htm

U.S. Department of Justice. (2012, January 16). *Attorney General Eric Holder announces revisions to the Uniform Crime Report's definition of rape: Data reported on rape will better reflect state criminal codes, victim experiences.* Washington, DC: U.S. Department of Justice, Office of Public Affairs.

U.S. Department of Labor Bureau of Labor Statistics. (2010). *Employment characteristics of families—2010.* Retrieved January 22, 2012, from http://www.bls.gov/news.release/ pdf/famee.pdf

U.S. Department of State. (2001). *Afghanistan: Country Reports on Human Rights Practices, Bureau of Democracy, Human Rights, and Labor.* Retrieved November 7, 2009, from http://www. state.gov/g/drl/rls/hrrpt/2000/sa/721.htm

U.S. Department of State. (2012). *Trafficking in persons report.* Washington, DC: U.S. Government Printing Office. Retrieved October 12, 2012, from http://www.state.gov/j/tip/ rls/tiprpt/2012/

U.S. Department of State: Bureau of Consular Affairs. (2011). *Intercountry adoption: Country information.* Retrieved from http://adoption.state.gov/country_information.php

U.S. Senate. (1974). *Hearings before the Subcommittee on Indian Affairs of the Committee on Interior and Insular Affairs,* 99th Cong., 2nd Session (testimony of William Byler). Washington, DC: U.S. Government Printing Office.

Uluorta, H. M. (2008). Welcome to the "All-American" fun house: Hailing the disciplinary neo-liberal non-subject. *Millennium: Journal of International Studies, 36*(2), 51–75.

UNAIDS. (2008). *2008 Report on the global AIDS epidemic.* Geneva. Retrieved from www.unaids.org

United Nations [UN]. (1948, December 9). *General Assembly, Prevention and punishment of the crime of genocide,* A/RES/260. Retrieved November 5, 2012, from http://www.unhcr.org/ refworld/docid/3b00f0873.html

United Nations [UN]. (2008, June 19). Security Council, 5916th Meeting. "Resolution 1820 [Sexual Violence as a War Tactic]". In *Resolutions and Decisions of the Security Council 2008* (S/RES/1820, pp. 51–52). Official Record. New York, 2008.

United Nations [UN]. (2013). *Somalia famine killed nearly 260,000, half of them children—reports UN.* UN News Centre [Press Release]. Retrieved from http://www.un.org/apps/news/ story.asp?NewsID=44811#.UddbtD7714E

United Nations Children's Fund [UNICEF], U.S. Agency for International Development. (2004). *Children on the Brink 2004: A joint report of New Orphan Estimates and a framework for action.* The Joint United Nations Programme on HIV/AIDS. New York: United Nations Children's Fund.

United Nations Children's Fund [UNICEF]. (2007, November 27). *UNICEF's position on inter-country adoption* [Press Release]. Retrieved from http://www.unicef.org/media/media_41918.html

United Nations Department of Peacekeeping Operations [UNDPKO]. (2010). *Review of the sexual violence elements of the judgments of the international criminal tribunal for the former Yugoslavia, the International Criminal Tribunal for Rwanda, and the special court for Sierra Leone in the light of Security Council Resolution 1820.* Retrieved from http://www.unrol.org/files/32914_Review%20of%20the%20Sexual%20Violence%20Elements%20in%20the%20Light%20of%20the%20Security-Council%20resolution%201820.pdf

Urban Institute. (2000). *A new look at homelessness in America.* Retrieved August 6, 2010, from Urban Institute Web site: http://www.urban.org

USCIS Immigration and Nationality Act 101(a) 41. Retrieved from http://www.uscis.gov/ilink/docView/SLB/HTML/SLB/0-0-0-1/0-0-0-29/0-0-0-101/0-0-0-195.html

Utsey, S. O., Payne, Y. A., Jackson, E. S., & Jones, A. M. (2002). Race-related stress, quality of life indicators, and life satisfaction among elderly African Americans. *Cultural Diversity and Ethnic Minority Psychology, 48*(3), 224–233.

Vanderbleek, L. M. (2004). Engaging families in school-based mental health treatment. *Journal of Mental Health Counseling, 26*(3), 211–224.

Van Hoeken, D., Seidell, J., & Hoek, H. (2003). Epidemiology. In J. Treasure, U. Schmidt, & E. van Furth (Eds.), *Handbook of eating disorders* (2nd ed., pp. 11–34). Chichester, UK: Wiley.

VanHook, Cortney R. (2012). *Racial disparity in the diagnosis of conduct disorder* (Undergraduate Research Awards, Paper 12). Retrieved from http://scholarworks.gsu.edu/univ_lib_ura/12

Van Slyke, D. M. (2003). The mythology of privatisation in contracting for social services. *Public Administration Review, 63*(3), 296–315.

Vearnals, S., & Campbell, T. (2001). Male survivors of male sexual assault: A review of psychological consequences and treatment. *Sexual and Relationship Therapy, 16*(3), 279–286.

Victim's Rights Act of 1998, 42 U.S.C. § 10606(b) (West 1993).

Vigil, J. M. (2003). Urban violence and street gangs. *Annual Review Anthropology, 32*, 225–242.

Violent Crime Control and Law Enforcement Act of 1994, Pub. L. No. 103-322, Title IV, § 40001 *et seq.*, 108 Stat. 1902 (1994).

Vohs, K. D., Voelz, Z. R., Pettit, J. W., Bardone, A. M., Katz, J., Abramson, L. Y., et al. (2001). Perfectionism, body dissatisfaction, and self-esteem: An interactive model of bulimic symptom development. *Journal of Social & Clinical Psychology, 20*, 476–497.

Von Hartz, J. (1978). *New York street kids.* New York: Dover.

Vörös, V., Fekete, S., Hewitt, A., Osváth, P. (2005). Suicidal behavior in adolescents—psychopathology and addictive comorbidity. *Neuropsychopharmacol Hung, 7*(2):66–71. Hungarian. PMID: 16167457 [PubMed—indexed for MEDLINE]

Vörös, V., Osváth, P., & Fekete, S. (2004). Gender differences in suicidal behavior. *Neuropsychopharmacol Hung, 6*, 65–71.

Vourlekis, B. S., Edinburg, G., & Knee, R. (1998). The rise of social work in public mental health through aftercare of people with serious mental illness. *Social Work, 43*, 567–575.

Waite, A., Bebbington, P., Skelton-Robinson, M., & Orrell, M. (2004). Life events, depression and social support in dementia. *British Journal of Clinical Psychology, 43*, 313–324.

Walcott, D. D., Pratt, H. D., & Patel, D. R. (2003). Adolescents and eating disorders: Gender, racial, ethnic, sociocultural, and socioeconomic issues. *Journal of Adolescent Research, 18*, 223–243.

Walker-Barnes, C. J., & Mason, C. A. (2001). Ethnic differences in the effect of parenting upon gang involvement and gang delinquency: A longitudinal, HLM perspective. *Child Development, 72*, 1814–1831.

Warr, P., Butcher, V., & Robertson, I. (2004). Activity and psychological well-being in older people. *Aging & Mental Health, 8*(2), 172–183.

Warren, A. (1995). *Orphan Train rider: One boy's true story.* Boston: Houghton Mifflin.

Weaver, H. N. (1999). Through indigenous eyes: Native Americans and the HIV epidemic. *Health & Social Work, 24*(1), 27–34.

Weaver, R. K., Shapiro, R. Y., & Jacobs, L. R. (1995). The polls—trends: Welfare. *Public Opinion Quarterly, 59*(4), 606–627.

Weber, M. (1958). *The Protestant ethic and the spirit of capitalism* (T. Parsons, Trans.). New York: Charles Scribner's Sons. (Original work published 1905.)

Weikart, R. (1998). Laissez-faire social Darwinism and individualist competition in Darwin and Huxley. *The European Legacy, 3*(1), 17–30.

Weil, M. O. (1996). Community building: Building community practice. *Social Work, 41*(5), 481–499.

Weiss, I. (2003). Social work students and social change: On the link between views on poverty, social work goals and policy practice. *International Journal of Social Welfare, 12*, 132–141.

Weiss, I. (2005a). Interest in working with the elderly: A cross-national study of graduating social work students. *Journal of Social Work Education, 41*(3), 379. Retrieved September 14, 2009, from MasterFILE Premier database

Weiss, I. (2005b). Is there a global common core to social work? A cross-national comparative study of BSW graduate students. *Social Work, 50*(2), 102–110.

Wells, K. (1991). Long-term residential treatment for children: Introduction. *American Journal of Orthopsychiatry, 61*, 324–326.

West, W. (2002). Some ethical dilemmas in counseling and counseling research. *British Journal of Guidance & Counseling, 30*(3), 261–268.

Whitbeck, L. B., Hoyt, D. R., & Ackley, K. A. (1997). Abusive family backgrounds and later victimization among runaway and homeless adolescents. *Journal of Research on Adolescents, 7*(4), 375–392.

The White House. (2010). *A more secure future: What the new health law means for you and your family.* Retrieved from http://www.whitehouse.gov/healthreform/healthcare-overview#healthcare-menu

White House, Office of the Press Secretary. (2009, February 5). *Obama announces White House Office of Faith-based and*

Neighborhood Partnerships [Press Release]. Retrieved March 8, 2012, from http://www.whitehouse.gov/the_press_office/ObamaAnnouncesWhiteHouseOfficeofFaith-basedand-NeighborhoodPartnerships/

Whitley, D. M., & Kelley, S. J. (2007, January). *Grandparents raising grandchildren: A call to action* (Prepared for the Administration for Children and Families, Region IV.) Retrieved January 20, 2012, from http://www.acf.hhs.gov/opa/doc/grandparents.pdf

Whitlock, J. L., Purington, A., & Gershkovich, M. (2009). Influence of the media on self injurious behavior. In M. Nock (Ed.), *Understanding non-suicidal self-injury: Current science and practice* (pp. 139–156). Washington, DC: American Psychological Association Press.

Wolfelt, A. (1996). Healing the bereaved child: Grief gardening, growth through grief, and other touchstones for caregivers. Fort Collins, CO: Companion Press.

World Health Organization. (1998). *Female genital mutilation—an overview*. Geneva.

Wright, T. (2000). Resisting homelessness: Global, national and local solutions. *Contemporary Sociology, 29*(10), 27–43.

Yoder, K. A., Whitbeck, L. B., & Hoyt, D. R. (2001). Event history analysis of antecedents to running away from home and being on the street. *American Behavioral Scientist, 45*(1), 51–65.

Young, T., Turner, J., Denny, G., & Young, M. (2004). Examining external and internal poverty as antecedents of teen pregnancy. *American Journal of Behavior, 28*(4), 361–373.

Zakour, M. J., & Harrell, E. B. (2004). Access to disaster services: Social work interventions for vulnerable populations. *Journal of Social Service Research, 30*(2), 27–54.

Zhan, Y., Wang, M., Liu, S., & Shultz, K. S. (2009). Bridge employment and retirees' health: A longitudinal investigation. *Journal of Occupational Health Psychology, 14*, 374–389.

Zucchino, D. (1999). *The myth of the welfare queen: A Pulitzer-prize winning journalist's portrait of women on the line*. New York: Touchstone.

Index